RECORDS OF EARLY ENGLISH DRAMA

Records of Early English Drama

OXFORD

EDITED BY JOHN R. ELLIOTT, JR, and ALAN H. NELSON (University)
ALEXANDRA F. JOHNSTON and DIANA WYATT (City)

2
Editorial Apparatus

THE BRITISH LIBRARY

and

UNIVERSITY OF TORONTO PRESS

© University of Toronto Press Incorporated 2004
Toronto Buffalo
Printed in Canada

First published in North America in 2004 by University of Toronto Press Incorporated
ISBN 0-8020-3905-7
and in the European Union in 2004 by
The British Library
96 Euston Road
London NW1 2DB

British Library Cataloguing in Publication Data
A catalogue record for this title is available from The British Library

ISBN 0-7123-4856-5

Printed on acid-free paper

National Library of Canada Cataloguing in Publication

Oxford / edited by John R. Elliott ... [et al.].

(Records of early English drama)
Includes bibliographical references and index.
Contents: 1. The records – 2. Editorial apparatus.
ISBN 0-8020-3905-7

1. Performing arts – England – Oxford – History – Sources.
2. Theater – England – Oxford – History – Sources. 3. Oxford
(England) – History – Sources. i. Elliott, John R. ii. Series.

PN2596.O93O93 2004   790.2'09425'74   C2004-900153-1

The research and typesetting costs of
Records of Early English Drama
have been underwritten by the
National Endowment for the Humanities and the
Social Sciences and Humanities Research Council of Canada

Contents

Figure 1 Christ Church hall. Reproduced from Joseph Skelton, *Oxonia antiqua restaurata*, vol 2 (Oxford, 1823), plate 107, by permission of the Library of the Pontifical Institute of Mediaeval Studies, Toronto.

Historical Background

The City

Oxford was an important centre of trade and government long before the scholars arrived in the late twelfth century (see below, p 597). It lies at the heart of southern England where the Thames curves round to the east and is joined by the River Cherwell. In Anglo-Saxon times the site of Oxford was the meeting point of three contending communities – the kingdom of the West Saxons to the south, Mercia to the north of the Thames, and the Danelaw encroaching from the east through Buckinghamshire.[1] Two ancient trackways, one coming down from the west off the height of the Berkshire Downs and the other coming along the valley from the south, crossed the river near the present site of the city.[2] One ford was at North Hinksey but it is probably the other one at the confluence of the Thames and the Cherwell that gave the settlement its name, since it was here that the original religious community dedicated to St Frideswide was established.[3]

John Blair in *Anglo-Saxon Oxfordshire* suggests that the borough of Oxford was laid out at the instructions of Æthelflæd, Lady of Mercia, daughter of King Ælfred. She 'ruled Mercia in name from 911' at the death of her husband, Æthelred, and 'perhaps in reality for several years earlier.'[4] Blair argues that there is strong evidence to suggest that Oxford, like London, was built by the Mercian rulers around the turn of the tenth century 'in the vain hope of preserving an autonomous Mercia.'[5] At about the time the town was laid out the configuration of the marshy flood plain to the south of the town 'was altered by gathering the waters into a new cutting tight round the south wall,' thus giving the new town water defences on three sides.[6] The importance of the town can be seen from the statement in the Anglo-Saxon Chronicle that Edward the Elder succeeded to 'London and Oxford and all that belonged to them.'[7]

Once established, the town grew and flourished, becoming a rare medieval centre that had no Roman predecessor.[8] There is archaeological evidence that the town was the site of a royal mint.[9] The Thames, navigable at this time from Oxford to the sea, linked the town with London and, almost as important, there were roads coming west from London and north from Southampton. The road from Southampton intersected with the main road to the southwest from London at Newbury and then continued north to Oxford. There it intersected both with the river and the main London road to the Midlands, which followed the ancient route from London northwest through Henley. These routes reflected 'the establishment of Oxford as a strategic centre. Land and water transport systems were complementary.'[10]

Shortly after the town was established the region was once again devastated by Danish raids from the east. In 1009 the army of King Swein of Denmark burned the town.[11] It was rebuilt on the grid established by Æthelflæd with the High Street and Queen Street running east-west and Cornmarket and St Aldate's running north-south – converging at Carfax.[12] At this major crossroad St Martin's Church was built and became the centre of the life of the community that continued to flourish. The building of the first bridge over the Cherwell at Pettypont (about the site of Magdalen Bridge) greatly facilitated passage to and from London, and Oxford became a place where national meetings were held.[13]

After the Conquest Oxford maintained its strategic importance. The Norman governor, Robert d'Oilly, built the large motte-and-bailey castle in the west end of the town to increase his control of the region. Also shortly after the Conquest a bridge was built over the Thames at Grandpont (the site of Folly Bridge) facilitating travel to the south. During this period the town began to grow outside its defences with the establishing of suburbs. As early as 1230 the sheriff of Oxfordshire was using the castle as a county jail, making Oxford one of four leading towns outside London that 'had a distinct character as seats of royal government in their shires, as indicated by the presence of royal castles, county courts and gaols.'[14]

By 1086 the burgesses of Oxford held in common a large tract of land, Port Meadow, to the northwest of the town. These men probably represented what was to become the Guild Merchant, formed to safeguard the interests of the merchants and the emerging craft guilds, particularly the two that formed the core of the town's prosperity, the clothmakers and the leatherworkers.[15] In 1147 'the "citizens of Oxford of the commune of the city and of the guild of merchants" could convey land belonging to the community' and in 1199 it was the Guild Merchant that purchased the fee-farm of the borough.[16] Trade both in the town and farther afield flourished. Markets were held twice weekly on Wednesday and Saturday with an extra market on Sunday in harvest time.[17] By the mid-twelfth century the market was centred on Carfax with stalls spilling out into the adjacent streets, a custom dating from Anglo-Saxon times.[18] In 1155 the king granted the Guild Merchant a charter that allowed its members to trade free of all tolls in England and Normandy with the same privileges as the citizens of London.[19] Oxford had become an important centre of trade and commerce but it slipped into relative political obscurity under the Normans. There were no more parliaments and 'the Norman barony centred on Oxford was a minor one.'[20] The royal interest in Oxfordshire shifted away from Oxford under Henry I to the hunting grounds at Woodstock, where it remained until the Civil War of the seventeenth century. However, if royal interest waned, Oxford's central location and thriving commerce did make it an attractive venue for the establishment of the institutions that would radically change the direction of the town's development.

THE LATER MIDDLE AGES

This period saw three interdependent waves of immigration to Oxford with the establishment

of three different but related institutions – the monasteries, the University, and the friaries
(see below, pp 588, 591). The effect on the life of the town was mixed. The increase in population inevitably helped the economy of the town, which experienced a period of growth and
prosperity from the late twelfth century to the early fourteenth century, but the presence of the
scholars, in particular, created major problems. The residential colleges so familiar from the
early modern period did not yet exist; instead, scholars were lodged with the townsfolk. By
1192 the townsmen were complaining that it was hard to provide food for so many scholars.
Unscrupulous landlords charged exorbitant rents and scholars bitterly condemned the quality
of food for sale at very high prices. Rioting between the townsfolk and the scholars was a
common occurrence, growing in ferocity and organization. The first town record in these
volumes involves such an incident where a clerk (a scholar) was killed in a conflict with townsfolk on Midsummer Eve 1306 when the crowd was out celebrating the festival.

At the same time as the town was being transformed by the newcomers, its relationship with
the Crown was changing. With the purchase of the fee-farm in 1199 the Crown no longer held
the town directly but rented that right to the Guild Merchant as tenant-in-chief in return for
an annual fee-farm rent of £63 5d.[21] Two bailiffs were chosen to collect the rent and pay it
directly to the king. Before 1229, when a new guildhall was built on the site of the present
one near the corner of St Aldate's and the High Street, the Guild Merchant had met across
the street in a house adjacent to St Martin's. By 1172 the larger 'portmanmoot' was meeting
in St Martin's churchyard.[22]

The town declined during the later Middle Ages with a shift from 'manufacturing and
commerce to service trades dependent on the University ... well advanced by 1381.'[23] The
Black Death contributed to this shift. Although both the University and town were hard hit,
properties left derelict by the death of citizens were acquired by academic foundations,
particularly to the east of St Mary the Virgin and south of the High Street, thus obliterating
some historic parishes and altering others (see below, p 593). Tensions between the townspeople and the scholars grew more strained and, although the old view that the coming of the
scholars reduced the citizens of Oxford to 'helots or subjects of a conquering people' is somewhat exaggerated, there is no doubt that the growing size and complexity of the University
created problems for the town and its people.[24] Three writs in particular issued by Henry III
exacerbated the relationship. In 1231 he fixed the rents on scholars' dwellings in both Oxford
and Cambridge and as one scholar has put it 'in a time of rising prices, the pegging of rents
for the benefit of scholars was a source of ill-feeling between town and gown.' In 1244 the
chancellor's court was given jurisdiction over disputes concerning rents. In 1324 the chancellor
was given joint custody with the mayor and council over the assizes of bread, ale, and wine.[25]

The periodic town-gown riots that continued almost always led to an erosion of the rights
of the town. At the heart of the issue was the legal distinction between the scholars and the
townsfolk. The scholars were all in minor orders and so subject not to the civil courts but to
the ecclesiastical courts, in this case the chancellor's court. The culmination of the troubles was
the St Scholastica's Day riots, 10–13 February 1354/5, in which three scholars and several
townsfolk were killed with much destruction of property. The riots began in Swindlestock
Tavern standing in Carfax directly opposite St Martin's, when (according to the town's account)

two University men, beneficed clerics, threw wine in the face of the tavernkeeper.[26] There was an inquiry that lasted a full year, during which the town was placed under interdict, closing all the churches. The king (Edward III) took the University's part and the mayor and bailiffs were deposed, all property was restored to the scholars, and the town was ordered to pay an additional £250 in damages.[27] More lasting grievances were caused by giving the chancellor sole custody of the assizes of bread, ale, and wine – in effect allowing the customers to set the price of the basic commodities rather than the vendors. The University was also given control over weights and measures, and the chancellor's court was given jurisdiction over any towns-folk involved in a fracas with members of the University. The incoming mayors were required to take an oath to uphold the liberties and privileges of the University. Until 1825 the mayor and council processed from the guildhall down the High Street to St Mary the Virgin on the anniversary of the riots where they were required to offer a silver penny and, at least before the Reformation, to pray for the souls of the victims.

THE EARLY MODERN PERIOD

Two population indicators 150 years apart help us understand the changing demographics of the town. The poll tax return of 1377 listed 2,357 taxpayers in Oxford. By 1440 the citizens complained to the Crown that they could no longer pay the fee-farm, claiming that only one-third of the lay population had inhabited the town when the fee-farm was set while the rest of the inhabitants, scholars and their servants, were exempt.[28] Almost eighty years later the second population indicator, the lay subsidy for 1524, listed only between 431 and 442 taxpayers, the majority in the distributive trades – that is, dealers in merchandise supplying the colleges and their scholars with food, drink, candles, and clothing.[29] Throughout the sixteenth and early seventeenth centuries the victualling trades held a position of prominence in both numbers and representation as members of the city council. Unlike other provincial centres such as York, Oxford had no wealthy primary producers or great merchants. The economy of the city was based on the service trades and was thus dependent upon the University for its prosperity. Although the 'university-based economy provided fairly secure employment at all levels' and the city 'escaped any prolonged recession between 1500 and the Civil War,' the fact that the colleges and the University were the major source of income for the townsfolk inevitably affected the relationship between town and gown.[30]

A further complexity was the presence of a large number of 'privileged persons' who were (normally) not freemen of the town nor scholars but employed one way or another by the University and enjoyed its privileges.[31] These people are mentioned as early as 1290 and were the subject of an agreement between the town and the University in 1459.[32] They were bedels, manciples, cooks, barbers, the personal servants of the scholars, and sometimes members of the building trades such as masons, carpenters, plumbers, and slaters, who were employed by the colleges for the management and maintenance of their affairs and their properties. On the whole, 'privileged persons' were not freemen of the town and claimed the jurisdiction of the chancellor's court rather than the municipal one.

Yet although it functioned much as an ecclesiastical court, by the sixteenth century the chancellor's court was, like the municipal court, ultimately under royal jurisdiction: 'public authority in Oxford, rather than being the monopoly of one body ... was divided between two sets of royal officers, those of the borough and those of the university.'[33] Royal officers, particularly in troubled times, could use this double jurisdiction to their own advantage. In the early sixteenth century the University feared its long-standing privileges would be eroded by a reinvigorated town government.[34] The University authorities appealed in 1514 to their diocesan, Thomas Wolsey, bishop of Lincoln, requesting a new royal charter. During the next fourteen years while Wolsey was busy establishing his new Cardinal College in St Aldate's, work on the new charter took its tortuous course. The provisions of what came to be known as 'Wolsey's charter' were finally made public on 14 July 1528.

The town attempted to appeal the charter to the first session of the 'Reformation parliament' in 1529 after Wolsey's fall. The highly public dispute between the University and the town coincided with the national crisis generated by the king's desire for a divorce from Katherine of Arragon. When asked about the validity of the king's marriage the University, led by the aging chancellor William Warham, archbishop of Canterbury, pronounced the marriage valid. Henry was furious and, as Thomas Cromwell grew in power, he openly took the side of the town, threatening to revoke many of the University's privileges. In May 1534 when the king again asked the advice of the University, this time about the 'powers of the bishop of Rome in England,' the University knew what answer it had to give – that no foreign bishop, including the bishop of Rome, had any powers in England.[35]

The ancient tensions between the University and the town had been used by Cromwell as a means to advance royal policy. Even after Cromwell's fall the privy council emerged 'as a body ready and able to deal with town-gown disputes on a regular basis.'[36] In this context the royal appointments of the chancellors of the University on the one hand and the high stewards of the town on the other came to be of key importance. Cromwell was apparently himself involved in creating the office of high steward as a position closely tied to the Crown.[37] The high stewards in the early modern period who have been identified were Charles Brandon, duke of Suffolk, a close adviser of Henry VIII by at least 1535; the Catholic John Williams, Lord Williams of Thame during Mary's reign (1553–8); Francis Russell, earl of Bedford (1559–63); Sir Francis Knollys (1563–92); Henry Carey, Lord Hunsdon (1592–6); Robert Devereux, earl of Essex (1596–1601); Sir Thomas Egerton, Lord Ellesmere (1601–10), who resigned when he became chancellor of the University; William Knollys, Lord Knollys (1611–31); and Thomas Howard, earl of Berkshire (1631–49).[38] Oxford 'used its costly high stewards as arbitrators in internal disputes and relied heavily on their support in struggles against the university or the Crown.'[39] The best example in these Records of the way the stewards mediated quarrels with the University is the settlement of the potentially nasty riot of 1597–8 by the earl of Essex on behalf of the city and Chancellor Thomas Sackville, Lord Buckhurst, on behalf of the University (see p 246 and p 1112, endnote to Hatfield House Library: Cecil Papers MS 62/16 single sheet).

However strained the relationship between town and gown was in the Middle Ages, Carl Hammer has argued that by the sixteenth century a 'symbiotic relationship' had evolved 'between the burghal host and the academic guest.'[40] Although the constitutional relationship was not always harmonious, the University and the town came to be mutually dependent in practical matters. The University 'provided essential services to the town through the administration of local franchises such as the assize of bread and ale, the enforcement of sanitary provisions and the night watch.'[41] It also served as a major local employer and the customer of the many goods and services provided by the citizenry. The presence of two competing jurisdictions within a single community was bound to create tensions and frictions, particularly when a large number of the inhabitants had the boisterous belligerence of youth and virility. Nevertheless, particularly after the legal skirmishing over Wolsey's charter, the major divisions between the University and the town found a mode of redress that avoided costly arbitration.

By the sixteenth century Oxford had taken on much of the geographical form that its central core has today. The Dissolution of the monasteries brought about the demolition of the great monastic buildings in the suburbs, providing new sites for the increasing number of secular colleges and building materials for others.[42] Of the four wards the westerly two were largely (though not exclusively) occupied by townsfolk while the 'eastern section of the town (particularly from St Mary's onwards) ... formed a virtual *pagus academicus*.' Although the number of taxpayers may seem remarkably low in 1524, modern scholars estimate the actual 'non-privileged population in the mid-sixteenth century (1547) [to be] about 5,500–6,000.'[43]

The town gradually shook off the economic decline of the late medieval period. In a time of profound social and religious change the old medieval community dominated by the friars and the great local religious houses was swept away. It was replaced by a 'vigorous, opportunistic, and eventually better-educated urban community,' which by the seventeeth century found its social outlets at one extreme in the multitudinous alehouses and at the other in the sombre, city-subsidized Puritan lectures. The solid citizen looked to the craft guild and the city to provide a measure of his status and to indulge his liking for ceremonial.[44] In 1542 Oxford was created a city when Christ Church Cathedral became the see of the newly created diocese of Oxford. Roads were improved, its charters were confirmed and clarified, and in 1605 the city received a royal charter. In the early seventeenth century the Thames that had silted up since the Anglo-Saxon period was again made navigable all the way to Oxford. The royal hunting lodge at Woodstock became a favourite resort, first of Elizabeth and then of the early Stuarts.[45]

The renewed prosperity of the city is reflected in the records cited in these volumes. The relevant city records survive only from 1554 when the chamberlains' accounts record the first payment to the king's minstrel. Except for the controversy over Wolsey's charter, there is little to indicate religious and political turmoil. The events that led to the foundation first of Cardinal College and eventually of Christ Church on the same site are nowhere in the records, although Wolsey's great scheme caused the disappearance of one parish church and the alteration of a major street, St Aldate's. That Princess Elizabeth was held prisoner in nearby Woodstock during her sister's reign is nowhere mentioned and the trial and execution of the 'Oxford Martyrs' appears most prominently through the complaints of the two bailiffs for that year, Anthony Welles and Thomas Winkell, that they had not been paid for the expenses they incurred feeding the prisoners.[46] Yet these events of national significance must have affected the city and its inhabitants. The high steward, Lord Williams of Thame, was responsible for Elizabeth during her stay in Woodstock and escorted her there from the Tower in 1554.[47] Archbishop Cranmer and Bishops Latimer and Ridley were tried for heresy in the University church of St Mary the Virgin. After the trials Lord Williams, as high steward, presided with the mayor, John Wayte, over the burnings, first of Latimer and Ridley on 16 October 1555 and then of Cranmer on 20 March 1555/6 just outside the city walls.[48]

The Records end in the year that Charles I returned to the city where he had been so lavishly welcomed in 1636, this time to take up residence with his court. In the troubled years leading up to the Civil War the court had been increasingly at Woodstock, and the city and parish records frequently refer to the ringing of bells as the king passed through the city on his journey from London. The years of the Civil War were extraordinary ones in the life of the city. 'From the king's arrival in 1642 until its surrender in 1646 Oxford was the royalist capital of England housing not only the king and his court, but also the central law courts, the exchequer, parliament and a mint.'[49] For the first time since before the Conquest, Oxford held centre stage in the life of the nation, and the townsmen and scholars joined forces in a grim effort to survive the deprivations of the war.

CIVIC GOVERNMENT

The civic government that evolved during the sixteenth century grew naturally from the structure of the medieval Guild Merchant. The system was based on councils drawn from the ranks of the freemen and a hierarchy of officers elected by the councils. Only freemen were allowed to trade or pursue a craft within the liberties of the city and to take part in the series of councils that constituted Oxford's civic government.

In theory, after 1554, the civic government of Oxford was based on 'a hierarchy through which ... men progressed with the accumulation of experience or of years, the common council being recruited from freemen who had served as constables, the chamberlains from among the common councillors, the bailiffs from the chamberlains, the assistants from the bailiffs, and the mayor and aldermen from the assistants.'[50] Although the theory did not always hold, largely because of the provision for 'compounding' or buying a higher rank, a sense of the functioning of each level of the hierarchy helps one understand the complex workings of Oxford's civic government. The officers of the lowest rank were the four constables responsible for working with the bailiffs to exercise 'police functions ... in each of the borough's four wards.'[51] Their work was inevitably shared with the University bedels. The members of the council of Twenty-four were normally chosen from among former constables.

The next level of service was the oversight of the finances of the town. The chamberlains served for one year only and that office was the first important step up the ladder of civic office. Although former chamberlains continued as members of the common council, most moved on to become bailiffs. Although the two bailiffs were ranked lower than the mayor, they had clearly defined and independent powers. In origin they had been royal officials appointed to collect the fee-farm. This continued to be one of their responsibilities and as long as the farm was paid they were not responsible to the town for the funds they collected. Among their other duties were keeping the peace and maintaining the town prison in the Bocardo at the North Gate. After their term in office the former bailiffs remained members of the common council

and by the seventeenth century they were listed at the beginning of each year's minutes in order
of seniority after the bailiffs serving that year. The next step up for a freeman after serving as
bailiff was to become a member of the council of Thirteen, usually as one of the 'assistants.'
In the council of Thirteen, the 'assistants' worked with the more senior aldermen. Unlike many
other towns Oxford had only four aldermen, one for each ward. For a time in the sixteenth
century the mayor was chosen only from among the aldermen but later, after the pool of
candidates was widened to include the assistants, former mayors often became aldermen.

The chief officer of the town was the mayor who was elected annually by the council from
a restricted pool of candidates. In the sixteenth century men often served more than once. For
example, Ralph Flexney served four times and Richard Atkinson five times. In the seventeenth
century, as the religious troubles increased, several men including John Wilmot (1625, 1630),
Oliver Smith (1630), William Boswell (1630, 1633), and William Blake (1633) refused to
serve when elected and paid their fines.[52] They did not, however, lose their place among the
Thirteen by their refusal.

Carl Hammer in his 'Anatomy of an Oligarchy: The Oxford Town Council in the Fifteenth
and Sixteenth Centuries' has argued that the Oxford town government functioned as a 'porous
oligarchy,' maintaining a solid core of experienced governors while at the same time providing
for the renewal of the system through the provision of 'compounding.'[53] There were instances
of men coming from other towns such as William Matthew, the former mayor of Abingdon,
who 'compounded' for a bailiff's place upon his arrival in Oxford in 1558 and was mayor by
1564. Such circumstances were unusual, however, and once a freeman entered the system by
election or payment he remained part of the governing elite. The major criterion for membership in the governing elite was wealth. This is clear from the lay subsidy of 1524 where virtually
all the council for that year appear on the lists. The aldermen (including the sitting mayor)
'have an average assessment of well over £60 and the bailiffs about half that, slightly over £30.
The chamberlains, in turn, were assessed at about half the bailiffs' level or slightly more than
£15 whilst the average for the Common Council is about two-thirds of that for the chamberlains or somewhat over £10.'[54] Occupation was also an important criterion for membership
on the council and most of the councillors were members of one or another of the powerful
craft guilds. Finally, Oxford's system of government where one office followed from another
ensured an experienced body of men as governors but it also ensured an elderly body of men
as governors. 'In 1584–5 the average age of the mayors' councillors was 59, of bailiffs 52, and
of common councillors 49; the youngest mayor's councillor was 44 years old.'[55]

Religious History

Oxfordshire formed an important part of the episcopal see founded, with St Birinus as the
first bishop, at Dorchester-on-Thames in the seventh century. The Norman Conquest brought
no immediate change but later in the eleventh century the bishop's seat was transferred to
Lincoln. (The connection of Lincoln with Oxford is reflected in the fifteenth-century foundation of Lincoln College.) Not until the sixteenth century did Oxford itself become the centre
of a diocese, with the foundation of Christ Church both as a college of the University and as

a cathedral. However, from the Saxon period Oxford had grown both as a religious centre and as an urban and commercial settlement. It has been noted that the Saxon minsters, like St Frideswide's Minster, were generally extensive and complex establishments, centred on a church and religious community but interacting economically with the surrounding district. They also undertook pastoral care in that district, the 'parochia' – a system of pastoral care that preceded the later medieval organization of urban parishes.[56] St Frideswide's Minster probably encouraged the settlement that was later formalized with its characteristic grid plan and fortified by the Saxons. Thereafter the town's commercial and strategic importance grew alongside its importance as a religious settlement.

In the immediate post-Conquest period Oxford attracted an impressive number of religious and scholarly foundations, which came in three identifiable waves – monastic, scholarly, and mendicant.[57] The Augustinian priory of St Frideswide, the successor to the Anglo-Saxon minster, was founded early in the twelfth century. Its church had probably been rebuilt by 1180 when the relics of St Frideswide were translated, but ten years later the priory buildings were burnt. The church (which in the sixteenth century became, and still remains, the cathedral of the diocese of Oxford) was the first building to be restored in the early thirteenth century. A second Augustinian priory was founded by Robert d'Oilly in 1129 on his manor of Osney southwest of the town; it was elevated to an abbey around 1154. A later addition was Rewley Abbey, established in 1280 on the west bank of the river northwest of the town as a house of study for Cistercian monks. The need for such a house was the result of the second major wave of immigrants to the town – scholars who had begun to gather in Oxford in the late twelfth century, attracted by the increasing reputation of Oxford schools for advanced learning in theology and law.[58] The third group of newcomers, the friars, began to arrive after 1221, attracted by the growing academic community. All four major mendicant orders had houses in the suburbs of Oxford – the Dominicans to the south, the Franciscans just south of the castle, the Carmelites in the northwest, and the Austin friars in the north. Two minor orders of friars – the friars of the Sack or Penance and the Trinitarian friars – arrived in the thirteenth century while the Crutched friars arrived in 1342. There were also two hospitals established in the twelfth century, St John the Baptist and St Bartholomew's leper hospital, both outside the East Gate.

In the two hundred years between the mid-twelfth century and the mid-fourteenth century Oxford had been transformed from a trading and administrative centre favoured by the royal house to a major religious and educational centre. H.E. Salter has cautioned, 'The religious houses of Oxfordshire were not remarkable for wealth, antiquity or learning.'[59] But wills, including those of Oxford residents, reflect the importance of the religious houses to lay people, and lay piety is equally reflected in the number of chantries established by Oxford people in the parish churches of the town.[60] The eight religious foundations, according to Barrie Dobson, 'constituted an agglomeration of varied monastic and mendicant settlement unsurpassed elsewhere in England.' Only St Frideswide and the later Benedictine community of Canterbury College were actually within the walls of the town. All but one, a small house of Trinitarian friars outside the East Gate, 'were ranged in a great arc around the western and northern perimeters.'[61] Little trace beyond Christ Church Cathedral remains of these large establishments but their presence during the period until Dissolution was a major factor in the life and economy of the town.

The site of Christ Church is rich in historical layers, dating from the Anglo-Saxon foundation that was succeeded by St Frideswide's Priory. In 1524 the priory was suppressed (and, incidentally, the nearby parish church of St Michael at the South Gate also demolished) to accommodate Thomas Wolsey's grandiose design for Cardinal College. However, his fall in 1529 left the buildings incomplete and the great plan for a college that would form the heart of the University's organization was left in abeyance. In 1532 Cardinal College was refounded as King Henry VIII College. During the next decade plans were formed to create a new bishopric of Oxford although the cathedral was established initially in 1542 at Osney, where the abbey had been dissolved in 1539. The last abbot of Osney, Robert King, was appointed the first bishop of Oxford. Within a very few years these two separate foundations – the college on the site of St Frideswide's and the new cathedral at Osney – were merged. On the same day in 1545 both the cathedral and King Henry VIII College were surrendered to the Crown, and in November 1546 'the college and cathedral, now united, were founded again,' when a charter of foundation was granted to the cathedral church of Christ in Oxford – the beginning of Christ Church on its present site.[62] Although, as James McConica notes, the charter 'did not lay down the foundation of the academic college' as such, it did effectively mark the establishment of the unique double identity of Christ Church as both university college and city cathedral.[63] The former priory church of St Frideswide, still remaining within the new buildings, became both the college chapel and the cathedral church.

The relationship between the two identities of Christ Church could be delicate although from the start the dual identity seems to have been recognized. By 1847 'the cathedral was criticised for being primarily a college chapel from whose worship the laity was excluded.'[64] The extremely delicate balance of the civic and University functions, although found only at Christ Church, is perhaps dimly reflected in the relationship between the colleges and the Oxford parishes in the medieval and early modern period, when colleges owned the livings of so many parishes. (In 1326, for example, the bishop of Lincoln acquired the advowsons of All Saints, St Michael at the North Gate, and St Mildred – the last was suppressed to make way for Lincoln College in 1427.)

The increased prosperity in the twelfth and thirteenth centuries mentioned above (p 591) was reflected in renewed building not only of colleges, monastic foundations, and dwelling houses but also of churches. Altogether nineteen medieval Oxford parishes are recorded although not all were within the town liberties: St Giles and St Mary Magdalen, both to the north of the city, were in Northgate hundred and so strictly not in Oxford. H.E Salter notes, however, that from 1349 onward wills dealing with property in those two parishes were proved not in the hundred court but in the mayoral court. (The city eventually purchased Northgate hundred in 1592.)[65]

Five parish churches are recorded in the eleventh century: St Ebbe, St Martin, St Mary the Virgin, St Michael at the North Gate, and St Peter in the East.[66] St Frideswide's Minster was also in existence at that period (the earliest certain record is of 1004).[67] St Frideswide's Church evidently retained a parochial function until the late thirteenth century, when its parochial functions and the associated revenues were transferred to St Edward's, the contiguous parish to the north, on the south side of the High Street.[68] St Michael at the North Gate and St Peter in the East, which functioned as parish churches by 1086, may originally also have been minsters. Both were wealthier than other parish churches in Oxford at the time; St Peter's also seems to have been designed as a potential centre for pilgrimage: architectural evidence reveals that the crypt was built to accommodate the display of an important relic.[69] John Blair, noting this evidence, also draws an analogy with other late-Saxon foundations, noting that 'the existence of two or more minsters seems a characteristic feature of the late Anglo-Saxon Mercian towns.'[70] Although the available evidence is very inconclusive it does indicate the established importance of Oxford and its religious life by the immediate post-Conquest period.

Four more eleventh-century foundations are recorded: St Edward the Martyr, St George in the Castle, St Mary Magdalen, and St Mildred. By 1200 there were nine more: All Saints, St Aldate, St Budoc (refounded after the destruction of the original church during the building of the castle barbican), St Cross Holywell, St Giles, St John the Baptist, St Michael at the South Gate, St Peter le Bailey, and St Thomas, built by Osney Abbey in the western suburbs.[71]

Surveys and tax assessments from the thirteenth to the sixteenth centuries show fluctuations in the relative wealth of the parishes, which in turn reveal aspects of the varying prosperity of the town and the University. All Saints and St Martin – both located in the town centre, and St Martin in addition being the church used by the town corporation – were consistently the wealthiest, although St Martin's relative prosperity declined slightly in the sixteenth century. St Peter le Bailey, almost as rich as All Saints in the fourteenth century, had suffered a dramatic decline by the sixteenth, attributed to movement of wealthier residents out of the parish. Conversely, the suburban parishes of St Thomas, to the west of Oxford, and St Mary Magdalen, to the north, showed a decided rise in prosperity by the mid-sixteenth century, as wealthier townspeople increasingly settled there. Local economic change may be reflected here: the victualling trades, especially brewing, had grown increasingly important.[72]

Both the churches of St Martin and St Mary the Virgin held places of peculiar importance in local life – the former as the church adopted by the town government for ceremonial use and the latter as the 'University church,' where congregations and degree ceremonies were regularly held from the thirteenth century onward. The town corporation shared responsibility with the parish for the upkeep of St Martin's Church, as the University helped to support St Mary's, although town-gown friction seems to have existed, unsurprisingly, in both parishes.[73] But townspeople no doubt had mixed views, at best, of the fact that several churches were demolished and parishes reformed by landowning founders of colleges. The building of Merton College resulted in the takeover of the parish church of St John the Baptist in 1292 as the college chapel.[74] The bishop of Lincoln, when Oxford was still within the Lincoln diocese, acquired the advowsons of three town churches – All Saints, St Michael at the North Gate, and St Mildred – in 1326; in 1427, when Lincoln College was built, the three were combined into a collegiate church and St Mildred's was suppressed.[75] Wolsey's grandiose plans for his proposed Cardinal College involved the demolition, in 1525, of the church of St Michael at the South Gate and the merging of its parish with the contiguous St Aldate's.[76] Barrie Dobson has suggested that the town (like contemporary Cambridge) might have taken a less than positive view of this evidence of the University's health: 'The multiplication of academic colleges ... is so far from supporting a thesis of urban prosperity that it could be seen by the burgesses as an objectionable symptom of their own decay.'[77]

The histories of both the churches of St Martin and St Mary the Virgin reflect the difficult relationship between the town and the University. St Martin's, often surnamed Carfax after its central location, was one of the wealthiest and most prominent Oxford churches, and certainly among the early foundations. Wood claims that it is 'of a most ancient erection and beyond all record'; certainly the exact date of its foundation is not known, but King Cnut granted it to Abingdon Abbey in 1032.[78] Its location and early establishment may have contributed to St Martin's becoming, by the late twelfth century if not earlier, the official town church, appropriated by the town corporation for its regular worship and ceremonial use, with seats being reserved for the mayor and councillors. In recognition of this status the corporation assisted the parish in maintaining it. The parish historian Carteret Fletcher suggests that the church's identification with the town as a corporate body made it a focus for town-gown dissension: 'The church was used by the citizens as a fortress.... In 1321 complaint was made to the king that the citizens had raised the walls of the aisles and crenellated them.'[79] It may not be a coincidence that the crucial riots of St Scholastica's Day 1354/5 began at the Swindlestock Tavern, which stood at Carfax directly opposite the church. At any rate the church maintained its official position, as a 1579 decree of the city council reflects: all freemen of the city, with their families, were to 'come to the sermon at Carfoxe' every Sunday and holiday on pain of a fine of 12d.[80] The city lectureship was also established at St Martin's in 1586.

St Mary the Virgin, located on the High Street to the east of the town centre, occupied an equally and perhaps (in town and parish terms) more equivocally special position: recorded first in the Domesday Book, it seems to have been appropriated as the official University church from the mid-thirteenth century or earlier.[81] The University congregation met there for four hundred years until the new convocation house was built in 1637. (When the original was converted into a café in the late twentieth century, mindful of history, it retained the name 'The Old Convocation House.') The chancellor's court, Acts, and degree ceremonies were held in the church until the mid-seventeenth century; University sermons have been given there weekly since the fifteenth century. The parish did benefit from the special position of St Mary's in that the University and also Oriel College, which held the advowson from 1326, assisted considerably in the maintenance and repair of the church.[82] Nonetheless, there was evidently friction too, as the parish historian E.S. Ffoulkes has pointed out: 'Parishioners had no right of entry to the Congregation House; nor to any part of the church in which University services and sermons, or Oriel services and sermons, were then going on.' (Parishioners did however have an equal right with Oriel and any other college within the parish boundary to burial within the precincts; other members of the University had to ask the permission of the parish. Ffoulkes remarks drily that in the circumstances 'the parish might seem to have had small power of refusing; and now and then its consent was secured by a bequest.')[83] On the other hand, the parish was home to the confraternity of St Thomas the Martyr, which acted as a focus for both 'town' and 'gown' parishioners and is discussed in more detail below.

In general the parish records reflect a range of responsibilities undertaken by the parishes as part of the administration of the life of the town: churchwardens' accounts record regular expenses on the purchase and repair of church goods, the maintenance of the building and the ground surrounding it, charitable support of the poor and sick, and the raising of arms and, on occasion, soldiers. All the parish churches benefited from parishioners' wills, and numerous chantries, chapels, masses, and lights were maintained by private bequests as well as by parish fraternities and craft guilds.

Among the parishes whose records have been extracted for these volumes, most had guilds and fraternities that variously maintained chantries and lights and provided for needy members: the religious guilds were dedicated variously to God, the Holy Trinity, and a range of saints including the Blessed Virgin, St Andrew, St Clement, St George, St Michael, and St Thomas. Records of the guilds date generally from the fourteenth and fifteenth centuries although at least one guild at St Peter le Bailey is recorded in 1270.[84] The religious guilds and the various craft guilds also recorded as maintaining lights and regular masses at a number of Oxford churches were not open to all: the poorest were inevitably excluded because membership demanded the payment of dues. Despite this, Eamon Duffy has argued that such guilds functioned very much as part of parish life.[85] The overall prosperity of the parish of St Michael at the North Gate presumably benefited from the chantries of St Clement and St George, which are interesting as having individual proctors, hosting their own annual ales and keeping their own accounts.

In the parish of St Mary the Virgin, the confraternity of St Thomas the Martyr from its foundation in response to the Black Death in 1350 was one of the few places in Oxford where the three distinct 'classes' – members of the University, privileged persons, and townsfolk – came together in acts of communal piety. For two hundred years this confraternity served as a neutral meeting ground for all inhabitants of the town. Carl Hammer, in his analysis of the surviving evidence of the guild, has concluded that 'there was no institution in Oxford which in its origins, aims, ongoing connections and composition so clearly reflected the interlocking of "Town" and "Gown" as did the guild (and the chantry) of St Thomas the Martyr.'[86] Another aspect of the life of the parish that reflected civic rather than University life appears in the records of the light maintained in the church by the fifteenth century Cooks' guild.[87]

In addition most of the churches owned property that brought in at least a little rent. But the regular recording by the churchwardens of income from ales and hockings shows how, in many if not all parishes, the interests of traditional festivity and of fundraising went hand in hand.

The maintenance of festive as well as strictly religious traditions was of course severely challenged by the Reformation. Eamon Duffy's comprehensive study has shown very strikingly how profound and pervasive was the impact of religious change, enforced by government, on the lives of ordinary people and on the communal life of parishes throughout the country. On the purely financial level the strain of replacing many items of church furnishings and vestments – not once but several times under different regimes – was considerable. But Duffy also argues that the cumulative changes enforced on traditions of worship – the dropping of popular saints' days and holidays from the calendar, the banning of lights before saints' images, the dissolution of chantries, and the suppression of religious guilds – must inevitably have caused profound disturbance to communities.[88] Parish records – both churchwardens' accounts and inventories – suggest the drawn-out struggle to steer a safe course through the religious and political storms of the sixteenth and seventeenth centuries. On the whole, churches in Oxford inclined to conformity with the established religion, despite inevitable confusion and dispute as the country lurched from Henry VIII to Edward VI to Mary to Elizabeth in one century, and through civil war in the next. It is hard to be certain from surviving parish records exactly what the attitudes of parishioners were and how far the acceptance of change in any one parish reflects genuine conviction among individuals (incumbents or parishioners) rather than political caution. Extant inventories of St Martin's, for instance, show a parish making sedulous efforts to keep up with the alarming changes and reverses of official religious opinion from the mid-sixteenth century – although these inventories do not necessarily show that St Martin's was more eager to conform than other city parishes.[89] The inventory of 1547 includes mass books, altar cloths, and a mention of Our Lady's shrine; in 1552 these are replaced by communion tables, communion books, and no mention of the Virgin; shortly after Queen Mary's accession (20 November 1553) a longer inventory lists 'goods and ornaments gevyn to the churche ageyn by Mr Alderman Tryssher hys wyffe' as well as other goods brought in (presumably from safe keeping in private houses) by parishioners, including altar cloths, altar stones, mass books, and a 'sakryng bell' from Richard Whittington, who, incidentally, became mayor from 1558 to 1566.[90]

The incumbents of St Mary Magdalen seem also to have inclined to conformity with the religious establishment: under John Baker, vicar in the early Elizabethan period, altars were removed, wall paintings whitewashed, and tables of the commandments bought. The sale of 'an olde saye coot of grene wyche was made for wettsontyd' – identified by the *vch* as 'presumably a vestment'– may in fact indicate another aspect of parish life: since the record also states that the coat was made 'for the lord,' it may refer to the lord in a summer game (see p 108).[91] In this particular parish it is also just possible that it was made for the lord of the hundred, who donated it back to the parish for fundraising purposes – which would remove its possible religious significance.

St Mary the Virgin showed the characteristic local efforts at conformity, whether because of the church's official University status or not is not certain: the churchwardens sold plate and vestments under Edward VI, restored altars and repaired a defaced statue under Mary, and under the vicar William Powell conformed to the Elizabethan settlement in 1558. The last vicar before the Civil War, Dr Morgan Owen, being chaplain to Archbishop Laud, demonstrated Laudian tendencies in restoring the south porch, with a statue of the Virgin and Child above it; the statue was mutilated in 1642.[92]

St Michael at the North Gate also seems from its records to have attempted religious conformity, although the changes as elsewhere were gradual and so perhaps reluctant. Laudian and Puritan influences seem to have alternated in the seventeenth century: the chancel was re-arranged and new altar rails installed in 1634–5 but these changes were reversed in 1641.

It has been suggested that Puritanism was a feature in the parish of St Peter le Bailey more, and earlier, than in other Oxford parishes: an instance of possible puritan vandalism is recorded in 1584 and 'by 1593 the parishioners had adopted the puritan practice of sitting for communion.' Parish opinion was evidently not by any means uniform, however, and old practices continued – although not without objections. In 1634, for instance, two parishioners were proceeded against for causing a disturbance when the May Day garland was brought into church, and for trying to stop the Whitsun festivities, as well as for refusing to bow at the name of Jesus.[93]

By contrast the records of St Peter in the East, although they suggest the usual Oxford attempts to conform with the religious establishment of the time, also indicate unreformed and traditionalist feeling in that parish at least.[94]

The University

ORIGINS

It is not possible to affix a firm date to the moment at which the group of individual teaching masters who had assembled in the late twelfth century at a provincial town on the upper reaches of the River Thames became incorporated as a 'university,' after the model of Paris and Bologna, from which most of them came.[95] In the Middle Ages Oxford was part of the diocese of Lincoln and it was the bishops of Lincoln who were empowered by the pope to appoint Oxford's chancellors.[96] While Robert Grosseteste has traditionally been regarded as the first occupant of this office c 1225, an earlier document from c 1214 accords this honour to Geoffrey de Lucy.[97] Royal confirmation of Oxford's corporate status, extending the chancellor's jurisdiction to many aspects of life in the town as well, followed in a series of charters issued by Henry III as noted above (p 585).[98]

Why the town was chosen as the site of such an institution can only be a matter of conjecture. Richard Southern points to Oxford's importance in the twelfth century as a centre for the trying of ecclesiastical court cases, thus affording masters and students the opportunity of studying both the theory and practice of canon and Roman law.[99] This circumstance may explain why Oxford, and shortly thereafter its eastern offspring Cambridge, developed along essentially secular lines, despite both universities' dependence in their early centuries on the patronage of the church. They existed not as seminaries but as centres of what we today would call 'higher learning.' While most Oxford students were expected to take holy orders eventually, their stay at the University, especially if limited to an undergraduate course of study, was intended to give them a general education in the liberal arts that led, as often as not, to a civil rather than to an ecclesiastical career.

The early chancellors of the University were picked from among the resident masters and exercised their duties in person. In time, however, it became the custom to delegate the chancellor's powers to one or more deputies ('commissarii'), the chief of whom was the vice-chancellor, who was elected by 'congregation,' an assembly of 'regent masters' (that is, resident teachers holding the MA).[100] After the Reformation the chancellor was appointed by the king, who usually chose him from among his privy councillors. By this time the position had come to be regarded as largely ceremonial, with the actual job of running the University being performed by the vice-chancellor. Congregation also appointed other officers such as the two proctors, elected annually, whose duties were manifold but can best be described as disciplinary; and the six bedels, divided into three 'esquire bedels' and three 'yeoman bedels,' who were servants of the proctors and whose duties lay generally in assisting them in enforcing the statutes, customs, and privileges of the University. Yet another deliberative body called 'convocation,' consisting of both regent and non-regent masters, exercised the final authority of framing statutes and of settling matters unresolved by congregation.[101] Although this assembly rarely met more than once or twice a year, it functioned, in theory at least, as the supreme governing body of the University. (Today it meets solely for the purpose of electing the Professor of Poetry.)

CURRICULUM

Throughout the period covered by these volumes, academic instruction in Oxford was in the hands of the four 'faculties,' those of arts, theology, law, and medicine. The vast majority of Oxford students were associated with the arts faculty since the last three subjects could be read only after the student had received his MA. Upon admission a student's name was recorded in a ledger-book, often called a 'buttery-book,' of the college or hall in which he resided so that a daily record might be kept of his consumption of food and drink. (Such of these books as have survived are often our only way of knowing the names of the men who lived in a college or hall at any given time.) The student then enrolled under a specific master, from one of the faculties, who became his tutor and who theoretically taught him all of the subjects in the curriculum until he received his degree. In the sixteenth century the introduction of specialized lecturers and Regius Professors added a new dimension to an Oxford education, but the old idea of a single continuous relationship between master and pupil survives to this day in the institution of the 'moral tutor.'[102] After the choice of tutor had been made the student was required by the statutes to appear before the vice-chancellor and sign his name in the University matriculation book. As a fee was required for this, however, students frequently put off formal matriculation until shortly before they were ready to 'supplicate' for their BA degree. Matriculation books, therefore, rarely tell us when a student actually entered Oxford. Indeed, if a student failed to take a degree, his name may not appear in any official University document.

The curriculum studied by the undergraduate at Oxford was much the same throughout the period covered by these volumes. The medieval 'trivium' – grammar, rhetoric, and logic – formed its core and was studied over a mandatory period of residence of four years. Bachelors were expected to stay another three years until they became masters and for this they studied the 'quadrivium' – arithmetic, geometry, astronomy, and music. All seven subjects were taught both theoretically through lectures and practically through exercises called 'disputations,' in which the student would practise orally what he had learned, either as an 'opponent' (who proposed the subject of debate) or as a 'respondent' (who answered it). The question put to one of the candidates for a doctorate in Civil Law in 1593, for example, was 'Whether actors be disreputable' ('An histriones sint infames?'), to which the respondent answered in the affirmative ('Sunt').[103]

By the late sixteenth century statutory requirements concerning such matters as residence, attendance at lectures, and participation in exercises had become so numerous and complicated that virtually no student could truthfully claim to have fulfilled all of them. Consequently almost every degree required a 'grace' or 'dispensation' from congregation or convocation, so that 'supplication' for 'grace' to proceed to a degree became itself a statutory requirement. Degrees were conferred at a July commencement ceremony called 'the Act.' This, however, was not the end of the matter since the BA degree did not become official until the candidate 'determined' on 'Egg Saturday' (the Saturday before Ash Wednesday) of the following year, while the MA degree was not official until the candidate 'incepted' at the following Act.[104] Both 'determination' and 'inception' consisted of further disputations, requiring further fees, although both the exercises and the fees might occasionally be waived by the obtaining of further 'graces.' Candidates for doctorates in law, medicine, and theology faced similar procedures.

Once the new MA had completed his 'inception' he was admitted to membership in congregation and entered a period of either one or two years of 'necessary regency,' during which he was obliged to give lectures, preside over disputations, and perform other duties prescribed by congregation. His necessary regency completed, the regent master was then expected, usually as a condition of his college fellowship, to join one of the faculties of law, medicine, or theology in order to obtain either a second baccalaureate or a doctorate. At this point he became a non-regent master, losing his seat in congregation but gaining one in convocation. Some five to seven years might be spent in obtaining these further degrees, for a total of fourteen to sixteen years' residence in Oxford. In the sixteenth century only about three per cent of MAs went on to study law since those seriously intent on becoming lawyers preferred to move on to the Inns of Court in London. The faculty of medicine had even less business, conferring on average fewer than two degrees per year over the whole century. Only theology, which attracted some ten per cent of Oxford students to take higher degrees, can be said to have flourished.[105] These figures are hardly surprising given the fact that during most of this century only a quarter of the entering students made it as far as the BA. Of some two thousand total members of the University in 1600, the overwhelming majority were undergraduates who stayed in Oxford for less than four years.

HALLS AND COLLEGES

Until 1488 the University itself possessed only one building, or rather one part of one building. Congregation House consisted of a single large room on a lower level of the church of St Mary the Virgin, on the High Street, with another room above it used as a library.[106] The church itself, although known as 'the university church,' was actually the property of Oriel College. In 1488 construction was completed on the University's second building, the Divinity School on the ground floor and Duke Humfrey's library above. The latter, and subsequently the Bodleian, were called 'the public library' because both were open to all members of the University as well as to qualified visitors. The addition of the Bodleian quadrangle constructed between 1613 and 1621, greatly expanding the library space while providing new 'schools' for the faculties, completed the building works undertaken by the University during the period covered by the present volumes.

From this it will be seen that the University made no provision of any sort for the housing of its members. In the early years of Oxford's existence students lived either in private halls, of which there were more than a hundred in the fourteenth century, or in lodgings with towns-people, like Chaucer's Nicholas in *The Miller's Tale*. Students in Nicholas' situation, con-temptuously referred to in an early University statute as 'chamberdeacons,' were encouraged to take up residence in an official hall or college.[107] Endowed colleges were first founded in the mid-thirteenth century (University, Balliol, Merton), although it was not until the sixteenth century that they came to dominate the University's academic life and to house most of its students. By 1505 the number of Oxford halls had fallen to fifty-two, by 1537 to eight, accommodating only about 260 students.[108] By 1642 the number of Oxford colleges had risen to eighteen, variously founded by members of the royal family, charitable prelates, and pious merchants. (Three other colleges, all associated with the religious orders – Canterbury, Durham, and Gloucester Colleges – failed to survive the Reformation.)[109]

Each college was headed by a master who might bear the title of president, provost, warden, principal, dean, or rector, depending on the whim of the founder. Collectively the masters were known as the 'heads of houses' and from the mid-sixteenth century on the vice-chancellor was always chosen from their number. Each college provided a number of fellowships for the cleverer students and stipends (called 'exhibitions') for poor scholars. Fellows and exhibitioners were thus said to be 'on the foundation.' Most colleges also made room for paying customers or 'commoners,' who matriculated in increasing numbers toward the end of the sixteenth century and included many offspring of the nobility.[110] Indeed, the influx of commoners succeeded in doubling the size of some colleges, such as Queen's, in only a few years' time. The wealthier colleges also provided for boy choristers to sing in their chapels and in three instances (Christ Church, Magdalen, and New College) set up separate grammar schools for their instruction. (The word 'chorister' in Oxford parlance referred exclusively to boys; adult members of a choir were called 'singing-men.') Meals were taken in the hall, with the master and senior fellows (sometimes accompanied by noble 'commoners') typically seated at a high table on a raised platform while the junior members sat at lower tables.[111] Masters were required to reside in their colleges (in the medieval colleges their quarters were always located directly above the main gate), and their lodgings were often spacious enough to include a second, private hall. It is probably these private halls that are referred to in documents recording plays 'in the president's lodgings.' Such smaller, originally private halls survive at Magdalen, Merton, and St John's, although the 'warden's hall' in Merton has been converted into a 'middle commonroom' (that is, a graduate student lounge).

By far the wealthiest college was Christ Church, the only royal foundation in Oxford. (Queen's College, named after Queen Philippa, was not founded by her; Balliol was named after a king of Scotland but founded by his widow.) Begun by Cardinal Wolsey in 1525 Christ Church was refounded in 1546 by Henry VIII, who merged it with the chapter of the cathedral church in nearby Osney, where the diocese of Oxford had first been created in 1542. It is for this reason that the word 'college' is never used as part of Christ Church's name. Next in wealth of endowment, although barely half as rich as Christ Church, came Magdalen and New College. Then, with another drop of fifty per cent, came All Souls, Corpus Christi, Merton, Queen's, and St John's, followed far behind by Balliol, Brasenose, Exeter, Lincoln, Oriel, Trinity, and University. (Three colleges are omitted from consideration here – Jesus,

Pembroke, and Wadham – because they were all founded shortly before 1642: of these, only Jesus appears in the Records, beginning in 1622.) Christ Church was also by far the largest of the colleges, with over one hundred men on the foundation and by 1605 a total membership of over three hundred. (At Christ Church fellows were called 'Students,' always with a capital 'S.') In the sixteenth and early seventeenth centuries, the main period represented by the records in this collection, the other colleges with the largest number of members were Brasenose, Exeter, Magdalen, New College, Queen's, and St John's.[112] Some colleges drew their members primarily from geographical areas designated by their founders – Exeter from the west country, Jesus from Wales, Lincoln from its county namesake, and Queen's from Cumberland and Westmorland. Others gave preference to particular grammar schools – Christ Church to Westminster, New College to Winchester, and St John's to Merchant Taylor's.[113] The frequent references in the diary of Thomas Crosfield, fellow of Queen's, to sending letters or loaning costumes 'to the North' constitute an example of the use to which such knowledge can be put in understanding the records in the present collection.

Further historical notes on individual colleges may be found in the Document Descriptions below.

Drama, Music, and Ceremonial Customs

Drama in the Colleges and University

In addition to the analytical account given here, readers are referred to Professor Elliott's essay 'Drama' in *The History of the University of Oxford*.[1] Elliott observes (p 642) that complaints by such opponents of theatre as Stephen Gosson and John Rainolds had no practical effect on the performance of academic plays in Oxford. Anti-theatrical discourse as it bears on Oxford is considered in Appendix 11.

COLLEGE PLAYS, 1485 TO 1565

The sole Oxford college known to have engaged in plays before the reign of Henry VIII is Magdalen, where records of performances survive in relative abundance from 1485–6, following a less certain entry for 1483–4. An entry in 1486–7 for 'le capp mayntenaunce' may suggest a court satire but we are on more solid ground with *King Solomon* – evidently written by Thomas More and performed *c* 1495 – and with *St Mary Magdalene* (patron saint of the college) – written by John Burgess, performed in 1506–7, and perhaps revived in 1517–18.[2] (Edward Watson composed a play to earn an academic degree in 1511–12.) Magdalen mounted interludes occasionally from 1502–3 ('interlude' may or may not have been another word for 'play'). Its dramatic performances in the early years are most often associated with Christmas when datable within the year, less often with Easter (1495–6, 1509–10, 1519–20) – a logical occasion for a play of *St Mary Magdalene*. Plays were performed in the college's hall from 1531–2 (and doubtless earlier), and certain ones are designated as comedies from 1534–5 and as tragedies from 1539–40. Through the reign of Henry VIII internal evidence for plays outside of Magdalen occurs only for Lincoln and Merton Colleges in 1512–13, New College in 1524–5, and Cardinal College (a comedy) in 1529–30.

In a notebook entry for 1541–2 Alexander Nowell of Brasenose College refers, somewhat enigmatically, to 'my play in Englishe.' Far more substantial, measuring by the survival of texts and allusions, are plays from the pen of Nicholas Grimald, associated with Balliol and Merton, speculatively dated to the 1540s (see Appendix 6:1–2). Of his eight known titles – *Archipropheta*, *Christus Redivivus*, *Athanasius sive Infamia*, *Christus Nascens*, *Fama*, *Protomartyr*, *Troilus*, and 'De Puerorum in Musicis Institutione' – texts of only the first two survive, in continental imprints.

After Henry VIII's reign, Exeter College produced comedies in 1547–8 and 1550–1; New College produced plays in 1552–3. Trinity College seems to have borrowed costumes for a play in 1556–7, before producing Terence's comedy *Andria c* 1559 and a spectacle in 1564–5 (on Trinity Sunday, its feast day). In 1554–5 the dean and chapter of Christ Church decreed that henceforth comedies would be supported to the extent of two per annum at £1 each, while tragedies would be supported to the extent of two at £2 each, for a maximum of four plays per academic year, with equal emphasis on Latin and Greek; if fewer than four, then in similar proportions. (No record survives of any Oxford play written or performed in Greek.) The decree constitutes evidence of a flourishing dramatic tradition not recorded in financial records.

Magdalen College performed comedies and tragedies with some regularity to 1561–2. In 1550–1 and 1551–2 the college paid for the construction of a theatre, probably a set of demountable scaffolds erected in its hall exactly in the manner of contemporary Cambridge colleges (see below, p 608). In 1559–60 a new term, 'spectacul*orum*,' enters the Oxford college records: the spectacle at Magdalen for 1560–1 may have been John Bale's *Three Laws*.

COLLEGE AND UNIVERSITY PLAYS, 1566 TO 1591

Queen Elizabeth's royal visit to Oxford in August 1566 set its academic plays on a new course, following a pattern established by a royal visit to Cambridge in 1564.[3] Even more than Cambridge, however, Oxford University as a corporate body became the 'producer' of plays for royal visits, in the sense that the vice-chancellor and his deputies selected the plays and oversaw their financing, furnishing, and mode of production. The arrangements made for 1566 were followed – with variations – for royal visits in 1592, 1605, and 1636. Preparations usually began with an official letter from the chancellor to the vice-chancellor requesting the provision of suitable entertainments. The letter stressed that each college and hall, as well as each student (with the exception of poor scholars), was to bear an appropriate share of the financial burden. The chief beneficiary of this stipulation was Christ Church, exempted in 1635–6 from making even a proportional contribution in exchange for the use of its facilities. Christ Church apparently won its privilege because as a royal foundation it traditionally acted as host to the sovereign, and because its hall was exceptionally capacious. Accordingly, although actors were drawn from various colleges, Christ Church men tended to predominate.

John Bereblock, writing in Latin, gives short plot synopses of the three plays presented during Queen Elizabeth's 1566 visit but fails to name their titles or authors. Miles Windsor's account, in English, lists the three plays as *Marcus Geminus*, a Roman history play in Latin by Tobie Matthew of Christ Church; *Palamon and Arcite*, a dramatization of Chaucer's *Knight's Tale* by Richard Edwards, master of the children of the Chapel and a former Oxford student; and *Progne*, a Latin tragedy by James Calfhill, a doctor of Christ Church. Windsor, who performed in Edwards' play, appears not to have attended the other two productions but provides a list of the actors who appeared in all three plays. This list includes the name of Tobie Matthew, who may be presumed to have acted in his own play, a practice not uncommon among academic playwrights. Windsor also provides a wealth of amusing detail about the queen's reaction to *Palamon and Arcite*, principally in the draft version of his work, which only came to light in the preparation of the present collection.[4]

The years immediately following the 1566 royal visit witnessed a noticeable increase in play activity among Oxford colleges. Merton performed plays in 1566–7 (*Wylie Beguylie* and Terence, *Eunuchus*) and 1567–8 (Plautus, *Menaechmi*, and Edwards, *Damon and Pithias*). Corpus mounted its single recorded play in 1572–3 (apparently for Lord Strange), as did Exeter in 1585–6. Queen's put on two plays (a tragicomedy at Christmas 1572–3 and Wotton's *Tancredo* in 1585–6), as apparently did All Souls (1574–5, 1579–80?). More important, St John's now joined Christ Church and Magdalen as a principal producer of plays, and financed the construction of a hall-theatre in 1568–9. After 1585–6 no Oxford college other than Christ Church, Magdalen, and St John's is known from financial records to have mounted plays, although all continued to give support, financial or otherwise, for royal visits.

Colleges also cooperated with the University to offer plays for visits by noblemen, especially for visits by Robert Dudley, earl of Leicester, who served as chancellor from 1564 to his death in 1588.[5] On 5 May 1569 Thomas Cooper, dean of Christ Church, wrote to thank Leicester for his determination 'to see your Vniuersitie, as I am informed, the fifteenth of this present moneth': 'We haue also in readinesse a playe or shew of the destruction of Thebes, and the contention betwene Eteocles and Polynices for the gouernement therof. but herein I thinke we shall be forced to desyre your Honours fauorable healpe for prouision for som*m*e apparaile and other thinges needefull.' A visit by Leicester in 1582, with his nephew Sir Philip Sidney in tow, gave rise to a huge – and well-documented – burst of dramatic activity, recalled in a sermon by Laurence Humphrey. A year later, on 10–13 June 1583, Oxford received a visit from Albert Laski, palatine of Siradia, duke of Poland. New construction was undertaken on the Christ Church stage, while the professional poet and dramatist George Peele was paid for his services on 26 May. A lengthy description of the event was published by Holinshed in the second edition of his *Chronicles* (1587). In January 1584/5 Leicester made a final appearance, generating elaborate expense lists in the Christ Church accounts for both a tragedy and a comedy. Christ Church also paid for the carriage of 'stuffe fro*m* ye reuills and backe agayne.'

While agreeing in 1583–4 to restrict professional playing at Oxford, Leicester, apparently on his own initiative, intervened to protect and even encourage college plays (see p 195):

As I like and alowe all thease statut*es* and articl*es* aboue writt*en* and namelye in the fiuth article do thinke the p*r*ohibicio*n* of com*m*on stage players very requisite so wolde I ∧⌐not⌐ haue it meant theare bye theat the tragedies com*m*odies & other shewes of exercises of learninge in that kinde vsed to be sett foarth by vniu*er*sitye me*n* should be forbedde*n* but acceptinge the*m* as com*m*endable and greate furderances of learninge do wish the*m* in anye wise to be co*n*tinuid at set times and incresed ... and the youth of the vniu*er*sitye by good meanes to be incurragid to the decent and freque*n*t settinge fourth of the*m*.

Accordingly, students of certain colleges continued to perform 'tragedies com*m*odies & other shewes of exercises of learninge in that kinde' until the eve of the Civil War.

COLLEGE AND UNIVERSITY PLAYS, 1592 TO 1604

The Records are relatively silent about the plays performed for the royal visit of Elizabeth in September 1592. The only surviving eyewitness account is that of a Cambridge 'spy,' Philip Stringer, who did not write up his notes until eleven years later. By then he seems to have forgotten everything except the names of the two plays and his impression that they were 'but meanly performed' (see p 223). Other evidence (see pp 222–4) tells us, however, that one of the plays was Leonard Hutten's Latin comedy *Bellum Grammaticale*, not printed until 1635 but originally performed in Christ Church as early as 1581 (the 1592 version was fitted out with two new prologues and an epilogue by William Gager); the other play was Gager's own *Rivales*, a Latin comedy (now lost) that was first performed in 1583 for the state visit of the Polish prince palatine, and, like *Bellum Grammaticale*, revived as a Shrovetide entertainment in Christ Church a few months before the queen's visit. The fact that Christ Church recorded expenses of only £31 2s 2d for the 'stage & towardes plaies' suggests that they were indeed more 'meanly' set forth than in 1566, while resort to two plays already in the year's repertory may indicate that inadequate warning of the queen's visit was given to the University.

The royal visit of 1592 seems to have exhausted the colleges. Not until 1596–7 did St John's resume its dramatic activities, beginning with a comedy, but as if to make up for lost time, it scarcely missed another year between then and 1640. Christ Church resumed activities for a single year, 1598–9. (Christ Church had produced its first of many 'nil' entries for comedies and tragedies in 1583–4; with a few exceptions these must be read as evidence of non-performance.)

COLLEGE AND UNIVERSITY PLAYS, 1605 TO 1635

King James, Queen Anne, and the young prince Henry all participated in a royal visit to Oxford in August 1605. The Records show that four plays were presented in Christ Church, three in Latin for the king, all written or adapted by Oxford men, and one in English especially written for the queen and prince by the queen's favourite court poet, Samuel Daniel. Costumes were imported from the master of the revels in London. The Latin plays seem to have been chosen to demonstrate the three 'kinds' of classical drama as labelled by Vitruvius.[6] *Alba*, co-authored by Robert Burton of Christ Church, was a satyr play featuring shepherdesses, hermits, various gods and goddesses, and a magician. A cast of students exclusively from Magdalen College presented *Ajax Flagellifer*, a Latin play based upon Sophocles' tragedy. Finally Matthew Gwinne of St John's provided an allegorical comedy, acted by the students of that college, called *Vertumnus sive Annus Recurrens*, known in English as 'The Year About.' At *Vertumnus* the king 'was soe overwearied ... that after a while he distasted it, and fell a sleepe, when he awaked, he would have bene gone, sayinge I marvell what they thinke mee to be, with such other like speeches shewinge his dislike thereof, yet he did tarrye till they had ended yt, which was after one of the clock. The queene was not there that night' (see p 299).

A quasi-royal visit occurred in 1612–13, when Count Palatine Frederick v, who had married into the royal family, attended a comedy at Magdalen College supervised by Thomas Oates. For this event we have, unfortunately, no more than the bare record.

Meanwhile St John's College maintained its playing tradition in full force. Christ Church resumed its dramatic activities irregularly from 1605–6 to 1618–19. From 1616–17 comes a rich list of expenses for the theatre in the hall, including stage and scaffold; for a quire of paper to write out the play (a tragedy) twice; and finally, 18s paid for vizards lost and broken, and for the loan of other(s). Magdalen College mounted spectacles in 1606–7 and plays irregularly from 1612–13 to 1619–20, with one final play in 1634–5. Documentary evidence for college performances in the Records, limited after 1620 almost exclusively to St John's, is supplemented by bibliographical information concerning surviving or lost play texts from various colleges as noted in Appendix 6:1–3.

Of all plays performed by students of Oxford through 1642, the most notorious by a wide margin was Barten Holyday's *Technogamia*, which earned its dubious fame not for its original performance at Christ Church on 13 February 1617/18 but for a repeat performance before James I and his court at Woodstock on 26 August 1621, a Sunday. In the wake of the performance, sarcastic comments and satirical verses circulated in such abundance that they are segregated here in Appendix 2.

THE ROYAL VISIT OF 1636

The opulence of the 1605 plays at Christ Church was perhaps more than matched by the entertainment of Charles I at the same hall in 1636, the last occasion on which plays were presented to a monarch in Oxford. The plays were William Strode's *The Floating Island* and William Cartwright's *The Royal Slave*. Between performances the king and queen were treated to George Wild's *Love's Hospital*, performed in St John's hall. This was the only time that a royal party ventured out of Christ Church to see a play. Archbishop Laud, a former president of the college, financed the play from his own funds to celebrate the college's new quadrangle. (A fourth play, Jasper Mayne's *The City Match*, was written for the occasion but not performed.) The two Christ Church plays inspired perhaps the most vivid eyewitness appreciation to be found in this collection, that of Brian Twyne (pp 543–5). It is important to note, however, that the 1636 royal plays, although written and acted by Oxford men, were in all other respects the product not of Oxford but of the king's purveyors of court entertainment. The scenery and costumes were provided by the office of the works and the office of the revels; the music was written by William and Henry Lawes and performed by the king's musick and other professional musicians; student actors were specially coached by Joseph Taylor, leader of the king's men at the Globe; candelabra were brought from Whitehall Palace and reassembled in Oxford to provide lighting. In contrast to the choice of learned, academic plays for King James, all of the 1636 plays were comedies, and all, by royal command, were written in English, thus confirming William Cartwright's remark in the epilogue to *The Royal Slave*:

> There's difference 'twixt a Colledge and a Court;
> The one expecteth Science, the other sport.

Perhaps because of this, *The Floating Island*, a political allegory extolling monarchy, was generally dismissed as incomprehensible by the courtiers, despite its scenic wonders. *The Royal Slave*, however, an exotic romance about a Persian prisoner miraculously rescued from a pagan sacrificial altar, got a warm reception from the entire court, especially the queen, who asked to see it again performed at Hampton Court. What she saw both there and in Oxford, however, was not representative of Oxford culture but an imitation of the usual type of Stuart court entertainment.

THE FINAL YEARS

In a 1636 letter to the University (see p 539) Archbishop (and Chancellor) Laud advised that the scenery and costumes left over from the royal performances be 'laid up in some place fit,' so that if any 'are willing to set forth, need the use of any, or all of these things, it shall be ... lawful, and free for them to have and to use them.' Laud proposed that one copy of an inventory be kept at Christ Church, another elsewhere for safe keeping (he suggested the University Registry). He thought that members of a later student generation might wish to revive the performance tradition and would need an inventory to recreate the theatre from the parts that now went into storage. (A similar inventory, dated 1640, has survived at Cambridge.)[7] But when Charles I took up residence in Christ Church in 1642, there is no evidence that he ever requested further dramatic entertainment.

AFTERMATH

At the Restoration of Charles II a revival of the custom of royal dramatic entertainments was contemplated in Oxford but soon abandoned. Timothy Halton, a fellow of Queen's, tells us that in July 1661 a committee was formed to plan the reception of the new king in Oxford and that 'the play is made by Dr. Llewellyn.' He fears, however, that the plan cannot be carried out because 'they are so in want of actors' and may have to make use of the professional players from the Red Bull theatre, then in Oxford.[8] Halton undoubtedly was referring to the lack of experienced student actors engendered by the eighteen-year hiatus in dramatic activities, rather than any shortage of willing volunteers. While the professional companies in London – including the one at the Red Bull – quickly reorganized at the Restoration, Oxford's academic drama never recovered from this break in its traditions. Charles II returned to Oxford in September 1663 and James II in September 1687, but neither University nor Christ Church accounts list any payments for drama. In 1664 Christ Church attempted to revive the custom of Christmas revels by staging a comedy called *The Tricks* composed by a student named Richard Rhodes. This, however, according to Anthony Wood, led only to extensive damage to the hall and general 'drunkenness and wantonness.' Wood adds that Jasper Mayne, the unperformed playwright of 1636, tried to encourage the cast by saying 'he liked well an acting student,' but the college accounts reveal that this was the last such play to be performed in Christ Church hall.[9] It was, indeed, virtually the last student play to be performed in Oxford until the founding of the Oxford University Drama Society more than two centuries later.

Academic Play Venues

Oxford college comedies, tragedies, and interludes were almost all performed either privately in the master's lodging, or publicly in the college hall. While little is known about private performances, public performances can be reconstructed in some detail.

Most Oxford halls known to have been used for the public performance of plays survive more or less intact. These include the medieval halls of Magdalen (72' 6" x 29' 3"), Merton (78' x 27'), New College (79' x 32' 8"), and Trinity (59' 6" x 30' 6").[10] The hall of St John's was built c 1500 but increased by the length of one bay in 1616 (its final dimensions were 82' 6" x 26' 6").[11] The available floor space of all these halls was reduced by the depth of their entrance screens. Christ Church hall (114' 6" x 39' 9"), completed in 1529, has no internal entrance screen, so its entire length was available to the theatrical designer.[12] The surviving hall of Exeter (75' 6" x 27' 6") was built in 1618, long after its known play performances (1547–8, 1550–1).[13] The surviving hall of Queen's, which produced a tragicomedy in 1572–3, was built as late as 1714.[14]

Only the halls of Christ Church (Figures 1 and 4), Magdalen (Figure 2), Merton, and St John's (Figure 3) served as academic drama venues of any significant duration. Of the three smaller venues, most – but not much – is known about how Magdalen's hall was transformed into a theatre for a few days each year. Account entries employ suggestive nomenclature, including 'proscenium' in 1538–9 and 1551–2, 'scenam' in 1552–3, and 'theatrum' from 1553–4 onward. Carpenters spent from three to eleven days removing (and subsequently replacing) dining tables and installing (and subsequently removing) theatrical scaffolding. Rope and candles or lamps were purchased, doubtless for performances at night. The expenditures on wood and on sawyers, which continue from year to year, suggest a work in progress.

For want of sufficiently detailed evidence, perhaps the only way to reconstruct a typical Oxford college theatre is to assume a substantial similarity to the typical academic theatre at Cambridge, characterized by a stage platform across the width of the hall near the high-table end; a pair of stage houses facing one another across the length of the stage platform; raised scaffolding for the seating of distinguished guests behind the stage; raised scaffolding for lesser spectators along the lower end and side walls; and standing room or sitting room along the floor.[15]

Back in Oxford, Magdalen College paid painters to write names for the performance in 1560–1 and purchased 'hair for women' or a wig in 1561–2. In 1556–7 some college, probably Trinity, borrowed costumes from the master of the revels in London, providing for three kings, two dukes, six counsellors, one queen, three gentlewomen, one young prince, six maskers, and four torch-bearers.

More abundant information survives from the royal visit of Queen Elizabeth in August 1566, when a theatre was specially constructed in Christ Church hall. Workmen included the very carpenters who had perfected their art in the construction of the Magdalen College theatre since 1551–2. Although college accounts do not clearly distinguish work on the theatre from other college works (see pp 113–23), they do reveal that carpenters helped 'to take downe the stage & scaffolde' (see p 119) and that Goodwife Davis supplied board and studs 'about the

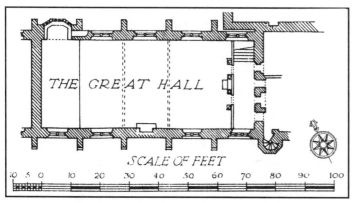

Figure 2 Ground plan of Magdalen College. Adapted from *Historical Monuments in the City of Oxford*, opposite p 72.

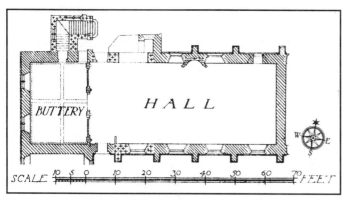

Figure 3 Ground plan of St John's College. Adapted from *Historical Monuments in the City of Oxford*, opposite p 104.

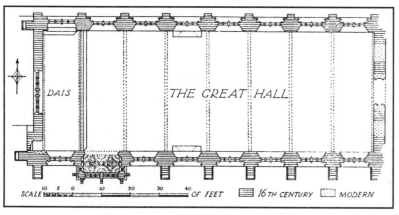

Figure 4 Ground plan of Christ Church hall. Adapted from *Historical Monuments in the City of Oxford*, p 34.

houses of ye stage' (see p 120). John Bereblock (see pp 136–41), who observed the end result, describes the walls and the ceiling of the hall as lined with gold panelling to create the effect of an ancient Roman palace ('veteris Romani Palatij'). While scaffolds for the audience were placed at one end of the hall and along the side walls, boxes for the more important spectators were built at the top of the scaffolds, and ordinary spectators ('populus') stood around the stage. The stage platform may have been placed at the west end of the hall, opposite the screen, with a throne for Elizabeth, who sat facing the audience.[16] Scenery for the plays consisted of classical stage houses, resembling magnificent palaces ('magnifica palatia'), which also served as the actors' dressing rooms. This may have been a typical academic theatre, elaborated with a throne for the queen behind the stage; nevertheless, information to support a full reconstruction is wanting.

Observers of the 1566 Christ Church plays commented on two further matters. First, a doorway was pierced at the level of the first storey through the end wall of the east range of the main quadrangle; then a gallery was hung within the stairwell leading to the antechamber of the hall. This tremendous engineering feat was undertaken merely so the queen could walk from her lodgings to the hall without descending to ground level.[17] (Though the doorway was closed up again, its outline can still be traced in the north wall of the corner stairwell.) Second, the crowd pressed so unrelentingly on a stairway near the hall – perhaps in the same stairwell – that three people were killed by falling masonry and others injured. (The queen sent her surgeon, but the play went on.)

Very little information survives concerning the plays performed for the royal visit of 1592 apart from the fact that the venue was Christ Church hall. In all probability the stage was taken out of storage at the last minute and set up as in 1566.

A great deal of information, by contrast, survives about the theatre erected for the royal visit of James i and his family in August 1605. This time an entirely new theatre, with a fresh and contemporary design by Inigo Jones, was constructed in Christ Church hall under the direction of Simon Basil, the king's comptroller (subsequently surveyor of the works), and by consultation with Sir Thomas Chaloner. While the Records (see pp 277–321) testify to much activity and expense (including a cost of £177 for 'the Kings comminge') as well as to the participation of Jones, who is reported to have been paid £50 for his efforts (see p 301), the crucial document for understanding the new theatre is an architectural drawing in the British Library, identified and analysed at length by John Orrell (see Appendix 1). Jones created a perspectival theatre – the first known in England – enhanced by the use of periaktoi. Spectators expressed amazement that the stage picture could change 'not only for the change for each show each day but also for the change of scene in one and the same play' (see p 306, as translated).

Unusually for a college theatre, the stage platform (at the upper end of the hall) was raked. Moreover, three sides of the stage were closed off by the periaktoi, which by coordinated rotation produced three different scenic backdrops. The main seating scaffolds at the lower end of the hall were also raked, with benches curving round in roughly concentric arcs. At the centre-point of those arcs stood a platform for the king's throne. For this particular king, however, the innovation was not a success. Perspective theory locates the privileged viewing point at the 'point of sight,' along the principal axis and somewhere in the middle of the audience. But James had never been planted in the middle of any audience and refused to sit where he ought. At his own insistence his seat was moved farther from the stage – but too far back for easy hearing. Thus he neither saw nor heard as Jones intended. Some of the 1605 plays were nevertheless a hit, helped no doubt by costumes secured from London (see pp 288– 93).

Inigo Jones served once more as principal designer for the royal visit of Charles I and his consort in August 1636.[18] The scaffolding of 1605 may well have been recycled, but Jones replaced the antique periaktoi with modern stage shutters thrust out in successive pairs from stage left and stage right to create even more astonishing scenic transformations, which were even more dependent on perspective theory. We have noted above (see pp 606–7) the contribution made by court professionals, Brian Twyne's rapturous description of the end result, and the queen's desire to revive Cartwright's *The Royal Slave* at Hampton Court. William Laud's reminiscence captures nicely the degree to which drama had become visual effect: 'I caused the University to send both the Clothes, and the Perspectives of the Stage' (see p 541).

Meanwhile, an occasional glimpse may be gained of dramatic activity in St John's College hall, as for example during the performance of The Christmas Prince over the winter of 1607-8. Events were first organized around a fire blazing there as well as in the college parlour over several successive nights in late October and early November. Thomas Tucker, elected Christmas prince, was carried in triumph about the hall and thence to his chamber (see p 342). A prefatory show called *Ara Fortunae* 'was not thought worthye of a stage or scaffoldes, and therfore after supper ye tables were onlye sett together, which was not done without great toyle & difficullty by reason of ye great multitude of people (which by ye default of ye Dore-keepers, and diuers others, euery mann bringinge in his freindes) had fild ye Hall before wee thought of it' (see p 347).

Subsequent projects were deemed worthy of a complete theatre, although a performance that should have gone forward on Holy Innocents' Day (28 December) had to be deferred a day, 'the Carpenters beeing no-way ready with the stage or scaffold's' (see p 355). A subsequent 'Bill of expences' – a rich source of theatrical information – includes an expenditure of £5 'to the Carpenters for setting up the stage scaffolds twise and lending boardes etcætera' and £1 'for nayles' (see pp 359–60). Other plays were performed privately 'in the lodging' (see pp 361–2.) The academic term was to have begun on Monday, 11 January, but because of frost, 'as also by reason the hall was still pestered with the stage and scaffolds which were suffered to stand still in expectation of the Comedy,' the president simply postponed the beginning of term for one week (see p 362).

In 1636 Henry Burton published the story of a carpenter who, 'undertaking to mend a Stage in S. Iohns Colleidge on the Saturday night,' worked into Sunday morning 'that the Stage might be ready against the Munday following.' Suffering divine punishment he 'fell backward from the Stage, being not farre from the ground, and brake his neck, and so ended his life in a fearfull Tragedy' (see p 558). Nevertheless, Archbishop Laud selected the hall for the performance of a supplementary play for the royal visit of August 1636, at a cost to himself 'for the stage & Comedy' of £394 13s (see p 531).

All in all, the plays presented in St John's College hall on its 'stage and scaffolds' were more representative of academic drama at Oxford than the extravaganzas presented for royal consumption at Christ Church.

Entertainment in the Colleges and University

For almost the whole of the period covered by the Records, academic prohibitions alternated with college or University sponsorship of public or private entertainment. The earliest known prohibition by the University is dated c 1300. University College enacted prohibitions by statute in 1292, Queen's in 1340, New College c 1398, All Souls in 1443, Magdalen in 1483, Merton in 1484–5, Balliol in 1507, Corpus in 1516–17, Brasenose in 1521, and Christ Church c 1546 and c 1550. Merton College enforced its prohibitions by order in 1499–1500, the University in 1500–1. A comprehensive restriction against performances by professional acting companies, promulgated by the University in 1584, is discussed elsewhere (see below, p 614).

Academic sponsorship of entertainment is exemplified for the early years by Exeter's support of a play in 1360–1 and Merton's payment for a 'mayynge' in 1386–7. The play in this instance was probably extramural, while the 'mayynge' was probably a festive repast provided by the college on or about the first of May. The two events may be taken as representing two hypothetically distinguishable kinds of activity – on the one hand academic support for extramural performers, whether the performance occurred outside or within the college, and on the other hand support for activities in which members of the college were the performers.

Extramural entertainers hired by the colleges or University for intramural performances are discussed below under 'Travelling Entertainers' and 'Music and Dance: Town and Gown.' Here it may simply be noted that external musicians were listed in academic accounts with much scribal ingenuity, not only as the familiar 'buccinatores,' 'histriones,' 'musici,' 'tibicines,' and 'tubicines,' but also as 'fidicines,' 'fistulans,' 'spondiales,' and 'symphonisti.' Such performers are recorded at Merton from 1431–2, New College from 1460–1, All Souls from 1467–8, and Queen's from 1541–2. The University as distinct from its colleges paid performers from as early as 1471–2 (the king's trumpeters). Players or musicians were recorded at All Souls from 1467–8, at Magdalen from 1485–6, and at Queen's from 1541–2. In addition 'satrape' from the town provided vocal music to Merton College from at least 1505–6 and possibly to Magdalen College as early as 1485–6.

BOY BISHOPS AND COLLEGE LORDS

On 5 December (St Nicholas' Eve) or less commonly on 28 December (feast of the Holy Innocents) at least four colleges sponsored ceremonies of the boy bishop: Durham College from 1399–1400, All Souls from c 1440, Lincoln from 1456–7, and Magdalen from 1482–3. Magdalen maintained the tradition until at least 1529–30, Lincoln until at least 1539–40.[19]

Many Oxford colleges appointed a 'lord,' often for the Christmas season, following the ancient and popular tradition of the 'lord of misrule.'[20] A king of beans ('Rex fabarum'), apparently celebrated on the vigil of the feast of St Edmund (19 November), is recorded at Merton College from 1485–6 to 1539–40. Entries in the same accounts record an annual 'fire,' evidently a festive gathering at which members of the college enjoyed the wintertime comforts of a good fire and refreshments. (Judging from variations in the names of the principals over successive years, the 'fire' was distinct from the king of beans.) Further evidence concerning Merton's king of beans is gathered in Appendix 5.

A useful description of a college lord occurs in a Magdalen school exercise book (c 1512–27): 'this boye playd the lord yester day a mong his companyounce a poyntyng euery man his office. oon he mayd his carver an other his butlere: an other his porter. an other bi cause ... he wold not do as he commandyd hym he toke and ... to bete hyme ...' (the phrase 'to bete hyme' means 'beat him thoroughly'). Magdalen account books contain an enigmatic reference to a lord in 1559–60. John Ponet's *Apologie* (1554–5) alludes to a (possibly fictional) New College lord and minion from an earlier decade. An antiquarian note here dated c 1559 refers to a 'Princeps Natalicius' or 'Christmas Prince' at Trinity College, while a letter of 3 April 1599 reveals that Christ Church usually chose an emperor but that year chose a boy of evidently feminine aspect as empress. Richard Carnsew's diary (1574–5) alludes to the appointment of a lord at Broadgates Hall (later Pembroke College), while Richard Madox's diary notes under January 1581/2 Richard Latewar's 'oration in ye name of kyng aulrede' and a 'savage who ... yelded his hollyn club.' Peter Heylyn reports (1617–18): 'November 20 Mr Holt chosen Lord (Christmas Lord of Magdalen college) & solemnly inaugurated on ye 2d of Ianuary following: In which I represented the Embassador of the Universitie of Vienna.' No doubt this was a jocular rather than a formal representation of the University of Vienna.

Events at St John's College over the 1607/8 festival season (30 October to 13 February) are recorded in extraordinary detail in a manuscript text dubbed by modern editors, appropriately enough, 'The Christmas Prince.' Enterprising students resurrected a ceremony that had lain dormant for thirty years (since 1577–8), when John Case was lord. Thomas Tucker was elected prince by ballot on 30 October 1607 after John Towse refused the office. The full season comprised eight plays or playlets, followed by a ninth *(Periander)* that was probably an independent event. Meanwhile Christ Church responded with a satirical play called *Yuletide*. The full text of The Christmas Prince provides an unrivalled view of the festive life of an early seventeenth-century Oxford college.[21]

OTHER ENTERTAINMENT

Oxford colleges indulged in further varieties of entertainment, some familiar from more secular venues, some defying exact definition. Canterbury College funded degree feasts beginning in 1395. All Souls paid for a hobby horse in 1467–8. 'Spectacles' are recorded at Magdalen from 1559–60 to 1606–7. Trinity College paid for a spectacle in 1564–5. Christ Church provided masques (or 'maskes') and mummings in 1598–9, while the records of St John's, from 1586–7 onward, are replete with shows, sports, interludes, merriments, masques, and a 'mock-show,' while a 'founders show' is recorded with some frequency from 1621–2 onward. Another event, called an 'exercise,' appears in the accounts from 1598–9 to 1601–2, described in 1600–1 as 'An exercyse of the Studentes in Latin Verse acted in Master presidentes Lodging.' From 1593–4 comes a single reference to a 'salting': judging from more elaborate records surviving at

Cambridge, this was a mock-academic ceremony characterized by general irreverence and sophomoric humour.[22] Finally, probate records, beginning as early as 1427–8, occasionally record the private ownership of musical instruments by individual members of various colleges.

Travelling Entertainers

The first travelling entertainers known to have been paid by the colleges were anonymous 'histrionibus' paid by Canterbury College in 1410–11. The first entertainer or entertainers whose patron is named visited Merton in 1431–2 under the patronage of Humphrey, duke of Gloucester. In the over one hundred years between these visits and 1541 we have evidence of fourteen more patronized troupes, four sets of entertainers, and a number of anonymous troupes identified in the University records by their place of origin. No other entry for playing companies (as opposed to trumpeters and pipers) appears in the University records until 1575–6 when the players of the chancellor of the University, the earl of Leicester, were paid 20s by Magdalen College. Three years later in 1578–9 the players of Leicester's second wife, Lettice Knollys, countess of Essex, were paid 10s 'for paines taken in the quire the last holie daies.'

In 1584, in a move similar to one taken in Cambridge in 1575, Convocation decreed:

> that no common stage players be permitted to vse or do anye such thinge with in the precincte of the vniuersitye And if it happen by extraordinarye meanes yat stage players shall gett or obtane leaue by the maior or other wayse yet it shall not be lawfull for anye master bachiler or scholler aboue the age of eighteene to repaire or go to see anye such thinge vnder paine of imprisonment And if any vnder the age of eighteene shall presume to do anye thinge contrarye to this statute the partye so offendinge shall suffer open punishment in St Maries Church according to the discrecion of the vichauncellor or Proctors (see p 195).[23]

From this time on players were regularly paid by the University not to play. Only three records may indicate that travelling companies were paid to play thereafter by University officials. The first is a payment to the lord admiral's men in 1587–8, which follows immediately after an entry in which Leicester's men were paid the same amount (20s) 'vt cum suis ludis sine maiore Academiæ molestia discedant' ('so that they would depart with their plays (or pastimes) without greater trouble to the University'). The second is a payment to Queen Anne's men in 1613–14 and the third is to the king's men in 1615–16, where, among a total of five payments by the vice-chancellor to performers related to the royal family, there appears a payment of 40s to the players. Neither of these last entries is followed by a qualifying proviso.

Despite the 1584 statute, it is clear that 'common stage players' still found ready clients in the city itself. The University could not enforce a prohibition against players in the city and the decree made it clear that it was the individual members of the University who were to be punished if they attended plays sponsored by the mayor and council, not the city officials. The presence of players in the city and the apparent laxness of the University in enforcing its own decree have allowed the survival of such eyewitness accounts as Henry Jackson's touching and immensely informative description of a contemporary performance of Shakespeare's *Othello* in 1609–10 by the king's men (see Appendix 10), as well as the extraordinary information from Thomas Crosfield that in 1633–4 players lodging in the King's Arms had brought fourteen plays with them (see p 514).

Although Crosfield's diary records many kinds of entertainers that were on the road during the 1620s and 1630s, there is no record of payment in the city accounts after 1617. Two circumstances may explain the disappearance of the evidence. One is the increasing tendency to give the mayor what amounts to a petty cash allowance. This is revealed by studying the accounting patterns in the audited corporation accounts. By 1640 the allowance had become an advance of £5 to the incoming mayor and a repayment to the outgoing mayor of £35.[24] The players may have been paid from this purse, after which the payment was noted in accounts that do not survive. Another place where such payments and other payments to entertainers may be hidden is in items for the recorder and other civic officials of repayment for 'entertainment at the assizes.'[25]

The city and the University shared the same geographical space and just as citizens and tourists today attend concerts in the Sheldonian Theatre and plays in the colleges while members of the University support local cultural activities, so in the sixteenth and seventeenth centuries members of the University went to plays in the city while citizens were invited to shows in the colleges (see p 371). The colleges also hired local musicians for their special events and sometimes for their college plays. The performances of *Othello* and *The Alchemist* by the king's men described by Henry Jackson in 1610 were sponsored by the city who paid 20s for the performance on 5 August. Crosfield's diary tells us that there was much to be seen 'for money in ye City' in 1630–1, beginning with plays and going on to animal acts – a list of entertainment possibilities familiar from the Coventry records in the same period.[26] Crosfield also records two performances each of two well-known puppet plays – William Sands' *The Chaos of the World* and William Gosling's *Destruction of Jerusalem* between 1628 and 1635.

The city fathers of Oxford were consumers rather than producers of culture. Unlike their counterparts in many other important provincial cities, they seem not to have ventured into sponsoring pageantry or drama. They were, however, generous patrons of itinerant entertainers. In the sixteenth and early seventeenth centuries they were particularly generous to those attached to the royal house who were frequently in the city because of the royal residence in nearby Woodstock. Of the over eighty payments to travelling entertainers from 1554 to 1617, over sixty per cent were to performers associated with the reigning monarch. Queen Mary's players performed in the guildhall in 1556–7. Queen Elizabeth's jester entertained the mayor and council three times between 1560 and 1567.[27] Her bearwards – first Richard Dorrington and then Ralph Bowes – were paid fourteen times between 1560 and 1581 and again in 1597.[28] The first baiting was part of the entertainment for the earl of Bedford, then the high steward of the city. Entertainers travelling under Elizabeth's patronage visited four times between 1565 and 1572, and the newly formed queen's men played in the city nine times between 1585 and 1599, and on three occasions (in 1589–90, 1594–5, and 1598–9) they were paid by the University not to play. There were thirteen visits of three Jacobean royal troupes. The king's men were in Oxford eight times from 1603 to 1622. Anne of Denmark's troupe visited four times and Prince Charles' once. The 'kinge*s* Mynstrelle*s*' were paid in 1554–5 even though Mary had been on the throne since 19 July 1553, and her minstrels were paid as the 'quenes Mynstrells' in 1556–7.

The last category of royal servants paid by both the council and the colleges consisted of men who were as much civil servants as they were entertainers. These were the trumpeters who first appear at the end of Elizabeth's reign and with increasing frequency during the Stuart period. It was the practice of the trumpeters to demand fees from the city and the colleges when the monarch simply passed through the city on the way to Woodstock. Thomas Crosfield notes that the city fathers refused to pay the trumpeters in 1630–1 when they 'demanded some fee from ye towne as due' as they had 'ye time also of their being there before' to the displeasure of the lord chamberlain. Some years later the city formalized its refusal to pay such fees by an order taken on 3 September 1638:

> Item whereas som*m*e of the kinges servants in respect the kinge by accident rode through this Cittie in his progresse doe demaund ffees of Ma*ste*r Maio*ur* The opinion of this house is That the kinge not Com*m*inge in State noe ffees are due vnto them It is therefore agreed that if m*aste*r Maio*ur* be questioned concerninge the same that hee shalbee defended at the Cittie chardge.[29]

The colleges, however, continued regular payments to the Stuart trumpeters leading to the impression that the travellers were exploiting the desire of the University to curry royal favour to their own advantage.

Leicester's men were the most frequent non-royal players paid by the city. They were paid by the city five times, twice while his players were still styled 'Lord Robert Dudley's players' before he became chancellor of the University in 1564, and an additional two times by the University. In only one year, the year of his death in 1588, was the company paid by both the city and the University. In 1585–6 the city paid his musicians rather than his players. This was in the period immediately after the establishment of the queen's men when Leicester's acting company, deprived of some of its star actors, seems to have been somewhat in eclipse.[30] The admiral's men made five visits between 1586 and 1596, including the one to the University in 1587–8.

The players of Leicester's second wife, Lettice Knollys, visited three times between 1576 and 1580. On one occasion (1576–7) the city not only paid the company but also spent what appears to be 6s on a banquet. During the Christmas season in 1578–9, as we have seen, the company helped out the choir at Christ Church. The same company under the patronage of the new earl of Essex, Robert Devereux, may have come in 1585–6 but were definitely in Oxford in 1589–90 and again in 1596–7, the year he became high steward. The players of the earl of Sussex came twice, 1572–3 and 1575–6, and were paid in March 1573 under the name of the lord chamberlain's players after he was made lord chamberlain. Single visits were also made by the players of the earls of Oxford (1556–7), Warwick (1561–2), Pembroke (1595–6), Derby (1595–6), and Hertford (1605–6), and Lords Strange (1592–3) and Morley (paid to play by the city but to go away by the University in 1594–5).

CIVIC PLAY VENUES

Little is known about the conditions under which visiting entertainers performed in Oxford. There are three specific references to playing in the guildhall. The first two are for Queen Mary's players in 1556–7 and Warwick's men in 1561–2. On 17 February 1579/80 the council passed an order 'that no Mayor of this Cytie or his deputie frome henceforth/ shall geve leave to any players/ to playe within the Guilde hall or the Lower hall/ or in the Guilde hall courte withowt consent of the Counsell.' This argues that all three areas of the guildhall may have been used by players. Possibly as a result of this order, no acting companies were paid by the council until 1585–6 when the ban was lifted for a possible performance by the earl of Essex's players. No playing place is mentioned in subsequent entries although the guildhall remained the logical place for the performances for the city and it has been suggested that Henry Jackson's description of *Othello* and *The Alchemist* in 1610 argues for an indoor theatre such as the guildhall.[31] Two inns are also associated with plays. In 1559–60 Dudley's players performed 'at mr Cogans.' H.E. Salter has identified Coggan's establishment as the King's Head, an inn run by the Coggan family from 1556. Salter describes it as 'a second class inn with an approach from Cornmarket and another from Sewy's Lane, and it had a large yard where the plays could be given' (Figure 5, p 618).[32] From the evidence of Crosfield's diary, a second inn, the King's Arms that still stands at the corner of Holywell and Parks Road, became popular as a playing place in the seventeenth century.[33]

Music and Dance: Town and Gown

The complex interrelationship between the musicians who performed for both the University and the city is perhaps best understood from the vantage point of 1631–2. By that year the demand for secular music in Oxford was great enough that a second troupe of waits was set up solely for the benefit of the University. This troupe was led by John Gerrard, a former city wait, who secured permission from the vice-chancellor to recruit six others to form the 'university music.' In return they promised to perform both 'loude musicke in ye Wynter morninges' to wake up the students in all the colleges and halls and 'very commendable lowe musicke' whenever it should be wanted. In addition they were allowed to perform one benefit concert each year in each of the colleges and halls. Besides Gerrard, the University musicians at this time were John Pollie, Thomas Hallwood, John Stacy, Thomas Jones, and their boys Francis Taylor, Thomas Curtise, William Rogers, and John Moore, making a total of nine, although in his original agreement with the vice-chancellor Gerrard had specified seven as the 'befittinge number for a right broken consort' (see p 502).

The establishment of the second official troupe of musicians was a major innovation and one that was not welcomed by the city musicians. Until 1632 musicians from the city had provided music for the colleges. The records of five colleges show regular annual payments to musicians while six others show occasional payments. Magdalen paid regularly for music at the bursar's feast, settling to an annual 5s by 1593–4. In 1603–4 New College began a regular payment of 6s 8d to 'musicis oppidanis.' Merton provided a similar sum from 1590–1, and

Figure 5 The King's Head Inn (1863), by permission of the Bodleian Library.

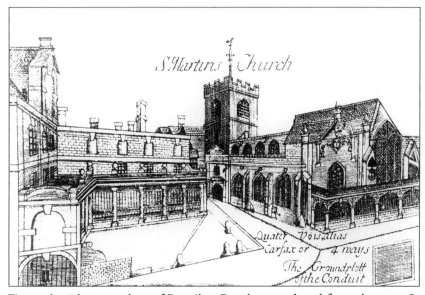

Figure 6 17th-c. woodcut of Penniless Bench, reproduced from the *VCH: Oxford*, vol 4, p 333, by permission of the General Editor.

from 1592–3 Queen's normally spent at least 10s a year on wind players. St John's, however, was the greatest patron of music, spending sometimes over £7 in a year on music that was often associated with their plays. This rich source of patronage may have been one of the reasons William Gibbons (father of the composer Orlando) for the decade of the 1580s returned to his native city of Oxford from Cambridge, where he had been head wait of both the town and the University.

Brian Twyne's Notes on the History of the University Music, compiled in 1632, gave three arguments for the establishment of University musicians. The first was an appeal to historic precedent. Citing a court case heard before the chancellor's court in 1501 involving a musician (a 'stranger') and two sets of Oxford musicians, Twyne concluded (with no evidence beyond the fact that the case was tried in the chancellor's court) that 'there were .2. companies of Musitians in Oxford; ye one for ye Vniuersities vse, ye other for ye Townes vse' (see p 499). His second argument was that music was one of the liberal sciences; men of the city had no right to practise it since 'ye profession of ye liberall sciences belongeth wholly to ye vniuersitie' (see p 503). His third argument again cited historic precedent. City musicians had been paid by the members of the University on a regular basis and were therefore to be considered 'priuiledged persons.' However spurious the arguments, the University musicians were established and St John's seems to have taken on the responsibility of providing their livery. The Jesus College accounts, which begin in 1631–2, include regular payments of 10s to the 'University music.' Both New College and Queen's continued to pay the city musicians until 1635–6 after which they switched their payments to 'musicis academicis.'

In addition to their prescribed duties, the University musicians agreed to make themselves available for 'all occasions of ye vniuersitie' (see p 502). One such occasion seems to have been the royal visit of 1636. Although the music for the plays themselves was composed by the court musicians Henry and William Lawes, £2 for 'Vniuersity Musicke' appears at the end of the extensive Christ Church expense account for the event and Archbishop Laud paid £1 to both the 'Vniuersity Waytes' and the 'Towne Waytes' for their performances at St John's. Perhaps the local musicians provided incidental music for the plays. On earlier occasions the Records show numerous payments to local musicians in connection with college plays.

The opportunity to earn significant money from sources other than the city explains the unusual arrangements between the city musicians and the city. In some towns, such as York, Exeter, or Norwich, the waits were recognizable town servants with regular payments for their wages and their liveries.[34] This was not the case with the Oxford waits. Indeed it was not until 1632–3, the year after the establishment of the University musicians, that the issue of payment to the city musicians was systematically addressed and provision made for their 'Cloakes.' At that time the city council minutes stated that the waits were to be paid for playing 'to this Citty on the Kinges Hollidayes and when the Mayor cometh from London and other publicke meetinges.'

This decree formalized the long-standing custom of civic-sponsored music on the occasion of civic ceremonies. Music was frequently part of the entertainment at the election of the new mayor and bailiffs that took place on the Monday before St Matthew's Day (21 September). The serjeant at mace rang the great bell of St Martin's Church summoning the burgesses to a service of morning prayer. The election was then held and if funds were available, there followed an election dinner for all the freemen – sometimes as many as six hundred in the seventeenth century.[35] A few days after the election the mayor then went to London where he took his oath before the barons of the exchequer. On his return to Oxford he was sometimes (as in 1561) greeted by a trumpeter.

Music was regularly part of the 'riding the franchises' that took place, weather permitting, in August or September. Rather than riding or walking the franchises, the mayor and his party circumnavigated the city largely by boat. The trip began on the Cherwell at Magdalen Bridge and travelled first south, then west across Christ Church Meadow to the Isis, and then north to Godstow. There refreshments were traditionally served and music was often played. The mayor and party then left the boats and walked across Port Meadow and beyond to the Cherwell where they once again took to the river, finally arriving back where they had begun at Magdalen Bridge.

Music was also part of the 17 November Accession Day celebrations held for Elizabeth in 1573–4, 1574–5, and 1576–7. In 1575–6 the same payment was specified as for her 'Coronation daye.' An unusual entry for 1585–6 speaks of musicians for the 'daye of Tryvmphe.' The official musicians played at the proclamation of King James in 1603. An ordinance of 1632–3 makes clear the nature of the music at civic occasions: 'Musitions to haue such allowance for playinge on the kinges hollidaies & other tymes to the Citty as the mayor & thirteene shall thinck fitt.' The musicians traditionally played at Penniless Bench at St Martin's, Carfax (Figure 6, p 618; see p 1110, endnote to OCA: C/FC/1/A1/001 ff 337v, 338). They also frequently played at guild dinners.

The terminology relating to musicians in Oxford is, as so often elsewhere, slippery. From time to time the term 'wait' does appear in these payments but the payment was equally or more likely (especially in guild accounts) to 'musicians' or for 'musicke.' In 1602–3 an order was given that no musicians but waits were to play 'within this Cytie & suburbes.' Any other musician was to be imprisoned. Yet from that year until 1628–9, when a new group of musicians was admitted freemen and named 'waits,' the term was used only once in 1606–7. During the same period, there were two payments for 'musicians' at the Tailors' election dinners (1610–11 and 1619–20). The chamberlains also recorded payments for 'Musitions' at the Accession Day ceremonies in 1605–6 and when the mayor 'rode the ffranchises' that same year. Music was again paid for at the franchise ceremonies in 1613–14 and 1614–15 ('trumpeters') and in 1618–19 ('Musicke'), and most significantly 'the Towne Musick' was ordered to be present at Penniless Bench during the civic celebration marking 'the happie & safe Retorne of the Prince' in 1623–4. Clearly some, if not all, of these references (if the order of 1602–3 was still in effect) were to the waits. The last record of an election of a wait, that of William Stronge in 1639–40, refers to the event as an election of 'one of the Musitions of this Cittie.' We can be sure that a record involved waits if the term was used but the fact that the term was not used does not mean that payment was not to a wait.

The first musicians to be named as town waits were George Ewen and George Buckner in 1577–8, when they had apparently been relieved of their positions and asked to hand in their 'scutchins' or silver medallions of office 'vntill suche tyme as farther order shoulde be taken.'[36]

The keykeepers duly recorded the receipt of the scutcheons in their accounts. In lieu of a regular retainer or livery the scutcheons were the only official indication of which musicians were, indeed, the city musicians. Ewen had been named in the records four times: in 1573–4 for playing at Accession Day, in 1574–5 for playing at the election dinner, in 1575–6 for both the election dinner and coronation festivities, and once in 1576–7 for the Accession Day events. Nothing more was recorded but the difficulties seem to have been resolved since the 'waytes' played at the election dinner in 1579–80.

In 1582–3, when William Gibbons arrived from Cambridge, he was made a freeman of the city, paying the officer's fee of 4s 6d, and given the 'Scuttchins of oure Waytes.' Apparently he had been made chief wait and had charge of all the scutcheons, a fact duly noted by the keykeepers in the next year. Gibbons rented a tenement in St Martin's parish from William Frere, a wealthy member of the town council.[37] Young Orlando, who would gain national fame as a musician himself, was baptized at St Martin's in December 1583.[38]

In 1587–8 George Buckner became head wait and the three scutcheons were to be delivered to him. In particular, 'mr Gybbons is to make one more to be likewise Delivered to the said George.' Nothing more is heard of Gibbons as a wait or musician in Oxford. He returned to Cambridge in 1589 and by 1591 was apparently once again University wait and head town wait. Despite the order that Buckner was to receive the scutcheons from Gibbons in 1587–8, the keykeepers continued to record that they were in Gibbons' possession. Indeed, the notation continued until 1615–16, twenty years after Gibbons' death in Cambridge in 1595. Subsequent appointments of Oxford waits made a great point of requiring that the new waits supply their own scutcheons, which they were to leave to the city when they left office. Evidently Gibbons never gave the scutcheons to Buckner but sold them or took them with him to Cambridge. George Buckner was made free in 1596–7, along with another musician, Leonard Major, but Buckner was dead by his own hand by August 1599. He had been living in a property in the parish of St Mary Magdalen owned by the University; as a suicide his entire estate of £18 19s 10d was forfeit to the University (see p 258).

The next wait to be admitted was John Baldwin the elder, made free on the payment of the officer's fee and 2s 6d for 'a leather buckett' in 1602–3. That year the waits played for the proclamation of James I. There follows a long silence in the records but in 1628 Baldwin was once again named as wait with his son John Baldwin the younger.[39] The other waits named were Sampson Stronge, who had been an apprentice, and three others who paid the officer's fee and the price of the leather bucket. These were John Gerrard (who later founded the University music), Philip Golledge, and Richard Burren. Details surrounding these appointments included the requirement that each wait produce a scutcheon before he receive his first payment at Christmas and that all waits hand in their scutcheons once a year as was the custom with the serjeants at mace and their maces. The council specified that they had the right to name replacements. Possibly in the long period where no new waits were named, the waits themselves had been naming replacements. During this period a man named George Payne seems to have been named a wait. In 1637–8 William Stronge (referred to only as 'Sampsons sonne') and William Hilliard and his eldest son were also named as waits. Stronge's official appointment appeared in the 1639–40 minutes where he was to replace Payne. In 1638 it was decided to limit admission to the waits to those who had first served an apprenticeship, perhaps a roundabout way of ensuring that the job could pass freely from father to son. The names of two other city musicians who do not appear in the Records – William Higgins (1608) and Thomas Bennett (1636) – can be recovered from the records of the chancellor's court for this period.[40]

Although REED volumes cover only secular music, it should be kept in mind that all of the musicians named here had other sources of income, some of which would have involved them in liturgical music. In addition, among the University waits, John Gerrard was a licensed alehousekeeper and also ran a musical instrument and book shop. The inventory of his shop compiled at his death in 1635 gives a good idea of the variety of instruments available in Oxford (see p 530). Francis Jones became an assistant to the first Heather Professor of Music, Richard Nicholson, and Thomas Curtise was an organist at Magdalen College. Many of the city waits also ran taverns. All of these musicians gave private lessons to students wishing to learn the gentlemanly arts of playing the lute or the viol.[41]

One of the other gentlemanly arts in the early seventeenth century, especially if a student had pretentions to become a courtier, was dancing. The need for a dancing master is listed in a seventeenth-century Christ Church document along with the necessity of engaging a riding master, fencing master, and master of instrumental and vocal music.[42] The dancing schools of Oxford were so renowned in this period 'as to influence a father in the choice of a university.'[43] The most prominent school (and the one that appears in these records) was in the Bocardo, the building near the North Gate that belonged to the city and served as a jail. The school was begun before 1606 by John Bosseley, a musician of the city. His son, also John, was still teaching dance there in 1661. Among the courtiers trained at the school were Lord Percy of Alnwick, John Evelyn, and Prince Charles (after the battle of Edge Hill).[44] The school is first mentioned in a council minute for 18 September 1606, when John Harington was seeking to sublet part of the property from Bosseley. The latter was given a new lease in May 1610 for thirty-one years at the annual rent of 26s 8d. An indenture drawn up at the same time details the property. One restriction put on its use was that no one was to dance 'in and vppon the said Demysed Roome Sollere or Chamber ... betweene the Howres of twoe of the clocke in the afternoon and ffive of the Cloke in the fforenoone.' In the next year Bosseley was granted a licence to transfer his lease to Thomas Charles, musician. Bosseley senior seems to have died between this date and 1626–7 when Charles was instructed not to let the school to a Mr Sett. In 1635–6 Bosseley's son John and William Stokes, who is said to have 'bredd vpp the said Iohn Bossely thexecutor and other the Children of the said Iohn Bossely Deceased,' sought a new lease. The property was viewed in order to adjust the rent. The indenture that accompanies the new lease allowed the school to hold classes all day, with hours of silence from 10 PM to 5 AM.

Local Entertainment

From the convent of Benedictine nuns at Godstow we have rare and early evidence of an abbess of misrule tradition on the feast of the Holy Innocents contained in a letter written to the

abbess by Archbishop Pecham in 1284. The other religious houses that were so much a part
of the life of Oxford in the later Middle Ages have left us little evidence of entertainment
activity. None of the three men's houses that could be considered within the geographic scope
of this collection – the Cistercian abbey of Rewley or the two houses of Augustinian canons,
Osney and St Frideswide – has left any trace of their day to day activities in 'household'
accounts that survive.

By contrast the abundance of evidence from Oxford parishes dating back to 1423 is remarkable. It is as if the scholars who served the parishes understood the value of the written records
and encouraged their churchwardens to preserve them on parchment rolls, not in the paper
books favoured by the wardens in the country parishes. Similarly, generations of scholarly
parishioners preserved the accounts, in some cases lovingly pasting them into large guard
books.[45] It is to the scholarly instincts of generations of Oxford churchmen that we owe such
a wealth of detail.

The Records tell us little of the kind of parish drama that was a feature of the country parishes
in the surrounding areas.[46] Despite the popular picture from Chaucer's *Miller's Tale* of thriving
parish drama in Oxford, little evidence of such activity survives. Only St Peter in the East has
any hint of true drama. Merton College paid players from the parish for a performance in
Holywell in 1469. There is also evidence from the St Peter's churchwardens' accounts that they
rented out their costumes in 1488–9 and 1495–6. But if they did not pursue the performance
of plays, Oxford parishes were seemingly unusual in the enthusiasm with which they pursued
the custom of gathering money at Hocktide – the second Monday and Tuesday after Easter.
The custom was that groups of young men or women of the parish would go into the streets,
capture members of the opposite sex, and hold them to mock ransom until they had given
them money. The young people would then move on to their next victim. Although there is
some evidence of men engaged in hocking in Oxford, the overwhelming number of entries is
for young women undertaking the gathering. The reason for this is not far to seek. The number
of well-to-do young men attending the University clearly made the game worthwhile. An
eyewitness account of an early sixteenth-century Oxford hocking survives in a Magdalen school
exercise book, *c* 1512–27, where the writer complains that 'wether I wold or no I was fayne
to giue them su*m*what.'

The survival of hocking customs of the parishes into the seventeenth century reflects the
unique situation of Oxford as a University town.[47] Clearly the presence of the students meant
that the parishes were unwilling to give up such an easy source of income. St Michael at the
North Gate was still sending its women into the streets on Hock Monday and holding a
Whitsun ale in 1642. The parishioners of St Martin, St Mary Magdalen, and St Peter in the
East were hocking until 1640. There is even a rare entry in the late Jesus College records of
2s 6d being given 'To the hocking women' in 1635–6.

All the parishes with surviving evidence held ales at Whitsun and only the evidence of St Mary
the Virgin lacks indication that the event included some form of music or customary activity.
The only years when no ales were recorded in these records were the years of Edward VI's reign
and 1626 when an order was issued 20 April prohibiting them 'by reason of the tyme of
infection and danger.' Some parishes occasionally leased a house in which to hold their ales.

For example in 1517–18 St Peter in the East paid George Coke 3s 8d 'for hys hows at wytsontyd' and in 1576–7 St Mary Magdalen paid one of their own tenants, Dr John Case, 4s 'for the use of his howsse at Whytsontyde.' In 1610–11 Thomas Burnham asked the parish for 10s for the use of his house 'for the Church ale.' St Mary Magdalen specified the use of their church house for the ale in 1614–15. The lease of the church house of St Aldate drawn up on 30 January 1569/70 specifies that the tenant, Richard Williams, must vacate the premises 'for the space of fifteine dayes yearely at or aboute the feaste of Penthecost yf church ale or whiteson ale for the whole parish of saynte Tolles aforesayde shalbe at the sayde feaste Penthecost there be kept in the same house.'[48]

All five parishes with extended runs of records – St Martin, St Mary Magdalen, St Michael at the North Gate, St Peter in the East, and St Peter le Bailey – noted payments to minstrels for their ale and the only roll from St Michael at the South Gate also recorded payment of 2s to a minstrel in 1501–2. Only St Michael at the North Gate does not specifically name a May or summer pole.

An antiquarian record gives All Saints a 'kinge game' in 1482–3. St Peter le Bailey twice recorded expenses for mending the 'gowne and kyrtell' (1537–8, and 1540–1) of the queen – presumably the May queen. In 1561–2 St Mary Magdalen sold for a shilling 'an olde saye coot of grene wyche was made for the lord for wettsontyd.' Finally, the early records of St Peter le Bailey speak of a pageant lion and dragon (1468–9). Although scattered among many entries that simply record the profits from the Whitsun ales, this evidence argues that the parishes of Oxford had annual festivities with many of the features of the country parishes elsewhere in the Thames Valley.[49] The only activity missing from these records is the custom of Robin Hood gatherings, although they were part of the Whitsun events in nearby Woodstock.[50] Most of the parishes were still holding occasional ales in the 1630s. This is considerably later than in most other parts of the country, although the pattern for ales is similar in much of the equally conservative surrounding countryside in north Berkshire and Oxfordshire.

Blood sports, although they appear infrequently in the Records, seem to have been a constant part of the life of the town. Bearbaiting, particularly when the queen's bearward was in town, was a popular entertainment. There is no mention of a bear pit but a reference from the Magdalen school copy book (c 1495) places the baiting inside the precincts of the castle. There was a bullring at an unspecified location as early as 1414, one in Carfax until 1616, and another 'outside the North Gate,' which was inside the parish bounds of St Mary Magdalen.[51] Thomas Crosfield provides a graphic description of a bullbaiting in St Clement's parish in 1635–6.

Aside from the apparent popularity of blood sports, the picture one gains from the entertainment records of Oxford is one of great decorum.[52] Yet underlying this decorum the constant town-gown tension occasionally found expression during traditional celebrations. Three instances of rowdy confrontation between scholars and townsfolk during festive activities occur in these records. The earliest, for 1306, took place on Midsummer Eve when a clerk, Gilbert Foxlee, was killed. The second was the 1598 May game confrontation between some youth of the town, including the mayor's son, William Furness, and the authorities of the University.

The description includes cross-dressing, a woman decked out as a May queen, and morris dancing. The third instance took place in 1617 when 'Actors in the Rydeing Company disguised vpon May day' were held to be in contempt, not of the University but of the mayor and council. These last two references may speak to a traditional May game riding that was not part of the licensed celebrations of the city or the parishes but rather a more subversive activity. The Holywell prosecution involving a maypole incident in 1641 also attests to an undercurrent of rowdiness and dispute more familiar in records from the countryside and other parts of England.[53]

Institutions and Documents

Most of the documents that provide evidence for dramatic and secular musical performance in Oxford may be assigned to particular institutions, organized here under Colleges, The University, and civic, guild, ecclesiastical, and legal headings. Institutional documents are listed under the institutions to which they logically belong, rather than under the libraries where they are currently housed.

Documents that cannot be linked to a particular institution are described under supplementary headings: these include court or diplomatic documents, private correspondence, personal records, histories and reminiscences, play texts, and poems and songs. To enable the reader to locate document descriptions where the category is not obvious, marginal codes have been supplied as a finding aid: see Symbols (p 2) for explanations.

While most documents are described in considerable detail, an exception may be made for any item currently housed in the Bodleian Library, most of whose manuscripts are already described in print. Thus Ashmole and Rawlinson MSS are described in nineteenth-century 'Quarto' catalogues, while others, including those from the important Anthony Wood collections, are described in the *Summary Catalogue of Western Manuscripts in the Bodleian Library*, Falconer Madan (ed), 7 vols (Oxford, 1895–1953).[1] The number assigned to each manuscript by the *Summary Catalogue* is here given after its shelf-mark, preceded by the symbol '*sc.*'[2] No attempt is made to tabulate the complete contents of poetic or antiquarian miscellanies. Relationships between REED entries that occur in more than one manuscript or later printed texts are generally analysed in full.

Duke Humfrey's Library, which has retained a separate identity within the Bodleian Library, is shortened in academic parlance to 'Duke Humfrey': 'in Duke Humfrey' thus means 'on the reference shelves of Duke Humfrey's Library within the Bodleian Library.'

The histories and archives of many Oxford institutions, academic as well as civic, are available in an ongoing series of volumes published by the Oxford Historical Society.

The Colleges

All Oxford colleges founded before 1642 retain physical custody of their archives with the single exception of All Souls, whose archives are housed in the Bodleian Library. College archives are generally housed in a muniment room that is physically and administratively separate from the library. Cataloguing ranges from the meticulous (New College, St John's) to the minimal (Lincoln, Oriel, Trinity). College libraries are the likely repository of materials of a literary character, such as letters and diaries.

Most Oxford colleges had at least two bursars, sometimes more, who had separate areas of responsibility but who also checked each other's work. It is not unusual, therefore, to find multiple hands in a given document and multiple entries for the same expense. Some accounts are annual, others semi-annual, quarterly, or weekly. The accounting year usually began at Michaelmas (29 September) but there are important exceptions to this rule, such as The Queen's College, whose accounting year began in July. Where quarters were indicated they almost always began on Michaelmas (29 September), Christmas (25 December), Lady Day (25 March), and the nativity of St John the Baptist (24 June). Sometimes the terms are named ('Terminus Natalitii'), more often they are numbered ('Terminus 2us'). Unless the actual calendar date is given, an expense may be datable only within the accounting period. An audit of each term's accounts was held in the first week of the following term, culminating in a formal dinner often accompanied by musical entertainment.

Bursars' accounts were kept in stages, from rough notes to 'engrossed' accounts prepared for an audit, which usually occurred in November: the amount of detail available for extraction is generally in inverse proportion to the degree of refinement. The weekly accounts preserved at St John's, for example, or the quarterly disbursement books at Christ Church, are a good deal more chatty than the final accounts, which tend to lump individual payments into such categories as 'Other expenses' ('Varia Expensae'), which are of little or no value to a REED editor. The paucity of information about dramatic activities at such colleges as Brasenose and University is largely due to the fact that only the final accounts have survived. Any generalizations about the amount of dramatic activity in a particular college must take such facts into consideration.

Readers requiring a more detailed understanding of college accounting practices are referred to Sir William Blackstone's *Dissertation on the Accounts of All Souls College Oxford* (London, 1898), composed in 1753 for the benefit of the future bursars of All Souls (Blackstone had been bursar in 1747 and 1751). Blackstone aptly concludes that the accounts are, as Alexander Pope said of man's world in the first epistle of his *Essay on Man* (1.6), 'a mighty maze, but not without a plan.'

Unless noted otherwise, the descriptions that follow are based on 'Oxford,' in *Encyclopaedia Britannica*, 11th ed; and *VCH: Oxford*, vol 3. For ease of reference colleges are listed here in alphabetical order rather than by date of foundation.

ALL SOULS COLLEGE

All Souls College was founded in 1438 by Henry Chichele, archbishop of Canterbury. (The name is now commonly spelled without the apostrophe.) Its head is a warden. It is the only Oxford college with no undergraduates (except four Bible clerks).

Most of the archives were deposited in the Bodleian Library in 1966 (ownership and control of access remain with the college). New shelf-marks conform to the new storage arrangements:

see E.F. Jacob, 'All Souls College Archives,' *Oxoniensia* 33 (1969), 89–91. The general Bodleian shelf-mark for the material is 'MS. D.D. All Souls'; 'c.' stands for 'carton.' Access is via Charles Trice Martin, *Catalogue of the Archives in the Muniment Rooms of All Souls' College* (London, 1877), of which a copy, annotated with the new shelf-marks, is kept in Duke Humfrey.

All Souls College Inventory

The inventory is of goods given to the college by its founder, Henry Chichele, archbishop of Canterbury.

Oxford, Bodleian Library, MS. D.D. All Souls c.268, no 210; *c* 1440; Latin; parchment; 2 mbs sewn together in roll form; mb 1: 600mm x 277mm, mb 2: 580mm x 288mm; writing on both sides in 2 and 3 cols.

All Souls College Foundation Statutes

Oxford, All Souls College Archives; 1443; Latin; 42 + iii (following flyleaves are uncut: the number represents 3 'double' leaves), ff 1–40 have needle marks on the outer edges, suggesting that they were previously sewn in a different format (upside down?), then unstitched and resewn; 308mm x 219mm (204mm x 122mm); unnumbered; excellent condition; decorated initial capitals, the opening initial is absent, suggesting original plans for an illumination, headers are enlarged and written in red ink; contemporary leather binding, 45mm x 42mm seal pendant.

All Souls College Bursars' Accounts

These are on parchment, and constitute the final annual accounts. There are also some paper rolls, comprising draft accounts. Those examined proved identical with the final accounts. For some years only the draft rolls survive. Accounts of one or the other type survive for all years since 1446, except the following: 1461–2, 1463–4, 1466–7, 1468–9, 1471–3, 1475–9, 1482–3, 1485–9, 1490–1, 1492–4, 1496–8, 1503–4, 1512–13, 1548–9, 1566–7, 1569–70, and 1581–2.

The accounting year began on 2 November (All Souls' Day). There is no division into quarters or terms. For a detailed analysis of how the accounts were compiled, see the treatise of Blackstone, cited on p 627.

Excerpts have been taken from the following rolls within the boxes listed.

Oxford, Bodleian Library, MS. D.D. All Souls c.278; 12 rolls in box including accounts for:

1467–8; Latin; parchment; 8 mbs attached serially; 390–707mm x 268–306mm (324–662mm x 210–75mm); unnumbered; accounts written on recto only, bursars' names and year-end date on dorse of first and last mbs; first mb badly frayed. The draft account for this year also survives as a paper roll and is included in this box.

1479–80; Latin; paper; 15 sheets attached serially; 215–400mm x 294–310mm (176–350mm x 170–294mm); modern pencil numbering; accounts written on recto only, bursars' names and year-end date on dorse of last sheet; sheet 1 in poor condition; wrapped with modern paper label and tied with ribbon.

Oxford, Bodleian Library, MS. D.D. All Souls c.283; 14 rolls in box including account for:

1567–8; English and Latin; parchment; 8 mbs attached serially; 388–660mm x 242–50mm (378–660mm x 217–50mm); unnumbered; accounts written on recto only, bursars' names and year-end date on dorse of first and last mbs; tied with white ribbon.

Oxford, Bodleian Library, MS. D.D. All Souls c.284; 15 rolls in box including accounts for:

1572–3; Latin; parchment; 6 mbs attached serially; 250–742mm x 161–200mm (164–738mm x 155–200mm); unnumbered; accounts written on recto only, bursars' names and year-end date on dorse of first and last mbs; tied with string.

1574–5; Latin and English; parchment; 7 mbs attached serially; 331–536mm x 198–207mm (125–525mm x 171–207mm); unnumbered; accounts written on recto only, bursars' names and year-end date on dorse of first and last mbs; tied with white ribbon.

1576–7; English and Latin; parchment; 6 mbs attached serially; 457–528mm x 204–19mm (415–520mm x 187–219mm); unnumbered; accounts written on recto only, bursars' names and year-end date on dorse of first and last mbs; tied with pink ribbon.

1578–9; Latin and English; parchment; 5 mbs attached serially; 255–644mm x 230–9mm (207–635mm x 201–27mm); unnumbered; accounts written on recto only, bursars' names and year-end date on dorse of first and last mbs; tied with white ribbon.

1579–80; English; parchment; 5 mbs attached serially; 533–743mm x 242–51mm (481–724mm x 182–248mm); unnumbered; accounts written on recto only, bursars' names and year-end date on dorse of first mb; tied with pink ribbon.

Oxford, Bodleian Library, MS. D.D. All Souls c.286; 8 rolls in box including accounts for:

1591–2; English and Latin; parchment; 15 mbs attached serially; 528–789mm x 246–55mm (410–789mm x 217–55mm); unnumbered; accounts written on recto only, bursars' names and year-end date on dorse of last mb; tied with contemporary parchment tab and tie attached to final mb.

1592–3; English and Latin; parchment; 18 mbs attached serially; 478–720mm x 242–58mm (396–720mm x 212–58mm); unnumbered; accounts written on recto only, bursars' names and year-end date on dorse of last mb; tied with contemporary parchment tab and tie attached to final mb. The draft account for this year also survives as a paper roll and is included in this box.

Oxford, Bodleian Library, MS. D.D. All Souls c.287; 9 rolls in box including accounts for:

1597–8; English and Latin; parchment; 11 mbs attached serially; 545–652mm x 255–64mm (505–648mm x 225–64mm); unnumbered; accounts written on recto only, bursars' names and year-end date on dorse of first and last mbs; tied with pink ribbon.

1599–1600; Latin and English; parchment; 12 mbs attached serially; 540–652mm x 225–40mm (160–640mm x 195–240mm); unnumbered; accounts written on recto only, bursars' names and year-end date on dorse of first and last mbs; tied with white ribbon.

1600–1; English and Latin; parchment; 11 mbs attached serially; 303–770mm x 315–25mm (303–760mm x 243–310mm); unnumbered; accounts written on recto only, bursars' names and year-end date on dorse of first and last mbs; tied with white ribbon.

Oxford, Bodleian Library, MS. D.D. All Souls c.288; 9 rolls in box including accounts for:

1602–3; English; parchment; 8 mbs attached serially; 550–800mm x 290–300mm (180–800mm x 240–95mm); unnumbered; accounts written on recto only, bursars' names and year-end date on dorse of first and last mbs; tied with white ribbon.

1604–5; English; parchment; 9 mbs attached serially; 540–785mm x 295–310mm (540–785mm x 240–310mm); unnumbered; accounts written on recto only, bursars' names and year-end date on dorse of first and last mbs; tied with white ribbon.

Oxford, Bodleian Library, MS. D.D. All Souls c.289; 8 rolls in box including accounts for:

1607–8; English; parchment; 15 mbs attached serially; 250–640mm x 290–8mm (250–640mm x 233–98mm); unnumbered; accounts written on recto only, bursars' names and year-end date on dorse of first and last mbs; tied with pink ribbon.

1609–10; English and Latin; parchment; 14 mbs attached serially; 240–758mm x 305–21mm (196–758mm x 275–315mm); unnumbered; accounts written on recto only, bursars' names and year-end date on dorse of first and last mbs; tied with pink ribbon.

Oxford, Bodleian Library, MS. D.D. All Souls c.290; 8 rolls in box including account for:

1613–14; English and Latin; parchment; 13 mbs attached serially; 418–800mm x 290–300mm (298–800mm x 246–300mm); unnumbered; accounts written on recto only, bursars' names and year-end date on dorse of first and last mbs; tied with twine.

Oxford, Bodleian Library, MS. D.D. All Souls c.291; 7 rolls in box including accounts for:

1615–16; English and Latin; parchment; 14 mbs attached serially; 459–640mm x 290–310mm (360–640mm x 236–300mm); unnumbered; accounts written on recto only, bursars' names and year-end date on dorse of first and last mbs; tied with string.

1616–17; English; parchment; 12 mbs attached serially; 400–722mm x 295–300mm (220–722mm x

248–300mm); unnumbered; accounts written on recto only, bursars' names and year-end date on dorse of first and last mbs; tied with string.

Oxford, Bodleian Library, MS. D.D. All Souls c.292; 9 rolls in box including accounts for:

1618–19; English; parchment; 13 mbs attached serially; 198–804mm x 288–98mm (198–804mm x 243–98mm); unnumbered; accounts written on recto only; tied with string.

1620–1; English; parchment; 11 mbs attached serially; 250–708mm x 293–303mm (250–708mm x 243–99mm); unnumbered; accounts written on recto only; tied with string.

Oxford, Bodleian Library, MS. D.D. All Souls c.293; 10 rolls in box including accounts for:

1623–4; English; paper; 17 sheets attached serially; 370–406mm x 302–10mm (80–406mm x 168–310mm); unnumbered; accounts written on recto only, bursars' names and year-end date on dorse of first and last sheets; tied with white ribbon.

1626–7; English; parchment; 11 mbs attached serially; 242–688mm x 298–310mm (242–678mm x 278–310mm); unnumbered; accounts written on recto only, bursars' names and year-end date on dorse of first mb.

1627–8; English; parchment; 12 mbs attached serially; 85–748mm x 300–5mm (85–748mm x 190–302mm); unnumbered; accounts written on recto only, bursars' names and year-end date on dorse of first and last mbs; tied with white ribbon. The draft account for this year is a paper roll stored in the box catalogued as MS. D.D. All Souls c.294.

Oxford, Bodleian Library, MS. D.D. All Souls c.294; 10 rolls in box including accounts for:

1628–9; English; parchment; 13 mbs attached serially; 133–674mm x 298–305mm (93–674mm x 246–305mm); unnumbered; accounts written on recto only, bursars' names and year-end date on dorse of first and last mbs; tied with string.

1629–30; English; parchment; 11 mbs attached serially; 274–765mm x 298–301mm (text area varies, maximum 765mm x 190mm, mb 11 is blank); unnumbered; accounts written on recto only, bursars' names and year-end date on dorse of first and last mbs; mbs 8 and 9 decayed; tied with string.

1630–1; English; parchment; 11 mbs attached serially; 330–820mm x 305–12mm (330–820mm x 290–312mm); unnumbered; accounts written on recto only, bursars' names and year-end date on dorse of first and last mbs; tied with string.

Oxford, Bodleian Library, MS. D.D. All Souls c.295; 10 rolls in box including accounts for:

1632–3; English; parchment; 13 mbs attached serially; 424–598mm x 309–15mm (332–598mm x 232–312mm); unnumbered; accounts written on recto only, bursars' names and year-end date on dorse of last mb; tied with pink ribbon. The draft account for this year also survives as a paper roll and is included in this box.

1633–4; English; parchment; 16 mbs attached serially; 298–738mm x 298–305mm (298–738mm x 225–305mm); unnumbered; accounts written on recto only, bursars' names and year-end date on dorse of last mb; tied with white ribbon.

1635–6; English; parchment; 11 mbs attached serially; 413–740mm x 303–7mm (334–728mm x 212–305mm, mb 11 blank); unnumbered; accounts written on recto only, bursars' names and year-end date on dorse of last mb; tied with string. The draft account for this year also survives as a paper roll and is included in this box.

1636–7; English; parchment; 12 mbs attached serially; 359–672mm x 305mm (264–672mm x 202–305mm); unnumbered; accounts written on recto only, bursars' names and year-end date on dorse of first mb; tied with pink ribbon. The draft account for this year also survives as a paper roll and is included in this box.

1637–8; English; parchment; 11 mbs attached serially; 356–712mm x 310mm (356–712mm x 268–310mm); unnumbered; accounts written on recto only, bursars' names and year-end date on dorse of last mb; tied with pink ribbon.

BALLIOL COLLEGE

Balliol College was founded *c* 1263 by John de Baliol. Its head is a master.

Access to the archives is via John Jones, 'The Records of Balliol College Oxford: A List of Records in the Custody of the Archivists' (1981 typescript). The earliest known bursars' accounts, 1544–68, were loaned to the Rev. Andrew Clark in 1909 and never returned. Clark's translation of excerpts, now Bodl.: MS. Top.Oxon e.124/9–10 (*sc* 35441), contains nothing of REED interest. Extant accounts were rebound in 1920.

Battells books 1576–1642, in fair condition, were consulted but yielded no REED items. Buttery books 1598–1642 (1600–1, 1603–6, 1608–10 missing) were too fragile to be consulted.

Balliol College Statutes

Oxford, Balliol College Archives, Statutes 1; *c* 1507 (near contemporary copy of 1507 college statutes); Latin; vellum; i + 47; 292mm x 197mm (232mm x 154mm); unnumbered; enlarged and decorated opening capitals plus closing design; good condition; leather bound on wood studded with detailed tooled design, loop on bottom of spine for chain, 2 clasps, both of which are broken.

Balliol College Register

The register contains various notes regarding college business and meetings, correspondence, and notes on miscellaneous matters relating to the college.

Oxford, Balliol College Archives, First Latin Register; 1514–1682; Latin and English; paper; iv + 188; 348mm x 228mm (338mm x 192mm); partial contemporary ink pagination; late 17th-c. leather binding, original binding of late 14th c.–early 15th c. made from illuminated parchment psalter pages preserved within the later binding front and back.

Balliol College Bursars' Accounts

In all three of these volumes, the accounts were kept semi-annually, the first half-year comprising 18 October to 7 July, the second half-year comprising 7 July to 18 October.

Oxford, Balliol College Archives, Computi 1568–1592; 1568–92; Latin; paper; iii + 117 + iii; 210mm x 580mm; modern pencil foliation; bound in parchment, modern ink title written on front cover: 'No 22 Bursar's Accounts. (1559–) 1568 to 1592.'

Oxford, Balliol College Archives, Computi 1592–1614; 1592–1614; Latin; paper; 118 leaves; 210mm x 580mm; modern pencil foliation; bound in parchment, 17th-c. ink title written on front cover: 'No 23 Liber Bursar: Ab Ann: Dom: 1592. Ad 1614.'

Oxford, Balliol College Archives, Computi 1615–1662; 1615–62; Latin and English; paper; 229 leaves; 210mm x 580mm; partial modern pencil foliation (1–157); bound in parchment, 17th-c. ink title written on front cover: 'No 24 Liber Bursar: Ab Ann: Dom: 1615 Ad 1662.'

Persons, Briefe Apologie

The passage excerpted in this volume is Persons' own translation into English of a Latin original, now lost, in an autobiography he started writing in 1598. A mid-seventeenth-century transcript by Fr. Christopher Grene survives in the library of Stonyhurst College, Lanc (Collectanea P, vol 1, ff 222–33). It has been published in J.H. Pollen, sj (ed), 'The Memoirs of Father Robert Persons,' *Miscellanea, ii*, Catholic Record Society (London, 1906), 12–36 (with an English translation).

[Robert Persons.] A BRIEFE | APOLOGIE, | OR DEFENCE OF THE CA- | tholike Ecclesiastical Hierarchie, & subordi- | nation in England, erected these later yeares by our holy Father Pope Clement the eyght; and im- | pugned by certayne libels printed & publi- | shed of late both in Latyn & English; by some vnquiet persons vnder the | name of Priests of the | Seminaries. | *VVritten and set forth for the true information and | stay of all good Catholikes, by Priests vnited in due subordination to the Right Reuerend Arch- | priest, and other their Superiors.* | Hebr. 13. vers. 17 | *Obedite praepositis vestris, & subiacete eis, &c.* | Obey your Superiors, and submit your selues vnto | them. | 1. Thess. 5. | *Rogamus vos fratres, corripite inquietos.* | We beseech yow brethren represse those that are vn- | quiet amongst yow. | [device] | Permissu Superiorum. | [Antwerp, 1601]. *stc*: 19392.

Ely, Certaine Briefe Notes

[Humphrey Ely.] CERTAINE | BRIEFE | NOTES VPON A | BRIEFE APOLOGIE SET | out vnder the name of the Prie- | stes vnited to the Archpriest. | *Dravvne by an vnpassionate secular Prieste* | *friend to bothe partyes, but more* | *frend to the truth.* | VVherunto is added a seuerall ansvveare | vnto the particularites obiected | against certaine Persons. | FORTE EST VIRUM, FORTIOR EST | REX, SED SVPER OMNIA VIN- | CIT VERITAS ET MANET IN | ETERNUM. 3. Esd. 3. | [device] | Imprinted at Paris, by PETER | SEVESTRE. | [rule] | *VVith Priuiledge.* [1602]. *STC*: 7628.

The excerpt comes from a separately paginated section following the half title on p 313: [device] | AN ANSVVEAR OF | M. DOCTOR BAGSHAW | to certayne poyntes of a li- | bell called. | *An Apologie of the subordination* | *in England.*

BRASENOSE COLLEGE

Brasenose College was founded *c* 1509 by William Smith, bishop of Lincoln, and Sir Richard Sutton of Prestbury, Cheshire. Its head is a principal. No archives survive from its predecessor, Brasenose Hall.

Access to the archives is via a catalogue prepared by the National Register of Archives (1966 typescript), of which an annotated copy is available in the library. Further documents are described by Jeffery, 'The Bursars' Account Books,' pp 19–30. The accounting year began and ended on 21 December (St Thomas' Day).

A complete set of final bursars' accounts survives for 1516–1662 on parchment rolls now bound flat. Limited to general categories of expense, these have yielded no REED entries.

Alexander Nowell's Notebook

This manuscript was bought by Brasenose College in 1859 from the Dawson Turner sale (no. 353), and deposited in the Bodleian in 1891. A table of contents made shortly thereafter is keyed to the old ink foliation and a note on the flyleaf points out correctly that 'some of the leaves seem to have been inserted at wrong places.' The manuscript was subsequently repaired and refoliated, though not reorganized or rebound.

The current folio 45 was once a loose sheet and has no connection with the remainder of the contents, which constitute a scrapbook of miscellaneous papers in Nowell's hand, including three undated prose prologues to Westminster School plays by Terence and Seneca. The leaf is primarily devoted to a list of books with prices. It can be dated by its numerous references to printed books and to Oxford contemporaries of Nowell, who was a student and fellow of Brasenose College (1520–43) and became headmaster of Westminster School in 1543.

Oxford, Bodleian Library, Brasenose College MS. 31; *c* 1535–61; Latin and English; paper; xiv + 35 + iv; 150mm x 210mm; modern pencil foliation superseding 2 earlier foliations, one in pencil, the other in ink; some leaves have 2 or 3 cols; 19th-c. leather and board binding, title stamped on spine: 'Noelli Litere &c.'

Brasenose College Bursars' Roll of Account

Due to its poor condition BNC Arch: U.B.21 is no longer produced for examination.

Oxford, Brasenose College Archives, U.B.21; 1582, 1634–8; English; paper; 96 leaves; 190mm x 310mm; modern pencil foliation; 17th-c. stamped calf and board binding, badly worn. The accounts are bound in random order.

Brasenose College Senior Bursars' Accounts

Oxford, Brasenose College Archives, A.2.41; 1631–2; English; paper; 41 leaves; 190mm x 305mm; partial modern pencil foliation (1–20, last approximately 20 leaves blank, with a few notes of expenses for 1638); bound in original vellum, title in ink on front cover faded and largely illegible.

Brasenose College Junior Bursars' Accounts

The accounts survive in an eleven volume series (A.8.1–11) covering the period 1611–12 and 1627–41, with some gaps.

Oxford, Brasenose College Archives, A.8.5; 1631–2; English and Latin; paper; i + 96 + i; 600mm x 222mm (566mm x 212mm); partial modern pencil foliation; good condition; modern card binding.

Oxford, Brasenose College Archives, A.8.7; 1634–5; English and Latin; paper; 69 leaves; 591mm x 222mm (570mm x 200mm); partial modern pencil foliation; generally good condition with some wear to outer leaves; 3 separate smaller vols sewn together, each retaining its contemporary leather binding with ink title.

Oxford, Brasenose College Archives, A.8.10; 1639–40; English and Latin; paper; 72 leaves; 590mm x 225mm (566mm x 218mm); partial modern pencil foliation; generally good condition with some wear to outer leaves; 3 separate smaller vols sewn together, each retaining its contemporary leather binding with ink title.

Oxford, Brasenose College Archives, A.8.11; 1640–1; English and Latin; paper; 85 leaves; 596mm x 223mm (576mm x 213mm); partial modern pencil foliation; generally good condition with some wear to outer leaves; 4 separate smaller volumes sewn together, each retaining its contemporary leather binding with ink title.

Brasenose College Statutes (A)

This manuscript is a copy of the 1521 statutes for Brasenose College amended by Sir Richard Sutton.

Oxford, Brasenose College Archives, A.2.3; 1681; Latin; parchment; ii + 27 + iii; 235mm x 164mm (187mm x 93mm); contemporary ink pagination; margins marked in red, some title capitals; good condition; contemporary leather binding with blind tooled decoration.

CANTERBURY COLLEGE

Canterbury College was founded in 1363 by Simon Islip, archbishop of Canterbury, with the concurrence of the Cathedral Priory of Christ Church, Canterbury. It stood on the site of what is now Canterbury Quadrangle in Christ Church. Its head was a warden. Shortly after its dissolution in 1540 it was incorporated into Christ Church (see p 637).

Expenses for Inception at Canterbury College

These expenses are excerpted from the register of William Molash, prior of Christ Church, Canterbury. A number of entries in the register appear to have been copied from earlier registers or other documents, including the one transcribed here, with their dates left approximate or incomplete.

Oxford, Bodleian Library, MS. Tanner 165; 1427–57; Latin; parchment; ii + 177 + i; 220mm x 300mm; modern pencil foliation replacing contemporary foliation; 17th-c. leather and board binding, badly worn at corners.

Expenses for a Degree Feast at Canterbury College (AC)

A history of the college, with transcriptions of documents, is Pantin's *Canterbury College*. Professor Elliott failed to trace 'Cant Cathedral Archives: Cart. Ant. O.151.3.b' and indeed some ten per cent of the materials transcribed by Pantin were marked 'not found' in the course of a 1974 search of Canterbury Cathedral archives.

W.A. Pantin (ed), *Canterbury College, Oxford*, vol 3, Oxford Historical Society, ns, 8 (Oxford, 1950 for 1943–4).

CARDINAL COLLEGE

Cardinal College was founded by Cardinal Wolsey in 1525 on the site of what is now Christ Church. Dissolved in 1530 after Wolsey's fall from power, it was refounded in 1532 as King Henry VIII College and subsequently incorporated into Christ Church (see p 637).

The only surviving account book, now in the PRO, covers the last full year of the college's existence under its original name.

Cardinal College Expense Book

The accounting year ran from 1 November to 1 November; the accounts are complete for all four terms.

London, Public Record Office, E/36/104; 1529–30; Latin; parchment; vi + 28 + vi; 390mm x 300mm; 19th-c. stamped ink foliation (1–24, omitting a fragmentary leaf and the cover leaf at beginning), also 18th- and 19th-c. ink pagination (1–54, omitting first fragmentary leaf); original cover leaf (pp 1–2) now bound backwards; 19th-c. leather and board binding, stamped on spine: 'Expences Of Cardinal College Oxon,' on p 1 in contemporary ornamental hand: 'Expen*cae* Collegij Cardinalis Oxon.' Folio 3 of the document gives the date: 'Primus Terminus Quinti Anni,' ie, 1529, the fifth year after foundation of the college in 1525.

CHRIST CHURCH

Christ Church was founded in 1546 by Henry viii, consolidating Canterbury and Cardinal Colleges (see p 636 and also p 592). Thoroughly idiosyncratic, Christ Church is both a cathedral and an academic foundation: it is never called a 'College'; its members are called Students (always with a capital 'S'); its head is a dean; it has always admitted substantially more scholars than any other Oxford college; and it is considered Oxford's only royal foundation.

Archives are housed in a muniment room in Blue Boar Quadrangle. Financial and administrative records are accessed via E.G.W. Bill, 'Catalogue of Treasury Books' (1955 typescript). A supplement, begun by Mrs. J. Wells, awaits completion.

Treasurers' (or treasury) accounts run from Michaelmas to Michaelmas, divided into four thirteen-week terms (numbered). Some accounts removed by Anthony Wood in the 1660s survive in the Bodleian Library.

Statutes

Christ Church Cathedral and College Foundation Statutes

Statutes survive in a single ms comprising Henry viii foundation statutes, three versions of Edward vi statutes (ff 47–60v, 65–114, 115–56v), and notes and drafts pertaining to each. The first of the Edward vi statutes bears internal marks of collation – here ignored – against the statutes of Corpus Christi College.

Oxford, Christ Church Archives, D.P.vi.b.1; *c* 17th c.; Latin and English; paper; v + 209 + ii; 309mm x 209mm (264mm x 206mm); modern pencil foliation for whole collection, some items within the collection bear contemporary ink foliation; good condition; antiquarian(?) calf binding.

Financial Documents

Christ Church Treasurers' Accounts

Rolls were prepared each December for the audit, totalling all receipts and expenses for the year. They contain draft accounts later copied into the engrossed computi and are excerpted here only when the computi are not extant. Substantive differences are noted in the endnote to each record. ChCh Arch: iii.c.1 contains the accounts for 1528–9, 1545–8, 1597–8, 1602–6, 1609–15, 1617–20, 1622–3, and 1629–30.

Oxford, Christ Church Archives, iii.c.1; 1527–1630; Latin; paper; 286 leaves; 390mm x 470mm; modern pencil foliation; originally rolls, now bound in vellum and board.

Oxford, Bodleian Library, MS. Top.Oxon c.23 (sc 30777); 1581–2; Latin; paper; 6 leaves; 340mm x 210mm; foliated 43–8 in ink; originally rolls, now bound with miscellaneous Christ Church papers.

Christ Church Disbursements

Individual volumes survive for 1548–9, 1577–87, 1589–1631, and 1641–4 (another series takes over after this date). They list both internal and external expenses and were kept quarterly, with specific dates usually assigned to each expense.

Oxford, Christ Church Archives, xii.b.21; 1578–9; English and Latin; paper; ii + 87 + ii; 297mm x 191mm (245mm x 190mm); modern pencil foliation; generally good condition; contemporary leather rebound onto modern board, title on spine: 'DISBURSEMENTS 1578–1579.'

Oxford, Christ Church Archives, xii.b.24; 1581–2; English and Latin; paper; ii + 86 + i; 290mm x 196mm (286mm x 181mm); partial modern pencil foliation; good condition, some cutting apparently to remove entries; some enlarged title capitals; contemporary leather rebound onto modern board, contemporary ink title on front cover, antiquarian ink title on spine, modern embossed title on spine: 'DISBURSEMENTS 1581–1582.'

Oxford, Christ Church Archives, xii.b.25; 1582–3; English and Latin; paper; ii + 91 + i; 294mm x 199mm (210mm x 183mm); modern pencil foliation (2 folio 65s, labelled 'a' and 'b'); good condition, some cutting of leaves to remove entries; some decorated capitals; contemporary leather rebound onto modern board, contemporary ink title on front cover, modern embossed title on spine: 'DISBURSEMENTS 1582–1583.'

Oxford, Christ Church Archives, xii.b.27; 1584–5; English and Latin; paper; ii + 80 + ii; 294mm x 196mm (290mm x 185mm); modern pencil foliation; good condition; contemporary leather rebound onto modern board, contemporary ink title on front cover, antiquarian ink title on spine, modern embossed title on spine: 'DISBURSEMENTS 1584–1585.'

Oxford, Christ Church Archives, xii.b.28; 1585–6 plus cancelled fragments from 1586–7; English and Latin; paper; i + 87 + i; 295mm x 201mm (292mm x 163mm); partial modern pencil foliation; good condition; contemporary leather rebound onto modern board, contemporary ink title on front cover, modern embossed title on spine: 'DISBURSEMENTS 1586.'

Oxford, Christ Church Archives, xii.b.29; 1586–7; English and Latin; paper; ii + 114 + ii; 291mm x 198mm (273mm x 153mm); modern pencil foliation; good condition; contemporary leather rebound onto modern board, contemporary ink title on front cover, modern embossed title on spine: 'DISBURSEMENTS 1[6]586–1[6]587.'

Oxford, Christ Church Archives, xii.b.31; 1588–9; English and Latin; paper; ii + 135 + ii; 303mm x 195mm (246mm x 155mm); partial modern pencil foliation; fair condition, some pages cut to remove entries, and some pages torn, water damage to final leaves, no substantial loss of information; contemporary leather rebound onto modern board, contemporary ink title on front cover, modern embossed title on spine: 'DISBURSEMENTS 1588–1589.'

Oxford, Christ Church Archives, xii.b.32; 1589–90; English and Latin; paper; ii + 77 + i; 297mm x 200mm (251mm x 159mm); partial modern pencil foliation; good condition; contemporary leather rebound onto modern board, contemporary ink title on front cover, modern embossed title on spine: 'DISBURSEMENTS 1589–1590.'

Oxford, Christ Church Archives, xii.b.33; 1590–1; English and Latin; paper; ii + 90 + i; 288mm x 193mm (264mm x 179mm); modern pencil foliation; good condition; contemporary leather rebound onto modern board, contemporary ink title on front cover, modern embossed title on spine: 'DISBURSEMENTS 1591.'

Oxford, Christ Church Archives, xii.b.34; 1591–2; English and Latin; paper; ii + 89 + i; 294mm x 194mm (277mm x 172mm); modern pencil foliation; good condition; contemporary leather rebound onto modern board, modern embossed title on spine: 'DISBURSEMENTS 1592.'

Oxford, Christ Church Archives, xii.b.35; 1592–3; English and Latin; paper; ii + 115 + i; 291mm x 195mm (265mm x 149mm); modern pencil foliation; good condition; contemporary leather rebound onto modern board, contemporary ink title on front cover, modern embossed title on spine: 'DISBURSEMENTS 1592–1593.'

Oxford, Christ Church Archives, xii.b.43; 1598–9; English and Latin; paper; i + 82 + i; 298mm x 192mm (292mm x 179mm); modern pencil foliation; fair condition, some cutting of leaves to remove entries, water damage to initial and final leaves destroying up to ⅓ of damaged folio, paper conservation; contemporary leather rebound onto modern board, contemporary ink title on front cover, modern embossed title on spine: 'DISBURSEMENTS 1598–1599.'

Oxford, Christ Church Archives, xii.b.44; 1599–1600; English and Latin; paper; i + 70 + i; 304mm x 198mm (279mm x 168mm); modern pencil foliation; fair to poor condition, water damage causing destruction of initial and final leaves, all leaves have washed/running ink, paper conservation; modern leather rebound onto board, modern pencil title on front cover, modern embossed title on spine: 'DISBURSEMENTS 1599–1600.'

Oxford, Christ Church Archives, xii.b.45; 1600–1; English and Latin; paper; ii + 82 + i; 323mm x 210mm (306mm x 173mm); partial modern pencil foliation; good condition; contemporary leather rebound onto modern board, contemporary ink title on front cover, antiquarian ink title on spine, modern embossed title on spine: 'DISBURSEMENTS 1600–1601.'

Oxford, Christ Church Archives, xii.b.49; 1604–5; English and Latin; paper; i + 84 + i; 330mm x 203mm (293mm x 187mm); partial modern pencil foliation; good condition; contemporary leather rebound onto modern board, contemporary ink title on spine, modern embossed title on spine: 'DISBURSEMENTS 1605.'

Oxford, Christ Church Archives, xii.b.50; 1605–6; English and Latin; paper; ii + 74 + i; 349mm x 220mm (341mm x 178mm); partial modern pencil foliation; good condition; contemporary leather rebound onto modern board, contemporary ink title on front cover, antiquarian ink title on spine, modern embossed title on spine: 'DISBURSEMENTS 1606.'

Oxford, Christ Church Archives, xii.b.52; 1607–8; English and Latin; paper; ii + 74 + i; 294mm x 198mm (291mm x 179mm); partial modern pencil foliation; good condition; contemporary leather rebound onto modern board, contemporary ink title on front cover, antiquarian ink title on spine, modern embossed title on spine: 'DISBURSEMENTS 1607–1608.'

Oxford, Christ Church Archives, xii.b.53; 1608–9; English and Latin; paper; ii + 74 + i; 315mm x 198mm (298mm x 158mm); partial modern pencil foliation; good condition; contemporary leather rebound onto modern board, contemporary ink title on front cover, antiquarian ink title on spine, modern embossed title on spine: 'DISBURSEMENTS 1608–9.'

Oxford, Christ Church Archives, xii.b.57; 1612–13; English and Latin; paper; ii + 80; 316mm x 197mm (306mm x 175mm); partial modern pencil foliation; generally good condition, second flyleaf loose, some minor insect damage; contemporary leather, leather ties partially preserved, contemporary ink title on front cover, antiquarian ink title on spine, modern ink title on spine: 'DISBURSEMENTS 1612–13.'

Oxford, Christ Church Archives, xii.b.60; 1615–16; English and Latin; paper; iv + 91 + i; 310mm x 194mm (272mm x 168mm); modern pencil foliation; good condition; contemporary leather rebound onto modern board, contemporary ink title on front cover, modern title printed on spine: 'DISBURSEMENTS 1615–16.'

Christ Church Computi

These rolls, now deteriorated, contain the final accounts, copied from the Christ Church treasurers' accounts, after they had been approved at the audit. Rolls survive for 1549–51, 1560–3, 1569–72, 1575–85, 1587–8, 1590–2, 1596–1608, 1611–13, 1615–16, and 1619–24.

Oxford, Christ Church Archives, iii.c.6(b.); 1581–2; Latin; parchment; 3 mbs sewn at top; 655mm x 345mm (648mm x 330mm); unnumbered; enlarged and decorated title capitals; good condition.

Oxford, Christ Church Archives, iii.c.6(c.); 1583–5; Latin; parchment; 3 mbs sewn at top; 701mm x 262mm (658mm x 258mm); unnumbered; enlarged and decorated title capitals; good condition.

Oxford, Christ Church Archives, iii.c.6(f.); 1591–2; Latin; parchment; 3 mbs sewn at top; 790mm x 342mm (740mm x 243mm); unnumbered; enlarged and decorated title capitals; good condition, tear to bottom of mb 1.

Oxford, Christ Church Archives, iii.c.7(a.); 1597–8; Latin; parchment; 5 mbs sewn at top; 785mm x 363mm (732mm x 243mm); unnumbered; enlarged and decorated title capitals; good condition.

Oxford, Christ Church Archives, iii.c.7(b.); 1598–9; Latin; parchment; 4 mbs sewn at top; 824mm x 381mm (754mm x 322mm); unnumbered; enlarged and decorated title capitals; written front to back, text on dorse written upside down with respect to text on front to enable reading of entire col without turning roll; good condition.

Oxford, Christ Church Archives, iii.c.7(c.); 1600–1; Latin; parchment; 5 mbs (4 large mbs sewn at top plus a smaller mb with a contemporary tie sewn to foot of mb 4, lesser mb blank save for regnal date, seems to have served as a wrapper); 780mm x 335mm (694mm x 329mm); unnumbered; enlarged and decorated title capitals; written front to back, text on dorse written upside down with respect to text on front to enable reading of entire col without turning roll; good condition.

Oxford, Christ Church Archives, iii.c.7(d.); 1601–2; Latin; parchment; 5 mbs (4 large mbs sewn at top plus a smaller mb with a contemporary tie sewn to foot of mb 4 and serving as a wrapper); 702mm x 321mm (625mm x 310mm); unnumbered; enlarged title capitals; written front to back, text on dorse written upside down with respect to text on front to enable reading of entire col without turning roll; good condition.

Oxford, Christ Church Archives, iii.c.7(e.); 1603–4; Latin; parchment; 5 mbs (4 large mbs sewn at top plus a smaller mb with a contemporary tie sewn to foot of mb 4 and serving as a wrapper); 750mm x 357mm (723mm x 339mm); unnumbered; enlarged and decorated title capitals; written front to back, text on dorse written upside down with respect to text on front to enable reading of entire col without turning roll; good condition.

Oxford, Christ Church Archives, iii.c.7(g.); 1605–6; Latin; parchment; 5 mbs (4 large mbs sewn at top plus a smaller mb sewn to foot of mb 4 and serving as a wrapper); 695mm x 286mm (656mm x 275mm); unnumbered; enlarged and decorated title capitals; written front to back, text on dorse written upside down with respect to text on front to enable reading of entire col without turning roll; good condition.

Oxford, Christ Church Archives, iii.c.8(a.); 1606–7; Latin; parchment; 5 mbs (4 large mbs sewn at top plus a smaller mb with a contemporary tie sewn to foot of mb 4 and serving as a wrapper); 744mm x 342mm (735mm x 336mm); unnumbered; enlarged and decorated title capitals; written front to back, text on dorse written upside down with respect to text on front to enable reading of entire col without turning roll; good condition.

Oxford, Christ Church Archives, iii.c.8(b.); 1607–8; Latin; parchment; 5 mbs (4 large mbs sewn at top plus a smaller mb with a contemporary tie sewn to foot of mb 4 and serving as a wrapper); 720mm x 357mm (669mm x 338mm); unnumbered; enlarged and decorated title capitals; written front to back, text on dorse written upside down with respect to text on front to enable reading of entire col without turning roll; good condition.

Oxford, Christ Church Archives, iii.c.8(d.); 1611–12; Latin; parchment; 4 mbs (3 large mbs sewn at top plus a smaller mb originally sewn to foot of mb 3, but now detached, and serving as a wrapper);

716mm x 311mm (715mm x 301mm); unnumbered; enlarged and decorated title capitals; written front to back, text on dorse written upside down with respect to text on front to enable reading of entire col without turning roll; fair condition.

Oxford, Christ Church Archives, iii.c.8(e.); 1612–13; Latin; parchment; 4 mbs (3 large mbs sewn at top plus a smaller mb with a contemporary tie sewn to foot of mb 3 and serving as a wrapper); 820mm x 315mm (818mm x 315mm); unnumbered; enlarged and decorated title capitals; written front to back, text on dorse written upside down with respect to text on front to enable reading of entire col without turning roll; generally good condition, some minor insect damage.

Oxford, Christ Church Archives, iii.c.8(f.); 1615–16; Latin; parchment; 3 mbs sewn at top; 755mm x 365mm (729mm x 354mm); unnumbered; enlarged and decorated title capitals; written front to back, text on dorse written upside down with respect to text on front to enable reading of entire col without turning roll; good condition.

Oxford, Christ Church Archives, iii.c.9(a.); 1619–20; Latin, English, and French; parchment; 5 mbs sewn at top; 690mm x 330mm (644mm x 329mm); unnumbered; enlarged and decorated title capitals; written front to back, text on dorse written upside down with respect to text on front to enable reading of entire col without turning roll; fair condition, rodent damage to mb 4 causing some loss of information, some minor insect damage.

Oxford, Christ Church Archives, iii.c.9(b.); 1620–1; Latin; parchment; 5 mbs sewn together at top; 615mm x 340mm (570mm x 328mm); unnumbered; enlarged and decorated title capitals; written front to back, text on dorse written upside down with respect to text on front to enable reading of entire col without turning roll; good condition.

Oxford, Christ Church Archives, iii.c.9(c.); 1621–2; Latin; parchment; 5 mbs sewn together at top; 785mm x 370mm (755mm x 360mm); unnumbered; enlarged and decorated title capitals; written front to back, text on dorse written upside down with respect to text on front to enable reading of entire col without turning roll; fair condition, rodent and insect damage to mb 5, some material wear (ink lost).

Oxford, Christ Church Archives, iii.c.9(d.); 1622–3; Latin; parchment; 5 mbs sewn together at top; 670mm x 400mm (610mm x 383mm); unnumbered; enlarged and decorated title capitals; written front to back, text on dorse written upside down with respect to text on front to enable reading of entire col without turning roll; generally good condition, some material wear leading to loss of ink.

Christ Church Battells Books

These are weekly records of commons, kept from early September, usually from the second Friday of the month, the week being divided from Friday through Thursday. The accounts for each week are followed by a category of 'Extra Expenses.'

Oxford, Christ Church Archives, x(i).c.43; 1606–7; English and Latin; paper; iii + 55 + i; 578mm x 214mm (565mm x 202mm); partial modern pencil foliation; good condition; contemporary leather rebound onto modern board, contemporary ink title and modern pencil year date on front cover, some contemporary ink calculations on front cover, modern embossed title on spine: 'MICH. 1606 to MIDS. 1607.'

Oxford, Christ Church Archives, x(i).c.44; 1607–8; English and Latin; paper; ii + 55 + i; 600mm x 222mm (577mm x 220mm); partial modern pencil foliation; good condition; contemporary leather rebound onto modern board, modern pencil year date on front cover, modern embossed title on spine: 'MICH. 1607 to MIDS. 1608.'

Oxford, Christ Church Archives, x(i).c.48; 1611–12; English and Latin; paper; ii + 56 + i; 565mm x 202mm (542mm x 195mm); modern pencil foliation; fair condition, minor insect damage plus water damage causing loss of information; modern board, embossed title on spine: 'SEPT. 1611–SEPT. 1612.'

Oxford, Christ Church Archives, x(i).c.50; 1613–14; English and Latin; paper; ii + 58 + i; 568mm x 210mm (543mm x 205mm); modern pencil foliation; fair condition, water, insect, and mould damage, some loss of information; contemporary leather rebound over modern board, contemporary ink title on front cover, modern embossed year date on spine.

Christ Church Receipts

Individual volumes survive for 1593–4, 1596–1617, 1620–1, 1623–7, 1629–31, and 1641–2. These were kept quarterly, with specific dates usually assigned to each receipt.

Oxford, Christ Church Archives, xi.b.16; 1613–14; English; paper; ii + 59 + i; 340mm x 218mm (318mm x 213mm); modern pencil foliation; generally good condition, water damage has led to warping of binding, no loss of information apparent; contemporary leather rebound over modern board, contemporary ink title and antiquarian pencil year date on front cover, modern embossed title on spine: 'RECEIPTS 1613.'

Royal Visit Expenses

Christ Church Expenses for the Royal Visit

The sheets of Bodl.: MS. Rawlinson C.878, originally loose, appear to be rough accounts, with many deletions and obliterations, and to have been transcribed in edited form onto the sheets now contained in Bodl.: MS. Top.Oxon e.9. The latter comprises loose sheets that were given to Anthony Wood by the treasurer of Christ Church in 1667, along with other Christ Church documents. They appear to be a fairer copy of the rough accounts contained in Bodl.: MS. Rawlinson C.878, ff 1–9 (see p 1098, endnote to Bodl.: MS. Rawlinson C.878 ff 1–9, for discussion of substantive variants).

Oxford, Bodleian Library, MS. Rawlinson C.878 (sc 12712), 1566; English; paper; 9 leaves; 210mm x 150mm. Bound into an 18th-c. volume of 'English Historical Miscellanies' and foliated 1–9.

Christ Church Expense Sheet

This sheet is composed in the first person and the figures match the expenses reimbursed to Robert Mooneson in Bodl.: MS. Rawlinson C.878. The document is perhaps Mooneson's personal expense account.

Oxford, Bodleian Library, MS. Top.Oxon c.22 (sc 30776); 1566; English; paper; single sheet; 340mm x 210mm; writing on one side only. Bound with a collection of papers borrowed from Christ Church by Anthony Wood in 1667 and foliated 55 in ink.

Christ Church Expense Account for Plays

This document was prepared by a scribe for Dr Samuel Fell, treasurer of Christ Church, to be submitted to the University for reimbursement of Christ Church's expenses on the plays for the royal visit of 1636. The sheet was discovered among the deanery papers when the archives were moved to their present location in 1969. For a fuller description and analysis of this document, see John R. Elliott and John Buttrey, 'Royal Plays at Christ Church,' pp 93–109.

Oxford, Christ Church Archives, D.P.iii.c.1, item 27; 1636; English; bifolium; 290mm x 380mm; unnumbered; accounting entries written across the full width of the 2 inner pages; stored in a box of loose sheets. On the back of the sheet, in addition to the signatures of the 3 delegates, are 4 endorsements. One reads: 'The Account for the Vniuersity. Wherby there is due to Dr. ffell 243 li. 15 s. 6 d.' Another, initialled by Fell, reads: 'Christschurch found only the carpenters worke for the stage & scaffoldes.' The other two appear to have been added later, at different times. One reads: 'Charge of Entertaining the King by the University. 1636.' The other, probably the last to be written, gets the year wrong: 'The chardge of the vniuersitye plays exhibited to his maiesty anno 1638.'

Dean and Chapter Documents

Christ Church Chapter Book

This volume was called 'The Black Book' by Dean Liddell, who made extracts from it in the nineteenth century (ChCh Arch: D&C.i.b.1). The first eighty-six pages are blank. On page 87 occurs the following title in a sixteenth-century hand: 'Registrum eorum quae acta sunt in Domo nostra Capitulari per Decanum vel Subdeacanum et Canonicos omnes aut eorum maiorem partem in Ecclesia Christi Oxoniae … Anno domini 1549 octavo die Marcij./' The remainder of the volume contains decrees and official correspondence of the dean and chapter of Christ Church to 1646.

Oxford, Christ Church Archives, D&C.i.b.2; 1549–1646; Latin; paper; 449 leaves; 210mm x 310mm; modern pagination; bound in 17th-c. leather, written inside front cover in an 18th-c. hand: 'The Subdean's Book.'

Letter of the Dean and Chapter of Christ Church to the Chancellor

Cambridge, Magdalene College, Pepys Library, MS 2502/15; 10 December 1566; English; paper; bifolium; 312mm x 225mm (265mm x 160mm); addressed to the earl of Leicester, chancellor of the University. Bound in a guardbook and paginated 651–4 in modern pencil.

Letter of Thomas Cooper, Dean of Christ Church, to the Chancellor

Cambridge, Magdalene College, Pepys Library, MS 2503/273; 5 May 1569; English; paper; bifolium; 310mm x 220mm (235mm x 180mm); addressed to the earl of Leicester, chancellor of the University. Bound in a guardbook and paginated 273–6 in modern pencil.

Memorandum of the Dean and Chapter of Christ Church

Oxford, Christ Church Archives, D.P.ii.c.1, item 6; 4 January 1605/6; English and Latin; paper; bifolium; 310mm x 200mm (173mm x 152mm); modern pencil numbering; good condition; stored in a box of loose sheets.

Miscellaneous Documents

William Withie's Notebook

Withie, who was a fellow of Christ Church, kept this notebook from 1578 to 1581.

London, British Library, MS Sloane 300; 1578–81; Latin and English; paper; iv + 60 + iv; 295mm x 195mm; 19th-c. ink foliation; 19th-c. leather and board binding (before f 1 is an unfoliated fragment of the original vellum cover).

William Gager's Commonplace Book

This manuscript contains miscellaneous literary works by Gager, including fragments of scenes from *Oedipus* and *Dido*. The earliest datable piece is from 1578, the latest from December 1590.[3]

London, British Library, MS Additional 22583; 1578–90; Latin and English; paper; ii + 102 + i; 210mm x 175mm; contemporary ink foliation; 19th-c. stamped leather and board binding, stamped on spine: 'Poems of William Gager.'

Letter of Bishop of Llandaff to Sir Thomas Lake

The bishop of Llandaff from 1601 to 1617 was Francis Godwin. The letter concerns his son Thomas Godwin, who had matriculated at Christ Church in 1604.

London, Public Record Office, SP/15/37; 3 November 1605; English; paper; bifolium; 200mm x 305mm; addressed in scribal hand: 'To the Right Worshipfull our very loving ffreind Sir Thomas Lake Knight'; endorsed in a different hand, probably Lake's: 'Thomas Godwyn for a Schollers place in Christes Church in Oxford. 3o November 1605.' Bound in a guardbook and foliated 128–9.

Letter of King James to Christ Church

The letter is a copy of the original in the hand of Sir Thomas Lake. Folios 134–5 of this volume contain a letter of thanks from the bishop of Llandaff to Lake, dated 20 November 1605, for procuring the royal letter. Thomas Godwin proceeded BA from Christ Church in 1608.

London, Public Record Office, SP/15/37; 14 November 1605; English; single sheet; paper; 190mm x 280mm; endorsed: 'xiiijo November 1605. Thomas Godwin for a Schollers place in Christes Church Oxon.' Bound in a guardbook and foliated 130.

CORPUS CHRISTI COLLEGE

Corpus Christi College was founded in 1517 by Richard Fox, bishop of Winchester. Its head is a president. Archives are housed in an underground vault beneath the Fellows' Building, near the library.

No single catalogue of the contents of the archives, perhaps the largest in Oxford, was available at the time of inspection. One is currently in progress, to be published in microform.

The college manuscript collection, arguably the richest in Oxford and housed in the Bodleian Library until 1985, was transferred to the archive vault pending repairs to the Bodleian stacks. The archives and the manuscripts remain distinct collections. For library documents cited in this volume, see under Miles Windsor's Narrative (p 696) for CCC: MS 257; Letter of Henry Jackson to D.G.P. (p 648) for CCC: MS 304; and Appendix 11 for CCC: MS 352.

Corpus Christi College Statutes

Oxford, Corpus Christi College Archives, A/4/1/1; 13 February 1527/8; Latin; parchment; iii + 94; 344mm x 232mm (271mm x 175mm); contemporary ink foliation; some enlarged title capitals; good condition; contemporary calf binding with blind tooling, founder's seal on oval pendant (90mm x 60mm).

Corpus Christi College Bursars' Accounts

The bursars' accounts at Corpus are contained in the so-called 'Libri Magni.' Most of these were originally parchment booklets but were bound in leather by the Bodleian in 1931, each volume containing ten to twelve years of accounts and foliated at that time. The accounting year, divided into four numbered terms, ran from Michaelmas to Michaelmas.

An analysis of selected accounts may be found in G.D. Duncan, 'An Introduction to the Accounts of Corpus Christi College,' Appendix 2, *History of the University*, vol 3, pp 574–96.

Oxford, Corpus Christi College Archives, C/1/1/4; modern leather binding, tooled with clasps, embossed title on spine: 'C.C.C. LIBRI MAGNI IV 1558–1564 1566–1570.'

Extracts from:

f [9]: 1565–6; English and Latin; parchment; 15 leaves; 338mm x 206mm (305mm x 160mm); unnumbered apart from continuous modern pencil foliation of volume; excellent condition.

f [7]: 1568–9; English and Latin; parchment; 9 leaves; 275mm x 277mm (247mm x 187mm); unnumbered apart from continuous modern pencil foliation of volume; good condition.

Oxford, Corpus Christi College Archives, C/1/1/5; modern leather binding, tooled, embossed title on spine: 'C.C.C. LIBRI MAGNI V 1571–1580.'

Extract from:

f [8v]: 1572–3; English and Latin; parchment; 12 + i; 338mm x 276mm (312mm x 246mm); unnumbered apart from continuous modern pencil foliation of volume; good condition.

Oxford, Corpus Christi College Archives, C/1/1/6; 1581–99; modern leather binding, tooled, embossed title on spine: 'C.C.C. LIBRI MAGNI VI 1581–1599.'

Extract from:

f [10]: 1582–3; English and Latin; parchment; i + 9 + ii; 336mm x 225mm (307mm x 215mm); unnumbered apart from continuous modern pencil foliation of volume; good condition.

Oxford, Corpus Christi College Archives, C/1/1/8; modern leather binding, tooled, embossed title on spine: 'C.C.C. LIBRI MAGNI VIII 1611–13 1615–24.'

Extracts from:

f [9]: 1611–12; English and Latin; parchment; 11 + i; 383mm x 316mm (322mm x 270mm); unnumbered apart from continuous modern pencil foliation of volume; good condition.

f [10]: 1615–16; English and Latin; parchment; 14 + i; 389mm x 310mm (350mm x 260mm); unnumbered apart from continuous modern pencil foliation of volume; good condition.

f [14]: 1617–18; English and Latin; parchment; 15 + i; 362mm x 291mm (258mm x 207mm); unnumbered apart from continuous modern pencil foliation of volume; good condition.

f [11]: 1618–19; English and Latin; parchment; 12 + ii; 341mm x 341mm (301mm x 326mm), 2 cols; unnumbered apart from continuous modern pencil foliation of volume; good condition.

f [11]: 1619–20; English and Latin; parchment; 12 leaves; 351mm x 295mm (332mm x 288mm), 2 cols; unnumbered apart from continuous modern pencil foliation of volume; good condition.

f [11]: 1622–3; English and Latin; parchment; 12 + ii; 345mm x 243mm (317mm x 203mm), 2 cols; unnumbered apart from continuous modern pencil foliation of volume; good condition.

Oxford, Corpus Christi College Archives, C/1/1/9; modern leather binding, tooled, embossed title on spine: 'C.C.C. LIBRI MAGNI IX 1625–1628 1630–1641.'

Extract from:

mb [9]: 1635–6; English and Latin; parchment; 10 mbs; 420mm x 360mm (413mm x 359mm), 2 cols; unnumbered apart from continuous modern pencil foliation of volume; good condition.

Episcopal Visitation to Corpus Christi College

21M65/A1/26 is the register of Robert Horne, bishop of Winchester, from which the charges and replies of the episcopal visitation to Corpus are excerpted. This manuscript also yields records pertaining to visitations to New College (see p 146).

Winchester, Hampshire Record Office, 21M65/A1/26; 1560–79; Latin and English; parchment; ii + 119 + i; 405mm x 302mm (text area varies); contemporary ink foliation; good condition; bound in brown calf over boards with an 18th-c.(?) red calf spine, title on board cover and on second flyleaf: 'Horne 1560 to 1579.'

Letter of Henry Jackson to D.G.P.

Jackson's letter is in a volume compiled by William Fulman (1632–88) sometime after 1662, as materials toward a history of the college. This forms the current volume 10 of Fulman's collection of papers. Folios 79–207 are devoted to copies of the works of Henry Jackson (1586–1662), folio 79 bearing the heading 'Liber Henrici Jacksoni, Oxon. Coll. Corp. Chr. Alumni, 1600.' Extracts from sixty-nine letters written by Jackson are given, together with miscellaneous information about his life, the first half of which was spent as a student and fellow of Corpus. The originals of these letters, including the one describing performances of *Othello* and *The Alchemist* at Oxford in 1610, have not survived.

Oxford, Corpus Christi College, MS 304; *c* 1662; English; paper; 207 leaves; 215mm x 160mm; modern foliation; original board binding, endorsed in William Fulman's hand on f 1: 'Historiae Collegii Corporis Christi Lib. III. De Viris Illustribus, et Scriptoribus.'

DURHAM COLLEGE

Durham Priory first sent monks to study at Oxford in the late thirteenth century. About 1380

Prior Robert Walworth and Bishop Thomas Hatfield oversaw the founding of Durham College, later refounded as Trinity College (see p 677). While Dobson's estimate that over a period of 150 years nearly half of all Durham monks studied here may be overblown, its educational importance to the Priory was clearly very great. Landless and deriving its entire income from appropriated churches, the college was nevertheless expected to provide shelter, sustenance, and books for eight monks and eight secular scholars. Its support of boy bishops occurred during a brief period in which it was in financial difficulty.[4]

Accounts survive among the muniments of Durham Cathedral.

Durham College Accounts

Account rolls are extant for 1389–1537, yielding relevant material only for 1399–1402. The accounting year in this period normally began and ended on the day after the Ascension.

Durham, Durham University Library, Durham Cathedral Muniments Oxford Ac.1399–1400; 1399–1400; Latin; parchment; single mb; 600mm x 280mm (text area varies); unnumbered.

Durham, Durham University Library, Durham Cathedral Muniments Oxford Ac.1401–2; 1401–2; Latin; parchment; single mb; 835mm x 270mm (text area varies); unnumbered.

EXETER COLLEGE

Exeter College was founded in 1314 by Walter de Stapledon, bishop of Exeter. First known as Stapledon Hall, it became known subsequently as Exeter Hall and finally as Exeter College. (A secondary foundation occurred in 1566 under Sir William Petre.) Its head is a rector. Its account books, among the earliest in Oxford, provide the basis for the history of the college contained in Boase, *Registrum Collegii Exoniensis*, pp i–clxxxiii.

Archives, housed in a former kitchen beneath the rector's lodgings, are consulted in the library. A.V. Bradley and J.M. Cockayne, Archives of Exeter College, Oxford, 2 vols (1977), is available in Duke Humfrey as Bodl.: MS. R.Top 671.

Battells books 1600–35 (EC Arch: A.IV.15–21) and a weekly expense book for 1596–8 (within EC Arch: B.I.16) yielded no REED entries.

Exeter College Rectors' Accounts

Oxford, Exeter College Archives, A.1; 10 July–17 October 1361; Latin; parchment; single mb; 280mm x 694mm; written on 1 side only; endorsed at top: 'Compotus Roberti de Clyste Rectoris domus de stapildonhall Oxonia super receptis suis & expensis ∧⌈in officio Rectorie⌉, a die sabbati proxima post festum translacionis Sancti Thome martiris anno domini millesimo CCCmo. seximo. primo vsque ad proximam diem sabbati post festum sancti dionisij proximam post sequentem anno supradicto.' This document was misdated '1360' by H.T. Riley, 'Exeter College, Oxford,' Historical Manuscripts Commission, *2nd Report*, Appendix (London, 1871), 128–9.

Oxford, Exeter College Archives, B.i.16:

1547–8; Latin; parchment; single mb; 540mm x 840mm; unnumbered; written on both sides, entries are in linear blocks with no headings or marginal rubrics. Contains the accounts for the whole year, with two quarters on each side. Exact dates are given for each of the four quarters, which begin at Michaelmas.

1550–1; Latin; parchment; single mb; originally measuring approximately 540mm x 840mm, but half is now torn away; unnumbered; written on both sides, 2 quarters on each side. Entries referring to expenses for comedies belong to a term of which the heading is partially torn but which appears to have run from approximately Christmas to Easter.

Oxford, Exeter College Archives, A.ii.9; 1566–1639; Latin; paper; 367 leaves; 200mm x 300mm; modern pencil foliation; bound in vellum and board, on spine in 17th-c. hand: 'Rector's Accounts 1566 1639,' front cover inscribed 'H.' The accounting year ran from All Saints' Day to All Saints' Day and was audited on 2 November.

GLOUCESTER COLLEGE

Gloucester College was founded in 1298 to educate the Benedictine monks of Malmesbury Abbey on the site of a former establishment belonging to Gloucester Abbey. It was dissolved in 1541, purchased by St John's College in 1560, renamed Gloucester Hall, and leased out as a student residence. During Elizabeth's reign it continued to be noted for Catholic sympathies. In 1714 it was refounded as Worcester College. Very little remains of its records.

Letter of Richard Croke to Thomas Cromwell

Richard Croke had been Greek tutor to Henry viii in 1517 and was later appointed as special envoy to Italy from 1529 to 1531 to gather opinions of canon lawyers on the validity of the king's marriage. From 1532 to 1545 he was canon and subdean of King Henry viii College in Oxford.
     No year is given but it may be deduced from internal references to current events.

London, Public Record Office, SP/1/82; 26 January 1533/4; English; paper; bifolium; 285mm x 175mm; later red cloth binding on boards gilded at corners and spine, remains of red wax seal on f 122. F [1] has 2 signatures by Richard Croke and is endorsed in the same hand as the text: 'rede thys laste To the right honorable and my synguler good Maister Maister Cromwel,' f [1v] is dated 'thys night ⌐the¬ xxvj of Ianuary at Oxforde.' Now bound in a volume of letters to Cromwell with Croke's notes, memoranda, and drafts; foliated 122–3v in modern pencil and stamped 106–7.

JESUS COLLEGE

Jesus College was founded in 1571 by Queen Elizabeth, acting under the persuasion of Hugh Price. Its head is a principal.

Archives are kept in a muniment room above the library. The college possesses no financial or administrative records before 1631. A handlist by D.L. Evans and J.N.L. Baker is available from the archivist.

Jesus College Statutes (A)

This manuscript is an antiquarian copy of the 1622 statutes.

Oxford, Jesus College Archives, ST4; 18th c.; Latin; parchment; ii + 68 + iii; 296mm x 200mm (225mm x 129mm); contemporary ink pagination; excellent condition; contemporary calf binding, now rather worn, with some decoration, embossed title on front cover: 'STATUTA COLL: IESU OXON.'

Jesus College Bursar's Book

The accounting year runs from 30 November to 30 November. There is no division into terms.

Oxford, Jesus College Archives, BU:AC:GEN:1; 1631–50; English; paper; vi + 205 (final 105 leaves blank); 200mm x 300mm; modern pagination; bound in stamped calf, text on spine faded and illegible.

LINCOLN COLLEGE

Lincoln College was founded in 1427 by Richard Fleming, bishop of Lincoln. Its head is a rector.

Archives, formerly kept in the Gate Tower, are now in the Senior Library (in the decommissioned All Saints' Church).

The earliest surviving accounts date from 1455. Pre-1600 accounts are called 'Computi'; post-1600 accounts, 'Calculi.'

Lincoln College Computi

The accounting year runs from 21 December to 21 December and is divided into quarters.

Oxford, Lincoln College Archives, Computus 1; 1456–1513; Latin and English; paper; iii + 182 + iii; 299mm x 103mm (260mm x 87mm); intermittent contemporary ink foliation (some folios have no visible numbers but are included in this sequence) which is followed here, occasional antiquarian ink foliation for some years; generally good condition; modern board binding with leather spine, ink title on spine.

Oxford, Lincoln College Archives, Computus 2; 1486–1510; Latin and English; paper; ii + 282 (originally 7 separate booklets of 27, 43, 49, 33, 39, 43, and 48 leaves) + ii; 390–420mm x 120–30mm (350mm x 110mm); contemporary ink pagination of each booklet separately, with modern pencil letters 'a' and 'B–F' to distinguish number sequences; much wear and damage along inner edges but little text lost, generally legible except for fading in F; modern cloth-covered board binding with leather spine and ties.

Oxford, Lincoln College Archives, Computus 3; 1511–25; Latin and English; paper; iv + 145 + iv; 443mm x 159mm (408mm x 135mm); modern pencil foliation (occasional contemporary ink foliation for some years); modern board and leather binding. Contains the accounts for 1511–13, 1514–17, 1519–21, and 1523–5.

Oxford, Lincoln College Archives, Computus 4; 1525–38; Latin and English; paper; i + 161; 430mm x 157mm (388mm x 119mm); modern pencil pagination (occasional contemporary ink foliation for some years); fair condition, water damage has resulted in substantial loss of information for many folios; modern board covers with modern leather spine, ink title on spine.

Oxford, Lincoln College Archives, Computus 5; 1538–60; Latin and English; paper; iv + 172; 429mm x 149mm (424mm x 128mm); modern pencil foliation (occasional contemporary ink foliation for some years); occasional decorated initial capitals; generally good condition, previous water damage, now restored; modern board binding with leather spine, ink title on spine.

Oxford, Lincoln College Archives, Computus 6; 1560–80; Latin and English; paper; iv + 149 + iv; 418mm x 151mm (400mm x 124mm); modern pencil foliation (occasional contemporary ink foliation for some years); occasional decorated title capitals; generally good condition, previous water damage, now restored; modern board binding with leather spine, ink title on spine.

Oxford, Lincoln College Archives, Computus 7; 1580–90; Latin and English; paper; v + 158 + iii; 425mm x 152mm (401mm x 111mm); modern pencil foliation (occasional contemporary ink foliation for some years); modern board and leather binding.

Oxford, Lincoln College Archives, Computus 8; 1590–1600; Latin and English; paper; ii + 172 + ii; 412mm x 137mm (394mm x 121mm); modern pencil foliation (occasional contemporary ink foliation for some years); modern board and leather binding.

Oxford, Lincoln College Archives, Computus 10; 1576–7; English; paper; 11 + v; 300mm x 100mm (289mm x 98mm); unnumbered; fair condition, previous severe water damage, leading to substantial loss of information, repaired; modern leather binding over contemporary leather binding with notes of various expenses on its front cover, ink title on front cover of modern binding.

Lincoln College Calculi

Sheets formerly were bound but now exist in loose gatherings for each year. Some are badly deteriorated and do not yet possess genuine shelf or class numbers. The calculus for 1610–11, now missing, was seen by Andrew Clark, Notes from Lincoln College Accounts, 8 vols (Bodl.: MS. Top.Oxon e.109–16), a partial translation and summary of the college financial records. The calculus for 1617–18, containing, according to Clark, a reference to William Davenant and other references to musicians, is now too fragile to touch. Other missing calculi are 1600–1, 1601–2, 1611–12, 1617–20, 1622–3, and 1628–40.

Oxford, Lincoln College Archives; 1604–5; English and Latin; paper; 14 leaves; 407mm x 152mm

(395mm x 147mm); modern pencil foliation; generally good condition, previous water damage, now restored.

Oxford, Lincoln College Archives; 1607–8; Latin and English; paper; 16 leaves; 457mm x 178mm (448mm x 157mm); modern pencil foliation; generally good condition, previous water damage, now restored.

Oxford, Lincoln College Archives; 1612–13; Latin and English; paper; 19 + i; 423mm x 166mm (407mm x 149mm); modern pencil foliation; good condition.

Oxford, Lincoln College Archives; 1613–14; Latin and English; paper; i + 21 + ii; 404mm x 153mm (385mm x 129mm); modern pencil foliation; generally good condition, previous water damage, now restored.

Oxford, Lincoln College Archives; 1614–15; Latin and English; paper; 16 leaves; 413mm x 162mm (375mm x 148mm); modern pencil foliation; good condition.

Oxford, Lincoln College Archives; 1616–17; Latin and English; paper; 16 leaves; 391mm x 154mm (366mm x 146mm); modern pencil foliation; fair condition, considerable physical damage to ff 13–16, leading to loss of information, rest of MS water damaged and fragile.

Oxford, Lincoln College Archives; 1641–2. No longer available for examination.

MAGDALEN COLLEGE

Magdalen College was founded by William of Waynflete, bishop of Winchester, with a charter in 1448, expansions from 1458, and statutes in 1480. (Note distinction in spelling between Magdalen College, Oxford, and Magdalene College, Cambridge.) Its head is a president.

Archives are divided between the Muniment Tower and the Founder's Tower (readers are accommodated in the latter). The earliest surviving bursar's roll (discovered in 1980) dates from 1478–9, while regular accounts date from 1481 (with some gaps). Draft accounts were kept on paper rolls, formal computi on parchment rolls: both, bound flat in the nineteenth century, lack shelf-marks. The accounting year ran from Michaelmas to Michaelmas, only rarely divided into terms.

Not systematically catalogued, internal financial and administrative records are briefly described in C.M. Woolgar, 'A Catalogue of the Estate Archives of St. Mary Magdalen College,' vol 1 (1983 typescript), 60–2 (part of a 7-volume set), available as Bodl.: MS. R. Top. 680a.

Magdalen College Statutes

Oxford, Magdalen College Archives, MS 277; 15th c.; Latin; parchment; vii + 53 + ii; 291mm x 226mm (224mm x 167mm); contemporary ink foliation; decorated initial capitals; good condition; modern leather binding over board, original cover preserved, 2 modern clasps top and bottom.

The version of the statutes found in MC Arch: MS 277 has been collated with:

Oxford, Magdalen College Archives, MS 276; 15th c.; Latin; parchment; i + 52 + ii (modern paper fly-leaves); 306mm x 223mm (235mm x 135mm); unnumbered; enlarged title script, decorated initial capitals; good condition; modern parchment binding, ink title on front cover, embossed title on spine.

Oxford, Magdalen College Archives, MS 278; 15th c.; Latin; parchment; i + 61; 301mm x 239mm (208mm x 135mm); contemporary ink foliation; illuminated initial capital, initials of capitula are decorated; good condition; contemporary wood binding bound over with embossed leather, 2 clasps, both broken.

Magdalen College Battells Books

There survive three volumes of weekly lists of those dining in hall, including guests. They were originally loose bifolia and were bound together, with other fragmentary accounts, in the nineteenth century. The year is seldom given and must be deduced from internal evidence.

Oxford, Magdalen College Archives, CP 8/49; 1477–86; Latin and English; paper; i + 111 + ii; 300mm x 105mm; 19th-c. pencil foliation (several blank leaves); many leaves bound out of order; 19th-c. leather and board binding, stamped in gold on red on spine: 'Bursary Book Magd. Coll. Oxon. 1477–86.' Contains summaries of the bursars' annual accounts for 1476–7 and 1483–4, and the battells accounts for 1485–6 and 1486–7 (complete).

Oxford, Magdalen College Archives, CP 8/50; 1490–7; Latin; parchment and paper; i + 137 + i; leaves of varying sizes, averaging 310mm x 110mm; 19th-c. pencil foliation; 19th-c. leather and board binding, stamp on spine 'Bursary Book Magd. Coll. Oxon. 1490–99.' Contains the battells accounts for 1490–1 (complete), 1493–4 (lacking Term 2), 1494–5 (Term 4 only), and 1496–7? (Term 4 only).

Oxford, Magdalen College Archives, CP 8/51; 1501–8; Latin and English; paper; ii + 123 + ii; leaves of varying dimensions, typically 350mm x 130mm; 20th-c. pencil foliation (some leaves blank, some leaves bear notes on dating, in ink, in the hands of antiquarians Anthony Wood, John Rouse Bloxam, and William Macray); 19th-c. binding, stamped 'Bursary Book Magd. Coll. Oxon. 1501–7.' Contains the battells accounts for 1501–2? (Terms 1 and 4 only), 1502–3? (Terms 1 and 4 only), 1506–7, and 1507–8 (both complete). In both of the latter years the start of the academic year was delayed because of plague: the first term began on 8 November.

Magdalen College Libri Computi

Libri computi 1482–1620, formerly bound into large guardbooks, have been (or are being) reconstituted as individual parchment booklets, identifiable by date.

Oxford, Magdalen College Archives, Liber Computi; 1482–3; Latin; parchment; 18 leaves; 308mm x 216mm (240mm x 169mm); modern pencil foliation; good condition; modern card binding.

Oxford, Magdalen College Archives, Liber Computi; 1483–4; Latin; parchment; 20 leaves; 303mm x 255mm (218mm x 138mm); modern pencil foliation; good condition; modern card binding.

Oxford, Magdalen College Archives, Liber Computi; 1485–6; Latin; parchment; i + 17; 284mm x 183mm (194mm x 164mm); modern pencil foliation; good condition; contemporary parchment binding, resewn but with original cover, contemporary and antiquarian ink year dates on front cover (plus some contemporary rough account notes).

Oxford, Magdalen College Archives, Liber Computi; 1486–7; Latin; paper; 10 leaves; 295mm x 218mm (225mm x 187mm); modern pencil foliation; good condition; modern card binding.

Oxford, Magdalen College Archives, Liber Computi; 1487–8; Latin; parchment; 14 + i; 286mm x 203mm (207mm x 177mm); modern pencil foliation; good condition; contemporary parchment cover bound within modern card cover, contemporary ink title on cover plus some rough workings.

Oxford, Magdalen College Archives, Liber Computi; 1488–9; Latin; parchment; 13 + i; 287mm x 207mm (208mm x 137mm); modern pencil foliation; good condition; modern card binding.

Oxford, Magdalen College Archives, Liber Computi; 1490–1; Latin; parchment; 14 leaves; 315mm x 227mm (255mm x 188mm); modern pencil foliation; good condition; modern card binding.

Oxford, Magdalen College Archives, Liber Computi; 1495–6; Latin; parchment; 13 + iii; 279mm x 197mm (233mm x 152mm); modern pencil foliation; good condition; modern card binding.

Oxford, Magdalen College Archives, Liber Computi; 1496–7; Latin; parchment; 12 leaves; 298mm x 225mm (230mm x 155mm); modern pencil foliation; good condition; modern card binding.

Oxford, Magdalen College Archives, Liber Computi; 1502–3; Latin; parchment; 13 + i; 310mm x 216mm (233mm x 166mm); modern pencil foliation; decorated initial capital on f 1; good condition; modern card binding.

Oxford, Magdalen College Archives, Liber Computi; 11 November 1506–11 November 1507; Latin; parchment; 15 + i; 304mm x 246mm (249mm x 214mm); modern pencil foliation; good condition; modern card binding.

Oxford, Magdalen College Archives, Liber Computi; 1507–8; Latin; parchment; 16 leaves; 300mm x 220mm (252mm x 187mm); modern pencil foliation; good condition; modern card binding.

Oxford, Magdalen College Archives, Liber Computi; 1508–9; Latin; parchment; 15 leaves (final leaf is uncut at top, so ff 15 and 16 are joined); 319mm x 226mm (257mm x 195mm); modern pencil foliation; good condition; modern card binding.

Oxford, Magdalen College Archives, Liber Computi; 11 November 1509–11 November 1510; Latin; parchment; 16 leaves; 342mm x 240mm (293mm x 209mm); modern pencil foliation; good condition; modern card binding.

Oxford, Magdalen College Archives, Liber Computi; 1510–11; Latin; parchment; 11 + i; 336mm x 228mm (265mm x 218mm); modern pencil foliation; good condition; modern card binding.

Oxford, Magdalen College Archives, Liber Computi; 1511–12; Latin; parchment; 12 + ii; 335mm x 224mm (279mm x 207mm); modern pencil foliation; good condition; modern card binding.

Oxford, Magdalen College Archives, Liber Computi; 1512–13; Latin and English; parchment; 11 + i; 333mm x 228mm (254mm x 163mm); modern pencil foliation; good condition; modern card binding.

Oxford, Magdalen College Archives, Liber Computi; 1517–18; Latin; parchment; 15 + i; 332mm x 218mm (291mm x 170mm); modern pencil foliation; good condition; modern card binding.

Oxford, Magdalen College Archives, Liber Computi; 1519–20; Latin; parchment; 19 + v; 324mm x 267mm (267mm x 213mm); modern pencil foliation, partial contemporary ink foliation; good condition; modern card binding.

Oxford, Magdalen College Archives, Liber Computi; 1520–1; Latin; parchment; iii + 18; 358mm x 277mm (335mm x 250mm); modern pencil foliation; good condition; modern card binding.

Oxford, Magdalen College Archives, Liber Computi; 1529–30; Latin; parchment; 23 + i; 330mm x 285mm (288mm x 273mm); modern pencil foliation; good condition; modern card binding.

Oxford, Magdalen College Archives, Liber Computi; 1530–1; Latin; parchment; ii + 13; 418mm x 284mm (412mm x 255mm); modern pencil foliation; good condition; modern card binding.

Oxford, Magdalen College Archives, Liber Computi; 1531–2; Latin; parchment; 18 + ii; 397mm x 259mm (327mm x 231mm); modern pencil foliation; good condition; modern card binding.

Oxford, Magdalen College Archives, Liber Computi; 1533–4; Latin; parchment; i + 26; 330mm x 248mm (248mm x 236mm); modern pencil foliation; good condition; modern card binding.

Oxford, Magdalen College Archives, Liber Computi; 1534–5; Latin; parchment; 12 + ii; 356mm x 254mm (315mm x 235mm); modern pencil foliation; good condition; modern card binding.

Oxford, Magdalen College Archives, Liber Computi; 1535–6; Latin; parchment; 11 leaves; 350mm x 265mm (304mm x 222mm); modern pencil foliation; good condition; modern card binding.

Oxford, Magdalen College Archives, Liber Computi; 1537–8; Latin; parchment; i + 14 + ii; 380mm x 288mm (295mm x 216mm); modern pencil foliation; good condition; modern card binding.

Oxford, Magdalen College Archives, Liber Computi; 1538–9; Latin; parchment; 12 + v; 393mm x 287mm (252mm x 222mm); modern pencil foliation; good condition; modern card binding.

Oxford, Magdalen College Archives, Liber Computi; 1539–40; Latin; parchment; 10 + i; 418mm x 302mm (388mm x 255mm); modern pencil foliation; good condition; modern card binding.

Oxford, Magdalen College Archives, Liber Computi; 1540–1; Latin; parchment; 11 leaves; 412mm x 300mm (293mm x 224mm); modern pencil foliation; good condition; modern card binding.

Oxford, Magdalen College Archives, Liber Computi; 1541–2; Latin; parchment; i + 13; 404mm x 295mm (301mm x 211mm); modern pencil foliation; excellent condition; modern binding.

Oxford, Magdalen College Archives, LCE/5; 1543–59; Latin; parchment; i + 244 + i; 336–518mm x 239–346mm (292–495mm x 150–279mm); modern pencil foliation; good condition; guardbook with parchment binding of original accounts, embossed title on spine: 'LIBRI COMPUTI S. M. MAGD. COLL. 1543–1559.'

Oxford, Magdalen College Archives, LCE/6; 1559–80; Latin; parchment; i + 258 + i; 535mm x 350mm (467mm x 317mm); partial modern pencil foliation; reasonable condition, substantial water damage leading to loss of information; modern white parchment binding, title embossed on spine: 'LIBRI COMPUTI S. M. MAGD. COLL. 1559–1580.'

Oxford, Magdalen College Archives, LCE/7; 1586–1605; Latin; parchment; i + 173 + i; 598mm x 365mm (428mm x 269mm); partial modern pencil foliation; decorated initial capitals; good condition; modern white parchment binding, title embossed on spine: 'LIBRI COMPUTI S. M. MAGD. COLL. 1586–1605.'

Oxford, Magdalen College Archives, LCE/8; 1605/6–19/20; Latin; parchment; i + 125 + i; 396–570mm x 305–60mm (361–536mm x 230–307mm); partial modern pencil foliation; some accounts in 2 cols; generally good condition, damage to some final leaves resulting in loss of information; modern white parchment binding, title embossed on spine: 'LIBER COMPUTI S. M. MAGD. COLL. 1606–1620.'

Oxford, Magdalen College Archives, LCE/9; 1621–2; Latin; parchment; 8 leaves; 547mm x 345mm (511mm x 290mm); unnumbered; good condition; contemporary parchment binding, original leather ties, contemporary ink date on front cover.

Oxford, Magdalen College Archives, LCE/10; 1622–3; Latin; parchment; 8 leaves; 572mm x 362mm (499mm x 304mm); unnumbered; good condition; contemporary parchment binding, original leather ties, contemporary ink date on front cover.

Oxford, Magdalen College Archives, LCE/11; 1623–4; Latin; parchment; 8 leaves; 530mm x 343mm (502mm x 317mm); unnumbered; good condition; contemporary parchment binding, contemporary ink date on front cover.

Oxford, Magdalen College Archives, LCE/12; 1624–5; Latin; parchment; i + 8 + i (paper flyleaves); 535mm x 340mm (513mm x 300mm); unnumbered; good condition; contemporary parchment binding, original leather ties, contemporary ink title on front cover.

Oxford, Magdalen College Archives, LCE/13; 1625–6; Latin; parchment; 8 leaves; 528mm x 335mm

(510mm x 310mm); unnumbered; good condition, minor insect damage; contemporary parchment binding, original leather ties, contemporary ink title on front cover.

Oxford, Magdalen College Archives, LCE/14; 1626–7; Latin; parchment; i + 8 + i (paper flyleaves); 508mm x 336mm (482mm x 300mm); unnumbered; good condition; contemporary parchment binding, leather ties partially extant, contemporary ink title on front cover.

Oxford, Magdalen College Archives, LCE/15; 1627–8; Latin; parchment; i + 6 + i (paper flyleaves); 492mm x 360mm (480mm x 287mm); unnumbered; good condition, some insect damage; contemporary parchment binding, leather ties partially extant, contemporary ink title on front cover.

Oxford, Magdalen College Archives, LCE/16; 1629–30; Latin; parchment; i + 7 + i (paper flyleaves); 507mm x 360mm (484mm x 308mm); unnumbered; good condition; contemporary parchment binding, original leather ties, contemporary ink title on front cover.

Oxford, Magdalen College Archives, LCE/16a; 1630–1; Latin; parchment; 6 leaves; 513mm x 356mm (476mm x 262mm); unnumbered; poor condition, considerable water and insect damage, leading to loss of information. Bound with LCE/16.

Oxford, Magdalen College Archives, LCE/17; 1631–2; Latin; parchment; i + 6 + i (paper flyleaves); 523mm x 347mm (488mm x 323mm); partial modern pencil foliation; good condition; contemporary parchment binding, leather ties partially extant, contemporary ink title on front cover, antiquarian ink year dates on front cover.

Oxford, Magdalen College Archives, LCE/18; 1632–3; Latin; parchment; i + 6 + i (paper flyleaves); 495mm x 350mm (450mm x 310mm); unnumbered; good condition, minor insect damage; contemporary parchment binding, leather ties partially extant, contemporary ink title on front cover.

Oxford, Magdalen College Archives, LCE/19; 1633–4; Latin; parchment; i + 6 + i (paper flyleaves); 490mm x 360mm (449mm x 320mm); partial modern pencil foliation; good condition; contemporary parchment binding, leather ties partially extant, contemporary ink title on front cover.

Oxford, Magdalen College Archives, LCE/20; 1634–5; Latin; parchment; i + 5 + i (paper flyleaves); 489mm x 351mm (446mm x 308mm); unnumbered; good condition; contemporary parchment binding, leather ties extant, contemporary ink title on front cover.

Oxford, Magdalen College Archives, LCE/21; 1635–6; Latin; parchment; i + 6 + i (paper flyleaves); 502mm x 366mm (443mm x 323mm); unnumbered; good condition; contemporary parchment binding, leather ties partially extant, contemporary red ink title on front cover (plus contemporary ink note, written upside down on front cover, but unrelated to title).

Oxford, Magdalen College Archives, LCE/23; 1637–8; Latin; parchment; i + 6 + i (paper flyleaves); 516mm x 366mm (494mm x 334mm); unnumbered; good condition; contemporary parchment binding, leather ties partially extant, contemporary ink title on front cover.

Oxford, Magdalen College Archives, LCE/24; 1638–9; Latin; parchment; i + 5 + i (paper flyleaves); 510mm x 362mm (480mm x 287mm); unnumbered; good condition, minor insect damage; contemporary parchment binding, leather ties partially extant, contemporary ink titles on front cover.

Oxford, Magdalen College Archives, LCE/25; 1639–40; Latin; parchment; i + 5 + i (paper flyleaves); 516mm x 390mm (488mm x 332mm); unnumbered; good condition, minor insect damage; contemporary parchment binding, leather ties partially extant, contemporary ink title on front cover.

Oxford, Magdalen College Archives, LCE/27; 1641–2; Latin; parchment; i + 6 (paper flyleaf); 507mm x 366mm (464mm x 307mm); unnumbered; good condition, minor insect damage; contemporary parchment binding, leather ties extant, contemporary ink title on front cover.

Magdalen College Draft Libri Computi

The draft computi are cited in the present volume only if they differ significantly from the computi or supply missing years.

Oxford, Magdalen College Archives, LCD/1; 1552–79; Latin; paper; i + 502 + i; 405mm x 275mm (343mm x 231mm); partial modern pencil foliation; generally good condition, minor insect damage and wear to some papers, certain leaves wholly or partially cut out; contemporary(?) leather binding with blind tooling, later embossed title on spine: 'LIBER COMPUTI S. M. MAGD. COLL. 1552–1578.'

Oxford, Magdalen College Archives, LCD/2; 1582–1614; Latin; paper; i + 186 + i; 421mm x 278mm (410mm x 240mm); partial modern pencil foliation; some accounts in 2 cols; good condition; antiquarian tooled leather binding, embossed title on spine: 'LIBER COMPUTI S. M. MAGD. COLL. 1582–1614.'

Oxford, Magdalen College Archives, LCD/3; 1621–42; Latin; paper; i + 328 + i (many of final 167 folios blank); 428mm x 281mm (410mm x 195mm); partial modern pencil foliation; some accounts in 2 or 3 cols; good condition; antiquarian cloth on board, embossed title on spine: 'LIB COMP 1617–1643.'

Magdalen School Copy Book

This volume was apparently compiled by a Magdalen School grammarian. It consists chiefly of personal letters and school exercises, the latter comprising short English passages to be translated into Latin and probably composed c 1495–9. See Nelson (ed), *A Fifteenth Century School Book*. The letter of Thomas More on folio 85v has been edited by E.F. Rogers, *The Correspondence of Sir Thomas More* (Princeton, 1947), 3–4.

London, British Library, MS Arundel 249; c 1495–9; Latin and English; parchment and paper; ii + 120 + iii; 170mm x 220mm; modern pencil foliation; bound in stamped leather and board in 1967.

Episcopal Visitation of Magdalen College

Folios 44–74 of this volume contain the report of an examination of the fellows of Magdalen by a commissary of Richard Fox, bishop of Winchester, on 20–7 January 1506/7.

A transcript of this report made in 1900 constitutes MS 787 in the Magdalen College Archives and claims to contain a collation with a second copy of the Register found at Farnham Castle in 1899, whose present location is unknown.[5]

Winchester, Hampshire Record Office, 21M65/A1/18; 21 September 1506–June 1510; Latin; parchment; ii + 150 + iv; 280mm x 380mm; modern foliation; leather-cased parchment cover.

Magdalen School Exercise Book

Folios 35–49 of this volume comprise a fragmentary set of Latin/English exercises, probably composed by a Magdalen school master.[6]

London, British Library, MS Royal 12.B.xx; c 1512–27; Latin and English; paper; ii + 49 + ii; 145mm x 215mm; modern pencil foliation; bound in stamped leather and board in 1930.

Magdalen College Vice-President's Register

Oxford, Magdalen College Archives, VP1/A1/1; 1547–1839; Latin and English; paper; i + 520 + i; 305mm x 200mm; partial modern foliation; bound in leather and board, in ink on flyleaf: 'Incipit hoc Registrum ann. 1547. sc. 1mo Edw. 6ti.' Contains miscellaneous records of college administration.

Letters of Complaint Regarding Abuses at Magdalen College

These letters are included in a collection of sixteenth to nineteenth century manuscripts pertaining to Magdalen College presidents compiled in the nineteenth century by Dr John Rouse Bloxam.

Oxford, Magdalen College Archives, MS 655a; 19th c.; paper; English and Latin; 348mm x 212mm (text area varies); contemporary ink and pencil pagination, some parts of which may indicate the sequence of a previous compilation; 19th-c. paper over board, embossed title on spine: 'The Presidents of S. M. Magdalen College Vol. 1.'

Excerpts from:

Complaint of Edward Gellibrand: c 1584; English and Latin; paper; bifolium; 296mm x 204mm (288mm x 193mm); originally unnumbered; good condition. Now bound within guardbook and paginated 321–4 in modern pencil.

Complaint of William Cooke: c 1584; English; paper; bifolium; 266mm x 177mm (212mm x 160mm);

originally unnumbered; good condition. Now bound within guardbook and paginated 329–32 in modern pencil.

Complaint of Simeon Pett: *c* 1584; English; paper; bifolium; 295mm x 200mm (275mm x 190mm); originally unnumbered; good condition. Now bound within guardbook and paginated 337–40 in modern pencil.

Letter of Nicholas Bond to Lord Treasurer Dorset

Bond was president of Magdalen College; the earl of Dorset was Thomas Sackville, lord treasurer of England and chancellor of the University.

Maidstone, Centre for Kentish Studies, U269 C1; 11 September 1592; English; paper; bifolium; 300mm x 195mm; unnumbered; writing on 2 inner pages only; endorsed in later hands.

MERTON COLLEGE

Merton College was founded in 1264 (at the latest) by Walter de Merton, then translated to Oxford in 1274. Its head is a warden. It is unique among Oxford colleges in having maintained for nearly three hundred years a daily chronicle known as the college register.

Archives are preserved in a designated space but produced for readers in the library. Accounts have been preserved from 1276. Access is via W.H. Stevenson, 'Merton College Calendar of Records,' 2 vols (1891 typescript), available as Bodl.: MS. Top.Oxon d.461/1 and 461/2. This has been supplemented by a handwritten list, in three volumes, photocopied by the National Register of Archives in 1961.

The following yielded no REED entries:

1/ 4278. Paper roll, in Latin, listing rewards over two years to various persons. Dated *c* 1525 by Stevenson but more likely 1487–8. Contains some Cambridge references.

2/ 4305d. A bundle of miscellaneous letters, inventories, and fragments in Latin. Includes a room inventory by Edmund Bunny.

3/ 4600–25. Annual computi of John Wylyot's foundation for poor scholars, or 'Portionists,' to 1550, in Latin.

4/ 3964–4048. Subwarden's accounts, 1276–1642, in Latin.

5/ 4283. Receipts for payments by the college, 1608–39, in Latin.

6/ Miscellaneous proctors', chaplains', and supervisors' accounts, in Latin.

Merton College Supervisors of Founders' Kin Accounts

Oxford, Merton College Records, 4109; 1386–7; Latin; parchment; single mb; 578mm x 213mm (552mm x 208mm); unnumbered; good condition.

Oxford, Merton College Records, 4114; 1400–1; Latin; parchment; single mb; 733mm x 272mm

(676mm x 263mm); unnumbered; generally good condition, some physical damage leading to minor loss of information.

Oxford, Merton College Records, 4115; 1410–11; Latin; parchment; single mb; 380mm x 203mm (329mm x 197mm); unnumbered; good condition.

Merton College Bursars' Accounts

Merton's accounting system is unique among Oxford colleges. Instead of the usual four terms, Merton divided its accounting year into three four-month periods. Moreover, a different bursar was responsible for each period, yielding the following system (with each period beginning and ending on the Friday before the dates listed with the exception of the 1489–90 account in which the periods begin and end on the Friday after):

    1st bursar: 1 August–25 November

    2nd bursar: 25 November–25 March

    3rd bursar: 25 March–1 August

Each of three bursars kept his accounts on a separate roll, the third – the senior bursar – compiling a 'Computus Generalis,' in which he audited the work of his juniors and added their totals to his. Thus some 1,098 rolls would have been produced from 1276 to 1642. Up to 1360, however, rolls survive only in fragments; from 1360 to 1400 at least one roll survives for about half the years; from 1400 to 1479 some years are represented by all three rolls; early Tudor rolls survive in irregular numbers; from 1537 to 1585 almost every year is represented by at least one roll; and from 1585 to 1642 all rolls survive complete. Pre-1585 rolls (MCR: 3612–3965), mostly parchment but some on paper, survive in various degrees of preservation; post-1585 rolls, all parchment, have been bound flat into two volumes.

Oxford, Merton College Records, 3754; 1431–2; Latin; parchment; 2 mbs; 602mm x 302mm (527mm x 285mm); unnumbered; written on front only, contents of roll noted on dorse; reasonable condition with some rodent damage.

Oxford, Merton College Records, 3785; 1469–70; Latin; parchment; single mb; 631mm x 310mm (511mm x 295mm); unnumbered; written on front only; good condition with some insect damage.

Oxford, Merton College Records, 3808; 1489–90; Latin; parchment; 2 mbs; 615mm x 287mm (570mm x 284mm); unnumbered; written on front only; antiquarian notes on dorse; fair condition with significant loss of text due to rodent damage.

Oxford, Merton College Records, 3932d; 1566–7; Latin; parchment; single mb; 580mm x 387mm (481mm x 384mm); unnumbered; written on front only, reasonable condition with some damage.

Oxford, Merton College Records, 3932e; 1567–8; Latin; parchment; single mb; 583mm x 476mm (536mm x 465mm); unnumbered; written on front only; reasonable condition with some damage.

Oxford, Merton College Records, 3944c; 1572–3; Latin; parchment; single mb; 683mm x 505mm (530mm x 485mm); unnumbered; written on front only; good condition, minor insect damage.

Oxford, Merton College Records, 3.1; 1585–1633; Latin; parchment; i + 262 + ii; 410mm x 300mm; modern pencil foliation; late-17th-c. tooled leather binding, repaired in 19th c., on spine in gold leaf on red background: 'Liber Rationarius Coll: Mert: I. 1585–1633.'

Oxford, Merton College Records, 3.2; 1633–52; Latin; parchment; ii + 126 + ii; 380mm x 230mm; modern pencil foliation; rebound in 1975, preserving the gold leaf text on red background on spine of original binding: 'Liber Rationarius Coll: Mert: II 1633–1652.'

Merton College Registers

Register 1.2 has been published in two volumes by the Oxford Historical Society: Salter (ed), *Registrum Annalium Collegii Mertonensis 1483–1521*; and Fletcher (ed), *Registrum Annalium Collegii Mertonensis 1521–67*. The first 202 pages of Register 1.3, containing the annals to 1603, have been published by the Oxford Historical Society: Fletcher (ed), *Registrum Annalium Collegii Mertonensis 1567–1603*. The archives contain a handwritten 'Subject Index to the Merton College Register Vol. II A.D. 1567 to 1730' (MCR: 1.5.S), compiled anonymously about 1890.

Oxford, Merton College Records, 1.2; 1483–1567; Latin; paper; 357 leaves; 270mm x 380mm (text area varies); modern foliation; originally written on loose sheets, now bound in 16th-c. oak boards, on spine: 'Coll: Merton Registrum Vetus. 1482–1567.'

Oxford, Merton College Records, 1.3; 1568–1731; Latin; paper; iv + 400 + xxv; 260mm x 390mm (text area varies); modern pencil pagination; inside margins heavily cropped in 19th c. rebinding, note at the top of f [i] reads: 'Registrum commune Domus sive collegij scholarium de Merton in Oxon' 1567. precium xiij s. iiij d.'

NEW COLLEGE

New College was founded by William of Wykeham in 1379. Its head is a warden. Its bursars' accounts are more or less continuous from 1381–2.

Archives, housed in the Muniment Tower built at the time of foundation for that purpose, are accessed via Francis W. Steer (ed), *The Archives of New College, Oxford* (London, 1974).

New College Statutes

Oxford, New College Archives, 9429; 14th c.; Latin; parchment; iii + 44 + iii; 411mm x 294mm (318mm x 209mm); contemporary ink foliation; illuminated initial capital, decorated title capitals for each section, title script for each section highlighted in red; excellent condition; contemporary parchment binding with 3 plaited cord ties partially extant, founder's seal pendant (111mm x 63mm).

The version of the statutes found in NC Arch: 9429 has been collated with:

Oxford, New College Archives, 9431; 14th c.; Latin; parchment; i + 43; 408mm x 293mm (311mm x 224mm); contemporary ink foliation; illuminated initial capital, decorated initial capitals for each chapter, title script, foliation, and chapter number given in red ink; generally good condition, some minor water damage to initial leaves; modern brown leather binding.

New College Hall Books

Hall books are notebooks of weekly accounts of commons, with the names of all visitors at meals. They were kept by the seneschal or steward. Several notebooks are bound into each modern volume. Weekly accounts run Saturday to Friday – but there are many gaps, both of weeks and entire years, and actual years are often conjectural (inserted slips mark the probable break between years).

Oxford, New College Archives, 5527; 1396–1418; Latin; paper; ii + 145 + iii; 301mm x 109mm (271mm x 90mm); contemporary pagination of some individual years; 2 cols; good condition; 17th-c. leather binding over board with modern replacement ties, antiquarian ink title on spine.

Oxford, New College Archives, 5529; 1478?–99; Latin; paper; 278 + i (paper inserts indicating change of year not included in count); 310mm x 106mm (298mm x 104mm); unnumbered; 2 cols; generally good condition, some paper torn, minor insect damage; 17th-c. leather on board with modern ties, antiquarian ink title on spine.

Oxford, New College Archives, 5530; undated (antiquarian dating: 1501?–44); Latin; paper; iii + 289 + i (paper inserts indicating change of year not included in count); 311mm x 100mm (302mm x 80mm); unnumbered; 2 cols; generally good condition; 17th-c. leather on board with modern ties, fragments of original parchment MS binding preserved, antiquarian ink title on spine.

New College Bursars' Accounts

The accounts were kept from Michaelmas to Michaelmas. Headings such as 'Internal' and 'External Expenses' are subdivided into the usual four terms.

Oxford, New College Archives, 7713; 1460–1; Latin; parchment; 6 mbs sewn to form continuous roll; 3,299mm x 295mm (3,162mm x 274mm); unnumbered; good condition.

Oxford, New College Archives, 7720; 1469–70; Latin; parchment; 5 mbs sewn to form continuous roll; 3,509mm x 281mm (3,447mm x 277mm); unnumbered; condition generally good, some rodent damage leading to loss of information.

Oxford, New College Archives, 7722; 1479–80; Latin; parchment; 8 mbs sewn to form continuous roll; 4,157mm x 238mm (3,992mm x 193mm); unnumbered; condition generally good although initial mb(s) now lost, minor damage leading to loss of information.

Oxford, New College Archives, 7477; 1524–5; Latin; parchment; 9 mbs sewn to form continuous roll; 5,441mm x 238mm (5,279mm x 193mm); unnumbered; good condition.

Oxford, New College Archives, 7488; 1533–4; Latin; parchment; 11 mbs sewn to form continuous roll; 5,383mm x 370mm (5,306mm x 365mm); unnumbered; good condition.

Oxford, New College Archives, 7489; 1534–5; Latin; parchment; 10 mbs now unstitched and glued to form continuous roll; 4,366mm x 340mm (4,295mm x 302mm); unnumbered; good condition, original initial mb now absent.

Oxford, New College Archives, 7493; 1536–7; Latin; parchment; 8 mbs sewn to form continuous roll; 3,770mm x 349mm (3,564mm x 345mm); unnumbered; good condition.

Oxford, New College Archives, 7495; 1537–8; Latin; parchment; 6 mbs sewn to form continuous roll; 4,636mm x 316mm (4,593mm x 312mm); unnumbered; good condition, rodent damage leading to minor loss of information.

Oxford, New College Archives, 7522; 1552–3; Latin and English; parchment; 10 mbs unstitched and glued to form continuous roll; 4,430mm x 288mm (4,393mm x 282mm); unnumbered; condition generally good, insect damage leading to minor loss of information.

Oxford, New College Archives, 7553; 1575–6; Latin; parchment; 11 mbs (the 11th of which is blank) stitched to form continuous roll; 5,744mm x 317mm (5,126mm x 307mm); unnumbered; good condition.

Oxford, New College Archives, 7556; 1578–9; Latin; parchment; 8 mbs unstitched and glued to form continuous roll; 4,352mm x 287mm (4,124mm x 229mm); unnumbered; good condition.

Oxford, New College Archives, 7563; 1582–3; Latin; parchment; 9 mbs sewn to form continuous roll; 4,762mm x 291mm (4,743mm x 241mm); unnumbered; good condition.

Oxford, New College Archives, 7564; 1583–4; Latin; parchment; 12 mbs sewn to form continuous roll; 7,339mm x 291mm (7,195mm x 222mm); unnumbered; good condition.

Oxford, New College Archives, 7576; 1590–1; Latin; parchment; 11 mbs sewn to form continuous roll; 7,340mmm x 277mm (7,318mm x 221mm); unnumbered; good condition.

Oxford, New College Archives, 7586; 1597–8; English and Latin; parchment; 8 mbs sewn to form continuous roll; 5,102mm x 280mm (4,792mm x 213mm); unnumbered; good condition.

Oxford, New College Archives, 7588; 1599–1600; Latin; parchment; 10 mbs sewn to form continuous roll; 5,542mm x 258mm (5,274mm x 230mm); unnumbered; good condition.

Oxford, New College Archives, 7590; 1600–1; Latin; parchment; 7 mbs sewn to form continuous roll;

4,460mm x 252mm (4,179mm x 222mm); unnumbered; decorated initial capital in MS header; good condition.

Oxford, New College Archives, 7593; 1602–3; English and Latin; parchment; 5 mbs sewn to form continuous roll; 3,759mm x 297mm (3,651mm x 268mm); unnumbered; decorated initial capital and enlarged title script in MS header; good condition.

Oxford, New College Archives, 7595; 1603–4; Latin; parchment; 6 mbs sewn to form continuous roll; 4,314mm x 280mm (4,126mm x 277mm); unnumbered; decorated initial capital and enlarged title script in MS header; good condition.

Oxford, New College Archives, 7596; 1604–5; Latin; parchment; 5 mbs sewn to form continuous roll; 3,969mm x 221mm (3,721mm x 219mm); unnumbered; decorated initial capitals and enlarged title script in MS header; good condition.

Oxford, New College Archives, 7599; 1605–6; Latin; parchment; 8 mbs sewn to form continuous roll; 5,126mm x 296mm (5,012mm x 289mm); unnumbered; decorated initial capitals and enlarged title script in MS header; certain notes made in a second hand throughout; good condition.

Oxford, New College Archives, 7600; 1606–7; Latin; parchment; 11 mbs sewn to form continuous roll; 4,882mm x 287mm (4,768mm x 282mm); unnumbered; decorated initial capitals and enlarged title script in MS header; generally good condition, minor insect damage leading to negligible loss of information.

Oxford, New College Archives, 7603; 1607–8; Latin; parchment; 9 mbs sewn to form continuous roll; 4,806mm x 299mm (4,732mm x 296mm); unnumbered; decorated initial capitals and enlarged title script in MS header; good condition.

Oxford, New College Archives, 7604; 1608–9; Latin; parchment; 11 mbs sewn to form continuous roll; 5,411mm x 268mm (5,375mm x 265mm); unnumbered; decorated initial capitals and enlarged title script in MS header; good condition.

Oxford, New College Archives, 7606; 1609–10; Latin; parchment; 13 mbs sewn to form continuous roll; 6,764mm x 333mm (6,683mm x 330mm); unnumbered; decorated initial capitals and enlarged title script in MS header; generally good condition.

Oxford, New College Archives, 7611; 1612–13; English and Latin; parchment; 11 mbs sewn to form continuous roll; 6,536mm x 294mm (6,507mm x 289mm); unnumbered; enlarged title script in MS header; good condition.

Oxford, New College Archives, 7614; 1613–14; English and Latin; parchment; 13 mbs sewn to form continuous roll; 6,218mm x 311mm (5,991mm x 309mm); unnumbered; enlarged title script in MS header; generally good condition.

Oxford, New College Archives, 7615; 1614–15; English and Latin; parchment; 14 mbs sewn to form

continuous roll; 6,759mm x 309mm (6,749mm x 307mm); unnumbered; decorated initial capitals and enlarged title script in MS header; good condition.

Oxford, New College Archives, 7617; 1615–16; English and Latin; parchment; 10 mbs sewn to form continuous roll; 4,919mm x 307mm (4,819mm x 304mm); unnumbered; enlarged title script in MS header; generally good condition, some physical damage.

Oxford, New College Archives, 7619; 1616–17; Latin and English; parchment; 8 mbs sewn to form continuous roll; 3,907mm x 292mm (3,846mm x 262mm); unnumbered; good condition; modern cataloguing mark on label tied to roll.

Oxford, New College Archives, 7621; 1617–18; Latin and English; parchment; 12 mbs sewn to form continuous roll; 5,583mm x 306mm (5,517mm x 305mm); unnumbered; decorated initial capitals and enlarged title script in MS header; good condition; modern cataloguing mark on label tied to roll.

Oxford, New College Archives, 7623; 1618–19; Latin and English; parchment; 8 mbs sewn to form continuous roll; 4,684mm x 305mm (4,566mm x 285mm); unnumbered; enlarged-title script; good condition; modern cataloguing mark on label tied to roll.

Oxford, New College Archives, 7624; 1619–20; Latin and English; parchment; 8 mbs sewn to form continuous roll; 4,720mm x 305mm (4,704mm x 297mm); unnumbered; enlarged title script in MS header; good condition; modern cataloguing mark on label tied to roll.

Oxford, New College Archives, 7626; 1620–1; Latin and English; parchment; 11 mbs sewn to form continuous roll; 4,737mm x 303mm (4,579mm x 297mm); unnumbered; good condition; modern cataloguing mark on label tied to roll.

Oxford, New College Archives, 7629; 1621–2; English and Latin; parchment; 9 mbs sewn to form continuous roll; 4,285mm x 308mm (4,110mm x 306mm); unnumbered; enlarged title script in MS header; good condition; modern cataloguing mark on label tied to roll.

Oxford, New College Archives, 7631; 1622–3; Latin and English; parchment; 10 mbs sewn to form continuous roll; 5,202mm x 304mm (4,641mm x 302mm); unnumbered; decorated initial title capital and enlarged title script in MS header; good condition, minor insect damage to mb 1; modern cataloguing mark on label tied to roll.

Oxford, New College Archives, 7633; 1623–4; English and Latin; parchment; 10 mbs sewn to form continuous roll; 4,771mm x 304mm (4,751mm x 298mm); unnumbered; good condition.

Oxford, New College Archives, 7635; 1624–5; English and Latin; parchment; 13 mbs sewn to form continuous roll; 5,528mm x 255mm (5,496mm x 253mm); unnumbered; enlarged and decorated title script in MS header, some decorated initial capitals in main body of text; good condition.

Oxford, New College Archives, 7637; 1625–6; English and Latin; parchment; 14 mbs sewn to form

continuous roll; 5,599mm x 280mm (5,444mm x 276mm); unnumbered; enlarged title script in MS header; good condition.

Oxford, New College Archives, 7638; 1626–7; English and Latin; parchment;13 mbs sewn to form continuous roll; 6,574mm x 299mm (6,439mm x 277mm); unnumbered; enlarged title script and decorated capitals in MS header; good condition.

Oxford, New College Archives, 7640; 1627–8; English and Latin; parchment; 13 mbs sewn to form continuous roll; 7,130mm x 304mm (6,995mm x 249mm); unnumbered; illuminated initial capitals and enlarged title script in MS header; good condition.

Oxford, New College Archives, 7642; 1628–9; English and Latin; parchment; 10 mbs sewn to form continuous roll; 5,294mm x 305mm (5,109mm x 279mm); unnumbered; good condition.

Oxford, New College Archives, 7645; 1630–1; Latin and English; parchment; 14 mbs sewn to form continuous roll; 6,516mm x 301mm (6,386mm x 296mm); unnumbered; illuminated initial capitals and enlarged title script in MS header; good condition.

Oxford, New College Archives, 7647; 1631–2; English and Latin; parchment; 13 mbs sewn to form continuous roll; 7,193mm x 298mm (6,833mm x 295mm); unnumbered; illuminated initial capital, decorated title capitals, and enlarged title script in MS header; good condition.

Oxford, New College Archives, 7650; 1632–3; English and Latin; parchment; 15 mbs sewn to form continuous roll; 8,093mm x 297mm (7,666mm x 266mm); unnumbered; illuminated and decorated initial capitals and enlarged title script in MS header; good condition.

Oxford, New College Archives, 7651; 1633–4; Latin and English; parchment; 13 mbs sewn to form continuous roll; 7,046mm x 296mm (6,721mm x 274mm); unnumbered; illuminated initial capitals, other decorated capitals, and enlarged title script in MS header; good condition.

Oxford, New College Archives, 7653; 1634–5; English and Latin; parchment; 11 mbs sewn to form continuous roll; 6,315mm x 288mm (6,202mm x 271mm); unnumbered; illuminated and decorated initial capitals and enlarged title script in MS header; good condition.

Oxford, New College Archives, 7655; 1635–6; English and Latin; parchment; 12 mbs sewn to form continuous roll; 6,295mm x 300mm (6,237mm x 281mm); unnumbered; illuminated initial capital, decorated title capitals, and enlarged title script in MS header; generally good condition, rodent damage leading to negligible loss of information.

Oxford, New College Archives, 7656; 1636–7; English and Latin; parchment; 14 mbs sewn to form continuous roll; 6,880mm x 298mm (6,848mm x 280mm); unnumbered; illuminated initial capital, decorated initial capitals, and enlarged title script in MS header; good condition.

Oxford, New College Archives, 7657; 1637–8; English and Latin; parchment; 13 mbs sewn to form

continuous roll; 7,386mm x 287mm (7,013mm x 276mm); unnumbered; decorated initial capitals and enlarged title script in MS header; good condition.

Oxford, New College Archives, 7660; 1638–9; English and Latin; parchment; 14 mbs sewn to form continuous roll; 7,159mm x 293mm (6,639mm x 277mm); unnumbered; decorated initial capitals and enlarged script in MS header; excellent condition.

Oxford, New College Archives, 7661; 1639–40; English and Latin; parchment; 14 mbs sewn to form continuous roll; 7,376mm x 291mm (7,164mm x 271mm); unnumbered; decorated initial capitals and enlarged script in MS header; generally good condition, minor rodent damage.

Oxford, New College Archives, 7663; 1640–1; English and Latin; parchment; 15 mbs sewn to form continuous roll; 8,333mm x 289mm (8,167mm x 266mm); unnumbered; illuminated initial capital in header, enlarged title script in header and other parts of MS; good condition.

Oxford, New College Archives, 7665; 1641–2; English and Latin; parchment; 16 mbs sewn to form continuous roll; 8,055mm x 295mm (7,361mm x 277mm); unnumbered; enlarged title script in MS header; good condition.

New College Bursars' Long Book

These are draft accounts kept by the bursar and supply one entry for the year 1629–30, for which the annual account is missing. A similar volume containing drafts for some of the years between 1621 and 1634 (Steer 1126) yielded no REED entries.

Oxford, New College Archives, 4200; 1626–31; Latin; paper; i + 256; 160mm x 460mm; unnumbered; bound in original vellum.

Episcopal Visitation to New College

See under Episcopal Visitation to Corpus Christi College (p 648) for Hampshire Record Office: 21M65/A1/26.

Robert Townshend's Expenses

These accounts were kept for Robert Townshend, who matriculated at New College in 1593 at the age of twelve as a private pupil of the warden, Arthur Lake, whose hand appears on some pages.

Oxford, New College Archives, PA/L2; 1592–5; English; paper; 21 loose sheets; 210mm x 150mm average (text area varies); unnumbered; some sheets worn and defective.

Letter of Arthur Lake to Lady Townshend

Oxford, New College Archives, PA/L2; 3 April 1594; English; paper; single sheet; 229mm x 209mm (152mm x 180mm); unnumbered; fair condition.

ORIEL COLLEGE

Oriel College was founded by Edward II in 1326. Its head is a provost.

Archives, housed in a muniment room underneath the treasury, are produced for readers in the library. The internal financial records remain under the administrative authority of the treasurer.

Annual treasurers' accounts, called 'The Style,' survive from 1409 but are missing from 1416 to 1449 and 1527 to 1582. Access is via C.L. Shadwell, 'Treasurers' Accounts from 1409 to 1526,' 10 vols (1878–99 handwritten transcript), available in the library, and a card index.

Accounts were kept from Michaelmas to Michaelmas.

Oriel College Treasurers' Accounts

This volume appears to have been kept in book form from the beginning rather than as rolls or loose sheets, as a note on folio 9 refers to it as 'hoc novo libro chartaseo.'

Oxford, Oriel College Archives, S.I.C.1; 1583–1649; English; paper; 391 leaves; 235mm x 350mm; modern foliation; bound in vellum, written on cover, in modern hand: 'Oriel College [Rental] ⌐Accounts⌐ from 1583 to 1649'; stamped on spine: 'Oriel College Oxford Style 1583 to 1649.'

THE QUEEN'S COLLEGE

The Queen's College was founded in 1341 by Robert Eglesfield, chaplain of Philippa, queen consort of Edward III (the article, insisted on by purists, is sometimes omitted in this collection; also compare The Queen's College, Oxford, and Queens' College, Cambridge). Its head is a provost.

Archives, housed in a muniment room near the bursary, are produced for readers in the library. Access is via N. Denholm-Young, 'Calendar of the Archives of the Queen's College,' 4 vols (1931 typescript), available as Bodl.: MS. R. Top. 694. A transcript of the computus rolls (or 'Long Rolls') 1340–1470, by C.L. Stainer and J.R. McGrath, 10 vols, is library MS 453 (vols 9–10 are indexes to vols 1–8).

The Queen's College Long Rolls, 1340–1592

The surviving accounts begin in 1340 and continue throughout our period with some gaps. A few of the rolls are in deteriorated condition and could not be examined. Until 1592 the accounts survive as individual rolls; after that, in three bound volumes. They are divided into subject headings but not into terms. The accounting year is 7 July to 7 July.

Oxford, The Queen's College Archives, 2P131; 1541–2; Latin; parchment; single mb; 888mm x 575mm (708mm x 561mm); unnumbered; sections of 4 cols, otherwise 1 col, dorse is in 2 cols; fair condition, some physical damage leading to actual loss of information.

Oxford, The Queen's College Archives, 2P146; 1558–9; Latin; parchment; single mb; 950mm x 672mm (781mm x 655mm); unnumbered; 1 section of 4 cols, the rest 1 col only; reasonable condition, some wear to central portion of mb.

Oxford, The Queen's College Archives, 2P150; 1563–4; Latin and English; parchment; single mb; 930mm x 610mm (858mm x 604mm); unnumbered; 1 section of 4 cols, the rest 1 col; good condition.

Oxford, The Queen's College Archives, 2P156; 1572–3; Latin; parchment; single mb; 836mm x 603mm (762mm x 567mm); unnumbered; 1 section of 4 cols, the rest 1 col; fair condition, some damage to left side of mb leading to minor loss of information, minor insect damage.

Oxford, The Queen's College Archives, 2P161; 1583–4; Latin; parchment; single mb; 797mm x 663mm (667mm x 598mm); unnumbered; 1 section of 4 cols, the rest 1 col; good condition.

Oxford, The Queen's College Archives, 2P162; 1584–5; Latin; parchment; single mb; 770mm x 626mm (562mm x 591mm); unnumbered; good condition, some wear to central section of mb.

Oxford, The Queen's College Archives, 2P163; 1585–6; Latin; parchment; single mb; 803mm x 570mm (661mm x 545mm); unnumbered; good condition.

Oxford, The Queen's College Archives, 2P164; 1586–7; Latin; parchment; single mb; 900mm x 668mm (779mm x 610mm); unnumbered; generally good condition, some physical damage.

Oxford, The Queen's College Archives, 2P165; 1589–90; Latin; parchment; single mb; 845mm x 662mm (795mm x 636mm); unnumbered; good condition.

Oxford, The Queen's College Archives, 2P167; 1591–2; Latin; parchment; single mb; 810mm x 668mm (745mm x 624mm); unnumbered; fair condition, water damage causing some loss of information to top right of roll.

The Queen's College Long Rolls, 1592–1657

The accounts are divided into subject headings but not into terms. Some entries continue past the 7 July close of the accounting year; see, for example, p 408 under 1614–15.

Oxford, The Queen's College Archives, LRA; 1592–1610; Latin and English; parchment; i + 38 + i; 396mm x 268mm (375mm x 222mm); modern pencil foliation; 1 and 2 cols; good condition; contemporary binding, embossed leather binding (very worn) with restored spine.

Oxford, The Queen's College Archives, LRB; 1610–28; Latin; parchment; ii + 45 + i; 393mm x 270mm (370mm x 261mm); modern pencil foliation; 2 cols; good condition; contemporary embossed leather binding (very worn) with replacement spine, modern rebinding.

Oxford, The Queen's College Archives, LRC; 1628–57; Latin; parchment; i + 58; 392mm x 298mm (380mm x 285mm); partial modern pencil foliation; 2 cols; good condition; contemporary embossed leather binding with modern (replacement) cloth ties, replaced spine.

The Queen's College Statutes (A)

This is an antiquarian copy of the 1340 statutes for The Queen's College.

Oxford, The Queen's College Archives; 1583; Latin; parchment; i + 48 + i; 335mm x 242mm (243mm x 161mm); contemporary ink pagination; good condition; contemporary leather binding with elaborate blind tooling to front and back covers.

ST JOHN'S COLLEGE

St John's College was founded in 1555 by Sir Thomas White. Its head is a president.

Archives, housed and consulted extramurally, preserve virtually complete accounts from 1568–9 forward. Access is via a card index. A guide to the index, by H.M. Colvin and M.G.A. Vale (1983 typescript), is available in Duke Humfrey as Bodl.: MS. R. Top.700.

Archival items found to be without REED interest include chest books, buttery books, miscellaneous early correspondence, other college registers, visitation documents, inventories, building accounts, and antiquarian scrapbooks.

St John's College Register

This volume contains records of benefactions, elections to fellowships, and decrees of the governing body.

Oxford, St John's College Archives, Admin.I.A.1; 1557–91; English and Latin; paper; iii + 310 + vii; 371mm x 273mm; contemporary ink foliation; some enlarged and illuminated capitals; written front to back; good condition; modern calf binding with some embossing on front and back covers, title on spine: 'I Register 1557–1591.'

St John's College Computus Annuus

The accounting year was from Michaelmas to Michaelmas, divided into the usual four terms. The annual audit was held on 20 November and expenses between 29 September and the audit are sometimes included in the account for the previous accounting year. The volumes in this series are uniformly labeled 'Computus Annuus.' Twenty-four volumes survive for the period

1568–1642. Some contain a single year's accounts, some more than one. Missing are 1572–8, 1588–98, and 1604–16.

Oxford, St John's College Archives, Acc.i.A.l; 1569–72; English and Latin; paper; xvi + 14 + xx; 340mm x 152mm (323mm x 135mm); contemporary ink pagination; written front to back; good condition, lower part of each page missing, possibly rodent damage; modern board binding with brown cloth cover, title on spine: 'COMPUTUS ANNUUS 1568–72.'

Oxford, St John's College Archives, Acc.i.A.2; 1578–81; English and Latin; paper; i + 41; 405mm x 148mm (400mm x 142mm); modern pencil pagination; written front to back; good condition; contemporary leather binding with cloth ties, rebound within modern board binding, title on spine: 'COMPUTUS ANNUUS 1579–80.'

Oxford, St John's College Archives, Acc.i.A.3; 1581–2; English and Latin; paper; ii + 32 + i; 418mm x 140mm (384mm x 95mm); modern pencil foliation; written front to back, verso of folios often blank; good condition; contemporary leather binding, rebound within modern board binding, title on spine: 'COMPUTUS ANNUUS 1581–82.'

Oxford, St John's College Archives, Acc.i.A.4; 1582–3; English and Latin; paper; i + 27; 419mm x 149mm (387mm x 133mm); modern pencil foliation; written front to back; good condition; contemporary leather binding with leather ties, rebound within modern board binding, title on spine: 'COMPUTUS ANNUUS 1582–83.'

Oxford, St John's College Archives, Acc.i.A.5; 1583–4; English and Latin; paper; iv + 45 + ii (first 2 opening flyleaves are modern, others contemporary inserted pages, end flyleaves are modern); 443mm x 168mm (412mm x 121mm); partial modern pencil foliation; good condition; modern board with leather spine (possibly remnants of contemporary binding?).

Oxford, St John's College Archives, Acc.i.A.6; 1584–5; English and Latin; paper; ii + 26 + xx; 488mm x 171mm (481mm x 107mm); modern pencil foliation; written front to back; good condition, some water damage; contemporary leather binding, leather ties lost, rebound within modern board binding, title on spine: 'COMPUTUS ANNUUS 1584–5.'

Oxford, St John's College Archives, Acc.i.A.8; 1586–7; English and Latin; paper; 22 leaves; 496mm x 169mm (468mm x 100mm); modern pencil foliation; written front to back; good condition, some insect damage; contemporary leather binding, leather ties lost, rebound within modern board binding, title on spine: 'COMPUTUS ANNUUS 1586–7.'

Oxford, St John's College Archives, Acc.i.A.10; 1598–1604; English and Latin; paper; 174 leaves; 445mm x 172mm (409mm x 130mm); modern pencil foliation; written front to back; fair condition, some insect and water damage; contemporary leather binding, leather ties lost, rebound within modern board binding, title on spine: 'COMPUTUS ANNUUS 1598–1604.'

Oxford, St John's College Archives, Acc.i.A.11; 1616–17; English and Latin; paper; ii + 30 + ix; 566mm x 215mm (562mm x 182mm); contemporary ink pagination and modern pencil foliation; written front to back; fair condition, somewhat fragile, cover worn; contemporary leather binding, wording on cover largely worn.

Oxford, St John's College Archives, Acc.i.A.12; 1617–28; English and Latin; paper; i + 274 + v; 389mm x 150mm (367mm x 127mm); modern pencil foliation; written front to back; decorated capitals on cover; good condition; contemporary leather binding with ties, contemporary ink title on cover worn.

Oxford, St John's College Archives, Acc.i.A.15; 1628–34; English and Latin; paper; iii + 174 + i; 383mm x 140mm (357mm x 141mm); modern pencil foliation; written front to back; very poor condition, severe water damage, rebound with conservation but most leaves are at best only partially extant or legible; modern board binding, title on spine: 'COMPUTUS ANNUUS 1629–34.'

Oxford, St John's College Archives, Acc.i.A.16; 1631–2; English and Latin; paper; 31 + xiv; 545mm x 204mm (524mm x 179mm); contemporary ink foliation; written front to back; enlarged capitals in headings on f 1; fair condition, some water damage; contemporary leather binding with dates (largely illegible) on cover, rebound within modern board binding, title on spine: 'COMPUTUS ANNUUS 1631–32.'

Oxford, St John's College Archives, Acc.i.A.17; 1633; English and Latin; paper; 31 leaves; 568mm x 210mm (520mm x 137mm); contemporary ink foliation; written front to back; enlarged capitals in headings on f 1; good condition; contemporary leather binding with '1633' on cover in contemporary ink, ties lost, rebound within modern board binding, title on spine: 'COMPUTUS ANNUUS 1633.'

Oxford, St John's College Archives, Acc.i.A.18; 1633–4; English and Latin; paper; ii + 32 + x; 577mm x 210mm (478mm x 134mm); partial contemporary ink foliation covering used leaves only; written front to back; enlarged capitals in headings on f 1; good condition; contemporary leather binding with leather ties, contemporary ink title on cover: '39 Computus Annuus 1633'4.'

Oxford, St John's College Archives, Acc.i.A.19; 1634–5; English and Latin; paper; iii + 32 + xiv; 560mm x 215mm (516mm x 189mm); modern pencil foliation; written front to back; enlarged capitals in headings on f 1; good condition; contemporary leather binding with leather ties partially preserved, contemporary ink title on cover: '40 Computus Annuus 1634'5.'

Oxford, St John's College Archives, Acc.i.A.20; 1635–6; English and Latin; paper; ii + 34 + iii; 564mm x 207mm (476mm x 184mm); contemporary ink foliation to f 29, then modern pencil foliation to end; written front to back; enlarged capitals in headings on f 1; good condition; contemporary leather binding with leather ties partially preserved, contemporary ink title on cover: '41 Computus Annuus 1635'6 1635 1636.'

Oxford, St John's College Archives, Acc.i.A.21; 1636–7; English and Latin; paper; ii + 40 + ii; 580mm x 214mm (540mm x 205mm); incomplete contemporary ink foliation; written front to back; enlarged capitals in headings on f 1; good condition; modern board cover.

Oxford, St John's College Archives, Acc.i.A.22; 1637–8; English and Latin; paper; iii + 41 + iv; 574mm x

215mm (514mm x 165mm); incomplete contemporary ink foliation; written front to back; enlarged capitals in headings on f 1; good condition; contemporary leather binding with leather ties, contemporary ink title on cover: '43 Computus Annuus For ye yeares 1637'8,' later ink title on spine: '1637–8.'

Oxford, St John's College Archives, Acc.i.A.23; 1638–58; English and Latin; paper; i + 138 + xiv; 407mm x 155mm (356mm x 113mm); modern pencil foliation; written front to back; fair condition, early pages badly water damaged and illegible, later pages in good condition, paper conservation has taken place; modern board cover, title on spine: 'COMPUTUS ANNUUS 1638–58.'

Oxford, St John's College Archives, Acc.i.A.24; 1639–40; English and Latin; paper; i + 38; 577mm x 211mm (505mm x 147mm); modern pencil foliation; written front to back; enlarged capitals in headings on f 1; fair condition, some water damage but little text lost; contemporary leather binding with contemporary ink title on cover: '(.)6 Computus Annuus ad 1639'40.'

Oxford, St John's College Archives, Acc.i.A.25; 1640–1; English and Latin; paper; i + 42 + xi; 564mm x 206mm (513mm x 122mm); incomplete modern pencil foliation; written front to back; enlarged capitals in headings on f 1; good condition; contemporary leather binding with ties, contemporary ink title on cover: '44 Computus Annuus 1640'1.'

Oxford, St John's College Archives, Acc.i.A.26; 1641–2; English and Latin; paper; ii + 42 + vi; 576mm x 214mm (501mm x 164mm); incomplete modern pencil foliation; written front to back; enlarged capitals in headings on f 1; good condition; contemporary leather binding with ties partially preserved, contemporary ink title on cover: '45 Computus Annuus ad Festum Michaelis 1641'2,' later ink title on spine: '1641.'

St John's College Computus Hebdomalis

Accounts are divided into four numbered terms per year, each term of thirteen (or so) numbered weeks. There is no division into subject headings. All weeks run Monday to Sunday. The first week of the first term was identified as the one that included Michaelmas but the weeks that included the three subsequent term-days (Christmas, Lady Day, St John's Day) were holidays. As a consequence the first weeks of Terms 2–4 were identified as the ones that followed their term-days. What otherwise would have been the 'first' weeks of Terms 2–4 were counted instead as the last weeks of Terms 1–3. Thirteen volumes cover the period from 1593 to 1642. Missing are 1623–5, 1626–7, 1628–30, 1633–7, and 1639–42.

Oxford, St John's College Archives, Acc.v.E.l; 1593–8; Latin and English; paper; i + 67; 440mm x 174mm (391mm x 155mm); modern pencil foliation; written front to back; good condition; contemporary leather binding with leather ties partially preserved, contemporary ink title on cover: '20 Computus hebdomadalis Liber computus hebdomadalis 1593 Liber Hebdomadalis Incipit 1593 Michaelmas Explicit 1598 Michaelmas.'

Oxford, St John's College Archives, Acc.v.E.2; 1598–1604; Latin and English; paper; i + 82 + ix; 452mm x 163mm (417mm x 157mm); modern pencil foliation; written front to back; fair condition, some insect damage; contemporary leather binding with contemporary ink title on cover: '21 Computus Hebdomadalis Liber Hebdomadalis anno domino 1603 1598 1599 1600 1601 1602 1603 1604.'

Oxford, St John's College Archives, Acc.v.E.3; 1600–1; Latin and English; paper; iii + 53; 439mm x 166mm (424mm x 132mm); modern pencil foliation; written front to back; good condition; contemporary leather binding with contemporary ink title on cover: 'Computus Hebdomadalis Michaelmas ⟨...⟩ 160⟨.⟩,' bound within modern board binding with title on spine: 'Computus Hebdomadalis Michaelmas 1600–1601.'

Oxford, St John's College Archives, Acc.v.E.4; 1604–14; Latin and English; paper; i + 132 + i; 406mm x 162mm (385mm x 148mm); modern pencil foliation; written front to back; fair condition, some significant wear; contemporary leather binding with leather ties partially preserved, contemporary ink title on cover: '22 Computus Hebdomadalis Liber Hebdomadalis Incipit 1604 Michaelmas 1604 ad Explicit 1613 Annunciatio 1614.'

Oxford, St John's College Archives, Acc.v.E.6; 1614–23; Latin and English; paper; i + 133 + i; 410mm x 156mm (386mm x 151mm); modern pencil foliation; written front to back; fair condition, some insect damage; contemporary leather binding with contemporary ink title on cover: '23 Computus Hebdomadalis Liber Hebdomadalis Incipit 1614 Annunciatio Beatae Explicit 1623 Michaelmas.'

Oxford, St John's College Archives, Acc.v.E.8; 1627–8; English and Latin; paper; ii + 52; 446mm x 176mm (435mm x 162mm); modern pencil foliation; written front to back; fair condition; contemporary leather binding with leather ties, contemporary ink title on cover: '4 Computus Hebdomadalis Michaelmas 1627 ad Michaelmas 1628.'

St John's College Christmas Prince

See Appendix 6:1 for modern editions.

Oxford, St John's College Library, MS 52; 1607–8; English and Latin; paper; ii + 265; 304mm x 190mm (284mm x 173mm); contemporary ink pagination (in 2 sequences); coloured illuminations and ink drawings; excellent condition; contemporary leather binding, embossed and set with gold leaf. Though the entire MS is conventionally called 'The Christmas Prince,' the first part, with its own pagination sequence, consists of a verse history of the college. By the same token 'The Christmas Prince' is sometimes identified as MS 52, Part 2.

St John's College Short Books

These are drafts of the final accounts but often more detailed. They are labelled on the spine 'Bursar's Private Accounts' in a modern hand and are also referred to as 'Short Books.' Three volumes cover the period 1616–42. Missing are 1623–5, 1626–9, 1631–3, 1634–5, 1636–8, and 1639–40.

Oxford, St John's College Archives, Acc.III.D.1; 1616–22; English and Latin; paper; i + 96; 400mm x

144mm (346mm x 137mm); modern pencil foliation; written front to back; good condition; modern board binding, title on spine: 'BURSAR'S PRIVATE ACCOUNTS 1616–22.'

Oxford, St John's College Archives, Acc.III.D.2; 1625–31; English and Latin; paper; i + 123 + i; 402mm x 157mm (393mm x 152mm); partial contemporary ink pagination, then modern pencil continuation; written front to back; excellent condition; contemporary leather and board binding with leather ties, antiquarian title on cover: '2 Bursar's Private Accompt 1625'6 1629-3[0]1.'

Oxford, St John's College Archives, Acc.III.D.4; 1633–46; English and Latin; paper; ii + 207; 390mm x 146mm (363mm x 126mm); incomplete modern pencil foliation; written front to back; good condition; contemporary leather and board binding with contemporary ink title on cover: '1633 to 1645 1633'4 1636 1639 1644 1645 1646 °from 1633'4 … 1646°,' antiquarian ink title also on cover: '3 Bursar's Private Accompt.'

Letter from the Vice-Chancellor to the Chancellor

The vice-chancellor at this time was Richard Baylie, president of St John's, and the chancellor was Archbishop Laud.

London, Public Record Office, SP/16/344; 16 January 1636/7; English; paper; 2 leaves, originally bifolium; 175mm x 295mm; unnumbered; writing on first 3 pages; endorsed on f [2v]: 'The History of Turners – Printing. &c. 16. Ian*uary* .1636.' Baylie has dated the letter 'Ian*uary* 16 .1636.' Now bound in a guardbook and numbered 20.

TRINITY COLLEGE

Trinity College was founded in 1555 by Sir Thomas Pope, incorporating grounds and buildings of Durham College (see p 649). Its head is a president.

Most archives are kept in a muniment tower but financial records are housed in the bursar's office under his jurisdiction. Access is via manuscript handlists, including one compiled by the National Register of Archives and another by the History of the University project.

Trinity College Bursars' Books

These books contain annual accounts kept from Michaelmas to Michaelmas, divided into the usual four terms.

Oxford, Trinity College Archive, I/A/1; 1556–1600; Latin; parchment and paper; 436 leaves; 260mm x 380mm; modern pencil foliation; bound in leather in 1799, embossed antiquarian title on spine: 'Computi Bursariorum Ab Anno Fundationis Ad Ann. Dom. MDC.' The volume is complete except for the absence of the accounts for 1557–8, 1558–9, and 1559–60 (see p 678).

Oxford, Trinity College Archive, I/A/2; 1600–31; Latin; paper; iii + 345 + iii; 300–45mm x 192–231mm (264–304mm x 149–222mm); continuous modern pencil foliation (individual accounts have contemporary ink foliation in some cases); generally good condition; antiquarian leather binding, some tooling on front and back covers, embossed antiquarian title on spine: 'Computi Bursariorum Ab Anno MDC. Ad Annum MDCXXXI.'

Oxford, Trinity College Archive, I/A/3; 1631–95; Latin; paper; iii + 384 + ii (f 384 is partial and blank); 291–387mm x 183–246mm (274–380mm x 136–206mm); modern pencil foliation; generally good condition; antiquarian leather binding, some tooling front and back, embossed antiquarian title on spine: 'Compvti Bvrsariorvm Ab. Anno MDCXXXI Ad. Annum MDCXCV.' From our period of interest, the years 1639–42 are missing.

Notes on a Trinity College Bursar's Book (AC)

Missing bursar's accounts (1557–8, 1558–9, 1559–60) may have been borrowed by Thomas Warton (the accounts were unbound before 1799), now the sole authority for a performance of Terence in 1559 (see p 101). A fellow of Trinity until his death in 1790, Warton has gained a reputation for forgery.[7]

Thomas Warton, *The History of English Poetry From The Close of the Eleventh To The Commencement of the Eighteenth Century. To Which Are Prefixed Two Dissertations. I. On The Origin of Romantic Fiction In Europe. II. On the Introduction Of Learning Into England.* Vol. 2 (London, 1778).

UNIVERSITY COLLEGE

University College, believed to be the oldest college in Oxford, was founded *c* 1249. Its head is a master.

Archives are maintained in a specially designated site. While no finding aids have been published, a catalogue is currently in progress. As each segment is completed, a copy is deposited with the National Register of Archives. Bursars' accounts, transcribed and edited by A.D.M. Cox and R.H. Darwall-Smith, have recently been published by the Oxford Historical Society, ns, 39 (1999): 1381/2–1470/1, and 40 (2001): 1471/2–1596/7.

University College Statutes

The statutes exist in three copies, each contained in the chancellors' registers. The transcription in this collection is taken from OUA: NEP/Supra/A, which is described below (see under University Registers, p 680). It represents the earliest, if not a contemporary, version of the statutes.

The version of the statutes found in OUA: NEP/Supra/A has been collated with the versions registered in the following:

Oxford, Oxford University Archives, NEP/Supra/C; 14th c.; Latin; parchment; ii + 159 + ii; 334mm x 218mm (240mm x 166mm); contemporary ink foliation; decorated capitals and markers throughout, illuminated capitals; good condition; antiquarian calf binding with blind tooling, antiquarian ink and modern embossed titles on spine.

Oxford, Oxford University Archives, NEP/Supra/B; 15th c.; Latin; parchment; ii + 141 + ii; 335mm x 225mm (225mm x 179mm); contemporary ink foliation; decorated capitals and coloured markers throughout, illuminations; generally good condition; antiquarian calf binding with blind tooling, antiquarian ink and embossed title on spine.

University College Bursars' Accounts

The college retains nearly two hundred bursars' rolls dating from 1381 to 1616. These were all examined and yielded only one entry of interest (1578–9), due to the fact that the expenses were not itemized beyond very general categories.

Oxford, University College Archives, BU1/F/171; 1578–9; Latin; parchment; single mb; 794mm x 620mm (766mm x 540mm); unnumbered (modern pencil catalogue reference on dorse); 3 cols; written on recto only; good condition; contemporary ink note on dorse: 'Rich*ard* Jennins An*n*o 1578.'

University College Bursar's Journal

Oxford, University College Archives, BU3/F1/2; 1623–38; English and Latin; paper; 96 leaves; 378mm x 146mm (375mm x 129mm); unnumbered; generally good condition; contemporary leather binding, ties extant, rough accounts worked on front and back covers, contemporary ink and modern pencil titles on front cover.

University College General Accounts

Oxford, University College Archives, BU2/F1/1; 1632–67; English and Latin; paper; i + 223 + i; 422mm x 174mm (404mm x 145mm); contemporary ink pagination (first page of MS labelled p 9); good condition; antiquarian calf binding, title embossed on spine.

Oxford University

The history of Oxford University is summarized above (pp 597–601). The Oxford University Archives (OUA) are housed in the main tower of the Bodleian Schools Quadrangle. Individual documents are produced for readers in Duke Humfrey. In lieu of a catalogue access is via a shelf-list compiled by Strickland Gibson (1929–45 typescript) available in Duke Humfrey as Bodl.: MS. R.Top. 628M/1–3. For a general description of documents by type, see T.H. Aston and D.G. Vaisey, 'University Archives,' in Paul Morgan (comp), *Oxford Libraries Outside the Bodleian*, 2nd ed (Oxford, 1980), 200–5; see also Reginald Lane Poole, *A Lecture on the History of The University Archives* (Oxford, 1912).

Generally speaking, only the more formal administrative and financial documents remain in OUA. Many items that might be expected to be housed there, or that were in fact once housed there, are now in the Bodleian Library. Examples are the antiquarian collections of the first two keepers of the archives, Brian Twyne (1633–43) and Gerard Langbaine (1644–58), and the numerous manuscripts left behind by the University's first historian, Anthony Wood (1631–95). Some documents, notably the early registers of matriculation and degrees, of the chancellor's court, and of congregation and convocation, have been published by the Oxford Historical Society.

UNIVERSITY REGISTERS

Chancellors' Registers

The volume OUA: NEP/Supra/A is the oldest extant University register. It was copied beginning *c* 1350 as an official record of statutes and privileges, from documents dating from the thirteenth and early fourteenth centuries. It continued in use for some 250 years, being several times rearranged and rebound.

The manuscript has been edited in part by Anstey, *Munimenta Academica*, and by Gibson, *Statvta Antiqva Universitatis Oxoniensis*.

This register also contains the University College statutes transcribed in this collection (see p 4) and collated with the versions registered in OUA: NEP/Supra/B and OUA: NEP/Supra/C (see pp 678–9).

Oxford, Oxford University Archives, NEP/Supra/A; *c* 1350–1600; Latin; parchment; i + 125 + i; 315mm x 206mm (224mm x 197mm); contemporary ink foliation superseding a partial system in contemporary ink and some modern pencil foliation; good condition; contemporary brown calf binding (repaired in 1886 and resewn in 1941) tooled with the royal arms on front and back covers, antiquarian embossed title on spine.

Oxford, Oxford University Archives, Hyp/A/1, Register Aaa; 1434–69; Latin and English; paper; v + 273 + vi; 307mm x 215mm (274mm x 155mm); contemporary ink foliation, plus partial modern pencil foliation; good condition; contemporary calf covers, antiquarian replacement spine, holes for clasps at top and bottom of covers, simple decoration at the edges, embossed title on spine.

Oxford, Oxford University Archives, Hyp/A/2, Register D (or D reversed); 1498–1506; Latin; paper; i + 238 + iii; 303mm x 201mm (250mm x 181mm); contemporary and antiquarian ink foliation; good condition; contemporary leather binding with punched scrolling design on front and back covers, spine repaired, modern ink title on spine.

Chancellor's Court Register

Oxford, Oxford University Archives, Hyp/A/4, Register EEE (or B reversed); 1527–43; Latin; paper; i + 405 + i; 230mm x 370mm (227mm x 312mm); 17th-c. ink foliation; original leather and board binding, repaired in 1971.

Registers of Congregation and Convocation

Oxford, Oxford University Archives, NEP/Supra/G; June 1505–27 November 1517; Latin; paper; iii + 321 + iv; 210mm x 300mm (170mm x 230mm); 17th-c. ink foliation; bound in 17th-c. leather, on spine: 'Vniv: Oxon: Arch: G 6 1505. 1516.,' title on f 1 in Brian Twyne's hand: 'Registrum .G. Ab Anno. Regis Henrici Septimi [vijo.] xxjo. ad annum Regis Henrici Octaui .8um. viz. ab Anno Domini 1505. ad annum Domini 1516. Acts of Congregation for ye most part, with a fewe Acts of Conuocation here & there intermixed./'

Oxford, Oxford University Archives, NEP/Supra/L; 1582–94; Latin and English; paper; iii + 298 + iii; 230mm x 335mm (text area varies); 17th-c. ink foliation, with a second f 1 added by Brian Twyne; many leaves repaired in 19th c.; original leather and board covers, modern stamped leather spine, original spine pasted onto inner front cover, stamped on current spine: 'Vniv. Oxon. Arch. L 10 1582 1594.'

Oxford, Oxford University Archives, NEP/Supra/N; 1615–28; Latin and English; paper; vi + 270 + iii + 1 loose unnumbered sheet; 184mm x 296mm (text area varies); 17th-c. ink foliation; original leather and board covers, modern stamped leather spine: 'Acta Convocationis Universitatis Oxon: Arch: N 23 1615 1628.'

Oxford, Oxford University Archives, NEP/Supra/R; 1628–40; Latin and English; paper; ii + 282 + v; 205mm x 355mm (text area varies); 17th-c. ink foliation; original leather and board covers, modern leather spine, title stamped on spine: 'Acta Convocat: Univ: Oxon: ARCH: R24 1628–1640.'

Shortly after OUA: NEP/Supra/R was bound this volume came into the hands of the Puritan William Prynne, who mutilated parts of it. A note in Langbaine's hand on f 1 says: 'Note yat where ye see any Letters of Chancellor Laud scored with a pen underneath, or marked in ye Margin thus X. ye must take notice twas maliciously done by William Prinne–.' These marks are ignored in the transcriptions in the present volume.

Another copy of ff 132–2v, the 'Orders for the Royal Entertainment' of 1636, without significant variants, survives in CCC: MS 301, f 127. Other relevant texts include a version of the order of the committee that met in the Tower of the Schooles (ff 133v–4v of OUA: NEP/Supra/R) and of the 'Advertisements' (ff 134v–5) in Bodl.: MS. Twyne 17, pp 187–90 (see under Entertainment of King Charles I, p 703). Substantive differences in the latter manuscript have been collated.

UNIVERSITY FINANCIAL DOCUMENTS

Proctors' Accounts

This is an audited annual account, unlike the more informative proctors' draft books that survive at Cambridge. The fifteen rolls that survive between 1464–5 and 1496–7 at Oxford have been edited by Salter, *Mediaeval Archives of the University of Oxford*, vol 2, pp 272–358. These record receipts for degrees, rents, fines for breaches of the peace, and expenses for entertainments, 'recreations,' salaries, and rents. Miscellaneous annual accounts from 1561–2 to 1743–4 survive (some in later copies only) in OUA: NW/6/1–5 but yield no REED entries.

Oxford, Oxford University Archives, NW/5/3; 1471–2; Latin; parchment; single mb; 460mm x 700mm (350mm x 682mm); unnumbered; writing on both sides.

Vice-Chancellors' Accounts

This volume contains annual, or sometimes biannual, statements of receipts and payments, prepared by the vice-chancellor for a delegacy of convocation, who scrutinized and allowed or disallowed them. Each account was written in three copies, one kept by the vice-chancellor, one placed in the archives as a parchment roll, and one entered into a large folio paper book, which, with the single exception listed below, is the only surviving copy.

The dates of the accounting year (or half-year) vary and are given here in the subheading for each entry.

Oxford, Oxford University Archives, WP/β/21(4); 1547–1666; Latin and English; paper; 189 leaves; 225mm x 330mm; modern pencil foliation 1–7, contemporary ink pagination 1–358 beginning on f 8; bound in 17th-c. leather, written on f 1: 'Liber Computi Vicecancellarii Oxon.'

Vice-Chancellors' Draft Accounts

The expenses recorded on these sheets were copied into the vice-chancellors' annual accounts (OUA: WP/β/21(4), ff 99–102), see above, with which they are collated here.

Oxford, Oxford University Archives, WP/β/S/1; 1583; English; paper; 2 bifolia within an otherwise blank parchment mb headed 'Computi Vicecancellarii 1583'; unnumbered; writing on the first 3 pages of each sheet, with endorsements on the fourth page.

sheet 1: 287mm x 190mm (255mm x 177mm); written in black ink; endorsed 'Expensae – Recepti Palatini Siradiensis.'

sheet 2: 336mm x 230mm (289mm x 219mm); written in brown ink with ornamental lettering; endorsed 'Expensae ab Academia Oxoniensi factae in Susceptione Alberti Lacei Comitis Palatini Siradiensis poloni. 1583'; at the bottom of f [2v] is written 'Examinas et allocat' 19. Decembris.'

STATUTES, ORDERS, AND PROCLAMATIONS

Vice-Chancellor's Proclamation

This document is one of a miscellaneous collection of vice-chancellors' proclamations from 1556 to 1630, having to do with University-city relations. Some are drafts and some fair copies. All bear notes in the hand of Brian Twyne and were evidently collected by him.

Oxford, Oxford University Archives, SEP/T/7/g; 1593; English; paper; bifolium; 300mm x 400mm (296mm x 199mm); writing begins on f [2], continues onto f [1v], and then f [1]; f [2v] blank except for endorsement in the hand of Brian Twyne: 'August: 1593. 35ᵗᵒ Eliz: A proclamacion by Dr Lilly ViceChancellor & Henry Dodwell Mayor, of severall Orders for the Government of the University & towne, especially in relacion to the Sicknesse.'

Cardinal Pole's Statutes

Oxford, Bodleian Library, MS. Top.Oxon b.5; early 17th c.; Latin; paper; iv + 153; 415mm x 283mm (347mm x 187mm); contemporary ink foliation; good condition; contemporary leather binding, tooled, with some gilding front and back, 2 clasps (now broken).

Orders of the Delegates of Convocation for the Royal Plays

This document appears to be a draft of the minutes of several meetings of congregation held during June and July 1605 to prepare for the king's visit in August. A partial copy of this document, or of a common source, appears in Bodl.: MS. Twyne 17, pp 181–3. Of this copy Twyne says: 'All this yat followeth [is taken] touchinge ye entertainement was taken out of a loose note which/ Merricke had, then Registrary of ye Vniuersitie. & I had this of Mr Estcott Warden of Wadham College.' Although the copy made by Twyne omits some passages, the 'loose note' that came into his possession may have been the present document, which would explain its presence in the archives. A collation of Bodl.: MS. Twyne 17 (see under Entertainment of King Charles I, p 703) is given here.

A copy of the section contained on f 3v, entitled, 'Advertisementes for the heades of houses,' survives in CCC: MS 301, f 93v, but has not been collated here. A version of the 'Advertisements' also appears in Cambridge University Library: MS Additional 34 (see under Narratives by Cambridge Men, p 699) which has been collated here.

MS 301 was compiled by William Fulman (see under Letter of Henry Jackson to D.G.P., p 648). As now catalogued it forms volume 7 of his collected papers. Most of the documents are copies in Fulman's hand but some are of earlier date. The copy of the 'Advertisements for Heads of Houses' for the royal entertainment of 1605, on f 93v, is in Fulman's hand. The copy of the 'Orders' for the royal entertainment of 1636, on f 127, is in a contemporary hand and is signed by 'Ric: Baylie Vicecan: Oxon' and witnessed by John Frenche, registrar of the University.

Oxford, Oxford University Archives, WP/γ/19/1; 1605; English; paper; 3 bifolia; 300mm x 200mm; unnumbered; writing in ink on both sides of each of the first 4 leaves, ending on f [5]; endorsed on f [6v], in a different hand from that of the main scribe: 'Anno Domini 1605. Orders about ye enterteynment of King James in Oxford.' The first page is dated 'Sexto die Iunij 1603' and gives a list of 45 delegates to oversee the king's visit.

Chancellor Laud, Corpus Statutorum

This is an annotated copy kept in the Bodleian Library (Bodl.: N 1.12 Jur.Seld.).

CORPVS | STATVTORVM | VNIVERSITATIS | OXON. | SIVE | PANDECTES

CONSTITVTIONVM | ACADEMICARVM, E LIBRIS PVBLICIS | ET REGESTIS VNIVERSITATIS | CONSARCINATVS. | [device] | *OXONIÆ* | Excudebant Iohannes Lichfield & Guilielmus | Turner, *Academiæ celeberrimæ Typographi*. | *M.DC.XXXIV. stc*: 19005.

The Great Charter

Oxford, Oxford University Archives, Long Box xix; 1636; Latin; parchment; 14 mbs sewn at top; approximately 670mm x 855mm; contemporary ink foliation; first mb richly illuminated, decorated title capitals used throughout; excellent condition; permanently stored flat in a case.

INVENTORIES

Chancellors' Court Inventories

Excerpts have been printed from inventories on the following folios within the boxes listed below. For ease of reference the main foliation (ie, the sequential modern pencil foliation of each item within the Hyp/B series) is offered here along with the name of the individual whose inventory is excerpted.

Oxford, Oxford University Archives, Hyp/B/10:

ff 21–2v (Ralph Allen ('Mr Alyne') of Balliol College): 17 October 1561; English; paper; bifolium; 312mm x 205mm (282mm x 172mm); good condition.

ff 111–11v (William Battbrantes of Christ Church): 23 March 1571/2; English; paper; single sheet (originally long bifolium); 307mm x 210mm (304mm x 101mm); good condition.

ff 164–5v (Nicholas Bond of Magdalen College): 21 February1607/8; English and Latin; parchment; 2 mbs originally sewn at top, now separated; mb 1: 585mm x 123mm (554mm x 117mm), mb 2: 267mm x 122mm (248mm x 120mm); enlarged title script; good condition.

Oxford, Oxford University Archives, Hyp/B/11:

ff 119–25v (Nicholas Clifton): 19 January 1578/9; English; paper; 7 mbs originally sewn to form continuous strip, now separated; mbs 1–6: 348mm x 133mm (339mm x 130mm), mb 7: 171mm x 133mm (83mm x 127mm); modern pencil numbering of inventory itself alongside main foliation; enlarged script for headers; good condition.

Oxford, Oxford University Archives, Hyp/B/12:

ff 44–5v (Giles Dewhurst): 15 October 1577; English; paper; long bifolium; 415mm x 154mm (395mm x 140mm); good condition.

ff 62–7v (Robert Dowe): 1 May 1588; English and Latin; paper; 6 mbs (no evidence of attachment);

381mm x 143mm (362mm x 133mm); contemporary ink and modern pencil foliation of inventory itself alongside main foliation; enlarged title script for headers; good condition, minor physical damage, but no loss of information.

ff 78–9v (John Dunnet): 18 April 1570; English; paper; long bifolium; 410mm x 150mm (384mm x 146mm); good condition.

Oxford, Oxford University Archives, Hyp/B/13:

f 5 (John Gerrard, University musician): 12 October 1635; English; paper; single sheet; 400mm x 154mm (376mm x 146mm); good condition.

ff 112–15v (Robert Harte): 18 March 1570/1; English; paper; 2 long bifolia; 414mm x 159mm (388mm x 147mm); modern pencil foliation of inventory itself alongside main foliation; good condition.

Oxford, Oxford University Archives, Hyp/B/14:

ff 66–8v (Henry Hutchinson): 2 August 1573; English; paper; single sheet (f 66) and 1 bifolium (ff 67–8v); f 66: 413mm x 155mm (384mm x 133mm), ff 67, 68: 314mm x 210mm (302mm x 149mm); modern pencil foliation of inventory itself alongside main foliation; good condition, some minor insect damage.

Oxford, Oxford University Archives, Hyp/B/15:

ff 134–4v (Richard Ludbye): 6 February 1566/7; English; paper; single sheet; 420mm x 157mm (388mm x 138mm); good condition.

Oxford, Oxford University Archives, Hyp/B/17:

ff 67–8 (Thomas Pope): 5 April 1578; English; paper; 2 single mbs originally sewn to form continuous strip, now separated; 325mm x 157mm (304mm x 123mm); modern pencil foliation of inventory itself alongside main foliation; good condition.

ff 78–9v (Ambrose Powell): 25 January 1624/5; English and Latin; paper; bifolium; 291mm x 194mm (273mm x 187mm); good condition.

Oxford, Oxford University Archives, Hyp/B/18:

ff 12–15v (James Reynolds): 21 October 1577; English; paper; 2 bifolia (no evidence of attachment); 379mm x 130mm (348mm x 122mm); modern pencil foliation of inventory itself alongside main foliation; good condition.

f 140 (William Smalwood): 10 June 1572; English; paper; single sheet; 415mm x 155mm (388mm x 148mm); good condition.

ff 215–16v (John Simpson): 31 August 1577; English; paper; long bifolium; 415mm x 156mm (384mm x 143mm); good condition.

Oxford, Oxford University Archives, Hyp/B/19:

ff 48–9v (Christoper Tillyard): 31 July 1598; English and Latin; paper; long bifolium; 390mm x 151mm (363mm x 149mm); fair condition, some physical damage and loss of information.

MISCELLANEOUS

University Response to Town Complaints of a Riot

Oxford, Oxford University Archives, SEP/Y/12a; 24 February 1297/8; English and French; parchment; 7 mbs sewn at top (original order of mbs unknown, mbs now arranged to form an apparently chrono-logical sequence of complaints and replies); 218mm x 187mm (150mm x 177mm); modern pencil numbering; generally good condition, some wear.

Laurence Humphrey's Ash Wednesday Sermon

IESVITISMI | PARS PRIMA: | SIVE | DE PRAXI ROMANÆ CVRIÆ | contra Resp, & Principes: Et De noua le- | gatione Iesuitarum in Angliam, προθεράπεια | & præmunitio ad ANGLOS. | Cui ADIUNCTA EST CONCIO | eiusdem Argumenti, Laurentio Humfredo | Sacrae Theologiæ in Academia Oxoni- | ensi professore Regio; Autore. | Rogo vos, Fratres, vt speculemini eos, qui sediciones & offen- | siones præter doctrinam, quam vos didicistis, excitant. &c. Ro. 16. | Tertullianus in Apologetici capitulo 13. Circuit cauponas Religio mendicans. | Athanasius contra Arrianos Oratione 1. Syncera & simplicia Apostolicorum | virorum ingenia sunt. | [device] | LONDINI, | Excudebat Henricus Middletonus | impensis G. B. | 1582. STC: 13961.

The secondary title-page on p 161 reads: PHARISAISMVS | VETUS ET NOVVS: SIVE DE | FERMENTO PHARISÆORVM | ET IESVITARVM, | LAVRENTII HVMFREDI | CONCIO IN FESTO CINE- | RVM ANNO DOMINI 1582. | Februarij vltimo Apud Acade- | micos Oxonienses: | Eidem nobilissimo Comiti, | Leicestrensi, Academiæ summo Can- | cellario dedicata. | Matth. 16. | Videte & cauete à Fermento Pharisæorum & | Sadduceorum. | LONDINI, | Excudebat H. Middletonus, | impensis G. B. | ANNO DOMINI 1582.

Letter of the Mayor and Aldermen of Oxford to the High Steward of Oxford

Hatfield, Hatfield House Library, Cecil Papers MS 62/14; 3 June 1598; English; paper; bifolium; 300mm x 200mm (272mm x 195mm); good condition except for portion of document torn away when the seal was removed affecting 6 lines of text; addressed: 'To the Right honourable our verie good Lord the Erle of Essex Earle Marshall of England'; endorsed: 'The Maior & Aldermen of Oxford 3 Iune 98 Complayning of an outrage offerd vnto some of ye Town by certen schollers./.' Foliated '14' in red ink and bound into guardbook c 1830; volume repaired and rebound in half goatskin in 1994 with title on spine: 'CECIL PAPERS VOL. 62.'

Report of the University to the High Steward of Oxford

Hatfield, Hatfield House Library, Cecil Papers MS 62/16; 9 June 1598; English; paper; single sheet; 324mm x 205mm (312mm x 175mm); good condition. Numbered '16' in red ink and bound into guardbook *c* 1830; volume repaired and rebound in half goatskin in 1994 with title on spine: 'CECIL PAPERS VOL. 62.'

Costumes and Props for the Plays for King James

This document has been published by F.S. Boas and W.W. Greg (eds), 'James I at Oxford in 1605. Property lists from the University Archives,' *Collections* [1], Part 3, Malone Society (Oxford, 1909; rpt 1965), 247–59, who have identified the persons named. The present edition adopts a different ordering of the loose sheets from that given by Boas and Greg in an attempt to make their possible relationship clearer.

The intended order, if any, of these five loose sheets is unclear. All five are in the hand of Bernard Banger, chief esquire bedel of the University in 1605, but the entries were made at different times, using a variety of pens and hands ranging from cursive secretary to set italic. The following leaves are blank except for endorsements in another hand: sheet [1], f [1v]; sheet [2], ff [2, 2v]; sheet [3], ff [1v, 2v]; sheet [4], ff [2, 2v]; sheet [5], f [1v]. Sheet [1] appears to be a list of requirements for the plays and at the end contains receipts for payments to Matthew Foxe and Thomas Kendall. Sheet [2] is a partial inventory of goods provided, copied from shéet [1]. It is written in brown ink, with accounting symbols and marginalia added in a darker ink. The endorsement on f [2v] reads 'ffor the Playes att the King*es* co*m*minge. 1605.' Sheet [3] is a list of requirements sent to Edward Kirkham, with further requirements from Kendall. Sheet [4] is an inventory of goods received from Kendall, partially copied from sheet [3] and partially from 'lettres of mr Daniels.' Sheet [5] continues the inventory without specifying the source. The endorsement on f [2v] reads: 'A note of players apparell. at K*ing* James be*ing* here.'

Oxford, Oxford University Archives, WP/β/P/5/3; 1605; English; paper; 5 bifolia; 200mm x 300mm (200mm x 296mm); unnumbered.

Archbishop Laud's Expenses for the Royal Visit

This expense account was prepared for Laud by one of his servants, Adam Torless, who has signed his initials at the end. Torless was awarded an honorary MA at a special convocation held at Oxford on 31 August 1636 after the king had left.

London, Public Record Office, SP/16/348; February 1636/7?; English; paper; 4 sheets, originally bifolia(?); 300mm x 200mm; unnumbered; writing on both sides, except for f [1v], which is blank; endorsed on f [4v]: 'The whole Chardge of the K*ing* & Queen's Entertaynment at Oxford. In Aug*ust* 29. 1636. All payed' (on the same page, in a 19th-c. hand: 'Feb. 1636/7'). Now bound in a guardbook and numbered 85.

COURT AND DIPLOMATIC DOCUMENTS

Financial Accounts

Wardrobe of the Robes Day Book

This manuscript is now part of the PRO collection called 'Duchess of Norfolk Deeds.' It has been published by Janet Arnold, *'Lost from Her Majesties Back': Items of Clothing and Jewels Lost or Given Away By Queen Elizabeth I Between 1561 and 1585, Entered in One of the Day Books Kept for the Records of the Wardrobe of Robes*, The Costume Society (np, 1980).

London, Public Record Office, C/115/L2/6697; 1561–85; English; paper; 390 leaves (296 blank); 298mm x 209mm; partial modern pencil pagination 1–86; original vellum binding, badly damaged, title in ink on cover faded and illegible.

Treasurer of the Chamber's Account

London, Public Record Office, E/351/542; 29 September 1579–3 July 1597; English and Latin; parchment; 222 mbs, attached at head probably with original (vellum?) lace; 620–820mm x 470mm (580–780mm x 390–460mm); modern pencil numeration at foot of each mb; written front to back; monotone ink capital embellishment at beginning of main heading; moderately serious loss at lower right corners, some damage at edges and feet, a little rubbing on mb 1, tears on mb 222.

Master of the Revels' Annual Engrossed Account

London, Public Record Office, AO/1/2046/11; 1604–5; English and Latin; paper and parchment; roll of 5 sheets + 2 mbs; 250mm x 340mm; unnumbered; writing on 1 side only.

Diplomatic Letters

Letter of Guzmán de Silva to the King of Spain

An English translation of the entire letter may be found in A.S. Hume (ed), *Calendar of Letters and State Papers Relating to English Affairs, Preserved Principally in the Archives of Simancas (1558–1567)* (London, 1892), 577–8.

Simancas, Archivo General de Simancas, Estado, legajo 819; 6 September 1566; Spanish; paper; 2 bifolia; 170mm x 270mm (text area varies); written in a scribal hand on both sides of f [1] and the top quarter of f [2], with Guzmán's signature at the bottom; endorsed on f [2v]: 'A su M*aje*sta*d*, Diego Guzman de Silva vj. de Septiembre 1566 Sacada en relacion Recebida a xxiiij. del mismo Resp*o*nd*i*da a iij de octub*re*.'

Letter of the Venetian Ambassador Nicolò Molen to the Doge

English translations of the letters may be found in Horatio F. Brown (ed), *Calendar of State Papers and Manuscripts Relating to English Affairs, Existing in the Archives and Collections of Venice, and in other Libraries of Northern Italy (1603–1607)* (London, 1900), 265, 270.

Venice, Archivio di Stato, Senato, dispacci ambasciatori, Inghilterra, filza ɪᴠ; 10 August and 14 September 1605; Italian; paper; 2 bifolia; 235mm x 340mm; writing in a scribal hand on first 3 pages of each sheet, with Molen's signature at the bottom and endorsements of receipt by the Venetian chancellery on the back. Part of letter 27 is written in cipher. Now bound in a guardbook stamped and numbered '23' (10 August) and '27' (14 September).

Jurisdictional Documents

Privy Councillors' Letter to the Master of the Revels

This letter, from Robert Rochester, Francis Englefield, and John Bourne, privy councillors, to Sir Thomas Cawarden, master of the revels, was originally part of the Loseley manuscripts. It is one of fourteen miscellaneous papers of various dates sewn together for no apparent reason, some belonging to the office of the revels and some to the office of the tents. For discussion of its date and other problems of interpretation, see Feuillerat, 'Performance of a Tragedy,' pp 96–7; and Elliott, 'A "Learned Tragedy" at Trinity?' pp 247–50.

This document was published by Feuillerat, *Documents Relating to the Revels*, p 250. See p 1096, endnote to Surrey History Centre: LM/41/8 f [1], for a summary of the dating of this record.

Woking, Surrey History Centre, LM/41/8; 19 December 1556; English; paper; bifolium; 280mm x 185mm; unnumbered; writing on inner 2 pages only; endorsed: 'Revylls fro*m* Ma*s*ter Controwl*er* and Mr Engllfeld' and addressed: 'To Mr Cawerden knyght/ M*aster* of the Revell*es* & to eanye of the offycers thereof & to eu*er*ye of them at the blake ffryers.'

Robert Gill's Petition

London, Public Record Office, SP/16/304; 18 December 1635; English; paper; single sheet; 290mm x 180mm (195mm x 155mm); some loss of text on lower edge, some paper repairs to verso; 2 later pencil endorsements reading '1635 De*cember* 18.' Now bound in a guardbook and stamped 115.

PRIVATE CORRESPONDENCE

Letter Recommending a Father Remove His Son from Oxford

ᴍꜱ Royal 17.B.xlvii is a miscellany of documents including sample letters for use in London, poems on health, regulations governing apprenticeship, purgation, the computation of scutage, and land purchase, and ownership notes and deeds.

London, British Library, MS Royal 17.B.xlvii; 14th c.; Latin; paper; iv + 173 + iii; 210mm x 140mm (165mm x 115mm); modern pencil foliation, some contemporary ink foliation; good condition; modern cloth binding, leather corners and spine, with gilt coat of arms on front cover; raised bands and gilding on spine, with title: 'Collections on Dictamen with legal and Other Commonplaces.'

Letter of John Foxe to Laurence Humphrey

The text of the letter to Humphrey occupies ff [1–1v]. The text of f [1] was apparently cancelled due to the arrival of a letter from Humphrey (now lost), to which f [1v] was drafted, and presumably sent, as a response. The cancelled text has been translated by J.F. Mozley, *John Foxe and His Book* (London, 1940), 66.

John Foxe (1516–87) was a famous martyrologist: for his *Christus Triumphans* see Appendix 9. Laurence Humphrey (1527?–90), an exile with Foxe in Switzerland during the reign of Queen Mary, was president of Magdalen College from 1561 to 1590.

London, British Library, MS Harleian 416; January(?) 1561/2; Latin; paper; bifolium; 310mm x 205mm; modern pencil foliation. Bound in a guardbook labelled 'Papers of John Fox' and foliated 140–40v.

Letter of Dudley Carleton to John Chamberlain

London, Public Record Office, SP/12/270; 3 April 1599; English; paper; bifolium; 200mm x 300mm; modern foliation; writing on inner 2 pages only; addressed: 'To my very assured frend Mr. Iohn Chamberlain at Doctor Gilberts house on St Peters hill neer Paules London'; before Carleton's signature on f [3] is the valediction 'from Ricott .Aprill 3ᵈ. 99.' Now bound in a guardbook and numbered 71.

Letter of Robert Burton to his brother, William Burton

The original letter was cut in half by William Burton to be used as note paper, only the lower half of the sheet surviving. The fragment was subsequently joined to the bottom edge of a fragment of another letter, not by Burton, to make up a single foolscap sheet. For further discussion of this document, see Nichols, *Progresses of King James*, vol 4, p 1067; and Nochimson, 'Robert Burton's Authorship of Alba,' pp 325–31. The text is published here by permission of the current owner, the earl of Shrewsbury.

Stafford, Staffordshire Record Office, D649/1/1; 11 August 1605; English; paper; single sheet; 202mm x 150mm (168mm x 133mm); unnumbered; writing in Robert Burton's hand on 1 side of the sheet, writing in William Burton's hand on the other; fragmentary. Now bound in a volume with approximately 200 other sheets containing antiquarian notes by William Burton.

Letter of Sir Thomas Bodley to Sir John Scudamore

This autograph letter, along with four others to Scudamore now preserved in the same PRO bundle, has been published by Trevor-Roper, 'Five Letters of Sir Thomas Bodley,' pp 134–9. Scudamore (1566–1616) was gentleman usher to Queen Elizabeth, a member of the council for the marches of Wales, and a member of five parliaments for the county of Hereford. He was a close friend of Bodley and a contributor to his library. On the interest of the Scudamore family in plays, see J.P. Feil, 'Dramatic References from the Scudamore Papers,' *Shakespeare Survey* 11 (1958), 107–15.

London, Public Record Office, C/115/M20, no 7594; 20 September 1605; English; paper; bifolium; 195mm x 300mm; unnumbered.

Letter of John Chamberlain to Ralph Winwood

Examined in photocopy only, supplied by the Northamptonshire Record Office, the letter is in the fourth (vol 37) of eleven volumes now constituting volumes 34–44 of the Montagu (Boughton) Miscellaneous mss. The letter is a holograph, signed by Chamberlain.

Kettering, Northamptonshire, Boughton House, Winwood Papers, vol 4; 12 October 1605; English; paper; bifolium; 305mm x 408mm; unnumbered. Now bound in an 18th-c. volume of leather-covered boards with gold tooling and lettering, on spine: 'Winwood's Orig State Papers Volume 4 1605 1606.'

Letter of George Garrard to Viscount Conway

London, Public Record Office, SP/16/331; 4 September 1636; English; paper; 2 bifolia; 185mm x 300mm; writing on ff [1–3v] of the second. Now bound in a guardbook and numbered 14.

Letter of Thomas Read to Sir Francis Windebank

London, Public Record Office, SP/16/331; 8 September 1636; English; paper; bifolium; 195mm x 285mm; writing on f [1] only; addressed on f [2v]: 'To the right honorable my very worthy good Vncle Sir ffrancis Windebank knight principall Secretary of State and one of his Maiesties most honorable priuy Counsell,' at bottom left of f [1v], in Windebank's hand: '8: September 1636/ My Nephew: Thomas Reade.' Now bound in a guardbook and numbered 24.

Letter of Edward Rossingham to Sir Thomas Puckering

This letter is bound into one of eighteen volumes of letters (mss Harleian 6989–7006) collected by Thomas Baker in the early eighteenth century. Several surrounding letters in the same hand are signed 'E.R.' The identification of the author and recipient given in the transcript of this letter made by Thomas Birch (bl: ms Additional 4178, ff 402–5) and published in *The Court and Times of Charles The First*, R.F. Williams (ed), vol 2 (London, 1848), 263–6, has been accepted here.

London, British Library, ms Harleian 7000; 11 January 1636/7; English; paper; bifolium; 210mm x

315mm; modern pencil foliation; writing on both sides of each leaf, both horizontal and vertical. Now bound in a guardbook and numbered 198.

PERSONAL RECORDS

Richard Carnsew's Diary

Richard Carnsew was a student at Broadgates Hall, now part of Pembroke College. His diary also lists some expenses for his brother Matthew, who 'entred into commons at Christchurche' on 6 August 1574 (f 216v). The brothers were from Cornwall.

Each page of the diary is divided into several vertical columns: the leftmost gives the day of the month, the next the number of pages read in various books, the next the titles of other books, the central and widest column the principal events of the day, and the right column expenses incurred. The leaves are bound into the present PRO volume in what appears to be random order. The exact dates of some of the entries can therefore not be determined with certainty. Each page is headed with the name of a month, the year sometimes being added by a different but contemporary hand; some pages are signed by a George Grenville. Datable references are few.

London, Public Record Office, SP/46/15; *c* April 1572–*c* December 1575; Latin and English; paper; 8 leaves; 145mm x 195mm; modern pencil foliation. Now bound in a guardbook and foliated 212–19 (ff 213v, 214v, 218v blank).

Richard Madox's Diary

The majority of this work is devoted to describing Madox's travels in Africa and South America in 1582. The entries for January and February record his life in Oxford, where he was a fellow of All Souls. The work has been edited by E.S. Donno, *An Elizabethan in 1582. The Diary of Richard Madox, Fellow of All Souls*, Hakluyt Society, 2nd series, vol 147 (London, 1976).

London, British Library, MS Cotton Appendix 47; 1582; English; parchment; iv + 50 + v; 190mm x 275mm; modern pencil foliation superseding contemporary ink foliation; most leaves repaired, 2 extra leaves added, margin of f 3 badly worn, with holes and tears near the edge, obliterating portions of words at the ends of lines; bound in stamped leather and board in 1884.

Baron Waldstein's Diary

Vatican, Biblioteca Apostolica Vaticana, Reg. lat. 666; 1597–1603; i + 369 + i; 154mm x 90mm (120mm x 70m); 18th-c. ink foliation; good condition; bound in white parchment, gold stamped title on front cover.

Dr Howson's Interrogation

This document is a scribal copy, unsigned, of a report written by John Howson, canon of Christ Church, of his interrogation before King James by Archbishop George Abbot in 1615 on charges of papist leanings. The interrogation reached back to Howson's behaviour during the royal visit of 1605, at which time Abbot was vice-chancellor.

London, Public Record Office, SP/14/80; 1615; English; paper; 5 leaves; 190mm x 285mm; writing on both sides; modern numbering; endorsed on f [5v]: '1615 Dr Howson answers to the Lord ArchBishop of Canterbury Abbott his accusations before King Iames'. Now bound in a guardbook, foliated '65' in modern pencil, and stamped '175–9' in ink.

William Ayshcombe's Memoirs

No author's name appears in the manuscript. The work was erroneously attributed to John Pym by the Historical Manuscripts Commission, 10th Report, Appendix 6 (1887), 82–3, but was correctly assigned to William Ayshcombe by the *DNB* in its article on John Pym (1584–1643). The author refers to 'my uncle William Ayshcombe' and to 'my uncle Oliver Ayshcombe.' Though called a diary by both the Historical Manuscripts Commission and the *DNB*, the work is actually a memoir cast into the form of a diary probably copied or condensed from an original diary, and covering the years 1591–1620.

Ayshcombe matriculated at St John's in 1601 but did not take a degree.

San Marino, Huntington Library, MS HM 30665; *c* 1620; English; paper; 20 + ii; 155mm x 105mm; modern pencil foliation; unbound with modern stitching, title on f 1: 'Memorable Accidententes.'

Hentzner's Travels in England

Pauli Hentzneri, JC. | ITINERARIUM | Germaniæ, Galliæ, | Angliæ, Italiæ: | Cum indice Locorum, Rerum, atq' Verborum | commemorabilum. | *Huic libro accessére novâ hâc editione* | *I.* | Monita Peregrinatoria | duorum doctissimorum | Virorum: | Itemq', | *II.* | *Incerti Auctoris Epitome Præcognito-* | *rum Historicorum, antehac non edita.* | [device] | NORIBERGæ | Typis ABRAHAMI Wagenmanni, | sumptibus sui ipsius & Johan. Güntzelii. | [rule] | ANNO M. DC. XXIX.

Robert Ashley's Autobiography

Robert Ashley (1565–1641) arrived in Oxford in 1580 and attended successively Hart Hall, Alban Hall, and Magdalen College, of which he became a fellow in 1584. In addition to his dramatic activities there, he tells of having acted in 'ludi literati' at Corfe Castle (f 16v) and in a 'Comedie' at Christmas, perhaps in the same place (f 17). For commentary on this work, see Wood, *Athenae*, vol 3, cols 19–20; Macray, *Register*, vol 3, pp 92–7; and Boas, *University Drama*, p 196.

London, British Library, MS Sloane 2131; *c* 1622; Latin and French; paper; 5 leaves; 220mm x 310mm; modern pencil foliation. Bound in a guardbook and foliated 16–20; title on f 16: 'Vita RA ab ipso conscripta.'

Thomas Crosfield's Diary

This invaluable manuscript is a codicologist's nightmare. The work as currently bound appears to be an amalgamation of at least two separate notebooks of Crosfield's, made up with no particular care. The second, more complete foliation may be in the hand of Matthew Hutchinson who has written in the same colour ink his name and the date '24 Dec. 1674' on what is now the first leaf. Hutchinson may also have been responsible for the binding, but if so it was only after he had lost and jumbled many of the leaves he had foliated. It is not known how Hutchinson acquired the manuscript or how and when it found its way back to The Queen's College. The transcripts follow the second foliation sequence, despite its inaccuracy.

The diary entries occupy ff 16–81v, 84v, 87–92v, and 173v–7. The remaining leaves contain various notes on books read, almanacs, transcripts of sermons, etc. The diary entries are for the following dates: 6 January 1625/6–9 November 1638; 15 November 1638–25 December 1638; the month of January 1639/40; 2 February 1652/3–1 February 1653/4; 1 November 1632–10 September 1638 (ie, a second set of entries for those years). Most of the diary was written while Crosfield (1602–63) was a student and fellow of Queen's, from 1618 to *c* 1640.

Excerpts from this work have been edited by F.S. Boas, *The Diary of Thomas Crosfield, M.A., B.D., Fellow of Queen's College, Oxford* (London, 1935). This is a simplified and partially modernized edition of 'about three-fourths of the Diary proper,' with useful explanatory notes. The manuscript is currently kept in a box along with the transcript by J.R. Magrath, used for Boas' edition.

Oxford, The Queen's College Library, MS 390; 1626–54; English, French, Latin, and Greek; paper; 192 leaves (at least 5 missing from front, at least 9 from end); 130mm x 182mm; 2 sets of ink foliation, the first, on some leaves only, in Crosfield's hand, the other, in a slightly later hand, on most leaves, beginning '5' and ending '228,' but with many leaves missing and out of order; pages often laid out in 2 or 3 cols; original leather and board binding, badly damaged. The author's name nowhere appears in the volume, only the initials 'T.C.'

Robert Woodforde's Diary

Robert Woodforde (1606–54), steward of Northampton, had no connection with Oxford other than through his visit there on business during the Act of 1639.

Oxford, New College Archives, 9502; 1637–41; English; paper; ii + 291 + i; 140mm x 90mm (text area varies); unnumbered; entries separated by horizontal rules; original vellum binding.

Peter Heylyn's Memoirs

The manuscript mentioned by Wood (see p 886) has not survived. Wood's transcript occupies folios 20–8 in Part III of the current volume, bearing the original number '98.' The volume is composed of what were originally four different manuscripts, mostly in Wood's hand, containing copies of documents relating to the history of the University. The transcript has been published by John R. Bloxam (ed), *Memorial of Bishop Waynflete Founder of St Mary Magdalen College, Oxford*, Caxton Society 14 (1851), x–xxiv.

Oxford, Bodleian Library, MS. Wood E.4; 1673; English; paper; i + 421; 185mm x 250mm; 17th-c. ink foliation; on f 20 in Anthony Wood's hand: 'Out of an account of Dr Heylyns Life, written by him self to Apr. 8. 1645'; note in right margin of same page, in Wood's hand: 'Mr Henry Heylyn of Minster Lovell his son, lent me ye ms. 8. July. 1673.'

Laud, Diary of His Own Life

THE | HISTORY | OF THE | TROUBLES | AND | TRYAL | OF | *The Most Reverend Father in God,* | *and Blessed Martyr,* | WILLIAM LAUD, | Lord Arch-Bishop of *Canterbury.* | [rule] | *Wrote by* HIMSELF, | *during his* | *Imprisonment in the* Tower. | [rule] | To which is prefixed | THE DIARY OF HIS OWN LIFE | *Faithfully and entirely Published from the Original Copy:* | And subjoined | A SUPPLEMENT to the Preceding HISTORY: | The Arch-Bishop's *Last Will*: His *Large Answer* to the Lord SAY's | *Speech* concerning *Liturgies*; His *Annual Accounts* of his Province deli- | vered to the King; And some other Things relating to the History. | [rule] | IMPRIMATUR, | *Martij*: 7: 1693/4. JO: CANT. | [rule] | *LONDON*: | Printed for **Ri. Chiswell**, at the *Rose* and *Crown* in St. *Paul's* | Church-Yard, MDCXCV. Wing: L586.

Laud, Historical Account

AN | Historical Account | OF ALL | **Material Transactions** | Relating to the | UNIVERSITY | OF | OXFORD, | FROM | ARCH-BISHOP LAUD'S | Being ELECTED | CHANCELLOR | To his RESIGNATION of that | OFFICE. | [rule] | Written by Himself. [rule].

Printed with separate title-page and separate pagination in: **The Second Volume** | OF THE | REMAINS | OF THE | Most Reverend Father in God, | And Blessed *MARTYR,* | WILLIAM LAUD, | Lord Arch-Bishop | OF | CANTERBURY. | [rule] | Written by HIMSELF. | [rule] | Collected by the late Learned Mr. *Henry Wharton,* | And Published according to his Request by the Re- | verend Mr. *Edmund Wharton,* his Father. | [rule] | LONDON, | Printed for *Sam. Keble* at the *Turk's-Head* in *Fleet-street, Dan.* | *Brown* without *Temple Bar, Will. Hensman* in *Westminster-Hall,* | *Matt. Wotton* near the *Inner-Temple Gate,* and *R. Knaplock* at | the *Angel* in St. *Paul's Church-yard.* 1700. Wing: L596.

HISTORIES AND REMINISCENCES

Continuatio Eulogii

London, British Library, Cotton MS Galba E.VII; *c* 15th c.; Latin; parchment; v + 104 + iv; 360mm x 250mm (text area varies); modern (19th-c.?) pencil foliation, earlier cancelled ink foliation, 1 folio less (ie, '193' in ink for '194' in pencil); 2 cols; blue and red capitals and paragraph divisions; some damage and loss (not to text) at edge of ff throughout, considerable peripheral damage to early ff including some loss of text; modern calf binding, gilded and stamped, gilt coat of arms on front cover, raised bands containing green leather with gilt lettering on spine: 'Cronica Breuis A Christi Nat. Ad. Ann. 1364 – Eulogium. Historia Universitatis A Mundi Creatione Add. Ann. 1413.'

Ponet, Apologie

AN APOLO | GIE FVLLY AVNSVVERINGE BY SCRI- | *ptures and aunceant Doctors| a blasphemose book gatherid by | D. Steph. Gardiner| nou Lord chauncelar and D. Smyth of Ox | ford| and other Papists| as by ther books appeare| and of late | set furth vnder the name of Thomas Martin Doctor of the Ci- | uile lawes as of himself he saieth| against the godly mariadge | of priests. wherin dyuers other matters whiche the Papists | defend be so confutid| that in Martyns ouerthrow | they may see there own impudency | and confusion. | [device] | By IOHN PONET Doctor of diuinitie and | busshop of winchester. | The author desireth that the reader will content him- | self with this first book vntill he may haue leasure to | set furth the next| whiche shalbe by | Gods grace shortly. | It is a hard thing for the to spurn aga- | inst the prick. Act. 9.* [Strasburg, 1555]. *STC*: 20175.

Miles Windsor's Narrative

This manuscript is part of Brian Twyne's collection of documents on the history of Oxford University, formed while he was a fellow of Corpus Christi College and keeper of the archives in 1634. It contains both original documents, antiquarian copies in other hands, and copies in Twyne's hand. The volume contains two versions of Miles Windsor's 'The Receiving of the Queen's Majesty into Oxford in 1566': one is a fair copy in Windsor's own hand and initialled by him, occupying folios 104–14; the other is a draft, also in Windsor's hand, with corrections and additions by him made in a darker ink, occupying folios 115–23. A nineteenth-century hand has added occasional marginal transcriptions of headings and proper names, ignored in the present text.

The draft copy has been selected as the authoritative text here, with collations of Windsor's fair version. Twyne's later copy of the fair text (Bodl.: MS. Twyne 17) is not collated, nor are two contemporary abridgements of Windsor's work contained in Bodl.: MS. Twyne 21 and Folger Shakespeare Library: MS V.a.176, ff 167–74 (see p 1099, endnote to CCC: MS 257). These abridgements are the source of the published versions of the work in Nichols' *Progresses of Queen Elizabeth*, vol 1, pp 206–17, Wood's *History and Antiquities*, vol 2, pp 154–63, and Plummer's *Elizabethan Oxford*, pp 195–205.

Windsor, who names himself as one of the actors in the royal plays of 1566, was an undergraduate at Corpus at the time of the queen's visit. The omission of some material in the draft version from the fair copy would appear to be his deliberate attempt to show the acting in a better light.

Windsor's narrative has sometimes been misattributed by modern scholars to Thomas Neal (eg, Boas, *University Drama*, p 98) (see p 697, under Nicholas Robinson's 'Of the Actes Done at Oxford').

Oxford, Corpus Christi College, MS 257; *c* 1566; English and Latin; paper; i + 178 + v; 150mm x

210mm; 19th-c. pencil foliation, some leaves have 17th-c. ink pagination (incomplete); bound in original vellum.

Nicholas Robinson's 'Of the Actes Done at Oxford'

This manuscript was compiled by Nicholas Robinson, bishop of Bangor, originally to commemorate the royal visit to Cambridge in 1564, at which he was present. The Cambridge material occupies the first 154 leaves, written in several hands, all in Latin.

Washington, DC, Folger Shakespeare Library, MS V.a.176; *c* 1566; Latin and English; i + 174; 215mm x 150mm; modern pencil foliation; bound in stamped leather and board in 1827. Originally Phillips MS 4827. Robinson added in 1566 the following accounts of the royal visit to Oxford:
1/ ff 154–66v: 'Of the Actes Done at Oxford,' in Latin, written by Robinson. This was later copied into BL: MS Harleian 7033, ff 142–9, by Thomas Baker, which served as the text for the published versions of Nichols' *Progresses of Queen Elizabeth*, vol 1, pp 229–47 and Plummer's *Elizabethan Oxford*, pp 171–91. None of these later versions has any independent authority and they are not collated here.
2/ ff 167–74: title on f 167: 'A.D. 1566./ A brief rehearsall of all suche thinges as were/ doonne in th'vniversitie of Oxford, during the Queenes/ Maiesties abode there.' Marginal note on same page: 'This exhibited by Richard Stephens as an extract drawn oute/ of a longer treatise made by Mr Neale reader of Hebrew at Oxford.' It is likely that the mistaken attribution of the longer work to Thomas Neal arose from the fact that another work of Neal's, the *Dialogus in aduentum Reginae*, was copied by the same scribe immediately before the anonymous abridged account of the royal visit in Bodl.: MS. Twyne 21, ff 792–800, which is Robinson's source. In fact the author of the original was Miles Windsor (see p 696). Richard Stephens was a contemporary of Miles Windsor at Corpus Christi College. This is the only reference to his authorship of the 'Brief Rehearsal.' While mainly an abridged copy of Windsor's account, the 'Brief Rehearsal' occasionally furnishes details not in the original and omits others.

Bereblock's Commentary

The front flyleaf of this MS has the signature of Thomas Hearne, with the date 29 August 1727 and a statement that the manuscript was a gift from Thomas Ward of Warwick, knight. On the same flyleaf a later note in Hearne's hand reads: 'I have printed this MS at the End of Vita Ricardi II.' The note refers to Hearne's edition of the *Historia Vitae et Regni Ricardi II* (Oxford, 1729), 253–96. Hearne's edition was reprinted by Plummer, *Elizabethan Oxford*, pp 111–50, who added a collation with Bodl.: MS. Additional A.63.

Oxford, Bodleian Library, MS. Rawlinson D.1071; *c* 1566–71; Latin; paper, vellum flyleaves; v + 25 + iii; 140mm x 200mm; modern pencil pagination; grey paper-covered board binding.

The transcription from MS. Rawlinson D.1071 has been collated with the following manuscripts, which appear to have been copied separately (ie, none is the copy of the other), although the Folger Shakespeare Library manuscript may have a more common ancestry with the Rawlinson manuscript. Bodl.: MS. Additional A.63 appears to have more errors and omissions, and both it and the Folger Shakespeare Library manuscript have emendations by correctors of uncertain identity.

Washington, DC, Folger Shakespeare Library, MS V.a.109; *c* 1566–71; Latin; paper; ix + 24 + iv; 144mm x 184mm; modern pencil foliation 1–24; modern (1959) tan cloth binding, previously in an 18th-c. binding, bound in with several other MSS and printed works. The manuscript must have been copied between 1566, the year of the events it describes, and 1571, the year of the death of one of its two dedicatees, William Petre.

Oxford, Bodleian Library, MS. Additional A.63 (*sc* 28864); *c* 1566; Latin; paper; ii + 22; 170mm x 125mm; modern pencil foliation; modern red leather binding. There is no title-page and no indication of an author or title. The only heading is the date '1565' written at the top of f 1, a mistake for 1566. This manuscript was described by Thomas Tanner in the 18th c. as belonging to Thomas Rivers, fellow of All Souls.[8]

Stow, Chronicles

A Sum- | *marye of the Chroni-* | **cles of Englande, from the** | first comminge of Brute into | **this Lande, Vnto this pre** | sent yeare of Christ. | 1570. | *Diligentlye collected,* | **and nowe newly corrected** | and enlarged, by Iohn Stowe, | **Citizen of London. | ℂ Seene and allowed according to the Queenes Maiestyes | Iniunctions.** | *Imprinted at London* | *in Fleetestreate by Tho-* | *mas Marshe.* STC: 23322.

Visit of the Prince of Siradia

Washington, DC, Folger Shakespeare Library, MS L.b.606; *c* 1583; English; paper; single sheet; 210mm x 305mm, written on both sides; written in late 16th-c. secretary hand; kept in a folder marked 'Loseley Manuscripts.' This sheet is a rough draft with many corrections. A 19th-c. hand has numbered the two sides of the leaf '72' and '72v.'

Holinshed, Third Volume of Chronicles

THE | Third volume of Chronicles, be- | *ginning at duke William the Norman* | commonlie called the Conqueror; and | *descending by degrees of yeeres to all the* | kings and queenes of England in thier | orderlie successions: | *First compiled by Raphaell Holinshed,* | *and by him extended to the* | *yeare 1577.* | *Now newlie recognised, augmented, and* | *continued (with occurrences and* | *accidents of fresh memorie)* | *to the yeare 1586.* | *Wherein also are conteined manie matters* | *of singular discourse and rare obser-* | *uation, fruitfull to such as be* | *studious in antiquities, or* | *take pleasure in the* | *grounds of anci-ient histories.* | With a third table (peculiarlie seruing | this third volume) both of | names and matters | memorable. | *Historiae placeant nostrates ac peregrinae.* [London, 1587]. STC: 13569.

Bunny, A Briefe Answer

A | Briefe Answer, vnto those | idle and friuolous quarrels of | R.P. against the late edition of | the RESOLVTION: | By | *Edmund Bunny.* | *Wherunto are præfixed the booke* | of Resolution, and the treatise of | Pacification, perused and noted in | the margent, on all such places as | are misliked of R.P. shewing in | what Section of this Answer fol- | lowing, those places are | handled. | PSALM. 120.7. | I labour for *peace: but when* to | that ende *I speake* vnto them, | *they* prepare themselues | *vnto warre.* | AT LONDON. | Printed by Iohn Charle- | wood, *Anno. Dom.* | 1589. *STC*: 4088.

Harvey, Four Letters

[Harvey, Gabriel.] FOVRE LETTERS, | and certaine Sonnets: | *Especially touching* Robert Greene, *and other parties,* | *by him abused*: | But incidentally of diuers excellent persons, | and some matters of note. | *To all courteous mindes, that will voutchsafe the reading.* | [device] | LONDON | Imprinted by Iohn Wolfe, | 1592. *STC*: 12900.

Harington, Metamorphosis of Ajax

[Sir John Harington.] A NEVV DIS- | COVRSE OF A STALE | SVBIECT, CALLED THE | Metamorphosis of AIAX: | *Written by* MISACMOS, *to his friend* | *and cosin* PHILOSTILPNOS. | [device] | AT LONDON, | Printed by Richard Field, dwelling | in the Black friers, | 1596. *STC*: 12779.

Narratives by Cambridge Men

Folios 3–9 of the following MS are in the hand of Philip Stringer, fellow of St John's College, Cambridge, who along with Henry Mowtlowe, fellow of King's College, was sent by his university to observe the royal entertainment at Oxford in 1592. Stringer wrote out the 1592 narrative for Mowtlowe on 3 May 1603 in Cambridge, based on 'notes' he had made at the time, asking him to 'alter' them as he saw fit 'for the vse of the vniuersity here.' No corrections or additions appear in the manuscript, however. The date of composition of the description of King James' visit to Oxford in 1605 (ff 28–45v) is not given. The description is in a different hand, possibly Mowtlowe's, as the author was clearly a King's College man.

This manuscript was copied by Thomas Baker in the eighteenth century into BL: MS Harleian 7044, ff 97–107. Baker's transcript was published by Nichols in *Progresses of Queen Elizabeth*, vol 3, pp 149–60, and *Progresses of King James*, vol 1, pp 530–59. As these versions have no independent authority, they are not collated here.

Cambridge, Cambridge University Library, MS Additional 34; English; 1603–*c* 1605; paper; 145mm x 185mm; modern foliation; bound in original leather, badly damaged. A note in a different hand on f 87v reads: 'This Manuscript found in Mr Bucks Study 1722.' John Buck, a University bedell, died in 1680.

Nixon, Oxfords Triumph

[Anthony Nixon] OXFORDS | Triumph: | In the Royall Enter- | *tainement of his moste Excellent* | Maiestie, the Queene, and | the Prince: the 27. of *August* | last, 1605. | With | *The Kinges Oration deliuered to the* | Vniuersitie, and the incorpo- | rating of diuers Noble-men, | Maisters of Arte. | [device] | *LONDON* | Printed by *Ed. Allde,* and are to bee solde in | Paules Church-yard by Iohn | *Hodgets. 1605. STC:* 18589.

Wake, Rex Platonicus

This editon of *Rex Platonicus* has been collated with the subsequent editions *STC*: 24939.5; *STC*: 24940; *STC*: 24941; *STC*: 24942; and *STC*: 24942.5.

REX PLATONICVS: | Sive, | DE POTEN- | TISSIMI PRINCIPIS | IACOBI BRITANNIARVM | Regis, ad illustrissimam Academiam | *Oxoniensem, adventu, Aug. 27.* | Anno. 1605. | *NARRATIO* | *AB ISAACO WAKE, PVBLICO A-* | *cademiæ ejusdem Oratore, tum temporis* | *conscripta, nunc verò in* | *lucem* | *edita, non sine authoritate* | *Superiorum.* | [device] | *OXONIÆ,* Excudebat Iosephus Barnesius, | *Anno Dom.* 1607. *STC*: 24939.

Armin, A Nest of Ninnies

A | Nest of Ninnies. | Simply of themselues without | Compound. | *Stultorum plena sunt omnia.* | By *Robert Armin* | [device] | LONDON: | Printed by *T.E.* for *Iohn Deane.* 1608. | *STC*: 772.7.

A Letter to Mr T.H. from Sir Edward Hoby

A | LETTER | TO Mr. T. H. | LATE MINISTER: | Now Fugitiue: | FROM SIR Edvvard | Hoby Knight. | IN ANSWERE OF HIS | *first Motiue.* | [rule] | Hebr..3.12. | *Take heed, Brethren, lest at any time there be in any* | *of you an euill heart, and vnfaithfull, to depart* | *away from the liuing God.* | [rule] | [ornament] | *AT LONDON,* | Imprinted by *F.K.* for *Ed. Blount* and *W. Barret,* | and are to be sold at the signe of the blacke | *Beare in Pauls Church-yard.* | 1609. *STC*: 13541.

Theophilus Higgons' Answer to Sir Edward Hoby

THE | APOLOGY | OF | THEOPHILVS HIGGONS | LATELY MINISTER, | NOW CATHOLIQVE. | Wherein | THE LETTER | OF | SIR EDVV. HOBY KNIGHT | directed vnto the sayd T.H. in answere of his | FIRST MOTIVE, is modestly | examined, and clearely refuted. | [ornament] | *Patior, sed non confundor.* | 2. Timoth. I. 12. | [ornament] | ROAN. | BY Iohn Machvel, dwelling in the streete | of the Prison, ouer the Crowne of Orleans. | 1609. *STC*: 13452.

Camden, Annales

ANNALES | RERVM ANGLICARVM, | ET HIBERNICARVM, | REGNANTE | ELIZABETHA, | *AD* | ANNVM SALVTIS | M. D. LXXXIX | Gvilielmo Camdeno | Avthore. | Londini, | Typis

Guilielmi Stansbij, Impensis *Simonis Watersoni,* | ad insigne CORONÆ in Cœmeterio | PAVLINO. | [rule] | M. DC. XV. *STC*: 4496.

Wallington, 'God's Judgement on Sabbath Breakers'

London, British Library, Sloane MS 1457; 1618–58; English; paper; ii + 107 + ii; 195mm x 150mm (190mm x 140mm); modern pencil foliation, contemporary ink pagination; good condition; modern cloth-covered cardboard binding, leather corners and spine.

Burton, Anatomy of Melancholy

This volume contains transcription from the second edition of *Anatomy of Melancholy* collated with the 1621 first edition (*STC*: 4159).

[Robert Burton] *THE* | ANATOMY OF | MELANCHOLY: | *VVHAT IT IS.* | VVITH ALL THE KINDES, CAV- | SES, SYMPTOMES, PROGNOSTICKS, | AND SEVERALL CVRES OF IT. | *IN THREE MAINE PARTITIONS,* | with their seuerall SECTIONS, MEM- | BERS, and SVBSECTIONS. | PHILOSOPHICALLY, MEDICI- | NALLY, HISTORICALLY | *opened and cut vp,* | BY | DEMOCRITVS *Iunior.* | With a Satyricall PREFACE, conducing to | the following Discourse. | *The second Edition, corrected and aug-* | *mented by the Author.* | MACROB. | Omne meum, Nihil meum. | [device] | AT OXFORD, | Printed by IOHN LICHFIELD and IAMES SHORT, | for HENRY CRIPPS, *Aᵒ Dom. 1624.* *STC*: 4160.

Camden, Tomus Alter Annalium

TOMVS ALTER | ANNALIVM | RERVM | ANGLICARVM, | *ET* | HIBERNICARVM, | *REGNANTE* | ELIZABETHA, | Qui nunc demum prodit: | *SIVE* | PARS QVARTA. | *AVTURE* | GVIL. CAMDENO | [rule] | LONDINI, | Excudebat *Guil. Stansby,* Impensis *Simonis* | *Waterson.* 1627. *STC*: 4496.5.

Brian Twyne's Notes on the History of the University Music

This volume contains a collection of transcripts of documents on the history of the University, most of them in the hand of Brian Twyne, with some annotations by Gerard Langbaine. The contents are miscellaneous and bound in no particular order. There is no calendar or index. A brief description of the contents may be found in Clark, *The Life and Times of Anthony Wood*, vol 4, pp 217–18.

Oxford, Bodleian Library, MS. Twyne-Langbaine 4; *c* 1630–44; Latin and English; paper; ii + 318 + iv; leaves of various sizes, averaging 190mm x 305mm; modern pencil foliation 1–318, some leaves have marginal rules, some blank; 18th-c. leather and board binding, title stamped on spine: 'Collectanea B. Twyne Langbaine &c.'

Burton, For God and the King

FOR | GOD, and the KING. | *THE* | SVMME OF TWO SERMONS | Preached on the fifth of November last | in St. MATTHEWES FRIDAY- | STREETE. 1636. | [rule] | By HENRY BVRTON, Minister of Gods Word | there and then. | [rule] | 1. PET. 2.17. | *Feare GOD. Honour the KING.* | 2. TIM. 4.1,2,3. | *I charge thee before God, and the Lord Iesus Christ, who shall* | *judge the quicke and the dead at his appearing, and his* | *Kingdome: Preach the Word, be instant, in season, out of* | *season, reproove, rebuke, exhort with all long suffering and* | *doctrine. For the time will come, when they will not endure* | *sound doctrine, &c.* | Bernard. in Dedic. Ecclæ. Ser. 3. | *Non miremini, fratres, si durius loqui videor:* | *Quia veritas neminem palpat.* | [rule] | Printed, Anno Dom. 1636. *STC*: 4141.

Burton, A Divine Tragedie

[Henry Burton] A DIVINE TRAGEDIE | LATELY ACTED, | *Or* | A Collection of sundry memorable exam- | ples of Gods judgements upon Sabbath-breakers, and other | like Libertines, in their unlawfull Sports, happening within | the Realme of England, in the compass only of two yeares | last past, since the Booke was published, worthy to be | knowne and considered of all men, especially such, who are | guilty of the sinne or Arch-patrons | thereof. | *Psal. 50. vers. 22.* | Now consider this, ye that forget God, least he teare you in peeces, | and there be none to deliuer you. | *Gregorius M. Moraliu. lib. 36. c. 18.* | Deus, etsi quaedam longanimiter tolerat, quaedam tamen in hac vita | flagellat, & hic nonnunquam ferire inchoatur quos aeterna | damnatione consumat. | *Tibullus Elegiarum. lib. 3. Eleg. 7-* | –Foelix quicunque dolore | Alterius disces posse carere tuo. | *Concil. Paris. 2. lib.3.c.5.* | Salubriter admonemus cunctos fideles, ut diei Dominico debitum hono- | rum & reverentiam exhibeant. Quoniam hujus dehonoratio, & | à Religione Christiana valde abhorret, & suis violatoribus anima- | rum perniciem proculdubio generat. | *Alex. Alensis ex Hieron.P.3.Q. 32. M.4. Art.1. Resol.* | Quis dubitat Sceleratiùs esse commissum, quod graviùs est punitum? ut | Num.15.35. ibid. | [device] | Anno M.DC.XXXVI. *STC*: 4140.7.

Heylyn, A Briefe and Moderate Answer

A BRIEFE and | Moderate | ANSWER, | TO | The seditious and scandalous Chal- | lenges of *Henry Burton,* late of | *Friday-Streete;* | In the two *Sermons,* by him preached on the | Fifth of *November.* 1636. And in the | *Apologie* prefixt before them. | *BY* | PETER HEYLYN. | 1. Pet. 2. 13, 14. | *Submit your selves to* every ordinance of man for the | Lords sake, whether it be to the King as supreame: or unto Go- | vernors, as unto them which are sent by him, for the punish- | ment of evill doers, and for the praise of them that doe well. | [rule] | LONDON: | Printed by *Ric. Hodgkinsonne;* and are to be sold by *Daniel* | *Frere,* dwelling in *little-Brittan,* at the signe of the | *red-Bull. Anno Domini* 1637. *STC*: 13269. The imprimatur by the archbishop of Canterbury, on p (ii), is dated 23 June 1637.

H.L., Jests from the Universitie

Until 1967 only two copies (BL and Rosenbach) of this book were known, both incorrectly dated '1628' with the correct date of '1638' written in ink. The Bodleian copy, purchased in 1967 from Christie's, bears the correct printed date.

Gratiæ Ludentes. | IESTS, | FROM THE | VNIVERSITIE. | [rule] | By *H.L. Oxen.* | [rule] | Mart. *Dic mihi quid melius de sidiosus Agas.* | [device] | Printed at London by *Tho. Cotes,* for | *Humphrey Mosley.* 1638. *STC*: 15105.

Entertainment of King Charles I

The whole of this manuscript is in the hand of Brian Twyne, first keeper of the University archives (1634–44). The section relevant here is that called 'Entertainmentes,' occupying pages 147–203. The pages now numbered 147–90 also bear an earlier ink foliation (1–42).

This manuscript is the source of the collation of the excerpts from OUA: NEP/Supra/R (see under Registers of Congregation and Convocation, p 681) and OUA: WP/γ/19/1 (see under Orders of the Delegates of Convocation for the Royal Plays, p 683).

Oxford, Bodleian Library, MS. Twyne 17; *c* 1640; Latin and English; paper; 243 leaves; 304mm x 205mm; modern pagination; 17th-c. leather and board binding; ink title on spine in Gerard Langbaine's hand: 'De Statutis Uni*ver*sitatis Orders occasionall. Enterteynm*ents*. Iurisdictio sp*irit*ualis. Circa incontinentes. &. Testamentorum proba*tio*/ &c.'

Walton, 'Life of Henry Wotton' in Reliquiae Wottonianae

Izaak Walton's 'Life of Henry Wotton,' in: *Reliquiae Wottonianæ.* | [rule] | OR, | A COLLECTION | *Of* LIVES, LETTERS, POEMS; | *With* | CHARACTERS | OF | Sundry PERSONAGES: | *And other* | Incomparable PIECES | of *Language* and *Art.* | [rule] | *By* The curious PENSIL of | the Ever Memorable | Sr *Henry Wotton* K^t, | Late, | Provost of *Eton Colledg.* | [rule] | LONDON, | Printed by *Thomas Maxey*, for *R. Marriot,* | *G. Bedel,* and *T. Garthwait.* 1651. Wing: W3648.

Wilson, History of Great Britain

This copy of Arthur Wilson's book, now TC Library: N.7.5, was owned by Edward Bathurst and bequeathed to Trinity College on his death in 1668. Bathurst was a student at Trinity from 1629 to 1634. Wilson's own autobiography survives in Cambridge University Library: MS Additional 33 and indicates that his plays were all written before he entered Oxford in 1630, at the age of 32. Both documents were published by Philip Bliss in *The Inconstant Lady, A Play* (Oxford, 1814), Appendices 3 and 4. They disagree on the date that Wilson entered Oxford and the length of his stay there. See also Wood, *Athenae,* vol 3, cols 318–23, and Bentley, *The Jacobean and Caroline Stage,* vol 5, pp 1267–8.

A manuscript note by Edward Bathurst on the flyleaf of the Trinity College copy describes performances by the king's men of Wilson's plays in Oxford while Wilson was a student at Trinity.

THE | HISTORY | OF | Great Britain, | BEING | THE LIFE AND REIGN | OF | King JAMES | THE FIRST, | RELATING | To what passed from his first Access to | the Crown, till his Death. | [rule] | By *ARTHUR WILSON*, Esq. | [rule] | [device] | [rule] | *LONDON*, | Printed for *Richard Lownds*, and are to be | sold at the Sign of the *White Lion* near Saint *Paul's* | little North-door. 1653. Wing: W2888.

Heylyn, Cyprianus Anglicus

CYPRIANUS ANGLICUS: | OR, THE | HISTORY | OF THE | Life and Death, | OF | The most Reverend and Renowned PRELATE | WILLIAM | By Divine Providence, | Lord Archbishop of *Canterbury*, Primate of all | *ENGLAND*, and Metropolitan, Chancellor of the | Universities of *Oxon.* and *Dublin*, and one of the | Lords of the Privy Council to His late most | SACRED MAJESTY | King CHARLES the First, | Second MONARCH of *Great Britain. CONTAINING ALSO* | The Ecclesiastical History of the Three Kingdoms | of *ENGLAND, SCOTLAND,* and *IRELAND* | from His first rising till His Death. | [rule] | By P. *Heylyn* D.D. and Chaplain to *Charles* the | first and *Charles* the second, Monarch of *Great Britain.* | [rule] | ECCLUS. 44 VERS. 1, 3. | 1. *Let us now praise Famous Men and our Fathers that begat Vs.* | 3. *Such as did bear Rule in their Kingdoms, Men Renowned for their Power,* | *giving Counsel by their Vnderstanding, and Declaring Prophesies.* | [rule] *LONDON*: | Printed for *A. Seile*, MDCLXVIII. Wing: H1699.

Burnet, Life of Sir Matthew Hale

THE | **Life and Death** | OF | *Sir* MATTHEW HALE, Kᵗ. | SOMETIME | *LORD CHIEF IUSTICE* | OF | His Majesties Court | OF | KINGS BENCH. | [rule] | Written by | *GILBERT BURNETT*, D.D. | [rule] | *LONDON,* | Printed for *William Shrowsbery*, at the | Bible in *Duke-Lane*, 1682. Wing: B5828.

Langbaine, English Dramatick Poets

AN | ACCOUNT | OF THE | English Dramatick | POETS. | OR, | Some OBSERVATIONS | And | *REMARKS* | On the Lives and Writings, of all those that | have Publish'd either Comedies, Trage | dies, Tragi-Comedies, Pastorals, Masques, | Interludes, Farces, or Opera's in the | *ENGLISH TONGUE.* | [rule] | *By* GERARD LANGBAINE. | [rule] | *OXFORD*, | Printed by *L.L.* for GEORGE WEST, | and HENRY CLEMENTS. | [rule] | *An. Dom.* 1691. Wing: L373.

PLAY TEXTS, SYNOPSES, AND PART BOOKS

A Twelfth Night Play at St John's

See Appendix 6:1 under *Narcissus.*

Vertumnus *Plot Synopsis*

See Appendix 6:1 under *Vertumnus.*

Robert Burton's Philosophaster

The transcription from Harvard Theatre Collection: MS Thr.10 has been collated with Folger Shakespeare Library, MS V.a.315. For both manuscripts see Appendix 6:1 under *Philosophaster.*

An Actor's Part Book

See Appendix 6:1 under 'The Part of Poore.'

Poem by Thomas Goffe

See Appendix 6:1 under *The Courageous Turk.*

Emily's Lament from Palamon and Arcite

See Appendix 6:2 under *Palamon and Arcite.*

PROLOGUES, PREFACES, DEDICATIONS, AND EPILOGUES

Dedicatory Epistle to Gilbert Smith, Archdeacon of Peterborough

See Appendix 6:1 under *Christus Redivivus.*

Epilogue to Caesar Interfectus

See Appendix 6:2 under *Caesar Interfectus.*

Gager, Meleager

See Appendix 6:1 under *Meleager.*

Gwinne, Vertumnus

See Appendix 6:1 under *Vertumnus.*

Holyday, Technogamia

See Appendix 6:1 under *Technogamia.*

Daniel, Whole Workes

THE | WHOLE | VVORKES OF | Samvel Daniel Esquire | *in Poetrie.* | [rule] | [device] | [rule] | LONDON, | Printed by Nicholas Okes, for | Simon Waterson, and are to be | sold at his shoppe in *Paules* Church- | yard, at the Signe of the Crowne. 1623. *stc:* 6238.

POEMS AND SONGS

Poem on Mercurius Rusticans

See Appendix 6:1 under *Mercurius Rusticans.*

Poem on the Royal Visit

The anonymous poem on the royal visit of 1605 was numbered '272' among the items in the volume by W.H. Black, who catalogued the Ashmole collection in 1845. The volume is a poetic miscellany of about 330 poems, songs, and verses, partly in the handwriting of Elias Ashmole.

Oxford, Bodleian Library, MS. Ashmole 3637 (*sc* 6917); *c* 1640; paper; English; vi + 327 + vi; modern pencil foliation; 17th-c. leather and board binding.

Verses Spoken in St John's Library

These verses are included in a poetic miscellany signed by Edmund Malone on folio 1, who has also written on the spine: 'Manuscript Poems 1644.'

Oxford, Bodleian Library, MS. Malone 21 (*sc* 20569); *c* 1640–50; English; paper; i + 121 + i; 175mm x 110mm; contemporary ink foliation; original vellum binding.

Mr Moore's Revels

See Appendix 6:1 under 'Mr Moore's Revels.'

Verses on the Comedians of Oxford and Cambridge

Oxford, Bodleian Library, MS. Malone 19; early 17th c.; English and Latin; paper; ii + 163 + ii; 181mm x 138mm (162mm x 119mm); modern pencil foliation, partial contemporary ink foliation; good condition; modern board binding with leather spine, embossed title on spine.

Civic Records

The records of the city of Oxford, with one exception, remain in the possession of the city and are housed in the city hall.[9] They are brought on the request of the county archivist to the Oxfordshire Record Office for consultation. They consist of the legislative and financial records of the city. The earliest documents (from 1275) are found pasted in the city memorandum book. However, the vast majority of the records survive only from the sixteenth century – the hannisters' registers from 1514, the council minutes from 1528, and the financial records from 1553.

CITY MEMORANDUM BOOK

The city memorandum book consists of three volumes containing property leases, bonds, indentures, lists of civic officials, etc, for the period of 1275–1649.

Oxford, Oxford City Archives, D.5.2; 1583–4; English and Latin; parchment (now mounted on a paper stub); single sheet; 121mm x 223mm (105mm x 200mm). Bound in a guardbook, numbered '181,' and foliated 190–90v; in a brown cloth binding with leather corners and spine, stamped title on spine: 'OXFORD CITY RECORDS vol II 1505–1584.'

HANNISTERS' REGISTERS

The term 'hannister' is unique to Oxford. According to W.H. Turner it was derived from the Latin 'hanisterius,' which he says, 'seems to be the Latinized form of the old German and Latin *Hansa, societas mercatorum* "a corporation of merchants"....'[10] The registers are what, in other jurisdictions, would be called freemen's registers, recording the entry of men into the freedom of the city. Admission to the freedom was open to freemen's sons, to those who had been apprenticed to freemen, or to those who paid a fee for the privilege. The number of freemen in the sixteenth century 'must have totalled several hundreds, perhaps a third or even a half of the adult male population.'[11] Among other things, freemen were required 'to obey the city's officers, to keep its liberties, to share in its taxation and other burdens, to join no guild without the council's consent, to report to city officers any foreign merchant "that useth any craft buying or selling."'[12] The further obligation of a freeman was to serve in office. Some freemen, especially as the political climate grew difficult in the seventeenth century, refused to serve and were fined accordingly. On the other side, the privileges of a freeman were the ancient right to trade outside the city, to elect the city's chief officers from constable to mayor, to take part in the festive and ceremonial occasions, to share the valuable pasture of Port Meadow, and to use the city's municipal charities including the freemen's school.[13]

Oxford, Oxford City Archives, A.5.3; 1514–1608; English and Latin; paper; v + 419 + iii; 394mm x 276mm (text area varies); contemporary ink foliation (bound so folios run 1–23, 401–9, 24–394, 413–19, 395–400, 411–12, 423); brown suede binding, 4 red leather patches on spine tooled with gold and lettered: (1) 'ENROLMENT OF APPRENTICES. 1514–1591. LISTS OF COUNCIL 1520–1528,' (2) 'SECTATORES 1520–1591 HANNISTERS 1520–91,' (3) 'MAYORS COURT. (PROCEEDINGS) 1528–1535 HUSTINGS COURT PROCEEDINGS HEN.VIII TO ELIZ.TH,' (4) 'PURCHASE OF CATTLE (INROLLED) 1569–1608.'

Oxford, Oxford City Archives, L.5.1; 1590–1614; Latin; paper; iv + 302 + v; 383mm x 255mm (text area varies); 19th-c. ink foliation; some ff damaged and repaired; brown suede binding, red leather patch on spine tooled in gold: 'HANNISTERS 1590–1614.'

Oxford, Oxford City Archives, L.5.2; 1613–40; Latin; paper; ii + 421 + iii; 434mm x 285mm (377mm x 261mm); modern ink foliation (ff 335–8 numbered but blank, ff 339–421 written from the end of the book forward and inverted); some damage and repair; 19th-c. brown suede binding upside down and backward, both boards detached from spine, red leather patch on spine tooled in gold: 'HANNISTERS. 1613.–1640.'

CITY COUNCIL MINUTES

The city council minutes survive in two overlapping series: C/FC/1/A1 and C/FC/1/A2. The relationship between the two series is difficult to determine precisely. C/FC/1/A1 is not merely a duplicate fair copy of C/FC/1/A2 although the C/FC/1/A1 books do seem to be fair copies of important material contained in the C/FC/1/A2 series. In general they are of a better quality, more neatly, formally, and often more ornamentally written and in better condition. Where they do duplicate the C/FC/1/A2 series, the entries are often corrected versions. For example a clause crossed out in C/FC/1/A2/1, f 5, has simply been omitted in C/FC/1/A1/001, f 37. The C/FC/1/A2 versions are clearly the first ones, possibly written during the meetings themselves. Many C/FC/1/A2 items do not appear at all in C/FC/1/A1, indicating that the more careful series was meant to be a digest of only those items that the council wanted to keep for future reference or permanent record. One feature of the C/FC/1/A1 series that is missing from the C/FC/1/A2 series is the annual lists of the newly elected council officers. Indeed for a few years around 1560 C/FC/1/A1/001 contains little other than these lists.

C/FC/1/A1/002 bears a similar relationship to the C/FC/1/A2 series as C/FC/1/A1/001, with formal lists of elected officers and, on the whole, fewer running minutes of council business. However, in one instance, C/FC/1/A1/002 usefully fills the gap in C/FC/1/A2/1 where the latter covers the business between 1583 and 1586 in a few scrappy dog-eared notes (ff 165–6), not in chronological order, and then jumps to 1600. C/FC/1/A1/002 covers the missing years. By 1600, on the other hand, C/FC/1/A1/002 seems to have become a fair copy of C/FC/1/A2/1, recording the same material with the emendations incorporated. Some material is reorganized and the lists of councillors' names are featured with display letters (eg, ff 58v–9). It is possible that the C/FC/1/A2 series began as single sheets used to take notes at the meetings, which were later copied as the C/FC/1/A1 series, and that some of the gaps in the C/FC/1/A2 series can be explained by the possibility that the sheets were bound later after some of them had been lost.

Oxford, Oxford City Archives, C/FC/1/A1/001; 1528–92; English; paper; ii + 371 + i; 289mm x 410mm (245mm x 350mm); 19th-c. ink foliation; brown leather blind-stamped binding.

Oxford, Oxford City Archives, C/FC/1/A1/002; 1591–1628; English; paper; ii + 322 + i; 265mm x 398mm (215mm x 370mm); contemporary ink foliation; brown reversed calf binding.

Oxford, Oxford City Archives, C/FC/1/A2/2; 1615–34; Latin and English; paper; ii + 310 + ii; 210mm x 320mm (190mm x 300mm); contemporary and later ink foliation; original brown calf binding with decorative stamp. This volume is double foliated throughout by contemporary hands. Careful examination revealed that the first system of foliation is the more accurate and it has been followed in these extracts.

Oxford, Oxford City Archives, C/FC/1/A1/003; 1628–63; English with some headings in Latin; paper; iv + 345 + xix (+ 7 reversed, containing other material); 300mm x 430mm (270mm x 380mm); contemporary foliation; blind-tooled reversed calf binding with contemporary label.

Oxford, Oxford City Archives, C/FC/1/A2/3; 1635–67; English; paper; ii + 329 + v; 225mm x 310mm (135mm x 275mm); 19th-c. ink foliation; brown suede binding decorated with blind stamp.

Oxford, Oxford City Archives, E.4.5; 1635–1715; English with some Latin headings; paper; v + 336 + ii; 90mm x 80mm, (text area varies); 19th-c. ink foliation; order of writing generally chronological with occasional exceptions when later material is inserted in blank spaces; some damage and crumbling on edges, some folios near the end have been bound in upside down; apparently later brown suede binding with decorative leaves stamped on front cover corners, red leather label with gold tooling: '1635–1715. CIVIL WAR. CHARITIES. GENERAL MINUTES.' Contains a table of contents by George P. Hester dated 1841.

AUDITED CORPORATION ACCOUNTS

The finances of the city were the responsibility of two separate sets of officials – the chamberlains and the keykeepers. The chamberlains served for only one year and were in charge of the city's 'current account' – that is, the normal receipts and expenditures for their year in office. Payments for entertainment and later for public sermons came from the chamberlains' accounts. The chamberlains were also responsible, among other duties, for repairs to public buildings, the gallows, and the fire-fighting equipment. The five keykeepers or 'keepers of the chest with five keys' were the city's more permanent financial officers during the sixteenth century, consisting of the mayor 'pro tem' and senior councillors.[14] They were in charge of the overall finances of the city, including monitoring outstanding debts and arrearages both in cash and plate (such as William Gibbons' obligation for his wait's scutcheon (p 621)). The keykeepers were also ultimately responsible for the accounts of Castle Mill (accounted for twice a year), the accounts of the Frideswide and Austen fairs until 1571, and charitable bequests.

The accounts were audited annually although the audit was often not done at the end of the accounting year but sometime later. Sometimes the lateness of the audit date is quite conspicuous, eg, the 1554–5 account was not audited until 16 December 1556, the 1556–7 account was audited 12 January 1558/9, and the 1559–60 account was audited 29 January 1560/1. Thereafter the annual accounts were routinely audited in November or December of the same year in which they ended.

Oxford, Oxford City Archives, P.5.1; 1553–91; English; paper; i + 274 + i; 400mm x 270mm; modern ink foliation; modern brown suede binding, red leather patch on spine with 'AUDIT ACCOUNTS 1553–1591' stamped in gold. The accounts end on f 240. The rest of the volume was begun as a record of indentures and other legal notes followed by a record of payments for the lottery of 1568. The numbering of this part of the volume was begun as if this was the beginning of the book. The 34 folios are written 'upside down' – that is, the book was reversed when the audit accounts were begun. The pages at this end are tabbed (ie, cut away in order) as if for easy reference.

Oxford, Oxford City Archives, P.5.2; 1592–1682; English; paper; i + 406; 385mm x 200mm; modern ink foliation; some display headings; some intrusive show through after f 55; modern brown suede binding, red leather patch on spine stamped in gold: 'AUDIT ACCOUNTS 1592–1682.'

KEYKEEPERS' ACCOUNTS

Oxford, Oxford City Archives, P.4.1; 1555–1664; English and Latin; paper; ii + 263 + i; 350mm x 250mm; modern ink foliation; some display headings; some show through; modern dark brown leather binding stamped and tooled, red leather patch on upper spine stamped in gold: 'KEYKEEPERS ACCOUNTS 1555–1664.'

INDENTURES AND LEASES BOOKS

These two books contain the seventeenth-century leases for the famous dancing school in the Bocardo. Both were placed in evidence in a case in Chancery in November 1873 involving a dispute between the city and a man named Muir. Notes to this effect are pasted on the covers.

Oxford, Oxford City Archives, D.5.5; 1578–1636; English; paper; i + 508 + v; 420mm x 255mm (text area varies); contemporary ink foliation; some display capitals; 19th-c. brown kid binding, red leather patch on spine tooled in gold: 'LEDGER 1578–1636.'

Oxford, Oxford City Archives, D.5.6; 1636–75; English; parchment; 436mm x 264mm (400mm x 202mm); iii + 563 + vi; original ink foliation; good condition; 19th-c. brown suede binding with a red leather patch on the spine tooled in gold: 'LEDGER. 1636.–1675.'

CITY WAITS' OBLIGATIONS

These obligations are among miscellaneous documents mounted on stubs in a guardbook. It begins with documents from the sixteenth century but items are not in date order. A note signed 'GH' or 'George Hester' inside the front cover indicates that the documents were collected over the period 1839–53 and bound by order of the council at the time.

Oxford, Oxford City Archives, F.5.2, 16th c.–19th c.; English and Latin; paper; vii + 283 (including 20 leaves of 19th-c. index) + i; 205mm x 310mm; trace of the seal remains on f 51; 19th-c. brown binding with calf corners and spine, title stamped in gold on front cover: 'CITY OF OXFORD,' title stamped in gold on the spine: 'SUNDRY DOCUMENTS AUTOGRAPHS, etc I.'

CHAMBERLAINS' ACCOUNTS (AC)

Brian Twyne was a seventeenth-century antiquarian and the first keeper of the archives in the Bodleian Library. Just as he extracted material from the University and college archives, so he made notes from the city records that, in some cases, are no longer extant. Twyne's transcriptions are now the only evidence that has survived of particular events. Two extracts are included here. One from 1414 gives us early information about a civic bullring. The second from 1490–1 gives us the traditional order of the civic procession at the time of the newly sworn mayor's return from London.

Oxford, Bodleian Library, MS. Twyne 23; *c* 18 May 1657; Latin and English; paper; ii + 334 + i; 202mm x 154mm (194mm x 120mm); contemporary ink pagination (some confusion in pagination); uniform margin ruled top to bottom; fair condition, some pages brittle or worn; contemporary green leather and board binding, now detached from spine, contemporary and antiquarian numbers in ink on spine.

Guild Records

The financial records of only two guilds, the Cordwainers or Shoemakers and the Tailors, survive from the period. They are deposited in the Bodleian.

The Cordwainers' accounts were rendered in mid-November, suggesting that the accounting year was based on the company election date, the Monday next after the feast of St Luke the Evangelist (18 October).

The dating of the Tailors' accounts is less straightforward. When expressed, the accounting year in MS. Morrell 9 runs from the Monday after the feast of St John the Baptist to the same in the next year. The MS. Rolls Oxon 66 follows a Michaelmas to Michaelmas accounting year.

CORDWAINERS' MINUTES

Oxford, Bodleian Library, MS. Morrell 20; 1534–1645; English; paper; i + 109; 200mm x 290mm (text area varies); 19th-c. pagination; contemporary brown leather binding with decorative stamping, title on spine: 'THE CORDWAYNOR OF OXFORD ANNUAL MEETINGS ACCOMPTS ETC 1534–1645.'

TAILORS' WARDENS' ACCOUNTS

The accounts of the Tailors' Company are preserved in what appears to be two radically different formats. Some accounts in the sequence are now pasted into a nineteenth-century guardbook (Bodl.: MS. Morrell 9). Others are bundled together and stitched at the top (Bodl.: MS. Rolls Oxon 66). There are no duplicate accounts and one set does not appear to be a rough draft of the other. There are needle marks in the membranes of MS. Morrell 9 similar to the marks that would appear in the membranes of MS. Rolls Oxon 66 if the bundle was disassembled. It appears likely that the membranes represent what once was a single series bundled together but that in the nineteenth century the bundle came apart with some of the loose membranes pasted into a guardbook and others simply sewed back together again.

Oxford, Bodleian Library, MS. Morrell 9; 1511–1620; English and Latin; parchment and paper; i + 34 + i; 285mm x 420mm; modern pencil foliation with some folios missing and some sequences paginated rather than foliated; sheets pasted into 19th-c. guardbook bound in tan leather and board, both covers now detached, gold stamp on spine: 'TAYLORS COMPANY OXFORD ACCOMPTS.'

Extracts from:

f 8, piece 4: 1512–13; single mb; 418mm x 278mm (315mm x 260mm).

f 9, piece 5: 1513–14; single mb; 385mm x 250mm (355mm x 247mm).

f 33, piece 19: 1567–8; 2 mbs; 720mm x 180mm (592mm x 150mm).

f 37, piece 22: 1573–4; detached third mb of roll for 1573–4 pasted on ff 35–7; 235mm x 260mm (96mm x 230mm).

f 46, piece 30: 1619–20; detached last 2 mbs of roll pasted on ff 42–6; 756mm x 235mm (735mm x 228mm).

Oxford, Bodleian Library, MS. Rolls Oxon 66; 1575–1712; English; parchment; 12 rolls stitched together at top and rolled as 1, fastened with modern pink string.

Extracts from:

roll 2: 1578–9; 2 mbs; 1,143mm x 270mm.

roll 3: 1591–2; 2 mbs; 1,000mm x 223mm.

roll 4: 1595–6; 2 mbs; 955mm x 222mm.

roll 5: 1597–8; 2 mbs; 945mm x 220mm.

roll 6: 1598–9; 2 mbs; 1,057mm x 205mm.

roll 8: 1610–11; 3 mbs; 1,428mm x 255mm.

Monastic Documents

ARCHBISHOP PECHAM'S REGISTER

London, Lambeth Palace Library, MS Archbishop Pecham's Register; 1279–92; Latin; parchment; i + 249 (with some irregularities including inserted sheets); irregular size leaves, the maximum being 340mm x 215mm (maximum 250mm x 155mm); foliated; many individual leaves cockled; bound in dark brown decorated leather over boards, prominent wormholes, much repaired, written on spine: 'PECKHAM 1279.'

Parish Records

ALL SAINTS CHURCHWARDENS' ACCOUNTS

All Saints was one of the original medieval parishes, the church standing on the corner of the High Street and Turl Street. On the foundation of Lincoln College in 1427, the parish was amalgamated with those of St Michael at the North Gate and St Mildred; the church became the collegiate church. It was made redundant in 1971 and is now the college library.

Manuscripts survive from the 1230s. The records were deposited with the Bodleian Library from 1967 and subsequently with the ORO. The collection was recatalogued in 1996.

The accounting year for the one account excerpted here ran from the Wednesday after Easter to the same in the next year.

Cowley, Oxfordshire Record Office, PAR 189/4/F1/1, item 1; 23 April 1606–8 April 1607; English; parchment; single mb; 642mm x 265mm (600mm x 248mm). Roll now numbered '1' in pencil and mounted with other individual rolls in paper guardbook, covered in brown leather, brown calf spine, stamped on spine: 'CHURCHWARDENS ACCOUNTS | FROM 1605 | to 1716.'

ALL SAINTS CHURCHWARDENS' ACCOUNTS (AC)

This is an antiquarian collection of notes and transcriptions from various church accounts (All Saints, St Aldate, St Martin, St Mary Magdalen, St Michael, and St Peter in the East) and miscellaneous college material (registers, statutes, muniments, etc).

Oxford, Bodleian Library, MS. Wood D.2; c 1665; English and Latin; paper; viii + 318; 202mm x 161mm (text area varies); mixed ink and pencil pagination (pages numbered 1–666 but some numbers used 2 or 3 times, pencil numbering adjusted to bridge gaps in ink numbering); some page edges damaged; parchment over cardboard binding with holes in front and back covers equidistant from edges suggesting there once was a clasp, spine covering cracked and faded, labelled in ink: 'V D.2 53 8513,' burgundy patch with gold lettering: 'WOOD 2 D.'

ST ALDATE CHURCHWARDENS' ACCOUNTS

Records survive from 1394. The collection includes churchwardens' accounts of 1501–2 from St Michael at the South Gate, one of the parishes amalgamated with St Aldate in 1524 when St Michael's Church was demolished for the building of Cardinal College (see p 592).

From 1536–7 forward the accounting year began on St Aldate's Day (4 February) with the exception of 1587–8 (which began 2 February). From 1604–5 the accounting year began and ended within the week of Easter from one year to the next.

The rolls in each series have been dated and shelf-marked by Bodleian librarians and packed in flat boxes.

Oxford, Oxfordshire Record Office, DD Par. Oxford St Aldate c.15; 1410–1590; English; parchment.

Extracts from:

c.15/2; 1535/6–6/7; 3 mbs; 1,650mm x 200mm (1,600mm x 170mm), written on dorse; slight tearing at left margin.

c.15/11; 1581/2–2/3; 2 mbs; 1,050mm x 175mm (900mm x 150mm).

c.15/15; 1586/7–7/8; single mb; 570mm x 420mm (350mm x 330mm); 2 cols; some decoration; 2 small paper notes pinned to corner.

c.15/17; 1588/9–89/90; 2 mbs; 750mm x 200mm (650mm x 160mm); 3 small paper notes pinned to bottom.

Oxford, Oxfordshire Record Office, DD Par. Oxford St Aldate c.16; 1592–1609; English.

Extracts from:

c.16/1; 1591/2–2/3; parchment; 2 mbs; 1,090mm x 200mm (940mm x 170mm).

c.16/4; 1594/5–5/6; parchment; 2 mbs; 700mm x 145mm (670mm x 120mm); some writing on dorse.

c.16/5; 1595/6–6/7; 4 fragments (2 were once a roll of 2 mbs, 2 paper accounts); fragment containing the record: 280mm x 174mm (260mm x 150mm); tear immediately below relevant entries.

c.16/10; 1602/3–3/4; parchment; 2 mbs; 510mm x 125mm (500mm x 125mm); some writing on dorse.

c.16/11; 1604–5; parchment; single mb; 600mm x 150mm (580mm x 130mm).

c.16/12; 1605–6; parchment; single mb; 700mm x 140mm (670mm x 125mm).

c.16/13; 1606–7; parchment; 2 mbs; 1,520mm x 310mm (1,320mm x 250mm).

c.16/14; 1607–8; parchment; single mb; 400mm x 120mm (380mm x 105mm).

c.16/15; 1609–10; parchment; single mb; 790mm x 320mm (640mm x 280mm).

Oxford, Oxfordshire Record Office, DD Par. Oxford St Aldate b.17; 1610–42; English; parchment.

Extracts from:

b.17/1; 1610–11; 2 mbs; 1,050mm x 315mm (1,000mm x 280mm).

b.17/3; 1612–13; 2 mbs; 1,040mm x 310mm (1,015mm x 270mm).

b.17/4; 1616–17; single mb; 1,380mm x 275mm (1,290mm x 260mm).

b.17/5; 1618–19; 2 mbs; 820mm x 290mm (700mm x 250mm; dorse 450mm x 200mm); written on both sides.

b.17/6; 1619–20; 2 mbs; 1,058mm x 442mm (1,025mm x 399mm).

b.17/7; 1620–1; 2 mbs; 935mm x 498mm (850mm x 443mm).

b.17/8; 1621–2; 2 mbs; 1,218mm x 531mm (1,139mm x 454mm).

b.17/9; 1622–3; 2 mbs; 970mm x 200mm (940mm x 165mm).

b.17/10; 1623–4; 2 mbs; 1,300mm x 468mm (1,274mm x 424mm).

b.17/11; 1625–6; single mb; 620mm x 430mm (575mm x 402mm); 2 cols.

LEASE OF ST ALDATE'S PARISH HOUSE

Oxford, Oxfordshire Record Office, MS. DD. Par. Oxford St Aldate c.24/1; 30 January 1569/70; English; parchment; single indented mb; 77–90mm x 478mm; some display capitals, lower 28mm of mb turned up to allow for red wax seal (arms not decipherable) 18mm in diameter; tab parchment strip 15mm wide, endorsed: 'Sealed and ⟨...⟩ in the presence of Iohn Burkesdall William Furnes and Phillip cooles the wryter/.'

ST MARTIN CHURCHWARDENS' ACCOUNTS

The records of St Martin's, Carfax, were handed over to All Saints when St Martin's Church was demolished in 1896; in 1967 they were transferred to the Bodleian Library and subsequently to the ORO. A long series of churchwardens' accounts survives (from 1540) as well as a large collection of churchwardens' bills and receipts from the sixteenth century to the nineteenth.

PAR 207/4/F1/1 comprises account rolls and some inventories. The accounting years were organized as follows: from 1543–4 onward they began and ended on St Catherine's Day (25 November); from 1574–5 onward they began and ended on the Sunday after the feast of St Catherine; from 1603–4 onward it was Eastertide to Eastertide. St Martin accounts for 1623–4, 1624–5, and 1631–2 through to 1635–6 explicitly state the fiscal year was Easter week to Easter week. For the rest only the days and months on which the accounts were made (ie, ended or rendered) are known, but these dates do suggest an Easter to Easter framework. Up to 1625 the rendering dates were as early as the day after Easter and as late as Trinity Sunday.

The accounts were mounted in a guardbook in 1860. The 'item' here refers to the guardbook number as well as the number on the original artifact, as they match (ie, the modern piece numbers are the same as the folio/stub numbers and empty stubs are also given folio numbers).

Oxford, Oxfordshire Record Office, PAR 207/4/F1/1; 1540–1680: English; parchment, some paper; 238 leaves; 540mm x 360mm; generally good condition; bound in brown cloth with leather spine and corners (front cover now loose), spine tooled, title on spine: 'ST MARTINS CHURCHWARDENS ACCOUNTS. 1540–1680.'

Extracts from:

item 6; 1543–4; single mb; 670mm x 362mm (630mm x 347mm); 2 cols.

item 8; 1544–5; single mb; 530mm x 248mm (recto: 522mm x 235mm, dorse: 420mm x 182mm).

item 9; 1546–7; 2 mbs; 1,162mm x 270mm (recto: 1,010mm x 255mm, dorse: 590mm x 203mm).

item 22; 1553–4; single mb; 668mm x 238mm (recto: 638mm x 237mm, dorse: 525mm x 235mm).

item 25; 1554–5; single mb; 764mm x 208mm (recto: 734mm x 202mm, dorse: 278mm x 183mm).

item 28; 1557–8; single mb; 761mm x 235mm (recto: 745mm x 233mm, dorse: 55mm x 185mm).

item 30; 1558–9; single mb; 775mm x 255mm (735mm x 253mm).

item 37; 1564–5; 3 mbs; 800mm x 130mm (760mm x 128mm).

item 39; 1565–6; 2 mbs; 972mm x 167mm (710mm x 147mm).

item 41; 1566–7; single mb; 529mm x 78mm (recto: 525mm x 65mm, dorse: 65mm x 43mm).

item 17; 1568–9; 2 mbs; 677mm x 185mm (650mm x 152mm).

item 48; 1574–5; 2 mbs; 686mm x 240mm (627mm x 205mm).

item 55; 1578–9; 2 mbs; 1,052mm x 190mm (recto: 1,042mm x 170mm, dorse: 25mm x 160mm). Dorse not part of an account, indicating reused parchment.

items 56–9; 1579–80; 2 mbs of single roll now detached and bound separately: item 56 (mb 1): 404mm x 170mm (392mm x 138mm), item 59 (mb 2): 392mm x 172mm (324mm x 160mm). The relevant entries are on item 56.

item 63; 1581–2; 2 mbs; 852mm x 190mm (820mm x 180mm).

item 65; 1582–3; single mb; 508mm x 192mm (505mm x 170mm).

items 67–9; 1583–4; 2 mbs of single roll now detached and bound separately: item 67 (mb 1): 470mm x 192mm (375mm x 179mm), item 69 (mb 2): 490mm x 190mm (315mm x 179mm). The relevant entry is on item 67.

item 73; 1584–5; single mb; 750mm x 228mm (630mm x 212mm).

item 74; 1585–6; 2 mbs; 834mm x 195mm (725mm x 177mm).

item 77; 1588–9; single mb; 512mm x 193mm (505mm x 152mm).

item 81; 1589–90; 2 mbs; 752mm x 168mm (707mm x 150mm).

item 82; 1590–1; 2 mbs; 802mm x 218mm (790mm x 195mm).

item 85; 1592–3; single mb; 532mm x 184mm (528mm x 165mm).

item 89; 1594–5; 2 mbs; 1,252mm x 185mm (1,235mm x 178mm).

item 94; 1597–8; 2 mbs; 880mm x 195mm (recto: 700mm x 178mm, dorse: 280mm x 180mm).

item 96; 1598–9; single mb; 620mm x 250mm (570mm x 225mm).

item 98; 1600–1; single mb; 525mm x 260mm (450mm x 240mm).

item 99; 1601–2; single mb; 528mm x 259mm (525mm x 228mm).

item 100; 1602–3; single mb; 564mm x 248mm (555mm x 214mm).

item 102; 27 November 1603–1 April 1605; single mb; 685mm x 345mm (648mm x 328mm).

item 103; 1605–6; single mb; 525mm x 195mm (522mm x 170mm).

item 105; 1606–7; single mb; 530mm x 195mm (525mm x 168mm).

item 107; 1608–9; single mb; 772mm x 194mm (705mm x 185mm).

item 110; 1609–10; single mb; 542mm x 198mm (490mm x 192mm).

item 112; 1610–11; single mb; 696mm x 252mm (625mm x 248mm).

items 113–15; 1611–12; 2 mbs of single roll now detached and bound separately: item 113 (mb 1): 408mm x 175mm (recto: 402mm x 173mm, dorse: 224mm x 152mm), item 115 (mb 2): 327mm x 200mm (296mm x 170mm). The relevant entry is on item 113.

item 116; 1612–13; 3 mbs; 1,115mm x 220mm (1,065mm x 200mm).

item 118; 1613–14; 2 mbs; 1,110mm x 195mm (1,065mm x 170mm).

item 119; 1614–15; 3 mbs; 1,630mm x 225mm (1,542mm x 205mm).

item 121; 1615–16; 2 mbs; 1,180mm x 222mm (995mm x 200mm).

item 123; 1616–17; 2 mbs; 1,140mm x 183mm (1,115mm x 170mm).

item 124; 1617–18; 2 mbs; 945mm x 125mm (935mm x 123mm).

item 125; 1618–19; 2 mbs; 865mm x 163mm (850mm x 146mm).

item 127; 1619–20; single mb; 800mm x 160mm (787mm x 141mm).

items 134–6; 1620–1; 3 mbs of single roll, 2 now detached from the third and bound separately: item 134 (mbs 1 and 2): 518mm x 175mm (508mm x 155mm), item 136 (mb 3): 292mm x 170mm (198mm x 165mm). The relevant entry is on item 134.

items 138–40; 1621–2; 3 mbs of single roll, 2 now detached from the third and bound separately; item 138 (mb 1): 648mm x 158mm (630mm x 144mm), item 140 (mbs 2 and 3): 445mm x 170mm (428mm x 153mm). The relevant entry is on item 138.

items 141–7; 1622–3; 5 mbs of single roll, now in 4 pieces and bound separately: item 141 (mbs 1 and 2): 665mm x 198mm (632mm x 174mm), item 142 (mb 3): 683mm x 200mm (660mm x 180mm), item 145 (mb 4): 796mm x 200mm (700mm x 168mm), item 147 (mb 5): 340mm x 200mm (272mm x 195mm). The relevant entry is on item 141.

item 148; 1623–4; single mb; 532mm x 470mm (530mm x 455mm); 2 cols.

item 151; 1624–5; single mb; 498mm x 420mm (480mm x 400mm); 2 cols.

item 153; 1625–6; single mb; 743mm x 362mm (722mm x 342mm); 2 cols.

item 155; 1626–7; single mb; 705mm x 360mm (638mm x 332mm); 2 cols.

item 157; 1627–8; single mb; 662mm x 436mm (632mm x 405mm); 2 cols.

item 159; 1628–9; single mb; 525mm x 495mm (520mm x 465mm); 2 cols.

item 161; 1629–30; single mb; 528mm x 415mm (520mm x 406mm); 2 cols.

item 163; 1630–1; single mb; 524mm x 415mm (520mm x 406mm); 2 cols.

item 165; 1631–2; single mb; 740mm x 527mm (735mm x 500mm); 2 cols.

item 167; 1632–3; single mb; 485mm x 432mm (438mm x 425mm); 2 cols.

item 169; 1633–4; single mb; 635mm x 340mm (625mm x 320mm); 2 cols.

item 171; 1634–5; single mb; 530mm x 440mm (520mm x 425mm); 2 cols.

item 173; 1635–6; single mb; 707mm x 470mm (672mm x 440mm); 2 cols.

item 175; 1636–7; single mb; 672mm x 498mm (648mm x 480mm); 2 cols.

item 179; 1638–9; single mb; 660mm x 475mm (655mm x 465mm); 2 cols; substantial tear upper right segment.

item 181; 1640–1; single mb; 448mm x 415mm (445mm x 413mm); 2 cols.

ST MARY MAGDALEN CHURCHWARDENS' ACCOUNTS

The medieval parish of St Mary Magdalen lay outside the medieval walls of Oxford, to the north, but was generally treated as part of Oxford (see p 592). Records survive from 1430; most were deposited in the Bodleian Library in 1954 before being transferred to the ORO.

The accounting year for 1560–1 onward is not specified but the accounts were usually rendered on Rogation Sunday. As of 1605–6 the accounts were rendered on the Tuesday after Easter.

Oxford, Oxfordshire Record Office, PAR 208/4/F1; 1560–1650; English; parchment; generally good condition (some have areas of damaged parchment or faded ink).

Extracts from:

PAR 208/4/F1/2; 1560–1; single mb; 750mm x 425mm (675mm x 385mm).

PAR 208/4/F1/3; 1561–2; 2 mbs; 730mm x 270mm (700mm x 225mm).

PAR 208/4/F1/6; 1564–5; single mb; 580mm x 315mm (485mm x 305mm); chewed at edges by a rodent.

PAR 208/4/F1/7; 1565–6; single mb; 690mm x 310mm (590mm x 290mm); considerable repair on left side.

PAR 208/4/F1/8; 1567–8; single mb; 560mm x 323mm (500mm x 275mm); special account to buy new bell and repair old one rolled in with larger account.

PAR 208/4/F1/9; 1568–9; single mb; 630mm x 345mm (540mm x 343mm); written right to the left edge.

PAR 208/4/F1/10; 1569–70; single mb; 715mm x 350mm (680mm x 343).

PAR 208/4/F1/11; 1570–1; single mb; 640mm x 368mm (570mm x 360mm).

PAR 208/4/F1/15; 1575–6; single mb; 690mm x 460mm (682mm x 447mm).

PAR 208/4/F1/16; 1576–7; single mb; 640mm x 485mm (543mm x 462mm).

PAR 208/4/F1/17; 1577–8; single mb; 640mm x 500mm (555mm x 475mm); rent roll pinned to the bottom.

PAR 208/4/F1/18; 1578–9; single mb; 618mm x 485mm (595mm x 480mm); rent roll rolled inside.

PAR 208/4/F1/19; 1579–80; single mb; 610mm x 490mm (520mm x 450mm).

PAR 208/4/F1/20; 1580–1; single mb; 695mm x 490mm (620mm x 460mm).

PAR 208/4/F1/21; 1581–2; single mb; 645mm x 520mm (510mm x 490mm); rent roll pinned to the bottom.

PAR 208/4/F1/22; 1583–4; single mb; 580mm x 403mm (490mm x 387mm).

PAR 208/4/F1/23; 1584–5; single mb; 690mm x 430mm (665mm x 390mm); 2 rent rolls pinned to the bottom and notices of debts recorded on the dorse.

PAR 208/4/F1/24; 1585–6; single mb; 880mm x 435mm (720mm x 410mm); rent roll and account pinned to the bottom.

PAR 208/4/F1/25; 1587–8; single mb; 775mm x 433mm (665mm x 420mm); loose rent roll rolled inside and another sewn to the side at the bottom.

PAR 208/4/F1/26; 1588–9; single mb; 920mm x 435mm (740mm x 370mm).

PAR 208/4/F1/27; 1590–1; single mb; 790mm x 525mm (720mm x 490mm); rodent holes.

PAR 208/4/F1/28; 1591–2; single mb; 700mm x 580mm (622mm x 570mm); rent roll rolled inside.

PAR 208/4/F1/29; 1593–4; single mb; 805mm x 605mm (720mm x 565mm).

PAR 208/4/F1/30; 1594–5; single mb; 780mm x 455mm (700mm x 310mm); rent roll pinned to larger account.

PAR 208/4/F1/31; 1595–6; single mb; 605mm x 435mm (565mm x 355mm).

PAR 208/4/F1/32; 1596–7; single mb; 745mm x 490mm (705mm x 375mm).

PAR 208/4/F1/33; 1597–8; single mb; 670mm x 390mm (658mm x 322mm); heading torn; inventory on dorse.

PAR 208/4/F1/34; 1598–9; single mb; 594mm x 377mm (460mm x 320mm); rent roll pinned to the bottom; a receipt for 1599 and an inventory on the dorse.

PAR 208/4/F1/35; 1599–1600; single mb; 730mm x 480mm (530mm x 395mm).

PAR 208/4/F1/36; 1602–3; single mb; 710mm x 555mm (695mm x 530mm); tear in the heading.

PAR 208/4/F1/37; 1604–5; single mb; 650mm x 530mm (520mm x 460mm).

PAR 208/4/F1/38; 1605–6; single mb; 590mm x 450mm (535mm x 440mm).

PAR 208/4/F1/39; 1606–7; single mb; 730mm x 615mm (675mm x 515mm).

PAR 208/4/F1/40; 1608–9; single mb; 620mm x 445mm (560mm x 430mm); rent roll pinned to the bottom.

PAR 208/4/F1/41; 1609–10; single mb; 580mm x 450mm (520mm x 410mm).

PAR 208/4/F1/42; 1610–11; single mb; 650mm x 485mm (570mm x 370mm).

PAR 208/4/F1/43; 1612–13; single mb; 720mm x 480mm (640mm x 390mm); inventory on dorse.

PAR 208/4/F1/44; 1613–14; single mb; 630mm x 532mm (590mm x 515mm).

PAR 208/4/F1/45; 1615–16; single mb; 615mm x 415mm (570mm x 405mm).

PAR 208/4/F1/46; 1616–17; single mb; 640mm x 470mm (550mm x 390mm); rent roll attached.

PAR 208/4/F1/47; 1617–18; single mb; 700mm x 410mm (610mm x 390mm).

PAR 208/4/F1/48; 1619–20; single mb; 540mm x 380mm (515mm x 335mm).

PAR 208/4/F1/49; 1620–1; single mb; 790mm x 410mm (610mm x 385mm); half of bottom 200mm are cut away from the right side; inventory on dorse.

PAR 208/4/F1/50; 1621–2; single mb; 750mm x 400mm (710mm x 400mm).

PAR 208/4/F1/51; 1622–3; single mb; 680mm x 430mm (640mm x 420mm); rent roll sewn to bottom right edge, roll shaved after writing.

PAR 208/4/F1/52; 1623–4; single mb; 740mm x 423mm (545mm x 410mm).

PAR 208/4/F1/53; 1624–5; single mb; 650mm x 515mm (590mm x 435mm); rent roll pinned to larger account.

PAR 208/4/F1/54; 1625–6; single mb; 670mm x 490mm (660mm x 425mm).

PAR 208/4/F1/55; 1626–7; single mb; 670mm x 533mm (635mm x 410mm); small parchment roll stitched to the bottom.

PAR 208/4/F1/56; 1627–8; single mb; 645mm x 525mm (535mm x 490mm); small parchment roll stitched to the bottom.

PAR 208/4/F1/57; 1628–9; single mb; 710mm x 563mm (645mm x 525mm); small parchment roll stitched to the bottom.

PAR 208/4/F1/58; 1629–30; single mb; 630mm x 440mm (610mm x 375mm).

PAR 208/4/F1/59; 1630–1; single mb; 780mm x 540mm (695mm x 510mm); damaged and repaired.

PAR 208/4/F1/60; 1631–2; single mb; 520mm x 500mm (495mm x 470mm); 2 cols.

PAR 208/4/F1/62; 1635–6; 2 mbs; 990mm x 300mm (930mm x 295mm).

PAR 208/4/F1/64; 1639–40; single mb; 705mm x 430mm (695mm x 405mm); left edge shaved off after writing, increasing slightly from top to bottom.

PAR 208/4/F1/65; 1640–1; 2 mbs; 875mm x 450mm (850mm x 420mm).

ST MARY MAGDALEN CHURCHWARDENS' ACCOUNTS (AC)

See under All Saints Churchwardens' Accounts (p 713) for Bodl.: MS. Wood D.2.

ST MARY THE VIRGIN CHURCHWARDENS' ACCOUNTS

Records survive from 1530. Some were deposited at the ORO directly from the parish in 1935; others went to the Bodleian Library or Hertford College and most were transferred from there to the ORO in the 1980s. The collection was recatalogued by the ORO in November 1998.

The fiscal year began on Michaelmas in 1538–9 and 1559–60 onward, St Andrew's Day (30 November) as of 1584–5, and Easter as of 1605–6.

Oxford, Bodleian Library, MS. Rolls Oxon Box 1, #15; 1538–9; English; paper; 3 sheets pasted together serially; 976mm x 213mm (972mm x 178mm average); written only on recto; stitched at the top to a 19th-c. paper wrapper labelled: 'Oxfordshire. Oxford – St Mary the Virgin churchwardens' accounts 30–31 Hen. VIII,' tied with cloth ribbon and tagged: 'B.13 Oxfordshire Oxford. St Mary's Par. No. 15.'

Oxford, Oxfordshire Record Office, PAR 209/4/F1; English; parchment.

Extracts from:

PAR 209/4/F1/1; 1553–4; 2 mbs attached serially; 1,065mm (+ 299mm modern extension at foot) x 320mm (1,000mm x 250mm); good condition; later list (17th c.?) of other accounts now lost in this series on dorse (for 1509, 1522, 1528, 1531, 1534, 1537, and 1554).

PAR 209/4/F1/2; 1559–60; single mb; 695mm x 215mm (555mm x 175mm); written 1 side only; 2 small holes in parchment (not affecting relevant material), otherwise good condition.

PAR 209/4/F1/12; 1584–5; single mb; 680mm x 275mm (630mm x 220mm); written 1 side only; ink faded throughout, worst at top.

PAR 209/4/F1/18; 1601–2; single mb; 640mm x 310mm (515mm x 275mm); written 1 side only; some marginal tearing down left side.

PAR 209/4/F1/19; 1602–3; single mb; 610mm x 310mm (515mm x 275mm); written 1 side only; 1 small hole but generally good condition.

PAR 209/4/F1/21; 30 November 1604–20 April 1606; single mb; 720mm x 305mm (630mm x 260mm); written 1 side only; hole at the bottom right, otherwise good condition.

PAR 209/4/F1/24; 1609–10; single mb; 750mm x 350mm (575mm x 275mm); written 1 side only; a little marginal tearing.

PAR 209/4/F1/25; 1611–12; single mb; 730mm x 340mm (600mm x 260mm); written 1 side only; good condition.

PAR 209/4/F1/27; 1623–4?; single mb; 770mm x 350mm (750mm x 300mm); list of other accounts on dorse, some now lost, once held with this series (for 1602–8, 1610, 1612, 1617, 1623, 1624, 1626–8); good condition.

Oxford, Bodleian Library, ms. Ch. Oxon. a.11, item 192; 1612–13; English; paper; single sheet; 413mm x 292mm (390mm x 273mm); unnumbered; considerably stained and scored, some loss of text at left and bottom from cropping; now mounted in a large guardbook with a blue cover, leather corners, and spine, gold tooling and decoration on spine: 'MS Charters Oxon. a. 11.,' title on cover: 'OXFORDSHIRE (Charters) MISCELLANEOUS 139–204.'

ST MARY THE VIRGIN CHURCHWARDENS' ACCOUNTS (AC)

ms. Wood D.3 is a miscellany of antiquarian transcriptions from registers of congregation and convocation, vice-chancellors' registers, Act books and visitation articles, and miscellaneous parish accounts from as early as 1461 to as late as 1629.

The relevant transcriptions begin on page 250 with the heading, 'Out of diuers accompts or rentalls belonging to ye church of s maries in oxon, in ye Custody of ye churchwardens of ye same parish.' That these are copies from now lost rolls of the parish of St Mary the Virgin can be surmised from a payment on page 274: 'I*tem* to Georg hall for pauing in a Lane in ye North side of ye church going to Catstreete 16 s. 1 d. ob.' Catte Street runs north from the High Street to Broad Street between St Mary the Virgin and All Souls College. The present day Radcliffe Camera is immediately north of the church with the Bodleian Library the next complex of buildings north of the Camera on the west side of Catte Street.

The entries in the manuscript are out of chronological order.

Oxford, Bodleian Library, MS. Wood D.3; 17th c.; English and Latin; paper; i + 143 + iii; 198mm x 52mm; contemporary ink pagination; top 44mm of spine covering torn away revealing booklet gatherings, second tear at bottom of spine; bound in white parchment, stamped in gold on red leather patch: 'WOOD 3 D.'

ST MICHAEL AT THE NORTH GATE CHURCHWARDENS' ACCOUNTS

The collection of churchwardens' papers from St Michael at the North Gate includes a series of accounts beginning in 1403 – the earliest in the county. The collection was recatalogued in May 1998.

Until 1468–9 accounts run from Epiphany to Epiphany (6 January); from 1468–9 to 1471–2 they run from March to March (undefined start and end dates). They run in two streams as of 1471–2: Christmas to Christmas and Purification to Purification (2 February). As of 1490–1 they again follow a March to March year (accounts beginning and ending sometimes on the Thursday before the feast of St Gregory and sometimes on the Thursday after). As of 1529–30 they begin and end exactly on the feast of St Gregory (12 March) and beginning in 1604–5, they follow an Easter to Easter year.

Each separate roll has a piece or 'item' number and is pasted into a large guardbook on the right page only. The corresponding pages from the printed edition (Salter (ed), *Churchwardens' Accounts*) are pasted on the left page up to the year 1562.

Oxford, Oxfordshire Record Office, PAR 211/4/F1/1; 1404–99; Latin and English; parchment; ii + 39 + ii; 765mm x 680mm; modern pencil foliation (guardbook paper pages); generally good condition; title stamped on spine in gold: 'ST. MICHAEL AT THE NORTH GATE, OXFORD CHURCHWARDENS' ACCOUNTS 1403–1499.' The accounts are in chronological sequence, with chantry chapel accounts and churchwardens' accounts interspersed.

Extracts from:

item 5; 1422/3–3/4; single mb; 410mm x 335mm (336mm x 303mm).

item 25; 1456/7–7/8; single mb; 418mm x 222mm (385mm x 130mm); continued on dorse from bottom to top; very faded.

item 33; 1463/4–4/5; single mb; 708mm x 222mm (660mm x 178mm); continued on dorse from top to bottom.

item 38; 1467/8–8/9; single mb; 490mm x 222mm (380mm x 185mm).

item 39; 1468/9–70; single mb; 515mm x 183mm (450mm x 145mm).

item 42; 1469/70–70/1; single mb; 395mm x 210mm (345mm x 178mm); tear from bottom right corner (100mm x 200mm at largest).

item 43; 1471–2; single mb; 440mm x 255mm (385mm x 215mm); continued on dorse from bottom to top; slightly faded.

item 46; 1472/3–3/4; single mb; 497mm x 280mm (463mm x 242mm); continued on dorse from top to bottom.

item 49; 1474/5–5/6; single mb; 395mm x 210mm (370mm x 190mm); tear in bottom left corner (100mm x 50mm).

item 50; 1475–6; single mb; 352mm x 242mm (297mm x 230mm).

item 53; 1477/8–8/9; single mb; 508mm x 247mm (438mm x 210mm).

item 54; 1478–9; single mb; 420mm x 282mm (388mm x 242mm).

item 55; 1479–80; single mb; 590mm x 242mm (533mm x 203mm).

item 59; 1481–2; single mb; 367mm x 235mm (292mm x 203mm); tear in bottom left corner.

item 62; 1483/4–4/5; single mb; 387mm x 262mm (362mm x 242mm).

item 67; 1489/90–90/1; single mb; 482mm x 238mm (457mm x 215mm).

item 69; 1491–2; single mb; 312mm x 242mm (260mm x 215mm); continued on dorse from bottom to top.

item 70; 1492–3; single mb; 342mm x 228mm (285mm x 197mm); small irregular tear on right margin.

Oxford, Oxfordshire Record Office, PAR 211/4/F1/2; 1500–1601; ii + 49 + i; English, with a little Latin; 750mm x 700mm; modern pencil foliation (guardbook pages); generally good condition; title stamped on spine in gold: 'ST. MICHAEL AT THE NORTH GATE, OXFORD CHURCH-WARDENS' ACCOUNTS 1500–1600.' The accounts are in chronological sequence, the numbering continuous with PAR 211/4/F1/1, with chantry chapel accounts and churchwardens' accounts interspersed until the chantry chapel accounts end in 1534.

Extracts from:

item 77; 1499/1500–1500/1; parchment; single mb; 400mm x 226mm (360mm x 190mm).

item 90; 1511/12–12/13; parchment; single mb; 585mm x 290mm (565mm x 255mm).

item 94; 1514/15–15/16; parchment; single mb; 510mm x 275mm (445mm x 220mm).

item 96; 1515/16–16/17; paper; 4 sheets labelled 96–1, 96–2, 96–3, and 96–4; 310mm x 210mm (270mm x 185mm).

item 97; 1517–18; paper; 9 sheets in 3 booklets labelled 97–1 (6 sheets), 97–2 (1 sheet), and 97–3 (2 sheets); part 1, f [4]: 550mm x 225mm (275mm x 202mm); part 3, f [1]: 310mm x 215mm (280mm x 85mm).

item 100; 1518/19–19/20; parchment; single mb; 620mm x 255mm (500mm x 190mm).

item 101; 1522/3–3/4; parchment; single mb; 600mm x 370mm (500mm x 300mm).

item 104; 1524/5–5/6; parchment; single mb; 625mm x 415mm (490mm x 360mm); memos on dorse.

item 105; 1525/6–6/7; parchment; single mb; 620mm x 440mm (receipts: 580mm x 375mm, expenses: 580mm x 220mm); memos on dorse.

item 106; 1526/7–7/8; parchment; single mb; 770mm x 445mm (680mm x 380mm); memos on dorse.

item 108; 1528/9–9/30; parchment; single mb; 700mm x 250mm (660mm x 210mm); memos on dorse.

item 110; 1529/30–30/1; parchment; single mb; 685mm x 260mm (600mm x 210mm).

item 111; 1530/1–1/2; parchment; single mb; 685mm x 240mm (600mm x 210mm); memos on dorse.

item 113; 1531/2–2/3; parchment; single mb; 745mm x 240mm (730mm x 195mm); repair accounts and memos written on dorse bottom to top.

item 114; 1532/3–3/4; parchment; single mb; 560mm x 245mm (515mm x 205mm); end of accounts and memos written on dorse bottom to top.

item 116; 1534/5–5/6; parchment; single mb; 685mm x 365mm (645mm x 280mm); memos on dorse.

item 117; 1535/6–6/7; parchment; single mb; 650mm x 240mm (630mm x 200mm); end of accounts and memos written on dorse bottom to top.

item 119; 1543/4–4/5; parchment; single mb; 730mm x 260mm (690mm x 220mm); end of accounts and memos written on dorse bottom to top.

item 120; 1544/5–5/6; parchment; single mb; 670mm x 245mm (630mm x 210mm); end of accounts and memos written on dorse bottom to top; repaired heavily in upper left margin.

item 121; 1546/7–7/8; parchment; single mb; 490mm x 290mm (420mm x 230mm); memos on dorse.

item 126; 1555/6–6/7; parchment; single mb; 465mm x 380mm (405mm x 340mm); memos on dorse.

item 127; 1556/7–7/8; parchment; 2 mbs; 1,040mm x 270mm (980mm x 235mm).

item 129; 1557/8–8/9; parchment; single mb; 565mm x 280mm (540mm x 240mm).

item 130; 1560/1–1/2; parchment; single mb; 530mm x 260mm (510mm x 230mm).

item 135; 1566/7–7/8; parchment; single mb; 705mm x 240mm (660mm x 225mm).

item 136; 1568/9–9/70; parchment; single mb; 510mm x 245mm (495mm x 225mm).

item 137; 1569/70–70/1; parchment; single mb; 495mm x 270mm (465mm x 250mm).

item 138; 1570/1–1/2; parchment; single mb; 520mm x 220mm (510mm x 200mm).

item 141; 1574/5–5/6; parchment; single mb; 715mm x 225mm (700mm x 200mm).

item 146; 1579/80–80/1; parchment; single mb; 620mm x 220mm (600mm x 205mm).

item 147; 1580/1–1/2; parchment; single mb; 400mm x 215mm (375mm x 195mm).

item 148; 1582/3–3/4; parchment; single mb; 770mm x 230mm (765mm x 210mm).

item 149; 1585/6–6/7; parchment; single mb; 500mm x 190mm (490mm x 175mm).

item 150; 1586/7–7/8; parchment; single mb; 670mm x 270mm (600mm x 230mm).

item 151; 1587/8–8/9; parchment; 2 mbs; 890mm x 265mm (880mm x 225mm).

item 152; 1588/9–9/90; parchment; single mb; 720mm x 205mm (700mm x 180mm).

item 153; 1589/90–90/1; parchment; 2 mbs; 880mm x 220mm (825mm x 210mm).

item 154; 1592/3–3/4; parchment; single mb; 525mm x 200mm (485mm x 165mm); written on dorse top to bottom.

item 155; 1593/4–4/5; parchment; 2 mbs; 900mm x 205mm (800mm x 185mm).

item 158; 1595/6–6/7; parchment; 3 mbs; 1,230mm x 160mm (1,205mm x 145mm).

item 159; 1596/7–7/8; parchment; single mb; 680mm x 275mm (640mm x 245mm).

item 162; 1598/9–9/1600; parchment; single mb; 690mm x 425mm (680mm x 380mm).

item 163; 1599/1600–1600/1; parchment; single mb; 650mm x 415mm (580mm x 360mm).

Oxford, Oxfordshire Record Office, PAR 211/4/F1/3; 1601–59; English, with a little Latin; parchment; ii + 62 + ii; 745mm x 715mm; modern pencil foliation (guardbook pages); generally good condition; title stamped on spine in gold: 'ST. MICHAEL AT THE NORTH GATE, OXFORD CHURCHWARDENS' ACCOUNTS 1600–1659.' The accounts are in chronological sequence, the numbering continuous with PAR 211/4/F1/1 and 211/4/F1/2.

Extracts from:

item 165; 1601/2–2/3; single mb; 610mm x 260mm (600mm x 190mm); memos on dorse.

item 166; 1602/3–3/4; single mb; 625mm x 245mm (615mm x 210mm); memos on dorse.

item 167; 1604–5; single mb; 750mm x 300mm (740mm x 250mm); memos on dorse.

item 168; 1605–6; 2 mbs; 970mm x 265mm (960mm x 220mm).

item 169; 1606–7; 2 mbs; 1,210mm x 210mm (1,190mm x 185mm).

item 170; 1607–8; 2 mbs; 995mm x 195mm (950mm x 165mm); written on dorse.

item 171; 1608–9; single mb; 600mm x 275mm (575mm x 210mm); written on dorse.

item 172; 1609–10; single mb; 540mm x 340mm (530mm x 290mm).

item 174; 1611–12; single mb; 700mm x 280mm (660mm x 215mm); written on dorse.

item 175; 1612–13; single mb; 805mm x 295mm (550mm x 225mm); written on dorse.

item 179; 1615–16; single mb; 580mm x 530mm (550mm x 510mm).

item 180; 1616–17; single mb; 660mm x 320mm (520mm x 200mm).

item 181; 1617–18; 2 mbs; 1,100mm x 235mm (880mm x 200mm).

item 182; 1618–19; single mb; 730mm x 250mm (700mm x 215mm).

item 184; 1619–20; 2 mbs; 900mm x 205mm (880mm x 175mm).

item 185; 1620–1; 2 mbs; 1,040mm x 260mm (1,000mm x 240mm).

item 186; 1621–2; single mb; 730mm x 265mm (710mm x 235mm).

item 187; 1622–3; single mb; 700mm x 315mm (675mm x 275mm).

item 188; 1623–4; single mb; 660mm x 385mm (600mm x 335mm).

item 189; 1624–5; single mb; 630mm x 385mm (555mm x 345mm).

item 190; 1626–7; single mb; 565mm x 465mm (525mm x 390mm).

item 191; 1627–8; single mb; 560mm x 390mm (500mm x 300mm); 2 cols.

item 192; 1629–30; single mb; 540mm x 455mm (480mm x 420mm); 2 cols.

item 193; 1630–1; single mb; 650mm x 445mm (540mm x 320mm); 2 cols.

item 195; 1634–5; single mb; 520mm x 445mm (450mm x 370mm); 2 cols.

item 197; 1635–6; single mb; 580mm x 440mm (470mm x 360mm); 2 cols.

item 199; 1636–7; single mb; 545mm x 425mm (480mm x 390mm); 2 cols.

item 204; 1642–3; single mb; 580mm x 335mm (560mm x 290mm); 2 cols.

ST MICHAEL AT THE SOUTH GATE CHURCHWARDENS' ACCOUNTS

When the church of St Michael at the South Gate was demolished to make way for Cardinal College, its parish was merged with St Aldate's. This parish account is among St Aldate papers catalogued as 'Miscellaneous and stray papers 1394–1963.'

Oxford, Oxfordshire Record Office, DD Par. Oxford St Aldate, c.33, item l; 8 December 1501–8 December 1502; English; parchment; 2 mbs; 790mm x 215mm (770mm x 190mm); mb 2 text in 2 cols; dog-eared down left side but no loss of text, parchment discoloured.

ST PETER IN THE EAST CHURCHWARDENS' ACCOUNTS

This was one of the oldest of the medieval parishes. The church is now the library of St Edmund Hall. The parish records were transferred to the Bodleian Library in batches from the 1930s to the 1960s, and subsequently to the ORO.

The fiscal year was Michaelmas to Michaelmas from 1443–4 onward, based on the feast of the Conception (8 December) as of 1474–5, and Easter to Easter as of 1605–6.

There is a single manuscript mounted on every other sheet. Sheet numbers are in reference to the guardbook numbering and are retained here as a finding aid. The transcriptions in the Records show the membrane numbering of the original document.

There are no extant accounts for the period from 1444 to 1461.

Oxford, Oxfordshire Record Office, PAR 213/4/F1/1; 1443–1600 (with major gaps); Latin and English (from 1520); parchment; ii + 101 (individual single mb rolls mounted on separate paper leaves); 572mm x 458mm; modern pencil foliation; bound in boards covered in brown cloth, kid corners, spine tooled, title stripped away; stamped on front in black leather patch with tooling: 'ST PETERS IN THE EAST CHURCH WARDENS ACCOUNTS. 1444–1599.'

Extracts from:

sheet 1: 1443–4; 490mm x 285mm (475mm x 225mm); 180mm x 25mm lost at bottom left corner.

sheet 3: 1461–2; 560mm x 360mm (510mm x 280mm); several holes in parchment, top right and bottom left corners gone.

sheet 7: 1474–5; 490mm x 218mm (380mm x 185mm); several holes in parchment.

sheet 9: 1480–1; 670mm x 255mm (635mm x 170mm); top right and 340mm x 120mm of bottom right lost.

sheet 11: 1481–2; 600mm x 185mm (570mm x 150mm); some holes especially at lower right side.

sheet 13: 1482–3; 600mm x 225mm (520mm x 180mm); good condition except for a few tears at the top.

sheet 15: 1488–9; 620mm x 230mm (560mm x 195mm); some holes but little text lost.

sheet 17: 1495–6; 600mm x 285mm (520mm x 205mm); edges chewed by rodents.

sheet 21: c 1496–1502; 440mm x 370mm (360mm x 265mm); parchment torn at top and left side.

sheet 25: 1503–4; 450mm x 310mm (410mm x 260mm); somewhat dog-eared but otherwise good condition.

sheet 27: 1504–5; 460mm x 300mm (400mm x 240mm); fair condition.

sheet 29: 1505–6; 740mm x 340mm (recto: 610mm x 265mm, dorse: 150mm x 265mm); fair condition.

sheet 31: 1507–8; 535mm x 290mm (420mm x 240mm); blotched and faded.

sheet 33: 1508–9; 540mm x 295mm (480mm x 240mm); blotched and faded.

sheet 35: 1509–10; 430mm x 340mm (360mm x 270mm); discoloured and faded, nibbled by rodents on right side.

sheet 39: 1510–11; 460mm x 275mm (400mm x 240mm); blotched, ink faded toward the bottom.

sheet 37: 1511–12; 430mm x 225mm at widest (400mm x 185mm); fragmentary, several holes, tapers toward bottom.

sheet 41: 1512–13; 520mm x 260mm (460mm x 200mm); both margins missing from the bottom.

sheet 43: 1517–18; 720mm x 245mm (660mm x 195mm); blotched but generally legible.

sheet 45: 1519–20; 670mm x 305mm (560mm x 240mm); extensive staining.

sheet 47: 1520–1; 530mm x 250mm (420mm x 210mm); some holes, parchment very dark but legible.

sheet 49: 1522–3; 560mm x 305mm (515mm x 215mm); blotched but generally legible.

sheet 51: 1523–4; 555mm x 310mm (530mm x 235mm); blotched and dark, very little text lost but hard to read.

sheet 53: 1526–7; 290mm x 335mm (270mm x 280mm); fragment (top half only; bottom half bound into book on guardbook sheet 23), dirty but legible.

sheet 55: 1530–1; 555mm x 240mm (520mm x 200mm); dark but legible, holes at edges.

sheet 57: 1540–1; 640mm x 225mm (605mm x 200mm); some discolouration but in generally fair condition.

sheet 59: 1544–5; 555mm x 245mm (520mm x 200mm); holes at edges, dark.

sheet 61: 1545–6; 590mm x 320mm (550mm x 235mm); generally good condition.

sheet 69: 1581–2; 400mm x 525mm (340mm x 500mm); 2 cols; generally good condition.

sheet 71: 1582–3; 410mm x 510mm (390mm x 480mm); 2 cols; generally good condition.

sheet 79: 1587–8; 450mm x 460mm (435mm x 420mm); 2 cols; good condition.

sheet 81: 1588–9; 490mm x 465mm (430mm x 400mm); 2 cols; good condition.

sheet 83: 1589–90; 515mm x 525mm (400mm x 445mm); 2 cols; good condition.

sheet 87: 1591–2; 610mm x 270mm (540mm x 220mm); good condition.

sheet 89: 1594–5; 510mm x 400mm (350mm x 340mm); 2 cols; good condition.

sheet 91: 1595–6; 490mm x 380mm (350mm x 330mm); 2 cols; good condition.

sheet 93: 1596–7; 490mm x 380mm (380mm x 340mm); 2 cols; ink faded, fair condition.

sheet 95: 1597–8; 520mm x 465mm (460mm x 390mm); 2 cols; left edge much torn and repaired.

sheet 97: 1598–9; 470mm x 420mm (350mm x 360mm); 2 cols; fair condition.

sheet 101: 1599–1600; 480mm x 420mm (350mm x 360mm); 2 cols; good condition.

Oxford, Oxfordshire Record Office, PAR 213/4/F1/2; 1600–40; parchment (occasional paper); single mbs or sheets; iii + 27; 510mm x 377mm; written mostly in 2 cols; modern pencil foliation; mounted on paper and bound in a single volume in boards covered in black leather, purple spine, guard, and corners (back now broken and front cover detached), preserved between separate archival boards, title on front cover stamped in gold: 'ST. PETER'S IN THE EAST CHURCHWARDENS ACCOUNTS 1600–1640 CHURCHWARDENS 1868 J. JENKINS & F.W. ANSELL.'

Extracts from:

f 1: 1600–1; highly irregular shape averaging 387–690mm x 225–490mm (text area varies).

f 2: 1602–3; 585mm x 425mm (505mm x 380mm); damaged at edges.

f 4: 1605–6; irregular shape, 448–500mm x 375mm (approximately 480mm x 315mm); damaged at right edge.

f 5: 1606–7; 480mm x 435mm (444mm x 390mm); damaged at edges.

f 6: 1607–8; 485mm x 392mm (430mm x 385mm).

f 7: 1608–9; paper; 450mm x 280mm (338mm x 250mm).

f 8: 1609–10; 315mm x 335mm (235mm x 320mm).

f 9: 1612–13; 500mm x 345mm (395mm x 310mm).

Oxford, Oxfordshire Record Office, PAR 213/4/F1/3; 1614–85; English; paper; 158 leaves; 296mm x 210mm (275mm x 145mm); modern pencil foliation; contemporary parchment binding, title in contemporary script on front cover: 'The Booke of accomtes for the churchwardens of Saint Peter in the Easte Anno domini 1613.' This is a paper copy of ORO: PAR 213/4/F1/2.

ST PETER IN THE EAST CHURCHWARDENS' ACCOUNTS (AC)

This is a collection, compiled by H.E. Salter, of St Peter in the East churchwardens' accounts, with an expository essay. The booklet is written in brown ink and made up of miscellaneous sheets of recycled, lined paper (similar to school scribblers) with unrelated material on reverse. Some sheets are inverted.

Oxford, Bodleian Library, MS. Top.Oxon c.403; 1948?; Latin; paper; i + 103 + i; ff 1–36: 254mm x

203mm, ff 37–103: 325mm x 203mm (text area varies); pencil foliation 1–102 (10 repeated), circled pencil foliation 1–50 for ff 38–89 (29 repeated); good condition; bound in modern blue cover with small pasted tab in lower left corner showing shelf-mark; title on spine: 'H.E.SALTER – ST. PETER IN THE EAST.'

ST PETER LE BAILEY CHURCHWARDENS' ACCOUNTS

The churchwardens' accounts date from 1453. At a date probably in the nineteenth century the accounts from 1453 to 1702 were mounted in five guardbooks but removed, recatalogued, and stored separately in September 1998.

The accounting year was Michaelmas to Michaelmas from 1465–6 forward; St Catherine's Day to St Catherine's Day (25 November) as of 1499–1500; the Sunday after the Conception of the Virgin in December as of 1545–6; and Easter to Easter as of 1603–5.

Oxford, Oxfordshire Record Office, PAR 214/4/F1; 1453–1642. Formerly mounted within a guard-book the Latin and English accounts have been reconstituted and recatalogued as individual artifacts.

Extracts from:

PAR 214/4/F1/3; 1464–5; parchment; 630mm x 160mm (610mm x 135mm).

PAR 214/4/F1/4; 1465–6; parchment; 560mm x 180mm (480mm x 175mm); some writing on dorse.

PAR 214/4/F1/5; 1466–7; parchment; 820mm x 160mm (535mm x 130mm); some writing on dorse.

PAR 214/4/F1/6; 1467–8; parchment; 680mm x 160mm (630mm x 130mm); some writing on dorse.

PAR 214/4/F1/7; 1468–9; parchment; 795mm x 155mm (750mm x 150mm).

PAR 214/4/F1/8; 1471–2; parchment; 710mm x 150mm (580mm x 130mm).

PAR 214/4/F1/9; 1473–4; parchment; 650mm x 140mm (610mm x 130mm).

PAR 214/4/F1/10; 1475–6; parchment; 750mm x 160mm (630mm x 135mm).

PAR 214/4/F1/11; 1476–7; parchment; 850mm x 145mm (400mm x 125mm).

PAR 214/4/F1/12; 1477–8; parchment; 520mm x 180mm (500mm x 155mm); some writing on dorse.

PAR 214/4/F1/13; 1479–80; parchment; 700mm x 160mm (658mm x 135mm); some writing on dorse.

PAR 214/4/F1/14; 1499–1500; parchment; 670mm x 160mm (recto: 625mm x 150mm, dorse: 330mm x 115mm).

PAR 214/4/F1/15; 1506–7; paper; 430mm x 300mm (405mm x 265mm); damaged and repaired top left corner.

PAR 214/4/F1/16; 1529–30; paper; 518mm x 340mm (495mm x 275mm); repaired.

PAR 214/4/F1/17; 1530–1; paper; 2 sheets; 690mm x 314mm (645mm x 270mm); receipt sheet torn bottom right corner and repaired.

PAR 214/4/F1/18; 1531–2; parchment; 835mm x 265mm (700mm x 223mm).

PAR 214/4/F1/19; 1534–5; parchment; 765mm x 235mm (640mm x 195mm).

PAR 214/4/F1/20; 1535–6; parchment; 600mm x 240mm (560mm x 180mm).

PAR 214/4/F1/21; 1537–8; parchment; 650mm x 250mm (640mm x 200mm).

PAR 214/4/F1/22; 1538–9; parchment; 740mm x 235mm (690mm x 215mm).

PAR 214/4/F1/23; 1539–40; parchment; 1,065mm x 190mm (975mm x 170mm).

PAR 214/4/F1/24; 1540–1; parchment; 900mm x 278mm (845mm x 230mm).

PAR 214/4/F1/26; 1542–3; parchment; 2 mbs; 760mm x 220mm (745mm x 175mm).

PAR 214/4/F1/27; 1545–6; parchment; 3 mbs; 993mm x 165mm (983mm x 140mm).

PAR 214/4/F1/29; 1556–7; paper; 3 sheets; 873mm x 213mm (758mm x 180mm).

PAR 214/4/F1/31; 1560–1; paper; 410mm x 300mm (350mm x 245mm).

PAR 214/4/F1/32; 1563–4; paper; 422mm x 312mm (385mm x 255mm).

PAR 214/4/F1/34; 1572–3; paper; 415mm x 310mm (385mm x 263mm).

PAR 214/4/F1/35; 1576–7; paper; 413mm x 310mm (327mm x 265mm).

PAR 214/4/F1/37; 1586–7; paper; 558mm x 440mm (438mm x 330mm).

PAR 214/4/F1/38; 1587–8; paper; 325mm x 443mm (318mm x 440mm); 2 cols.

PAR 214/4/F1/39; 1588–9; paper; 458mm x 360mm (428mm x 320mm); 2 cols.

PAR 214/4/F1/40; 1589–90; paper; 420mm x 310mm (375mm x 270mm); 2 cols.

PAR 214/4/F1/41; 1590–1; paper; 585mm x 430mm (505mm x 300mm).

PAR 214/4/F1/42; 1592–3; parchment; 510mm x 386mm (430mm x 343mm).

PAR 214/4/F1/43; 1593–4; parchment; 415mm x 283mm (338mm x 250mm).

PAR 214/4/F1/44; 1594–5; parchment; 375mm x 235mm (360mm x 225mm).

PAR 214/4/F1/45; 1597–8; parchment; 495mm x 243mm (480mm x 210mm).

PAR 214/4/F1/46; 1598–9; parchment; 590mm x 365mm (570mm x 320mm).

PAR 214/4/F1/47; 1599–1600; parchment; 530mm x 215mm (420mm x 185mm).

PAR 214/4/F1/48; 1600–1; parchment; 660mm x 452mm (630mm x 330mm).

PAR 214/4/F1/49; 1601–2; parchment; 730mm x 207mm (497mm x 190mm).

PAR 214/4/F1/50; 1602–3; paper; 400mm x 332mm (380mm x 270mm).

PAR 214/4/F1/51; 1603–5; paper; 412mm x 308mm (380mm x 295mm); damaged and repaired.

PAR 214/4/F1/52; 1605–6; parchment; 561mm x 285mm (516mm x 280mm).

PAR 214/4/F1/53; 1606–7; parchment; 540mm x 416mm (515mm x 400mm).

PAR 214/4/F1/54; 1607–8; parchment; 3 mbs; 2,030mm x 315mm (1,810mm x 305mm).

PAR 214/4/F1/55; 1608–9; parchment; 2 mbs; 1,015mm x 232mm (1,000mm x 227mm).

PAR 214/4/F1/56; 1609–10; parchment; 600mm x 230mm (378mm x 220mm).

PAR 214/4/F1/57; 1610–11; parchment; 495mm x 235mm (430mm x 230mm).

PAR 214/4/F1/58; 1611–12; parchment; 445mm x 245mm (375mm x 245mm).

PAR 214/4/F1/59; 1612–13; parchment; 650mm x 225mm (615mm x 225mm).

PAR 214/4/F1/60; 1613–14: parchment; 375mm x 150mm (360mm x 150mm); 1614–15: parchment; 380mm x 150mm (365mm x 145mm).

PAR 214/4/F1/61; 1615–16; paper; bifolium; 313mm x 210mm (295mm x 175mm); written on both sides of f 1.

PAR 214/4/F1/62; 1617–18; paper; bifolium; 305mm x 200mm (285mm x 175mm); written on both sides of f 1.

PAR 214/4/F1/63; 1618–19; paper; bifolium; 310mm x 195mm (290mm x 175mm); written on both sides of f 1.

PAR 214/4/F1/64; 1619–20; paper; bifolium; 300mm x 190mm (285mm x 180mm); written on both sides of f 1.

PAR 214/4/F1/65; 1620–1; paper; bifolium; 284mm x 181mm (270mm x 174mm); modern pencil foliation.

PAR 214/4/F1/66; 1621–2; paper; bifolium; 295mm x 195mm (285mm x 175mm); written on both sides of both folios.

PAR 214/4/F1/67; 1624–5; parchment; 972mm x 202mm (892mm x 180mm).

PAR 214/4/F1/68; 1625–6; parchment; 670mm x 290mm (630mm x 253mm).

PAR 214/4/F1/76–7; 1633–4?; parchment; 2 mbs, now detached; 1,265mm x 170mm (1,263mm x 142mm); expenses only.

PAR 214/4/F1/78; 1634–5; parchment; 370mm x 180mm (365mm x 167mm); written on both sides.

ST PETER LE BAILEY CHURCHWARDENS' ACCOUNTS (AC)

This antiquarian collection contains excerpts from Oriel College statutes and parish material from All Saints, St Mary, and St Peter le Bailey. The parish accounts range from 1338 to 1539 in date.

Oxford, Bodleian Library, MS. Wood C.1; 17th c.; paper; English and Latin; iii + 46; ink pagination; some leaves torn at the end; bound in heavy white parchment with small red leather patch on spine stamped in gold: 'WOOD. C. 1.'

Ecclesiastical Court Documents

ECCLESIASTICAL COURT PROCEEDINGS

Oxford, Oxfordshire Record Office, MS.Oxf. Dioc. papers Oxon.c.2; 24 April 1630–28 November 1631; English and Latin; paper; i + 375 + i; 315mm x 190mm (text area varies); contemporary ink and modern pencil foliation (modern system followed); pages badly scuffed at edges; bound in white vellum over boards (now virtually separated from book except for a few threads), written on front cover: 'W.H. 1630–31.' Contemporary table of contents up to f 145, index attempted ff 361–74v.

ARCHDEACON'S COURT BOOK

Oxford, Oxfordshire Record Office, MS.Oxf.Arch. papers Oxon.c.13; 13 May 1637–23 February 1637/8;

Latin and English; paper; 396 leaves; 312mm x 210mm; modern foliation; contemporary leather and board binding.

Legal Records

GAOL DELIVERY ROLL

London, Public Record Office, JUST 3/180; 1389–95; Latin; parchment; 61 mbs; 690–860mm x 240–60mm (590–790mm x 210–30mm); modern pencil numbering; attached at top with leather thong; some damage at right edge resulting in loss of text, lower right of mb 21 torn away.

CITY QUARTER SESSIONS

Like the legislative and financial records of the city, these legal records are kept in the city hall and were consulted in the ORO where they were brought on request.

Oxford, Oxford City Archives, QSC/A2/001; 1614–38; English; paper; iv + 283 + x; 230mm x 360mm; contemporary ink pagination; some engrossing; modern brown suede binding, some tooling, red leather patch on spine stamped: 'SESSION ROLL 1614 1631.'

INVENTORY OF THE GOODS OF JOHN STACY

Oxford, Oxfordshire Record Office, I 60/1/28; 10 August 1627; English, with some Latin; parchment; single mb; 408mm x 171mm (350mm x 168mm); unnumbered; good condition.

INVENTORY OF THE GOODS OF GEORGE PAYNE

Oxford, Oxfordshire Record Office, I 144/3/13; 28 January 1635/6; English, with some Latin; parchment; single mb; 382mm x 149mm (375mm x 135mm); unnumbered; good condition.

A REPORT ON THE INQUEST INTO THE DEATH OF GILBERT FOXLEE (AC)

MS. Twyne 4, like many of the antiquarian collections of Brian Twyne and his contemporary Anthony Wood, is drawn from both college and city accounts.

Oxford, Bodleian Library, MS. Twyne 4; 17th c.; Latin and English; paper; vii + 355 + ii; generally 275–315mm x 180–95mm (text area varies); 2 systems of later ink pagination (pp 665–709 blank); some damage and repair; irregular booklets now bound together in heavy white parchment over boards, title on cover, small yellow patch at the base of the spine bearing the shelf-mark.

PROCEEDINGS REGARDING GEORGE BUCKNER (A)

MS. Twyne-Langbaine 3 comprises some transcriptions as well as some original documents pasted in on stubs. Gerard Langbaine succeeded Brian Twyne as the keeper of the archives in the Bodleian, serving in that capacity from 1644 to 1658. Both keepers worked on this collection.

Oxford, Bodleian Library, MS. Twyne-Langbaine 3; 17th c.; English and Latin; paper; ii + 127; 309mm x 207mm (ruled side margins 35mm, text area 308mm x 190mm); pencil foliation; pages brittle and frayed, evidence of damage by worms or rodents; light brown calf binding tooled front, back, and spine, small paper sticker with shelf-mark at base of spine, title on spine: 'COLLECTANE B.TWYNNE LANGBAINE &C.'

Miscellaneous Records

ORDER FOR RECEIVING THE MAYOR

See under Chamberlains' Accounts (pp 710–11) for Bodl.: MS. Twyne 23.

ANTIQUITIES OF OXFORD

Oxford, Bodleian Library, MS. Wood F.29(a); 1661–6; English and Latin; paper; iii + 505; 108–312mm x 143–91mm (97–296mm x 138–89mm); partial contemporary ink foliation, partial modern pencil foliation; good condition; modern leather binding on board, tooling to covers and spine, embossed title on spine.

Editorial Procedures

Principles of Selection

This collection embraces the whole of Oxford, including colleges, halls, University, town government, parish churches, guilds, and civil and ecclesiastical courts. The late medieval and early modern royal borough of Oxford covered an area of some ninety acres and in 1336 a royal charter extended the boundary beyond the city walls to all the extramural suburbs by about a mile in each direction, specifically to Cowley and Shotover on the east, to Botley on the west, to Bagley Wood in Kennington (Berks) on the south, across the River Thames, and to Godstow Bridge in Wolvercote on the north. It is for this reason that contemporary descriptions of royal entries as excerpted in these volumes always begin with the sovereign's arrival in Wolvercote (when the sovereign, as usually happened, came from Woodstock Palace five miles north of Oxford) and end with his or her departure from Shotover. The priory of Godstow lay across the river at the extreme northwest boundary. Because the city fathers regularly had refreshments and listened to music at Godstow when they perambulated the franchise, we have deemed Godstow to be within the boundaries and so include the very early reference to an abbess of misrule in the priory. Visitation records warn the nuns against too much contact with the Oxford students, again supporting the idea that the priory was considered part of Oxford. On the other hand, although a part of the parish of Marston was inside the boundaries on the northeast edge of the jurisdiction, most of that parish lay outside and we do not include those parish records here. The only extramural parish within the franchise – whose records survive – is St Mary Magdalen.

All the dramatic, musical, and ceremonial activities recorded in the present collection fall within the geographical boundaries described above, with the exception of two student plays that originated in Oxford but were later taken to the royal palaces at Woodstock or Hampton Court by royal request. Other evidence of entertainment in these two venues will be dealt with in appropriate REED county volumes. Oxford-educated professional playwrights such as John Lyly, whose name does not occur in the Records, and George Peele, whose name does, are briefly listed in Appendix 14.

Consistent with REED principles of selection, our intention has been to include only musical activity for secular occasions in this collection. The only references to musicians that do not directly relate to performance occur in records of apprenticeship. Documents concerning the teaching of music within the Faculty of Arts, and private instrumental lessons to students, are omitted.[1] On the other hand evidence concerning the popular seventeenth-century dancing school run by professional musicians is included. Ownership of instruments by individuals other than professionals has been recorded only when the relevant documents (eg, wills and inventories) were made known to us through printed sources. Otherwise such personal papers have not been systematically searched.

Boy bishops are found in the records of All Souls, Magdalen, and Lincoln Colleges. We have noted above the abbess of misrule at Godstow priory. College plays during the Christmas season were sometimes given under the auspices of a lord of misrule, whose title varied from college to college but who is known generically as a Christmas lord or Christmas prince, although the election of such a lord did not guarantee that plays would be involved, as the lord's more general duties were to oversee the costs and conduct of feasts throughout the Christmas vacation.

The Christmas festivities in colleges were paralleled by spring and summer festivals in the parishes. References to parish ales have been included if there is evidence that they customarily, or at one time, featured plays or such activities as the election of summer lords and ladies, music, morris dancing, or the erection of summer poles. All references in the parish records to hocking have been included.

Oxford hosted four official royal visits in 1566, 1592, 1605, and 1636. All preparations for such visits including the orders and acts for the reception of the monarch, the construction of stages and making or borrowing of costumes for plays, and the repairs, alterations, and new construction of roads and buildings in both the colleges and the city (which were in themselves 'the sets' for much of the ceremonial business) are included. The ceremonial welcomings by both city and University officials have also been included, along with both prose and verse descriptions of the entertainments. Omitted are details pertaining to convocations, debates and disputations, services and sermons, feasts and banquets where no musical or mimetic activity took place, and details of the accommodation of the court. Members of the royal family passed through Oxford frequently at various other times, as Oxford lay on the direct route from London to Woodstock, a favourite royal retreat during the month of August. Transcriptions from the vice-chancellors' accounts (OUA: WP/β/21(4)) where the presence of performers ('buccinatoribus' primarily) in Oxford likely relates to the monarch's passage to Woodstock have been included with additional context to make clear the reason for their presence. The bells of parishes and certain colleges, such as Merton, were frequently rung to mark the royal passage through the city and on occasion gifts were given by either the University or the city. These records have not been transcribed. Also omitted are references to jousts and tournaments in the fourteenth century because there is no evidence that these ceremonies involved mimetic display.[2]

Interest in classical plays is often witnessed by college and University library lists or by individual purchase or ownership of texts. Such records, although of great potential interest, are excluded here on the grounds that the mere existence or ownership of a text constitutes no evidence of performance.[3] Original Oxford play texts, listed in Appendix 6, are not cited in the Records except on the rare occasion that they shed light on performance venues. Latin plays deriving from Oxford have been reproduced in facsimile in *Renaissance Latin Drama in England*, Martin Spevack, J.W. Binns, and Hans-Jürgen Weckermann (eds), 1st series, nos 1–13 (Hildesheim and New York, 1981–6), with introductions and plot summaries.

Some but not all Oxford plays in English have been published, whether individually or in a series. Title-page information, which often bears on the date or location of performances, is presented in full in Appendix 6. One complete text, the previously unknown masque 'Mr Moore's Revels,' discovered in the preparation of this work, appears in the Records (see pp 560–4). The 'Anti-theatrical Controversy' that erupted in Oxford in the 1590s spawned numerous documents, some of which were eventually published in John Rainolds' *Th' Overthrow of Stage-Playes* (1599). These have been deemed too lengthy and tendentious to be included here, though they contain many incidental references to Oxford plays, performances, and performers. A guide to the extant documents, with excerpts, is given in Appendix 11.

With the exception of the years of the royal visits, University and college ceremonies, including disputations and commencement exercises, though often quasi-theatrical, have been omitted. College and University statutes often prohibited 'unseemly games' ('ludos inhonestos'). The authorities normally had in mind not dramatic plays but card games, gambling, and physical activities such as ball playing, which might result in damage to buildings. Restrictive statutes and disciplinary cases mentioning game playing are therefore included only when the language specifically refers to plays or shows. Entertainment involving the baiting or display of animals has been included but references to fencing schools, along with mentions of sports such as tennis and football, have been omitted.

Chronology

The collection has been organized on an overall Michaelmas to Michaelmas chronology (29 September to 29 September) based on the predominant administrative year used by the colleges and city. Nine of the sixteen colleges from which records are drawn follow this year as do the Oxford civic accounts. Exceptions include individual city parishes, whose fiscal years also changed over time (see Institutions and Documents for summaries of individual parish accounting practices). Usually, however, the excerpted parish entries have a specific internal event date, such as Hocktide or Pentecost, which makes it possible to assign the record to the appropriate Michaelmas to Michaelmas year.

A general description of the college and University fiscal year may be found in Institutions and Documents (see p 627). A more detailed account of each college's practices is supplied as appropriate in the headnote for that college. Of the seven colleges that employed fiscal years other than Michaelmas to Michaelmas, those that began their college year on a date after 29 September are placed under the Michaelmas to Michaelmas year already in progress. Thus, for example, an account for 1 November 1498–1 November 1499 will appear under '1498–9.' In this way the larger portion of the college's year falls within the appropriate year. If, however, an excerpted passage is specifically dated for an event occurring in the final months of the college's fiscal year (ie, in the above example, between 29 September and 1 November 1499) it will be positioned according to the event date.

Similarly, colleges that began their fiscal year on a date before 29 September are placed under the year heading of the Michaelmas to Michaelmas period that is about to commence, with the like exception in those instances when a record is specifically dated for an event occurring in the opening months of the college's fiscal year.

For the parishes and the colleges without term divisions the accounting year (when other than Michaelmas to Michaelmas) is supplied in the editorial subheading and reiterated in the document descriptions. For any college with stable term or week divisions the precise week or month date range is supplied in the record subheading.

Reminiscences or allusions to events in years gone by are normally assigned to the year of the event. When possible, documents of uncertain date have been assigned to a likely year or to the year of publication, and the problems are discussed in endnotes.

Even though 1 January was celebrated as New Year's Day the change in the calendar year was usually recorded from 25 March. Thus a document dated 18 February 1639 refers, by modern reckoning, to 18 February 1640. Such dates are rendered as, for example, 18 February 1639/40. Where documents are dated by regnal year C.R. Cheney's *Handbook of Dates for Students of British History* has been used as a guide.

Many events are dated in the source documents by feast day rather than by day and month. Many of the feast days remain familiar (eg, Christmas) or are easily established. Others depended on local custom and may be beyond recovery. Appendix 15 gives the dates of most feasts named in the documents or, for movable feasts, directions for discovering the dates in a given year. Dates that cannot be discovered by reference to Appendix 15 are given in headings, footnotes, or endnotes as occasion dictates.

Many dramatic and musical events at Oxford are referred to as having taken place 'at the Act,' that is, at the commencement ceremonies held in July. Technically 'the Act' (Latin 'Comitia') took place each year on the first Monday after 7 July but the phrase might also refer to the ceremonies and celebrations beginning on the preceding Saturday, sometimes more specifically referred to as 'Act Saturday.'[4] Where no actual date is given, the inferred date of the Act that year is supplied in a footnote. References to 'Act Week' or 'Act Time' refer to the period from the Saturday before the Act to the following Friday.

Layout

Each entry in the Records is preceded by a name or descriptive title, along with a brief identification of its source. On a separate line the folio, page, or membrane number is given, along with the precise date of the entry (where known) and an abbreviated English version of the manuscript account heading (where available). Within each year documents are arranged with the college and University records first, followed by the city records. Documents from academic institutions precede those from civic institutions. Academic documents are arranged in the order of college (in alphabetical order), University, and miscellaneous. Civic documents are arranged in the order of civic government, guild, parish, legal, and miscellaneous. For all categories, annual accounts precede administrative documents. For categories that are not immediately obvious, codes in the left margins of the Records serve as aids to locating the documents in Institutions and Documents (see Symbols, p 2). Miscellaneous documents follow the order of Institutions and Documents, when they are few, or chronological order, when they are numerous and form a narrative sequence.

Within practical limits the general layout of the originals has been preserved. Headings, marginalia, and account totals are printed in the approximate position they occupy in the source. Right-hand marginalia have had to be set in the left margin of the printed text, a transposition indicated by the symbol ®. The lineation of the original has not been observed in passages of continuous prose. Where the layout of the original is idiosyncratic (eg, a diagonal left margin) no attempt has been made to reproduce that format. Marginalia too long or too cumbersome to set in the margin have been set within the body of the text and marked with a dagger symbol.

Dittography and obvious scribal errors are noted in the footnotes. Administrative cancellations (such as those for loans of money repaid or costumes returned) as distinguished from cancellations used by scribes to correct errors in writing are noted in endnotes. Decay, damage, and other problems that adversely affect the clarity of the original are briefly noted in footnotes or discussed in endnotes. Problems of dating and provenance are discussed in endnotes. An asterisk in the subheading line will alert the user to the existence of an endnote.

Text with Multiple Copies

Where records exist in multiple copies we have attempted to select the 'most authentic' copy as the base text. Two cases deserve special attention. First, where a letter was transmitted from one party to another and copies were made by sender, recipient, or both, preference is given to the letter that was actually sent (often distinguished by fold marks, seals, etc). If the transmitted document does not survive, a registered copy is used as base text. Second, where accounts exist both in rough (or draft) form and in neat (or finished) form, preference is given to the neat version, which may be considered more 'official,' unless the rough text preserves details lost in the neat text. When two or more copies of the same document survive we have recorded the location of the copies and noted any substantive variants in the endnotes. Multiple copies which appear to have independent authority are collated and substantive variants are listed in the collation notes. The collated MSS are described in Institutions and Documents. Differences in spellings, capitalization, forms of abbreviation, word division, or punctuation are not noted in collations.

Other Editorial Conventions

Manuscript punctuation has been retained, except that excessive scribal pointing is usually ignored. Virgules are indicated as / and //. Most manuscript braces and all line fillers have been overlooked. Capitulum marks and other marginal marks in financial accounts and inventories have for the most part not been transcribed. The spelling of the original has been preserved, along with the capitalization. The letters 'ff' have been retained for 'F'; the standard and elongated forms of 'I' are uniformly transcribed as 'I' except where clearly distinguished as a 'J' in later and printed documents. Ornamental capitals and display letters have been transcribed as ordinary letters but are noted. Arabic '1' has been substituted for 'i' in numbers other than sums.

Abbreviated words have been expanded with italics to indicate letters supplied by the editor. Where manuscripts yield insufficient evidence to judge individual scribal habits, abbreviations are expanded to classical forms in Latin and modern British forms in English. First names have been expanded wherever possible. Where a single 'P' with a mark of abbreviation is used as an abbreviation for 'patet per,' the second 'p' has been italicized, yielding '*patet per.*' Italics and other special typefaces in printed sources are not observed; they are silently printed as roman in transcriptions within the Records. Abbreviations that are easily understood today ('li.,' 's.,' 'd.,' 'ob.' (for half-pence), 'q*ua*.' (for farthing), 'viz.,' and 'etc' or '&c'), and abbreviations cumbersome to expand, including those typical for weights and measures ('lb.' for 'pound' and 'di.' for 'half') are retained. 'Mr' and 'Dr' are expanded only when used as nouns or when occurring before another title (eg, M*aste*r Mayor); they are left unexpanded when introducing a proper name. 'Xp-' and 'xp-' are expanded as 'Chr*ist*-' and 'chr*ist*-.' The sign ⅄ has been expanded '*es*,' '*ys*,' or '*is*' according to scribal practice, except when it follows an 'e': in this case it is expanded as '*s*.' Where single minims are too many or too few by obvious scribal error, an editorially corrected version is supplied in the text and the textual oddity is footnoted. Otiose flourishes such as the barred 'ell' are ignored. Superlineated letters are lowered to the line except when used with numerals.

Where an unfoliated manuscript has a small number of leaves or membranes, these have been counted by hand and conjectural folio numbers placed in square brackets.

Notes

Historical Background

1   John Blair, *Anglo-Saxon Oxfordshire* (Oxford, 1994), 102.

2   *VCH: Oxford*, vol 4, pp 3–4.

3   Blair, *Anglo-Saxon Oxfordshire*, pp 87–92.

4   Blair, *Anglo-Saxon Oxfordshire*, p 101.

5   Blair, *Anglo-Saxon Oxfordshire*, p 101.

6   Blair, *Anglo-Saxon Oxfordshire*, p 104.

7   Quoted in Blair, *Anglo-Saxon Oxfordshire*, p 101.

8   Derek Keene, 'The South-East of England,' *The Cambridge Urban History of Britain*, vol 1: 600–1540, D.M. Palliser (ed) (Cambridge, 2000), 551. Although Oxfordshire is more commonly thought of as a Midland county, Keene includes it in his discussion of the 'South-East.' His comparison counties are Bedfordshire, Berkshire, Buckinghamshire, Essex, Hampshire, Hertfordshire, Kent, Middlesex, Surrey, and Sussex.

9   Grenville Astill, 'General survey 600–1300,' *The Cambridge Urban History of Britain*, vol 1, Palliser (ed), p 36.

10 Keene, 'The South-East,' p 550.

11 Blair, *Anglo-Saxon Oxfordshire*, p 168.

12 Following Blair, *Anglo-Saxon Oxfordshire*, p 147, the modern names of the streets are used to locate the site of the crossroads. Only the High Street retains its medieval name. During the period covered by the Records, Cornmarket was known as Northgate or North Street; Queen Street was called Great Bailey because it led to the castle; and St Aldate's was first called Fish Street and then South Street.

13 James Campbell, 'Power and authority 600–1300,' *The Cambridge Urban History of Britain*, vol 1, Palliser (ed), p 66.

14 Ralph B. Pugh, *Imprisonment in Medieval England* (Cambridge, 1968), 60. The quotation is from Keene, 'The South-East,' p 568. The other towns were Bedford, Canterbury, and Winchester.

15 Blair, *Anglo-Saxon Oxfordshire*, pp 153–4.

16 Richard Holt, 'Society and population 600–1300,' *The Cambridge Urban History of Britain*, vol 1, Palliser (ed), p 88; and Carl I. Hammer, Jr, 'Anatomy of an Oligarchy:

The Oxford Town Council in the Fifteenth and Sixteenth Centuries,' *The Journal of British Studies* 18 (1978), 2.

17 *VCH: Oxford*, vol 4, p 305.
18 Blair, *Anglo-Saxon Oxfordshire*, p 150.
19 *VCH: Oxford*, vol 4, p 50.
20 Blair, *Anglo-Saxon Oxfordshire*, p 172.
21 *VCH: Oxford*, vol 4, p 52.
22 D.M. Palliser, T.R. Slater, and E. Patricia Dennison, 'The topography of towns 600–1300,' *The Cambridge Urban History of Britain*, vol 1, Palliser (ed), p 176.
23 *VCH: Oxford*, vol 4, p 45.
24 Hastings Rashdall, *The Universities of Europe in the Middle Ages*, vol 3, F.M. Powicke and A.B. Emden (eds), 2nd ed (Oxford, 1936), 106.
25 C.H. Lawrence, 'The University in State and Church,' *The History of the University of Oxford*, vol 1, pp 134–7.
26 For a succinctly informative account of the St Scholastica's Day riots and their aftermath, see Hibbert, *Encyclopaedia of Oxford*, p 424. See also Pantin, *Oxford Life in Oxford Archives*, pp 99–102. Pantin comments that the February 1354/5 riots were not the first, but the extent and violence of that episode may have 'shocked men into common sense': bad feeling remained for centuries but never again exploded into violence.
27 *VCH: Oxford*, vol 4, p 56.
28 Carl I. Hammer, Jr, 'Oxford Town and Oxford University,' *The History of the University of Oxford*, vol 3, pp 70–1.
29 Carl I. Hammer, Jr, 'Some Social and Institutional Aspects of Town-Gown Relations in Late Medieval and Tudor Oxford,' PhD thesis (University of Toronto, 1973), 98. The complex relationship between two lists of taxpayers made at approximately the same time is discussed in great detail on pp 93–115.
30 *VCH: Oxford*, vol 4, p 110.
31 For a full and detailed discussion of the 'privileged persons' and their relationship with the city, see Hammer, 'Oxford Town and Oxford University,' pp 74–86.
32 Hammer, 'Oxford Town and Oxford University,' p 74.
33 Hammer, 'Oxford Town and Oxford University,' p 87.
34 The details that follow are taken from Hammer, 'Oxford Town and Oxford University,' pp 88–94.
35 Hammer, 'Oxford Town and Oxford University,' p 92.
36 Hammer, 'Oxford Town and Oxford University,' p 94.
37 Hammer, 'Some Social and Institutional Aspects of Town-Gown Relations,' pp 81–4.
38 Hammer, 'Some Social and Institutional Aspects of Town-Gown Relations,' pp 83–5; *VCH: Oxford*, vol 4, p 148; Salter (ed), *Oxford Council Acts 1583–1626*, pp 205–8; and Hobson and Salter (eds), *Oxford Council Acts 1626–1665*, p xvii.
39 *VCH: Oxford*, vol 4, p 148.
40 Hammer, 'Oxford Town and Oxford University,' p 69.
41 Hammer, 'Oxford Town and Oxford University,' p 115.

42   *vcH: Oxford*, vol 4, pp 364–8.

43   Hammer, 'Oxford Town and Oxford University,' pp 70–1.

44   *vcH: Oxford*, vol 4, p 74.

45   Hammer, 'Oxford Town and Oxford University,' p 69. Frequent visits to Woodstock by Elizabeth I and James I are reflected in records contained in this collection.

46   Turner (ed), *Selections from the Records of the City of Oxford*, pp 228–40, 317.

47   S.T. Bindoff (ed), *The House of Commons 1509–1558*, vol 3, The History of Parliament (London, 1982), 623.

48   Bindoff (ed), *The House of Commons 1509–1558*, vol 3, pp 561, 623.

49   *vcH: Oxford*, vol 4, p 80.

50   *vcH: Oxford*, vol 4, p 136.

51   Hammer, 'Anatomy of an Oligarchy,' p 4.

52   For Wilmot, see Salter (ed), *Oxford Council Acts 1583–1626*, p 333; and Hobson and Salter (eds), *Oxford Council Acts 1626–1665*, p 27. See the latter for Smith (p 27), Boswell (pp 27, 47) and Blake (p 47).

53   Hammer, 'Anatomy of an Oligarchy,' p 11.

54   Hammer, 'Anatomy of an Oligarchy,' p 12.

55   *vcH: Oxford*, vol 4, p 138.

56   See Gervase Rosser, 'The cure of souls in English towns before 1000,' *Pastoral Care Before the Parish*, John Blair and Richard Sharpe (eds) (Leicester, 1992), 267–84. In particular he notes of St Frideswide's (p 272) that 'the location of the shrine and a parochial altar, in the north transept of the twelfth century church, may indicate both the site of the Anglo-Saxon minster church and its pastoral function.'

57   The details of the following paragraph come from *vcH: Oxford*, vol 4, pp 364–8.

58   R.W. Southern, 'From Schools to University,' *The History of the University of Oxford*, vol 1, pp 1–36.

59   *vcH: Oxford*, vol 2, p 64.

60   Numerous bequests to the Dominicans in Oxford, to take one example, are listed in *vcH: Oxford*, vol 2, pp 119–20; benefactors include not only locally connected nobility, gentry, clerics, and academics but townspeople (the odd merchant, brewer, or widow, and others given no occupation or other title).

61   R.B. Dobson, 'The Religious Orders 1370–1540,' *The History of the University of Oxford*, vol 2, p 541.

62   *vcH: Oxford*, vol 2, p 32; pp 31–2 give a detailed account of the complicated process by which Christ Church came into being.

63   Valuable accounts of the foundation of Christ Church and its historical context are given in *vcH: Oxford*, vol 4, pp 369–70; and James McConica, 'The Rise of the Undergraduate College,' *The History of the University of Oxford*, vol 3, pp 1–68. See especially McConica, 'The Rise of the Undergraduate College,' p 33.

64   *vcH: Oxford*, vol 4, p 369.

65   Salter, *Medieval Oxford*, p 71.

66   *vcH: Oxford*, vol 4, p 23.

67 Blair, *Anglo-Saxon Oxfordshire*, p 61. Blair cites 'a grant in 1004 to "a certain minster situated in the town called Oxford where the most blessed Frideswide rests."'

68 John Blair, 'St. Frideswide's Monastery: Problems and Possibilities,' *Oxoniensia* 53 (1988), 255–6.

69 *VCH: Oxford*, vol 4, p 400.

70 Blair, *Anglo-Saxon Oxfordshire*, p 113.

71 The earliest record of St Frideswide's parish, as distinct from the priory church, is of the 1170s (*VCH: Oxford*, vol 4, p 381). By 1500 several church closures left a total of fourteen parish churches and three non-parochial chapels (*VCH: Oxford*, vol 4, p 70).

72 On fluctuations in the relative prosperity of Oxford parishes in the later medieval period, see Salter, *Medieval Oxford*, pp 88–9; and *VCH: Oxford*, vol 4, p 31.

73 For a generally positive interpretation of relations between the parishes and the University, however, see Hammer, 'Oxford Town and Oxford University,' especially pp 105–8.

74 *VCH: Oxford*, vol 3, p 95 and vol 4, p 384.

75 *VCH: Oxford*, vol 3, p 163 and vol 4, p 394.

76 *VCH: Oxford*, vol 3, p 229 and vol 4, pp 373, 397.

77 R.B. Dobson, 'Urban decline in late medieval England,' *The Medieval Town: A Reader in English Urban History 1200–1540*, Richard Holt and Gervase Rosser (eds) (London, 1990), 273.

78 Anthony Wood, *Survey of the Antiquities of the City of Oxford*, vol 2, Oxford Historical Society 17, Andrew Clark (ed) (Oxford, 1890), 80; and *VCH: Oxford*, vol 4, p 384.

79 Fletcher, *History of St Martin*, p 10.

80 Fletcher, *History of St Martin*, pp 22–3.

81 The Domesday reference is to two dwellings formerly held by Earl Aubrey (later the king's), which 'lie (with the lands of) St Mary's church and pay 28d.' See Morris (ed), *Domesday Book*, vol 14, p 154a.

82 *VCH: Oxford*, vol 4, p 391.

83 Ffoulkes, *History of S. Mary the Virgin*, pp 82–3.

84 For guilds associated with specific Oxford churches, see *VCH: Oxford*, vol 4, pp 370–406.

85 Eamon Duffy, *The Stripping of the Altars: Traditional Religion in England, c. 1400– c. 1580* (New Haven and London, 1992), 145.

86 Carl I. Hammer, 'The Town-Gown Confraternity of St. Thomas the Martyr in Oxford,' *Mediaeval Studies* 39 (1977), 475–6.

87 *VCH: Oxford*, vol 4, pp 391–2.

88 Duffy, *The Stripping of the Altars*, pp 377–564. Duffy (pp 524–64) underlines the inevitably disorientating effects on local communities, not only of radical changes to patterns of worship and outward manifestations of belief but of the confusing about-turn of Mary's reign, 1553–8. He also cites examples (none, however, from Oxford) of evident resistance to change in parishes, reflected not only in their frequent slowness in complying with new regulations but in the tendency to adapt as far as possible without jettisoning tradition

altogether. For example, statues of newly banned saints were on occasion 'transposed' into still-permitted ones: in Ashford, Kent, St Thomas Becket was iconographically transformed into St Blaise by 'taking his archiepiscopal cross from his hand and putting in its place a wool-comb' (p 419).

89 Fletcher, *History of St Martin*, Appendix 3. Inventories of 1547, 1552, 1553, and 1560 are fully transcribed.

90 Richard Whittington was also a churchwarden: his name appears on the account for 1552–3 (ORO: PAR 207/4/F1/1, item 19).

91 *VCH: Oxford*, vol 4, p 388.

92 *VCH: Oxford*, vol 4, pp 392–3.

93 Information in this paragraph comes from *VCH: Oxford*, vol 4, pp 395, 402.

94 The churchwardens' accounts express considerable determination to renew lapsed customs in the non-liturgical sphere of parish life: after a gap of over twenty years, receipts from hocking reappear in the accounts for 1663–4 and the following year hocking, the Whitsun ale, and the maypole are all recorded.

95 Information in this section is drawn chiefly from *The History of the University of Oxford*, vols 1, 2, 3.

96 *The History of the University of Oxford*, vol 1, pp 34–6.

97 *The History of the University of Oxford*, vol 1, pp 32, 47.

98 *The History of the University of Oxford*, vol 1, pp 134–40.

99 *The History of the University of Oxford*, vol 1, pp 12–13.

100 *The History of the University of Oxford*, vol 2, pp 730–1, and vol 3, pp 401–2.

101 *The History of the University of Oxford*, vol 3, pp 117–18.

102 *The History of the University of Oxford*, vol 3, pp 49–50.

103 Clark (ed), *Register*, vol 2, pt 1, *Introductions* (Oxford, 1887), p 183.

104 *The History of the University of Oxford*, vol 3, pp 182–3, 197.

105 These figures are averaged from figures given in *The History of the University of Oxford*, vol 3, pp 155–6.

106 *The History of the University of Oxford*, vol 3, p 599.

107 *The History of the University of Oxford*, vol 2, p 624.

108 *The History of the University of Oxford*, vol 3, p 52.

109 *VCH: Oxford*, vol 3, pp 235, 239, 253.

110 *The History of the University of Oxford*, vol 3, pp 668–72, 722–6.

111 *The History of the University of Oxford*, vol 3, pp 623–7.

112 For numbers, see *The History of the University of Oxford*, vol 3, pp 58–64.

113 See the entries for these colleges in *VCH: Oxford*, vol 3.

Drama, Music, and Ceremonial Customs

1 John R. Elliott, Jr, 'Drama,' *The History of the University of Oxford*, vol 4, pp 641–58. (Portions of Elliott's essay have been incorporated here with the free permission of Oxford University Press).

2 *OED*, 'maintenance,' sb. 6.

3 Nelson (ed), *Cambridge*, vol 1, pp 223–44.

4 Elliott, 'Queen Elizabeth at Oxford: New Light on the Royal Plays of 1566,' pp 218–29.

5 *The Historical Register of the University of Oxford* (Oxford, 1888), p 19: for the last three years of his life, 1585–8, the office was given to a deputy.

6 See Orrell, *The Theatres of Inigo Jones and John Webb*, p 30.

7 Nelson (ed), *Cambridge*, vol 1, pp 688–93; and Alan H. Nelson, *Early Cambridge Theatres: University, College, and Town Stages, 1464–1720* (Cambridge, 1994), 16–37.

8 *Calendar of State Papers, Domestic Series*, Charles II, vol 2 (1661–2), 32, July 4. The play in question may have been the same one Martin Lluelyn presented for his degree to Dean Fell of Christ Church back in 1640.

9 For Jasper Mayne's comment, see *The Life and Times of Anthony Wood*, vol 2, p 2.

10 *An Inventory of the Historical Monuments in the City of Oxford*, Royal Commission on Historical Monuments, England (London, 1939), 73–4 (Magdalen), 77 (Merton), 86–7 (New College), 113–14 (Trinity); plans opposite p 72 (Magdalen), opposite p 80 (Merton), opposite p 88 (New College), p 109 (Trinity); plates 133 (Magdalen), 153 (New College – 2 views). The dimensions given for New College hall (p 86) are by error those for Christ Church hall; corrected information in the Introduction has been supplied by the New College archivist.

11 *Historical Monuments in the City of Oxford*, pp 105–6, plan opposite p 104.

12 *Historical Monuments in the City of Oxford*, pp 33–4; plans opposite p 32 and on p 34.

13 *Historical Monuments in the City of Oxford*, pp 56–7; plan p 55; photo plate 111.

14 *Historical Monuments in the City of Oxford*, p 99.

15 Nelson, *Early Cambridge Theatres*, pp 16–76, 102–17.

16 Alan H. Nelson, 'Early Drama in the English Universities,' *Contexts for Early English Drama*, Marianne Briscoe and John Coldewey (eds) (Indiana, 1989), 143; and Elliott, 'Drama,' *The History of the University of Oxford*, vol 4, pp 644–5. Wickham, *Early English Stages*, vol 1, p 359 (with a diagram), situates the stage platform at the lower end of the hall, near the main door.

17 Reconstructed (with a diagram) by Wickham, *Early English Stages*, vol 1, p 357.

18 Elliott and Buttrey, 'The Royal Plays at Christ Church in 1636.'

19 The statutes of New College *c* 1398 (see p 12, ll.6–11) make provision for the involvement of boys in the divine services on Holy Innocents' Day.

20 Chambers, *The Mediaeval Stage*, vol 1, 403–19; on Oxford, see pp 407–12. See also Sandra Billington, *Mock Kings in Medieval Society and Renaissance Drama* (Oxford, 1991). The image in Billington's Fig. 4, from the beginning of the Statutes of St John's College (1562), is not 'a drawing of a king and queen pageant' (p 60) but the Holy Trinity.

21 See entry in Appendix 6:1.

22 Nelson (ed), *Cambridge*, vol 2, Appendix 12, pp 996–1001.

23 Nelson (ed), *Cambridge*, vol 1, pp 276–7.

24 OCA: P.5.2, f 252.

25 OCA: P.5.2, f 252v.

26 R.W. Ingram (ed), *Coventry*, REED (Toronto, 1981), 431–48.

27 In Nichols, *Progresses of Queen Elizabeth*, vol 1, p 270, Nichols records a payment to 'Robert Grene, the Quene's Fool' in an account of the 'Queen's Purse' from 1559 to 1569. Grene may have been the jester as early as 1560 although John Southworth dates Grene's tenure from 1565 in *Fools and Jesters at the English Court* (Stroud, Gloucestershire, 1998), 108. Southworth gives him the first name of 'Jack.' On pages 108 and 114, Southworth also suggests that Richard Tarlton, who was certainly the queen's fool by the 1580s, may have been introduced to the court by Robert Dudley, earl of Leicester, as early as 1565.

28 David Cook (ed), *Collections* 6, Malone Society (London, 1962 for 1961), xii.

29 OCA: C/FC/1/A1/003, f 85.

30 Scott McMillin and Sally-Beth MacLean, *The Queen's Men and their Plays* (Cambridge, 1998), 18–36.

31 Geoffrey Tillotson, '*Othello* and *The Alchemist* at Oxford in 1610,' p 494.

32 Salter (ed), *Oxford Council Acts 1583–1626*, p xxiv. The site is now the Clarendon Centre and its third exit is on to Shoe Lane, which is indeed the former Sewy's Lane. See VCH: *Oxford*, vol 4, p 438: 'An inn immediately to the north [sc of the Crown Inn close to the Carfax end of Cornmarket Street, on the west side], Pyry Hall in 1498, ... became the King's Head in the early 16th century, when it incorporated Sewys Lane; plays were performed in its galleried stable-yard in the 17th and 18th centuries.'

33 See also Salter (ed), *Oxford City Properties*, p 339.

34 See Alexandra F. Johnston and Margaret Rogerson (eds), *York*, 2 vols, REED (Toronto, 1979); John Wasson (ed), *Devon*, REED (Toronto, 1986); and David Galloway (ed), *Norwich, 1540–1642*, REED (Toronto, 1984), passim.

35 Salter (ed), *Oxford Council Acts 1583–1626*, pp xxxii–xxxiv.

36 Buckner is variously referred to as 'Bucknall,' 'Bucknold,' and 'Buckner.' He was called 'Bucknell' when he was finally admitted to his freedom in 1596–7, but he is most commonly called Buckner in the Records. From the various descriptions of the Oxford scutcheons in the Records they seem to have been very like the ones preserved from the sixteenth century in the Exeter guildhall. The Exeter ones are substantial silvered embossed medallions with heavy and intricate silver chains.

37 City Memorandum Book, OCA: D.5.2, f 190, records the agreement between Frere and Gibbons.

38 Salter (ed), *Oxford City Properties*, p 360.

39 A John Baldwin, musician, was fined for a misdemeanor the year before along with another musician, Thomas Charles (city quarter sessions, OCA: QSC/A2/001, pp 241, 243). It was probably John the younger. Charles was never named as a wait but was probably the 'yonge Charles' paid by St Peter le Bailey in 1604–5. He was subsequently associated with John Bosseley in the dancing school.

40 The names here are taken from a card index to the chancellor's court act registers from 1594–1664, excluding 1634–8, compiled by Walter Mitchell, and a similar index for the years 1634–8 compiled by Malcolm Underwood, kept in the Oxford University Archives. The entries themselves are not included in the Records since they consist simply

of the witness' name, followed by the word 'musician,' and have otherwise nothing to do with music.

41 On these and other aspects of music in Oxford, see John Caldwell, 'Music in the Faculty of Arts,' *The History of the University of Oxford*, vol 3, pp 201–2; and Penelope Gouk, 'Music in Seventeenth-Century Oxford,' *The History of the University of Oxford*, vol 4, pp 621–40.

42 ChCh Arch: D.P.ii.c.1, item 25.

43 *vch: Oxford*, vol 4, p 427.

44 *vch: Oxford*, vol 4, p 427.

45 These guardbooks have proved very difficult to store in modern archival conditions and the archivists in the Oxfordshire Record Office began to remove the rolls from the books in 2000 when the office moved to new quarters in Cowley.

46 See Alexandra F. Johnston, 'Summer Festivals in the Thames Valley Counties,' *Custom, Culture and Community: A Symposium*, Thomas Pettitt and Leif Søndergaard (eds) (Odense, 1994), 37–56; and Johnston and MacLean, 'Reformation and Resistance in Thames/Severn Parishes,' pp 178–200.

47 The contrast with the customs in the three parishes of the other substantial Thames Valley town, Reading, is striking. St Laurence Reading stopped its hocking practice in 1558–9, St Giles' in 1561–2, and St Mary's in 1566–7. For St Laurence see Berkshire Record Office: D/P 97 5/2, p 295; for St Giles see bro: D/P 96 5/1, p 116; for St Mary's see bro: D/P/98 5/1, p 67.

48 This is very similar to a 1571 lease of the church-house of the tiny neighbouring parish of Appleton just over the border in Berkshire where a period of ten days is specified. The Appleton leases are still held by the parish and have no shelf-marks.

49 Johnston, 'Summer Festivals in the Thames Valley Counties'; and Johnston and MacLean, 'Reformation and Resistance in Thames/Severn Parishes.'

50 oro: ms DD Par Woodstock c.12.

51 *vch: Oxford*, vol 4, p 426.

52 The one indecorous custom associated with the civic authorities was the lord of misrule or mock mayor called the 'king or judge of Slovens Hall.' The first witness to this was the antiquarian Twyne who stated that the custom was discontinued in 1651 but reinstated after the Restoration (Bodl.: ms. Twyne 9, p 154). No evidence survives for the custom before 1642.

53 See pp 578–9 and p 895 for evidence that the figure in the tub was a picture rather than a real person contrary to the implication of the account in the city council minutes (see p 579). This event is mentioned in *The Life and Times of Anthony Wood*, vol 1, p 49, which cites John Vicars' *A looking-glasse for malignants: or, God's hand against God-haters* (London, 1643), 13. Wing: V317.

Institutions and Documents

1 *Catalogi Codicum Manuscriptorum Bibliothecae Bodleianae*, 14 vols (Oxford, 1845–89). The Rawlinson Collection is catalogued in vol 5, the Ashmole Collection in vol 10.

2 An important exception to these rules is the collection of manuscripts compiled by Brian Twyne. These are not described in the Bodleian catalogues, as they were in the possession of the University archives when the catalogues were compiled. They are, however, fully described in *The Life and Times of Anthony Wood*, vol 4, pp 202–26.

3 For the date of the earlier fragment see the facsimile edition prepared and introduced by J.W. Binns, Renaissance Latin Drama in England, 1st ser, no 1 (Hildesheim and New York, 1981), 7–8.

4 *VCH: Oxford*, vol 3, p 238, citing, as the fullest account of the college, H.E.D. Blakiston (ed), *Some Durham College Rolls*, vol 3, *Collectanea*, Oxford Historical Society (Oxford, 1896). See also R.B. Dobson, *Durham Priory, 1400–1450*, Cambridge Studies in Medieval Life and Thought, 3rd ser, 6 (Cambridge, 1973), 348–9.

5 See Macray, *Register*, vol 1, p 35.

6 See Orme, 'An Early-Tudor Oxford Schoolbook,' pp 11–39.

7 See *VCH: Oxford*, vol 3, p 248.

8 Thomas Tanner, *Bibliotheca Britannico-Hibernica* (London, 1748), 82.

9 The exception is the set of hannisters' registers for 1590–1889 (OCA: L.5.1–L.5.6), which are so frequently requested that they are stored on a permanent basis at the ORO.

10 Turner (ed), *Records of the City of Oxford*, p 23.

11 Hammer, 'Anatomy of an Oligarchy,' p 2.

12 *VCH: Oxford*, vol 4, p 126.

13 *VCH: Oxford*, vol 4, p 126.

14 *VCH: Oxford*, vol 4, p 140.

Editorial Procedures

1 On these other aspects of music in Oxford, see John Caldwell, 'Music in the Faculty of Arts,' *The History of the University of Oxford*, vol 3, pp 201–12; and Penelope Gouk, 'Music in Seventeenth-Century Oxford,' *The History of the University of Oxford*, vol 4, pp 621–40.

2 See H.C. Maxwell Lyte, *History of the University of Oxford from the Earliest Times to the Year 1530* (London, 1886), 133; and *VCH: Oxford*, vol 4, p 425. Shakespeare makes reference to jousts and tournaments at Oxford (*Richard II*, v.ii.52).

3 On book ownership, see Ian Lancashire, *Dramatic Texts and Records of Britain* (Toronto, 1984), 241–7; and N.R. Ker, 'The Provision of Books,' *The History of the University of Oxford*, vol 3, pp 441–519.

4 See Clark (ed), *Register*, vol 2, Part 1, p 82.

Select Bibliography

This bibliography includes books and articles with first-hand transcriptions of primary documents relevant to this collection, together with a few essential reference works. No attempt has been made to list all works cited in the Introduction and Endnotes.

Alton, R.E. (ed). 'The Academic Drama in Oxford: Extracts from the Records of Four Colleges,' *Collections* 5. Malone Society (Oxford, 1960 for 1959), 29–95.

Anstey, Henry (ed). *Munimenta Academica, or Documents Illustrative of Academical Life and Studies at Oxford*. Part 1, *Libri Cancellarii et Procuratorum*. Part 2, *Libri Cancellarii et Procuratorum, Accedunt Acta Curiae Cancellarii et Memoranda ex Registris Nonnulla*. 2 vols. Rolls Series 50, 51 (London, 1868). [Facs Kraus rpt 1966.]

Bentley, Gerald Eades. *The Jacobean and Caroline Stage*. 7 vols (Oxford, 1941–68).

Bereblock, John. *Commentarii sivi Ephemerae Actiones Rerum Illustrium Oxonii Gestarum in Adventu Serenissimae Principis Elizabethae* [1566], in *Historia Vitae et Regni Ricardi II*. Thomas Hearne (ed) (Oxford, 1729), 253–96.

Birch, Thomas (compiler). *The Court and Times of Charles the First; Containing a Series of Historical and Confidential Letters*. Vol 2 (London, 1849).

Boas, F.S. 'The Early Oxford Academic Stage,' *The Oxford Magazine* 30 (1912), 240–1, 259–60.

– '*Hamlet* and *Volpone* at Oxford,' *The Fortnightly Review*, ns, 107 (os, 113) (1920), 709–16.

– '*Hamlet* at Oxford: New Facts and Suggestions,' *The Fortnightly Review*, ns, 94 (os, 100) (1913), 245–53.

– *Shakespeare and the Universities, and Other Studies in Elizabethan Drama* (Oxford, 1923). [Facs Benjamin Blom (New York, 1971).]

– 'Theatrical Companies at Oxford in the Seventeenth Century,' *The Fortnightly Review*, ns, 104 (os, 110) (1918), 256–62.

– *University Drama in the Tudor Age* (Oxford, 1914).

– (ed). *The Christmas Prince*: *An Account of St. John's College Revels Held in Oxford in 1607–8*. Malone Society Reprints (Oxford, 1922).

– and W.W. Greg (eds). 'James I at Oxford in 1605: Property Lists from the University Archives,' *Collections* 1.3. Malone Society (Oxford, 1909), 247–59.

Boase, Charles W. *Oxford*. 3rd ed (London and New York, 1890).

– (ed). *Register of the University of Oxford*, vol 1, *1449–63; 1505–71*. Oxford Historical Society 1 (Oxford, 1885).

– (ed). *Registrum Collegii Exoniensis. Register of the Rectors, Fellows, and Other Members of the Foundation of Exeter College, Oxford*. Oxford Historical Society 27 (Oxford, 1894).

Carnegie, David. 'Actors' Parts and the "Play of Poore,"' *Harvard Library Bulletin* 30 (1982), 5–24.

– 'The Identification of the Hand of Thomas Goffe, Academic Dramatist and Actor,' *The Library*, 5th ser, 26 (1971), 161–5.

Chamberlain, John. *The Letters of John Chamberlain*. Norman Egbert McClure (ed). 2 vols. Memoirs 12, 2 pts. The American Philosophical Society (Philadelphia, 1939).

Chambers, E.K. *The Elizabethan Stage*. 4 vols (Oxford, 1923; rpt 1974).

– *The Mediaeval Stage*. 2 vols (Oxford, 1903).

Clark, Andrew (ed). *The Colleges of Oxford: Their History and Traditions. XXI Chapters Contributed by Members of the Colleges* (London, 1891).

– (ed). *Register of the University of Oxford*, vol 2, *1571–1622*. 4 parts. Oxford Historical Society 10, 11, 12, 14 (Oxford, 1887–9).

Costin, W.C. *The History of St. John's College Oxford 1598–1860*. Oxford Historical Society, ns, 12 (Oxford, 1958 for 1951–2).

Cox, A.D.M., and R.H. Darwall-Smith (eds). *Account Rolls of University College, Oxford*, vol 2, *1471/2–1596/7*. Oxford Historical Society, ns, 40 (Oxford, 2001).

Crosfield, Thomas. *The Diary of Thomas Crosfield, M.A., B.D., Fellow of Queen's College, Oxford*. Frederick S. Boas (ed) (London, 1935).

'The Drama at Oxford in 1636,' *The Bodleian Quarterly Record* 2 (1917–19), 151–2.

Driscoll, John P. 'A Miracle Play at Oxford,' *Notes and Queries*, continuous series, 205 (1960), 6.

Elliott, John R., Jr. 'Degree Plays,' *Oxoniensia* 53 (1988), 341–2.

– 'Drama,' *History of the University of Oxford*, vol 4, pp 641–58.

– 'Drama at the Oxford Colleges and the Inns of Court, 1520–1534,' *Research Opportunities in Renaissance Drama* 31 (1992), 64–6.

– 'Early Staging in Oxford,' *A New History of Early English Drama*. John D. Cox and David Scott Kastan (eds) (New York, 1997), 68–76.

– 'Entertainments in Tudor and Stuart Corpus,' *The Pelican* (1982–3), 45–50.

– 'A "Learned Tragedy" at Trinity?' *Oxoniensia* 50 (1985), 247–50.

– 'Mr. Moore's Revels: A "Lost" Oxford Masque,' *Renaissance Quarterly* 37 (1984), 411–20.

– 'Plays, Players, and Playwrights in Renaissance Oxford,' *From Page to Performance: Essays in Early English Drama*. John A. Alford (ed) (East Lansing, MI, 1995), 179–94.

– 'Queen Elizabeth at Oxford: New Light on the Royal Plays of 1566,' *English Literary Renaissance* 18 (1988), 218–29.

– and John Buttrey. 'The Royal Plays at Christ Church in 1636: A New Document,' *Theatre Research International* 10 (1985), 93–109.

Ellis, William Patterson, and H.E. Salter (eds). *Liber Albus Civitatis Oxoniensis: Abstract of the Wills, Deeds, and Enrollments Contained in the White Book of the City of Oxford* (Oxford, 1909).

Emden, A.B. (ed). *A Biographical Register of the University of Oxford to A.D. 1500*. 3 vols (Oxford, 1957).

– (ed). *A Biographical Register of the University of Oxford, A.D. 1501 to 1540* (Oxford, 1974).

Evelyn, John. *The Diary of John Evelyn*. E.S. de Beer (ed). 6 vols (Oxford, 1955).

Feuillerat, Albert. *Documents Relating to the Revels at Court in the Time of King Edward VI and Queen Mary (The Loseley Manuscripts)*. Materialien zur Kunde des älteren Englischen Dramas 44 (Leuven, Leipzig, and London, 1914; rpt Kraus, 1968).

– 'Performance of a Tragedy at New College, Oxford, in the Time of Queen Mary,' *The Modern Language Review* 9 (1914), 96–7.

Ffoulkes, Edmund S. *A History of the Church of S. Mary the Virgin, Oxford, the University Church* (London, 1892).

Finnis, John, and Patrick H. Martin. 'An Oxford Play Festival in February 1582,' *Notes and Queries*, continuous series, 240 (2003), 391–4.

Firth, Charles. 'Annals of the Oxford Stage,' *The Oxford Magazine* 4 (1886), 66.

Fletcher, C.J.H. *A History of the Church and Parish of St Martin (Carfax) Oxford* (Oxford and London, 1896).

Fletcher, C.R.L. (ed). *Collectanea. First Series*. Oxford Historical Society 5 (Oxford, 1885).

Fletcher, John M. (ed). *Registrum Annalium Collegii Mertonensis 1521–1567*. Oxford Historical Society, ns, 23 (Oxford, 1974 for 1971–2).

– *Registrum Annalium Collegii Mertonensis 1567–1603*. Oxford Historical Society, ns, 24 (Oxford, 1976 for 1973–4).

Foster, Joseph (ed). *Alumni Oxonienses: The Members of the University of Oxford, 1500–1714*. 4 vols (Oxford and London, 1891–2).

Fowler, Thomas. *The History of Corpus Christi College with a List of its Members*. Oxford Historical Society 25 (Oxford, 1893).

Gibson, Strickland (ed). *Statuta Antiqua Universitatis Oxoniensis* (Oxford, 1931).

Green, Vivian. *The Commonwealth of Lincoln College 1427–1977* (Oxford, 1979).

Harbage, Alfred. *Annals of English Drama 975–1700*. 3rd ed. Sylvia Stolen Wagonheim (rev) (London and New York, 1989).

Heylyn, Peter. *Memorial of Bishop Waynflete, Founder of St Mary Magdalen College, Oxford*. John Rouse Bloxam (ed). Caxton Society Publications 14 (1851; rpt New York, 1967).

Hibbert, Christopher, and Edward Hibbert (eds). *Encyclopaedia of Oxford* (London, 1988).

The History of the University of Oxford. Aston, T.H. (ed). Vol 1, *The Early Oxford Schools*. J.I. Catto (ed) (Oxford, 1984). Vol 2, *Late Medieval Oxford*. J.I. Catto and Ralph Evans (eds) (Oxford, 1992; rpt with corrections 1995). Vol 3, *The Collegiate University*. James McConica (ed) (Oxford, 1986). Vol 4, *Seventeenth-Century Oxford*. Nicholas Tyacke (ed) (Oxford, 1997).

The Historical Manuscripts Commission. J.A. Bennett. 'The Diary of Robert Woodford, Steward of Northampton, Lib III,' *The 9th Report of the Manuscripts Commission*, Appendix, pt 2 (London, 1884), 493–9.

– Horwood, Alfred J. 'The Manuscripts of the Right Honourable The Earl de la Warr (Baron Buckhurst) at Knole Park, Co. Kent,' *The 4th Report of the Manuscripts Commission*, Appendix, pt 1 (London, 1874), 276–317.

– Maxwell Lyte, H.C. 'Report on the Manuscripts of Philip Pleydell Bouverie, Esq.,' *The 10th Report of the Manuscripts Commission*, Appendix, pt 6 (London, 1887), 82–98.

– Purnell, E.K. *Report on the Pepys Manuscripts, at Magdalene College, Cambridge* (London, 1911).

– Riley, Henry Thomas. 'Exeter College, Oxford,' *The 2nd Report of the Manuscripts Commission* (London, 1871), 128–9.

– [Riley, Henry Thomas.] 'Wadham College,' *The 5th Report of the Manuscripts Commission* (London, 1876), 479–81.

Hobson, M.G., and H.E. Salter (eds). *Oxford Council Acts 1626–1665*. Oxford Historical Society 95 (Oxford, 1933).

Jeffery, R.W. 'The Bursars' Account Books,' *The Brazen Nose* 4 (1924–9), 19–30.

Johnston, Alexandra F., and Sally-Beth MacLean. 'Reformation and Resistance in Thames/Severn Parishes: The Dramatic Witness,' *The Parish in English Life*. Katherine L. French, Gary G. Gibbs, and B.A. Kümen (eds) (Manchester, 1997), 178–200.

Jones, John. *Balliol College: A History, 1263–1939* (Oxford and New York, 1988).

Kimball, Elisabeth G. (ed). *Oxfordshire Sessions of the Peace in the Reign of Richard II*. Oxfordshire Record Society 53 (Banbury, Oxfordshire, 1983).

Lawrence, W.J. '*Hamlet* at the Universities: A Belated Reply,' *The Fortnightly Review*, ns, 106 (os, 112) (1919), 219–27.

Lee, Margaret L. (ed). *Narcissus: A Twelfe Night Merriment Played by Youths of the Parish at the College of S. John the Baptist in Oxford, A.D. 1602*. The Tudor Library 4 (London, 1893), 1–27.

Macray, William Dunn. *A Register of the Members of St. Mary Magdalen College, Oxford, from the Foundation of the College*. 8 vols (London, 1894–1915).

Madox, Richard. *An Elizabethan in 1582: The Diary of Richard Madox, Fellow of All Souls*. Elizabeth Story Donno (ed). The Hakluyt Society, 2nd ser, no 147 (London, 1976).

Manning, Percy. 'Sport and Pastime in Stuart Oxford,' *Surveys and Tokens*. H.E. Salter (ed). Oxford Historical Society 75 (Oxford, 1923), 87–135.

Mitchell, W.T. (ed). *Registrum Cancellarii 1498–1506*. Oxford Historical Society, ns, 27 (Oxford, 1980 for 1979–80).

Morris, John (ed). *Domesday Book, vol 14: Oxfordshire* (Chichester, 1978).

Nelson, Alan H. (ed). *Cambridge*. 2 vols. REED (Toronto, 1989).

Nelson, William (ed). *A Fifteenth-Century School Book from a Manuscript in the British Museum (MS. Arundel 249)* (Oxford, 1956).

Nichols, John. *The Progresses and Public Processions of Queen Elizabeth*. 3 vols (London, 1823). [Facs Burt Franklin: Research and Source Works Series, no 117 (New York, nd).]

– *The Progresses, Processions, and Magnificent Festivities of King James the First*. 4 vols (London, 1828). [Facs Burt Franklin: Research and Source Works Series, no 118 (New York, nd).]

Nochimson, Richard L. 'Robert Burton's Authorship of Alba: A Lost Letter Recovered,' *Review of English Studies*, ns, 21 (1970), 325–31.

Orme, Nicholas. 'An Early Tudor Oxford Schoolbook,' *Renaissance Quarterly* 34 (1981), 11–39.

Orrell, John. 'The Theatre at Christ Church, Oxford, in 1605,' *Shakespeare Survey* 35 (1982), 129–40.

– *The Theatres of Inigo Jones and John Webb* (Cambridge, 1985).

Pantin, W.A. *Oxford Life in Oxford Archives* (Oxford, 1972).

– (ed). *Canterbury College, Oxford*. 4 vols. Oxford Historical Society, ns, 6, 7, 8, 30 (Oxford, 1947–85).

Plummer, Charles (ed). *Elizabethan Oxford: Reprints of Rare Tracts*. Oxford Historical Society 8 (Oxford, 1887).

Poole, A.L. 'A University Entertainment in 1583,' *The Oxford Magazine* 29 (1911), 85–6.

Rogers, J.E. Thorold (ed). *Oxford City Documents, Financial and Judicial, 1268–1665*. Oxford Historical Society 18 (Oxford, 1891).

Salgado, Gamini. *Eyewitnesses of Shakespeare: First Hand Accounts of Performances 1590–1890* (London, 1975).

Salter, H.E. *Medieval Oxford*. Oxford Historical Society 100 (Oxford, 1936).

– *Survey of Oxford*. Vol 1. W.A. Pantin (ed). Oxford Historical Society, ns, 14 (Oxford, 1960 for 1955–6). Vol 2. W.A. Pantin and W.T. Mitchell (eds). Oxford Historical Society, ns, 20 (Oxford, 1969 for 1965–6).

– (ed). *The Churchwardens' Accounts of St Michael in the North Gate*. Transactions of the Oxford Archaeological Society 78 (Oxford, 1933).

– (ed). *Mediaeval Archives of the University of Oxford*. 2 vols. Oxford Historical Society 70, 73 (Oxford, 1920–1).

– (ed). *Oxford City Properties*. Oxford Historical Society 83 (Oxford, 1926).

– (ed). *Oxford Council Acts 1583–1626*. Oxford Historical Society 87 (Oxford, 1928).

– (ed). *Registrum Annalium Collegii Mertonensis 1483–1521*. Oxford Historical Society 76 (Oxford, 1923).

– W.A. Pantin and H.G. Richardson (eds). *Formularies which Bear on the History of Oxford c. 1204–1420*. Vol 2. Oxford Historical Society, ns, 5 (Oxford, 1942).

Statutes of the Colleges of Oxford. 3 vols (Oxford, 1853).

Stevenson, W.H. and H.E. Salter. *The Early History of St. John's College Oxford*. Oxford Historical Society, ns, 1 (Oxford, 1939).

Stratman, Carl Joseph. 'Dramatic Performances at Oxford and Cambridge, 1603–1642.' PhD thesis (University of Illinois, Urbana, 1947).

Taylor, A.J. 'The Royal Visit to Oxford in 1636: A Contemporary Narrative,' *Oxoniensia* 1 (1936), 151–8.

Tillotson, Geoffrey. '*Othello* and *The Alchemist* at Oxford in 1610,' *Times Literary Supplement*, 20 July 1933.

Trevor-Roper, H.R. 'Five Letters of Sir Thomas Bodley,' *Bodleian Library Record* 2 (1941–9), 134–9.

Turner, William H. (ed). *Selections from the Records of the City of Oxford* (Oxford and London, 1880).

The Victoria History of the Counties of England. *A History of the County of Oxford*. Vol 2. William Page (ed) (London, 1907). *The University of Oxford*. Vol 3. H.E. Salter and M.D. Lobel (eds) (London, 1954). *The City of Oxford*. Vol 4. Alan Crossley (ed) (Oxford, 1979).

Wickham, Glynne. *Early English Stages 1300–1660*. 2 vols (London, 1959–73; 2nd ed, 1980).

Wood, Anthony. *Athenae Oxonienses. An Exact History of all the Writers and Bishops Who Have had Their Education in the University of Oxford. To Which Are Added The Fasti, or Annals of the Said University*. Philip Bliss (ed). 3rd ed. 4 vols (London, 1813–20).

— *The History and Antiquities of the University of Oxford, in Two Books: By Anthony à Wood, M.A. of Merton College. Now First Published in English, From the Original MS in the Bodleian Library*. John Gutch (ed). 2 vols (Oxford, 1792–6).

— *The Life and Times of Anthony Wood, Antiquary, of Oxford, 1632–1695*. Andrew Clark (compiler and ed). 5 vols. Oxford Historical Society 19, 21, 26, 30, 40 (Oxford, 1891–1900).

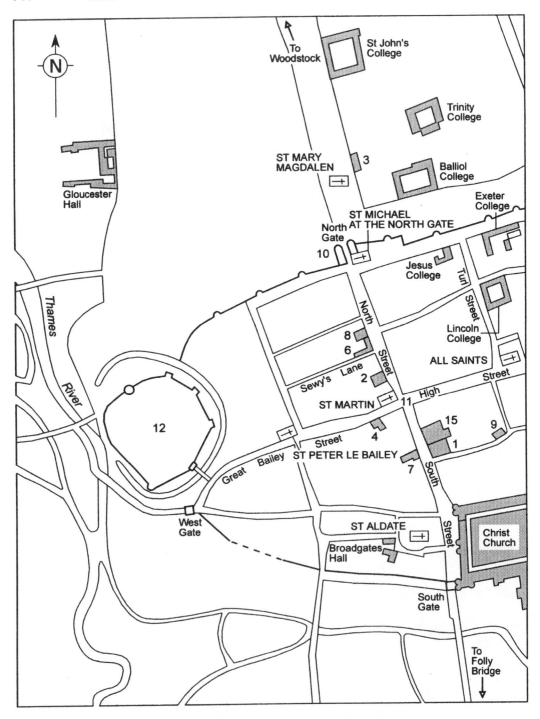

Map 1 Oxford, *c* 1578. See p 762 for Key to Map 1.

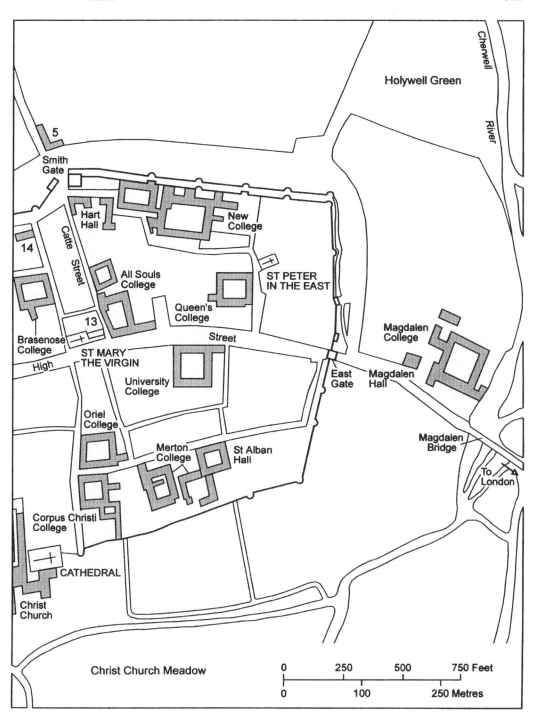

Cherwell

River

Holywell Green

5

Smith
Gate

Hart
Hall

New
College

14

Catte
Street

All Souls
College

ST PETER
IN THE EAST

13

Queen's
College

Magdalen
College

Brasenose
College

Street

ST MARY
THE VIRGIN

High

University
College

East
Gate

Magdalen
Hall

Oriel
College

Merton
College

St Alban
Hall

Magdalen
Bridge

To
London

Corpus Christi
College

CATHEDRAL

Christ
Church

Christ Church Meadow

0	250	500	750 Feet
0	100	250 Metres	

Key to Map 1

INNS AND TAVERNS

1 Blue Boar
2 Crown
3 Dolphin
4 Fleur de Luce
5 King's Arms
6 King's Head
7 Red Lion
8 Star
9 Bear

OTHER BUILDINGS

10 Bocardo
11 Carfax
12 Castle
13 Congregation House
14 Divinity School
15 Guildhall

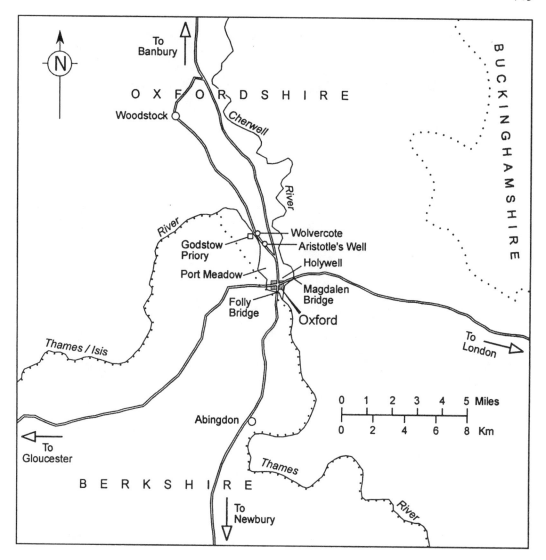

Map 2 Oxford and environs, with principal Renaissance routes.

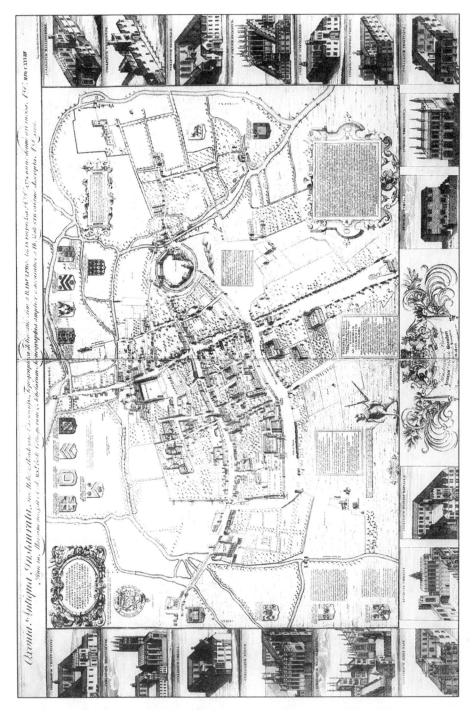

Map 3 Ralph Agas' Map of Oxford, 1578. Reproduced from Gough Maps Oxon 1 (Agas Map of Colleges and Halls), by permission of the Bodleian Library, University of Oxford.

APPENDIX 1

Architectural Drawing of Christ Church Theatre (1605)

The architectural drawing now classed as BL: MS Additional 15505, f 21, was identified by John Orrell in 1982 as the representation of a theatre installed in Christ Church hall at the royal visit of James I in August 1605 (see Records, 1604–5). Orrell has discussed the document at least four times: 'The Theatre at Christ Church,' pp 129–40; *The Quest for Shakespeare's Globe* (Cambridge, 1983), 129–38, 168–70; 'The Theatre at Christ Church Oxford,' *The Theatres of Inigo Jones and John Webb*, pp 24–38; and 'The Christ Church Theatre,' *The Human Stage: English Theatre Design, 1567–1640* (Cambridge, 1988), 119–29. See also R.A. Foakes, *Illustrations of the English Stage, 1580–1642* (London, 1985), 56–61; and John H. Astington, *English Court Theatre, 1558–1642* (Cambridge, 1999), 33–4, 84–7.

The document is a sheet of paper (381mm x 298mm) made up of two smaller sheets, slightly overlapped. The first sheet contains a plan, showing the theatre as from above; the second, a section, showing the theatre as from the side. The direction 'Verte folium' at the bottom right of the first sheet suggests that the document began life as a bifolium. Not visible in the photographs are dry-point drawing-compass arcs, swung from a clearly visible point near K on the plan, which assisted the draughtsman in laying out the rows of seats.

A note on the section exactly matches the (unique) dimensions of Christ Church hall: 'The hall is a 115 foote longe & 40 broade.' Three arguments support Orrell's claim that the occasion was August 1605. First, Isaac Wake describes, in a publication of 1607 concerning the royal visit two years earlier, a stage platform that sloped toward the front and 'in planitiem desinebat' ('came to an end in a level surface') (see p 306). The section shows precisely such a stage. Second, when James objected that his throne was placed too close to the stage, it was moved back some 14' (see p 770). Both plan and section reflect an (original) intent to situate the throne close to the stage. Third, the stage designed for the royal visit of Charles I in 1636 filled the upper end of the hall to the 'hearth' (see p 545 and Figure 4, p 609) while the stage implied by the drawings is relatively shallow.

Both drawings focus on what may be called the auditorium. The length of the plan is exactly twice its width: judging from the declared scale (1/10" = 1') the plan thus represents an area of 40' x 80'. While nicely fitting the width of the hall the plan comes 35' short of its length. Annotations reveal that the auditorium up to the front of the stage is 82' deep, the backstage and stage platform 33', for a total of 115'.

The section, read from left to right, shows an auditorium that rakes from a gap between it and the stage upward toward the back of the hall. The auditorium consists of a rail (C), seven rows of seats (D), a walkway (F), thirteen rows of seats (G), another rail (H), and finally a sloped platform (I, L) bisected by a rail (K). Near H is drawn a stylized eye from which proceeds a broken line showing an unobstructed line of sight to the front edge of the stage platform (raised 4' above the hall floor).

The plan (rotated 180°) likewise shows the gap to the left, and the auditorium to the right with the seating now clearly disposed in roughly concentric arcs. Embraced by the seven forward rows of seats stands the central 'Isl' or platform for the king (K), raised three steps and flanked by seats for lords against the side walls (L, LL). Behind the seven rows (meant for ladies and the king's servants) are a walkway (G) and thirteen more rows of seats, the latter disposed in relatively flat arcs. At ground level a passageway runs beneath the upper rows through a gallery or 'vault' and continues uncovered between the forward rows. Beyond the upper seats at the upper level is a 'slope scaffold' for standees, with rails to keep them from 'ouerpressing' one another. Beneath the 'slope scaffold' are false walls to prevent access to the space beneath the seats, and a pair of square stair houses (B) against the side walls for access to the standing room above. Note that C on the plan refers to 'the entrys on eyther side the skreene,' for Christ Church hall had two doorways into the lower end of the hall (each marked A in the plan) rather than one as in modern times. (It is unclear whether the 'skreene' was a feature of the hall or of the temporary structure.) Just within the doorways stood a kind of portico with lights inset to illuminate the foyer. A note on the section reveals that the auditorium was designed for 200 in the seven forward rows, 350 in the thirteen back rows, 130 standees in front of K, and as many again behind, for a total of 810 'without pressing.'

Further details are available in external documents (see pp 278, 295–6, 299, 301, 303–7, 314, and 329). From these we discover the project was supervised by the clerk of the works, identifiable as Simon Basil, with advice from Mr (Inigo) Jones (recently back from Italy).

External documents also reveal a change of plan. Although, as an observer noted, the designers wished the king to sit at the uniquely advantageous viewing point demanded by 'art perspective' (see p 295), the king and his advisors cared only that he be seen to best advantage. The same observer noted that the 'isle' was pushed back a full 28' from the stage: thus the seven forward rows, so carefully designed to conform to principles outlined by the Italian theatre architect Sebastian Serlio, must have been entirely rebuilt. (Orrell, *Quest*, p 133, speculates in an architectural drawing of his own on the appearance of the theatre after the changes had been carried out.) One result was that the king could neither see well nor hear well. Thus the earliest perspective theatre known in England, designed in part by Inigo Jones, was changed almost beyond recognition to accommodate the deeply rooted prejudices of the audience, particularly the king.

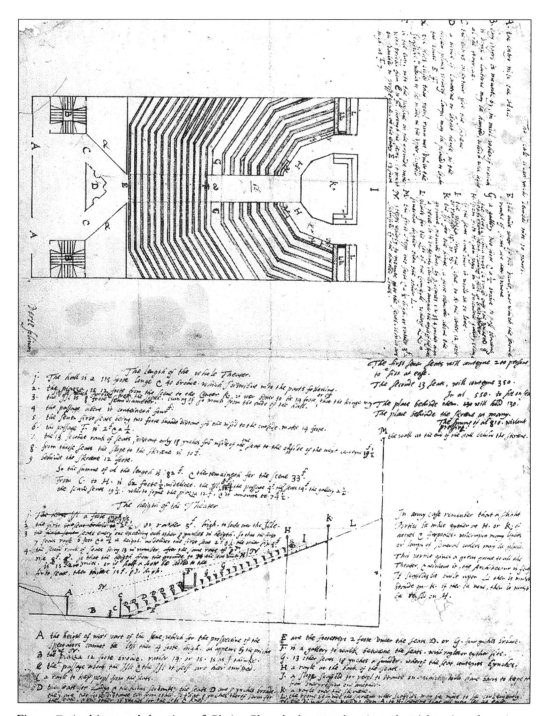

Figure 7 Architectural drawing of Christ Church theatre, showing plan (above) and section (below), with annotations.

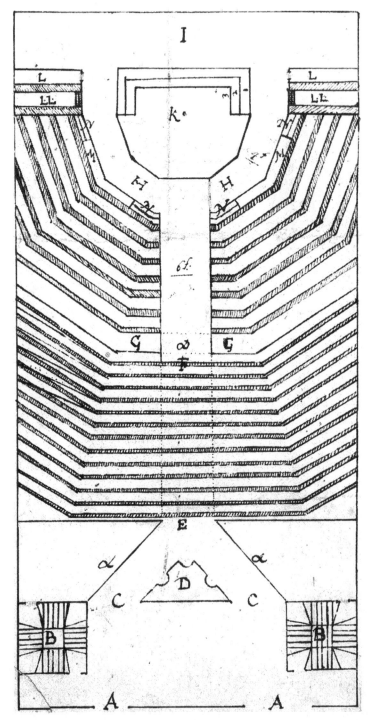

Figure 8 Plan of Christ Church auditorium (entrances at bottom and stage platform at top).

Transcription of the notes to the diagrams (the exact arrangement of the text in respect to the sketches has not been reproduced, but the relative positioning of the blocks of text has been indicated):

f [1]   *(Notes accompanying the plan)*

The scale is an ynch deuided into 10 parts.

A. the entry into the Hall.   5
B. easy stayrs to mounte by, in midl wherof which is voyde a lanterne may bee hanged, which will light al the stayrcase.
C. the entrys on eyther side the skreene.
D. a kinde of lanterne or light house, in the hollow places wherof lamps may bee placed to light the vaute E.F.   10
α. the sides closed that peopl runn not vnder the scaffolde. needles to bee made in the vpper scaffold.
E. is the entry into the passage on the grounde noted with pricks from E to F. through the seats. It must be vaulted in prospectiue, at the entry E 13 foote high at F. 7.   15
F. the ende [wher] of the vault, ouer which the seconde ranke of seats are heer drawne.
G. a gallery two foote & a ½ broade to pass betweene the seats, which must be raysed ouer the passage α, 8 y. to pass rounde about, leauing 7 foote at least-vnder.   20
H. from F. to H. you pass in an vncouered gallery because if the seats came ouer it would bee to lowe.
I. the piazza from the scene, to K. the center, 12 foote. or rather 14' or 15.
K. the Isl for the kinge, a foote eleuated aboue the grounde, mounted vnto   25 by 3 degrees 1.2.3[.] 4 ynches high a peece. it is vnæqualy deuided to aunswer the angls of the seats.
L. places for the Lords of the Counseyle wherof L.L. is somewhat higher then the other L.
M. the first stepp two foote & a ½ high. or rather 3 f.:   30
N. stepps whereby to mounte into the seats. which are signified by the hached lines.

Verte folium

35

f [2]   *(Notes above the section)*

The length of the whole Theater.

1. The hall is a 115 foote longe & 40 broade. which I distribut into the parts following.
2. the piazza is 12 foote from the scene to the Center K. it wer better to bee 14 foote, ∧⌈or 15⌉ that the kinge may sit so much further from the scene. cutting of so much from the ende of the hall.   5
3. the Isl is 8 foote ⌈in⌉ semi diameter.
4 the passage about it conteineth four f.:
5 the seuen first seats being two foote [broade] distant from the insid to the outside. make 14 foote.
6. the passage F. is 2 f. & a ½.   10
7 the 13 seconde rank of seats, distant only 18 ynches from inside of [the] ∧⌈one⌉ seat to the ou∧⌈t⌉side of the next conteyne 19 f. ½.
8. from thoose seats the slope to the skreene is 10 f.
9 behinde the skreene 12 foote.

> So the summe of al the length is 82 f. & ther remaineth for the   15
> scene 33 f.
> From C. to H. is 62 foote ½. uidelicet. the Isl [8 ½ f.] [f.] ∧⌈8 f.⌉ the passage 4 f. the ∧⌈7⌉ seats 14 f. the gallery 2 ½. the second seats 19 ½. wherto joyne the piazza 12 f., & it amounts to 74 f. ½.

20

The heigth of the Theater

1. [The Kings Isl a foote high]
2 the first [st⟨.⟩] seat behind [it] ∧⌈the Isle⌉ 2 f. ½: or rather 3 f. high. to looke ouer the Isle.
3 the [first seuen] seats euery one exceeding ech other 8 ynches in heigth. so   25 that the first 7 seats rayse 6 foot & a ½ in heigth. videlicet the first seat 2 f. & ½. the other six. 4 f.:
4. the second rank of seats being 13 in number, after the same rate of 8 yn., rise 8 f. 8 y. so that the heigth from the grounde to [H.] the seat vnder H is 15 f. [10] 2 ynches. or if half a foote bee added to the first seate,   30 then thyare 15 f. 8 y. high.

(Notes below the section)

A   the heigth of next part of the scene; which for the prospectiue of the   35 spectators cannot bee less then 4 foote high. as appears by the prickt line N.
B   the piazza 12 foote broade. rather 14. or 15. 15 as I thinke.
[C] the passage about the Isle and the Isl it self are heer omitted.
C   a rayle to keep peopl from the seats: 40

3–5/ it wer … the hall.: *added later in same hand*   23–4/ or rather … the Isle.: *added later in same*
23/ seat behind: *lightly cancelled (?)*   hand

D   the seats for Ladys & the Kings servants; the seats D are 8 ynches broade.
    they are two foote distante ech from other. so that 8 ynches therof serue
    for the seate, & the other 16 ynches for the legs & knes.
E   are the footesteps 2 foote vnder the seats D. or G. four ynches broade.
F. is a gallery to walk betweene the seats. with rayles on eyther side.   5
G. 13 other seats 18 ynches a sunder. wherof the seat conteyns 6. ynches.
H   a rayle at the back of the seats.
I   a slope scaffold for peopl to stande on. which should haue barrs to keepe
    them from ouerpressing one another.
K. a rayle ouer the skreene.   10
L. the roome behinde the skreene wher scaffolds may bee made to see
    conveniently.
M. the wall at the end of the Hall behind the skreene
N. the visual line passing from A. to H. shewing that all may see at ease.

                                                                                           15

(Notes above and to the right of the section)

The first seuen seats will conteyne 200 persons to sitt at ease.
The seconde 13 seats, will conteyne 350.
                        In al 550. to sitt on seats   20
The place behinde them. [130] will hold 130.
The place behinde the skreene as many.
                The summe of al 810. without pressing.

    In anny case remember that a slight Portico bee made eyther at H. or   25
    K. of hoopes & firrpooles. wherupon many lights or lamps of seueral
    coulers may bee placed.
    This portico giues a great grace to all the Theater, & without it, the
    Architectur is false.
    If scaffolds bee built upon L. then it must stande on K. if ther bee none,   30
    then it must bee reysed on H.

8/ slope: e *corrected over* p
13/ M. ... skreene: *part of key to section, but written adjacent to M where it appears on diagram*

APPENDIX 2
Technogamia, or The Marriages of the Arts at Woodstock (1621)

Poems

Barten Holyday's play *Technogamia, or The Marriages of the Arts*, first performed at Christ Church on 13 September 1618, was performed again before James I at Woodstock on 26 August 1621, a Sunday. Although the performance occurred outside the limits of Oxford, documents are included here by reason of its direct connection to Christ Church. This second performance ignited a furore in verse, in which contending wits capitalized on the fact that Sunday was a sacred 'holiday.'

Fourteen poems have been selected for presentation here in full, in an order determined by seven (A, C, D, E, G, I, J) that appear consecutively in BL: MS Sloane 542, ff 38–40.

With a single exception (Poem D), only one MS source has been selected for each poem (the sources are fully identified). Each poem transcribed here is followed by notes, by references, and by a list of libraries in which MS copies are known to survive. Since Cavanaugh (see below) provides highly detailed annotations of ten of the fourteen poems, only light annotation is attempted here. Notes on still other poems are presented in textual notes or in editorial notes following the transcriptions.

REFERENCE WORKS CITED:
Sister M. Jean Carmel Cavanaugh (ed), Technogamia *by Barten Holyday. A Critical Edition* (Washington, DC, 1942).
Margaret Crum (ed), *First-Line Index of English Poetry, 1500–1800, in Manuscripts of the Bodleian Library, Oxford*, 2 vols (Oxford, 1969).
Nichols, *Progresses of King James*, vol 4, pp 1109–12.

Copies in the Bodleian Library may be traced via Crum, others via internal first-line indexes: British Library, London (BL); Folger Shakespeare Library, Washington, DC (Folger); Harvard University, Houghton Rare Books Library (Harvard); National Library of Wales, Aberystwyth (NLW); and Yale University, Beinecke Rare Books Library (Yale).

A)   A Satyr made against Mr Holydayes Technogamia or rather
          Technobigamia, presented before ye kings ma*i*estie at woodstock   30

29/ Technogamia: *Cavanaugh, p xxxi, transcribes incorrectly as* Technogana on friday 26 of Aug*ust* 1621 by the students of Christchurch.

Quid dignum tanto ferat hic promissor hiatu?

Whoop holiday, why then twil nere be better   5
why al ye guard, that never saw a letter
Save those vppon their coates, whose wit consists
In Archyes, bobs, & Garrets, saucy iests,
Deride our *Christ Church* play and swear that they
Nere kept ye doore to such a midnighte play   10
why Cambridg Dulman pitcht beyond it far
They fell two barrs short of Albumasar
Besides they feasted with a hen that nighte
wherein ye L*or*d vicechancelour vsd their mighte
Now both their guts are empty and their eare   15
Could neither cause nor noise of Laughter heare |
Our hobby horse came short of theirs, but yet
wee did excel them in ye flash of wit
we had an Ape forsooth, bare three yeares old
Should doe more tricks then Colli westons could   20
An excellent ape god is my rightful iudge
A most fine Ape, could skip, & leape and trudge
Ly stil or caper most prodigious bouts
An active Ape and yet compos'd of clouts.
    Why how now saucy groome, go medle with   25
Your bil and holbeard, scour your rusty teeth
With the remainder of ye last kild steere
And scowre your nasty throates with bloxford beere
Do you deride his worth? who dare vphold you
No more, be husht, and say a freind hath told you   30
Els heele in fury come you naked strip
And scourge you with a Sixteen knotted whip.
Doe you not know, that al this was begot
(I speake my conscience) when it was his lot

3/ Quid ... hiatu?: *'What shall this promissor produce worthy of such a big mouth?'; cp Horace,* Ars Poetica *138*
10/ ye doore: *at Woodstock the king's guards rather than students served as doorkeepers*
11/ Dulman: *a character in George Ruggle's* Ignoramus, *performed for the king at Cambridge on 8 March and 13 May 1615; see Nelson (ed),* Cambridge, *vol 2, pp 865–78, 902–3*
12/ Albumasar: *a character in Thomas Tomkis'* Albumazar *of 9 March 1614/15, see above*
17–18/ Our hobby horse ... wit: *Cambridge's* Ignoramus *was famous for the appearance of a hobby horse: see* Poem M
20/ Colli westons: *Cavanaugh was unable to identify; possibly an ape-ward. Colly Weston is the name of a town in Northamptonshire*

To be at truce with study, that this mirth
At first edition was but fiue weekes birth.
Yet no abortiue. Set a higher price
Vppon his work at least let not your eyes
make an accute bad comment that which yee   5
Obiect was grosse was his best poetry
A Poet is a maker and tis more
To make an ape, then teach one [be] made [fo] before.
This answer'd, think you hard your captaine say
Silence or els you shall not eate to day.   10
So, now they are gonne but see more anger yet
Theres one hath begd monopolyes of wit
fastidious brisk ye Courtier, see it grinneth
A made a ballad and it did begin with
It is not full as yet a fortnight since   15
Christ Church at woodstock entertained ye Prince
And vented have a studyed toy (pray mark this)
Long as ye seige of Troy to please ye marquess
Good Sir a word for all your silk and sattin
Yet I may safely sweare you know no latin   20
And wil you talk sir None must iudge his parts.
But such as are wel skild in all the Arts
Nor is it fit you iest on him Sir, since
He late hath conquer'd a faire latin prince,
He hath a zelous sword if you he heares   25
Be sure heele cut of your rebellious eares,
fly to ye Globe or Curtaine with your trul,
Or gather musty phrases from ye Bul,
This was not for your dyet he doth bring
what he prepar'd for our Platonique King. | 30
Goe court your mistres sir hees likewise gon
And I am left halfe angry hear alone
Glad that I have ye Poet so commended
Mad that such dull inventions were commended
To such a sacred audience, was his muse   35
Tongue ty'de, or witt bound? that she did refuse
To lend new matter, or els did her deeme
Crambe bis cocta was of such esteeme?

18/ Long ... marquess: *reference is to a poem written on Cambridge plays of 1615; see Nelson (ed)*, Cambridge,
    vol 2, pp 866–7, ll.7–8
27/ Globe, Curtaine: *London theatres*
28/ ye Bul: *the Red Bull, a London theatre*

what though Ben Iohnson made some alteration
Yet stil he built vppon ye old foundation
Nay more tis feared ye second repetition
wil plague ye print, or els with a new edition
The title this, A pleasant Comedy   5
Lately presented to his maiesty.
The prince ye marques, & ye Courtiers prudent
At woodstock mannor by ye *Christ Church* student.
would once twere come to that, for then mighte wee
Be cleared from a general obloquy   10
for most beleiue, nor wil they change theire minde
That al ye vniversity combin'd
In ye performance, and with out al doubt
To countenance toy, twas so given out
Nor at ye court alone, more was ye pitty   15
Tis so beleiu'd in villadge towne and citty
Nay I haue hard ye Rascal black gard say,
Schollers run home, study and mend your play
Horrible Truth shall priuate weaknes bee
A slander to ye vniversity.   20
Giue Cambridge such occasion us to mock
And make poor Oxford a pure laughing stock
O fate of life, and can I hould my peace
Vrg'd thus, & from reueng so iust surcease
Twere but the wit of iustice now to raile   25
Vppon ye Poet, but twil not availe
And therefore out of mercy Ile be free
To pitty and giue counsel with out fee.
The better to digest his new disgrace
I would not haue him run to such a place   30
where it may bee preferment to endure
To teach some schools or els to starue some cure.
A milder course is better let him get
Commendatory letters and intrete
His worthy freind iudicious Mr Ley   35
To write a Persian censure on his play.

Source of this transcription: Folger: MS V.a.345, pp 140–2

1–2/ what though ... foundation: *the clear implication that Ben Jonson altered (improved?) the play has not
   been verified*
36/ a Persian censure: *ie, of Persius*

References: Crum W2255; Nichols, pp 1109–10 (first six lines only); Cavanaugh, pp xxxi–xxxvii

Note: Attributed to Peter Heylyn (see p 427). Followed in BL: MS Sloane 542, ff 38–9, by 'The Epigram' (Poem C)

Other copies: Bodl., BL, Folger, Harvard (followed by 'The King and the Court' – see p 789), Yale

B)   An Answere to ye Satyr.

> Thou that as yet hast no name of thine owne   10
> But hopest by traducing his to be knowne
> Enioy thy dear purchase, yet not without laughter.
> Be thy name halfe Holyday euer after
> for in learning and wit I would haue thee belieue
> Where Holyday comes thou art but his Eue.   15

Source of this transcription: Folger: MS V.a.345, p 142
References: Nichols, p 1112; Cavanaugh, p xxxvii
Note: Apparently unique. Attributed to Peter Heylyn (see Appendix 13, p 886)

C)   Mr Merideth on Christ Church Play

> Att Christ Church marriage act before the King
> That thos maiestes should not want an offering
> The King himselfe did offer; what I pray?   25
> Hee offred twice or thrice to goe away.

Source of this transcription: Folger: MS V.a.97, p 44
References: Crum C229, T392; Cavanaugh, pp xxix–xxxi
Note: Followed by Poem D. More copies survive of this poem than of any other that survives from the controversy. Crum A1341 identifies 'And you have offered too methinks, your pleasure' as an answer. See also Appendix 13, p 886.
Other copies: Bodl., BL, Folger, Harvard, NLW, Yale

D)   (1) Holyday of Christ Church his answere to it   35

> More trouble yet, twas but an organist
> And fooles & fidlers may do what they list,
> But could ye Chanter suffer him to play
> Such foolish verses on a holy day.   40

21/ Mr Merideth: *William Meredith, organist of New College, subject also of Crum H886*
37/ an organist: *William Meredith*

Source of this transcription: Folger: MS V.a.345, p 13
References: Crum M462
Note: Attributed in Poem D(2) to Holyday. Nichols, p 1109, cites as 'Our Arts...'

    (2) The Reply   5

    What more anger yet? twas but an Organist
    ffidlers and fooles may say what they list
    But would the Chanter giue him leaue to play
    Such idle Iigges vpon an Holliday.   10

Source of this transcription: Folger: MS V.a.97, p 44
References: Crum W615–16
Other copies: Bodl., BL, Folger, Yale

E)   Vpon Christ church play acted before King Iames at Woodstock

    Brag on old *Christ Church* neuer frett nor greeue,
    But in thy practise let proud Wolsey liue
    Who neuer thought he well performd that thing   20
    Was not about or els aboue ye King.
    His fault was ego first & then rex meus
    Thine greater when as rex is ioynd with deus,
    God nor ye Kinge seem'd to approuue that play
    That made his saboth lesse then holy day   25
           ye play was made by Holyday of *Christ Church*

Source of this transcription: Folger: MS V.a.345, p 12
References: Crum B520; Nichols, p 1111; Cavanaugh, p xxxix
Note: Answered by Poem F
Other copies: Bodl., BL, Folger, Yale

F)   If I can iudge a sick man by his fitt
    The Poet hath more heresie then witt
    for if the last verse of the 8th say true,   35
    What ever his country be he is a Iew.

Source of this transcription: Bodl.: MS. Rawlinson D.1048, f 61v
References: Crum I812; Nichols, p 1111; Cavanaugh, p xxxix (note)

    5/ The Reply: *ie, to Mr Merideth on Christ Church Play (Poem C)*
    36/ a Iew: *ie, Jewish because he considers the sabbath Saturday rather than Sunday*

Note: Answers Poem E
Other copies: Bodl., BL

G)   I could forgiue thy macharoing rimes
            Did they condemne mee ⌜onely⌝ and thes times.   5
            But how comes Wolsay in, why dost thou lay
            My faults on him? hee founded not my play.
            Nor doe wee in our Oxford Wolsey say
            When wee intend to rayle, but wee pray.
            And what hath Sunday done? Why dost thou spite   10
            God, for my sake? and rob him of his right?
            The Saboth in thy throat, better bee dumbe,
            Then by thy phrase deny yat Christ is come.

Source of this transcription: BL: MS Sloane 1792, f 64
References: Nichols, p 1111; Cavanaugh, p xxxix
Note: Attributed to Barten Holyday
Other copies: BL, Yale

H)   Cambridge men on Hollyday and his play before ye King/ terme newes   20
            from Cambridge

            Blame me not (muses) cause I often play
            for it is lawfull vppon a Hollyday
            shold I play more, I doe but what is fitt   25
            Play is a good subiect, for an idle witt
            Sith yat such playinge, I doe not affect
            But can, & will my idlensse correct
            which to prove true, my more yan three-bare verse
            Strange newes from out of Cambrige shall ∧⌜reherse⌝   30
            Cambridge schollers laugh, & laughinge say
            Christ Church men in Oxford made a play
            A brave play, a play fitt for the kinge
            Nay such a play ye like was never seene
            It ∧⌜cost⌝ them silver it cost ∧⌜them⌝ gold   35
            It made yem give great Tom a lesser mold
            It yem all soe poore, yat it is sed |
            yat they for thirst wold nothing eat but bred

12–13/ The Saboth ... is come: *ie, his critic fails to acknowledge that the Christian sabbath is Sunday*
28/ idlensse: *for* idlenesse
37/ It: *for* It left *or* It made (?)

for all their charges, & for all theire cost
wh⌈e⌉n all came to all, 'twas but labor lost
ye King, ye prince, ye Marquesse all his traine
were come, whome Christ Church men wold entertain
who with a play yet of ye last edition   5
scorning ye helpe of foole or of Physition
ye Marquest sent his Coach (as men say)
To fetch ye players royally away
Being come to Court, & by ye guard embraced
Vpp in ye highest cockloft they were placed   10
They had noe sooner brought ye prologue out
But streyght ye King begann to turne about
And asked ye Marquesse if they had not done
who stright replyed they had but new begun
with yat ye King slept 2 howers & more   15
ye nobles they runne tumblinge out of doore
they went (say Christ Church men to laugh willing
because they durst laugh before ye king
ye King begining now his 3 howers sleepe
Their mery bells such ginling nos'd did keepe   20
yat he awakid, & shaking of his head
wish'd them all hang'd for keping him from bed
he cold not laugh to see such foolish toyes
but cals his foole to mocke those Christ Church boyes
It did soe well content him that he swore   25
this is soe good, yat Ile see it noe more |
ye play being donne, he sent his noble men,
to know who 't was that worthy play did pen
they cold not ask'd for Hollyday did cry
Looke you for him yat made this play, 't was I   30
These be some blankes & here is pen & Inke
you [doe] come to give me a liuing as I thinge
Noe sayd ye nobles, which did his courage coole
ye king wol'd have you, shake bands bands with his foole
yee scholers, fy I meane you Christ Church men   35
As you like this, soe make a play agen
ye king to grace you more, gave you a marke
& bid you seeke your bedes in wod stocke parke

17/ (say ... men: *closing parenthesis omitted*
32/ a liuing: *earlier actors and playwrights had been granted a living by the monarch: see pp 130, 133; and*
Nelson (ed), Cambridge, vol 1, p 243 (Edward Halliwell)
32/ thinge: *for* thinke

There was a grace, to heer ye king thus say
I loved you well before you made this play
Nay ye blacke guard w*hi*ch knew noe letter
Cold say ye play was good, where there noe better
for shame leave of, if youle gett some prayes   5
study a while & read Ben Iohnsons playes.

Source of this transcription: BL: MS Egerton 923, ff 63v–4v
References: Crum B384
Note: Followed by Poem I
Other copies: Bodl., BL

I)   Barten Holiday to the Puritan on his Technogamia.

            'Tis not my person, nor my play,   15
            But my sirname, Holiday,
            That does offend thee, thy complaints
            Are not against me, but the Saints;
            So ill dost thou endure my name,
            Because the Church doth like the same,   20
            A name more awfull to the puritane
            Than Talbot unto france, or Drake to Spaine.

Source of this transcription: *Wits Recreations* (London, 1640; STC: 25870, No 485)
References: Nichols, p 1111; Cavanaugh, pp xxxix–xl
Note: Presumably by Barten Holyday
Other copies: BL, Yale

J)   An aunswere to A skandall layd
            on Mr Merideth. p:35:   30

            Nor Organist, nor ffidler, nor yet ffoole,
            Three termes equivalent in yo*ur*e learned schoole,
            Compos'd those lines, it was A Sparke y*at* had
            A strayne y*at* made your noble ffestus mad.   35
            It was noe antheame singer, though y*at* day
            did crave an antheame rather then A play.
            'Twas one y*at* wonders how A Poet can
            Make his free Muse to turne A iourney man.
            Six Miles his Muse did travell, this I thinke   40
            The cause y*at* made his verses feete to stinke.

4/ where: *for* were   30/ p:35: *Yale, Osborn Shelves, B200, p 35*

His play at first had not soe sweete A strayne,
But y*at* ye 2nd action was as vayne.
Seconds are Musicks discords, & their tone
Yeeldes at ye best, but harsh division.
Whiffling Tobacko, & Corinna's kisse   5
Being now growne stale were well-com'd w*i*th A Hisse.
Mongst his additions, 'tis not yet decided
Why his Ape Carrier had noe Wife provided.
Now, by my ffayth, & Troth, it is not well,
d'ee thinke he's willing to leade Apes to Hell?   10
Why was his Ape not married, since 'tis cleare
Artes are but Natures Apes, yet married are?
His Antequaries part I must vpholde
As well befitting any play y*at*s olde.
But I must pitty Greenes, & Euphues wrong   15
Brought in by Head, & Shoulders in A throng.
Whence had your Poet those distracted fits?
I thinke he ne're consulted w*i*th ye witts. |
I marvile how it came into his minde
To take ye Artes, & leave ye Witts behinde!   20
Some thinke y*at* his pure Genius did repine,
Because he once put Sugar in his Wine.
Thus ye grapes mixture w*hi*ch ye wits defy
Had made his braynes produce this Rapsody.
Now if heareafter he dare vndertake   25
To deale w*i*th Hymens torches, let him make
A constant vow allwayes to keepe them in,
And let them n'ere goe out, O 'tis A sinne;
Next time such Torches vnto Woodstock fly,
They'le scarce be knowne from Ignes fatui.   30
Those other notes, w*hi*ch he was branded with
Were never chaunted by Will Meredith.

Source of this transcription: Yale, Osborn Shelves, B200, pp 36–7
References: Crum N237b
Note: Answers Poem D. Bodl.: MS. Malone 21, f 73, lacks closing couplet. The couplet on
    p 780, ll.40–1, is cited separately in H.L.'s *Gratiae Ludentes. Jests from the Universitie*
    (London, 1638; *STC*: 15105) (see pp 788–9)
Other copies: Bodl., Yale

15/ Greenes: *Robert Greene, writer*
15/ Euphues: *protagonist of two popular prose works by John Lyly*

K)   On the play acted by the Oxford students at Woodstock before ye King: 1621

Rome for a new songe
Which shall bee as longe
   Almost as a Technogamia   5
If you thought it not pretty
Were the tune like the ditty
   I durst pockett vpp the ly=a |
Helpe yee bonny sweet faces
Of the gracefull graces   10
   And goldy locks Apollo,
Thou harmonius glee
Of the Muses thrice three
   Come hearken to my hallow.
On Woodstock high way   15
In garments most gay
   Goes Oxford amplest foundacion
With their horse & coach
Though without a caroach
   In Pontificiall fashion.   20
ffirst leavinge high street
As it was most meete
   They hurry through Bocardo:
Had they there still stayd
How had Oxford beene made   25
   Though now shee is not mard=o
Next know good people
That Maudlins steeple
   Brought Maudlin College in mind
Their scæne should not downe   30
They'le serue for the towne
   But these leaue them 2 leagues behind.
O but, had you seene
That angry spleene
   And sheepes eyes they cast at St Iohns.   35
When they passed by
Soe disdainfully
   T'would haue grieud you twice & once. |
St Iohns they sed
And shake their head   40

3/ Rome for a new songe: *ie, make room or make way for a new song*

Your actions quite forgott
Wee are those they
Goe to act a play
   ffoure miles beyond Woluercott.
Thus they passe to St Giles=es   5
Which not many miles is
   Soe farre they are on ye way:
To relate each toy
Hap't in their convoy
   Were as tedious as their play.   10
Now thinke they carowse
In his Maiesty's house
   Nere the bower of Rosamunda
And their play there they acted
ffor soe twas compacted   15
   On noe worse day then Sunday
What will it pra'vayle
Though the Puritanes rayle
   Hee knowes not what they did intend
They nere then had ventred   20
On the stage to haue entred
   Had not Sunday beene Holydayes friend.
To keepe the doore stifflier
They gott a Diuine whifflier
   Whose swearinge the company heard.   25
Who bore greater stroke
In his veluet cloake
   Then the best of his Maiestys guard.
On Sunday night
When ye tapers were light   30
   The Kinge was come into the hall. |
fforth a black gowne breaks
And tragically speakes
   A prologue Comicall.
Great Kinge quoth hee   35
Most humble wee
   Present vnto your gracious view
A most quaint straine
Past vulgar braine
   A refin'd play both old & new.   40

13/ Rosamunda: *character in* Don Quixote; *see also p 784, ll.23–4*

Now fye, fye, for shame
Giue a second name
   Hereticq*ue* Holyday:
Tis worth the listninge
That his second chrystninge   5
   Made an Anababtisticall play.
This or some other thinge
Did not please the kinge
   Who was as still as a Mouse is
Till the glasse made him cry   10
I feare I shall Dye
   In one of the best of my houses.
And now good Holyday
Alacke & welladay
   A ffauorable censure god send you   15
Else for all thy blancks
Thou wilt gett thee small thanks
   But goe home as thou cam'st & mend yee.
Yet this aboue all
Poeta his braule   20
   With gramm*a*r may not bee forgott:
Which disnobleth quite
The notorious fight
   Betwixt the Briscan & Don Quixott.
Nor may wee escape   25
The deuice of the Ape
   The Hobby=horse or Morrice
Which would make your diaphange
Your dialaughter ⟨.⟩oe to twange
   Had you beene as dull as a doore is.   30
And Astronomies health
Though it came in by stealth
   Was soe longe that ye kinge cryed out
By my soule I feare
Theyle drinke all my beare   35
   Before this health goe about.
The kniues inuention
Was a braue intention
   To their iuglinge tricks that next were

23–4/ The notorious ... Quixott: *this reference to the battle between Don Quixote and the Biscayan extends the Quixote allusion in the reference to Rosamunda (p 783, l.13)*
24/ Betwixt ... Quixott.: *for lack of space written to the right of (rather than below) the previous line*

To fitt it right
An Epithite
    Cannott bee found in Textor.
The length of the play
Had brought night to day   5
    And the *King* the leaues to number
Who when hee seene
Their lacke seauenteene
    In despayre hee fell in a slumber.
Oh! my dull brayne   10
That could not contayne
    One halfe of the thinges worth notinge
If in after tyme
Any iudge by my rime
    They may thinke the play worth nothinge.   15
Yett they were not well vsd
But I feare mee abusd
    Best thinges oft times Displease: |
Most that went in coach=boote
Returnd home on foote   20
    And I thinke twas not for their ease.
Lett that Ignoramus
The pure witt of Chamus
    His former prayers stint
Lett him yeeld the day   25
To his sport & play
    ffor this was a play in print.
And now to conclude
Though some thought it rude
    As who can stopp mens detraction?   30
Each one doth it singe
The court, guard, & Kinge
    Lord how famous is Christchurch action!
Yett before I doe goe
I will freely bestow   35
    This Epitaph on this dead play:
What a Sunday displayd
And a Holyday made
    Was scarce thought fitt for a workinge day.

7/ seene: *for* had seene
22/ Ignoramus: *the eponymous title of a 1615 Cambridge play*

Source of this transcription: Folger: MS V.a.162, ff 71v, 74–6
Note: Apparently unique. Previously printed in Bentley, *Jacobean and Caroline Stage*, vol 4,
   pp 591–5

L)   ON CHRIST-CHURCH PLAY AT WOODSTOCK.   5

         If wee, at Woodstock, haue not pleased those,
         Whose clamorous Iudgments lye in urging no'es,
         And, for the want of whifflers, have destroy'd
         Th' Applause, which wee with vizards hadd enjoy'd.   10
         Wee are not sorry; for such witts as these
         Libell our Windowes oftner, then our Playes;
         Or, if Their patience be moov'd, whose Lipps
         Deserve the knowledge of the Proctorships,
         Or iudge by houses, as their howses goe,   15
         Not caring if their cause be good or noe;
         Nor by desert, or fortune can be drawne
         To credit us, for feare they loose their pawne;
         Wee are not greatly sorry: but if any, |
         Free from the Yoake of the ingaged many,   20
         That dare speak truth even when their Head stands, by
         Or when the Seniors spoone is in the pye;
         Nor to commend the worthy will forbearer
         Though he of Cambridge or of Christchurch were,
         And not of his owne colledge; and will shame   25
         To wrong the Person, for his Howse, or Name;
         If any such be greiv'd, then downe proud spirit;
         If not, know, Number never conquerd Merit.

Source of this transcription: Richard Corbet, *Poëtica Stromata* ([Holland], 1648; Wing:
   C6273), 83–4
References: Nichols, p 1110; Cavanaugh, p xxxviii
Note: Printed in *The Poems of Richard Corbett*, J.A.W. Bennett and H.R. Trevor-Roper (eds)
   (Oxford, 1955), 70; discussed pp 140–3
Other copies: BL

M)   To his Friends of Christ-Church upon the mislike of the Marriage
           of the Arts acted at Woodstock.

           But is it true, the Court mislik't the Play,   40
           That Christ-Church and the Arts have lost the day;

That Ignoramus should so far excell,
Their Hobby-horse from ours hath born the Bell?

    Troth you are justly serv'd, that would present
Ought unto them, but shallow merriment; | 5
Or to your Marriage-table did admit
Guests that are stronger far in smell then wit.

    Had some quaint Bawdry larded ev'ry Scene,
Some fawning Sycophant, or courted queane;   10
Had there appear'd some sharp cross-garter'd man
Whom their loud laugh might nick-name Puritan,
Cas'd up in factious breeches and small ruffe,
That hates the surplis, and defies the cuffe:
Then sure they would have given applause to crown   15
That which their ignorance did now cry down.

    Let me advise, when next you do bestow
Your pains on men that do but little know,
You do no Chorus nor a Comment lack   20
Which may expound and construe ev'ry Act:
That it be short and slight; for if 't be good
Tis long, and neither lik't nor understood.

    Know tis Court fashion still to discommend   25
All that which they want brain to comprehend.

Source of this transcription: Henry King, *Poems, elegies, paradoxes, and sonnets* (London,
    1657; Wing: K501), 22–3
References: Crum B646; Cavanaugh, pp xl–xli
Note: BL: MS Additional 62134, f 16v, has been identified as King's original MS: 'But all
    is true....' Printed in *The Poems of Henry King*, Margaret Crum (ed) (Oxford, 1965), 67.
    Crum, p 196: 'These verses did not go beyond King's own family, and are not found with
    the satires and defences known to Nichols in manuscript miscellanies, though they are in
    Harl. (Cf. P. 57)'
Other copies: Bodl., BL

N)   In Concionem *Magist*ri Bartini Holiday
        in Cruce D*ivi* Pauli habitam Nov*ember* 5º.

    2/ Their Hobby-horse ... Bell: *Cambridge's* Ignoramus *was famous for the appearance of a hobby horse: see*
    Poem A

Woodstochiæ excepta est nullo tua Fabula risu:
   At jam cachinnos Concionator moves.
Si me audis, Bartine, tuas, aut in Cruce Pauli
   Comœdias dabis, vel in Scenâ Homilias./

5

Thy Comœdy at Woodstock wan no praise
But preaching thou movest every man to laughter
Dost heare me Bartin? in Pauls Crosse thy playes
Or on the Stage thy Sermons act hereafter./

Source of this transcription: Harvard: Houghton MS Eng. 699, f [10]
References: Cavanaugh, p xli, citing *Huth's Inedited Miscellanies* (unpaginated, 'Epigrams')
Note: Apparently unique

Other Commentaries and Poems Concerning Woodstock

1) From a 16 February 1621/2 letter from John Chamberlain to Dudley Carleton:

> ...Here be certain verses [of] made of Dr Corbet deane of christchurch who
> preaching before the king at woodstocke last sommer was so grauelled that he 20
> was faine to geue ouer, neither had he better lucke in his play then in his
> preaching, for thincking to mend the matter with a comedie of the mariage
> of the Arts, yt proued so tedyous as well for the matter as the action, that the
> king indured yt with great impatience, wherupon the very boyes and children
> flouted yt [⟨.⟩] with a rime. A mariage we had but offering there was none, 25
> saue that the king offered twise or thrise to be gone....
>
> ...

Source of this transcription: PRO: SP/14/127, f 140
Note: Chamberlain incorrectly attributes *The Marriages of the Arts* to Corbet rather than to
    Holyday. (Corbet composed Poem L.) Chamberlain refers to two poems: first, to 'certain
    verses,' which no longer accompany the letter but which are described at the end of this
    appendix; second, to Poem C

2) From H.L., *Gratiae Ludentes. Jests from the Universitie* (1638)

    ...

             At Woodstocke by Schollers.
King James, of Famous memory be-ling at Woodstocke, the Schollers of
Christ-Church, presented him with a play, named the Marriage of the Artes,
a Comedy very good, but not well taken by the Court, whereon one made 40
this disticke to the Authour.

8/ Pauls Crosse: *site of an outdoor pulpit next to St Paul's Cathedral in London*

Sixe miles thy Muse had travell'd that I thinke.
The cause that made thy verses feete to stinke.

Source of this transcription: *STC*: 15105, pp 102–3
Note: These two verses are excerpted from Poem J (p 780, ll.40–1)

3)   One speaking this in the play at Woodstocke

As at a banquett some meates haue sweet some saore tast

10

Hoskins of Oxford standing by
as a spectator rimes openly to it.

Euen soe your dubllett is to short in the waste.

Source of this transcription: Folger: MS V.a.162, f 59v

Not cited here at length, because it does not comment on Holyday's play, is 'The King and the Court desirous of sport' (Crum T844), entitled 'On the Kinges being at Woodstocke, 1621.' The poem is printed in (Sir) John Mennes, *Wit Restor'd* (London, 1658; Wing: M1719), 62–3; and in Nichols, pp 1110–11. The concluding lines, beginning 'The reverend Deane with his ruffe starched cleane,' a satire on Richard Corbet (author of Poem L), survive separately: see Crum A394 and BL: MS Egerton 293, ff 10v–11 ('A Reverent Deane').

APPENDIX 3

The Royal Slave at
Hampton Court (1636/7)

William Cartwright's play *The Royal Slave*, first performed at Christ Church on 30 August 1636, was performed again at Queen Henrietta Maria's own request at Hampton Court on 12 January 1636/7. Although the performance occurred outside the limits of Oxford and with professional actors, documents are included here by reason of its close connection to Christ Church.

Although lacking a date, the Lord Chamberlain's Playlist has, since it was discovered in the nineteenth century, been associated with the 1637 Lord Chamberlain's Warrant and probably accompanied it. On this document and the warrant, once suspected of being forgeries but now regarded as genuine, see A.E. Stamp, *The Disputed Revels Accounts* (Oxford, 1930).

George Chalmers' *An Apology for the Believers* is the only surviving record of a personal payment to Cartwright by the king. Its source is a now-lost office book of Sir Henry Herbert, master of the revels, to which Chalmers, like Edmund Malone, had access (N.W. Bawcutt, *The Control and Censorship of Caroline Drama: The Records of Sir Henry Herbert, Master of the Revels 1623–73* (Oxford, 1996), 15–17; record printed p 200, No 358).

Letter of Queen Henrietta Maria to the University
Oxford, Bodleian Library, ms. Rawlinson D.912; 6 December 1636; English; paper; single sheet; 225mm x 340mm; autograph signature. Now bound as f 66 into a collection of official letters to and from the University, entitled 'Papers Relating to the University of Oxford.'

Lord Chamberlain's Warrant Book
London, Public Record Office, LC/5/134; 1634–41; English; paper; 230 leaves; 240mm x 360mm; contemporary pagination; original vellum binding, repaired in 1959, title in ink on front cover: 'Warrants ab Anno 1634 Vsque ad Annum 1641.'

Royal Warrant
London, Public Record Office, SP/16/352; 11 April 1637; English; parchment; single mb; 145mm x 290mm; writing lengthwise on 1 side only; no titles or endorsements (the names 'William Hawkins' and 'Iohannis Chapman,' presumably clerks of the privy seal, written by the scribe at the end of the document). Now bound in a guardbook and numbered 55.

Lord Chamberlain's Playlist
London, Public Record Office, AO/3/908 (22); 1636–7; English; paper; bifolium; 200mm x 300mm;
writing on first folio only.

Lord Chamberlain's Warrant
London, Public Record Office, AO/3/908 (23); 12 March 1636/7; English; paper; bifolium; 200mm x
305mm; text on f [1], endorsement on f [2v]: 'Warrant for payment of 240 li. vnto the Kinges Players
for Playes Acted 1636 1637 Anno 1637' and 'ovjto Iuly 37 Received in parte of this warrant C li. et
more 20 december 37 L li. et more L li. per me Eyllaerdt Swanston.'

Royal Payment for *The Royal Slave* (AC)
[Chalmers, George.] *An Apology for the Believers in the Shakspeare-Papers, Which Were Exhibited in
Norfolk-Street* (London, 1797).

1636–7
Letter of Queen Henrietta Maria to the University
Bodl.: MS. Rawlinson D.912
single sheet   *(6 December)*

5

       To Our Trusty and Wellbeloved ye Vicechancellour and
          Convocacion of ye Vniversity of Oxford.
   (signed) Henrietta Maria Regina
Trusty and Welbeloved, Wee greet you Well. The Cloathes together with ye
whole furniture and Ornaments belonging to that Play wherewith wee were   10
so much pleas'd att our last being in Oxford wee have Received: and doe
acknowledge for no contemptible Testimony of your Respect to Vs ye
Vnfurnishing your Selfe of such Necessaries meerly for our Accommodation.
A thing which wee doe not ∧ʳonlyꞋ take very kindly, but are Ready to
Remember very Really, whensoever you will furnish Vs with any Occasion   15
wherein [⟨....⟩] our ffavour may bee vsefull vnto you. In ye Meane time you
may bee confident that no Part of these things yat are come to our hands,
shall bee suffered to bee prostituted vpon any Mercenary Stage, but shall bee
carefully Reserv'd for our owne Occasions and particular Entertainments att
Court: With which assurance, together with thankes, and our best Wishes for   20
ye perpetuall fflourishing of your Vniversity. Wee bidd you hartily ffarewell.
Given vnder our hand[s] at Hampton Court ye sixt day of December. 1636.

Lord Chamberlain's Warrant Book   PRO: LC/5/134
p 158   *(15 March)*   25
...

Players warrant   A Warrant for payment of 240 li. vnto his Maiesties Players (vizt) 210 li. for

21 playes Acted by them at 10 li. a play & 30 li. more for the new Play
called The royall Slaue. March 15. 1636
...

p 165   *(4 April)*   5

...

Reward for the   To ye E*arl* of Denbigh*shire*
Roiall slaue   M*aste*r of ye Wardrobe
Wheras ye Charge of ye alterations, reparac*i*ons & addition⟨.⟩ which were
made vnto ye scene, Apparell & propertyes that were imployed for the setting   10
forth of ye new Play called the Royall slaue, which was lately Acted &
presented before his M*ai*estye at Hampton Court, together *with* the Charge
of Dancers & composers of Musique which were vsed therin, amounteth to
ye sum*m*e of One Hundred fifty fower pound*es* appearing by the billes of ye
seuerall persons imployed therin. Theis are to pray & require you to p*re*pare   15
A Bill for his M*ai*esties royall signature for a priuy seale to bee directed to ye
Tr*e*asurer & Vnder Tr*e*asurer of ye Exchequ*er* requireing & authorizing them
out of his M*ai*esties receipt there to pay or cause to bee payd vnto ye seuerall
persons heerafter named (vizt) to Peter Lehuc Property maker the sum*m*e of
50 li. to George Portman Painter the sum*m*e of 50 li. & to Estienne Nau &   20
Sebastian La Pierre for themselues & twelue Dancers the sum*m*e of 54 li.
amounting in ye whole to ye aforesayd sum*m*e of 154 li. to bee payd vnto
them *with*out Account imprest or other Charges to be sett vpon them or their
Executors for ye same or any part therof: And this shall bee *your* warr*a*nt.
Aprill 4. 1637./   25
To ye Signett

Royal Warrant   PRO: SP/16/352
single mb   *(11 April)*

                                                                                         30
Charles by the grace of God King of England Scotland ffrance and Ireland
defendor of the ffaith &c. To the Tr*e*asurer and vnder Tr*e*asurer of our
Exchequ*er* for the time being, greeting. Whereas the charge of the Alterac*i*ons
reparac*i*ons and addic*i*ons which were mad⟨. ..... .⟩he Scene, Apparell and
properties that were imployed for the setting forth of the New Play called the   35
Royall Slaue which was lately acted and presented before vs at Hampton Court,
together with the charge of Dancers and Composers of Musique, which
were vsed therein amounteth to the som*m*e of One hundred and ffiftie foure
pounds, As by the Bills of the seuerall persons imployed therein appeareth,

2/ 1636: *underlined*
9/ addition⟨.⟩: *letter lost through cropping of right margin*

Our will and pleasure is, and wee doe hereby will and command you out of
our Treasure remayning in the Receipt of our said Exchequer to pay or cause
to be paid vnto the severall persons hereafter named, vizt, to Peter le Huc
Propertie maker the somme of ffiftie pounds; to George Portman, Painter
the somme of ffiftie pounds and to Estienne Nau and Sebastian la Pierre for   5
themselues and twelue dancers the somme of ffiftie foure pounds, amounting
in the whole to the aforesaid somme of One hundred and ffiftie foure pounds.
The same to be taken vnto them without accompt imprest or other charges
to be sett vpon them or their executors for the some or any part thereof. And
these our bids shalbe your sufficient warrant and discharge in this behalf.   10
Given vnder our Privy seale at our Pallace of Westminster the Eleuenth day
of Aprill in the Thirteenth yeare of our raigne.
...

Lord Chamberlain's Playlist   PRO: AO/3/908 (22)   15
f [1]

                    Playes acted before the Kinge and Queene
                        this present yeare of the lord. 1636./
...   20
16 The 12th. of Ianuary the new play from Oxford. the Royall slave.
...

Lord Chamberlain's Warrant   PRO: AO/3/908 (23)
f [1]   *(12 March)*   25

Wheras by virtue of his Maiesties Letters Patentes bearing date the 16th of
Iune 1625 made & graunted in confirmation of diuers Warrantes & priuy
seales vnto you formerly directed in the time of our late Souueraigne Lord
King Iames, you are Authorized (amongst other things) to make payment   30
for Playes Acted before his Maiestye. Thees are to pray and require you out
of his Maiesties Treasure in your Charge to pay or cause to bee payd vnto
Iohn Lowen and Ioseph Taylor or either of them for themselues & the rest of
the Company of his Maiesties Players the summe of °two hundred & tenne°
poundes (beeing after the vsuall & accustomed rate of Tenne poundes for   35
each play) for One and Twenty Playes by them Acted, before his Maiesty at
Hampton Court & else where within the space of a yeere ended in February
last: And that you likewse pay vnto them the summe of °thirtye° poundes
more for their paynes in studying & Acting the new Play sent from Oxford
called The royall slaue which in all amounteth to the summe of Two Hundred   40

21/ 16: *ie, the sixteenth play on the list*

& forty pound*es*: And thees together w*i*th their Acquittance for the Receipt
therof shall bee your warr*a*nt. Whitehall the 12th of March. 1636./
(signed) Pembroke & Montgomery.

To Sir William Vuedale kn*igh*t
Tr*easu*rer of his Ma*iesti*es Chamber./   5
°v^t: Iunij 1638

Rece*iv*ed the same day & yeare of Sir William Vuedale

kn*igh*t Tr*easu*rer of his Ma*ies*t*ie*s Chamb*er* the som*m*e of   CCxl li.°
(signed) Eyllaerdt Swanston

240 li.   10

AC   ***Royal Payment for The Royal Slave***   Chalmers: *Apology*
pp 507–8   *(12 January)*

…The acting of Cartwright's Royal Slave, on Thursday the 12th of January   15
1636/7, before the King at Hampton-court, cost one hundred and fifty-four
pounds, exclusive of forty pounds, I which Sir Henry Herbert says the King
gave the author.…

    …

2/ 1636: *underlined*
6/ 1638: *underlined*

APPENDIX 4
New College Warden's Progress

The following payments are presented here 'faute de mieux,' as volumes in this series are organized by place rather than dynamically by journey. Francis W. Steer (comp), *The Archives of New College, Oxford* (London, 1974), 127, dates this MS *c* 1600. Steer's dating is confirmed by internal evidence. The MS identifies the sexton of 'Newton Longfield' (presumably Newton Longville, Bucks), one Quartermain, as having been parson forty years: the dates of Quartermain's tenure, 1558–1613, suggest *c* 1598; the MS names the vicar of Hornchurch as Charles Ryves: his tenure in that office implies a range of 1597–1611. The peripatetic warden was apparently either Martin Colepeper (1573–99) or George Ryves (1599–1613). Since the latter bore the same last name as the vicar of Hornchurch, and may well have been a relative, he seems the more likely of the two candidate wardens.

Much more information might be forthcoming if the MS could be fully restored.

A Warden's Progress Book
Oxford, New College Archives, 910; *c* 1600; English, Latin, Greek; paper; approximately 36 leaves; 200mm x 148mm (197mm x 120mm); unnumbered; poor condition, fire and water damage, many leaves stuck together; contemporary parchment binding is a folio from what appears to be a 12th-c. psalter.

c **1600**
A Warden's Progress Book   NC Arch: 910
f [3v]
...
Musicians   xij d.   5
...

f [4]
...
to ye musicions in ye morninge   xij d. 10
& to ther playinge at Drinking at m*aste*r wardens
appoyntem*en*t   ij s.
...

f [7]   *(London (?))*

...

To the trumpeters of ye Duke of lyniox by
m*aste*r wardenes appoyntme*n*t   v s.

...   5

f [10v]

...

There to Takely

...   10

At wallricks Hall in Takeley

...

To musicions   nothing they not playinge before I was gone

...
                                                                       15

f [13]

...

To Ca*m*bridge fro*m* Thetford 28 miles, hither, a Saterday night by six a clocke
The Hoste ther mr Woolfe at the Rose.

...   20

Sundaye Dinner for m*aste*r Wardens menne – himselfe m*aste*r Steward
& I Dyninge with M*aste*r D*r* Nevile Deane of Ca*n*terburye & Master of
Trynitye Colledge

...

To ye musicions   xij d. 25

...

9, 11/ Takely, Takeley: *Tackley, Oxfordshire*
18/ Thetford: *Little Thetford, Cambridgeshire*
19/ the Rose: *the Rose Inn, which gave its name to the modern Rose Crescent (near the Market)*

APPENDIX 5
College Lords and Merton's King of Beans

College lords, for the most part Christmas lords including both the king of beans ('rex fabarum') from Merton (1485–6 to 1539–40) and the Christmas Prince from St John's (1576–7, 1607–8), are discussed in the Introduction (see pp 612–13) and are the subject of extracts printed in the Records. Here generalized and undated references are brought together.

Texts and ceremonies relative to Oxford college lords are discussed by the following:

Boas (ed), *University Drama*, pp 3–10, 196.
George C. Brodrick, *Memorials of Merton College*, Oxford Historical Society 4 (Oxford, 1885), 46, 245, 249, 279.
Bernard W. Henderson, *Merton College* (London, 1899), 267.
H.H. Henson, 'Letters Relating to Oxford in the 14th Century from Originals in the Public Record Office and British Museum,' Fletcher (ed), *Collectanea*, pp 39–49.
Pantin (ed), *Canterbury College*, vol 3, pp 68–72.
John Peckham, *Registrum Epistolarum Fratris Johannis Peckham*, Charles T. Martin (ed), vol 1, Rolls Series 77 (London, 1882), xlvii.
Salter (ed), *Formularies*, pp 351, 439.
Salter (ed), *Registrum Annalium*, pp xviii–xix.

Also of importance are references cited under 'The Christmas Prince' in Appendix 6:1 and evidence from Cambridge: see Nelson (ed), *Cambridge*, vol 2, Index, especially under 'Christmas lords, colleges.'

Wood's *Athenae Oxonienses*, vol 3, col 480, gives the following account, which begins with an allusion to St John's:

the custom was not only observed in that coll*ege*, but in several other houses, particularly in Mert*on* Coll*ege*, where, from the first foundation, the fellows annually elected, about S. Edmund's day in November, a Christmas lord, or lord of misrule, stiled in their registers rex fabarum and rex regni fabarum: Which custom continued till the reformation of religion, and then that producing puritanism, and puritanism presbytery, the professors of it looked upon such laudable and ingenious customs as popish, diabolical and antichristian.

Also in *Athenae Oxonienses*, vol 1, col 456, Wood attributes to David de la Hyde: 'De Ligno & Fœno. Spoken in praise of Mr. Jasper Heywood, who was in the time of qu*een* Mary, rex regni fabarum in Merton college; which was no other than a Christmas lord, or a lord, or king of misrule.'

Wood's *History and Antiquities*, vol 2, pp 136–7, contains another account of de la Hyde's activities at Merton, this time dated 1557:

> The subject was 'de ligno et foeno' in praise of Mr. Jasp*er* Heywood, about this time King, or Christmas Lord, of the said Coll*ege* being it seems the last that bore that commendable office. That custom hath been as antient for ought that I know as the College itself, and the election of them after this manner. On the 19 of Nov*ember*, being the Vigil of St. Edmund, K*ing* and Martyr, Letters under seal were pretended to have been brought from some place beyond sea, for the election of a King of Christmas, or Misrule, sometimes called with us of the aforesaid College, Rex fabarum. The said letters being put into the hands of the Bachelaur Fellows, they brought them into the Hall that night, and standing, sometimes walking, round the fire, there reading the contents of them, would choose the senior Fellow that had not yet borne that office, whether he was a Doctor of Divinity, Law or Physick, and being so elected, had power put into his hands of punishing all misdemeanours done in the time of Christmas, either by imposing Exercises on the juniors, or putting into the stocks at the end of the Hall any of the servants, with other punishments that were sometimes very ridiculous. He had always a chair provided for him, and would sit in great state when any speeches were spoken, or justice to be executed, and so this his authority would continue till Candlemas, or much about the time that the Ignis Regentium was celebrated in that college.

This account by Wood contains some exaggerations, especially as to the antiquity of the tradition, corrected by Boas (ed), *University Drama*, pp 5–6.

Some 'texts' pertaining to college lord election ceremonies in Oxford have survived in ASC Arch: 182, ff 91v, 94–4v; and BL: MS Royal 10.B.IX, ff 129–33. (Another text had been transcribed in Salter (ed), *Formularies*, p 439, but the reference, BL: MS Harleian 5398, ff 132v–3, is apparently incorrect.) Transcribed below is one mock letter, from among the small number that survive, to provide a taste of the mock pomposity and ceremony that characterized the activities of college lords. (See also excerpts from the Christmas Prince festivities at St John's College in 1607–8, pp 340–81).

The texts may be broken down approximately thus:

– six mock letters (*c* 1440) introducing Merton College's 'king of beans' (BL: MS Royal 10.B.IX, ff 129–33). Discussed in Salter (ed), *Registrum Annalium*, pp xviii–xix, where the first letter is also transcribed. A satiric letter (*c* 1414–30) relating to Canterbury College also appears in BL: MS Royal 10.B.IX, ff 32v–3v and is transcribed in Pantin (ed), *Canterbury College*, vol 3, pp 68–72. Pantin suggests that the letter was written 'to enliven the Christmas festivities' and notes that this letter appears in the same MS as the Merton king of beans letters. The connection remains unclear.

    – three letters relating to the custom of electing a Christmas king. Two are described by
Martin in Peckham, *Registrum*, vol 1, p xlvii. Martin's MS reference is ASC Arch: 182,
ff 91v, 94. He makes no mention of the third letter, which remains untraced. All three
letters are printed in Henson, 'Letters Relating to Oxford,' pp 39–49, but without a
full declaration of sources.

    Under the name of Jasper Heywood, Bliss has added a note of his own in his edition of
Athenae Oxonienses, vol 1, col 665: 'Heywood exercised the office of Christmas prince, or
lord of misrule in his college (Merton); and among Wood's MSS. in the Ashmole museum
is an oration praising his admirable execution of his office, written by David de la Hyde....'
Although Bodl.: MS. Wood D.32, f 315, col 2, in the hand of Brian Twyne, contains a passage
that may have given rise to Wood's observations as cited above, no text of 'de ligno et foeno'
has yet been traced.

c 1400–22

Mock Letter from Neptune to the Nobles of the Kingdom of Beans
BL: MS Royal 10.B.IX
f 129v

...   5

Celestis progenies neptunus & magne dyane filius a ditis palacio ad maximi
Iovis artem Rector, dominus & patronus? omnibus & singulis Regni fabe
proceribus. Salutem cum pace & ad perpetue polecie precepta aures erigere/
manus apponere. & tanquam alis pennatis affeccionis pedibus prope conuolare.
Summus cunctorum opifex & genitor causatorum/ orbem terrarum infimum   10
sub statu condicionis huiusmodi stabiliuit. quod quamuis sperarum omnium
quasi basis existat. et stabile fundamentum. in diuisionis puluerem subito
solueretur. nisi nostre magnifice largitatis continuo potiretur humore sic
quecumque regio/ nobilitate stabilita regali si quando priuetur eadem in
diuisionem vertitur & nititur in occasum. Hinc est quod nostris auribus nuperime 15
iam intonuit relacio fidedigna. quod Rex vester eximius/ celsi frater attlantis,
renunciaturus seculo. famosissimi regni vestri septrum resignauit & arma Ne
tante regionis communitas nobis ab inicio precipue peramanda tanquam gens
sine capite populus sine principe vel oues pastore sublato, in direpcionem
incidant pariter et ruinam. Vobis iniungendo mandamus quatinus omni mora 20
postposita/ ad eleccionem noui regis celeriter festinetis/ eo procedentes consilio
vt quater in fratris rabiem Gole temperante, vestre nauis remigium ad vniuoce
portum concordie feliciter applicetis Quicquid in premissis feceritis/ nobis
fideliter intimantes/ cum proximo iam illuxerit festiuitas clementina. Scriptum
in portu pelionis. Instanti? quo thetis vndique bacho gaudebat honore.   25

...

7/ artem: *for* arcem

Oxford Play Bibliography

Plays listed in this appendix have been divided into four groups:

    Group 1: surviving play texts certainly or probably performed at Oxford

    Group 2: lost plays certainly, probably, or possibly performed at Oxford

    Group 3: plays written at Oxford but not performed, and perhaps not meant for
            performance

    Group 4: plays sometimes attributed to Oxford, but for which there is no evidence
            for performance there, or positive evidence against

Plays originally composed for other venues but performed by Oxford students are listed in Appendix 9. The distinctions among the various groups are often not sharp.

    The following information – where available – is given for each play:

Title	Modern edition (usually one only)
Language	Reference work(s) (usually one or two only)
Author	Synopsis
Early printed edition(s)	History
Manuscript(s)	Note

    Information or conjecture concerning performance histories is based on the Records, evidence gathered in Appendix 8, title-pages, internal evidence, and University careers. Conclusions drawn by or recorded in Chambers, *Elizabethan Stage (ES)*, or Bentley, *Jacobean and Caroline Stage (JCS)*, are accepted unless specific objection is raised in a note. The modern edition accords with that indicated by Harbarge, *Annals (AED)*, unless a more recent edition is available.

    Printed title-pages, transcribed in full by W.W. Greg, *A Bibliography of the English Printed Drama to the Restoration*, 4 vols (London, 1939; rpt 1962), are presented more briefly; all information bearing on author, title, date, place of performance, and presence of dignitaries is retained. Greg lists stationers' register entries, which are not noted here. Also cited is M.A. Shaaber, *Check-list of Works of British Authors Printed Abroad, in Languages other than English, to 1641* (New York, 1975).

    Listed separately from modern editions are facsimile editions, whether of Latin plays in Renaissance Latin Drama in England, Marvin Spevack and J.W. Binns (gen eds) (RLDE), or English plays in Malone Society Reprints (MSR) or Tudor Facsimile Reprints (TFR).

Electronic editions of certain Oxford plays are currently available on the Web, and more are likely to be available over time. Five available at the time of publication, all edited by Dana F. Sutton, are *Iphis* by Henry Bellamy; *Nero* and *Tres Sibyllae* by Matthew Gwinne; *Thibaldus* by Thomas Snelling; and *Physiponomachia* by Christopher Wren. The first is posted at http://eee.uci.edu/~papyri/iphis/ while the others may be found by substituting the following for 'iphis': 'Nero,' 'sibyls,' 'snelling,' and 'wren.'

Reference works are generally limited to ES or JCS, and to AED. Entries in ES and JCS often contain much more information than is given here. AED references include the year to which its editors have assigned the plays: estimated limits are included where the exact year is in doubt. Problems with dates and questions of attribution and production are discussed in the notes.

A synopsis is named where one is available in a standard article or book. 'Boas' signifies Boas (ed), *University Drama*.

Appendix 6:1: Surviving Play Texts

Antoninus Bassianus Caracalla

AUTHOR: Unknown   LANGUAGE: Latin

MANUSCRIPTS:
– Bodl.: MS. Rawlinson C.590, ff 1–25v: Antoninus Bassianus Caracalla
– Harvard Theatre Collection: Thr.10.1, ff 8v–19v (actor's part for Antoninus). (No title)

MODERN EDITION: William E. Mahaney and Walter K. Sherwin (eds), Walter K. Sherwin and Jay M. Freyman (trans), *Antoninus Bassianus Caracalla*, Salzburg Studies in English Literature, Elizabethan and Renaissance Studies 52 (Salzburg, 1976)

FACSIMILE EDITION: RLDE 1.7 (2), prepared with an introduction by J.W. Binns (1983)

REFERENCE WORKS: JCS, vol 5, p 1291; George B. Churchill and Wolfgang Keller, 'Die lateinischen Universitäts-Dramen Englands in der Zeit der Königen Elisabeth,' *Shakespeare Jahrbuch* 34 (1898), 264–7; AED 1618

SYNOPSIS: RLDE, pp 9–11

HISTORY: Christ Church (?), 1617–19

NOTE: This play seems to have been written into the blank pages of a (reversed) volume originally containing notes on a Hebrew text. The fact that the Rawlinson MS is incomplete at the end is taken by JCS as evidence that the play was never finished and thus never performed; moreover, 'There is a note at the end in a much later hand, but so badly smeared as to be almost illegible.' The following may represent an improvement on the transcription given in JCS:

the End /

⟨...⟩ Reason why   because

⟨...⟩ he that writt this

did write no more.

But the survival of an actor's part in the Harvard MS implies a performance

Archipropheta

AUTHOR: Nicholas Grimald   LANGUAGE: Latin

EARLY PRINTED EDITION: ARCHIPROPHETA, TRAGOEDIA *Iam recèns in lucem êdita* (Cologne, 1548; Shaaber G393)

MANUSCRIPT:
– BL: MS Royal 12.A.xlvi (holograph (?)): Archipropheta Tragoedia. Authore Nicolao Grimoaldo

MODERN EDITION: L.R. Merrill (ed and trans), *The Life and Poems of Nicholas Grimald*, Yale Studies in English 69 (New Haven, 1925), 217–357

FACSIMILE EDITION: RLDE 1.9 (2), prepared with an introduction by Kurt Tetzeli von Rosador (1982)

REFERENCE WORKS: *ES*, vol 3, p 31; *AED* 1547

SYNOPSIS: RLDE, pp 17–22

HISTORY: Christ Church or Exeter, 1546–7

NOTE: Latin Biblical tragedy; adapted from Jacob Schoepper, *Johannes decollatus*. MS discussed by N.R. Ker, *Paste-downs in Oxford Bindings*, Oxford Bibliographical Society, ns, 5 (Oxford, 1954), 48, no 512a. For a comprehensive note on Grimald, see Appendix 14, p 898

Atalanta

AUTHOR: Philip Parsons   LANGUAGE: Latin

MANUSCRIPT:
– BL: MS Harley 6924, ff 1–19: ATALANTA. SCENA ARCADIA

MODERN EDITION: William E. Mahaney and Walter K. Sherwin (eds), Walter K. Sherwin,

Jay Freyman, and Eve Parrish (trans), *Two University Latin Plays: Philip Parsons'* Atalanta *and Thomas Atkinson's* Homo, Salzburg Studies in English Literature, Elizabethan Studies 16 (Salzburg, 1973)

FACSIMILE EDITION: RLDE 1.4 (2), prepared with an introduction by Hans-Jürgen Weckermann (1981)

REFERENCE WORKS: *ES*, vol 4, p 373; *AED* 1612

SYNOPSIS: RLDE, pp 12–17

HISTORY: St John's College, 1612

NOTE: Pastoral. MS carries dedication to William Laud

Bellum Grammaticale sive Nominum Verborumque Discordia Civilis

AUTHOR: Leonard Hutten   LANGUAGE: Latin

EARLY PRINTED EDITION: BELLVM *Grammaticale*, Sive, *Nominum Verborumq:* discordia civilis TRAGICO-COMŒDIA. Summo cum applausu olim apud *Oxonienses* in Scænam producta, & nunc in omnium illorum qui ad Grāmaticam animos appellunt oblectamentum edita (London, 1635; Greg L13; *STC*: 12417). Prologue and Epilogue printed in William Gager, *Meleager* (1592), sigs F6v–7 (see below, under *Meleager*)

MANUSCRIPT:
– BL: MS Harley 4048, f 74v (rev) (fragment with prologue): Comœdia inscripta bellum Gramaticale acta apud Oxonienses in Æde Cristi, Anno Domini 1581: Decembris 18. This MS page also bears the page number 106 (as numbered from the back, reversed)

MODERN EDITION: *Andrea Guarnas, Bellum Grammaticale und seine Nachahmungen*, Johannes Bolte (ed), Monumenta Germaniae Paedagogica 43 (Berlin, 1908)

FACSIMILE EDITION: RLDE 1.12 (1), prepared with an introduction by Lothar Cerny (1982)

REFERENCE WORKS: *ES*, vol 4, pp 373–4; *AED* 1582

SYNOPSES: Boas, pp 255–67; RLDE, pp 7–12

HISTORY: Christ Church, 18 December 1581; repeated 24 September 1592 (royal visit)

NOTE: Comedy. Subsequent editions: 1658, 1698, 1718, 1726, 1729. A dramatization of

Andreas Guarna, *Bellum grammaticale nominis & verbi regum, de principalitate orationis inter se contendentium* (Argentorat, 1512).

Note on title-page of Anthony Wood's copy of the 1635 edition, Bodl.: MS. Wood 76(4) (visible in RLDE): 'Dr Gardiner Can*on* of *Chri*stch*urch* hath often told me y*at* Dr Leonard Hutten was the author of this play. A. W.' See also epigram in William Gager's commonplace book, clearly datable to 1583 (p 183; RLDE, p 5). On the basis of multiple references to Hutten's authorship, and of the date supplied by BL: MS Harley 4048 (identified by Professor Elliott in 1987), authorship is presented here unqualified by a query mark and the history has been thoroughly revised. William Gager's Prologue and Epilogue composed for the 1592 royal visit are available in Dana F. Sutton (ed and trans), *William Gager: The Complete Works*, vol 2 (New York and London, 1994), 245–53

Caesar and Pompey, or Caesar's Revenge

AUTHOR: Unknown   LANGUAGE: English

EARLY PRINTED EDITIONS: THE TRAGEDIE OF Cæsar and Pompey OR CÆSARS Reuenge (London, [*c* 1606]; Greg 232; STC: 4339). The second edition is more informative: THE TRAGEDIE OF Cæsar and Pompey OR CÆSARS Reuenge. Priuately acted by the Studentes of Trinity Colledge in Oxford (London, 1607; STC: 4340)

MODERN EDITION: Wilhelm Mühlfeld (ed), 'The Tragedie of Caesar and Pompey or Caesars Reuenge. Ein Drama aus Shakespeares Zeit zum ersten Male neugedruckt,' *Jahrbuch der Deutschen Shakespeare-Gesellschaft* 47 (1911), 132–55, and 48 (1912), 37–80

FACSIMILE EDITIONS: MSR (1911); TFR (1913)

REFERENCE WORKS: ES, vol 4, pp 4–5; AED 1595

SYNOPSES: Boas, pp 267–78; see also W.W. Greg, 'Notes on the Society's Publications,' *Collections* 1, pts 4–5, Malone Society (Oxford, 1911), 290–4

HISTORY: Trinity College, *c* 1592–6

NOTE: Tragedy. On parallels with Shakespeare's *Julius Caesar*, see Geoffrey Bullough (ed), *Narrative and Dramatic Sources of Shakespeare*, vol 5 (London, 1964), 33–5

The Careless Shepherdess

AUTHOR: Thomas Goffe (?); revised by R. Brome (?)   LANGUAGE: English

EARLY PRINTED EDITION: THE Careles Shepherdess. A TRAGI-COMEDY Acted before the

KING & QUEEN, And at *Salisbury-Court*, with great Applause. Written by T. G Mr. of Arts (London, 1656; Greg 761; Wing: G1005)

REFERENCE WORKS: *JCS*, vol 4, pp 501–5; *AED* 1619

HISTORY: Christ Church (?), 1618–29 (rev *c* 1638)

NOTE: Pastoral. *JCS*, vol 4, p 502, suggests 'that the play was originally written for an Oxford audience between September 1618 ... and [Goffe's] death in July 1629,' then revised for one or more non-academic productions

Cephalus et Procris

AUTHOR: Joseph Crowther   LANGUAGE: Latin

MANUSCRIPT:
– SJC Library: MS 217. (No title)

FACSIMILE EDITION: RLDE 1.10 (2), prepared with an introduction by Bernfried Nugel (1982)

REFERENCE WORKS: *JCS*, vol 3, pp 183–5; *AED* 1627

SYNOPSIS: RLDE, pp 18–22

HISTORY: St John's College (?), 1626–8

NOTE: Comedy. MS gives synopses by scenes. MS dedicated to William Juxon, president of St John's 1621–33. See 'Note' under *Homo*, below, concerning similarities between this and certain other St John's plays and play MSS

The Christmas Prince

AUTHOR: Various   LANGUAGE: English and Latin

MANUSCRIPT:
– SJC Library: MS 52, pp 5–260: A True, and faithfull relation of the risinge and fall of THOMAS TUCKER Prince of Alba Fortunata, Lord of St. Iohns...

MODERN EDITION: Boas (ed), *The Christmas Prince*

FACSIMILE EDITION: RLDE 1.11, prepared with an introduction by Earl Jeffrey Richards (1982)

REFERENCE WORKS: *ES*, vol 4, p 71; *AED* 1607 (and 1608)

SYNOPSIS: RLDE, pp 6–35

HISTORY: St John's College, 1607–8

NOTE: Excerpted at length in Records, pp 340–81. The Christmas Prince was not a play per se but a sequence of plays and other 'Christmas lord' entertainments stretching over the 'Christmas season' from 31 October 1607 to 13 February 1607/8. Two plays mentioned in the documentation but not fully integral to the event were *Periander* (listed as a separate play below) and *Yuletide* (see Appendix 6:2). The following is an outline of the events, with dates and folio numbers. All authors are unknown.

Narrative (Election, &c)	31 October–30 November	pp 5–13
Ara Fortunae	30 November	pp 14–26
LANGUAGE: Latin		
Narrative	30 November–25 December	pp 26–39
Saturnalia	25 December	pp 40–7
LANGUAGE: Latin		
Narrative	26–9 December	pp 47–9
Philomela	29 December	pp 50–84
LANGUAGE: Latin		
NOTE: The end of *Philomela* overlaps the beginning of the next narrative		
Narrative	29 December–1 January	pp 83–5
Time's Complaint	1 January	pp 86–110
LANGUAGE: English		
NOTE: Page 88 skipped in pagination		
Narrative	1–10 January	pp 111–16
The Seven Days of the Week	10 January	pp 119–28
LANGUAGE: English		
NOTE: Pages 116–17 blank		
Narrative	10–15 January	pp 129–30
Philomathes	15 January	pp 131–68
LANGUAGE: Latin		
Narrative	15 January–9 February	pp 169–78
Ira Fortunae	9 February	pp 179–206
LANGUAGE: Latin		
Narrative	9–13 February	pp 206–8
Periander	13 February	pp 209–56
NOTE: See separate listing below		
Narrative	13 February	pp 256–60

Christus Redivivus

AUTHOR: Nicholas Grimald

LANGUAGE: Latin

EARLY PRINTED EDITIONS: CHRISTVS REDIVIVVS, COMOEDIA *Tragica, sacra & noua* (Cologne, 1543; Shaaber G394). 2nd ed (Augsburg, 1556; Shaaber G395)

MODERN EDITION: L.R. Merrill (ed and trans), *The Life and Poems of Nicholas Grimald*, Yale Studies in English 69 (New Haven, 1925), 55–215

FACSIMILE EDITION: RLDE 1.9 (1), prepared with an introduction by Kurt Tetzeli von Rosador (1982)

REFERENCE WORKS: *ES*, vol 3, p 31; *AED* 1540

SYNOPSIS: RLDE, pp 10–14

HISTORY: Brasenose College, *c* 1540–1

NOTE: Tragicomedy. On possible performance, see p 85 and RLDE, p 8. For a comprehensive note on Grimald, see Appendix 14, p 898

The Combat of Love and Friendship

AUTHOR: Robert Mead

LANGUAGE: English

EARLY PRINTED EDITION: THE COMBAT OF Love *and* Friendship, A Comedy, As it hath formerly been presented by the Gentlemen of Ch. Ch. in *OXFORD*. By *ROBERT MEAD*, sometimes of the same Colledge (London, 1654; Greg 735; Wing: M1564)

REFERENCE WORKS: *JCS*, vol 4, pp 851–2; *AED* 1638

SYNOPSIS: Laurens J. Mills, *One Soul in Bodies Twain: Friendship in Tudor Literature and Stuart Drama* (Bloomington, 1937), 357–62

HISTORY: Christ Church, 1634–42

NOTE: Tragicomedy. Date and conditions of performance are highly uncertain

The Converted Robber alias Stonehenge

AUTHOR: John Speed (?)

LANGUAGE: English

MANUSCRIPT:
– BL: MS Additional 14047, ff 44v–59v: The converted Robber. A Pastorall Acted by st. Iohns College. 1637. … The sceane Salisburye Playne (Greg 107)

REFERENCE WORKS: JCS, vol 5, pp 1181–4; AED 1635

HISTORY: St John's College, 1637 (?)

NOTE: Pastoral. See JCS on the probability that this was the same play as *Stonehenge*. On the first page of the MS occur titles in rough hands: 'Loves Hov,' 'The Royal slave' (several times), 'Loves Hospitall' (several times), 'Loues Labores Lost'

The Courageous Turk, or Amurath I

AUTHOR: Thomas Goffe   LANGUAGE: English

EARLY PRINTED EDITION: THE COVRAGIOVS TVRKE, Or, AMVRATH the First. *A Tragedie. Written by* THOMAS GOFFE Master of Arts, and Student of Christ-Church in OXFORD, and Acted by the Students of the same House (London, 1632; Greg 458; STC: 11977)

MANUSCRIPTS:
– Cheshire and Chester Archives: Tabley MS DLT/B 71, ff 1–25: The Tragædy of Amurath third Tyrant of the Turkes As it was publiquely presented to ye Vniversity of Oxon: By ye students of Christchurch Mathias day 1618
– Harvard Theatre Collection: Thr.10.1, ff 57–71 (actor's part for Amurath). (No title)

MODERN EDITION: Susan Gushee O'Malley (ed), *A Critical Old-Spelling Edition of Thomas Goffe's 'The Courageous Turk,'* Renaissance Drama (New York and London, 1979)

FACSIMILE EDITION: David Carnegie (ed), MSR (1974)

REFERENCE WORKS: JCS, vol 4, pp 505–7; AED 1619

HISTORY: Christ Church, 24 February 1618/19

NOTE: Tragedy. The Tabley MS includes a poem on the hoarseness that befell the actor playing Amurath, probably Thomas Goffe himself (see pp 434–6 and p 1126, endnote to Harvard Theatre Collection: MS Thr.10.1 f 2). On the flyleaf are the names 'Thomas' and 'Henrie' once each; inside the back cover, on paper pasted onto the parchment, is written, 'The Tragedy of Amurath,' with a signature of Thomas Pygott

Dido

AUTHOR: William Gager   LANGUAGE: Latin

MANUSCRIPTS:
- ChCh Library: 486: Dido Tragœdia Acta in Æde Christi Oxoniæ Pridie Idus Iunij Anno Domini 1583
- BL: MS Additional 22583, ff 34v–44v (acts 2 and 3 only, along with Prologue, *Argumentum*, and Epilogue): Prologus in Didonem tragædiam

MODERN EDITION: Dana F. Sutton (ed and trans), *William Gager: The Complete Works*, vol 1 (New York and London, 1994), 239–363

FACSIMILE EDITION: RLDE 1.1 (2), prepared with an introduction by J.W. Binns (1981)

REFERENCE WORKS: *ES*, vol 3, p 318; *AED* 1583

SYNOPSES: Boas, pp 183–91; RLDE, pp 9–11

HISTORY: Christ Church, 12 June 1583

NOTE: Tragedy. Performance described in Holinshed, *Chronicles* (see p 191). See RLDE, p 12, for further bibliographical information. Sutton (ed), *William Gager*, vol 1, pp 250–1, demonstrates that both surviving manuscripts of *Dido* are almost certainly in Gager's hand. Sutton presents evidence, necessarily tentative (pp 246–9), for considering George Peele or even Richard Edes as possible collaborators in the composition of the play. For more on *Dido*, see also J.W. Binns (ed and trans), 'William Gager's *Dido*,' *Humanistica Lovaniensia* 20 (1971), 167–254

Eumorphus sive Cupido Adultus

AUTHOR: George Wild   LANGUAGE: Latin

MANUSCRIPT:
- BL: MS Additional 14047, ff 60–96v: Sequitur Eumorphus sive Cupido-Adultus. Comœdia. Acta A Ioannensibus Oxon' Feb. 5º 1634. Authore Georgio Wilde eiusdem Coll. Soc. et Legum Baccalarius

MODERN EDITION: Heinz J. Vienken (ed and trans), *Eumorphus; sive, Cupido Adultus; A Latin Academic Comedy of the Seventeenth Century*, Humanistische Bibliothek, Reihe 2, Texte, 19 (Munich, 1973)

FACSIMILE EDITION: RLDE 1.3 (2), prepared with an introduction by Heinz J. Vienken (1981)

REFERENCE WORKS: *JCS*, vol 5, pp 1259–60; *AED* 1635

SYNOPSIS: RLDE, pp 11–16

HISTORY: St John's College, 5 February 1634/5

NOTE: Comedy. Wood, *Athenae*, vol 3, col 720: '*Hermophus*, a Com*edy* - written in Lat. and several times acted, but not printed'; however, there is no other evidence of a second performance

The Floating Island (Passions Calmed; Prudentius)

AUTHOR: William Strode   LANGUAGE: English

EARLY PRINTED EDITION: THE FLOATING ISLAND: A TRAGI-COMEDY, Acted before his Majesty at OXFORD, Aug. 29. 1636. By the Students of CHRIST-CHURCH. Written by WILLIAM STRODE, late *Orator* of the University of OXFORD. The *Aires* and *Songs* set by Mr. HENRY LAVVES, servant to his late Majesty in his publick and private Musick (London, 1655; Greg 746; Wing: S5983)

MODERN EDITION: Bertram Dobell (ed), *The Poetical Works of William Strode (1600–1645): … To Which is Added The Floating Island, a Tragi-Comedy* (London, privately published, 1907), 137–240

REFERENCE WORKS: *JCS*, vol 5, pp 1189–95; *AED* 1636

SYNOPSIS: Dobell (ed), *Works*, pp xli–xliii

HISTORY: Christ Church, 29 August 1636 (night); second performance for the University, 'Before whom it was afterwards acted,' 3 September (afternoon)

NOTE: Tragicomedy. Described by Laud and others (see pp 537, 543, 545–6)

Fuimus Troes (The True Trojans)

AUTHOR: Jasper Fisher   LANGUAGE: English

EARLY PRINTED EDITION: FVIMVS TROES. *Æneid*. 2. THE TRVE TROIANES, Being A Story of the *Britaines* valour at the Romanes first invasion: Publikely represented by the Gentlemen Students of Magdalen *Colledge in Oxford* (London, 1633; Greg 482; *STC*: 10886)

MODERN EDITION: Robert Dodsley (ed), *A Select Collection of Old Plays*, vol 7 (London, 1825–7), 377–456

REFERENCE WORKS: *JCS*, vol 3, pp 304–5; *AED* 1625

HISTORY: Magdalen College, *c* 1611–33

NOTE: History. In *Athenae*, vol 2, col 636, Wood identifies Jasper Fisher as the author of *Fuimus Troes*, published in 1633, adding: 'Before which time, it had been once, or more, publicly represented by the gentlemen-students of Magd. coll. in Oxon'

Grobiana's Nuptials

AUTHOR: Charles May   LANGUAGE: English

MANUSCRIPT:
– Bodl.: MS. Bodley 30, ff 13–25: Grobiana's Nuptialls

MODERN EDITION: Ernst Rühl (ed), *Grobianus in England. Nebst Neudruck der ersten Übersetzung 'The Schoole of Slovenrie' (1605) und erster Herausgabe des Schwankes 'Grobiana's Nuptials' (c. 1640) aus Ms. 30. Bodl. Oxf*, Palaestra 38 (Berlin, 1904)

REFERENCE WORKS: *JCS*, vol 5, pp 1054–6 (under Shipman, Roger); *AED* 1638

HISTORY: St John's College, 14 January 1636/7 (a Saturday)

NOTE: Mock-show. The authorship has been assigned to Roger Shipman, and the performance dated after Ben Jonson's death in August 1637 (*JCS*, vol 5, p 1056), but see p 556

Homo

AUTHOR: Thomas Atkinson   LANGUAGE: Latin

MANUSCRIPT:
– BL: MS Harley 6925, ff 1–11v: HOMO

MODERN EDITION: William E. Mahaney and Walter K. Sherwin (eds), Walter K. Sherwin, Jay Freyman, and Eve Parrish (trans), *Two University Latin Plays: Philip Parsons'* Atalanta *and Thomas Atkinson's* Homo, Salzburg Studies in English Literature, Elizabethan Studies 16 (Salzburg, 1973)

FACSIMILE EDITION: RLDE 1.4 (3), prepared with an introduction by Hans-Jürgen Weckermann (1981)

REFERENCE WORKS: *JCS*, vol 3, p 4; *AED* 1618 (1615–21)

SYNOPSIS: RLDE, pp 18–23

HISTORY: St John's College, 1615–21

NOTE: Tragedy. MS dedicated to William Laud. *JCS*, vol 3, p 4, suggests that four St John's College plays – *Mercurius* (by Blencow), *Cephalus et Procris* (by Crowther), *Iphis* (by Bellamy), and *Homo* (by Atkinson), which have much in common, may all represent a standard exercise of that college

Iphis

AUTHOR: Henry Bellamy   LANGUAGE: Latin

MANUSCRIPT:
– Bodl.: Lat. misc. e.17. On vellum cover: Iphis Comœdia Latina MS autore Henrico Bellamy

MODERN EDITION: Jay M. Freyman, William E. Mahaney, and Walter K. Sherwin (eds and trans), *Iphis*, Salzburg Studies in English Literature, Elizabethan and Renaissance Studies 107:1 (Salzburg, 1986)

FACSIMILE EDITION: RLDE 1.10 (1), prepared with an introduction by Bernfried Nugel (1982)

REFERENCE WORKS: *JCS*, vol 3, pp 19–20; *AED* 1626

SYNOPSIS: RLDE, pp 6–16

HISTORY: St John's College, 1621–33

NOTE: Comedy. Dedicated to William Juxon, president of St John's College 1621–33 (*AED*'s terminal date of 1623 is presumably an error for 1633). See 'Note' under *Homo*, above, concerning similarities between this and certain other St John's College plays and play MSS

Love's Hospital (Lovers' Hospital)

AUTHOR: George Wild   LANGUAGE: English

MANUSCRIPTS:
– BL: MS Additional 14047, ff 7–39: LOVES HOSPITALL. as it was acted before the Kinge

& Queens Majestyes [a] by the students of St. Iohn Baptists College in Oxon' Augustij 29o
1636. Authore GEORGIO WILDE *Legum* Bac*calarius*
– Folger Shakespeare Library: MS J.b.7 (fragment of 2 leaves only followed by 22 stubs with
evidence of writing in same hand): Lovers Hospitall

MODERN EDITION: Jay Louis Funston (ed), *A Critical Edition of* Love's Hospital *by George Wilde*,
Salzburg Studies in English Literature, Jacobean Drama Studies 13 (Salzburg, 1973)

REFERENCE WORKS: *JCS*, vol 5, pp 1260–4; *AED* 1636

HISTORY: St John's College, 30 August 1636 (afternoon)

NOTE: Comedy. Performed for a royal visit (see p 543). Bodl.: MS. Malone 21 contains Henry
Lawes' music for the play

Meleager

AUTHOR: William Gager   LANGUAGE: Latin

EARLY PRINTED EDITION: MELEAGER. Tragœdia noua: BIS PVBLICE ACTA IN *ÆDE
CHRISTI* Oxoniæ (Oxford, 1592; Greg L2; *STC*: 11515)

MODERN EDITION: Dana F. Sutton (ed and trans), *William Gager: The Complete Works*, vol 1
(New York and London, 1994), 27–221

FACSIMILE EDITION: RLDE 1.2 (1), prepared with an introduction by J.W. Binns (1981)

REFERENCE WORKS: *ES*, vol 3, p 318; *AED* 1582

SYNOPSES: Boas, pp 165–78, 192–5; RLDE, pp 8–9

HISTORY: Christ Church, first, 7 February 1581/2; second, January 1584/5 (in the presence
of the earls of Pembroke and Leicester, and of Sir Philip Sidney and other courtiers)

NOTE: Tragedy. Further information on the play appears in the Records (see pp 180–1)

Mercurius Rusticans

AUTHOR: Unknown   LANGUAGE: Latin

MANUSCRIPT:
– Bodl.: MS. Wood D.18, Pt 2: Mercurius Rusticans Scena Hyncksey vel Hincksie

MODERN EDITION: Ann J. Cotton (ed), *'Mercurius Rusticans': A Critical Edition'* (New York and London, 1988)

FACSIMILE EDITION: RLDE 1.7 (1), prepared with an introduction by J.W. Binns (1983)

REFERENCE WORKS: *JCS*, vol 5, pp 1373–4; *AED* Supplement I (contains further information)

SYNOPSIS: RLDE, pp 5–8

HISTORY: written 1605–18

NOTE: Comedy. The Bodleian *Summary Catalogue* (8557, under 8837) declares that the text was 'written in 1663' but gives no evidence for this evidently erroneous assertion. The action takes place in the village of Hinksey, just west of Oxford. The text includes several songs to tunes named in the margins: 'The hunt is up,' 'Whoop doe me noe harme,' and 'Bonny nell.' See p 392 for a poem penned into the play MS

Mercurius sive Literarum Lucta

AUTHOR: John Blencow   LANGUAGE: Latin

MANUSCRIPT:
– SJC Library: MS 218: Mercurius siue Literarum Lucta. (At conclusion of play: 'Ioannes Blenkow')

FACSIMILE EDITION: RLDE 1.3 (1), prepared with an introduction by Heinz J. Vienken (1981)

REFERENCE WORKS: *JCS*, vol 3, pp 29–30; *AED* 1633

SYNOPSIS: RLDE, pp 6–8

HISTORY: St John's College, 1629–38?

NOTE: Comedy. RLDE, p 6, proposes a date at the end of the 1620s. MS contains no dedication. See 'Note' under *Homo* above concerning similarities between this and certain other St John's College plays and play MSS

'Momus'

See *Panniculus Hippolyto Assutus*, 'Note'

'Mr Moore's Revels'

AUTHOR: Thomas Moore   LANGUAGE: English

MANUSCRIPT:
–Bodl.: MS. Ashmole 47, ff 122v–6: Mr Moores revells nere Eastgate in Oxon. 1636

MODERN EDITION: Elliott (ed), 'Mr. Moore's Revels,' pp 411–20

REFERENCE WORKS: *JCS*, vol 5, p 1375; *AED* 1636

SYNOPSIS: Elliott (ed), 'Mr. Moore's Revels,' p 412

HISTORY: Performed at East Gate, Oxford, 1636, over three nights

NOTE: Christmas revel (?). Bentley, in *JCS*, vol 5, p 1375, declares of the text, 'I do not know where it is,' but see the complete text, pp 560–4. Probably not a college play but one within the University play tradition

Narcissus, a Twelfth Night Merriment

AUTHOR: Francis Clarke (?)   LANGUAGE: English and Latin

MANUSCRIPT:
– Bodl.: MS. Rawlinson poet.212, ff 67–82 (rev): A Twelfe night merriment: anno 1602

MODERN EDITION: Lee (ed), *Narcissus*, pp 1–27

REFERENCE WORKS: *ES*, vol 4, p 36; *AED* 1603

SYNOPSIS: Boas, pp 278–85

HISTORY: St John's College, 5 January 1602/3

NOTE: Farce. *ES*, vol 4, p 36, infers Francis Clarke's authorship from, among other things, the name 'Francis' given to the Porter, a character in the play (for excerpts see pp 268–71). On the identity of Clarke, see p 1115, endnote to Bodl.: MS. Rawlinson poet.212 ff 82, 67. In addition to the play text the MS includes four letters, all by the same author: 'A speech made for ye foresaid porter...' (ff 84–2v, rev), transcribed in Records (see pp 269–71); 'A speech deliverd by ffrancis Clarke to ye Ladie Keneda' (ff 46–5v, rev); 'A Speech spoken by Francis Clarke in the behalfe of ye freshmen' (ff 44v–3v, rev); and 'A letter composd for Francke Clarke ye porter of St Iohn's, who in his brothers behalfe did breake ones head with a Blacke staffe' (ff 84v–5, rev). These four letters are printed by Lee (ed), *Narcissus*, pp 28–36

Oedipus (fragment)

AUTHOR: William Gager   LANGUAGE: Latin

MANUSCRIPT:
– BL: MS Additional 22583, ff 31–4. (No title)

MODERN EDITION: Dana F. Sutton (ed and trans), *William Gager: The Complete Works*, vol 1 (New York and London, 1994), 1–26

FACSIMILE EDITION: RLDE 1.1 (1), prepared with an introduction by J.W. Binns (1981)

REFERENCE WORKS: *ES*, vol 3, p 319; *AED* 1584

SYNOPSIS: RLDE, p 8

HISTORY: Christ Church (?), *c* 1577–92

NOTE: Tragedy. Binns, RLDE, p 8: '*Oedipus* consists of five short scenes, which may be either surviving scenes from a longer play, or the first attempt at what was intended to be a longer play, or a playlet complete in itself'

The Ordinary, or The City Cozener

AUTHOR: William Cartwright   LANGUAGE: English

EARLY PRINTED EDITIONS: THE ORDINARY, A Comedy, Written by WILLIAM CARTVVRIGHT, *M.A. Ch.Ch. Oxon* (London, 1651; Greg 702; Wing: C714). Also (Wing: C709)

MODERN EDITION: Robert Dodsley (ed), *A Select Collection of Old Plays*, vol 10 (London, 1825–7), 165–268

REFERENCE WORKS: *JCS*, vol 3, pp 132–4; *AED* 1635

HISTORY: Christ Church (?), 1634–5

NOTE: Comedy. *JCS* explicates an internal reference from which the play may be dated, gives an account of the play's subsequent career on the professional stage, and notes Henry Lawes' music for Priscilla's song in act 3, scene 2

Orestes

AUTHOR: Thomas Goffe   .   LANGUAGE: English

EARLY PRINTED EDITION: THE TRAGEDY *OF* ORESTES, VVritten by THOMAS GOFFE
Master of *Arts*, and *Student* of Christs Church in OXFORD: AND Acted by the STVDENTS
of the same HOVSE (London, 1633; Greg 485; *STC*: 11982)

MODERN EDITION: Norbert Frank O'Donnell (ed), 'The Tragedy of *Orestes* by Thomas Goffe:
A Critical Edition,' PhD thesis (Ohio State University, 1950)

REFERENCE WORKS: *JCS*, vol 4, pp 507–9; *AED* 1617

HISTORY: Christ Church, *c* 1613–18

NOTE: Tragedy

Panniculus Hippolyto Assutus (supplement)

AUTHOR: William Gager   LANGUAGE: Latin

EARLY PRINTED EDITION: Fragment of text in *Meleager* (see above), sigs E8–F5v: Panniculus
Hippolyto Senecæ Tragœdiæ assutus 1591. (Prologue and Epilogue printed with *Ulysses
Redux* (see below), sigs F2v–3)

MODERN EDITION: Dana F. Sutton (ed and trans), *William Gager: The Complete Works*, vol 2
(New York and London, 1994), 183–215

FACSIMILE EDITION: RLDE 1.2 (3), prepared with an introduction by J.W. Binns (1981)

REFERENCE WORKS: *ES*, vol 3, p 319; *AED* 1592

SYNOPSES: Boas, pp 198–201; RLDE, p 12

HISTORY: Christ Church, Tuesday, 8 February 1591/2

NOTE: Additions to Seneca's *Hippolytus*, the Latin play. *Panniculus ... assutus* means 'a patch ...
sewn (onto).' Sutton (ed), *William Gager*, vol 2, p 254, considers but casts doubt upon a
connection between Gager's text and a song by William Byrd. For the date of the performance, see 'Note' under *Ulysses Redux*, below. For more on *Panniculus*, see J.W. Binns (ed),
'William Gager's Additions to Seneca's *Hippolytus*,' *Studies in the Renaissance* 17 (1970),
153–91.

Published with *Ulysses Redux* was Gager's speech of Momus, presented as an afterpiece to *Panniculus*, which had nearly the standing of an independent play and triggered an important debate between Gager and the anti-theatrical polemicist John Rainolds (see Appendix 11). Momus' speech is edited and translated by Sutton (ed), *William Gager*, vol 2, pp 216–21

'The Part of Poore' (fragment)

AUTHOR: Unknown   LANGUAGE: English

MANUSCRIPT:
- Harvard Theatre Collection: MS Thr.10.1, ff 21–46v (actor's part for Poore). (No title)

MODERN EDITION: David Carnegie (ed), 'The Part of "Poore,"' *Collections* 15, Malone Society (Oxford, 1993), 111–69

REFERENCE WORK: *AED* 1618

HISTORY: Christ Church, 1617–19

NOTE: Moral

Periander

AUTHOR: John Sandsbury (?)   LANGUAGE: English

MANUSCRIPTS:
- SJC Library: MS 52, pp 209–56: A True, and faithfull relation of the risinge and fall of THOMAS TUCKER Prince of Alba Fortunata, Lord of St. Iohns…
- Folger Shakespeare Library: MS J.a.1, ff 134–57v (pamphlet ends f 160): *Periander*. Folio 134 (cover-leaf): Periander made bye Mr Iohn Sansburye

MODERN EDITION: Boas (ed), *The Christmas Prince*, pp 229–87

FACSIMILE EDITION: RLDE 1.11, pp 209–60, prepared with an introduction by Earl Jeffrey Richards (1982)

REFERENCE WORKS: *ES*, vol 4, p 71; *AED* 1607 (and 1608)

SYNOPSIS: RLDE, pp 6–35

HISTORY: St John's College, 13 February 1607/8

NOTE: *Periander* occurs in the manuscript of The Christmas Prince, following *Ira Fortunae*, the closing play in that sequence. This fact, along with the survival of the text in a second manuscript, suggests that *Periander* was an independent play. Discussed by R.H. Bowers, 'Some Folger Academic Drama Manuscripts,' *Studies in Bibliography* 12 (1959), 122

Philosophaster

AUTHOR: Robert Burton   LANGUAGE: Latin

MANUSCRIPTS:
- Folger Shakespeare Library: MS V.a.315: Philosophaster./ Comœdia noua./ Scripta Anno domini 1606. Alterata, [renovata] ⌈reuisa⌉, perfecta. Anno domini 1615. Acta demum et publicè exhibita Academicis In Aula Ædis Christi, et a Studiosis Ædis Christi Oxon' alumnis, Anno 1617 Februarij die decimo sexto, die lunæ ad horam sextam pomeridianam/ Auctore Roberto Burton, Sacræ Theologiæ Baccalaureo atque Ædis Christi Oxon' alumno 1617. Pages 4–7 contain an 'Argumentum.' (At conclusion of Epilogue, p 84: 'feb: 16to Æde Christi Oxon. 1617.' Page 85 contains 'Actorum nomina,' followed by 'Acted on Shrouemunday night 1617. feb: 16. die lunæ Oxon: It begane a bout 5: at night, and ended at eight. Auctore Roberto Burton Liniliaco Lecestrense.') (This volume, owned by Robert's brother William, is a virtual twin of the Harvard MS, though perhaps in a different hand.) (Cast list)
- Harvard Theatre Collection: MS Thr.10, pp 7–89: Philosophaster./ Comœdia noua./ [Inchoata] ⌈Scripta⌉ Anno domini 1606. Alterata, re[nouata] ⌈uisa⌉, [perfecta]. Anno domini 1615. Acta demum et publicè exhibita Academicis In aulâ Ædis Cristi, et a Studiosis ædis Cristi Oxon' alumnis, Anno 1617 Februarij [die] decimo sexto. die lunæ. ad horam sextam pomeridianam./ Auctore Roberto Burton Sacræ Theologiæ Baccalaureo atque Ædis Christi Oxon' alumno./ 1617. Pages 4–6 contain an 'Argumentum.' At conclusion of Epilogue, p 89: 'Feb: 16to Æde Cristi 1617.' Page 90 contains 'Actorum nomina,' followed by 'Acted on Shrouemunday night 1617. Feb: 16. die lunæ. It begane about 5. at night and ended at eight./ Auctore Roberto Burton Liniliaco Lecestrense./' Blank leaves following play text include modern notes identifying the actors. (This volume, evidently in Burton's own hand, is a virtual twin of the Folger MS.) (Cast list)
- Harvard Theatre Collection: MS Thr.10.1, ff 48–56 (actor's part for Polypragmaticus, in the hand of Thomas Goffe, including *Epilogus*, f 56). (No title.) (This volume has no apparent original connection with Harvard Theatre Collection: MS Thr.10)

MODERN EDITION: Connie McQuillen (ed and trans), *Philosophaster*, Medieval & Renaissance Texts & Studies 103 (Binghamton, 1993)

FACSIMILE EDITION: RLDE 1.8, prepared with an introduction by Marvin Spevack (1984). (From Harvard Theatre Collection: MS Thr.10)

REFERENCE WORKS: *JCS*, vol 3, pp 99–100; *AED* 1606

SYNOPSIS: RLDE, pp 9–18

HISTORY: Christ Church, composed 1606; revised 1615; acted 16 February 1617/18: 'It began about five at night and ended at eight'

NOTE: Comedy. The role of Polypragmaticus was played by Thomas Goffe: see MS Thr.10.1 above under 'Manuscripts,' and see Appendix 7 for cast list. Burton himself provides historical details of the composition and performance: see pp 427–8 and *JCS*

Physiponomachia

AUTHOR: Christopher Wren, Sr   LANGUAGE: Latin

MANUSCRIPT:
– Bodl.: MS. Bodley 30, ff 2–12: ΦΥΣΙΠΟΝΟΜΑΧΙΑ

FACSIMILE EDITION: RLDE 1.4 (1), prepared with an introduction by Hans-Jürgen Weckermann (1981)

REFERENCE WORKS: *ES*, vol 4, p 377; *AED* 1609

SYNOPSIS: RLDE, pp 6–10

HISTORY: St John's College, *c* 1609–11

NOTE: Comedy. MS carries dedication to John Buckeridge, president of St John's

The Queen's Arcadia (Arcadia Reformed)

AUTHOR: Samuel Daniel   LANGUAGE: English

EARLY PRINTED EDITION: THE QVEENES ARCADIA. A Pastorall Trage-comedie *presented to her Maiestie and* her Ladies, by the Vniuersitie of *Oxford in Christs Church*, in August last. 1605 (London, 1606; Greg 227; *STC*: 6262)

REFERENCE WORKS: *ES*, vol 3, p 276; *AED* 1605

HISTORY: Christ Church, 30 August 1605 (royal visit)

NOTE: Pastoral. On the play's reception see Letter of Chamberlain to Winwood (p 332).

The Raging Turk, or Bajazet II

AUTHOR: Thomas Goffe   LANGUAGE: English

EARLY PRINTED EDITION: THE RAGING TVRKE, OR, BAIAZET THE SECOND. A
  Tragedie vvritten by THOMAS GOFFE, Master of Arts, and Student of Christ-Church in
  Oxford, and Acted by the Students of the same house (London, 1631; Greg 447; *STC*:
  11980–1)

MODERN EDITION: Ahmed Alam El-Deen (ed), 'A Critical Edition of Thomas Goffe's
  The Raging Tvrke, or Baiazet the Second (1631),' PhD thesis (West Virginia University, 1984)

FACSIMILE EDITION: David Carnegie (ed), MSR (1974)

REFERENCE WORKS: *JCS*, vol 4, pp 509–10; *AED* 1618

HISTORY: Christ Church, *c* 1613–18

NOTE: Tragedy

The Royal Slave

AUTHOR: William Cartwright   LANGUAGE: English

EARLY PRINTED EDITIONS: THE ROYALL SLAVE. *A* Tragi-Comedy. Presented to the King and
  Queene by the Students of *Christ-Church* in Oxford. *August* 30. 1636. Presented since to
  both their Majesties at *Hampton-Court* by the Kings Servants (Oxford, 1639; Greg 570;
  STC: 4717). Subsequent edition (Oxford, 1640; *STC*: 4718)

MANUSCRIPTS:
– BL: MS Additional 41616 (Petworth sale), ff 1–24 (a pamphlet bound within the volume):
  The Royall Slaue A Tragicomedy The Scene Sardes Acted before the King at Oxford. Note
  bottom of page in later hand: This Play was written by *Willia*m Cartwright a Student of
  Christchurch & was first represented by the Students of that College before K*ing* Charles
  I & his Queen on the 30th of Aug*ust* 1636 – The Songs were set by Henry Lawes – Dr
  Busby – afterward Master of Westmr school performed a principal part with great applause
  he was at that time a Student of Christchurch...
– Bodl.: MS. Arch. Selden B26, pt E: The Royall Slaue A Tragi=Comedy
– Duke of Bedford: The Royall Slave A Tragi=Comedy
– Folger Shakespeare Library: MS V.b.212 (formerly 7044): The Royall Slaue A Trage=Comedy

MODERN EDITION: *Plays and Poems of William Cartwright*, G. Blakemore Evans (ed) (Madison, 1951)

REFERENCE WORKS: *JCS*, vol 3, pp 134–41; *AED* 1636

HISTORY: Christ Church, 30 August 1636 (evening); repeated 2 September (afternoon); played professionally 12 January 1636/7 at Hampton Court

NOTE: Tragicomedy. A lost fifth MS – Heber: 1043 – contained a cast list. On performance at Hampton Court, see Appendix 3. See frequent references in the Records (pp 529, 534 (as *The Persian Slave*), 538, 543–6, 556, and the related endnotes)

Technogamia, or The Marriages of the Arts

AUTHOR: Barten Holyday   LANGUAGE: English

EARLY PRINTED EDITIONS: ΤΕΧΝΟΓΑΜΙΑ: OR THE MARRIAGES *OF THE ARTS*. A Comedie, Written by BARTEN HOLYDAY, Master of Arts, and Student of *Christ-Church* in *Oxford*, and acted by the Students of the same House before the Vniuersitie, at *Shroue-tide* (London, 1618; Greg 353; *STC*: 13617). 2nd ed (London, 1630; *STC*: 13618). (Folger *STC*: 13617 carries MS corrections, apparently in the hand of the author)

MODERN EDITION: Sister M. Jean Carmel Cavanaugh (ed), Technogamia *by Barten Holyday. A Critical Edition* (Washington, DC, 1942). The text presented in this edition – heavily annotated in the editor's endnotes – is a photographic reprint of Folger *STC*: 13617

REFERENCE WORKS: *JCS*, vol 4, pp 589–96; *AED* 1618

SYNOPSIS: Cavanaugh (ed), '*Technogamia*,' pp lv–lxx

HISTORY: Christ Church, 13 February 1617/18; second performance at Woodstock, before the king, 26 August 1621 (a Sunday)

NOTE: Moral/comedy. On the play's venues and reception, see Peter Heylyn's *Memoirs* (p 427) and Appendix 2. See Appendix 7 for cast list

Thibaldus sive Vindictae Ingenium

AUTHOR: Thomas Snelling   LANGUAGE: Latin

EARLY PRINTED EDITION: THIBALDVS SIVE *VINDICTÆ INGENIVM*. TRAGOEDIA (Oxford, 1640; Greg L17; *STC*: 22888). Unsold sheets were later offered for sale with a new title-page: PHARAMVS *SIVE* LIPIDO VINDEX, Hispanica Tragoedia (Oxford, 1650; Wing: P1969)

FACSIMILE EDITION: RLDE 1.12 (2), prepared with an introduction by Lothar Cerny (1982)

REFERENCE WORKS: *JCS*, vol 5, p 1179; *AED* 1640

SYNOPSIS: RLDE, pp 14–19

HISTORY: St John's College, 1634–40

NOTE: Tragedy. Performance date is particularly uncertain

Titus et Gesippus

AUTHOR: John Foxe   LANGUAGE: Latin

MANUSCRIPT:
– BL: MS Lansdowne 388, ff 121–46, 112–16v (misbound in MS). (No title)

MODERN EDITION: John Hazel Smith (ed and trans), *Two Latin Comedies by John Foxe the Martyrologist: 'Titus et Gesippus'; 'Christus Triumphans,'* Renaissance Text Series 4 (Ithaca, 1973)

FACSIMILE EDITION: RLDE 1.6 (1), prepared with an introduction by John Hazel Smith (1986)

REFERENCE WORKS: *ES*, vol 2, p 15, and vol 4, pp 93, 152; *AED* 1545

SYNOPSIS: RLDE, pp 11–22

HISTORY: 1544/5 (or unacted (?))

NOTE: Comedy. While evidence of performance at court is strong (*ES*), a performance at Oxford can only be inferred

Ulysses Redux

AUTHOR: William Gager   LANGUAGE: Latin

EARLY PRINTED EDITION: VLYSSES REDUX Tragoedia Nova. IN AEDE CHRISTI OXONIAE *PVBLICE ACADEMICIS RECITATA, OCTAVO IDVS FEBRVARII*. 1591 (Oxford, 1592; Greg L4; *STC*: 11516)

MODERN EDITION: Dana F. Sutton (ed and trans), *William Gager: The Complete Works*, vol 2 (New York and London, 1994), 1–182

FACSIMILE EDITION: RLDE 1.2 (2), prepared with an introduction by J.W. Binns (1981)

REFERENCE WORKS: *ES*, vol 3, pp 318–19; *AED* 1592

SYNOPSES: Boas, pp 201–19; RLDE, pp 10–11

HISTORY: Christ Church, 6 February 1591/2 (first of several plays over a period of three days)

NOTE: Tragedy. Boas demonstrates (pp 196–7) that during this Shrovetide season *Ulysses Redux* was performed on Sunday, 6 February, while *Rivales* was revived on Monday, 7 February, and *Hippolytus* was performed on Tuesday, 8 February. Allusions to all three plays also appear in the Rainolds-Gager debate: see Appendix 11

Vertumnus sive Annus Recurrens (with *Tres Sibyllae*)

AUTHOR: Matthew Gwinne   LANGUAGE: Latin

EARLY PRINTED EDITION: VERTVMNVS SIVE ANNVS RECVRRENS OXONII, XXIX AVGVSTI, Anno. 1605. Coram IACOBO Rege, HENRICO Principe Proceribus. *A Ioannensibus in Scena recitatus* ab vno scriptus, Phrasi Comicâ *prope Tragicis Senariis* (London, 1607; Greg L6; *STC*: 12555; variant 12555.5)

MANUSCRIPT:
– Inner Temple Library: Petyt MS 538, vol 43, ff 293–3v (scenario only: see pp 310–12)

FACSIMILE EDITION: RLDE 1.5 (1), prepared with an introduction by Alexander Cizek (1983)

REFERENCE WORKS: *ES*, vol 3, p 332; *AED* 1605

SYNOPSIS: RLDE, pp 9–22

HISTORY: Acted by St John's College men at Christ Church, 29 August 1605

NOTE: The English title is 'The Yeare About.' On the play's reception, see Records under 1604–5 and related endnotes. For an additional ceremony performed by students of St John's, *Tres Sibyllae*, see p 298.
      Folios 284–303 of the Inner Temple Petyt MS comprise a poetic miscellany, all in the same early seventeenth-century italic hand. The contents include poems by Mary Sidney, Sir John Harington, and Thomas Nash, and several poems referring to Oxford, including

'A Dialogue betweene Constancie and Inconstancie/ Spoken before the Queenes Maiestie at Woodstock,' by Richard Edes of Christ Church (ff 299–300); 'The Melancholy Knight's Complaint in the Wood,' also by Edes (f 300v); and 'Bastards Libell of Oxeford,' by Thomas Bastard of New College (f 301), with references to William Gager. It can perhaps be assumed that the plot summary of *Vertumnus* was made between August 1605, the date of the only performance of the play, and 1607, when the play was printed, as there would have been no need for such a summary after publication of the text

Appendix 6:2: Lost Play Texts

Ajax Flagellifer

AUTHOR: Unknown   LANGUAGE: Latin

EVIDENCE: Reported by a visitor from Cambridge: see p 299

REFERENCE WORKS: *ES*, vol 1, pp 127, 130, 233; *AED* 1605

HISTORY: Christ Church, 28 August 1605 (royal visit); actors from Magdalen College

NOTE: Tragedy. *ES*, vol 1, p 130: 'not apparently a translation from Sophocles, but an independent play.' This was probably a different play from the *Ajax Flagellifer* performed at Cambridge in 1564 (see Nelson (ed), *Cambridge*, vol 2, Index)

Alba

AUTHOR: Robert Burton (and others (?))   LANGUAGE: Latin

EVIDENCE: Reported by a visitor from Cambridge: see p 298; also mentioned in a letter of Burton to his brother: see p 294

REFERENCE WORKS: *ES*, vol 1, p 130; *AED* 1605

HISTORY: Christ Church, 27 August 1605 (royal visit)

NOTE: Pastoral. For a comprehensive discussion of the evidence, see Nochimson, 'Robert Burton's Authorship of *Alba*,' pp 325–31

'Alexander and Bagoas'

AUTHOR: Unknown   LANGUAGE: Unknown

EVIDENCE: Noted in a sermon by Laurence Humphrey: see p 178

HISTORY: Acted by students of Christ Church or St John's (or possibly Magdalen)

NOTE: Identified by Finnis and Martin, 'Oxford Play Festival'

Andronicus Comnenus

AUTHOR: Samuel Bernard   LANGUAGE: Latin

EVIDENCE: See Appendix 14, p 899, for a comprehensive note on Bernard

REFERENCE WORKS: *JCS*, vol 3, p 26; *AED* 1618

HISTORY: Magdalen College, 1617–19 (*AED*)

NOTE: Tragedy. It is important to distinguish Bernard's play from BL: MS Sloane 1767, ff 17–66, a Jesuit neo-Latin tragedy with the same title (see Appendix 6:4)

'Anthony and Cleopatra'

AUTHOR: Unknown   LANGUAGE: Unknown

EVIDENCE: Noted in a sermon by Laurence Humphrey: see p 178

HISTORY: Acted by students of Christ Church or St John's (or possibly Magdalen)

NOTE: Identified by Finnis and Martin, 'Oxford Play Festival'

Astiages

AUTHOR: Unknown   LANGUAGE: Unknown

EVIDENCE: See p 245

REFERENCE WORK: *AED* 1598

HISTORY: St John's College, 1597–8 (in president's chamber)

NOTE: Tragedy

Athanasius sive Infamia

AUTHOR: Nicholas Grimald   LANGUAGE: Latin

EVIDENCE: Inferred from details of Grimald's life: see Appendix 14, p 898

REFERENCE WORK: *AED* 1547

HISTORY: Brasenose, Merton, or Christ Church, *c* 1540–7

Caesar Interfectus

AUTHOR: Richard Edes   LANGUAGE: Latin

EVIDENCE: Epilogue, in Latin prose, survives in Bodl.: MS. Top.Oxon e.5, f 359, where a later
    hand has supplied the date of 1582: see p 180

REFERENCE WORKS: *ES*, vol 3, p 309; *AED* 1582

SYNOPSIS: Boas, pp 163–5

HISTORY: Evidently Christ Church, February 1581/2

NOTE: Tragedy. Francis Meres, *Palladis Tamia* (1598, *STC*: 17834), sig Oo3, includes Edes
    among 'our best for Tragedie.' On the possible influence of this play on Shakespeare's *Julius
    Caesar*, see Geoffrey Bullough (ed), *Narrative and Dramatic Sources of Shakespeare*, vol 5
    (London, 1964), 33, 194–5, which also includes a translation (p 195). See also John Semple
    Smart, *Shakespeare Truth and Tradition* (London, 1928), 179–82.
        Bodl.: MS. Top.Oxon e.5 originally belonged to Robert Dowe, fellow of All Souls
    1575–88. It is a miscellany containing copies of various Latin orations, petitions, sermons,
    and speeches, Latin prayers, and Latin and English letters, all by various authors and
    mostly dating from the mid- to late sixteenth century.

Christus Nascens

AUTHOR: Nicholas Grimald   LANGUAGE: Latin

EVIDENCE: Inferred from details of Grimald's life: see Appendix 14, p 898

REFERENCE WORK: *AED* 1540

HISTORY: Brasenose College, 1540?

NOTE: 'Neo-miracle' (*AED*)

The Destruction of Thebes (The Contention between Eteocles and Polynices)

AUTHOR: Unknown   LANGUAGE: Unknown

EVIDENCE: Letter of Thomas Cooper: see p 150

REFERENCE WORKS: *ES*, vol 1, p 129, n 3, and vol 4, p 85; *AED* 1569

SYNOPSIS: Boas, p 158

HISTORY: Christ Church, projected for 15 May 1569

NOTE: Perhaps not performed

Doublet, Breeches, and Shirt

AUTHOR: Peter Heylyn   LANGUAGE: English

EVIDENCE: Heylyn's *Memoirs*: see p 440

REFERENCE WORKS: *JCS*, vol 4, p 551; *AED* 1620

HISTORY: Magdalen College, January 1619/20

NOTE: Christmas show

Fama

AUTHOR: Nicholas Grimald   LANGUAGE: Latin

EVIDENCE: Inferred from details of Grimald's life: see Appendix 14, p 898

REFERENCE WORK: *AED* 1547

HISTORY: Brasenose, Merton, or Christ Church, *c* 1540–7

NOTE: Tragedy

Hippolytus

AUTHOR: Unknown   LANGUAGE: Unknown

EVIDENCE: See p 276

REFERENCE WORK: *AED* 1604

HISTORY: St John's College, 13 February 1603/4

NOTE: Tragedy

Iphigenia

AUTHOR: George Peele   LANGUAGE: Unknown

EVIDENCE: Laudatory verses by William Gager, *In Iphigeniam Georgii Peeli Anglicanis versibus redditam*, printed by A.H. Bullen (ed), *The Works of George Peele*, vol 1 (London, 1888), xvii–xviii

REFERENCE WORKS: *ES*, vol 3, p 462; *AED* 1579

HISTORY: Christ Church (?), 1576–80

NOTE: Tragedy. Translation of Euripides

Julius et Gonzaga

AUTHOR: Samuel Bernard   LANGUAGE: Latin

EVIDENCE: See Appendix 14, p 899

REFERENCE WORKS: *JCS*, vol 3, pp 27–8; *AED* 1617

HISTORY: Magdalen College, 23 January 1616/17

NOTE: Tragedy

King Solomon

AUTHOR: Thomas More   LANGUAGE: Latin (?)

EVIDENCE: See p 37

REFERENCE WORK: *AED* 1495

HISTORY: Magdalen College, school, *c* 1495

NOTE: Comedy

Lucretia

AUTHOR: Unknown   LANGUAGE: Unknown

EVIDENCE: See p 281

REFERENCE WORK: *AED* 1605

HISTORY: St John's College, 11 February 1604/5

NOTE: Tragedy

Marcus Geminus

AUTHOR: Tobie Matthew   LANGUAGE: Latin

EVIDENCE: Reported in Miles Windsor's narrative: see p 131

REFERENCE WORKS: *ES*, vol 1, p 128; *AED* 1566

SYNOPSIS: Boas, pp 101–2

HISTORY: Christ Church, 1 September 1566 (royal visit)

NOTE: Comedy

Octavia

AUTHOR: Unknown   LANGUAGE: Latin

EVIDENCE: See p 213

REFERENCE WORK: *AED* 1591

HISTORY: Christ Church, 1590–1?

NOTE: Adaptation of Seneca (?)

Palamon and Arcite (Parts I and II)

AUTHOR: Richard Edwards   LANGUAGE: English

EVIDENCE: Reported in Miles Windsor's narrative (see pp 131–3) and elsewhere (see Index)

REFERENCE WORKS: *ES*, vol 1, p 128, and vol 3, p 311; *AED* 1566

SYNOPSES: Boas, pp 102–4; Ros King (ed), *The Works of Richard Edwards: Politics, Poetry and Performance in Sixteenth-Century England*, Revels Plays Companion Library (Manchester, 2001), 79–85

HISTORY: Christ Church, 2 and 4 September 1566 (royal visit)

NOTE: Comedy. Adaptation of Chaucer's *Knight's Tale*, conceivably through a Latin intermediary. Edwards' poem is the first of several Elizabethan poems copied into ff 106v–8v, which are otherwise devoted to the antiquities of Yorkshire, ie, extracts of charters, pedigrees, cartularies, etc, from the twelfth century onward but evidently entered into the volume no earlier than 1642. The hand is that of a professional scribe. This is the only surviving text for any of the 1566 royal plays. It was first printed by Hyder Rollins, 'A Note on Richard Edwards,' *Review of English Studies* 4 (1928), 204–6. See Appendix 7 for cast list

'Philarchus and Phaedra'

AUTHOR: Unknown   LANGUAGE: Unknown

EVIDENCE: Noted in a sermon by Laurence Humphrey: see p 178

HISTORY: Acted by students of Christ Church or St John's (or possibly Magdalen)

NOTE: Identified by Finnis and Martin, 'Oxford Play Festival'

Philotas

AUTHOR: Richard Latewar   LANGUAGE: Unknown

EVIDENCE: Reported by Samuel Daniel: see p 208

REFERENCE WORKS: *ES*, vol 3, pp 275–6; *AED* 1588

HISTORY: St John's College, *c* 1588–96

NOTE: Tragedy. Not the play of the same name by Samuel Daniel (see above, 'Evidence')

Phocas

AUTHOR: Samuel Bernard   LANGUAGE: Latin

EVIDENCE: See Appendix 14, p 899

REFERENCE WORKS: *JCS*, vol 3, p 28; *AED* 1619

HISTORY: Magdalen College, 27 January 1618/19

NOTE: Tragedy

Piscator sive Fraus Illusa

AUTHOR: John Hooker   LANGUAGE: Latin

EVIDENCE: John Bale, *Illustrium Maioris Brittanniae scriptorum* (Wesel, 1549; *STC*: 1296), 712.
    Information is reproduced by John Pits, *Relationum Historicarum de Rebus Anglicis* (Paris,
    1619), 730, and by Wood, *Athenae*, vol 1, col 138

REFERENCE WORK: *AED* 1539

HISTORY: Magdalen College, 1535–43

NOTE: Comedy

Progne

AUTHOR: James Calfhill   LANGUAGE: Latin

EVIDENCE: Reported in Miles Windsor's narrative: see p 133

REFERENCE WORKS: *ES*, vol 1, p 129, and vol 3, p 239; *AED* 1566

SYNOPSIS: Boas, pp 104–5

HISTORY: Christ Church, 5 September 1566 (royal visit)

NOTE: Tragedy. Probably an adaptation of Gregorio Corraro's *Progne* (1558)

Protomartyr

AUTHOR: Nicholas Grimald   LANGUAGE: Latin

EVIDENCE: Inferred from details of Grimald's life: see Appendix 14, p 898

REFERENCE WORK: *AED* 1547

HISTORY: Brasenose, Merton, or Christ Church, *c* 1540–7

NOTE: Tragedy. Evidently a play on St Stephen

'De Puerorum in Musicis Institutione'

AUTHOR: Nicholas Grimald   LANGUAGE: Latin

EVIDENCE: Inferred from details of Grimald's life: see Appendix 14, p 898

REFERENCE WORK: *AED* 1547

HISTORY: Possibly Brasenose, Merton, or Christ Church, *c* 1540–7

NOTE: Comedy

The Reformation

AUTHOR: Abraham Wright   LANGUAGE: English

EVIDENCE: Reported by Wood: see Appendix 13, p 893

REFERENCE WORKS: *JCS*, vol 5, p 1276; *AED* 1631

HISTORY: St John's College, 1629–33

NOTE: Comedy. Written and produced while Wright was an undergraduate

Rivales

AUTHOR: William Gager   LANGUAGE: Latin

EVIDENCE: Performance described by and play named in Holinshed, *Chronicles*: see p 191. Prologue printed in *Ulysses Redux* (see Appendix 6:1), sig F2. Facsimile in RLDE: 1.2 (2), prepared with an introduction by J.W. Binns (1981), p 7; see also Dana F. Sutton (ed and trans), *William Gager: The Complete Works*, vol 1 (New York and London, 1994), 223–38. For the 7 February 1591/2 performance date, see 'Note' under *Ulysses Redux*

REFERENCE WORKS: *ES*, vol 3, p 319; *AED* 1583

SYNOPSIS: Boas, pp 181–3, 197, 254–5

HISTORY: Christ Church, 11 June 1583; revived 7 February 1591/2, and again 26 September 1592 (royal visit)

NOTE: Comedy. Allusions to *Rivales* also appear in the Rainolds-Gager debate: see Appendix 11. Sutton (vol 1, p 227) suggests that the play was 'rustic' and probably stands in the background of George Peele's *Old Wives Tale*

St Mary Magdalene

AUTHOR: John Burgess   LANGUAGE: Unknown

EVIDENCE: See pp 46–7

REFERENCE WORK: *AED* 1507

HISTORY: Magdalen College, 1507

NOTE: Miracle play (?)

The Scholars

AUTHOR: Richard Lovelace   LANGUAGE: English

EVIDENCE: Prologue and Epilogue printed in *Lucasta* (London, 1649; Wing: L3240), 75–9; see also *JCS*, vol 4, pp 722–3

REFERENCE WORKS: *JCS*, vol 4, pp 722–4; *AED* 1634

HISTORY: Gloucester Hall (?), 1634–5?

NOTE: Comedy. Among works that Lovelace never published, Wood cites 'The Scholar,' which Lovelace 'composed at 16 years of age, when he came first to Glocester hall, acted with applause afterwards in Salisbury-Court' (*Athenae*, vol 3, col 462). Prologue and Epilogue indicate a performance at Whitefriars (probably Salisbury Court)

A Spanish Tragedy

AUTHOR: Unknown   LANGUAGE: English

EVIDENCE: Anecdote in Edmund Gayton, *Pleasant Notes upon Don Quixot* (London, 1654; Wing: G415), 94–5

REFERENCE WORKS: *JCS*, vol 5, pp 1411–12; *AED* 1636

HISTORY: Oxford, 1636–48?

NOTE: Tragedy, concerning Petrus Crudelis (Peter the Cruel)

Spurius

AUTHOR: Peter Heylyn   LANGUAGE: Latin

EVIDENCE: Reported in Heylyn's *Memoirs*: see p 422

REFERENCE WORKS: *JCS*, vol 4, p 552; *AED* 1617

HISTORY: Magdalen College, 8 March 1616/17 (acted privately in the president's chamber)

NOTE: Tragedy

Tancredo

AUTHOR: Henry Wotton   LANGUAGE: Unknown

EVIDENCE: Reported by Isaak Walton, *Reliquiae Wottonianae* (1651): see pp 202–3

REFERENCE WORKS: *ES*, vol 3, p 517; *AED* 1586

HISTORY: Queen's College, 1586–7

NOTE: Tragedy

Troilus

AUTHOR: Nicholas Grimald   LANGUAGE: Latin

EVIDENCE: Inferred from details of Grimald's life: see Appendix 14, p 898

REFERENCE WORK: *AED* 1547

HISTORY: Brasenose, Merton, or Christ Church, *c* 1540–7

NOTE: Comedy. Adaptation/translation, direct or indirect, of Chaucer *(Troilus ex Chaucero)*

Wylie Beguylie

AUTHOR: Unknown   LANGUAGE: English

EVIDENCE: See p 146

REFERENCE WORK: *AED* 1567

SYNOPSIS: Boas, p 157

HISTORY: Merton College, 3 January 1566/7 (at night)

NOTE: Comedy

Yuletide

AUTHOR: Unknown   LANGUAGE: English

EVIDENCE: Named in manuscript of The Christmas Prince: see p 364

REFERENCE WORKS: *ES*, vol 4, p 71; *AED* 1608

HISTORY: Christ Church, 21 January 1607/8

NOTE: Burlesque of The Christmas Prince

Appendix 6:3: Plays Written at Oxford, But Probably Not Performed

Antipoe

AUTHOR: Francis Verney   LANGUAGE: English

MANUSCRIPT:
– Bodl.: MS. Eng. poet. e.5: 'The tragedye of Antipoe with other poetical verses written by mee Nicolo Leatt Iunior in Allicant In Iune 1622'

REFERENCE WORKS: *ES*, vol 3, p 503; *AED* 1604

HISTORY: Trinity College (?), written 1603–8

NOTE: Tragedy. Dedicated to James I by 'Your graces most affectionate seruant to command Francis Verney.' There is no evidence that this play was ever performed

The Hunting of Cupid

AUTHOR: George Peele   LANGUAGE: English

EVIDENCE: Lost edition, *c* 1591 (Edward Arber (comp), *A Transcript of the Registers of the Company of Stationers of London, 1554–1640*, vol 2 (London, 1875–7), 591): 'A booke intituled the Huntinge of Cupid wrytten by George Peele, Master of Artes of Oxeford....' W.W. Greg (ed) has collected surviving 'fragments' in *Collections* 1, pts 4–5, Malone Society (Oxford, 1911), 307–14

REFERENCE WORKS: Greg 11; *ES*, vol 3, p 462; *AED* 1586

HISTORY: Oxford (?), written 1581–92?

NOTE: Pastoral. Any connection to Oxford must be speculative. There is indeed no certainty that this was a play

Liber Apologeticus

AUTHOR: Thomas Chaundler   LANGUAGE: Latin

MANUSCRIPT:
– Bodl.: New College MS. 288

MODERN EDITION: *Liber apologeticus de omni statu humanae naturae: A Defence of Human Nature in Every State (c. 1460): A Moral Play*, Doris Enright-Clark Shoukri (ed and trans), Publications of the Modern Humanities Research Association, vol 5 (London, 1974)

SYNOPSIS: Shoukri (ed), *Liber apologeticus*, pp 11–12

NOTE: Moral play in five acts. Thomas Chaundler (1418?–90) was warden of New College 1454–75. No independent evidence supports the idea of a performance, but the possibility cannot be entirely excluded. Fourteen accompanying illustrations are reproduced in Shoukri's edition

Lodovick Sforza

AUTHOR: Robert Gomersall   LANGUAGE: English

EARLY PRINTED EDITION: THE TRAGEDIE OF *LODOVICK SFORZA* DVKE OF *MILLAN* (London, 1628; Greg 418; *STC*: 11995)

MODERN EDITION: B.R. Pearn (ed), *The Tragedie of Lodovick Sforza, Duke of Millan, by Robert Gomersall*, Materials for the Study of the Old English Drama 8 (Louvain, 1933)

REFERENCE WORKS: *JCS*, vol 4, pp 512–14; *AED* 1622–8

NOTE: Tragedy. Dedicated to Francis Hyde, proctor of the University. A second edition was printed in 1633 (*STC*: 11993). *JCS*, vol 4, p 513: 'The play is probably only an academic exercise in dramatization'

Nero

AUTHOR: Matthew Gwinne   LANGUAGE: Latin

EARLY PRINTED EDITIONS: NERO TRAGÆDIA *NOVA*. MATTHÆO GWINNE Med. Doct. *Collegii Divi Ioannis Præcursoris* apud Oxonienses Socio *collecta* è Tacito, Suetonio, Dione, Seneca (London, 1603; Greg L5; *STC*: 12551). 2nd ed (1638; *STC*: 12552). Another issue (1639; *STC*: 12553)

FACSIMILE EDITION: RLDE 1.13, prepared with an introduction by Heinz-Dieter Leidig (1983)

REFERENCE WORKS: *ES*, vol 3, p 332; *AED* 1603

SYNOPSIS: RLDE, pp 10–15

HISTORY: St John's College, written *c* 1602–3

NOTE: Tragedy. Gwinne's Introduction addresses the question (sig ¶4, l.18), 'At cur non acta?' ('But why was it not acted?'). Some copies of the 1603 edition are dedicated to Elizabeth, others to James

Theomachia

AUTHOR: Peter Heylyn   LANGUAGE: Latin

EVIDENCE: Peter Heylyn's *Memoirs*: see p 426

REFERENCE WORKS: *JCS*, vol 4, pp 552–3; *AED* 1618

HISTORY: Magdalen College

NOTE: Comedy

Appendix 6:4: Plays Wrongly Attributed to Oxford

Andronicus Comnenus

AUTHOR: Unknown   LANGUAGE: Latin

MANUSCRIPTS:
– BL: MS Sloane 1767, ff 18v–66: Tragoedia [⟨…⟩] Andronicus Commenus

FACSIMILE EDITION: RLDE 1.6 (2), prepared with an introduction by John L. Klause
   (1986)

REFERENCE WORKS: *JCS*, vol 3, p 26; *AED* 1618 (but see 'Note' below)

SYNOPSIS: RLDE, pp 29–38

NOTE: Jesuit neo-Latin tragedy. This play text is quite unrelated to Oxford (despite its
   inclusion in RLDE), and should not be confused with the play of the same title by
   Samuel Bernard, listed in Appendix 6:2

Boot and Spur

AUTHOR: Unknown   LANGUAGE: English

MANUSCRIPT: Folger Shakespeare Library: MS J.a.1, ff 19–23

REFERENCE WORKS: *JCS*, vol 5, pp 1295–6; *AED* 1612

HISTORY: Unknown, 1611–20?

NOTE: 'Entertainment.' Probably not an Oxford play: see Nelson (ed), *Cambridge*, vol 2,
   p 892

'Phoenissae' (subject)

AUTHOR: Thomas Goffe   LANGUAGE: English

EVIDENCE: Unknown apart from listing in *AED*

REFERENCE WORK: *AED* 1619

HISTORY: Christ Church (?), *c* 1613–29

NOTE: Tragedy. Evidence for this play is quite uncertain

APPENDIX 7
Cast Lists

Comprehensive cast lists survive for two Oxford college plays: *Philosophaster* (1617) and *Technogamia* (1621). A list of actors, without identification of roles, survives for plays from the royal visit of 1566, including *Palamon and Arcite*. These three cast lists are given below. A fourth cast list, for *The Royal Slave* (1636), was lost with the disappearance of MS Heber 1043 in the nineteenth century: see William Cartwright, *The Plays and Poems of William Cartwright*, G. Blakemore Evans (ed) (Madison, 1951), 167.

In addition a few actors, sometimes with their roles, can be identified from the Records or other sources:

– Boas (ed), *University Drama*, pp 392–3, provides a list of 'some actors in Christ Church plays 1582–92,' including John King (tragic parts, probably including a part in *Meleager*), Thomas Crane (comic parts), Leonard Hutten (comic parts, probably including a part in *Bellum Grammaticale*), Francis Sydney (Ulysses in *Ulysses Redux*), and Tobie Matthew (Naïs in Gager's additions to *Hippolytus*). Boas bases several of his identifications on Gager's commonplace book (see pp 183–4). For evidence that Francis Sydney played Ulysses and James Weston Telemachus in Gager's *Ulysses Redux*, see Dana F. Sutton (ed and trans), *William Gager: The Complete Works*, vol 2 (New York and London, 1994), 18–21. The role of Phemius was played by the master of the choristers at Christ Church, William Maycock (see Appendix 11, p 864).

– Thomas Godwin, a commoner of Christ Church, acted in a comedy before James I in August 1605 (see p 329).

– Thomas Goffe evidently played the part of Amurath in his own *The Courageous Turk*, performed at Christ Church on 24 February 1618/19 (see p 1126, endnote to Harvard Theatre Collection: MS Thr.10.1 f 2).

– In *Love's Hospital*, acted at St John's on 30 August 1636 (see p 543), the author, George Wild, is reported to have taken the lead role (Comastes), while other roles were taken by Humphrey Brooke, Edmund Gayton, John Goad, and John Heyfeild (see Appendix 13, p 893).

– Richard Busby, subsequently master of Westminster School, was hailed as a second Roscius and is said, on uncertain evidence, to have played the part of Cratander in *The Royal Slave* on 30 August and 2 September 1636 (see p 547).

– John Case was the Christmas Prince of St John's in 1577–8 (see pp 341, 347).

– Some thirty members of St John's were assigned ceremonial roles in The Christmas Prince (1607–8), such as Prince of Alba Fortunata or Duke of Grove-land (see pp 348–50, 353). Thomas Tucker, as Christmas lord (or the Prince), took the 'ex officio' role of Princeps in *Ara Fortunae* (scenes 5 and 6) and *Ira Fortunae* (acts 2, 4, and 5); he also made an appearance in act 1 of *Time's Complaint* (see pp 357–8) and played Tereus in *Philomela* (see pp 355–6) and the title role in *Periander* (see p 379). Thomas Downer and John Towse took 'ex officio' roles in *Ara Fortunae* and *Ira Fortunae*; similarly, Richard Baylie, John Englishe, Joseph Fletcher, Richard Holbrooke, and Rowland Juxon took 'ex officio' roles in *Ira Fortunae*.

– Members of Merton College elected king of beans, from John Persons in 1485–6 to John Estwick in 1539–40, are too numerous to list here but may be identified by resort to the Index (see 'king of beans' under Merton College entry).

– Robert Ashley's *Autobiography* mentions his participation in various plays as a schoolboy (see Rosalind Conklin Hays and C.E. McGee/Sally L. Joyce and Evelyn S. Newlyn (eds), *Dorset/Cornwall*, REED (Toronto, 1999), 170, 339). In 1588–9 he was chosen Christmas lord of Magdalen (see p 209).

– Peter Heylyn notes in his memoirs that Thomas Holt was chosen Christmas lord of Magdalen College for 1617–18 (see p 426), John Stonehouse for 1619–20 (see p 440). In the former year Heylyn played the subsidiary role of ambassador of the University of Vienna, in the latter year, the duke of Helicon, first peer of the 'principalitie.'

– A Mr Moore, in what may have been a Christmas revel, cast himself in the role of Rex or Princeps in 1636 (see pp 560–4 and Appendix 6:1, p 815).

The three lists that follow are presented in chronological order. Original spellings of the names of characters and of last names of actors are preserved, but the lists are not otherwise intended as facsimiles of the originals and abbreviated names are silently expanded. The first name of the student actor, if editorially supplied, appears in parentheses. If the form of the last name found in the University Index is substantially different from that given in the base manuscript, the index form is also supplied in the parentheses. Doubt concerning the identification of a named student actor with a known member of the University is expressed by a question mark.

The title 'Sir' ('Dominus' or 'Ds.') normally refers to students who received the BA degree, while 'Mr' usually refers to a student with the MA degree. Sometimes, however, 'Mr' is assigned to students of whatever academic rank who had been admitted as fellow commoners or pensioners of a college. Corrections or supplementary information are occasionally taken from sources other than the base text: all such instances are noted in introductory or closing paragraphs. Names of characters not matched to named actors are omitted.

Palamon and Arcite and Other Plays (1566)

The cast list, from 'Miles Windsor's Narrative' (see p 135), is analysed by Boas (ed), *University Drama*, pp 390–2, using not the text transcribed in the Records (f 123v), but rather the fair version (f 107). Named individuals are of Christ Church unless noted otherwise. Boas suggests that 'Smithe nutrix' refers to the actor who played the Nurse in Calfhill's *Progne*, and 'Dalapers boye' refers to a servant who played the child.

Marbecke (Roger)	Mancell (George or John, MC)
Banes (Brian)	Wynsor (unidentified)
Badger (John)	Twyne (Thomas, CCC)
Rookes (William, MC)	Rainoldes (John, CCC)
Ball (John)	Pryn (unidentified)
Buste (John or Henry, MC)	Egerton (unidentified)
Bristoo (Richard Bristow)	Carewe (Peter, see below)
Penson (William)	Poll (John Paule or Rice Powell)
Mathewe (Tobie)	Yonge (Christopher, college unknown)
Potes (Thomas or Nicholas)	Dalapers boye
Thornton (Thomas)	Townsend (Stephen)
Pottes (Nicholas or Thomas)	Glasyer (Thomas)
Iones (Thomas)	Dorset (Robert)
Summers (Henry)	Graye (Henry)
Argall (John)	Fourde (John Forde)
Dalaper (John)	Romans (unidentified)
Danet (Audley)	Iutsam (Ralph, MC)
Edwardes (Richard)	Smithe nutrix (Robert)

Other sources reveal that John Rainolds played Queen Hippolyta (see Appendix 11, p 870); Roger Marbeck, Palamon (see pp 128–9); Brian Baynes, Arcite (see p 129); John Delabere, Trevatio (see p 129); and Peter Carew (a boy, son of the dean of Christ Church, George Carew), Emily (see Appendix 13, p 878).

Philosophaster (1617)

The cast list, heavily annotated in the hand of the original scribe, survives in two sister MSS in the Folger Shakespeare Library and the Houghton Library, Harvard (see p 428 and Appendix 6:1). In the latter, first names have been added in pencil, in an eighteenth-century hand. Those identifications are further amplified in W.E. Buckley's edition (Hertford, 1862), xv–xxi, upon which the following list is based.

Actors who also appeared in the 1621 performance of *Technogamia* at Woodstock (see below) are marked with an asterisk. First names that differ from Buckley's are marked with a dagger.

Desiderius Dux	Sir Kinge (Robert)
Eubulus	Mr Gorges (Timoleon)
Cratinus	Mr Bartlit (*Michael Berkeley (?))
Polumathes	Sir Bennet (*Matthew (?))
Philobiblos	Sir Haywood (Rowland)
Polupragmaticus	Mr Goffe (Thomas)
Æquiuocus	Mr Iohnson (William)
Simon Acutus	Sir ffortye (Robert)
Lodovicus pantometer	Sir Westlye (Thomas)
Pontamagus	Sir Osboston (*Lambert Osbaldeston)
Amphimacer	Limiter (*Charles)
Theanus	Sir Vauhan (*Richard)
Pedanus	Morly (*George)
Stephanio	Sir Arundall (Emanuel)
Polupistos	Sir Price (William)
Dromo	Hilsinge (Richard Heylyn (?))
	Sir Ingolsby (Anthony Ingoldsby)
	Harris (*John (?))
	Parsones (John)
Staphila	Benefeilde (*Robert Bedingfield)
Camaena	Price (*Francis†)
Tarentilla	Stroude (William)
Lictor promus	Sotton (Valentine† Sotherton)
	Portry (Alexander Portrey)
	Blunt (Robert)
	Serle (George)
	Hersen (unidentified†)

Burton seems consistent in distinguishing between undergraduates and bachelors through the use of the title 'Sir' for bachelors, a feature that enables us to date the composition of the cast list with some accuracy. The list cannot have been drawn up before 26 June 1618, for instance, when Haywood took his BA. And it cannot have been written after 17–19 December 1618, when Limiter, Morley, Bedingfield, and Sotherton all received their BAS.

Buckley, reading 'Sotton' as 'Cotton,' suggested Robert or John; but 'Sotton' seems to resolve the identification in favour of Valentine Sotherton. Reading 'Hersen' as 'Herser,' Buckley gives the first name William, but only on the uncertain authority of the eighteenth-century annotator.

Technogamia (1621)

Several of the actors in *Philosophaster* also acted in Barten Holyday's *Technogamia*, presented before King James at Woodstock in 1621. The cast list was printed by Nichols, *Progresses of King James*, vol 4, pp 1108–9, from a lost copy of the play said to have belonged to Joseph Haslewood. The following list is based on, but does not precisely follow, the work of Sister M. Jean Carmel Cavanaugh (ed), Technogamia *by Barten Holyday. A Critical Edition* (Washington, DC, 1942), 113–16.

Actors who also appeared in the 1617 performance of *Philosophaster* (see above) are marked with an asterisk. Dashes preceding last names indicate students who were not yet BA.

Politees	Mr. Vereer (Gerard)
Physica	Ds. Hide (Francis (?))
Astronomia	Ds. Berkley (*Michael (?))
Ethicus	Ds. Goodwin (John)
Geographus	Mr. Osbalston (*Lambert)
Geometres	Ds. Bennet (*Matthew (?))
Arithmetica	Ds. Guil. King (William)
Logicus	Mr. Stockwell ('Carrus')
Grammaticus	Ds. Morley (*George)
Poeta	Mr. Holden (William)
Historia	Ds. Needham (John)
Rhetorica	– Price (*Francis)
Musica	– Spencer (John or Thomas)
Medicus	Ds. Limiter (*Charles)
Causidicus	– Jones (unidentified)
Magus	Ds. Vaughan (*Richard)
Astrologia	Ds. Springham (Henry)
Phantastes	Mr. Collins (unidentified)
Melancholico	– Harrys (*John (?))
Choler	– Croft (James)
Sanguis	Ds. Beddingfielde (*Robert)
Phlegmatico	Ds. Smith (unidentified)
Physiognomus	– Clutterbooke (John Clutterbuck)
Cheiromantes	Ds. Phil. Kinge (Philip)

APPENDIX 8

Chronological List of College Performances

The following table presents a chronological list of plays, disguisings, shows, and other college performances whose dates can be established with some degree of certainty within a known academic year. The information is presented in five columns:

1 Year
2 Date
3 College (or other auspices)

4 Type
5 Title, author, producer, or other notes

Entries are listed alphabetically by college when dates within the year are unknown and chronologically when dates within the year are known, with editorial compromises when evidence is mixed. Italicized date ranges in column two signify the week in which payment occurred. 'Q' signifies the quarter in which payment occurred, 29 September to 24 December constituting Q1, and so forth. 'Christmas' signifies the Christmas season rather than 25 December. The abbreviations (roy) and (nob), in column four, signify royal or noble audiences. Titles (where known) are presented in italics. Names in column five given without play titles are those of producers.

The Records constitute the primary source of the abstracted information; the next most important source is Appendix 6. The Index should be consulted for details not found quickly in at least one of these three sources.

Year	Date	College	Type	Title, author, producer, or other notes
1485–6	Christmas	MC	player/s	
1486–7	6 Jan (?)	MC	play/players	'le capp mayntenaunce'; for play (?)
1487–8	Christmas	MC	players	
1490–1	Christmas	MC	plays	
1495–6	Christmas	MC	plays	
	Easter (3 Apr)	MC	play	
1496–7		MC	plays	
1502–3	Christmas	MC	interludes	
1506–7		MC	play	Burgess, *St Mary Magdalene*

1509–10	Easter (31 Mar)	MC	boy players	
1511–12		MC	interludes	
1512–13		LC	play	
	27 Dec	MC	interlude	
	6–13 Jan	MC	interlude	
1517–18		MC	play	Burgess, *St Mary Magdalene* (?)
1519–20	Easter (8 Apr)	MC	play	
1520–1	Christmas	MC	interludes	cancelled entry
1524–5	Christmas	NC	play	
1528–9		Crd	comedy	payment made in 1529–30 for previous year's play
1529–30	Christmas	MC	plays	
1530–1	Christmas	MC	interludes	
1531–2		MC	play (bachelors')	
1533–4	Christmas	Broadgates Hall	play	
		MC	plays (fellows' and scholars')	
1534–5		MC	comedy	Alard (?)
1537–8		MC	comedy	
1538–9		MC	comedy	
1539–40		MC	comedy, tragedy	
1540–1		MC	comedies	
1541–2		MC	comedies	
1542–3		MC	comedies	
1547–8		EC	comedy	
		MC	tragedies	
1550–1		EC	comedies	
		MC	play/s	theatre constructed
1551–2		MC	comedies	
1552–3		MC	comedies, tragedies, musical pastime	
		NC	plays	
1553–4	30 Jan	MC	tragedies	
1556–7		MC	tragedies	
	Christmas	TC (?)	tragedy	possibly 1555–6
1557–8		MC	play/s	theatre constructed
c 1559		TC	comedy	Terence, *Andria*
1559–60		MC	comedies, spectacles	
1560–1		MC	spectacle	Bale, *Three Laws* (?)
1561–2		MC	spectacles	

1564–5	Trinity Sun (17 June)	TC	spectacle	
1565–6	1 Sep	ChCh	history/comedy (roy)	Matthew, *Marcus Geminus*
	2 Sep	ChCh	comedy (roy)	Edwards, *Palamon and Arcite* I
	4 Sep	ChCh	comedy (roy)	Edwards, *Palamon and Arcite* II
	5 Sep	ChCh	tragedy (roy)	Calfhill, *Progne*
		MC	spectacles, comedy	
1566–7	3 Jan	MtC	comedy	*Wylie Beguylie*
	7 Feb	MtC	comedy	Terence, *Eunuchus*
1567–8		MC	comedy	
	21 Jan	MtC	comedy	Plautus, *Menaechmi*
		MtC	tragicomedy	Edwards, *Damon and Pithias*
1568–9	15 May	ChCh	tragedy	*Destruction of Thebes*; in readiness
		MC	play/s	theatre constructed
	Christmas	SJC	plays	
1572–3	Christmas	QC	tragicomedy	
		CCC	play (scholars')	
		MC	spectacles	
1573–4		MC	spectacles	
1574–5		ASC	play	
1578–9		TC	plays	
1579–80		ASC	play (?) ('players')	
		MC		theatrical expenses
1580–1		SJC	interlude (bachelors')	
1581–2	18 Dec	ChCh	comedy	Hutten, *Bellum Grammaticale* (1)
	8 Jan	TC	comedy	Gascoigne, *Supposes* (1)
	7 Feb	ChCh	tragedy	Gager, *Meleager* (1)
	15 Feb	ChCh	comedies, 3 tragedies	Browne and Heton
	(?) Feb	ChCh (?)	tragedy	Edes, *Caesar Interfectus*
	18–20 Feb	SJC	comedy, 2 tragedies	
		MC	spectacles	
			comedy	Plautus, *Menaechmi*
			comedy	Plautus, *Aulularia*
			tragedy	Seneca or Sophocles (?), *Oedipus*
			tragedy (?)	'Anthony and Cleopatra'
			tragedy (?)	'Alexander and Bagoas'
			tragedy (?)	'Philarchus and Phaedra'
1582–3	10 Feb	SJC	comedy, tragedy	
	26 May	TC	comedy	Gascoigne, *Supposes* (2)

	11 Jun	ChCh	comedy (nob)	Gager, *Rivales* (1)
	12 Jun	ChCh	tragedy (nob)	Gager, *Dido*
1583–4		ChCh	comedies, tragedies (nob)	Peele (among others)
	21 Jan	MtC	comedy (nob)	Plautus, *Captivi*
1584–5	(?) Jan	ChCh	comedy (1)	
	14 Jan	ChCh	comedy (2) (nob)	
	(?) Jan	ChCh	tragedy (nob)	Gager, *Meleager* (2)
		TC	plays	
1585–6		EC	play	possibly 1586–7
		QC	tragedy	Wotton, *Tancredo*
1586–7		ChCh	comedy	King and Crane (censors)
		SJC	show (students')	
1590–1		ChCh	tragedy (bachelors')	*Octavia*
1591–2	6 Jan	MC	plays	
	6 Feb (Sun)	ChCh	tragedy	Gager, *Ulysses Redux*
	7 Feb (Mon)	ChCh	comedy	Gager, *Rivales* (2)
	8 Feb (Tue)	ChCh	tragedy	Gager, *Hippolytus* (and 'Momus')
	24 Sep (Sun)	ChCh	comedy (roy)	Hutten, *Bellum Grammaticale* (2)
	26 Sep (Tue)	ChCh	comedy (roy)	Gager, *Rivales* (3)
1596–7	27 Dec–2 Jan	SJC	comedy	
1597–8	*16–22 Jan*	SJC	tragedy	*Astiages* (1: president's lodgings)
	23–9 Jan	SJC	tragedy	*Astiages* (2: hall)
1598–9	Shrovetide	ChCh	masques, mummings	
	5 Jan	SJC	'sporte'	Tuer and Groom
	15–21 Jan	SJC	spectacles	
	29 Jan–4 Feb	SJC	interlude	
	23–4 Feb	SJC	comedy, tragedy (scholars' and convicts')	
1599–1600	17 Nov	SJC	interlude	
	1 Jan	SJC	interlude	
1600–1	1 Jan	SJC	interlude (scholars' and convicts')	
1601–2	1 Jan	SJC	interlude	
	5 Jan	SJC	comedy	in hall
	23 Feb	SJC	tragedy	
1602–3	1 Jan	SJC	show	
	5 Jan	SJC	play/comedy/merriment	Clarke (?), *Narcissus*

	10–16 Jan	SJC	comedies	
1603–4	Christmas	SJC	shows	
	13 Feb	SJC	tragedy	*Hippolytus* (acted publicly)
1604–5	11 Feb	SJC	tragedy	*Lucretia* (acted publicly)
	24 Mar	ChCh	comedy	
	27 Aug	ChCh	pastoral/comedy (roy)	Burton (et al (?)), *Alba*
	27 Aug	SJC	show (roy)	*Tres Sibyllae*
	28 Aug	MC (and NC)	tragedy (roy, at ChCh)	*Ajax Flagellifer*, Castilion
	29 Aug	SJC	pastoral/comedy (roy, at ChCh)	Gwinne, *Vertumnus*
	30 Aug	ChCh	pastoral/comedy (roy)	Daniel, *Queen's Arcadia*
1605–6		ChCh	comedy (scholars')	Juckes and Blundell (censors)
	17–23 Feb	SJC	play	Vertue
1606–7		MC	spectacles	
1607–8	21 Jan	ChCh	comedy	*Yuletide*, Juckes and Osbaldeston (censors)
	31 Oct–13 Feb	SJC	comedies (various)	Christmas Prince (see Appendix 6:1)
	13 Feb	SJC		Sandsbury (?), *Periander*
1608–9		ChCh	plays	Juckes (censor)
1610–11	*11–17 Feb*	SJC	comedy, tragedy	
1611–12?		SJC	pastoral	Parsons, *Atalanta* (possibly 1612–13)
1612–13		ChCh	plays	
		MC	comedy (nob)	Oates
1613–14		ChCh	plays	Browne and Trulocke, Lancaster
1614–15		MC	pastoral/comedy (?)	Powell (in president's lodgings)
	13–19 Feb	SJC	comedy, tragedy	
1615–16		ChCh	2 comedies, tragedy	Iles
1616–17	1 Jan	SJC	show	
	13–19 Jan	SJC	comedy, tragedy	
	20–6 Jan	SJC	tragedy	
	23 Jan	MC	tragedy	Bernard, *Julius et Gonzaga*; in president's lodgings
	bef 8 Mar	MC	play	White; in president's lodgings
	8 Mar	MC	tragedy (poor scholars')	Heylyn, *Spurius*; in president's lodgings

1617–18	1 Jan	SJC	show	
	5 Jan	SJC	masque	
	26 Jan	MC	play	Bernard, *Andronicus*
	2 Feb	SJC	show	
	13 Feb	ChCh	comedy	Holyday, *Technogamia* (1)
	16 Feb	ChCh	comedy	Burton, *Philosophaster*
		MC	comedy, tragedy	
1618–19	1 Jan	SJC	show	
	27 Jan	MC	tragedy	Bernard, *Phocas*
	24 Feb	ChCh	tragedy	Goffe, *Courageous Turk*
	1–7 Mar	SJC	masque/show	
	19–25 Apr	SJC	masque	further payment for earlier masque (?)
		MC	tragedy	
1619–20	(?) Jan	MC	show	Heylyn, *Doublet, Breeches, and Shirt*
	Q2	SJC	shows	
1620–1	1 Jan	SJC	show	
	26 Aug	ChCh	comedy (at Woodstock)	Holyday, *Technogamia* (2)
1621–2	1 Jan	SJC	show	
	Q2	SJC	show (founders')	
	11–17 Mar	SJC	masque	
1622–3	1 Jan	SJC	show	
	3–9 Mar	SJC	masque	(late payment (?) Lent began 26 Feb)
1624–5	Q1	SJC	show	
	1 Jan	SJC	show	
1626–7	Q2	SJC	show	Stock
1627–8	1 Jan	SJC	show	
1629–30	Q2	SJC	show (founders')	
1630–1	Q2	SJC	show (founders')	
1631–2	Q1	SJC	show (founders')	
1633–4		SJC	show (founders')	carpenter paid Q3
1634–5	5 Feb	SJC	comedy	Wild, *Eumorphus*
	2–8 Mar (?)	SJC	tragedy	payment 22–8 Feb (but Lent began 11 Feb)
		MC	interlude (boys')	
1635–6	7 Dec	SJC	show	
	29 Aug (Mon)	ChCh	tragicomedy (roy)	Strode, *Floating Island* (1)
	30 Aug (Tue)	SJC	comedy (roy)	Wild, *Love's Hospital* (before 7 PM)

	30 Aug	ChCh	tragicomedy (roy)	Cartwright, *Royal Slave* (1) (after 7 PM)
	2 Sep (Fri)	ChCh	tragicomedy	Cartwright, *Royal Slave* (2) (afternoon)
	3 Sep (Sat)	ChCh	tragicomedy	Strode, *Floating Island* (2) (afternoon)
1636–7	Q2	SJC	3 plays	
	14 Jan (Sat)	SJC	mock-show	May, *Grobiana's Nuptials*; possibly 1 of 3 cited above
1637–8	Q2	SJC	show (founders')	
1638–9	Q2	SJC	show (founders')	
		SJC	plays	Atkinson
1639–40	Christmas	SJC	show (founders')	
	20–6 Jan	SJC	play	
1640–1	*29 Sept–* *20 Nov 1641*	SJC	plays	payment made in 1641–2 for previous year's plays

APPENDIX 9
College Plays from Extra-mural Sources

Classical play titles named in the Records are listed in the Index and cross-referenced to authors, including Plautus, Terence, and Sophocles or Seneca. Because classical plays were available in numerous manuscripts and printed editions, no bibliographical information is offered here.

Oxford colleges relied for some of their plays on graduates who had left the University to pursue careers elsewhere, including Samuel Daniel, Richard Edes, Richard Edwards, and George Peele. Plays by all four are listed in Appendix 6 on the understanding that the texts were newly commissioned for Oxford venues. Edwards' *Damon and Pithias*, however, seems to have had its first performance at court. Evidence for an Oxford performance of John Bale's *Three Laws* is admittedly obscure. Of the four playwrights listed below, Foxe and Edwards were Oxford men, while Gascoigne and Bale were Cambridge men.

References cited are Harbage, *Annals (AED)*, Chambers, *Elizabethan Stage (ES)* and *Mediaeval Stage (MS)*, W.W. Greg, *A Bibliography of the English Printed Drama to the Restoration*, vol 1 (London, 1939; rpt 1962), and M.A. Shaaber, *Check-list of Works of British Authors Printed Abroad, in Languages other than English, to 1641* (New York, 1975).

Christus Triumphans, by John Foxe

PERFORMANCE HISTORY: Prior history uncertain; Magdalen College, 1561–2?

FIRST EDITION: *Christus Triumphans, comoedia apocalyptica: autore Ioanne Foxo anglo. accessit, in Christum trimphantem, autoris eiusdem panegyricon* (Basel, 1556; Shaaber F180)

REFERENCE WORK: *MS*, vol 2, p 459

MODERN EDITION: *Two Latin Comedies by John Foxe the Martyrologist: Titus et Gesippus. Christus Triumphans*, John Hazel Smith (ed and trans), Renaissance Society of America, Renaissance Text Series 4 (Ithaca, New York, and London, 1973)

NOTE: Draft version is BL: MS Lansdowne 1045, ff 132–55v; see Nelson (ed), *Cambridge*, vol 2, pp 703, 969, 979

Damon and Pithias, by Richard Edwards

PERFORMANCE HISTORY: Presented to Queen Elizabeth at court, probably in 1564–5, by the children of the Chapel; revived at Merton College in 1568 (see pp 148–9)

FIRST EDITION: The excellent Comedie of two the moste faithfullest *Freendes, Damon and Pithias* (London, 1571; STC: 7514–15; Greg 58). (The title-page gives further information about the performance before the queen – see Greg – but no information about a performance at Oxford)

REFERENCE WORKS: *ES*, vol 3, pp 310–11; *AED* 1564

MODERN EDITION: Ros King (ed), *The Works of Richard Edwards: Politics, Poetry and Performance in Sixteenth-Century England*, Revels Plays Companion Library (Manchester, 2001), 109–84

NOTE: Tragicomedy. Edwards died in 1566, a few weeks after his play *Palamon and Arcite* was performed before the queen at Christ Church

Supposes, by George Gascoigne

PERFORMANCE HISTORY: Gray's Inn, London, 1566; Trinity College, 8 January 1581/2 (see p 179)

FIRST EDITION: SVPPOSES: A Comedie written in the Italian tongue by Ariosto, and Englished by George Gascoygne of Grayes Inne Esquire, and there presented. Printed in: *A Hundreth sundrie Flowres bounde vp in one small Poesie* (London, 1573, sigs A4–K1v; STC: 11635; Greg 60)

REFERENCE WORKS: *ES*, vol 3, p 321; *AED* 1566

MODERN EDITION: Lodovico Ariosto, *Supposes (I suppositi) (1509)*, George Gascoigne (trans), Donald Beecher and John Butler (eds), Carleton Renaissance Plays in Translation 33 (Ottawa, 1999)

NOTE: Translation of Ludovico Ariosto, *I Suppositi* (1509), subsequently printed in 1575 (STC: 11636–7), and with Gascoigne's *Whole Woorkes* in 1587 (STC: 11638)

Three Laws, by John Bale

PERFORMANCE HISTORY: Prior history uncertain; Magdalen College, 1560–1?

FIRST EDITION: A comedy concernynge thre lawes, of nature Moses, & Christ, corrupted by
the Sodomytes. Pharysees and Papystes (Wesel (?), 1548; *STC*: 1287; Greg 24)

REFERENCE WORKS: *MS*, vol 2, p 449; *AED* 1538

MODERN EDITION: *The Complete Plays of John Bale*, Peter Happé (ed), vol 2 (Woodbridge,
Suffolk, 1985–6), 64–124

NOTE: A payment of 3s 4d to a painter for painting names of the heresies in a spectacle (see
p 103) together with an enigmatic payment for 'portenta religioso*rum* in spectaculo baulino'
(see p 1097, endnote to MC Arch: LCE/6 f 17) may suggest this play. *Three Laws* was printed
in subsequent editions beginning in 1562 (*STC*: 1288)

APPENDIX 10

Town Plays by
Non-Oxford Authors

We have evidence suggesting the titles of eight plays performed in the town that were not by Oxford authors. Of these, four – *The Alchemist, Hamlet, Othello*, and *The Seven Deadly Sins* – were in the professional repertoire and two – *The Chaos of the World* and *The Destruction of Jerusalem* – were 'motions' or puppet plays popular in the 1630s. The other two – *Abraham and Isaac* and *Cupid's Whirligig* – were amateur performances. We have eyewitness accounts for all but the performance of *Hamlet*. The *Abraham and Isaac* performance is cited as hearsay by Edmund Bunny from an eyewitness. However, both Henry Jackson and Thomas Crosfield are direct witnesses. Henry Jackson (1586–1662) is best known as the editor of Hooker's 'Opuscula.' He was an Oxford-born divine, a fellow of Corpus Christi College, rector of the parish of Meysey Hampton in Gloucestershire (a parish associated with Corpus Christi), and a kinsman of Anthony Wood. His references to the performances of *The Alchemist* and *Othello* by the king's men in 1610 are preserved in copies made from their original manuscript fifty years after the event by his successor in the living of Meysey Hampton and another fellow of Corpus Christi, William Fulman (1632–88). Thomas Crosfield (1602–63) was associated with Queen's both as a student and a fellow from 1618 to *c* 1640 and was rector of the parish of Spennithorne, Yorkshire, from 1649 to 1663. The portion of his manuscript diary with relevant entries scattered among its eclectic selection of subjects runs from January 1625/6 to January 1639/40. He was a frequent observer of what went on in the city and provides us with considerable information in addition to his observations on the amateur productions and the two puppet plays. The only witness to the performance of *Hamlet* in Oxford is the title-page of the first quarto of 1603. The reference to Tarlton's *Seven Deadly Sins* appears in Gabriel Harvey's *Fovre Letters and certaine Sonnets especially touching Robert Greene, and other parties, by him abused*, published in 1592 (STC: 12900) as part of his running argument with Greene and Greene's friend Thomas Nash. A performance in Oxford is not certain but Harvey (a Cambridge man) says that it was a 'most liuely playe, I might haue seene in London: and was verie gently inuited thereunto at Oxford, by Tarleton himselfe…' (see p 222). Tarlton obviously intended to play the piece in Oxford although there is no supporting evidence that the performance took place.

For biographical information on Henry Jackson, William Fulman, and Gabriel Harvey, see *DNB*, and for Thomas Crosfield see Frederick S. Boas' introduction to Crosfield's *Diary*, pp xiii–xxviii.

Abraham and Isaac, Anonymous

Suggested dates of performance: *c* 1564–74 (see p 110)

A performance of an Abraham and Isaac play in Oxford was used by Edmund Bunny (1540–1618), a Protestant preacher, to attack the Jesuit Robert Persons (1546–1610), who was a member of Balliol College 1566–74. The reference occurs in Bunny's *A Briefe Answer vnto those idle and friuolous quarrels of R[obert] P[ersons] against the late edition of the Resolution* (London, 1589; *STC*: 4088), a response to Persons' *The First Booke of Christian Exercise, appertayning to resolution* (Rouen, 1582; *STC*: 19353) retitled in its second edition, *A Christian Directorie Guiding Men to their Salvation* (Rouen, 1585; *STC*: 19362). See Driscoll, 'A Miracle Play at Oxford,' p 6.

The Alchemist, by Ben Jonson

Suggested date of performance: 4 September 1610 (see p 387)

Henry Jackson describes the performance of a play attacking alchemists that also attacks Anabaptists. The king's men were in Oxford in August 1610. The single payment to them of 20s from the city chamberlains' accounts is dated 5 August 1610. The positive identification of the play as *The Alchemist* was made by Tillotson in 'Othello and *The Alchemist* at Oxford in 1610,' p 494.

The Chaos of the World, produced by William Sands

Suggested dates of performance: 16 July 1628, 11 July 1631 (see pp 474–7, 490)

This 'motion' or puppet show was licensed by Sir Henry Herbert on 27 August 1623 'to William Sands and others to show "the *Chaos of the World*;" to show a motion called "the Creation of the World"' (J.Q. Adams (ed), *The Dramatic Records of Sir Henry Herbert* (New Haven, 1917)). Thomas Crosfield saw the puppet show twice in three years. The episodes from the poem he recorded in 1628 include the Creation, the Fall, Cain and Abel, Abraham and Isaac, Nebuchadnezzar and the fiery furnace, the Nativity, the Wise Men, the Flight into Eygpt, the Slaughter of the Innocents, and Dives and Lazarus. In 1631 Crosfield mentions, in addition, 'Nineveh beseiged & taken.' This may have been a puppet show based directly on the text in the Book of Jonah or one of the two Renaissance dramatizations: *Nineveh's Repentance* (a lost play dated between 1570 and 1661 (Harbage, *Annals*, p 40; and Chambers, *Elizabethan Stage*, vol 4, p 402)) or Thomas Lodge and Robert Greene's *Looking Glass for London and England, c* 1590 (*Elizabethan Stage*, vol 3, p 328).

Sands, a Lancashire man, died in 1638 and bequeathed his 'Shewe called the Chaos, the Wagon, the Stage, & all the Ioyners tooles & other ymplementes & [p]appurtenances to the said Shewe belonging' to his son, John Sands (David George (ed), *Lancashire*, REED (Toronto, 1991), 87).

Puppet plays on biblical subjects occurred also in 1630 in two Dorset towns: Beaminster and Dorchester (see Rosalind Conklin Hays and C.E. McGee/ Sally L. Joyce and Evelyn S. Newlyn, (eds), *Dorset/Cornwall*, REED (Toronto, 1999), 121, 200). There was also a well-known puppet play of the Resurrection performed in nearby Witney (Ian Lancashire (ed), *Dramatic Texts and Records of Britain: A Chronological Topography to 1558* (Toronto, 1984), 286).

Cupid's Whirligig, by Edward Sharpham

Suggested date of performance: Christmas season, 1631–2 (see p 498)

This play was first performed by the children of the king's revels in 1607 (Harbage, *Annals*, p 95). It was published in 1607 (*STC*: 22380) and later editions appeared in 1611 (*STC*: 22381), 1616 (*STC*: 22382), and 1630 (*STC*: 22383) just before this amateur performance in Oxford as reported by Thomas Crosfield.

Destruction of Jerusalem, by William Gosling

Suggested date of performance: 15 July 1634 (see p 513)

The spectacle described by Thomas Crosfield was probably the same puppet version of the *Destruction* that Gosling showed the next year in Norwich. On 28 March 1635 he presented a licence from the master of the revels to the civic officials in Norwich 'dated the 9th day of August in the Tenth yeare of kinge Charles to shew the portraiture of the City of Ierusalem in all places for a yeare…' (David Galloway (ed), *Norwich 1540–1642*, REED (Toronto, 1984), 219).

Hamlet, by William Shakespeare

Suggested dates of performance: 1594–5, 1600–1

Evidence for an Oxford performance of *Hamlet* occurs in the title-page of the 1603 edition (*STC*: 22275):

> THE | Tragicall Historie of | HAMLET | *Prince of Denmarke* | By William Shake-speare.| As it hath beene diuerse times acted by his Highnesse ser-| uants in the Cittie of London: as also in the two V - | niuersities of Cambridge and Oxford, and else-where | [device] | At London printed for N.L. and Iohn Trundell. | 1603.

Of the two surviving copies of the 1603 edition, only the one at the Huntington Library preserves the title-page: a photoreproduction of the title-page can be found in G.R. Hibbard (ed), *Hamlet*, The Oxford Shakespeare (Oxford, 1987), 68. Boas discusses the possibilities of an Oxford performance in his '*Hamlet* at Oxford,' pp 245–53. He notes the long-standing prohibition about playing in the University and concludes that if a performance took place in Oxford it was under the sponsorship of the city. He notes that Lord Strange's men (with whom Shakespeare was at the time associated) performed in the city in 1593 and suggests that if *Hamlet* was performed at that time, it was in a version earlier than the 1603 quarto. He asks, 'Why should not *Hamlet*, as it appears in the First Quarto, have been written between 1592 and 1594?' This would mean that the play could have been performed in Oxford by Strange's men in 1593. However, a performance date of 1601 is more in keeping with the traditional understanding of the date of *Hamlet*. Since the notation of performance sites appears only in the first quarto and not in subsequent quartos, it is possible that the claim for performance at the universities may be 'a printer's groundless boast' as suggested in Nelson (ed), *Cambridge*, vol 2, p 985.

Othello, by William Shakespeare

Suggested date of performance: 5 September 1610 (see p 387)

This reference comes from Henry Jackson's letter to D.G.P. The last paragraph describes the death of Desdemona in moving terms, praising the character – and thus by implication the boy actor – when 'she appealed to the spectators' pity with her very expression.'

The Seven Deadly Sins, by Richard Tarlton

Suggested date of performance: before 1588 (see p 222)

Gabriel Harvey, the Cambridge man of letters, makes a passing comment that Richard Tarlton (d. 1588), the famous clown associated with Shakespeare, personally invited him to see the play at Oxford. The entry for Richard Tarlton in the *DNB* states, 'Tarlton was the contriver and arranger of the extempore play the "Seven Deadly Sins."' See Harbage, *Annals*, p 50; and Chambers, *Elizabethan Stage*, vol 3, pp 496–7.

The Anti-theatrical Controversy

At Christ Church on 6–8 February 1591/2, a Sunday, Monday, and Tuesday, three of William Gager's plays – *Ulysses Redux*, *Rivales*, and *Hippolytus* – were performed on the three successive nights. *Hippolytus* was the classical play with a supplemental scene by Gager and a satirical afterpiece featuring the character Momus. The satire comprised a thinly veiled attack on John Rainolds of Queen's College, whose anti-theatrical diatribes had become both notorious in Oxford and a thorn in Gager's flesh. When Gager published his afterpiece the following May as an appendix to *Ulysses Redux* and rather cheekily sent a copy to Rainolds, there ensued a war of words that eventually involved a third disputant, Alberico Gentili, Regius Professor of Civil Law.

Most of the letters and treatises that passed among these three men survive in a contemporary manuscript (described below) and in John Rainolds, *Th'overthrow of Stage-Plays* ([Middelburg], 1599; *stc*: 20616), which contains items 2, 4, and 6–9 below. Gentili published several of his contributions in continental imprints (see items 5 and 14 below), while others remain unpublished (see items 10–13 below). Several of Gentili's texts have been translated from the original Latin (see items 5 and 6 below).

Oxford, Corpus Christi College Library, ms 352; *c* 1592–9; English and Latin; paper; vi + 168; average 210mm x 300mm; late 17th-c. pagination, some sections with earlier, separate foliation, flyleaves in modern foliation; original vellum binding, in ink in Langbaine's hand on front cover: 'Mr Langbaine,' on spine: 'DDD Rainolds Gager Gentilis,' and on back inside cover: 'Mary Langbain.' In this 'Letter Book of John Rainolds' the letters of Gager and Gentili are mostly signed autographs, presumably the originals sent to Rainolds, while the Rainolds letters are scribal copies. Some bear headings and annotations in Langbaine's hand.

The Rainolds-Gager controversy has been discussed at length by Boas (ed), *University Drama*, pp 229–48; by Karl Young in 'An Elizabethan Defence of the Stage,' *Shakespeare Studies by Members of the Department of English of the University of Wisconsin* (Madison, 1916), 103–24, and 'William Gager's Defence of the Academic Stage,' *Transactions of the Wisconsin Academy of Sciences, Arts, and Letters* 18 (1916), 593–638; and by Dana F. Sutton (ed and trans), *William Gager: The Complete Works*, vol 2 (New York and London, 1994), vi–xiv. Also cited is M.A. Shaaber, *Check-list of Works of British Authors Printed Abroad, in Languages other than English, to 1641* (New York, 1975).

The following items make up the controversy insofar as texts survive:

1) Letter from Rainolds to Thomas Thornton, 6 February 1591/2. English.
MS 352, pp 11–14; Bodl.: MS. Tanner 77, ff 35–6v; Young, 'An Elizabethan Defence,'
pp 108–11.
2) Letter from Rainolds to Gager, 10 July 1592. English.
MS 352, pp 17–40; Rainolds, *Th'overthrow*, pp 1–27.
3) Letter from Gager to Rainolds, 31 July 1592. English.
MS 352, pp 41–65; Young, 'William Gager's Defence,' pp 604–37.
4) Letter from Rainolds to Gager, 30 May 1593. English.
MS 352, pp 71–179; CCC: MS 166, pp 9–67; Rainolds, *Th'overthrow*, pp 29–163.
5) Alberico Gentili, *Ad Tit. C. De Maleficis et Math. et ceter. similibus. Commentarius* (Oxford,
1593; STC: 11732) (Hanover, 1604; Shaaber G164). Latin. Translated by J.W. Binns, 'Alberico
Gentili in Defense of Poetry and Acting,' *Studies in the Renaissance* 19 (1972), 224–72.
6) Letter from Gentili to Rainolds, 7 July 1593. Latin.
MS 352, pp 183–4; Rainolds, *Th'overthrow*, p 164. Translated, along with items 7–9, by
Leon Markowicz, *Latin Correspondence by Alberico Gentili and John Rainolds on Academic
Drama*, Salzburg Studies in English Literature, Elizabethan and Renaissance Studies 68
(Salzburg, 1977).
7) Letter from Rainolds to Gentili, 10 July 1593. Latin.
MS 352, pp 185–7; Rainolds, *Th'overthrow*, pp 165–8.
8) Letter from Gentili to Rainolds, 15 July 1593. Latin.
MS 352, pp 191–3; Rainolds, *Th'overthrow*, pp 168–72.
9) Letter from Rainolds to Gentili, 5 August 1593. Latin.
MS 352, pp 195–208; Rainolds, *Th'overthrow*, pp 172–90.
10) Letter from Gentili to Rainolds, undated. Latin.
MS 352, pp 213–19. Unpublished.
11) Letter from Rainolds to Gentili, 25 January 1593/4. Latin.
MS 352, pp 221–72. Unpublished.
12) Letter from Gentili to Rainolds, 8 February 1593/4. Latin.
MS 352, pp 273–92. Unpublished.
13) Letter from Rainolds to Gentili, 12 March 1593/4. Latin.
MS 352, pp 295–307. Unpublished.
14) Alberico Gentili, *Disputationes Duae: 1. de actoribus et spectatoribus non notandis*
(Hanover, 1599; Shaaber G177). Latin.

In lieu of a full transcript of CCC: MS 352 and a fresh edition of *Th'overthrow* – both far beyond
the scope of the present publication – the following comments focusing on Oxford performance
practices and on details of the lost *Rivales* are excerpted from MS 352 (items 1–4). Italic script
for titles and for proper names in the MS is not observed, but display script to indicate quotation
is noted.

Letter from Rainolds to Thomas Thornton, 6 February 1591/2

Rainolds declines Thornton's personal invitation to the Christ Church plays

(pp 11–12): 'Syr because your curteous inviting of me yesterdaye againe to
your plaies dothe shewe you were not satisfied with my answer and reason
therof before geven, why I might not be at them … yow se that I, thinking
the thinge to be vnlawfull, shall [s⟨…⟩] ⌈sinne⌉ (yf I approved it) at least,
in doinge of that which is not of faith if not in hauinge fellowship with the   5
vnfruitfull workes of darkness, And this for that one circumstance which your
self mentioned, and toucheth (it may be) all your plaies.…'

Letter from Rainolds to Gager, 10 July 1592

10

Rainolds objects to the cost of plays and to use of the office of the revels
(p 39): '…But neither is it a good woorke or service vnto Christ, to spend
thirtie pownd in trimming vp a stage & borowing roabes out of the revils,
for feeding of that humour…'

15

Rainolds cites the negative opinion of a friend (Thornton (?)), and remarks
on being pressured to attend plays (p 39): '…as in part I knowe by a grave
learned man, your good frende & mine, who shewed me his dislike of the
representation of amorousnes & drunkennes, in Rivales, both; the former,
not in Rivales onely: in parte I coniecture by that I vnderstand that certaine   20
who came thither, came euen pressed to it by great importunitie; & as my
selfe by such meanes have bene overintreated to doo that sometimes which
I repented afterward…'

Letter from Gager to Rainolds, 31 July 1592   25

Gager acknowledges Rainolds' letter prompted by the gift of *Ulysses Redux*
(p 41): '…wheras, in the beginninge of your late Letter from or rather treatyse
to me, Master Doctor Rainoldes, you wryte, that you are muche to thanke me
for my letters, & Tragedye; it is as muche, at the most, as thay deserved; but   30
that you add, you are so to doe the more, for enlarginge the answere to
Momus, for yours, and others askinge, why thinges by hym obiected, weare
not answered, I ame rather the more to thanke you, for your takinge it in
so good parte.…'

35

In former years Rainolds wrote in reproof of 'Theatre-sightes and Stage-playes,'
including a letter to a mutual friend (item 1 above). Gager claims that he had
not read Rainolds' 'Theses, agaynst plays,' or if he had, it was during his
youth (p 41).

40

Gager declares his intention in creating Momus (p 42): '…to move delight

29–30/ to thanke … Tragedye: *in display script to mark quotation*

in the audytorye, with the noveltye of the invention and the person, beinge
nowe foreweryed and tyred with the tediusnes of the Tragedye…'

Gager notes that academic plays differ from professional plays in being not-
for-profit (p 43).   5

Gager rejects the appellation, 'Scenici, or Histriones' (p 47): '…for cum*m*inge
on the Stage once in a yeere, or twoe yeere, sevne, ten, or somtyme twentye
yeeres….'
                                                                                                        10
Gager on the difference between ancient professional and college plays (pp
47–8): '…thay did it with excessyve charge; we thriftely, warely, and allmost
beggerly; thay acted theire Playes in an other sorte then we doe, or can,
or well knowe howe; but so exquisytly, and carefully, that we may seeme,
compared with them, eyther for skill, or diligence, rather Recitare, which you   15
doe not dislike, then Agere…. we are vnlike them in the ende and effectes
of Playinge…. We contrarywise ∧⌜doe it⌝ to recreate owre selves, owre House,
and the better parte of the Vniuersitye, with some learned Poëme or other;
to practyse owre owne style eyther in prose or verse; to be well acquaynted
with Seneca or Plautus; honestly to embowlden owre yuthe; to trye their   20
voyces, and confirme their memoryes; to frame their speeche; to conforme
them to convenient action; to trye what mettell is in evrye one, and of what
disposition thay are of; wherby never any one amongst vs, that I knowe, was
made the worse, many have byn muche the better; Lastly, we differ from them
in many other circumstances as namely thay frequented the Stage; we doe it   25
seldome, somtyme not in seavne, ten, or twentye yeers; thay on the publick
theater, not of the Citie only, but of the whole worlde; we in a pryvate house,
and to a fewe, men of vnderstandinge; thay weare men growne, one of them
three score yeers oulde, Knightes, of noble houses, Patricij, and one of them
Emporour of the worlde; in vs beinge yunge men, boyes, poore Schollers, all   30
thes things are quyte contrarye….'

Gager on his *Ulysses Redux* and on patristic objections to plays (pp 48–9):
'…whoe ever would resemble owre Melantho, with your Laureolus? the on
represented by an ingenuus boye, and for her lewdnes imagined to be hanged 35
within; the other acted by Lentulus, a man noblye descended, expressinge
perhapps openly one the Stage, the deformytye of the same punishment.
what likenes is there betweene owre yonge men, puttinge on the personns of
Antinous, and the rest of Penelope's wooers; and betweene gentyllmen of the
noble race of Fabius, in their owne persons, not so muche cownterfettinge   40

15–16/ Recitare … Agere: *Rainolds was less disapproving of pure recitation so long as it was not accompanied
by action or personification*
23/ of: *corrected over other letters*

others, as expressinge their owne scurrilytyes? suche as owre Antinous, and the
rest of the woers, can not iustly be charged with; no not owre Irus, or Vlysses.
for thoughe Iuuenal thought it dishonorable and shamfull, as he well might,
that noble men shoulde take blowes and whirrytts openly, and that the peeple
should rather have pittyed, then liked suche behaviour in their nobylytye, yet   5
he thought so rather in respect of the actors, beeinge suche as thay weare, that
is, noble men (as it appeerethe by the whole drifte of his 8 Satyr, alleaged by
you so muche, which is not agaynst Playes, them he nowhere, that I knowe,
reprehendethe, but to shewe that trwe nobylytye is to be esteemed by the
vertues of the mynde, and not by bludd, or ancyent howses) then for any   10
other thinge, specialy if it weare no wurse; then is represented in owre Irus
or Vlysses. for neyther would Iuuenal hym selfe, if he weare alyve, reprehend
eyther the speeches thay vse, or the devyse of bringinge them in so meane
and beggerlye, because bothe are Homer's; neyther is their any suche thinge in
their partes, that may make vs base or ridiculous, or scurryle, for representinge   15
them. Vnhappy Vlysses, to whome as it was fatall ever to be in troble in his
life, so is he more hardly dealt withall after his deathe, that his person may
not honestly ˄⌈be⌉ resembled withowte note of infamye to the Actor. which
if I had knowne, howsoever he returned in Ithacam, he shoulde never have
cumme in Scenam by my means. Agayne, what resemblance is there betweene   20
owre Hippodamia only singinge, Eurymachus only sayinge, Phemius bothe
singinge and sayinge, all three represented by suche as thay weare; and betweene
Nero, playinge menn's, weemen's, and minstrells partes vpon the Stage in Rome?
lett vs therfor consider breefely the force of your arguinge. Many noble men,
and Nero hym selfe, weare infamous, for playinge, thoughe freely, menn's and   25
weemen's partes, and specialye Nero for singinge like a fidler on the Stage;
Ergo Schollers and the Students of Christchurche, are to be noted with a
marke of infamye, for playinge, thoughe gratis, suche partes as thay did in
Vlysse Reduce; and namely the master of owre Choristers, for playinge
Phemius; notwithstandinge for his honesty, modesty, and good voyce, he is   30
as wurthy [⟨.⟩] to be delyvered from infamye, as Phemius hym selfe is fayned
to be saved from deathe, for his excellent skill in Musicke, to say nothinge
of the rest....'

Gager on cross-dressing in plays (p 52): '...we doe it for an howre or twoe,   35
or three, to represent an others person, by one that is openly knowne to be
as he is in deede; it is not ill in vs to doe so, thoughe it be but in myrthe,
and to delyte...'

Gager on the same (p 53): '...for a boye to pray in the Churche openly, with   40
a caule, or a frenchehoode on his head, as you wryte, thoughe his mynd weare

---

29/ master of owre Choristers: *William Maycock*

never so chaste it weare a greate fault; but it followethe not that therfor it is so,
for a boy or a yonge man, to come on the Stage with a cawle or a frenchehood
on his head....'

Gager on the same and on dancing and kissing in plays (pp 54–6): 'Seeinge   5
therfor that, as I take it, it is not proved vngodly for a boy or a yuthe, to putt
on womanly rayment in owre case, it followethe that it is [not] ₐ⌈the lesse⌉
vnlawfull for suche a one also to imitate womanly speeche, and behaviour,
howe hardly so ever you thinke good to terme it.... yet a boy, by way of
representation only, may not indecently imytate maydenly, or womanly   10
demeannre. ffor as for all that tracte of your discourse, concerninge the danger
of wanton dansinge, of kissinge bewtifull boyes, of amatorye embracinges,
and effectuall expressinge of love panges, wherby bothe the spec₍ₐ⌈ta⌉tors
in behowldinge, and the actors in the meditation of suche thinges, are
corrupted ... owre younge men dansed only twoe solleme measures, withowte   15
any lyter galliarde, or other [⟨.⟩] danse, only for a decorum, to note therby
vnto the auditorye, what revelinge thay weare to imagin the wooers vsed
within. and yet truly if I might have over-ruled the matter, evne that littell
also, had byn lefte owte; because I feared lest it shoulde be ill taken, thoughe
I thought there was no ill in the thinge, as I nowe perceyve my feare was   20
not vayne. but what are the leadinge or treadinge of twoe Measures, to the
incommodytyes of dansinge which you insinuate? what Herode coulde be
inflamed? what Propertius ravished? what flame of lust kindled therby in
menns hartes? what woundes of love imprinted? whose senses coulde be
moved, or affections delyted more then ought to be, or may honestly be?   25
what enemyes of chastetye made by this sight? what stronge or constant harte
vanquished, nay what reede shaken therby? what so muche as flaxe or towe
sett on fyre? As for the danger of kissinge of bewtifull boyes, I knowe not
howe this suspition shoulde reache to vs. for it is vntrwe, whoesoever towlde
you so, that owre Eurymachus did kisse owre Melantho. I have enquyred of   30
the partyes them selves, [and thay constantly denye it,] whether any suche
action was vsed by them, and thay constantly denye it; sure I ame, no suche
thinge was taught. if you coniecture there was kissinge because Melantho
spake this verse, Furtiua nullus oscula Eurymachus dabit, you may perhapps
therby dislike my discretion for makinge a younge paynym Ladye, so to [take]   35
ₐ⌈bewayle⌉ her shamfull deathe (thoughe I can not thinke yet, howe I shoulde
mende it) yet, therby no kissinge can be proved agaynst vs, but that rather, that
thinge only in wordes was expressed, which was thought decent for suche a one
as she was, and in her case, to vtter....'

                                                                              40
Gager on Nero with his Sporus or Heliogabalus, ie, on homosexuality (p 56):

34/ Furtiua ... dabit: 'No Eurymachus will give stolen kisses'

'…we hartely abhorr them; and if I coulde suspecte any suche thinge to growe by owre Playes, I woulde be the first that should hate them, and detest my selfe, for gyvinge suche occasion….'

Gager on the moral influence of plays (p 56): '…I have byn often moved by   5
owre Playes to laughter, and somtyme to teares; but I can not accuse eyther my selfe, or any other of any such beastly thought, styrred vp by them. and therfore we should most vncharytably be wronged, if owre puttinge on of womanly rayment, or imytatinge of suche gesture, should eyther directly or indirectly be referred to the commandement, Thou shalte not [⟨.⟩] commit   10
adulterye. and yet if owre Eurymachus had kissed owre Melantho, thoughe Socrates had stood by, (and I would Socrates had stood by) he would perhapps have sayde he had done amysse, but not so dangerously as Critobulus did, because he might evydently perceyve, that no suche poyson of incontinencye could be instilled therby. As for the danger to the spectators in heeringe and   15
seeinge thinges lyvely expressed, and to the actors in the ernest meditation and studye to represent them; I grant that bad effectes doe fall owte in thos Playes, agaynst the which suche arguments are iustly to be amplyfyde; but there is no suche myscheefe to be feared to enswe of owres. wherin for owre penninge, we are base and meane as you see; and specialy for womanly   20
behaviour, we weare so careless, that when one of owre actors should have made a Conge like a woman, he made a legg like a man. in summ; owre spectators could not gretely charge owre actors with any such diligence in medytation and care to imprynt any passions; and so neyther of them coulde receyve any hurt therby. no not the nwe Nymphe in Hyppolitus whom you   25
so muche note, was any wittye wanton, or any so dangerous a woman, as that she brought fwell inoughe to heate a harte of yse or snowe. the poore wenche I perceyve hathe byn hardely reported of to you, and worse a greate deale then she deserved, as you and the worlde shall one day see. in whose person the devyse was, partly to sett owte the constant chastetye or rather   30
virginytye of Hippolytus, whoe neyther with honest love made to hym in the woods, nor with vnhonest attempts in the cyttye could be overcumme; partly to expresse the affection of honest, lawfull, vertuous, marriage meaninge love; for no other did she profer, and therfor me thinkes she is not, vnharde, to be reproched with the brode name of bawderye, wherof there is no one   35
syllable in worde or sense to be founde in all her speches….'

Gager on the moral effect of his plays (pp 57–8): '…Neyther doe I see what evill affections could be stirred vp by owre playes, but rather good. for in

10–11/ Thou … adulterye: *in display script to mark quotation*
12/ perhapps: h *corrected over another letter*
27/ she brought … snowe: *in display script to mark quotation*

Vlysse Reduce, whoe did not love the fidelytye of Eumæus, and Philætius,
towardes their [⟨.⟩] Master; and hate the contrary, in Melanthius? whoe was
not moved to compassion, to see Vlysses a greate Lorde, dryvne so hardly, as
that he was fayne to be a begger in his owne house? whoe did not wisshe hym
well, and all ill to the wooers, and thinke them worthely slayne, for their   5
bluddye purpose agaynst Telemachus, and other dissolute behaviour, not so
muche expressed on the Stage, as imagined to be done within? whoe did not
admyre the constancye of Penelope, and disprayse the lytenes, and bad nature
in Melantho, and [thoughte] thinke her iustly hanged for it? whoe did not
prayse the patience, wisdome, and secrecye, of Vlysses and Telemachus his   10
sonne? lastly whoe was not glad to see Vlysses restored to his wife, and his
goods, and his mortall enemyes overthrowne, and punished? In Riuales, what
Cato might not be delyted to see the fonde behaviour of cuntrye wooinge,
expressed by cyvill men, or the vanytye of a bragginge soldier? by the spectacle
of the drunken mariners, if there were any drunkard there, why might he   15
not the rather detest drunkenness by seeinge the deformytye of drunken
actions represented? possible it was not, that any man should be provoked to
drunkennes therby. the Lacedæmonians are commended for causinge their
slaves, beinge drunke in deed, to be brought before their children, that thay
seeinge the beastly vsage of suche men, myght the more lothe that vyce; but   20
we muche better ‸⌈expressinge⌉ the same intent, not with drunken, but with
sober men, counterfettinge suche vnseemly manners, are the lesse therfor to
be reprehended. In Hippolytus, what younge man did not wisshe hym selfe
to be as chast as Hippolytus, if he weare not so allreadye? whoe did not detest
the love of Phædra? who dide not approve the grave counsayle of the Nurse   25
to her in secrett? or whoe coulde be the worse for her wooinge Hippolytus,
in so generall termes? the drifte wherof, if it had byn to procure an honest
honorable marriage, as it was covertly to allure hym to inceste, he might
very well have listned to it. whoe wisshethe not that Theseus had not byn so
credulus? whoe was not sorrye for the crwell deathe of Hippolytus? thes and   30
suche like, weare the passions that weare, or might be moved, in owre Playes,
withowte hurte, at the leste, to any man....'

Gager on the character of his actors (p 58): '...Wherfor as the younge men
of owre house, are suche in deede, as I commended them for; so for me, or   35
for any thinge donne on the Stage, by the grace of God thay may so remayne
and continwe, and I hope shall ever be so reputed....'

Gager on the relative value of plays (pp 58–9): 'In your answere to my defence
of owre not mysspendinge tyme aboute Playes, I must needes saye, you spare   40

35/ are: r *corrected over another letter*

vs not a whitt. if you had but sayde that owre playes, are toyes, vnn⟨...⟩ssarye,
⟨.⟩ayne, or suche like; it had byn no more perhapps then in strict⟨..⟩s, trwe....
and I have harde a godly, and a learned preacher, whome you knowe, in the
pulpitt affirme, that owre declamations, oppositions, suppositions, and suche
scholasticall exercises, are no better then vayne thinges. but to compare owre   5
Playes, to ye wickednes of a foole committed in pastyme, to a madd mann's
castinge of fyrebrandes, arrowes, and mortall [⟨.⟩] thinges, as you doe before;
or to the hauntinge of a dycinge house, or taverne, or stwes, as in this place;
or to a Schollers playinge at stooleball amonge wenches, at mumchance, at
Mawe with idell lost companions, at Trunkes in Guile-halls, dansinge aboute   10
Maypoles, riflinge in alehouses, carrowsinge in taverns, stealinge of deere, or
robbinge of orchardes, as afterwarde; I say to compare oure Playes to no better
then thes thinges, it exceedethe the cumpasse of any tolerable resemblance.
I cowlde have wisht that suche comparisons had byn forborne, if not for the
Playes them selves, (thoughe also thay ought for the Playes them selves, beinge   15
thinges that savor of some witt, learninge; and iudgment, approved vnto vs by
longe continwance, recommended by owre cheefest governors, and donne in
a learned, grave, worshipfull, and somtyme honorable presence, with suche
convenient sollemnytye, honest preparation, ingenuous expectation, dwe
regarde, modest reverence, silent attention, and the generall, as it weare,   20
simmetrye and seemly carriage in them) yet in respecte of the actors, and owre
whole House; of the spectators that sawe them, and hartely approved them,
to whome it weare a foule shame, but to stand by as lookers on of thinges of
suche nature; and lastly, [for] ₐ⌐of⌐ thos reverend, famous, and excellent men,
for life, and learninge, and their places in the Churche of God, bothe of owre   25
house, and otherwise of the Vniuersitye, that have byn, and nowe are lyvinge,
with vs, and abrode, whoe have byn not only wryters of suche thinges them
selves, but also actors, and to this daye doe thinke well of them, to whome it
weare a greate reproche, at any tyme to have byn acquaynted with thinges of
so vyle, and base qualytye, and muche more, still to allowe of them....'   30

Gager on plays vs. sermons (p 59): '...Wheras I sayde that there was no more
tyme spent vpon owre Playes then was convenient, you replye that It may be
there was, evne some tyme that shoulde have byn spent in heeringe Sermons,
the very day that my Vlysses Redux came vpon the Stage. It may be there was   35
not; and for any thinge that can be proved, or for any thinge that any man
needed to be hindred from Sermons that daye for my Vlysses, it was not so in
deede. sure I ame, that the gentelman that playde Vlysses, was at Sermon, and
divers others of the actors, as if neede were thay coulde prove, perhapps the
rather, to avoyde suche a scandall. if any were awaye, thay might have other   40

6–12/ to ye wickednes ... orchardes: *in display script to mark quotation*
33–5/ It may be ... vpon the Stage: *in display script to mark quotation*

cause so to doe, thoughe (the more the pittye) it is no vnvsuall thinge, for
many other students, as well as owres, sometyme to mysse a sermon. and it
may be, that some of them that mysliked owre Playes, weare not there them
selves; it may be the same Sonday night thay were wurse occupied then owre
actors were; it may be, preventinge vs, playinge Momus parte in good ernest, 5
which we afterwarde did but for pastyme. and yet that accusation touchethe
my poore vnfortunate Vlysses only, not the other twoe....'

Gager on money spent on plays (pp 61–2): '...the mony bestowde on owre
Playes, was not, to add watstfullnes to wantonnes, but to procure honest 10
recreation, with convenient expence. surely if the Prodigall sonne, had byn as
moderatt, and as thriftye, in his spendinge at his boorde, as we weare in owre
Playes, he might well inoughe have sayde, to any niggarde, that shoulde have
vnwisely fownde falte with hym, as muche as you make hym to saye, not with
the note of a prodigall, but with the commendation of an ingenuous, and a 15
[b] liberall disposition.... Nero cowlde have as well spared suche huge summs
of mony, which he spent that way often, as owre House, with the cumpanye
in it, and belonginge to it (thanked be God) can, ons in many yeers, thirtye
powndes...'

20

Gager on whether his critics had attended his plays (p 62): '...I have not
done the Vniuersytye wronge, in producinge the iudgment therof, to the
approovinge of owre Playes. for thoughe, as you wryte, there weare some which
weare not present, because thay disallowed them, some disallowed them,
that weare present; yet, bothe thes putt together, if the greater parte may 25
denomynate the whole [bodye], which did with their hartye applause approve
them, I might withowte wronge, I ame sure, to the bodye of the Vniuersytye,
demand of Momus, Academiæ tu iudicia nihili facis?...'

Gager on gathering an audience for his plays (p 63): '...I may trulye saye, 30
that I never requested any man to owre Playes; neyther did I neede; thay woulde
cumme without biddinge, or sendinge for, more, and faster then somtyme we
would willingely [⌐then⌐] [thay shoulde] thay shoulde have donne. muche
lesse needed thay to be pressed to them, with greate importunytye. I beshrowe
them that did byd suche ghestes, whose roomthes, had byn better then their 35
cumpanyes. for of all men, I woulde thay that dislike Playes, had not byn at
owres...'

10/ to add ... wantonnes: *in display script to mark
  quotation*
10/ watstfullnes: *for* wastfullness
23–5/ there weare ... weare present: *in display script
  to mark quotation*

28/ Academiæ ... facis?: *'Do you make nothing of
  the judgments of the University?'*
32/ or: o *corrected over another letter*
34/ pressed ... importunytye: *in display script to
  mark quotation*

Gager on the numbers of those who took offence against his plays (p 63): '…I did not thinke, till I harde of the Preacher, and receyved your Letter, that there had byn so many as to make vp a number in this Vniuersitye, of whome owre Playes weare so mysliked, as nowe I perceyve there are, and yett but a number only. and to this daye, of my knowledge, I can not name [ay] any   5 man that is of your opinion, besyde you twoe….'

Letter from Rainolds to Gager, 30 May 1593

Rainolds objects to kissing in plays, even by implication (p 76): '…As namely   10 that I mentioned Eurymachus kissing of Melantho: a thing which I gathered to have bene doon by her owne woords: sith they were both intended to be alone secretly, when he had fowle vnmodest [speech] lascivious talke with her; & the musicke & dansing, whereof she speakes withall, was represented on the stage. But I named them onely for example sake; my drift being general against such   15 playes as expresse such actions: whether sett foorth presently by you, as your Rivales, in which some of the wooers perhaps kissed Phœda…'

Rainolds on being pressured to act – particularly female roles – in contravention of (divine) law (pp 84–5): '…ffor what if some of them knew not this point of   20 law? & were of such age too (which they were all perhaps, at least the players of wemens parts) as the lawe excuseth for ignorance thereof? what if others were commanded to play by their superiors, whom they durst not displease; & so were in a maner inforced thereunto … what if a third sort, or more, euen these also, have since repented their playing…'   25

Rainolds on having played a female role (Hippolyta in *Palamon and Arcite*) as a youth (p 85): '…wherefore having this perswasion of your players, even of them for whose parts I charged players most, namely Hippodamia, Melantho, the Nymph, Phædra, & her Nurse; if I should have noted them as infamous,   30 them I say, not their parts, these players & not players; I should have taken on me the iudgement that belongeth vnto the searcher of heartes & reines, & spoken against mine owne conscience. Which if you have made them beleeve I love them so ill, by reason of the bad conceit I have of them, that I would doo of spite & malice to discredit them: yet lett me intreat them to thinke I   35 love my selfe better, then that I would through their sides wounde mine owne; who, when I was about the age that they are, six & twentie yeares since, did play a womans part vpon the same stage, the part of Hippolyta….'

17/ Phœda: *for* Phœdra

APPENDIX 12
Degree Plays

In 1512 Edward Watson, college or hall unknown, was required by a grace of congregation to write one hundred songs in praise of the University and also a comedy in order to receive his BA (see p 54). In the mid-1540s Nicholas Grimald presented his *Archipropheta* to Dr Richard Cox of Christ Church as evidence of his abilities (L.R. Merrill (ed and trans), *The Life and Poems of Nicholas Grimald*, Yale Studies in English 69 (New Haven, 1925), 12).

Watson's case is the only known instance in University records of playwrighting as a statutory degree requirement. Other evidence, however, points to an informal tradition at Oxford of undergraduates presenting original dramatic compositions as part of the ritual of supplicating for their BAs.

The main evidence for such a suggestion comes from two poems written *c* 1640 by Martin Lluelyn, a student of Christ Church, printed in 1646 in a volume called *Men-Miracles. With Other Poemes* (Wing: L2625). The first poem, on p 77, is entitled, 'To my Lord B*ishop* of Ch*ichester* when I presented him a Play.' The second poem, immediately following on p 80 (78 and 79 are omitted in the pagination), is entitled, 'To Dr. F*ell* Deane of Ch*rist* Ch*urch* now Vicechancellour of Oxford, upon the Same occasion.' The first poem mentions 'single Leafes' and 'lesse papers' that the author had given the recipient 'foure yeares since' and that, because of the latter's encouragement, had now grown into the 'Prodigie' of a 'Play.' The second poem calls the play 'a Trifle' offered to the dean in order to 'begge degree' and 'receive a Hood,' adding that this is not a form of supplication 'as understood.'

From this information it is easy enough to reconstruct the date and the participants of this ritual. Martin Lluelyn matriculated as a student of Christ Church on 25 July 1636, at the age of eighteen. He took his BA on 7 July 1640. In that year the bishop of Chichester was Brian Duppa, who had been dean of Christ Church for the first two years of Lluelyn's residency. The table of contents to the volume confirms this by re-dedicating the first poem 'To my Lord B[ishop] of S[alisbury]' (sig A8), which was Duppa's title in 1646. The second poem is even more clearly addressed to Samuel Fell, who succeeded Duppa as dean of Christ Church in 1638, and who was also vice-chancellor of the University from 1645 to 1648, ie, at the time the poem addressed to him was finally published.

These poems, then, record a rite of passage enacted by an undergraduate about to receive his BA in the presence of the two men who had been heads of his house since he arrived in Oxford. The nature of the 'single Leafes' that Lluelyn had given Dean Duppa in 1636 remains mysterious, but he evidently felt in 1640 that a more substantial composition was now called for, and that it should be a play. There is no indication of what language it was written in and no suggestion that it was meant to be performed. The only hint as to its subject comes in the second poem, where the author asks Dean Fell to 'seat him high in his faign'd Queens view, High as her selfe, and yet both kneele to you' (p 81). All that can be made of this is that the central character in the play seems to have been a queen.

Lluelyn's career as a playwright did not end with his baccalaureate. Although he became a physician by profession, his attachment to Oxford and its cultural activities continued. In 1660 he was appointed both king's physician and principal of St Mary's Hall. In the following summer preparations were made for a visit to Oxford by the new king, Charles II, and we know from a letter of Timothy Halton, a fellow of Queen's, that 'the play [was] made by Dr. Llewellyn' (see p 607). Whether it was the same play he had written twenty years before we do not know, because it was never performed due to a 'want of actors.'

Taken together with the much earlier grace involving Edward Watson, the case of Martin Lluelyn, playwright, does not seem to be an isolated event. A number of Oxford plays, all of them in Latin, survive in MS copies for which there is no external evidence of performance and whose existence may be explained if we posit a circumstance like Lluelyn's. Thomas Atkinson's *Homo*, surviving in a fair copy dedicated to William Laud, president of St John's, would seem to be just such a degree play, although a few interpolated stage directions suggest that it may eventually have received a production. In the same category we can probably put Philip Parsons' *Atalanta*, also dedicated to Laud, and Christopher Wren's *Physiponomachia*, dedicated to John Buckeridge, Laud's predecessor. The fact that these plays, along with Henry Bellamy's *Iphis*, John Blencow's *Mercurius*, Joseph Crowther's *Cephalus et Procris*, and George Wild's *Eumorphus* were all written by St John's men has led Bentley to wonder whether they do not represent 'a standard St John's exercise' (*Jacobean and Caroline Stage*, vol 3, p 4). The survival of so many MSS from St John's is indeed suggestive of this, but Lluelyn's play, which was unknown to Bentley, may indicate that the practice they represent was more widespread throughout the University.

APPENDIX 13
Anthony Wood on Oxford

Anthony Wood (1632–95), an Oxford native, took advantage of his father's connections in Merton College and the University along with his mother's social connections in the county to make himself into Oxford's foremost – but crankiest – antiquary. (Among other things, he came to call himself Anthony à Wood, much to the torment of bibliographers.) Wood set himself the goal of producing a comprehensive history of Oxford. Given the abundance of available materials, he divided his project into three sections, covering the city, the University, and the colleges. Along the way he compiled hundreds and indeed thousands of individual biographies, and kept a personal diary.

Wood's antiquarian labours consisted to a considerable extent of copying out documents from the University archives. Although he borrowed wholesale from the papers of his predecessor Brian Twyne (1579?–1644), he made a considerable effort to trace Twyne's sources. A practitioner of the cut-and-paste method of composition, Wood several times destroyed one draft to create another. Although he published some of his work in his lifetime, particularly on the history of the University, much of his work was published posthumously and certain 'leavings' remain unpublished to this day.

Bodl.: ms. Wood F.1 is the last of several versions of the History or Annals of the University in Wood's own hand. The ms title is 'The History or Annals of the University of Oxford from the time of King Alfred till A.D. 1660.' Wood called this ms his 'last English copy' ('*Survey of the Antiquities of the City of Oxford*,' composed in 1661–6, by Anthony Wood, Andrew Clark (ed), vol 2, Oxford Historical Society (Oxford, 1889), 342). The printed edition, edited by John Gutch (2 vols, 1792–6), is based on this ms. The Gutch edition is a fairly faithful rendering of Wood's final intentions for the work, with a few typographical errors. It has been used to provide excerpts under 1612–13 and 1633–4 where the excerpts were not found in ms. Wood F.1. The first draft of Wood's History, finished c 1673, was cut up by Wood and is now lost, except for fragments pasted into other mss (*Life and Times*, vol 2, p 290, and vol 4, p 230). A copy of the first draft served as the basis for the Latin translation by R. Peers and R. Reeves that appeared in 1674. Wood called this 'the translator's copy' (*Life and Times*, vol 4, p 230). It too has been lost. Wood's personal copy of the printed Latin edition (Bodl.: ms. Wood 430) contains some marginal notes and corrections. A second draft of the History (Bodl.: ms. Wood F.38) c 1675, which Wood called his 'foul copy' (*Life and Times*, vol 2, p 290), survives. It has not been collated here.

Wood's *Athena Oxoniensis* or *Athenae Oxonienses*, covering approximately 1500–1690, was first published in two volumes over successive years, 1691–2 (Wing: W3382–3A). A second edition was published in 1721, and a third in 1813–20, in four volumes edited by Philip Bliss. Bliss began a fourth edition but of this only a single volume saw the light of day, in 1848. Because that edition was never completed the closest approximation to a definitive edition remains the third, of 1813–20. An understanding of how this complex but invaluable work is organized is necessary to make efficient use of it. The biographies of Oxford bishops and writers – which constitute the essence of the work for most users, including REED users – take up approximately the latter four-fifths of volume 1, the first two-thirds of volume 2, the whole of volume 3, and the first half of volume 4. Since entries are not alphabetical by last name but roughly chronological, an index is provided at the end of each part. More important, a comprehensive index is provided at the conclusion of the fourth part, roughly in the middle of volume 4. Meanwhile, the first one-fifth of volume 1 contains a life of Wood (with supporting materials), while the last third of volume 2 and the last half of volume 4 contain *Fasti Oxonienses* (third edition), which is indexed at the very end of volume 4.

For the modern editor of Oxford documents or historian of Oxford it is impossible to rely absolutely on Wood and equally impossible to proceed entirely without him. In recognition of that fact we present here certain materials from Wood's compilations, both printed and in manuscript.

For contemporary sources and parallel descriptions of the events described by Wood, readers are directed to the Records: for the royal (and noble) entertainments of 1566, 1583, 1605, and 1636, see pp 126–35, 190–1, 296–310, and 542–5; and for the maypoles at Holywell, see pp 578–9.

Wood's History or Annals of the University
Oxford, Bodleian Library, MS. Wood F.1 (*sc* 8463) ; 1678–85; English; paper; xx + 568; 280mm x 250mm; ink pagination in Wood's hand; proper nouns, names, and direct speech are typically under-lined; original leather binding dated 2 May 1678.

Gutch, *Wood's History and Antiquities*
The History and Antiquities of the University of Oxford, In Two Books: By Anthony à Wood, M.A. Of Merton College. Now First Published in English, From the Original MS in the Bodleian Library: By John Gutch, M.A. Chaplain of All Souls and Corpus Christi Colleges. Oxford, MDCCXCII.

Wood's *Historia et Antiquitates*
[Wood, Anthony.] HISTORIA I ET I ANTIQUITATES I UNIVERSITATIS I OXONIENSIS I Duobus Voluminibus Comprehensae. I [device] I OXONII, I E THEATRO SHELDONIANO. I [rule] I M.DC.LXXIV.

Wood's *Athenae Oxonienses*
Anthony a Wood, *Athenæ Oxonienses: An exact history of all the writers and bishops who have had their*

education in the University of Oxford. To which are added the Fasti, or Annals of the said University by Anthony A Wood. A new edition, with additions, and a continuation by Philip Bliss (London, 1813–20).

1565–6
Entertainment of Queen Elizabeth   Bodl.: MS. Wood F.1
pp 638–9   *(31 August)*

...

...In ye Euening came ye Queen with a noble retinew from Woodstock, & 5
at ye uttermost part of ye Universitie liberties near Wolvercote, the Earl of
Leycester [with] chancellour, four Doctors in ∧⌈their⌉ scarlet Habits namely
Kennall ye Vicechan*cellour* Humph∧⌈r⌉ey presid*ent* of Magd*alen* Coll*ege*
Godwyn Deane of Ch*rist* church & Whyte Warden of New College with
8 masters that were Heads of Houses in their Habits met ye Queen, & after 10
[ob] obeysance done to her, ye chancellour of ye Universitie, who before
her, received ye staves of the three Esquire Bedells then present, delivered
them up to her but shee no sooner had received, [them] but gave, them up
againe to ye chan*cellour* & he forthwith to ye Bedells. After this was done
an Oration was spoken before her by Marbeck ye ∧⌈late⌉ Orator ∧⌈now provost 15
of Oriel Coll*ege*⌉ beginning thus Multa sunt divina erga nos Comitatis &c
wh*ich* being finisht the Qu*een* said to him Wee have heard of y*ou* before but

Dedicus   now wee know y*ou*. The spanish Embassadour named Goseman, then with her,
Gosimannus   said also Non pauca multis sed multa paucis complexus est. Then ye Qu*een*
de Sylva   gave him her hand to kisse, as she did at ye same time to ye Vicechan*cellour* 20
Doctors & Masters but while Humphrey was doing y*at* complement ye Qu*een*
said Doctor Humphrey methinks this gowne & habit becomes y*ou* very well,
& I marvayle y*at* y*ou* are so straight laced in this point *(blank)* but I come
not now to chide

   These things being done, shee [with] ⌈and⌉ her nobility with ye chan*cellour* 25
Doctors, masters & Bedells before her, rid towards Oxford & being within
half a mile of it ye Mayor named Thom*as* Wyllyam*s* with ye Ald*er*men &
certaine Burgesses to ye number of 13, received her majestie. He then in ye
first place delivered up his mace to her wh*ich* shee forthwith returned againe;
then he [delivered] spake an English Oration & presented in ye name of ye 30
whole City a cup of silver, double gilt, worth 10 li., & in it about 40 li. in
old gold. This gift was ye first in money y*at* ever as I can yet learne, y*at* was
presented to a prince, for at ye com*m*ing of any one to ye University before
this time ye custome was y*at* ye citizens would give them five Oxen, as many
sheep, veales, lambes, & sugarloafes but this numerus quinarius was now 35

16/ Multa ... &c: *possibly, '(Your) divine kindnesses to us are many, etc.'*
18/ Goseman: *preceded by mark " to connect to marginal text*
19/ Non pauca ... est: *'He has grasped not a little with much but much with a little'*

altered by sir Francis Knollys ye Citie steward, & converted into money, which yet continueth. |

Afterwards entering into ye City ∧⌜in a rich chariot⌝ about 5. or 6 of ye clock at night, one Robert Deale of New college spake before [here] her at ye North gate called Bocardo, an oration in ye name of all ye scholars 5 yat stood one by one on each side of ye street from yat place [about] to Quartervois: which being finished shee went forward, ye scholars all kneeling & unanimously crying Vivat Regina which ye Queen taking verie kindly, answered oftentimes with a joyfull countenance [(sitting] Gratias ago gratias ago. 10

At her comming to Quartervois (commonly called Carfax) an oration was made in the Greek tongue by mr Lawrence ye kings professor of yat language at ye University which being finisht, shee seemed to be so well pleased with it, yat shee gave him thanks in ye Greek tongue, adding yat it was ye best oration yat ever shee heard in Greek & yat wee would answer you presently 15 but with this great company wee are somewhat abashed, wee will talke more with you in our chamber

From thence passing by ye Bachelaurs & Masters yat stood in like order as ye scholars, & in their formalities, shee came to ye Hall dore of Christchurch where another oration was spoken by Mr Kingsmyll Orator of ye Universitie, 20 whom she thanked & said you would have done well had you had good matter …

pp 640–4   (1–5 September)

25

…In the afternoon shee was present, but in ye morning absent upon some indisposition of body. At which time being in her privy chamber, there was

one Peter Carew was an exile tempore Mariæ Reginæ

brought into her presence a very pretty boy named Peter Carew (son as I think of Dr Carew late Deane of Christ Church) who making an oration to her in Latine with [2] ∧⌜two⌝ Greek verses at ye end, pleased her so much 30 yat she forthwith sent for secretary Cecyll to hear it, who being come, she commanded ye boy to pronounce it againe, saying before he began I pray god my fine boy thou maiest say it so well as thou didst to me just before – which being done according to her wish, she, ∧⌜with⌝ Cecyll & divers eminent persons then present were much taken as well with ye speech as ye Oratour. 35 At night was acted in Christ Church hall upon a larg scaffold erected, set about with stately lights of wax curiously wrought, a Latine play called Marcus Geminus, at which were present all ye Nobility, as also ye Spanish Embassador, who afterwards commended it so highly to ye Queen, being then absent, yat

p 875, l.32–p 876, l.2/ This gift … continueth.: *written in left margin and marked by # for insertion here*
35/ were much taken: *written into left margin*

she sayd In troth I will loos no more sport ‿⌈hereafter⌉ for ye good report yat
I hear of these your good doings – The Embassador also then said Multa
[vede] vidi sed hæc sunt admiranda, et sic referam ubi in patriam venero

The 2ᵈ of September being munday ... In ye afternoone ye Queen thought
to have heard disputations in Christ Church Hall, but ye stage taking up ye   5
roome, it could not well be, so yat keeping for ye most part within her lodging
Mr Thomas Neale ye Hebrew Professor presented to her Majestie a booke of
all ye prophets translated out of Hebrew by him, & a little book [containinge
ye description ⌈Effigies⌉ of every College, with Latine verses under [each] every
one of them describing theire respective Founders & times of Foundation.] of   10
Latine verses containing [⟨...⟩] the description of every college, public schooles
& Halls, with ye Names of ye respective founders ‿⌈of each College⌉ & time of
Foundations. [which [verses were] book was afterwards published by one Miles
Windsore in his intituled Europæ Orbis Academiæ printed in London 1591]
At night ye Queen heard ye first [ye first] part of an English play named   15
Palæmon ‿⌈or Palamon⌉ & Arcyte, made by Mr Richard Edwards, a Gentleman
of her chappel, acted with verie great applause in Christ Church hall. At ye
beginning of which play, there was by part of ye stage which fell, three persons
slaine, namely, (blank) Walker, a scholar of St Marie hall, one (blank) Pennie
a Brewer, and John Gilbert, Cook of Corpus Christi College beside five | yat   20
were hurt. Which disaster comming to ye Queens knowledge, ‿⌈she⌉ sent
forthwith ye Vicechancellour & her chirurgeons to help them, & to have a
care yat they want nothing for their recovery. Afterwards ye Actors performed
their parts so well, yat ye Queen laughed heartily thereat, and gave ye authour
of ye play great thanks for his paines.   25
...

The 4ᵗʰ of September being wednesday ... | At night the Queen was
present at the other part of ye play of Pal[⟨.⟩]‿⌈æ⌉mon & Arcyte, which should
have been acted ye night before, but deferred because it was late when ye
Queen came from disputations at St Maries. When ye play was ended she   30
called for Mr Edwards ye authour & gave him verie great thanks, with promises
of reward, for his paines: then making a pause, said to him, & her retinew
standing about her, this, relating to part of ye play, – By Palæmon I warrant
he dallieth not in love when he was in love indeed. By Arcyte, he was a right
martiall knight, having a swart countenance & a manly face. By Trecatio   35
‿⌈–⌉ gods pitty what a knave it is? By Perithous throwing St Edwards rich

2–3/ Multa ... venero: *'I have seen many things, but these are to be wondered at, and I will say so when I*
   return to my country'
10–14/ of Latine verses ... London 1591: *written into left margin and marked by # for insertion following* a
   little book; *of Latine verses ... Foundations.* to replace cancelled text on ll.8–10
35/ Trecatio: *in error for* Trevatio *as in* ccc: ms 257; *see p 129*
36/ St Edwards: *in error for* King Edwards *as in* ccc: ms 257; *see p 129*

cloake into ye funerall fier, which a stander by would have stayed by ye arme,
with an oath, goe foole ∧⌈–⌉ he knoweth his part ∧⌈I warrant–⌉ In ye said
play, was acted a cry of hounds in ye Quadrant, upon ye traine of a Fox in ye
hunting of Theseus, with which ye yong scholars, who stood ⟨..⟩ ye wind⟨....⟩
were so much taken ([some] ⌈[they]⌉ supposing it was reall) yat they [who   5
stood in ye windowes to see it] cryed out now now – there there – he's caught,
he's caught. – All which ye Queen merrily beholding said, O excellent! those
boyes in verie troth are ready to leap out of ye windowes to follow the hounds. –
This part it seems being [repeated] [afterwardes] repeated before certaine
courtieres [yat had been absent] in ∧⌈the Lodgings of⌉ Mr Roger Marbecks   10
[lodgings one of] ∧⌈one of⌉ the canons of christ church by ye players in [ye]
their Gownes (for they were all Scholars yat acted) before the Queen came to
Oxford, was by them so well liked, yat they said it farre surpassed Damon &
Pythias, than [ye] which, they thought, nothing could be better. Likewise
some said yat if ye authour did any more before his death, he would run   15
mad. But this comedie was ye last he made, for he died within few months
after[wards]. In ye acting of ye said play there was a [pretty] ⌈good⌉ part
performed by ye Lady æmilia, who, for gathering her flowers prettily in a

peter Carew
Knight see in
Sir Iohn
Cheeks Life
before the
rebell' at ye
end of ye life

garden then represented, & singing sweetly in ye time of March, received
8 angells for a gratious reward by her Majesties command. By whome yat   20
part was acted I know not, unless by Peter Carew, the pretty boy before
mentioned.

The 5 September being Thursday ... | she went to Christ church, & as
shee passed out of St Maries church dore, Mr Edrich somtimes Greek Reader
of ye University presented to her a book of greek verses, containing ye noble   25
Acts of her father, the which ye Queen having no sooner received & looked on
ye title, but Mr Edwards ye Comedian before mentioned said to ye Queen
Madam this man was my master, (meaning his Tutor in Corpus Christi college)
to whom ye Queen gave answer certainly he did not give thee whipping
enough – After ye Queen had refreshed her self with a supper, shee, with her   30
nobility went into Christ Church hall, where was acted before them a Latine
Tragedy, called Progne, made by Dr James Calfhill, Canon of Christ Church.
After which was done shee gave ye authur thanks, but it did not take half so
well as ye much admired play of Palamon & Arcyte.

The 6 of September being Friday ... a Latine sermon was made in ye   35
Cathedrall by Dr Iohn Piers, at which were present divers of ye Nobility but

4/ who stood ⟨..⟩ ye wind⟨....⟩: *written into right margin*
9/ repeated: *written into left margin*
19/ March: *in error for* May *as in* ccc: ms 257; *see p 133*
21–3m/ Sir Iohn ... life: *Sir John Cheke,* The true subiect to the rebell, or, The hurt of sedition *(1549),
reprinted and prefaced with a short life of the author by Gerard Langbaine (1641; Wing: C3778)*

ye Qu*ee*n not, because much wearied by attending disputations & ye Latine Tragedy ye day & night before. About dinner time ye Vicechancellour & Proctors presented to ye Queen in ye name of the whole University 6 pair of verie fine gloves, & to divers noble men & officers of ye Queens family, | some two, some one, pair, very thankfully accepted. After dinner, at ye   5 departure of ye Queen out of Ch*ri*st Church, Mr Tobie Mathew spake an oration before her, w*hi*ch she liking verie well, nominated him her Scholar. Then shee & her Nobility with ye retineu went from Ch*ri*st Ch*ur*ch to Carfax, & thence to East Gate: [before whom also went] ∧⌐with⌐ those members of ye Universitie & City ∧⌐going before⌐ y*at* brought her in. As shee passed   10 through ye streets ye Scholars stood in order Crying Vivat Regina: the walls also of St Maries Church, Allsoules and Universitie colleges were hung with innumerable sheets of verses, bemoaning ye Qu*eens* departure, [&] ∧⌐as⌐ [also] did ye countenances of the Layity (especially those of ye Female sex) y*at* then beheld her. W*he*n shee came to ye East bridge by Magd*alen* Coll*ege*   15 S*i*r Francys Knollys ye City Steward told her, y*at* their liberties reached no further, wherfore shee turned to ye Mayor [of] & his Brethren & bid them farewell with many thanks. W*he*n she came to ye forest of Shotover about two miles from Oxford, ye Earl of Leycester Chancellour of ye Universitie told her y*at* the Universitie liberties reached no farther y*at* way, whereupon   20 Mr Rog*er* Marbeck spake an eloquent Oration to her, containing many things relating to learning & ye encouragement therof by her, of its late ecclips and of the great probabilitie of its being now revived under ye government of so learned a princess, the which being done, shee gave him her hand to kisse, with many thanks to ye whole Universitie, speaking then these words (as tis   25 reported) with her face towards Oxford – Farewell ye worthie Universitie of Oxford, farewell my good subjects there, farewell my deare scholars, & pray god p*ro*sper your studies, farewell farewell

   Thus farre concerning this Entertainment : All y*at* I shall adde to it, is, y*at* her sweet, affable, & noble carriage left such impressions in ye minds   30 of scholars, y*at* nothing but emulation was in their studies, & nothing left untoucht by them wherby they thought they might be advanced by her & become acceptable in her eye.
   ...

                                                                                                        35
Life of Richard Edwards   Wood: *Athenae Oxonienses*, vol 1
cols 353–5
   ...
   RICHARD EDWARDS, a Somersetshire man born, was admitted scholar

14/ especially: *s corrected over* p

of Corpus Christi college under the tuition of George Etheridge, on the
eleventh of May 1540, 'and probationer fellow 11 August 1544,' student of
the upper table of Christ church at its foundation by King Henry 8, in the
beginning of the year 1547, aged 24, and the same year took the degree of
Master of arts. In the beginning of queen Elizabeth, he was made one of   5
the gentlemen of her chappel, and master of the children there, being
then esteemed not only an excellent musician, but an exact poet, as many
of his compositions in music (for he was not only skill'd in the practical
but theoretical part) and poetry do shew, for which he was highly valued
by those that knew him, especially his associates in Lincolns inn (of   10
which he was a member, and in some respects an ornament) and much
lamented by them, and all ingenious men of his time, when he died. He
hath written,

Damon and Pythias, a comedy; acted at court and in the university.

Palæmon and Arcyte, a comedy in two parts; acted before queen Elizabeth   15
in Christ Church hall 1566, which gave her so much content, that sending
for the author thereof, she was pleased to give him many thanks, with
promise of reward for his pains: and then making a pause, said to him
and her retinue standing about her, these matters relating to the said play,
which had entertain'd her with great delight for two nights in the said hall.   20
'By Palæmon – I warrant he dallied not in love, when he was in love indeed.
By Arcyte – he was a right marshal knight, having a swart countenance and a
manly face. By Trecatio – God's pity what a knave it is! By Pirithous his
throwing St. Edward's rich cloak into the funeral fire, which a stander-by
would have staid by the arm, with an oath, Go, fool - he knoweth his part I'll   25
warrant you,' &c. In the said play was acted a cry of hounds in the quadrant,
upon the train of a fox in the hunting of Theseus: with which the young
scholars who stood in the remoter parts of the stage, and in the windows,
were so much taken and surpriz'd (supposing it had been real) that they cried
out, there, there, - he's caught, he's caught. All which the queen merrily   30
beholding, said, O excellent! those boys in very troth are ready to leap out of
the windows to follow the hounds. This part being repeated before certain
courtiers in the lodgings of Mr Roger Marbeck one of the canons of Christ
Church by the players in their gowns (for they were all scholars that acted,
among whom were Miles Windsore and Thomas Twyne of Corpus Christi   35
College) before the queen came to Oxon., was by them so well liked, that

2/ fellow: *end of col 353*
14/ Damon and Pythias: *in italic font*
15/ Palæmon and Arcyte: *in italic font*
23/ Trecatio: *in error for* Trevatio *as in ccc: MS 257; see p 129*
24/ St. Edward's: *in error for* King Edward's *as in ccc: MS 257; see p 129*

they said it far surpassed Damon and Pythias, than which, they thought,
nothing could be better. Likewise some said that if the author did proceed
to make more plays before his death, he would run mad. But this it
seems was the last, for he lived not to finish others that he had lying
by him....   5

...

1582–3
Entertainment of the Prince of Siradia   Bodl.: MS. Wood F.1
pp 683–4   *(10 June)*   10

...

A noble & learned Polonian named Alb*er*tus [de Alasco,] Alaskie, or Laskie,
or de Alasco (so many [times] ⌈ways⌉ doe I find him written by our English
authors) being come to ye English Court to see ye Fashions & admire ye
wisdom of ye Queene, letters dated ye 13 May came from ye Chancellour   15
of ye Uniu*er*sitie by her majesties co*mm*and y*a*t ye memb*er*s thereof should
®Sirad   [pr*ou*ide] make pr*o*vision for ye reception of him according to his quality, being
a Prince & Palatine of Sirad[ia]. The day appointed for his reception was ye
10 of June, w*hich* being come, he, with our Chancellour and certaine noble
men appointed to attend him, came from Ricot, & appr*o*aching ye east part of   20
ye City met them Dr Humphrey, Dr Tob*ias* Mathew, Dr Arth*ur* Yeldard, Dr
Martin Culpepper & Dr Herb*ert* Westphaling in their scarlet gownes, the last
of whome made an oration to them, w*hich* was ansuered verie curteously in
ye Latine tongue by ye Prince. Co*mm*ing nearer Oxford met him ye Mayor,
Ald*er*men, & after ye Townclerk who was M*aster* of Arts, had spoken a short   25
Oration in ye Latine tongue, they presented to, [him] & ye noble men with,
him, gloves: w*hich* being done a consort of Musitians, y*a*t stood over ye East
Gate, played on their wind-musick till they ⌈were⌉ gone into ye City.

Going up ye High Street they were saluted from each side by all ye Degrees
of students in their formalities. At length co*mm*ing to S*t* Maries church, ye   30
Vicechanc*ellour* & seu*er*all Doctors in their scarlet, saluting them also, the
Insignia of ye Vicechanc*ellour* were by him surrendered up to ye Chancellour,
but soone after returned. Then ye Orator co*mm*ing forth spake before him an
eloquent oration, w*hich* being ended, a rich Bible with gloves therin were
presented to ye | Prince & other Gloves to ye noble men, received with great   35
demonstration of thankes.

From thence they went to Quartervois & so downe [ye South] ∧⌈Fish⌉ street
to Ch*rist* church gate, where received him & his company the Subdeane,
Canons & students who conducted them to their lodgings. soone after dark

1/ Damon and Pythias: *in italic font*
2/ could: *end of col 354 and page break*

night comming on strang fire works were shewed in ye great Quadrangle to
entertaine them.

The next day ... he supped at Christ church (which he did every night
yat he remained in ye Uniuersity) & then he with [his retinew] ⌈the Nobles⌉
and their respective retinews saw a pleasant Comedy acted in christ church   5
Hall by seueral of ye Uniuersity intituled Rivales, which giving them great
content, ye author, Dr William Gager had ye honur to receive from ye Prince
personall thanks.

...

10

pp 685–6   (11–12 June)
...

The Disputations being ended & the supper following at christ church,
he saw a verie stately Tragedy acted there, named Dido, wherein ye Queens
conquest, with Æneas his narration of ye destruction of Troy, was lively   15
described in a Marchpaine patterne. There was also a pleasant sight of Hunters,
with a full crie of a kennell of Hounds (partly as before when the Queen was
here) & Mercury & Iris descending & ascending from, & to, a high place.
The tempest also wherin it rained small comfits, rose water, & snew artificiall
snow was very strang to ye Beholders.   20

The third day ... he was invited to a costly banquet at St Johns college (the
gates & outward walls therof being couered with multitudes of verses & other
emblems of poetry) but his desire towards his journeys end, caused him not
to accept of it, only of a pithy Oration, delivered by a Fellow of yat House.

From thence he was accompanied with divers Doctors & Heads of Houses 25
in their scarlet gownes to ye Mile-stone or thereabouts, & then ye Uniuersity
Orator, speaking another oration, they all took their farewell of him, their
Chancellour, & ye rest of ye noble company. Some days after when they came
to London, they made such a good report of their entertainment to ye Queen,
yat shee ordered yat thankes should be sent to the Uniuersity, as if it had been   30
done to her, & | for her honor & credit. Such an entertainment it was,
yat ye like before or since was neuer made for one of his Degree, costing ye
Uniuersity [&] ∧⌈with ye⌉ colleges (who contributed towards ye entertainment)
about 350 li....

...   35

1591–2
Entertainment of Queen Elizabeth   Bodl.: MS. Wood F.1
pp 719–20   (22–8 September)
...   40

It being now 26 years since Queene Elizabeth visited our Uniuersitie, ∧⌈shee⌉

resolved this yeare to come again, yat shee might take her last farewell thereof,
& behold ye change & amendment of Learning & Manners yat had been
in her long absence made. The appointed day therefore appearing, which
was 22 September, shee with a splendid retinew came from Woodstock, &
approaching ye confines of ye Uniuersitie, was met by diuers Doctors, in their   5
skarlet robes, Heads of Houses, Proctors, & about 18 masters of Arts, besides
ye Vicechancellour & ⌜ye⌝ three Esquire Bedells. After a speech ⌜was spoke⌝
& a gift [were] delivered to her, which shee accepted verie kindly in ye latine
tongue, met her at ye end of St Gyles ye Mayer, Aldermen, Baylives, & others
of ye thirteen in their skarlet, who presenting themselves before her, ye   10
Recorder spake a speech, which ended, they in ye name of ye whole City
presented to her a silver-gylt Cup with 60 Angells therein.

Comming into ye City shee was received with great acclamations of ye
people, & from ye northgate to Quatervois & so to christchurch great gate
with yat of Vivat Regina, by Undergraduats, Bachelaurs and Masters of Arts.   15
From ye Undergraduats she [receiv] had an oration & verses spoken by two of
them, & from ye Bachelaurs & Masters the like: All which shee with brevity
answered in ye latine tongue & in ye conclusion gave them her benidiction.
At Quatervois, which is ye middle way between ye North, & christchurch
great gate, shee was saluted by ye Greek Reader with a Greek oration for which   20
shee thanked him in yat | yat language. At length shee alighting in christchurch
quadrangle, ye Orator of the Uniuersity welcom'd her in ye name of its
members....

As for other ceremonies yat were performed in her abode here, which was
till ye 28 September ye same method was used as in anno 1566 ... In ye nights   25
also were sometimes playes acted in christchurch Hall by seuerall students
of ye Uniuersity, but what they were or how applauded I know not. Every
College also prouided an oration to be spoken to ye Queene at her entrance
into them, some of which being performed, shee answered very readily with
great affability in ye latine tongue.   30
...

pp 722–3
...

...In ye afternoone shee left Oxford, & going through Fishstreet to Quatervois   35
& thence to | to ⌜ye⌝ East gate, receiued ye hearty wishes (mixt with teares)
of ye people, & casting her eyes on ye walls of S. Maries church, Allsoule,
Uniuersity & Magdalen Colleges which were mostly hung with verses &
emblematicall expressions of poetry, was often seen to giue gratious nods to

21/ yat | yat: *dittography (?); first yat does not appear to be a catchword*
36/ to | to: *dittography (?); first to does not appear to be a catchword*

ye scholars. W*hen* shee came to shotover hill (ye utmost confines of ye Uniu*er*sitie) accompanied with those Doctors & Masters y*at* brought her in, shee gratiously received a farewell oration fro*m* one of them, in ye name of ye whole Uniu*er*sity. W*hi*ch being done shee gave them many thanks & her hand to kiss, and then looking wistly towards Oxford said to this effect in ye latine tongue. Farewell farewell deare Oxford, God bless thee & increase thy sons in number, holiness & vertue, &c. & so went towards Ricote.   5

...

1604–5   10

Entertainment of King James   Bodl.: MS. Wood F.1
p 753   *(27 August)*
...

The 27 of Aug*ust* the King, Queen, Prince of Wales & a considerable number of the nobilitie, came from Woodstock to Oxford to ye end y*at* they   15
might see ye place & entertaine themselves with ye delights of the Muses. At ye end of the Uniu*er*sity limits northward, they were met & congratulated by ye chancellour, Vicechanc*ellour* Proctors & certaine heads of Houses in their formalities with an eloquent Oration w*hi*ch being done, they presented to [⟨...⟩] ⌈ye King⌉ Stephanus his Testament. com*m*ing nearer, ∧⌈they were   20
entertained⌉ by ye Mayor, Steward & ye cheifest of ye Citizens of Oxford; after whose complements finished also, they [presented] ⌈gave⌉ the said King a rich pair of gloves & as tis reported a purse of gold. At St Johns college gate they had ∧⌈a⌉ speech spoken to them by one of y*at* societie & ye veiw of divers copies of verses hanging on ye walls. w*hen* ye King came within the North   25
gate, he was saluted thence to christ church with great acclamations & shoutings of ye scholars (in numb*er* now 2254) besides laicks innumerable. At Quatervois he was stopt by Dr Perin, ye Greek Reader with an excellent greek oration from a pew or desk set up there for ye purpose. At christ church by Wake the ingenious Oratour, who, after he had pleased ye Auditory with   30
his Ciceronian stile, the King was conducted to ye cathedrall church under a canopie supported by Doctors in their scarlet habits....

...

pp 754–5   *(27–30 August)*   35

...After ye K*ing* Qu*een* & Prince had supped, ∧⌈they⌉ were conveyed to ch*rist* church hall, where they [say] saw a Latine Comedy [acted by ye students of] called Vertumnus acted by ye Students of y*at* House....

...   40

19–20/ w*hi*ch being done ... Testament: *written into left margin and marked by* ∧ *for insertion here*

The third day were disputations in Physick, performed also admirably well
by ye best of y*at* pro*f*ession in ye Uniu*er*sity: w*hi*ch being done, they went to
New college, where they were entertained with a royall feast and incomparable
Musick.... After supp*er* he & the King went to St Johns College, where they
were diverted with a play called Annus recurrens, penned by Dr Gwynne of   5
y*at* Society, which pleased his Majesty & ye Auditory verie much.

  The fourth & last day ‸⌜(30 Aug*ust*)⌝ the King, Prince and Court went
to ye publick Library, newly restored by S*ir* Thomas Bodley ... they went to
Brasenose, where ye Principall & fellowes received them at ye gate with a
speech.... After dinner, ye K*ing* being about to depart, ye Uniu*er*sity assembled   10
to take their leaves, & being admitted into his | presence ye junior proctor
gave him a farewell speech, [w*hi*ch] & being well accepted by ye king he
gave ye Academians his hand to kisse & then expressed many honorable
matters of ye Uniu*er*sity & his entertainment, with a p*r*omise y*at* he would
be a gratious soveraigne to it.   15

  Thus briefly concerning this entertainment if any are desirous to know
more the particulars of it, let him consult a book intituled Rex Platonicus,
written by ye ingenious Mr (since S*ir*) Isaac Wake of Merton coll*ege* [now]
‸⌜at this time⌝ Orator of ye Uniu*er*sity....

...   20

1612–13
Music at the Building of the Schools
Gutch: *Wood's History and Antiquities*, vol 2
p 790   *(30 March)*   25
...

  Thus far from the Will of Sir Thomas Bodley, concerning the third story
of the Schools and west part of the Library; the first was afterwards built,
though not furnished (only with Pictures) the other built and furnished. After
the said worthy person was interred (the manner of which I have elsewhere   30
told you) nothing remained to be done but of having the first hands put
to the said intended work. He was buried on Monday the 29 of March
1613, and the next day the first stone was laid in the north west end, where
afterwards the Moral and Civil Law Schools were built. Sir John Bennett was
present, and Mr. Seller, the Senior Proctor, delivered at that time an excellent   35
Oration. There was Music with voices, and other instruments, while Dr.
Singleton the Vicechancellor, and Sir John Bennett laid the first stone, who
having then offered liberally thereon, the Heads of Houses, Proctors, and
other followed....

4l he: *ie, the prince*

1620–1
Barten Holyday's Technogamia   Bodl.: MS. Wood F.1
pp 796–7   *(26 August)*
…

      This year ye King, Prince, and diuers of ye nobility came to woodstock,   5
to whome receeded ye Vicechancellour certaine Doctors & [ye] both the
Proctors, who being gratiously received by his Majestie, (to whome ye Orator
[m⟨...⟩ deli] spake a Speeech) they were dismissed, leaving then behind
them many paire of rich Gloves to be given to ye King Prince & ye cheif
of ye Nobility. It must be knowne now, yat on february 13. anno 1617 ye   10
comedie of Barten Holyday student of Christchurch ∧⌜called the Marriage
of Arts⌝ was acted publickly in Christchurch hall with no great applause,
& ye wits now of ye Uniuersity being minded to shew themselves before
ye King, | were resolved to act ye said comedie [before him:] at woodstock,
[whe⟨..⟩] wherefore ye author [adding] ⌜making⌝ some foolish alterations   15
in it, was accordingly performed on a sunday night 26. August but it being
too grave ⌜for ye king,⌝ & too Scholarlike for ye Auditory (or as some say yat
ye Actors had taken too much wine before) his Majesty after [2] ⌜two⌝ Acts
offered seuerall times to withdraw, but being perswaded by some of those
yat were neare him, to have patience till it was ended, least ye yong men   20
should be disencouraged, adventured it, though much against his will,
whereupon these verses were made by a certaine Scholar
At Christchurch Marriage done before ye King
Least yat those majestes should want an Offering
The King himself did offer, what I pray?   25
He offered twice or thrice to go away.

so also in Dr
peter Heylyns
diarie   There were seuerall witty copies of verses [came out] ⌜made⌝ on ye said
comedy, among which was yat by Peter Heylyn of Magdalen College called
Whoop Holyday. which giving occasion for ye making of [man] other
Copies pro et contra, Dr Corbet ye Deane of Christchurch, who had that   30
day preached (as it seems) before ye King with his band starcht cleane,
did put in for one, reproved by ye graver sort, but those yat knew him
well, not at all; for they have said it in my hearing, yat he loved to ye last,
Boyes-play verie well.
      As for Holyday ye Author, he was one highly conceited of his worth,   35
especially of his poetry & sublime fancy even to his last dayes…
      …

8/ Speeech: *for* Speech
27–9m/ Dr peter Heylyns diarie: *lost* MS; *see p 694*

1633–4
Affray at St John's   Bodl.: MS. Wood F.1
p 852 attachment

February 1634 the Vicech*a*nc*ellour*, Doct*o*rs & others ⌐being⌐ invited to see 5
a Tragedie acted by St Iohn's Scholars, certaine rude scholars disturbed them,
among w*h*ich were Io*h*n Baker, A.B. of Neuin a Determiner y*a*t lent Ioh*n*
Gaye & will*iam* Batenson Com*m*oners of Exeter, who through stones against
ye walls & gate, broke windowes & other mischeif, who being discou*e*red
were taken to ta⌐'s⌐ke by Dr. pink ye Vicechanc*ellour*, & forced to aske 10
forgiveness on y*e*r bended knees in ye north chappell of St Maries church,
March 21, before ye Vicechanc*ellour* Proctors & Determining Bachelaurs,
then promising faithfully & with weeping teares that they would neu*e*r act
act any thing hereafter contra bonos mores et pacem Academiae.
                    Gest*a* Vicecanc*ellarii* Pink. p. 14. 15
...

Music at the Building of Selden End
Gutch: *Wood's History and Antiquities*, vol 2
pp 939–40   *(13 May)* 20
...

On the thirteenth of May, being Tuesday, 1634, the Vicechancellor, Doctors,
Heads of Houses and Proctors, met at St. Mary's Church about 8 of the clock
in the morning; from thence each having his respective formalities on, came
to this place, and took their seats that were then erected on the brim of the 25
foundation. Over against them was built a scaffold where the two Proctors
with divers Masters stood. After they were all settled, the University Musicians
who stood upon the leads at the west end of the Library sounded a lesson on
their wind music. Which being done the singing men of Christ Church, with
others, sang a lesson, after which the Senior Proctor Mr. Herbert Pelham of 30
Magdalen College | made an eloquent Oration: that being ended also the
music sounded again, and continued playing till the Vicechancellor went to
the bottom of the foundation to lay the first stone in one of the south angles.
But no sooner he had deposited a piece of gold on the said stone, according
to the usual manner in such ceremonies, but the earth fell in from one side of 35
the foundation, and the scaffold that was thereon broke and fell with it, so
that all those that were thereon to the number of an hundred at least, namely

5/ ⌐being⌐: *text damaged by tear at top of sheet;*
  ⌐being⌐ *supplied by Wood below torn away area*
7/ Neuin: *ie, New Inn Hall*
13/ faithfully: *ully corrected over other letters*
13/ would: *uld corrected over other letters*

13–14/ act act: *dittography*
15/ Gesta Vicecanc*ellarii* Pink: *Robert Pinck, 'Gesta Vicecancellariatus sui', MS now lost*
25/ this place: *a piece of Exeter College ground on the northwest side of the library*

the Proctors, Principals of Halls, Masters, and some Bachelaurs fell down all
together one upon another into the foundation, among whom the under
Butler of Exeter College had his shoulder broken or put out of joint, and a
Scholar's arm bruised, as I have been informed.

The solemnity being thus concluded, with such a sad catastrophe, the breach   5
was soon after made up, and the work going chearfully forward, was in four
years space finished....

1635–6
Entertainment of King Charles   Bodl.: MS. Wood F.1   10
pp 859–60   *(29 August)*

...

®*Ibidem* in R. 124

The plague being now in seuerall parts of the nation, especially at London,
ye Act & Assizes were deferred, not onlie for ye security of the Scholars &
Citizens, but also ye King & court, who had intentions of visiting ∧⌈or seing⌉   15
ye Uniuersity. And being through ye great care of ye Chancellour & Proctors
kept cleer from ye infection, ye K*ing* Qu*een* & court came to Oxford 29.
Aug*ust* whose reception, entertainment & departure being memorable, I
shall therfore give *yo*u an account of it.

20

On ye same day therfore being Munday, towards ye evening, ye chancellour
(who c*a*me privatly into ye Uniu*er*sity 25. of ye said month) Vicechancellour,
divers Doctors & Masters, went from St. Johns Coll*ege* towards Wodstocke
to meet the King. The Chancellour, accompanied with Juxon ye Lord Treasurer,
Bishops of Winchester, Norwich & Oxford rode in a coach; ye Doctors &   25
Masters on horsback with foot-cloaths, & ye three Esquire Bedells before them.
Having rode as farr as ye way near Aristotles Well, they made a stay. After a
while, came ye King & Queen, Charles Prince Elector palatine & his Brother
Prince Rupert all in one coach. At whose appearance ye chancellour, Treasurer
& B*ishops* came out of their coach & ye Doctors & Masters alighted. [At]   30
⌈And⌉ drawing neare to y*a*t of ye Kings, ye Vicechancellour (with ye rest all |
kneeling) spake an eloquent oration, enduring about a quarter of an hour.
That being done the Chancellour gave up ye Bedells staves to the King, & ye
King againe to ye Chancellour, & he to ye Bedells. After this they drew forward
about a bow-shoot towards ye City, & then being met by ye Mayor, Ald*er*men   35
& certaine Citizens on horsback (some having Foot cloathes) a speech was
spoken by ye Recorder & ye Mace deliu*er*ed up & restored. That being done
also (ye Uniu*er*sity memb*er*s putting themselves into Ord*er* in ye mean time)
they marched into ye City (ye Citizens leading ye way) and making a stand

14m/ R. 124: *oua: NEP/Supra/R, f 124*
14/ deferred: *preceded by superscript* (w) *to connect to marginal text*

at St Iohns Coll*ege* gate, mr Tho*mas* Atkinson of y*at* house spake another
speech for ye King, very breif & very much appr*o*ved by his Majesty to ye
chancellour after the solemnity was over. Thence they went through Northgate-
street, then by Quatervois & so through Fishstreet, ye sides of wh*ich* though
loyned with scholars of all Degrees in their formalities, yet ∧⌈neither⌉ they,   5
nor ye Citizens made any expressions of joy or uttered as ye manner is Vivat
Rex. Deni

    Being come within christchurch gate, Strode ye Uniu*e*rsity Orator, saluted
them with a speech beginning thus. Maximorum optime, et optimorum   10
maxime R*e*x, si omnium Musarum linguae in me unum confluerent &c wh*ich*
speech being ended & appr*o*ued by many (especially those of chr*i*stchurch)
the chancellour in ye name of ye Uniu*e*rsitie presented to ye King a [costly
pair of gloves, to ye Queen a fair English Bible] ⌈Bible in folio with a velvet
cover, richly embroyd*e*red with ye Kings ar*m*es in ye midst & also a costly   15
pair of Gloves,⌉ to ye Prince Elector
Hookers books of Ecclesiasticall politie ⌈with gloves⌉ & to his brother Rup*ert*
Caesars Com*m*entaries in English, illustrated by ye learned Explanations &
discourses of S*ir* Clem*ent* Edmonds....

                                                                            20

pp 861–3 *(29–30 August)*
...

    That night, after ye K*ing* queen & two Princes had supped, they saw a
Comedie acted in Christ Church hall, but such an one it was, that had more
of ye moralist than poet, in it. And though it was well penned, yet it did not   25
take ∧⌈[so well]⌉ with ye Courtiers so well, as it did with ye togated crew. It
was intituled Passions Calmed or The Setling of the Floating Island, made
by Strode ye Orator & p*er*formed by ye scholars beyond expectation. It was
acted on a goodly stage, reaching from ye upp*er* end of ye Hall almost to ye
hearth place & had on it 3 or 4 openings on each side therof & par∧⌈ti⌉tions   30
between them, much resembling the deskes [&] ∧⌈or⌉ [pews] ∧⌈studies⌉ in a
library, out of wh*ich* the Actors issued forth. The said partitions, they could
draw in & out at their pleasire upon a suddaine, & thrust out new in their
places according to ye nature of ye sceen, wheron were represented churches,
dwelling houses, Pallaces, &c wh*ich* for its variety bred very great admiration. 35
Over all was delicat painting, resembling ye Sky, clouds &c At ye upp*er* end
a great fair shut of two Leaves y*at* opened & shut without any visible help.
Within wh*ich* was [was at] set forth ye emblem of ye whole play in a verie

---

7/ Deni: *false start; for* Denique, *ie, then (?)*
10–11/ Maximorum ... &c: *'Best king of the greatest and greatest of the best, if the tongues of all the muses*
   were to flow together into me as one, etc'
14–16/ Bible in folio ... of Gloves,: *written partly interlinearly and partly in the right margin*

sumptuous manner. Therin was ye perfect resemblance of ye billowes of ye |
Sea rolling, & an artificiall Island with churches & houses waving up & downe
& floating, as also rocks, trees & hills. Many other fine peices of work &
Landskips did also appeare at sundry openings therof & a chaire also seen to
come gliding on ye stage without any visible helpe. All these representations,   5
being ye first (as I have been enformed) yat were used on ye english stage, ⌈&
therfore⌉ giving [verie] great content, I have been therfore ye more punctuall
in describing them, to ye end yat posteritie might know yat ∧⌈what⌉ [was]
is ∧⌈now⌉ seen in ye playhouses at London belonging to his Majestie, & ye
Duke of York, is originally due to ye invention of Oxford scholars.   10
...

®This is true

    Soon after they all returned to Christ Church (the princes having before
seen some of ye fairest Colleges, especially | St Johns, where by his Majesties
Leave they were entered into ye buttery book) who having a desire to see ye
publicke library did, with ye Princes, Nobles, & Chauncellour of ye Uniuersity   15
go to yat place, (ye Queen being not yet ready) & [en] ⌈no⌉ sooner entered,
but were entertained with a speech spoken by William Herbert of Exeter
College, second son of ye Earl of Pembroke, then Lord chamberlaine: ...
word was brought yat ye Queen was come, so ye King went into her Coach
& forthwith proceeded to St Iohns College, where they saw ye new building   20
yat ye Chancellour had at his owne Charges lately erected. That done, ye
Chancellour attended them up ye Library staires, where, as soone as they began
to ascend, certaine Musitians above entertained them with a short song fitted
& tim'd to ye ascending ye staires. In ye library, they were welcom'd to ye
College with a short speech spoken by one of the Fellows called Abraham   25
wright....

pp 864–5   (30–1 August)
...

    When dinner was ended, he attended ye King & Queen toge[a]ther with ye   30
Nobles into seuerall withdrawing chambers, where they entertained themselves
for ye space of an hour. In the meane time he caused ye windowes of ye
common hall or Refectory to be shut, candles lighted, & all things to be made
ready for ye play, which was then to begin, called ye Hospitall of Lovers,
made for ye most part (as tis said) by Mr George Wild Fellow of St Iohns   35
College. When these things were fitted, he gave notice to ye King & Queen
& attended them into ye Hall, whethir, he had ye happiness to bring them by

12/ Soon after: *ie, soon after the convocation*
25–6/ called Abraham wright: *written in left margin and marked by* ∧ *for insertion here*
30/ he: *ie, the chancellor*

a way prepared from ye presence Lodgings to ye Hall without any ye least disturbance. He had ye Hall kept so fresh & coole yat there was not any one person when ye King and Queen came into it. The Princes, Nobles & Ladies entred ye same way with ye King & then presently another doore was opened below to fill ye Hall with ye better sort of Company. All being setled ye play 5 was began & [well] acted. The plot good & ye Action. It was merry & without offence & so gave a great deal of content, which I doubt cannot be said of any play acted in ye play-houses belonging to ye King & Duke, since 1660. In ye middle of ye play, ye Chancellour ordered a short banquet for ye King Queen [&] Lords & Ladies. And ye College was at yat time so 10 well furnisht, as yat they did not borrow any one Actor from any College in ye Uniuersity

The play ended ye King and Queen went to christ church, retired & supped privatly & about 8 of ye clock, went into ye Common hall there to see another Comedy called The Royall Slave made by Mr William 15 Cartwright of yat house. It contained much more variety than that of Passions Calmed. Within ye shuts were seen a curious Temple & ye sun shining over it, delightfull forests also & other prospects. Within ye great shuts mentioned before, were seen villages & men visibly appearing in them, going up & downe here & there about their business. The interludes therof 20 were represented with as much variety of sceens & motions as ye | great wit of Inigo Iones (well skill'd in setting out a court maske to ye best advantage) could extend unto. It was very well pen'd & acted, & ye strangness of ye Persian habits gave great content. All men came forth verie well contented, & full of applause of what they had seen & heard. It was ye day of St Felix 25 (as ye Chancellour observed,) & all things went happie.

The next day being Wednesday August 31. the Chancellour, Vicechancellour & Doctors attended about 8 in ye morning ye comminge forth of ye King & ye Queen. At their appearance [they] ye junior proctor (as I take it) made a farewell speech & then at ye conclusion their Majesties were 30 gratiously please to give ye Uniuersity a greate deale of thanks. After which, ye chauncellor in his owne name & yat of ye Uniuersitie, gave their Majesties all possible thanks for their great & gratious patience & acceptance of their poore & meane entertainment, & so they departed.
... 35

®In Diario suo, edito per Gulielmum Prinne

26/ observed: *preceded by superscript* (c) *to connect to marginal text*
27–9m/ In Diario … Prinne: *William Prynne,* A breviate of the life of VVilliam Laud, Arch-bishop of Canterbury *(1644; Wing: P3904), extracted from the manuscript of Laud's 'Diary'*

29–30/ ye junior proctor … their Majesties: *written in left margin and marked by* ∧ *for insertion here*

p 866   *(1–2 September)*

Upon Thursday after dinner ye chancellour departed from St Iohns to ye
Bishop of Oxfords new house at Cudesdon & then ye play which was acted
before ye King on Tuesday in ye afternoone, should have been represented   5
againe at ye same place to ye Uniuersity, & strangers yat were remaning in
ye City, but such was the unruliness of ye yong scholars in breaking in &
depriving ye Strangers of their places, yat nothing at all was done in it.
    On Friday in ye afternoone (Sept*ember* 2) was acted according to ye
chancellours appointment, The Royall Slave in christ church hall before ye   10
Uniuersity & strangers, & ye next day in ye afternoone Passions calmed.
Both which were acted very quietly & gave great content. In November
following, ye Queen sent to ye chancellour yat he would procure of christ
church ye Persian attire of ye Royall Slave & other apparell wherin it was
acted, to ye end yat shee might see her owne Players act it ouer againe, &   15
whether they could do it as well as 'twas done by ye Uniuersity. Wheruppon
ye chancellour caused ye cloaths & perspectives of ye stage to be sent to
Hampton Court in a waggon ˄ ⌈for which ye Uniuersity received from⌉ her
a letter of thanks. So yat all of it being fitted for use (the author therof being
then present) 'twas acted soon after, but by all mens confession, ye Players   20
came short of ye Uniuersity Actors. At ye same time ye Chancellour desired
of ye King & Queen yat neither ye Play or Cloaths nor Stage might come
into ye hands & use of ye common Players abroad, which was gratiously
granted. Mr Iasper Maine's Play called ye City Match, though not acted at
Christ Church before ye King & ye Court as was intended, yet it was sent   25
for to Hampton Court, & he went there about Christmas following to see
ye setting forth of his play. It took so well, yat it was afterwards acted before
ye King & Queen at Whitehall, & seuerall times by his Majesties Servants at
ye Black Fryers in London & at length published anno 1639. folio
30

Life of Abraham Wright   Wood: *Athenae Oxonienses*, vol 4
col 275
...
Abraham Wright ... was born in Black-swan-alley in Thames-street in the

(marginal note, lines 13–15): Vide Gesta Cancellariatus Laud p. 124, 128

(marginal note, lines 18–21): Register R at fol. 135, 138 &c.

4/ Cudesdon: *Cuddesdon, Oxfordshire*
13–15m/ Gesta ... Laud p. 124, 128: *a ms now lost, which served as the basis for the publication of Laud,*
    Historical Account, printed with separate title-page and separate pagination in The Second Volume of the
    Remains of William Laud *(1700; Wing: L596)*
13/ sent: *followed by superscript* (e) *to connect to marginal text*
18–19/ her a letter of thanks: *written in left margin as a continuation of interlineation*
19–21m/ Register R at fol. 135, 138 &c: *ou*: NEP/Supra/R, ff 135, 138
19/ letter: *preceded by superscript* (f) *to connect to marginal text*

parish of *St* James Garlickhith, in London, on the 23d of December 1611 ...
elected scholar of *Saint* John's coll*ege* an*no* 1629 by the endeavours of Dr.
Juxon president there, who finding him to be a good orator, especially in
proper and due pronunciation (which in his elderly years he retained in his
sermons and public offices) favoured him then and afterwards in his studies. 5
In 1632 he was elected fellow, and having then a genie which enclined him to
poetry and rhetoric, did, while bach*elor* of arts, make his collection of Delitiæ
Poetarum, being then esteemed also an exact master of the Latin tongue, even
to the nicest criticism. On the 30th of Aug*ust* 1636, at which time Dr. Laud
archb*ishop* of Canterbury entertained the king and queen at *Saint* John's 10
coll*ege* he spoke an English speech before them when they entred into the
library to see, and be entertained in, it at a dinner; and after dinner he was
one of the principal persons that acted in the comedy called Love's Hospital,
or The Hospital of Lovers, presented before their majesty's in the public
refectory of that house. The chief actor was the author Mr. George Wilde, and 15
the others, who were all of that house, were John Goad, Humphry Brook
(now one of the coll*ege* of physicians) Edmond Gayton, John Hyfield, &c...

col 277

... 20

...He hath also compleated other books, which are not yet printed, as (1)
A Comical Entertainment called The Reformation, presented before the
university at *Saint* John's coll*ege*. Written while he was an under-graduate....

Entertainment of King Charles   Wood: *Historia et Antiquitates* 25
p 343 col 2   *(29 August)*
...

Finitâ eadem nocte cœnâ, Comœdiæ Anglicanæ, quam in Aulæ suæ
Refectorio agebant Ædis Christi & aliorum Collegiorum Alumni, interfuere
Hospites augusti. Illam Strodus, quem sæpe diximus, Orator publicus 30
contexuit, & Passiones pacatae, seu Insula fluctuans in fixam conversa,
nomen fecit; verum ob argumentum serium nimis ac tetricum Aulicis æque
displicuit ac stoicæ quædam prælectiones, tametsi eandem tum Actorum
industria, tum amplissima Tabulati scenici structura (siquidem à supremâ
Refectorii parte ad focum pene pertingebat) sub hæc primitus usurpari 35
cœpta, plurimum commendaret.
...

12/ in, it: *for* in it,
22/ A Comical ... The Reformation: *a lost play text; see Appendix 6:2*
23/ while he was an under-graduate: *between September 1629, when Wright entered St John's College,
and 16 May 1633, when he took his* BA

p 344 cols 1–2   *(30 August)*

...

    Cum pransi hunc in modum essent, Regem ac Reginam atque Optimates
omnes, in conclavia seorsim varia deduxit Archipræsul, ubi horam integram
otio & colloquiis impendebant; ipse vero claudendas interea Refectorii   5
fenestras, accensisque lucernis quæ ad operas theatrales pertinerent paranda
curavit, ad Comœdiam utique animo intentus, à Magistro Georgio Wild,
Collegii Socio, maximam, ut perhibent, partem conscriptam, & Hospitium
Amatorum nuncupatam. Cum omnia essent in promptu Regem ac Reginam,
una cum Proceribus & Heroinis, viâ novâ, privatâ plane nullique molestiæ   10
obnoxiâ (siquidem a Regiæ, uti nos loquimur, Præsentiæ Camerâ ad Refectorium
patebat) incedentes comitatus est Cancellarius; exclusis, donec Ædes ipsi
spectaculis destinatas intrarent, aliis quibuscun*que* ne scilicet adaucto ex
confluentium multitudine fervore æstivo tantis Hospitibus injuriæ quicquam
fieret. Recluso deinceps Ostio inferiori, atque intromissis potioris notæ   15
Spectatoribus, prodibant in scenam Actores, ex unico illo Sodalitio desumpti;
qui cum ad Argumentum festivum & jucundum, neque tamen spurcum
aut inverecundum (de profano nihil dicam, ante annos enim paucissimos
inauditum erat Deum ac Religionem Ludos fieri) fabulam edendi peritiam
adferrent, magnâ omnes voluptate perfuderunt. Mediis quasi spectaculis Regi   20
ac Reginæ, necnon Dynastis omnibus, dapes conquisitissimas apponendas
curavit Archipræsul; peractâ vero Comoediâ illa, ad Ædem Christi redibant
Hospites augusti, & absolutâ privatim cœnâ, circa horam octavam ad Sodalitii
ejus Refectorium perrexere, à Ludo altero (Hunc Magister Gul*ielmus* Cartwright
conscripserat, & Captivum Regalem appellârat) oblectationem longe uberiorem   25
percepturi; quod prædictum & argumento, & ingenio, & theatrico præsertim
apparatu superaret. Pone valvas, interius & à tergo Proscenii collocatas (quas
quidem tum primitus fuisse usurpatas adnotandum) repagulis autem tam
affabre commissas, ut diduci quam citissime possent, latissimus juxta &
amœnus admodum patebat despectus: silvæ enim virentes, Templumque   30
speciosum, radiis solaribus desuper collustratum, spectantium oculos pascebant;
quibus & Oppidula quædam sese ingerebant, hominibus quibusdam ultro
citroque commeare, rerumque suarum satagere visis. Denique quamlibet Ludi
partem vividis locorum & personarum Imaginibus, reliquoque apparatu
adornandum curârat Ignatius, Iones, qui quidem spectacula omnigena, maxime   35
vero larvata illa quæ cum choreis celebrantur, Aulicorum ingenio quam
optime accommodabat. Pares etiam debebantur gratiæ *Magist*ro Busbeio; cui
Roscius palmam in scenâ concederet: tantam vero tum inde, tum ab Actoribus

---

8/ Collegii: *St John's College*
9/ promptu: *end of col 1*
35/ adornandum: *for* adornandam

35/ Ignatius,: *in the annotated Bodleian copy*
(Bodl.: G 2.5 Jur.), Wood has marked the comma
for deletion

exercitatissimis, & vestitu Persico novitatis pleno, voluptatem percipiebant
quotquot ibi aderant, ut pulchrius nil quicquam aut ingeniosius oculis
auribusve hausisse testarentur. Atque hic ejus diei exitus erat, quem *Sancto*
Felici dicatum fuisse, & quo prospere omnia successisse advertit Cancellarius.
...   5

1641–2
Maypoles at Holywell   Bodl.: MS. Wood F.1
p 876
                                                                            10
At ye salute of Flora two May-poles were set up in Holywell neare Oxforde in
despite of ye presisians. On ye top of one was placed a Tub & therin ye picture
of one Edw*ar*d Golledge or College a musitian & great Puritan living in ye
parish of st peters in Baylie, at whose house also were frequent conventicles.
And because he had form*er*ly stole wood (as 'twas reported) a little fagot was   15
tied to his back. This mockery had not stood a day or two but exciting much
ye precise people the scholars of New Inne & some of Magdalen hall came
armed & [pu] pluckt it downe, w*hi*ch giving great offence to ye parishioners
of Holywell, much harme would have followed, had not certaine Officers
interposed themselves.   20
...

4/ Cancellarius: *preceded by superscript* b *to connect to note in printed source, which reads* In Diaria suo.

Oxford Playwrights

Playwrights in the provisional list below were associated with Oxford either as graduates or as sometime students. Cambridge affiliations, which are noted in the University Index, are not listed here. Each name is followed by the appropriate college or colleges, approximate or inferable date of admission, and reference works. The latter include one or more of the following: Wood, *Athenae*, abbreviated as *Ath* (principal entries only); Chambers, *Mediaeval Stage*, abbreviated *MS* (names accessible through index in vol 2); Chambers, *Elizabethan Stage*, abbreviated *ES* (names given in alphabetical order in vol 3) or *ES(K)* (ie, Appendix K in vol 4); Bentley, *Jacobean and Caroline Stage*, abbreviated *JCS* (names given in alphabetical order in vols 3–5); and *DNB*. See the University Index for *Alumni Oxonienses* entries.

In *Athenae* references, the column number indicates the column in which the entry begins. *Athenae* includes entries for the following playwrights whose connection to Oxford is tenuous and who are not listed below: Francis Beaumont (vol 2, col 437), George Chapman (vol 2, col 575), Aston Cokayne (vol 4, col 128), William Davenant (vol 3, col 802), John Heywood (vol 1, col 348), Ben Jonson (vol 2, col 612), George Puttenham (vol 1, col 741), John Rastell (vol 1, col 100), Thomas Sackville (vol 2, col 30), and John Skelton (vol 1, col 49). Although James Shirley's connection to Oxford is similarly tenuous, *Athenae* supplies information that seems to be authoritative, so he is listed below.

At the end of the list appear short biographies of two Oxford playwrights – Nicholas Grimald and Samuel Bernard – concerning whose plays standard reference works have been deemed inadequate.

An asterisk indicates playwrights whose works are listed in Appendix 6 by title. Page numbers given in the University Index that fall within the range of Appendix 6 (pp 800–40) will assist the reader in matching playwrights to their plays.

Name	College	Date	References
*Atkinson, Thomas	SJC	1615	*JCS; DNB*
Badger, John	ChCh	1550	*ES*
Barnes, Barnabe	BNC	1586	*Ath*, vol 2, col 47; *ES*
Belchier, Daubridgcourt	CCC › ChCh	1598	*JCS; DNB*
*Bellamy, Henry	SJC	1621	*JCS*

Berkeley, William	QC › St Edmund Hall › MtC	1623	*Ath*, vol 3, col 1111; *JCS*; *DNB*
*Bernard, Samuel	MC	1607	*JCS*
*Blencow, John	SJC	1629	*JCS*; *DNB*
Braithwaite, Richard	OC	1605	*Ath*, vol 3, col 986; *JCS*; *DNB*
Browne, William	EC	1624	*Ath*, vol 2, col 364; *ES*; *DNB*
*Burgess, John	MC	1500?	
*Burton, Robert	BNC › ChCh	1593	*Ath*, vol 2, col 652; *JCS*; *DNB*
*Calfhill, James	ChCh	1548	*Ath*, vol 1, col 377; *ES*; *DNB*
Carew, Thomas	MtC	1608	*JCS*; *DNB*
*Cartwright, William	ChCh	1628	*Ath*, vol 3, col 69; *JCS*; *DNB*
*Chaundler, Thomas	NC	1435	
*Clarke, Francis	SJC	1603	*ES* (1603 is date of play)
Clavel, John	BNC	1619	*JCS*; *DNB*
*Crowther, Joseph	SJC	1626	*JCS*
*Daniel, Samuel	Magdalen Hall	1579	*Ath*, vol 2, col 268; *ES*; *DNB*
Davies, John	QC › MC	1585	*Ath*, vol 2, col 400; *ES*; *DNB*
Denham, John	TC	1631	*Ath*, vol 3, col 823; *JCS*; *DNB*
*Edes, Richard	ChCh	1571	*Ath*, vol 1, col 749; *ES*; *DNB*
*Edwards, Richard	CCC › ChCh	1540	*Ath*, vol 1, col 353; *ES*; *DNB*
*Fisher, Jasper	Magdalen Hall	1607	*Ath*, vol 2, col 636; *JCS*; *DNB*
*Foxe, John	BNC › MC	1533	*Ath*, vol 1, col 528; *MS*; *DNB*
Fulwell, Ulpian	St Mary Hall	1579	*Ath*, vol 1, col 540; *ES*; *DNB*
*Gager, William	ChCh	1574	*Ath*, vol 2, col 87; *ES*; *DNB*
*Goffe, Thomas	ChCh	1609	*Ath*, vol 2, col 463; *JCS*; *DNB*
*Gomersall, Robert	ChCh	1616	*Ath*, vol 2, col 590; *JCS*; *DNB*
Gosson, Stephen	CCC	1572	*Ath*, vol 1, col 675; *ES*; *DNB*
*Grimald, Nicholas	Various	1540?	*Ath*, vol 1, col 407; *MS*; *DNB*
*Gwinne, Matthew	SJC	1574	*Ath*, vol 2, col 415; *ES*; *DNB*
Heming, William	ChCh	1621	*Ath*, vol 3, col 277; *JCS*; *DNB*
*Heylyn, Peter	Hart Hall › MC	1613	*Ath*, vol 3, col 552; *JCS*; *DNB*
Heywood, Jasper	MtC › ASC	1547?	*Ath*, vol 1, col 663; *ES*; *DNB*
*Holyday, Barten	ChCh	1605	*Ath*, vol 3, col 520; *JCS*; *DNB*
*Hooker, John	MC	1525?	*Ath*, vol 1, col 138
*Hutten, Leonard	ChCh	1574	*Ath*, vol 2, col 532; *ES(K)*; *DNB*
Killigrew, Henry	ChCh	1628	*Ath*, vol 4, col 621; *JCS*; *DNB*
Kynaston, Francis	OC › St Mary Hall › TC	1601	*Ath*, vol 3, col 38; *JCS*; *DNB*
*Latewar, Richard	SJC	1580	*Ath*, vol 1, col 709; *DNB*
Lluelyn, Martin	ChCh	1636	*Ath*, vol 4, col 42; *DNB*
Lodge, Thomas	TC	1573	*Ath*, vol 2, col 382; *ES*; *DNB*
*Lovelace, Richard	Gloucester Hall	1634	*Ath*, vol 3, col 460; *JCS*; *DNB*
Lower, William	?	?	*Ath*, vol 3, col 544; *JCS*; *DNB*

Lyly, John	MC	1569	*Ath*, vol 1, col 676; *ES; DNB*
Marmion, Shackerley	Wadham	1618	*Ath*, vol 2, col 647; *JCS; DNB*
Marston, John	BNC	1592	*Ath*, vol 1, col 762; *ES; DNB*
Massinger, Philip	St Alban Hall	1602	*Ath*, vol 2, col 654; *JCS; DNB*
*Matthew, Tobie	UC (?) ›ChCh	1559	*Ath*, vol 2, col 869; *DNB*
*May, Charles	SJC	1634	
Mayne, Jasper	ChCh	1628	*Ath*, vol 3, col 971; *JCS; DNB*
*Mead, Robert	ChCh	1634	*Ath*, vol 3, col 342; *JCS; DNB*
*Middleton, Thomas	QC	1598	*JCS; DNB*
*Moore, Thomas	MtC	1627	*Ath*, vol 4, col 179; *JCS*
*More, Thomas	Canterbury Hall or St Mary Hall	1492?	*Ath*, vol 1, col 79; *MS; DNB*
Nabbes, Thomas	EC	1621	*JCS; DNB*
Nowell, Alexander	BNC	1526?	*Ath*, vol 1, col 716; *DNB*
*Parsons, Philip	SJC	1610	*ES(K); DNB*
*Peele, George	Broadgates Hall ›ChCh	1572	*Ath*, vol 1, col 688; *ES; DNB*
Percy, William	Gloucester Hall	1589	*ES; DNB*
Radcliffe, Ralph	BNC	1537?	*Ath*, vol 1, col 215; *MS; DNB*
Rastell, William	?	1525?	*Ath*, vol 1, col 343; *DNB*
Read, Thomas	NC	1624	*Ath*, vol 3, col 831; *DNB*
Salisbury, Thomas	JC	1625	*Ath*, vol 3, col 55; *JCS*
*Sandsbury, John	SJC	1593	*Ath*, vol 2, col 58; *DNB*
Sandys, George	St Mary Hall	1589	*Ath*, vol 3, col 97; *JCS; DNB*
Shirley, James	SJC	1615?	*Ath*, vol 3, col 737; *JCS; DNB*
*Snelling, Thomas	SJC	1634	*Ath*, vol 3, col 275; *JCS*
*Speed, John	SJC	1612	*Ath*, vol 2, col 660; *JCS; DNB*
*Strode, William	ChCh	1617	*Ath*, vol 3, col 151; *JCS; DNB*
Udall, Nicholas	CCC	1520	*Ath*, vol 1, col 211; *MS; DNB*
*Verney, Francis	TC	1600	*ES; DNB*
Watson, Edward	?	1512	
Watson, Thomas	?	?	*Ath*, vol 1, col 601; *ES; DNB*
White, Francis	Magdalen Hall ›MC	1607	*JCS*
*Wild, George	SJC	1629?	*Ath*, vol 3, col 720; *JCS; DNB*
Wilson, Arthur	TC	1631	*Ath*, vol 3, col 318; *JCS; DNB*
*Wotton, Henry	NC ›QC	1584	*Ath*, vol 2, col 643; *ES; DNB*
*Wren, Christopher, Sr	SJC	1608	*ES(K)*
*Wright, Abraham	SJC	1629	*Ath*, vol 4, col 275; *JCS; DNB*
Zouche, Richard	NC ›St Alban Hall	1607	*Ath*, vol 3, col 510; *JCS; DNB*

Notes on Selected Playwrights

Nicholas Grimald (1519?–62), probably of Leighton Bromswold, Huntingdonshire, began his academic career at Christ's College, Cambridge, where he attained his BA in 1540. He then migrated to Oxford, a member successively of Brasenose and Merton Colleges (1541–7), and finally of the newly founded Christ Church, having attained his MA on 24 March 1543/4. While Grimald's modern reputation rests primarily on his contributions to Richard Tottel's *Songes and Sonettes* of 1557 (*STC*: 13860), John Bale's contemporary bibliography *Scriptorum illustrium maioris Brytanniae Catalogus*, vol 1 (Basel, 1557), 701, assigns to Grimald several known or presumed plays. Two of these were published in his lifetime: *Christus Redivivus* (1543) and *Archipropheta* (1548). A MS of the latter, perhaps in Grimald's own hand, survives in the British Library. These two plays are listed, with details, in Appendix 6:1 (see also pp 85–6). Six other Grimald plays (*Athanasius sive Infamia, Christus Nascens, Fama, Protomartyr*, 'De Puerorum in Musicis Institutione,' and *Troilus*) – all lost – are listed in Appendix 6:2.

Both *Christus Redivivus* and *Archipropheta* were published not in Oxford or London, but on the continent. Similarly, evidence of performance abroad is stronger than evidence of performance in Oxford: see L.R. Merrill (ed and trans), *The Life and Poems of Nicholas Grimald*, Yale Studies in English 69 (New Haven and London, 1925), 11, 61–7. Our list of Grimald's eight plays follows Merrill's presumably definitive list, pp 24–7.

Samuel Bernard (*c* 1591–1657), whose academic career was spent at Magdalen College, matriculated on 3 July 1607 at the age of sixteen. He received his BA in 1610, his MA in 1613, his BD in 1621, and his DD in 1639. He was usher at Magdalen School in 1612 and master there from 1617 to 1625.

In his memoirs Peter Heylyn reports that on 8 March 1616/17 'My English Tragedy cald Spurius was acted privately (as Mr Whites & Mr Bernards plaies were) in the presidents Lodgings' (see p 422). This entry is supplemented by two entries in an eighteenth-century auction catalogue: Jacob Hooke (comp), *Bibliotheca Bernardiana: Or, A Catalogue Of the Library of the Late Charles Bernard, Esq; Serjeant Surgeon to Her Majesty. Containing a curious Collection of the best Authors in Physick, History, Philology, Antiquities, &c. With several MSS. Ancient and Modern which will begin to be sold by Auction on Thursday the 22d of March, 1710–11. At the Black-Boy Coffee-House in Ave-Mary-Lane, near Ludgate-Street* (London, 1711).

A copy preserved in the Bodleian Library (Crynes 701) has auction prices recorded in the margins. Lot 674 (p 217), which fetched 10s from an unknown buyer, was a folio-sized manuscript of tragedies by Charles Bernard's ancestor, Samuel Bernard, containing:

1) *Julius and Gonzaga*, performed in the president's house in Magdalen College, 23 January 1616/17 (this may be the play referred to by Peter Heylyn on 8 March 1616/17);
2) *Andronicus*, performed on 26 January 1617/18, in the Magdalen College hall; and
3) *Phocas*, performed on 27 January 1618/19, in the Magdalen College hall.

A second item, lot 925 (p 218) which fetched 2s, was a quarto-sized manuscript containing three tragedies and other poetical works by 'Sarm*ueli* Bernardi': since the plays are not named, it is uncertain whether or not these were the same three plays. Neither volume has been traced.

The three titles are listed in Appendix 6:2, where confusion concerning the supposed identity of *Andronicus* with a contemporary Latin play entitled *Andronicus Comnenus* is also noted (see also Appendix 6:4).

APPENDIX 15
Saints' Days and Festivals

The following list contains the dates for holy days and festivals mentioned in the Records. All days are entered under their official names but unofficial names occurring in the Records are also given in parentheses and repeated in their alphabetical place as required. Only feast days themselves are listed; if the night or eve of a feast or its tide or season (likely the feast day itself with its octave) is referred to, its date may be inferred from that of the feast. Exact dates for moveable feasts are included in textual notes to the Records. See also C.R. Cheney (ed) and Michael Jones (rev), *A Handbook of Dates for Students of British History* (Cambridge, 2000), 63–93.

Accession Day
    Elizabeth I   17 November
    James I   24 March
    Charles I   27 March
All Saints (All Hallows)   1 November
All Souls   2 November
Ascension Day (Holy Thursday)   Thursday following the fifth Sunday after Easter, ie, forty days after Easter
Ash Wednesday   the first day of Lent
Candlemas   2 February
Christmas   25 December
Circumcision   1 January
Coronation Day
    Elizabeth I   15 January
    Charles I   2 February
Easter   Sunday following the full moon on or next after 21 March
Egg Saturday   the Saturday before Shrove Tuesday
Epiphany (Twelfth Day)   6 January
Hock Monday, Tuesday   second Monday and Tuesday after Easter
Holy Cross
    Exaltation of   14 September
    Invention of   3 May

Holy Innocents	28 December
Holy Thursday	Thursday following the fifth Sunday after Easter, ie, forty days after Easter
King's Day	see Accession Day
Lady Day	25 March
Lent	the forty days before Easter, beginning with Ash Wednesday
May Day	on or about 1 May
Michaelmas	29 September
Midsummer	24 June
New Year's Day	1 January
Pentecost (Whit Sunday)	seventh Sunday after Easter, ie, fifty days after Easter
Queen's Day	see Accession Day
St Andrew	30 November
St Anne	26 July
St Bartholomew	24 August
St Catherine	25 November
St Clement	23 November
St Edmund, king and martyr	20 November
St Edward the Confessor, Translation of	13 October
St Felix	8 March
St James	25 July
St John the Baptist	
Beheading of	29 August
Nativity of (Midsummer)	24 June
St John the Evangelist	27 December
St Luke	18 October
St Mark	25 April
St Martin	11 November
St Mary Magdalene	22 July
St Mary the Virgin	
Annunciation to (Lady Day)	25 March
Assumption of	15 August
Purification of (Candlemas)	2 February
St Mathias	24 February
St Matthew	21 September
St Michael the Archangel (Michaelmas)	29 September
St Nicholas	6 December
Sts Peter and Paul	29 June
Sts Philip and James	1 May
Sts Simon and Jude	28 October

St Stephen	26 December
St Swithun, Translation of	15 July
St Thomas	21 December
Translation of	3 July
St Thomas the Martyr	29 December
Translation of	7 July
St Wulfstan	19 January
Shrove Sunday, Monday, and Tuesday	the Sunday, Monday, and Tuesday before Ash Wednesday, the start of Lent
Trinity Sunday	eighth Sunday after Easter
Twelfth Day	6 January
Whit Sunday	seventh Sunday after Easter, ie, fifty days after Easter

Translations

PATRICK GREGORY

The Translations are intended to be used in conjunction with the Records text and Latin Glossary. The documents have been translated as literally as possible. The order of the records in the Translations parallels that of the Records text. Place-names and given names have been modernized. The spelling of surnames in the Translations reflects the same principles used in the Index. Capitalization and punctuation are in accordance with modern practice. As in the Records text, diamond brackets indicate obliterations and square brackets cancellations. However, cancellations are not normally translated; they may be translated when a whole entry is cancelled, especially if it appears that a cancellation may be administrative rather than the correction of an error, or if they seem to be of special interest or relevance. Words not in the Latin text but needed in the English for grammatical sense or for clarification are enclosed in parentheses, as are alternative translations of ambiguous or difficult words and phrases. The translations of Latin verse are in prose but, where possible, they have been presented so that they correspond line for line or couplet for couplet with the verse original. No attempt has been made to duplicate the wordplay sometimes found in the more literary Latin texts, and all the Translations are intended for use in conjunction with the Records and Latin Glossary.

Not all the Latin in the text has been translated here. Some Latin passages are accompanied by contemporary English renderings in the Records and are therefore not included in the Translations. Latin tags, formulae, headings, very short entries, or other short sections in largely English documents are either translated in footnotes or not translated at all if the syntax and vocabulary are straightforward. In translated documents containing a mixture of Latin and English, the English sections are normally indicated with '*(English)*,' but in some cases, in which the syntax of English and Latin has become entangled, the English text appears in the translation in modern spelling. All Latin vocabulary not found in the *Oxford Latin Dictionary* is found in the glossary.

The Anglo-Norman 'University Response to Town Complaints of a Riot' (p 4) was translated by William Edwards, the Spanish 'Letter of Guzmán de Silva to the King of Spain' (p 125) by Josiah Blackmore, and the Italian 'Letters of the Venetian Ambassador Nicolò Molen to the Doge' (pp 293–4) by Dario Brancato. The Latin translations were checked by Abigail Ann Young and have benefitted greatly from her advice at every stage in their preparation.

1284-5
Archbishop Pecham's Register
Lambeth Palace Library: MS Archbishop Pecham's Register
f 223   *(November)*

...

® Godstow

® Regarding the
celebration of
the divine office

Brother John, by divine permission a humble servant of the church of Canterbury, Primate Of All England, (sends) greetings, grace, and blessing to (our)
beloved daughters in Christ, A.B. the abbess, and the convent of Godstow....
Namely, (we command) that you celebrate the ecclesiastical office in which
you have to speak with (your) bridegroom and receive his spirit at due times
with all reverence, at which time no one at all is allowed to be absent unless
she is obediently occupied in necessary tasks, not in conversations with outsiders. We order, moreover, that the office itself be sung precisely and in its
entirety. 'Precisely,' I say, so that, both in choir masses and in those of the
Blessed Virgin, irrelevant novelties be excluded throughout the whole year
and that nothing new be sung there except by the counsel of the master and
abbess equally and also the precentress, but that the old take precedence over
all the new. The office is also to be celebrated in its entirety, since all curtailment of the monastic office celebrated at Abingdon, as the presidents of the
chapter of the monks recently determined, is to be rejected. We permit, however, the children's observances that are customarily held on the feast of the
Innocents to begin only after vespers (on the feast) of St John, and they are
to be concluded completely on the next day, on (Holy) Innocents' Day itself.
For the governance of the convent, moreover, the abbess is obliged to call the
more mature and more discreet (members of the convent) for the internal
and external business of the house to be managed advantageously. But if
any (of them) should refuse to come after being called a second time, (her)
pittance shall be taken away from her at the following dinner. But if she
makes herself deaf to the one ordering by not coming the third time, bread
and water only shall be granted to her at the next dinner. We say the same
for all those who stick disobediently to their own will at any time, whoever
(they may be)....

1292
Chancellor's Register   OUA: NEP/Supra/A
f 55v   *(University College statutes)*

...

20.

Likewise all are to live honourably as clerics as befits the saints, not fighting,
not speaking scurrilous or shameful (words), not relating, singing, or willingly
listening to songs or tales about (their) mistresses or wanton things or things
conducive to licentiousness, not mocking or moving anyone to anger, not
shouting so that they keep students from study or rest....

1297–8
University Response to Town Complaints of a Riot OUA: SEP/Y/12a
mb [3]*

...

Concerning the conflict that took place Monday in the High Street, whereas according to those people (of) the town it was the work of the whole common-alty with bells and with horns and at a common cry, the armed bailiffs being present, and according to the clerks there were only a few individuals without authority and without a leader and without common cry, the University declares that the clerks can make a claim against the commonalty for the dam-ages they received to their persons or their goods before the chancellor, in form of law, and the laity who would make claims against the clerks (can do so) likewise before the chancellor; he will do right by them so that this lawsuit on both sides be made only as simple trespass, not of peril to life and limb....

...

c 1300
Chancellor's Register OUA: NEP/Supra/A
f 63* *(Decree against observance of local festivals)*

...

Regarding the manner of forbidding the feast days of the (student) nations By the lord chancellor's and the regent masters' authority with the non-regents' unanimous consent it has been decreed and established that from now on no feast day of any (student) nation shall be celebrated with a solemnity and customary convocation of masters and scholars or other well-known persons in any church whatever unless some persons wish to celebrate the feast of some

®°Diocesan festivals°

saint of their own diocese with devotion in the parishes where they are living, but not inviting masters, scholars, or any other well-known persons of another parish or their own, just as shall not happen on the feasts of St Catherine,

®°That pastimes in the public streets be prohibited°

St Nicholas, and similar (saints). We command also that this decree be observed by the same chancellor's authority under penalty of greater excommunication: that no one lead dances with masks or with any noise in churches or streets or go anywhere festooned or crowned with a crown made of the leaves of trees or of flowers or of anything else. We forbid (this) under penalty of excommunica-tion, which we establish from now on, and of a lengthy imprisonment.

...

1305–6
AC *A Report on the Inquest into the Death of Gilbert Foxlee*
Bodl.: MS. Twyne 4
pp 32–3*

...

'It happened on the Sunday next after the feast of the Assumption of the

Blessed Virgin Mary in the thirty-fourth year of the reign of King Edward (*ie*, Edward I) that Gilbert Foxlee, a cleric, died in his hostel where he was staying in the parish of St Peter in the East, Oxford, around the noon hour. And on the next Monday following he was seen by Thomas Lisewys, coroner of the lord king for the town of Oxford, and he had one wound in his left shin near his knee four inches wide all around and one-and-a-half inches deep. An inquest was taken afterward in the presence of the aforesaid coroner, by oath, etc.' Almost all the names of the jurors are lacking there. Then there follows: 'who say upon their oath that, on the Thursday, the eve of the Nativity of St John the Baptist immediately preceding, the tailors of Oxford and others from the town who were with them were keeping watch in their shops all through the night singing and making merry with harps and viols and various other instruments as is the usual custom to do there and elsewhere on account of the solemnity of that feast. And after midnight, since they understood that there was no one wandering there in the streets, they went out of their shops, and others who were there with them, and danced in the High Street opposite the Drapery. And, as they were playing in this way, the aforesaid Gilbert Foxlee appeared with a naked and unsheathed sword in his hand and immediately stirred up a quarrel against them wishing to break into that dance any way he could. Seeing (this), moreover, some of them | who were acquainted with him approached him and wished to take him away from them and asked him not to harm anyone. But that same Gilbert did not want to stop on this account, but at once jumped away from them and came back making an attack on one William de Cleydon. And he would have cut off his hand with his sword as he went in that dance if he had not quickly withdrawn. And Henry de Beaumont, corviser, Thomas de Bloxham, William de Ley, a servant of John de Ley, and the aforesaid William de Cleydon immediately rushed toward him. And the aforesaid Henry wounded him in his right arm with a sword and the aforesaid Thomas wounded him in the back with a misericord, but the aforesaid William de Cleydon wounded him in the head so that he fell. And immediately afterward William de Ley wounded him in his left shin with a kind of axe that is called a "sparth," and he gave him the aforesaid wound next to the knee from which he died on the aforementioned Sunday. But he lived for eight weeks and two and a half days and he received all his last rites.'
...

1340

A   ***The Queen's College Statutes***   QC Arch
p 18   (*Chapter 20*)
...

...And they are to assemble at the same time for dinner and supper, as much as they are conveniently able, at the hour of summoning for the same. The

summoning, moreover, is to be made by clarion in a suitable place by one
servant who is appointed to that (task), where he is more likely to be able to
be heard by all and each....

...

pp 26–7   *(Chapter 31)*
...

And since it is not appropriate for the poor, especially those living on alms,
to give the children's bread to dogs to eat, and (since) woe shall betide those
'that take their diversions with the birds of the air,' none of the scholars of
the said hall is to keep in the same (hall) or adjacent places a greyhound,
or hunting dog, or other personally owned (dog), hawk, or trained bird, or
possess any other kind (of bird). And since a large number (*or* the frequent
use) of musical instruments is apt often to provoke frivolity and insolence,
and to offer an occasion of distraction from study and progress, let the
aforesaid scholars know that the use of instruments of this kind within their
dwelling, except at times of common relaxation, is entirely forbidden for
them, and every kind of dice game and chess and every other game giving
occasion for the loss of money and coin of any kind in the hall, rooms, or
their dwelling, unless perhaps some person or persons should wish at any
time to amuse themselves decently and peacefully for the sake of recreation
outside the hall and without distracting themselves or the fellows from
study or the divine office. In this, games of dice and that kind of thing, from
which grounds for dispute are apt to arise and penury (is apt) frequently to
afflict the player, should especially be avoided. And let the chaplains, poor
(scholars), clerics, and all servants or residents at the said hall know that
they are bound to the avoidance of games of dice, according to the (same)
manner as the scholars, | under punishment to be inflicted by the provost.
But let the provost and his deputy know that they are bound by the bond of
their oath to stop all the aforementioned but only as far as necessity requires
or decency permits.

...

1360–1
Exeter College Rectors' Accounts   EC Arch: A.1
single mb*   *(10 July–17 October 1361) (Internal and external expenses)*
...

Likewise he accounts for 8d paid for expenses of parishioners of Long
Wittenham on the day of the Beheading of St John the Baptist, when there
was a play....

...

1378

Continuatio Eulogii   BL: Cotton MS Galba E.VII
f 194 col 2–f 194v col 1

…

In the same year a knight from the king's retinue (*or* household) came from Woodstock to Oxford. Some scholars came at night and stood before his hostel making a song in rhyming verse about him in English containing specific words against the king's honour. They also shot arrows at the window of the hostel.

Upon rising in the morning the knight complained to the king. The chancellor and his vice-chancellor were immediately called to London and were set before the chancellor of the realm and the king's council. And the chancellor of the University was asked why the mockers of the king were not punished. The chancellor replied | that he was afraid (of committing) a breach of canon law. And the chancellor of the realm (said) to him: 'You will prove that Oxford cannot be governed by a cleric. The king cannot be disdained in Oxford just as he cannot be elsewhere. And if you of Oxford cannot correct and chastise disdainers of the king because of (your fear of) a breach of canon law, as the chancellor says, it follows that Oxford cannot be governed by clerics but that the king ought to withdraw your privileges. You ought to defend the privileges of the University to the greatest extent both on account of your duty and also on account of your oath, and you speak against those very privileges. We depose you from your position.' The chancellor of the University replied: 'I have my position from the pope and from the king. What I have from the king, the king can take away, but not that which I have from the pope.' The chancellor of England (said) to him: 'And we relieve you of the royal part, disqualifying you for the said position, and then you shall see if you are able to rejoice in the pope's part. The king can remove the University and you from Oxford.'

The vice-chancellor, a monk, was condemned to prison because, as has been said above, at the pope's command he had imprisoned John Wycliffe who afterward was freed at the request of friends. The chancellor, concealing his deposition, although he had been deposed, resigned in convocation of his own free will, as he said, not being forced.…

…

1386–7

Merton College Supervisors of Founders' Kin Accounts   MCR: 4109
single mb dorse   *(1 August–1 August)* *(Necessary commons expenses)*
…

…Likewise for gaudies when all the fellows of the hall went out for maying, 2s.…

1389–90
Gaol Delivery Roll   PRO: JUST 3/180
mbs 2c–d*   *(18 February)*

Gaol delivery held at Oxford Castle before John Hulle and other JPs for Oxfordshire
...

Of Oxford   William Gymel and Peter Ardach arrested because they were charged before
Robert Cherlton and his fellows, the lord king's justices appointed to keep
the peace in the aforesaid county, because they together with other unknown
felons allied with them, armed (and) arrayed in a warlike manner, at Oxford
on the Thursday and Friday of the fourth week of Lent in the twelfth year
of the reign of the lord now king of England, appointed among themselves
specific captains and rulers to rise up against | *(blank)* some Welshmen
being in the town of Oxford, to shoot arrows before themselves in various streets and lanes, (and) to cry out, 'Ware, Ware, Ware. Slay the Welsh
dogs and their helps, and who so looketh out of his house, he shall be dead.'
And they killed some of them, as (named) below, and seriously injured some
and they forced some Welshmen to their knees (and) made them forswear the
town, leading them to the gates of the said town, and made them urinate on
those (gates) and kiss the gate and while kissing thus they struck their heads
against the gate so that sometimes blood came from the nose while tears came
from their eyes. And they feloniously broke into a certain hall in Oxford,
called Deep Hall, and in the same place they feloniously stole and took
away one book, one penner with a horn, one pair of breeches of William
Whetehull, and one sword and books of John Hoby, to the value of 38s.
And on the said Friday at night they feloniously broke into Thomas Frenche's
room situated in the same hall, and they feloniously stole and took away two
swords, one shield, two bows with twenty-six arrows, one jacket of fustian,
one red gown, two pairs of white sleeves (*or* cuffs), one pair of linen sheets
(*or* napkins), one lined cloak, five pairs of hose, two ells of canvas, one pair
of linen cloth, and other goods and chattels of Thomas Frenche himself at
the value of 60s. And on the aforesaid Friday they feloniously broke into other
rooms of various scholars staying in the aforesaid hall and they feloniously
stole the goods and chattels found there, namely, books, linen clothes, and
woollen clothes. And on the said Friday they feloniously broke into a hostel in
Oxford called Neville's Entry by night and feloniously stole and took away the
goods and chattels, namely, doors, windows, and grammar books and linen
and woollen clothing, of William Dannay, the principal of the same hostel,
of John Halkyn, a scholar there, and of other scholars remaining there, to
the value of 60s. And on the same Friday at night they feloniously broke into
a hall in Oxford called St Agase's Hall and feloniously stole the goods and
chattels found there, namely, linen and woollen clothes, grammar as well as
dialectic books, swords, bows, (and) harps, of William Gilton, John Mulle,

John Glove, and of other scholars being there, to the value of £4. And that on Saturday in the said fourth week of Lent in the abovesaid year, the aforesaid William Gymel and Peter together with other unknown felons feloniously broke into a hall in Oxford called Pyry Hall and feloniously stole goods of the principal of the same hall, Matthew Alco, and of Richard Oliver, namely, two swords, lined cloaks of various colours, one dagger, one axe, and bows and arrows to the value of £4, and they entered other halls and hostels there on the same day, namely, Mildred Hall, Hampton Hall, (and) Bastaples Entry, and feloniously stole various goods of various scholars staying in the said hall to the value of 50s. And that in the said uprising (men), namely, Edward Nuton, Geoffrey Hanlane of Wales, Thomas Repton, and John Boweman, were killed by the said felons. And that on the said Thursday, the aforesaid felons and various unknown (men) took doors, planks, and stones from the said despoiled halls into the High Street next to St Mary's Church and they seized laymen's timber, boxes, and doors against their will, and they closed themselves up from Charlton's Inn to Penchurch Lane and there they remained for the night.

They come before the justices, brought here in turn and having said how they wished to acquit themselves of the aforesaid felonies. They say that they are in no way guilty on that account and in this matter they entrust themselves to the jury for good or ill. Therefore let (a jury) be sworn in on that account. The jurors, who have been chosen, tried, and sworn for this (purpose), come. They say on their oath that the aforesaid William Gymel and Peter are not guilty of the aforesaid felonies nor have they ever withdrawn from the suit on this occasion.

(They are) acquitted

Therefore it has been decided that the aforesaid William Gymel and Peter should depart from here acquitted, etc.

…

mb 3d*

…And on the same Friday they feloniously broke into a hall in Oxford called St Agase's Hall by night and feloniously stole the goods and chattels found there, namely, linen and woollen clothes, grammar as well as dialectic books, swords, bows, (and) harps, of William Gilton, John Mulle, John Glove, and of other scholars being there, to the value of £4....

mb 5d*

…And on the same Friday he feloniously broke into a hall in Oxford called St Agase's Hall by night and feloniously stole the goods and chattels found there, namely, linen and woollen clothes, grammar as well as dialectic books, swords, bows, (and) harps, of William Gilton, John Mulle, John Glove, and of other scholars being there, to the value of £4....

1395

AC *Expenses for a Degree Feast at Canterbury College*
Pantin: *Canterbury College*, vol 3
p 56
…
Likewise given to pipers, 20s.
…

c **1396**

Letter Recommending a Father Remove His Son from Oxford
BL: MS Royal 17.B.xlvii
f 44v*
…

                         Another similar form
Most assured friend, although I have counselled you elsewhere that, taking an
example from the proverbs promulgated of old – 'what the head grasps when
young, it will savour when old' – you should send your son to the schools of
Oxford so that there he could be informed as much with knowledge as with
moral conduct, yet conceiving frequently from accounts that he will not
progress in learning but abandons detestable moral conduct – the highest
Lord be praised – and that he has been taught commendably both in scripture
and in playing the harp, I counsel you (now) with a pure heart that you
with discernment would direct him to serve in the court of the lord king or
the duke of Lancaster.
…

c **1398**

New College Statutes   NC Arch: 9429
ff 14–14v
…

® 18   On not delaying in the hall after dinner and supper
Likewise because after the refreshment of (their) bodies by the taking of food
and drink, people are commonly made more ready to perpetrate coarse jokes,
immodest speeches, and what is worse, back-bitings and quarrels, and likewise also other evils both numerous and dangerous, and (because) they, then
considering excesses of this kind less (important) than an empty stomach,
often move the souls of simple persons to arguments, insults, and other excesses,
we establish, ordain, and wish that every day after dinner and supper, when
thanksgiving to the Highest for things received has first been finished, thereafter without an interval of time, after the loving-cup has been provided for
those wishing to drink and after drinkings in the hall, at the hour of curfew
each of the seniors, of whatever estate or degree they be, are to move to their
studies or other | places. Nor shall they allow other juniors to delay there

further except on principal feasts and greater doubles, and except when house meetings, disputations, or other important (*or* difficult) business pertaining to the college has to be dealt with in the hall immediately afterward, or except when, on account of reverence for God or for his mother or for any other saint, a fire in the hall is provided for the fellows in wintertime after dinner- or supper-time; then scholars and fellows are permitted for the sake of recreation to make a suitable delay in the hall after dinner- or supper-time in songs and other decent diversions, and to study in a serious manner poems, chronicles, and marvels of this world and other things that are appropriate to the clerical estate.

...

f 16   (Chapter 24) (*Students and fellows not to leave the University without permission*)

...

...And that while they are absent in the country they are to be dressed as is appropriate for clerics and behave decently in moral conduct. And neither at that time nor while they are present in the University are the scholars and fellows or any others staying in the college itself to attend or frequent taverns, shows, or other disreputable places, but refrain entirely from suspect associations lest – which God forbid – scandal, injury, or prejudice should occur or in any way arise for our said college, (our) scholars, or the fellows of the same from (their) dishonourable or suspect social intercourse or otherwise from their shameless behaviour of whatever kind....

f 24*   (Chapter 42) (*Manner of saying mass, matins, and the other hours in the college chapel*)

...But on the other feasts written below – namely, (those) of St Stephen, of St John the Apostle, of the Holy Innocents, (and) of St Thomas the Martyr; and on the Monday, Tuesday, and Wednesday of Easter week and of Pentecost (week); and (those) of the Invention and Exaltation of the Holy Cross, of the Translation of St Thomas, of St Andrew and St Thomas the Apostles, of St Mathias, of St Mark, of the apostles Philip and James, and of St James the Apostle, of St Bartholomew, of St Matthew, of St Michael, of St Luke, of Sts Simon and Jude, of St Martin, of St Nicholas, of the Translation of St Swithun, of St Catherine, and of St (Mary) Magdalene – lesser and subordinate persons, the fellows of the college itself, when the regard and reputation due to these feasts and persons have been observed, are to perform the offices in due manner according to the greater or lesser status or dignity of the said feasts. We wish and command each and every (office) on each of these aforementioned days to be performed and carried out by the aforesaid scholars and fellows of the said college, in the aforesaid manner and form, the abovesaid feast of the Holy Innocents excepted, on which feast we allow that the boys may say and carry out vespers, matins, and the other divine offices in reading and singing according to the use and custom of the church of Salisbury....

...

ff 34v–5*

...

63

On dancing, wrestling matches, and other unlawful pastimes not to occur in the chapel or hall.

Likewise, because a certain stone wall in the middle of the chief or transverse wall of the chapel of our abovesaid college is known to lie between and also separate that chapel and the hall of that college, (and because) the image of the most holy and indivisible Trinity, the gibbet of the holy cross with the image of the crucified (Christ), the images of the most Blessed Virgin Mary and of many other saints, sculptures, glass windows, and various paintings, and a number of other sumptuous works finely crafted and adorned with diverse colours for the praise, glory, and honour of God and of his aforesaid mother, are devoutly placed and set in many ways on the said chapel's side (of that wall), (and because) that cross and images, sculptures, glass windows, paintings, and the other abovesaid works, indeed, could easily and accidentally and likely be harmed, disfigured, removed, broken, obstructed, or otherwise damaged from the inexperience, carelessness, and insolence of various fellows I and scholars (and) also of other persons by the various castings of stones, balls, or other things at the wall mentioned already on the aforesaid hall's side or by dances, wrestling matches, or other careless and irregular pastimes that would perhaps take place in the hall or in the chapel itself, (and because) the said wall also, in part or completely, could be made worse or even weakened, we indeed, desiring to provide for the safety of the images, sculptures, windows, and aforesaid works, strictly prohibit castings of stones and balls and also of any other things at the wall mentioned already, besides dances, wrestling matches, and any other careless and irregular games from taking place in the chapel or the aforesaid hall ever at any time, by which (activities), or any one of them, damage or loss could be inflicted on the images, sculptures, glass windows, paintings, or other aforesaid sumptuous works or the aforesaid chief wall in their construction or structure, in material or in form, by any means. Likewise because many different rooms are arranged below the aforesaid hall, which has been raised and built above ground in the manner of a solar, in which the scholars or fellows of our said college and also the priests, clerics, and servants and others who are obliged to serve in the chapel of this college ought to remain, lie down, rest, and also study, who can easily and likely be hindered by wrestling matches, round dances, formal dances, leaping dances, songs, shouts, commotions, and inordinate clamours, spills of water, ale, and of other liquors, and other tumultuous games that would perhaps take place in the same hall from their study, sleep, tranquillity, rest, and quiet, and otherwise sustain serious damages to their books, clothing, and other things, we indeed, desiring to provide for their convenience and their rest equally, strictly prohibit any wrestling matches of this kind, round dances, formal dances, leaping dances, songs, shouts, commotions, and inordinate clamours, spills of water, ale, and of all other liquors, and also tumultuous games and any other extravagances from taking place in the hall or aforesaid chapel ever at any time, by which (activities), or any one of them, the aforesaid students, priests, and others remaining together in the said rooms could in any way be hindered from their study, sleep, tranquillity, rest, or quiet, or otherwise sustain damage or injury to their books, clothing, or other things, or by which the hall itself, in its adornment or construction, below or above, inside or outside, in any part of it, may be disfigured or suffer injury or any damage. And if anyone is found guilty in the premises or any one of the premises, he shall appropriately make satisfaction for the damage he has caused. And notwithstanding, in order that the punishment of one be the fear of many, he shall be harshly punished without any partiality whatever by the loss of his commons or otherwise according to the discretion and determination of the warden, the vice-warden, the deans, and six other senior fellows of the said college according to the magnitude of the excess.

...

1399–1400

Durham College Accounts   Durham University Library:
  Durham Cathedral Muniments, Oxford Ac. 1399–1400
single mb*   *(3 or 7 July–28 May)* *(Expenses at Oxford)*

...

Likewise to the almonry bishop   2s

...

1400–1

Merton College Supervisors of Founders' Kin Accounts   MCR: 4114
single mb*   *(1 August–1 August)* *(Necessary expenses noted)*

...

...Likewise for May, 2d....

...

1401–2
Durham College Accounts   Durham University Library:
 Durham Cathedral Muniments, Oxford Ac. 1401–2
single mb   *(13 May–5 May)* *(Expenses at Oxford)*
...
Likewise to the almonry bishop   20d
...

1410–11
Expenses for Inception at Canterbury College   Bodl.: MS. Tanner 165
f 147*   *(Necessary expenses and wages)*
...
...Likewise in payment made to entertainers, 6s 8d....

Merton College Supervisors of Founders' Kin Accounts   MCR: 4115
single mb*   *(1 August–1 August)* *(Necessary expenses noted)*
...
...Likewise for gloves given for the triumph of versification (*or* for a feat of versification), 4d....
...

single mb dorse*
...
...Likewise for maying, 6d....
...

1414
AC *Chamberlains' Accounts*   Bodl.: MS. Twyne 23
p 242*
...
...Likewise for seven stone of lead for repair of the bullring, 7s 6d....
...

1427–8
Chancellor's Register   OUA: Hyp/A/1, Register Aaa
f 13   *(31 July)* *(Goods found in Thomas Cooper's study)*
...
...Likewise one old harp. Likewise one broken lute....
...

1431–2
Merton College Bursars' Accounts   MCR: 3754
mb 1   *(23 March–27 July)*
…
…Likewise to the lord duke of Gloucester's entertainer/s, 6d….
…

c 1440
All Souls College Inventory   Bodl.: MS. D.D. All Souls c.268, no 210
mb 2 col 1*   *(Contents of the vestry)*

…Likewise one shirt, one hood, and a mitre for the (St) Nicholas bishop.

1443
All Souls College Foundation Statutes   ASC Arch
ff [25–5v]   *(That fellows and scholars shall not leave the town without permission)*
…
…And that while they are absent in the country they are to be dressed as is appropriate for clerics and behave decently in moral conduct. And neither at that time nor while they are present in the University are the same scholars or fellows or any others whatsoever, chaplains staying in the college itself, to attend or frequent taverns, shows, or other disreputable places, | but refrain entirely from suspect associations lest – which God forbid – scandal, injury, or prejudice should occur or in any way arise for our said college, (our) scholars, or the fellows of the same from (their) dishonourable or suspect social intercourse or otherwise from their shameless behaviour of whatever kind….
…

1443–4
St Peter in the East Churchwardens' Accounts   ORO: PAR 213/4/F1/1
single mb   *(Receipts)*
…
…And of 13s 2d from the church ale….
…

1444–5
AC   *St Peter in the East Churchwardens' Accounts*
Bodl.: MS. Top.Oxon c.403
f 39   *(Receipts)*
…
…And of 12s (received) in the church ale at the feast of Pentecost….
…

1456–7
Lincoln College Computus LC Arch: Computus 1
f 3   *(21 September–21 December 1456)*   *(Offerings of All Saints' Church)*
...
Likewise on St Nicholas' Day   5½d
The remaining part, which comes to 6d, given, namely, to the bishop by
master rector's command.
...

f 14v   *(21 December 1455–21 December 1456)*   *(Necessary expenses)*

After the feast of St Michael the Archangel
...
Likewise to the clerk of St Michael's Church on
St Nicholas' Eve   6d
...

1460–1
New College Bursars' Accounts NC Arch: 7713
mb 5   *(External payments)*
...
...And paid to the lord king's entertainers for a reward given to them, 3s 4d....
...

1461–2
St Peter in the East Churchwardens' Accounts ORO: PAR 213/4/F1/1
single mb*   *(Receipts)*
...
And of 4s 3½d received among the parishioners at the feast of Pentecost for
a church ale....
...

1463–4
St Michael at the North Gate Churchwardens' Accounts
ORO: PAR 211/4/F1/1, item 33
single mb   *(6 January 1463/4–6 January 1464/5)*   *(Receipts)*
...
Likewise they received from the women
at Hocktide   4s 7d
...

1464–5
St Peter le Bailey Churchwardens' Accounts   ORO: PAR 214/4/F1/3
single mb* *(Receipts)*

...

Likewise received for ale at Pentecost   8s

...

1465–6
AC *St Peter in the East Churchwardens' Accounts*
Bodl.: MS. Top.Oxon c.403
f 42* *(Receipts)*

...

...And of 11s 2d received in ale sold against Pentecost....

...

St Peter le Bailey Churchwardens' Accounts   ORO: PAR 214/4/F1/4
single mb* *(Receipts)*

...

And (the churchwardens charge themselves) with 7s received at the feast of
Pentecost for ale.
And with 3s 3d received at Hock Tuesday.

...

1466
Chancellor's Register   OUA: Hyp/A/1, Register Aaa
f 236

...

Mr Robert Paslew has hired John Harris, harp-maker, as his servant, for a
gown or (its) price of 6s 8d, and the same John has been sworn to observance
of the privileges of the University, etc.

...

1466–7
St Peter le Bailey Churchwardens' Accounts   ORO: PAR 214/4/F1/5
single mb* *(Receipts)*

...

Likewise at the feast of Pentecost
for ale   6s 2d

...

1467–8

All Souls College Bursars' Accounts   Bodl.: MS. D.D. All Souls c.278
mb 4*   *(2 November–2 November)* *(Rewards)*

…

And of 2d given to one playing the hobby horse at Christmas time.

…

mb 5*   *(Various expenses)*

…

And of 16d paid to various (persons) playing in the hall at the time of the
Purification.

…

St Michael at the North Gate Churchwardens' Accounts
ORO: PAR 211/4/F1/1, item 38
single mb   *(8 March 1467/8–8 March 1468/9)* *(Receipts)*

…

Likewise they received at Hocktide   15s 8d

…

St Peter le Bailey Churchwardens' Accounts   ORO: PAR 214/4/F1/6
single mb   *(Receipts)*

…

Likewise on the day of Pentecost for ale	20s
Likewise on the day *(blank)* ale	23d
Likewise twice received for ale	5s 8d given to Pannuel

…

1468–9

St Michael at the North Gate Churchwardens' Accounts
ORO: PAR 211/4/F1/1, item 39
single mb   *(8 March 1468/9–29 March 1470)* *(Receipts)*

…

Likewise at Hocktide   15s

…

St Peter le Bailey Churchwardens' Accounts   ORO: PAR 214/4/F1/7
single mb*   *(Receipts)*

…

Likewise for ale given by John Rogers	17d
Likewise for ale given by Thomas Dalton	20d

…

Likewise at the feast of Pentecost for ale   20s

...

(Payments)
Likewise for the carrying of small cups with a lion
and a dragon at an ale   2d

...

1469–70
Merton College Bursars' Accounts   MCR: 3785
single mb   *(28 July–24 November)* *(External expenses)*

...

...Likewise in reward by the lord warden's order to players at Holywell for
the church of St Peter in the East, 12d....

...

New College Bursars' Accounts   NC Arch: 7720
mb 4   *(Necessary external costs)*

...

...And paid to the lord king's entertainers for a reward given to them, 2s....

...

St Michael at the North Gate Churchwardens' Accounts
ORO: PAR 211/4/F1/1, item 42
single mb*   *(20 March 1469/70–7 March 1470/1)* *(Receipts)*

...

Likewise at Hocktide one torch weighing thirty
pounds, at a price per pound (of)   4d total, and in coin, 1½d

...

1471–2
OUF   *Proctors' Accounts*   OUA: NW/5/3
single mb   *(29 April 1471–30 April 1472)* *(Payments)*

...

Likewise to the king's trumpeters for a reward, 3s 4d.

...

St Michael at the North Gate Churchwardens' Accounts
ORO: PAR 211/4/F1/1, item 43
single mb*   *(25 December–25 December)* *(Receipts)*

...

In receipt on Hockday   2s 6d

In receipt for ale sold in the week of Pentecost   14s

...

1472–3
St Michael at the North Gate Churchwardens' Accounts
ORO: PAR 211/4/F1/1, item 46
single mb*   (2 February 1472/3–2 February 1473/4)   (Receipts)

...

In receipt for ale sold in Pentecost week   17s 1d

...

In receipt for ale sold from John Rogers' gift   4s 6d

...

1473–4
St Peter le Bailey Churchwardens' Accounts   ORO: PAR 214/4/F1/9
single mb   (Receipts)

...

Likewise received at the feast of Pentecost for ale   14s

...

1474–5
St Michael at the North Gate Churchwardens' Accounts
ORO: PAR 211/4/F1/1, item 49
single mb*   (2 February 1474/5–2 February 1475/6)   (Receipts)

...

Likewise they received net for ale sold in Pentecost week   13s 6d
Likewise they received from ale sold from John Rogers'
gift on the feast of St Anne   2s 5d

...

St Peter in the East Churchwardens' Accounts   ORO: PAR 213/4/F1/1
single mb   (8 December–8 December)   (Receipts)

...

Likewise they received at Hocktide   8s 1d
Likewise for ale sold in Pentecost week   13s 7d

...

1475–6
St Michael at the North Gate Churchwardens' Accounts
ORO: PAR 211/4/F1/1, item 50
single mb   (25 December–25 December)   (Receipts)

...

...And of 4s 5d for ale sold.... And with 15d received on the day called

Hockday.… And with 15s 10½d for ale sold at the feast of Pentecost.…

…

St Peter le Bailey Churchwardens' Accounts   ORO: PAR 214/4/F1/10
single mb*   *(Receipts)*

…

Likewise received for ale at the feast of Pentecost	17s
Likewise received for ale given by John Holywode	3s 4d
Likewise received for ale given by Peter Schormolode	2s 8d
Likewise received for ale given by Richard Rust	3s
Likewise received for ale given by John Smith	5s
Likewise received for ale given by Thomas Dalton	3s 3d

…

1476–7

Lincoln College Computus   LC Arch: Computus 1
f 32v   *(21 September–21 December 1476)* *(Necessary expenses)*

…

Likewise to the clerk of St Michael's Church on St Nicholas' Eve	6d

…

St Peter le Bailey Churchwardens' Accounts   ORO: PAR 214/4/F1/11
single mb   *(Receipts)*

…

Likewise on the day of Pentecost for ale	13s

…

1477–8

St Michael at the North Gate Churchwardens' Accounts
ORO: PAR 211/4/F1/1, item 53
single mb   *(2 February 1477/8–2 February 1478/9)* *(Receipts)*

…

…And with 21d *(blank)* received on the day called Hockday. And with 17s *(?)* ½d in Pentecost week in ale sold.… And with 7s 8d received of money collected by the women on Hock Monday. And with 2s 3d received, which sum the young men collected from ale sold after the feast of Pentecost.…

…

St Peter le Bailey Churchwardens' Accounts   ORO: PAR 214/4/F1/12
single mb   *(Receipts)*

…

Likewise for ale at the feast of Pentecost   16s 6d

…

1479–80
All Souls College Bursars' Accounts   Bodl.: MS. D.D. All Souls c.278
sheet 9*   *(2 November–2 November)* *(Various expenses)*

…

And of 12d paid to those playing for the church of Evesham.

…

New College Bursars' Accounts   NC Arch: 7722
mb 7   *(Necessary external costs)*

…

…And in wine given to servants (*ie*, serjeants) of the town of Oxford on
the feast of the Circumcision, 6d. And in wine given to the lord prince's
entertainers, 12d. And in reward given to the same, 6s 8d.…

St Peter le Bailey Churchwardens' Accounts   ORO: PAR 214/4/F1/13
single mb*   *(Receipts)*

…

Likewise received from John Robyns by reason of
ale given   2s 8d

…

Likewise received for ale on the feast of Pentecost   11s 1d

…

1480–1
St Peter in the East Churchwardens' Accounts   ORO: PAR 213/4/F1/1
single mb*   *(Receipts)*

…

Likewise in coin at Hocktide   6s 8d
Likewise in ale sold in Pentecost week   16s 6d

…

1481–2
St Peter in the East Churchwardens' Accounts   ORO: PAR 213/4/F1/1
single mb*   *(Receipts)*

…

Likewise in coin at Hocktide   8s 6d

Likewise in ale sold in Pentecost week   9s 2d

…

1482–3
Magdalen College Liber Computi 1482–3   MC Arch
f 26v   *(Chapel costs)*

…Likewise on 5 December for the bishop's gloves on the feast of St Nicholas,
4d.…

St Peter in the East Churchwardens' Accounts   ORO: PAR 213/4/F1/1
single mb*   *(Receipts)*
…
Likewise in coin at Hocktide   9s
Likewise in ale sold in the week of Pentecost   10s 3d
…

1483
Magdalen College Statutes   MC Arch: MS 277
f 20v   *(That fellows and students should not leave town without permission)*
…
…And that while they are absent in the country they are to be dressed as is
appropriate for clerics and behave decently in moral conduct. And neither at
that time nor while they are present in the University are the same scholars
and fellows or any others whatsoever, chaplains or clerics staying in the college
itself, to attend or frequent taverns, shows, or other disreputable places, but
refrain entirely from suspect associations lest – which God forbid – scandal,
injury, or prejudice should occur or in any way arise for our said college,
(our) scholars, or the fellows of the same from (their) dishonourable or suspect
social intercourse or otherwise from their shameless behaviour of whatever
kind.…

f 38v

On not delaying in the hall after dinner
Likewise, because after the refreshment of the body by the taking of food
and drink, people are commonly made more ready to perpetrate coarse jokes,
immodest speeches, and what is worse, back-bitings and quarrels, and likewise
also other evils both numerous and dangerous, and (because) they, then considering excesses of this kind less important than an empty stomach, often
move the souls of simple persons to arguments, insults, and other excesses,
we establish, ordain, and wish that every day after dinner and supper, when
thanksgiving to the Highest for things received has first been finished, thereafter

without an interval of time, after the loving-cup has been freely provided for
those who wish (it) and after drinkings in the hall, at the hour of curfew, each
of the seniors, of whatever estate or degree they be, are to move to their studies
or other places. Nor shall they allow other juniors to delay there further except
when house meetings, disputations, or other important (*or* difficult) business
pertaining to the college has to be dealt with in the hall immediately afterward,
and also unless disputations or explanations of the chapters of the Bible read
at mealtimes by any theologian of the fellows to be appointed according to the
discretion of president, vice-president, or a senior then present and without
forewarning – indeed we wish that anyone thus appointed without warning,
if he is found refusing or much negligent in the said elucidation, to incur the
penalty of the kind which has been ordered for those abusing their tongues in
their maternal language, (and) indeed we wish these explanations to take place
every day it seems expedient to the president or in his absence the vice-president,
so that everyone present at the said reading be made more attentive – or except
when, on account of reverence for God or for his mother or for any other
saint, a fire – which we wish to be made from coal only – is provided in the
hall for the fellows; then fellows and scholars after dinner- or supper-time are
permitted for the sake of recreation to make a suitable delay in songs and
other decent diversions, and to study in a serious manner poems of kingdoms,
chronicles, and marvels of this world and other things that are appropriate to
the clerical estate.

1483–4
Magdalen College Liber Computi 1483–4   MC Arch
f 68   (*Chapel costs*)

…

x   …And paid for the bishop's gloves on the feast of St Nicholas and for his
cross-bearer, 8d.…

f 68v*

…And for bread suitable for consecration and for the men making the
prophet's tabernacle for the histories.…

1484–5
Merton College Register   MCR: 1.2
f 17v

…

Injunction made
to the junior
masters

On the same day the junior masters were enjoined there to beware of excessive
familiarity, arrogance, and presumption toward the senior masters under due
penalty. The same junior masters were also enjoined there not to utter shouts
or clamours hereafter on solemn nights (*ie*, on the eves of feast days (?)) to the

Injunction made
to Mr Esyngton

detriment of the house or the disturbance of the fellows on pain of loss of
commons. And Mr Esyngton had been enjoined there not to play musical
instruments hereafter within the quadrangle either before the *propositio tituli*
or after.

...

f 18*

...

'The regent
masters' fire'
® Regarding the
regents' fire

On the same day the regents' fire was held in the hall while Mr Woodward
was the senior regent, and this custom has passed into disuse for many
years (past).

...

f 18v*

...

Fire on
chapter day

On the same day a fire was held in the high hall after the last bever, because
from ancient times it was accustomed to take place on that day on which
the chapter is held if it is held before Lent, and for this reason the *propositio
tituli* was postponed until the following day.

...

1485–6
Magdalen College Battells Book MC Arch: CP 8/49
f 49 *(10–16 December)*

...

On Wednesday at dinner with the fellows: two bearwards of Lord Stanley....

...

f 83 col 1 *(22–8 July)*

Likewise on Saturday, namely, St Mary Magdalene's Day, at dinner
...And with the fellows at another table:... three singers....

...

On Sunday at dinner with the fellows: two youths, singers.... And at supper
with the fellows: one singer from Westbury....

...

Magdalen College Liber Computi 1485–6 MC Arch
f 100v* *(Other external expenses)*

...

...Paid 27 December to the mayor's officer for his pension also by ancient
custom, 2s 2d....

f 103   *(25 December–25 March) (Hall costs)*

…

…Paid in the second term to Mr Croft, the dean, for painting of gear (*or* costume/s) for the player/s at Christmas-time, as appears by his bill, 3s 5d….

Merton College Register   MCR: 1.2
f 22*

…

Mr Persons is elected king of the college †®

Persons is
elected king

°King°

On 18 November Mr John Persons was elected as the king of beans in the college according to the ancient custom and this (was) because he had then been preferred (to a post) at Eton College.

…

f 23*

…

® Regarding the
chapter fire

On the same day a fire, which is called 'the chapter fire,' was held in the high hall after supper.

…

New College Hall Book   NC Arch: 5529
f [90v]   *(15–21 July)*

…

On Wednesday (the following persons) came to supper with the fellows:… three performers of Lord Stanley….

…

1486-7
Magdalen College Liber Computi 1486-7   MC Arch
f 130v*   *(25 December–25 March) (Itemized hall costs)*

…

Paid on 6 January to harper/s and to performers at the time of the
play in the hall, by the deans' and bursars' consent, in reward   8d
• Paid for some gear for the players, called 'the cap of maintenance,'
as by the dean's bill   9d

…

Merton College Register   MCR: 1.2
f 30v

…

Mr Byrde was
elected as king
® °King°

On the preceding day, that is to say, 19 (November), Mr Byrde was promoted to king notwithstanding that at that time Hanchurche as a bachelor was promoted and in the same year Mr Ardern was proctor.

...

f 31v

...

The regents' fire   On the fifteenth day of the same month the regents' fire was in the high hall,
® °The regents'   Mr Ardern, the proctor, being then senior regent.
fire°

...

1487-8
Lincoln College Computus   LC Arch: Computus 2
p 20   *(21 December 1486-21 December 1487)* *(Necessary expenses and
   other costs)*

...

Likewise I paid to the clerk on the feast of St Nicholas   6⟨.⟩

...

Magdalen College Liber Computi 1487-8   MC Arch
f 145v   *(Hall costs)*

...

Paid for players' clothing at Christmas-time by the advice
of one dean as appears by Mr Radcliffe's bill ·   2s 2d

Merton College Register   MCR: 1.2
f 34v

...

On the nineteenth day of the same month Mr William Neal was elected
as king.

...

f 35v

...

The regents' fire   On the thirtieth day of the same ⟨month⟩ the regents' fire was in the high
hall, the senior regent being Mr Robert Ardern.

...

1488-9
Lincoln College Computus   LC Arch: Computus 1
f 89   *(21 December 1487-21 December 1488)* *(Necessary expenses)*

...

Likewise to the clerk of St Michael's on St Nicholas' Eve   6d

...

Magdalen College Liber Computi 1488–9 MC Arch
f 176v *(Chapel costs)*

...Paid to John Wynman for the writing of one book of the bishop's service for (Holy) Innocents' Day, 5d....

Merton College Register MCR: 1.2
f 39v

...

On the nineteenth day of the same month, with all the fellows' one consent, Mr Simon Mollond was elected as king.

...

On 18 December, that is to say, the eighth day before Christmas, a scrutiny was held in which deposition was made against the ill-advised manner of some masters toward the bachelors on St Edmund's Eve, allowed unpunished by the deans, and other things were deposed but none of great significance and the scrutiny was dissolved.

...

f 40

...

On the twentieth day of the same (month) the regents' fire was in the high hall, Mr Thomas Kent being the senior regent.

...

Margin notes:
Mollond was elected as king
® °King°

The month of December
Scrutiny held before Christmas

® The regents' fire

St Peter in the East Churchwardens' Accounts ORO: PAR 213/4/F1/1
single mb *(8 December–8 December) (Receipts)*

...

Likewise they received net at Hocktide   11s 1d

...

Likewise in Pentecost week they received net   13s 1d

...

Likewise from proceeds of one quart of ale and for players' garments   9d

...

1489–90
Merton College Bursars' Accounts MCR: 3808
mb 1 *(27 March–7 August) (External expenses)*

...

...For 12d (given) in reward to certain players at the warden's command....

...

Merton College Register   MCR: 1.2
f 43

…

® Harper was
elected as king

On the nineteenth day of the same (month), by the unanimous consent of the fellows, Mr Thomas Harper was elected as king.

…

1490–1
Magdalen College Battells Book   MC Arch: CP 8/50
f 30   *(26 March–1 April)*

On Sunday at supper with the fellows: one tenant at farm, called Philip Harris, and another (man), Venne, a singer. On Tuesday the same singer at dinner with the fellows. And on Friday the same (singer) at dinner with the fellows….

f 47   *(25 June–1 July)*

…On Thursday … at dinner with the fellows: a certain singer from Abingdon….
…

f 50   *(23–9 July)*

…On Friday at dinner in the hall:… Nicholas, a singer….

f 52   *(6–12 August)*

On Sunday … at supper with the fellows: one singer from London….
…

f 55   *(27 August–2 September)*
…
On Sunday at dinner with the fellows: two chapel singers of the lord bishop of Hereford….
…

Magdalen College Liber Computi 1490–1   MC Arch
f 11   *(Hall costs)*
…
…Paid for candles used at the time of the plays in Christmas, 6d….

Merton College Register   MCR: 1.2
f 47v

...

®°King°

Weldish is
elected as king

On the twentieth day of the same (month), by the unanimous consent of the
fellows, Mr George Weldish, the second of the four seniors, was elected as
king for the coming year.

...

1492–3
Lincoln College Computus   LC Arch: Computus 1
f 106v   *(21 December 1491–21 December 1492)* *(Necessary internal expenses)*

...

Likewise to the parish clerk on St Nicholas' Eve   6d

...

Merton College Register   MCR: 1.2
f 97v

...

®°King°

Rawlyns is
elected as king

On the twentieth day of the same month, by the unanimous consent of the
fellows, Mr Richard Rawlyns, the fourth of the four seniors, was elected as
king for the coming year because at that time he had been preferred.

...

New College Hall Book   NC Arch: 5529
f [166v]   *(8–14 June)*

...

On Sunday (the following persons) came to dinner with the fellows:... two
performers of the lord prince (and) two servants with them....

...

1493–4
Merton College Register   MCR: 1.2
f 101

°King of the
kingdom of
beans°

®Molder elected
as king

...

On the nineteenth day of the same month Mr John Molder had been elected
as king of the kingdom of beans.

...

New College Hall Book   NC Arch: 5529
f [179]   *(7–13 December)*

...

On Saturday (the following persons) came to dinner with the fellows:...

two performers who did not give warning of their coming.

…

f [182]   *(11–17 January)*

…

On Tuesday two performers came to supper with the fellows.

…

f [183v]   *(1–7 February)*

On Saturday (the following persons) came to dinner with the fellows:…
two performers.…

…

On Wednesday (the following persons) came to dinner with the fellows:…
one performer.…

…

1494–5
Merton College Register   MCR: 1.2
f 103v

…

®°King of beans°
Dale was
elected as king

On the same day, by the unanimous consent of each (of the fellows), Mr Robert Dale, at that time proctor of the University, was elected as king of the kingdom of beans.

…

c 1495
Magdalen School Copy Book   BL: MS Arundel 249
f 85v*   *(Letter of Thomas More to John Holt)*

…

Thomas More greets John Holt

We have sent you everything you wanted except those parts that we have added to that comedy that is about Solomon. I cannot send those to you now since they are not with me, (but) I will see to it that you receive (them) and anything else you want from my things next week.…

1495–6
Lincoln College Computus   LC Arch: Computus 1
f 123   *(21 December 1494–21 December 1495)* *(Necessary expenses)*

…

Likewise on the feast of St Nicholas to the clerk	6d
Likewise on wine to the bishop	2½d

…

Magdalen College Liber Computi 1495–6 MC Arch
f 41v *(Chapel costs)*

...

Paid to Henry Martin for linen, (that is,) a (length of) linen
(cloth), and other things bought for the play on Easter Day as
appears in the bill   17½d

...

f 42v *(Hall costs)*

...

x Paid for bread and drink consumed at the times of the plays
at Christmas   12d

...

Merton College Register MCR: 1.2
f 106v

...

Mr Thomas
Beaumont is
elected as king

®°King°

On the same day, by the unanimous consent and assent of each (of the
fellows), Mr Thomas Beaumont was elected as the king of our kingdom
of beans.

...

New College Hall Book NC Arch: 5529
f ˙[208v]* *(6–12 February)*

...

On Tuesday (the following persons) came to dinner with the fellows:... two
performers of the duke of Bedford....

...

St Peter in the East Churchwardens' Accounts ORO: PAR 213/4/F1/1
single mb *(8 December–8 December) (Receipts)*

...

Likewise on the feast of Hocktide   22s 2d
Likewise the said churchwardens received at the feast
of Pentecost   49s

...

c 1496–1502
St Peter in the East Churchwardens' Accounts ORO: PAR 213/4/F1/1
single mb* *(Receipts)*

...

Likewise on the feast of Hocktide they received net   20s

Likewise they received on the feast of Pentecost   46s 7d

...

1496–7
Magdalen College Liber Computi 1496–7   MC Arch
f 81v   *(Hall costs)*

...

Paid for coals and candles used at the time of the plays   3s 4d

...

Merton College Register   MCR: 1.2
f 109

...

°King°
® Claxton is
elected as king

On the nineteenth day of the same month, by the unanimous assent and consent of the fellows present, Mr Robert Claxton was elected as king, that is to say, of our kingdom of beans.

...

1497–8
Merton College Register   MCR: 1.2
f 113

...

°King°
® Walgrave is
elected as king

On the same day, with one vote (*ie*, ballot (?)) of all (the fellows), Mr John Walgrave was elected as king.

...

1498–9
Merton College Register   MCR: 1.2
f 117v

...

® °King°
Edward Bernard
is elected as king

On the nineteeth day of the same month Mr Edward Bernard was elected as king by one vote (*ie*, ballot (?)) of all (the fellows).

...

1499–1500
Merton College Register   MCR: 1.2
f 121

...

°King°
® Thomas King
was elected
as king

On the nineteenth day of the same month, with one vote (*ie*, ballot (?)) of all the fellows, Mr Thomas King was elected as king.

...

f 121v

…

Month of
February

On the fourth day of the same month, at 10 AM, the vice-warden called six seniors to the warden's lodgings to provide correction regarding a certain immoderate wake excessively held by Mr Ireland on the day of the Purification of St Mary at night, with shouts, clamours, and knocks at the fellows' and chaplains' doors, together with a certain indecent song. At this time a certain decree was shown, made in the second year of the reign of King Richard III, against foolish wakes of this kind, in which the junior masters were enjoined that henceforth on nights of recreation they not make foolish wakes of this kind, shouts, or clamours to the detriment of the house, or the disturbance of the fellows or chaplains, by which they would be less fit to celebrate the divine offices, under pain of loss of commons. A discussion was held there among the seniors about this (matter), (that is,) whether uncontrolled wakes of this kind were simply condemned under that penalty aforesaid. At this time some affirmed that they were not, if they were made on the authority of any dean and not extravagantly; all agreed, however, that the wakes recently held by Mr Ireland were done extravagantly and kept on his own authority

Injunction (to)
Ireland

only. On that account, with the unanimous consent of all the seniors, for his greater warning and as an example to others, he was enjoined to pay 6d for his commons. It was also decreed there, moreover, that none of the fellows of whatever estate or degree henceforth hold or keep wakes of this kind, shouts, or clamours to the disturbance of the fellows or chaplains under pain of loss of commons.

…

St Peter le Bailey Churchwardens' Accounts   ORO: PAR 214/4/F1/14
single mb*   *(25 November–25 November) (Receipts)*

…

Likewise of collections at Whitsontide   40s
Likewise at Hocktide   9s 6d

…

1500–1
Merton College Register   MCR: 1.2
f 126

…

® Goodhew is
elected king

On the nineteenth day of the same month, with the unanimous consent of the fellows, Mr John Goodhew was elected as king because he (was) preferred to (the post of) master of Wye College in Kent.

…

Chancellor's Register   OUA: Hyp/A/2, Register D (or D reversed)
f 93*   *(29 May)*

Proceedings of the court held before Thomas Bank, commissary
...

On 29 May a certain William Jannys, harper and stranger, came and complained that two men, namely Pittes and Hawkinse of the parish of St Michael at the North Gate, were keeping his harp unjustly, claiming service from him which he never owed to them or promised. And to prove this he brought John Huskinse of St Mary's Parish who promised and pledged surety that he would prove the same, namely, that the aforesaid William did not promise the aforesaid Pittes and Hawkinse any service but he promised service to himself, John Huskinse, and his fellow/s. And therefore both the aforesaid William and the aforementioned John asked me (*ie*, Thomas Bank) that it be registered that the oftensaid William promote his case before the commissary of the University lest he be unjustly harassed by the town bailiffs or by the town's mayor because he was a stranger, promising by his oath that he would reply, obey, do, and accept what justice requires if this was agreed upon, etc.
William Jannys, John Huskinse, Pittes, and Hawkinse.

1501–2
Merton College Register   MCR: 1.2
f 131
...

°Doctor of theology, king°

®Saunders was elected as king

On the nineteenth day of the same (month) Mr Hugh Saunders, a doctor of sacred theology, was elected as king by the consent of all the fellows, both because, although a senior, he had not previously undertaken the duty of king, and because he was preferred to the vicarage of the parish church of Meopham in the diocese of Canterbury.
...

f 131v
...

®Regarding the regents' fire

®°Fire°

On the seventeenth day of the same (month) the regents' fire was held with very entertaining interludes, Mr Thomas Scarsbrook being the senior.
...

New College Hall Book   NC Arch: 5530
f [26v]   *(29 January–4 February)*
...

On Wednesday (the following persons) came:... two performers to dinner with the fellows ... two performers to supper with the fellows.

On Thursday (the following persons) came:... one harper ... to dinner
with the fellows....

1502–3
Magdalen College Liber Computi 1502–3   MC Arch
f 126   *(External payments)*

...

 – Paid in expenses incurred in Christmas-time on bevers
after the interludes and other (events)   13s 4d

...

Merton College Register   MCR: 1.2
f 137

...

"King"
  ® Ireland was
  elected as king

On the same day the same Mr William Ireland by unanimous consent of all
the fellows was elected as our king for this year, in the first place because this
duty had come to him by reason of seniority, (and) then also because he had
been preferred this year to the rectory of Cuxham.

...

1503–4
Merton College Register   MCR: 1.2
f 144v

...

John Adams is
elected as king

"Vice-warden
as king"

On the nineteenth day of the same month, by the unanimous consent of all
the masters who were then present, who were very few for the cause which
has been given above, Mr John Adams, the vice-warden, at that time a senior
by reason of the new decree, which is set down above on the next folio
preceding, was elected as king.

...

f 145v

...

The regents' fire

On the thirtieth day of the same month Mr John Madstone, at that time senior
regent, entertained the masters and bachelors with the regents' fire and other
luxurious arrangements according to the ancient custom.

...

St Peter in the East Churchwardens' Accounts   ORO: PAR 213/4/F1/1
single mb   *(8 December–8 December)* *(Receipts)*

...

Likewise on the feast of Hocktide net   19s

Likewise on the feast of Pentecost   36s 8d

…

1504

AC *St Peter le Bailey Churchwardens' Accounts*   Bodl.: MS. Wood C.1
p 78*   *(Receipts)*

…

Of coin collected at Hocktide, 8s 4d.

…

1504–5
Merton College Register   MCR: 1.2
f 151v*

…

.A.

Gidding is
elected as king

°King°

On the nineteenth day of the same month Mr William Gidding by unanimous consent of all the fellows is elected as king of beans, both because he (is) senior fellow and because he has been preferred to the parish church of Meopham in the diocese of Canterbury.

…

St Peter in the East Churchwardens' Accounts   ORO: PAR 213/4/F1/1
single mb   *(8 December–8 December) (Receipts)*

…

Likewise on the feast of
Hocktide net   19s 3d
Likewise they received on
the feast of Pentecost net   30s 8d

…

1505–6
Merton College Register   MCR: 1.2
f 158

…

® Consaunt is
elected as king
conditionally

® °King°

On the nineteenth day of the same month, by the unanimous consent of all the masters and fellows and other bachelors who had been present at that time, Mr Nicholas Consaunt, vice-warden, is elected as king under the condition that if Mr Scarsbrook was inducted into a benefice, as was being said by many, he would undertake the duty, but if not, the aforesaid vice-warden was nevertheless the one pronounced (*ie*, as king) on the basis of those attending (the meeting), and ancient custom. And the condition was known only among the fellows.

...

f 158v

...

January

Regarding the town officers: how the noble granted of old as a gift was denied them

On the first day of that month town officers came to our college, as they were accustomed, to sing a song in the high hall and to receive from the bursar, from kindness and as a free gift, one noble. But on account of their ingratitude, and because they said they ought to receive (it) as an obligation and not from our generosity, we, for that reason, with suitable words and some sort of kindness shown to them, denied the said money to them on that occasion. And they thus withdrew to the college of St Mary Magdalen where, as we have heard, they received a similar response.

...

The regents' fire

On the fourteenth day of that month Mr John Wayte, at that time senior regent, entertained the masters and bachelors with the regents' fire and luxurious arrangements according to the ancient custom.

...

St Peter in the East Churchwardens' Accounts   ORO: PAR 213/4/F1/1
single mb   *(8 December–8 December)* *(Receipts)*

...

Likewise the said churchwardens received on the feast of Hocktide net	18s 2d
Likewise the said churchwardens received on the feast of Pentecost net	43s

...

1506–7
Lincoln College Computus   LC Arch: Computus 2
p 30   *(21 December 1505–21 December 1506)* *(Necessary internal expenses)*

...

Likewise to the clerk of St Michael's	6d

...

Magdalen College Battells Book   MC Arch: CP 8/51
f 63*   *(3–9 January)*

...

On Epiphany Day at dinner with the fellows in (their) mess:... at the fourth (mess) for meals, a harper....

...

Magdalen College Liber Computi 1506–7   MC Arch
f 200*   *(11 November–11 November)   (External payments)*
…

x   Paid to Sir Burgess for the writing of the play of
St Mary Magdalene   10d

…

x   Paid to the person leading songs by Mr Edward
Martin at the vice-president's command   8d

…

x   Paid to Kendall for his diligence in the play of St Mary
Magdalene at the vice-president's command   12d

…

f 201*

…

x   Paid to Sir Burgess for the notation of various songs at
the vice-president's command according to the bill   5s

…

f 201v

…

–   Paid for a performer's expenses in Christmas-time this year   4s

…

Episcopal Visitation of Magdalen College
Hampshire Record Office: 21M65/A1/18
f 47*   *(20 January)   (Interrogatories for Bishop Richard Fox's visitation taken
before John Dowman, LLD, vicar general)*

…

41. Likewise let them ask how books, ornaments, valuables, and other goods
were guarded by the said college.

…

45. Likewise let them ask whether any fellow or scholar of the said college uses
cloaks or liripipes outside the precinct of the college.

…

f 58v*   *(Reply of Mr John Burgess, MA)*

…

To the fortieth article he says that the sacrist is negligent in providing books
to the fellows for their cubicles and that in Christmas-time the players use
copes in interludes.

…

f 69*   *(Reply of Sir John Burgess, BA)*

…

…he says, moreover, that Pollarde, from the knowledge of that sworn witness, went out of the college in lay clothing and in the manner of one performing interludes…

Merton College Register   MCR: 1.2
f 165

…

® John Chambre
is elected as king

On the nineteenth day of the same month, by the consent of the masters and fellows, Mr John Chambre, a doctor of medicine who was at that time in Rome, was elected as king.

…

f 165v

…

[The regents' fire]
° The regents' fire°

On the eleventh day of that month Mr Wayte, the senior regent, entertained all the fellows with the regents' fire and other luxurious arrangements according to the ancient custom and usage.

New College Hall Book   NC Arch: 5530
f [157]   *(2–8 January)*

…

On the same day, at supper with the fellows, a certain performer….

…

1507
Balliol College Statutes   BC Arch: Statutes 1
f [31]   *(Concerning serious prohibitions)*

…We forbid also anyone at any place or time from frequenting indecent or suspect places or engaging in business or transactions forbidden to clerics, from immersing himself in persistent drinking and frequent drunkenness, from baiting or vexing anyone with injurious actions or opprobrious insults, from attending indecent or prohibited plays or those inciting vice or impeding doctrine and provoking contention, (and) from mixing with entertainers or jugglers. If he should be delinquent in these things thus prohibited by us or in other similar greater (offences), after being twice warned by the master or his deputy together with his dean, he shall be expelled if he offends a third time.

1507–8

Lincoln College Computus   LC Arch: Computus 2

p 23   *(21 December 1506–21 December 1507) (Necessary internal expenses)*

…

⟨…⟩ for wine, namely, for the St Nicholas bishop   5d
⟨…⟩ for the clerk of St Michael's   6d

…

Magdalen College Liber Computi 1507–8   MC Arch

f 216v   *(External expenses)*

+   Paid for a bever given to the bishop on St Nicholas' Eve,
    in wine 2½d, in ale 2½d, and in fire 2½d   6½d

…

Merton College Register   MCR: 1.2

f 175

…

® Wayte enter-
tained the fel-
lows as (his)
duty as king

On 10 January Mr John Wayte, as (his) duty as king, entertained all the
fellows with a fire and with other luxurious arrangements according to
ancient custom.

® Wyngar, the
senior regent,
entertained the
regents

Mr Wyngar, at that time senior regent, entertained all the regents on the
fifteenth day of the aforesaid month.

…

St Peter in the East Churchwardens' Accounts   ORO: PAR 213/4/F1/1

single mb   *(8 December–8 December) (Receipts)*

…

Likewise the said churchwardens received on the
feast of Hocktide net   17s
Likewise the said churchwardens received on the
feast of Pentecost net   40s

…

1508–9

Magdalen College Liber Computi 1508–9   MC Arch

f 231v   *(11 November–11 November) (External payments)*

…

Paid for wine given to the bishop, 2½d, and fire, 2d,
and a bever, 2d, on St Nicholas' Eve   6½d

…

Paid to the king's servant leading a bear to the college
by the vice-president's command   12d
...

Merton College Register   MCR: 1.2
f 191

...

°King°
® Mr Hill elected to duty as king

On the twenty-first day of this month, after a letter was read in the hall according to the ancient custom, all the fellows by unanimous consent elected Mr Hill king for the coming year.

...

f 194*

® Town officers
® °In no way as an obligation. See above f (blank) and below ff 242b and 256(.)°

® The king's banquet

...

On the first day of this month town officers came to our college to sing a song before the fellows in the high hall, at which time they received 6s 8d from the bursar in the college's name from kindness, to answer on our behalf in their house of convocation for our possession in the town.

Mr Hill, elected as king, entertained all the fellows with many luxurious arrangements on the eighth day of this month.

...

f 194v

°The regents' fire°

...

On the fifteenth day Mr Wyngar, the senior regent, entertained all the fellows with a fire at night according to the ancient usage.

...

The regents' fire

On the fifteenth day of this month the regents' fire was (held), Mr Wyngar being the senior regent.

...

f 195

°Chapter dinner°
® Chapter dinner
® °The chapter fire°

...

On the twentieth day of this month the second bursar held the chapter dinner for the dissolution of the chapter and in the great hall on the same night the chapter fire (was held).

...

ff 196–6v

® °Plays°

...

On the nineteenth day of the same month the senior bachelor, together with the junior, invited the warden to deign to see the diversions intended for his

'Feasts'

coming on the following night in the high hall of the college. Agreeing to this he took himself there with many other venerable men when the time for recreation had come. When the play was finished all the fellows | of the college, after they had been brought to the warden's lodgings with a good many other comrades of neighbouring halls, had a meal prepared with various confections. All the bachelors, coming (in) at the end of this (meal), sang rounds, each in his order (*or* one after another).

...

St Peter in the East Churchwardens' Accounts   ORO: PAR 213/4/F1/1
single mb   *(8 December–8 December) (Receipts)*

...

Likewise they received on the feast of Hocktide net   25s 6d
Likewise they received on the feast of Pentecost   £3 7s 7d

...

1509–10
Magdalen College Liber Computi 1509–10   MC Arch
f 6   *(11 November–11 November) (External payments)*

...

Paid to a performer in Christmas-time by
the vice-president's command   12d

...

f 6v

...

Paid for bread, food, and other things given
to boys performing on Easter Day by the
vice-president's command   17½d

...

Merton College Register   MCR: 1.2
f 204

...

The regents' fire   On 24 January Mr Wyngar, the senior regent, entertained all the fellows with a fire and banquet at night according to the ancient custom. And this was the end of that responsibility because the last year of his regency in the faculty of arts will now come to an end.

...

St Peter in the East Churchwardens' Accounts   ORO: PAR 213/4/F1/1
single mb   *(8 December–8 December)* *(Receipts)*
...
Likewise they received on the feast of Hocktide net   ⟨...⟩
Likewise they received on the feast of Pentecost   ⟨...⟩
...

1510–11
Magdalen College Liber Computi 1510–11   MC Arch
f 19   *(External payments)*
...
Paid to a certain performer in Christmas-time
in reward   8d
...

Merton College Register   MCR: 1.2
f 209
...
On St Wulfstan's Day Mr Wyngar, the king, entertained all the fellows with
many dishes of food.
...
On the tenth day of this month Mr Hewes, proctor (and) senior regent, held
the regents' fire and entertained the same (regents).
...

St Peter in the East Churchwardens' Accounts   ORO: PAR 213/4/F1/1
single mb*   *(8 December–8 December)* *(Receipts)*
...
Likewise they received on the feast of Hocktide net   23s
Likewise they received on the feast of Pentecost   53s 4d
...

1511–12
Magdalen College Liber Computi 1511–12   MC Arch
f 61*   *(Hall costs)*
...
Paid for bevers given to the fellows and scholars
after interludes   6s 8d 2s 8d
...

Register of Congregation and Convocation   OUA: NEP/Supra/G
f 143*

…

® Watson
® °See on the
next page°

On the same day cited above this (licence) was granted for Edward Watson,
scholar of grammar, to be admitted for teaching in the same faculty since (he
has completed) a course of four years with sufficient practice for teaching,
provided he compose one hundred poems (*or* songs) in praise of the University
and one comedy within a year after the position has been accepted.

…

f 143v*

…

Admission for
teaching in
grammar

Sir Edward Watson was admitted for teaching in grammar on the same day.

…

Merton College Register   MCR: 1.2
f 214

…

°King°
® Election of
the king

On the eve of St Edmund the King, when the ancient customs had been
completed and the letter read through, all the fellows by unanimous consent
elected Mr Morwent king for the coming year.

…

St Peter in the East Churchwardens' Accounts   ORO: PAR 213/4/F1/1
single mb   (*8 December–8 December*) (*Receipts*)

…

Likewise they received on the feast of Hocktide net	21s 4d
Likewise they received on the feast of Pentecost	56s 8d

…

1512–13
Magdalen College Liber Computi 1512–13   MC Arch
f 33v   (*11 November–11 November*) (*External payments*)

…

Paid to Peter Pyper for piping in the interlude on St John's Night	6d

…

f 34

…

+	Paid to John Tabourner for playing in the interlude in the octave of the Epiphany	6d

…

+ Paid to Robert Jonson for one coat for the interludes 4s

...

Merton College Register MCR: 1.2
f 218v

...

> Hewes was
> elected king

On the eve of St Edmund the King messengers came from distant parts bringing with them a letter for the electing of the king. When this was read through and other customs performed, by the unanimous consent of all, Mr Hewes was elected as king for the following year.

...

f 219

> °Symons,
> senior regent
> (and) proctor°
> ® The month of
> January
> ® °The regents' fire°

On the tenth day of this month Mr Symons, proctor and senior regent, entertained all the masters splendidly at night by means of a fire with many delicacies (and) with wine.

...

f 219v

> The master
> warden's banquet

On the twentieth day of this month the master warden entertained all the masters in his house at night and they had a very good play in the great hall.

> Mr Hewes'
> entertainment

On the twenty-fourth day of this month Mr Hewes, the present year's king, entertained all the masters at dinner and at night.

...

St Peter in the East Churchwardens' Accounts ORO: PAR 213/4/F1/1
single mb *(8 December–8 December) (Receipts)*

...

Likewise at Hocktide 19s 8d
Likewise on the feast of Pentecost 52s 4d

...

1513–14
Merton College Register MCR: 1.2
f 222

> °King°
> ® Symons was
> elected king

On the eve of St Edmund the King messengers came from remote parts bringing with them a letter for the electing of the king. When this was read

and other customs performed, by the unanimous consent of all, Mr Symons
was elected as king for the following year.

...

f 222v

...

The month of
February

The regents' fire

On 26 February Mr Richard Walker, at that time senior regent, entertained the
masters and bachelors with the regents' fire and other luxurious arrangements
according to ancient custom.

...

1514–15
Merton College Register   MCR: 1.2
f 227v

...

Poxwell
the king's
entertainment

On the twenty-ninth day of this month Mr Poxwell, the king, entertained all
the fellows at dinner with capons and wine, and honourably at night with a
fire and many dishes of food.

Walker the
senior regent's
entertainment

On 4 February Mr Walker, the senior regent, entertained all the fellows with
many dishes of food and with wine.

...

1515–16
Merton College Register   MCR: 1.2
f 230v

...

Knight was
elected as king

On the nineteenth day of the same month Mr William Knight, by the
unanimous consent of all the fellows, was elected as king for the coming year.

...

1516–17
Corpus Christi College Statutes   CCCA: A/4/1/1
ff 60–60v   (22 June)

...

On not delaying in the hall after meals
Immodest speeches, back-bitings, quarrels, coarse jokes, long-windedness, and
other vices of the tongue rarely accompany an empty stomach but often a
swelling and full one. Therefore we give a command in order to counter (such
things) at their beginnings, establishing that every day in our college after
dinner and supper, when thanksgiving to the Highest for things received has
first been finished and the loving-cup has been freely provided for those who
wish (it) and also after those drinkings which they call bevers, customary for

the time according to the usage of the University, each of the seniors, of whatever degree or estate they be, are to move immediately without any interval to their studies or other places. Nor shall they allow other juniors to delay there further, except when either house meetings or other important (*or* difficult) business pertaining to the college has to be dealt with immediately in the hall or when readings, disputations, or expositions and explanations of the Bible follow forthwith – when these also are completed and finished, they are to depart at once – or when for the reverence of God, of his glorious mother, or another saint, a fire is built for the diversion of each of the inhabitants there. For then the fellows and scholars of our college are permitted for the sake of recreation to make delay after the aforesaid meals and drinkings, modestly as is befitting to clerics, in songs and other suitable diversions, and to discuss amongst themselves, read, and recount poems, chronicles, and marvels of this world and other things of this kind.

On the disposition of bedrooms
We go out of the hall to the bedrooms as to places for rest and sleep and refuges after cares and labours. We establish therefore that everyone of our college conduct himself decently and modestly both with his room-mate and with other neighbours, and (act) in such a way that he hinder no one at any time from sleep, rest, or study by excessive shouts, laughs, songs, clamours, dances, (or) playing of musical instruments. But if at any time one is pleased to converse with others before the fire or elsewhere for the sake of relaxing the mind, the time is to be passed with moderate silence in those things which pertain to virtue and learning, and on those (occasions) there are not to be late feasts or drinkings, but temperate and salutary (meals).
…

1517–18
Magdalen College Liber Computi 1517–18   MC Arch
f 123v*   *(11 November–11 November)* *(External payments)*
…

+ Paid to one bringing a play coat from Mr Burgess   2d
…

f 126*   *(Chapel costs)*
…

Paid to Sir Perrott for the dyeing and making of the
coat for him who played the part of Christ and for
wigs for the women   2s 6d
…

Merton College Register   MCR: 1.2
f 239

...

® Pollen was elected as king

On the nineteenth day of the same month Mr John Pollen was elected as king for the coming year by the consent of all the fellows.

...

f 239v

...

December
°King°
Enjoining of the senior bachelor

On the tenth day of this month the warden, after he had heard of the senior bachelor's negligence in providing a letter with a seal according to the ancient custom for the election of the king, enjoined the same that Williot shall not receive one penny of (his) exhibition, nor shall he lay claim to the place and rank of a senior until he has testimony regarding his laudable penance, since on the eve of (St) Edmund the King, by his example and carelessness, the bachelors did not come at that same time wearing masks (and) in outlandish clothing.

...

St Peter in the East Churchwardens' Accounts   ORO: PAR 213/4/F1/1
single mb   *(8 December–8 December) (Receipts)*

...

| Likewise on the feast of Pentecost | £3 6s 8d |
| Likewise they received on the feast of Hocktide net | 22s |

...

1518–19
Merton College Register   MCR: 1.2
f 241

...

® Freindship elected as king

On the eve of St Edmund the King Mr Freindship was elected as king while two bachelors only, that is to say, a senior and junior, went around the fire with a letter and seal in the way it used to be done before, the (old) ceremonies being preserved.

...

f 241v

...

Note regarding town officers: under what condition they received one noble this year

On 1 January town officers came to our college, as they were accustomed, to sing a song in the high hall and they sang. Afterward one noble was given to the same (officers) by the bursar, the vice-warden being present. At which time it was made clear to them that this gift, that is, a royal, was not given to them by our college as an obligation of any kind, because for two or three years they have received nothing, but only from our kindness and generosity in order that we would be friends with each other as we used to be. And the speech pleased them and they withdrew.

1519–20
Magdalen College Liber Computi 1519–20   MC Arch
f 141   *(Chapel costs)*
…
Paid to Sir Magott for two pairs of gloves for the
St Nicholas bishop   4d
…

f 141v
…
Paid to Robert Payntar for the cross and crown and his
diligence about the play on Easter Day   8d
…

Merton College Register   MCR: 1.2
f 245
…

® Holdar elected as king

On the eve of St Edmund the King Mr Holdar was elected as king for this coming year while eight bachelors first went around the fire with a letter and seal in the way it used to be done before, the (old) ceremonies being preserved.
…

f 248v

January

On 1 January town officers came to the college to sing a song in the high hall. When it was finished one noble was given to them by Hooper, the second bursar. After they had gratefully accepted it they withdrew giving thanks.
…

1520–1
Magdalen College Liber Computi 1520–1   MC Arch
f 170v   *(External payments)*
…
[Paid for coals used on St Nicholas' Eve in the hall, 4d, and for coals used during various interludes in Christmas-time, 16d, and for candles used on the nights, 11d.]
…

1521

A ***Brasenose College Statutes***   BNC Arch: A.2.3
p 36   *(Chapter 23)*

...but in addition establishing that none of the fellows or scholars or
servants is to feed or keep any dog or bird of any kind, or any other
animal within the said college or outside it to the harm or detriment
of the same or to the annoyance, disquiet, or disturbance of any of the
fellows or scholars of the same college, nor shall he also hinder any fellow
or scholar of the said college whatever by song, clamour, shouting, a
musical instrument, or any other kind of tumult in any way from being
able to study or sleep....

...

1521–2
Merton College Register   MCR: 1.2
f 256

...

®A song by the
town officers

January

On 1 January town officers of Oxford came to the college, who afterward
according to custom sang a song in the common hall. They received 6s 8d
from kindness only and not as an obligation.

...

1522–3
Merton College Register   MCR: 1.2
f 257

...

On 1 January town officers came to the college according to custom, who also
sang a song in our hall. Afterward they received 6s 8d from the bursar, from
benevolence only and not as an obligation.

...

1523–4
Merton College Register   MCR: 1.2
f 258v

...

®January

On 1 January town officers came to the college, who according to ancient
custom sang a song afterward in the common hall. Gratefully receiving 6s 8d
from benevolence only and not as an obligation, they went away.

...

1524-5
Merton College Register   MCR: 1.2
f 261v

…

A noble

On the first day of this month town officers of Oxford came to the college to sing a song in the hall according to the ancient custom. When it was finished one noble was given to the same (officers) by Mr Ball, the second bursar, from the pure benevolence of the fellows. They accepted it in a grateful spirit and, giving thanks, they departed.

…

New College Bursars' Accounts   NC Arch: 7477
mb 4   *(Hall costs)*

…

…And paid to the steward on Christmas Day for the play, 4d.…

…

1525-6
Merton College Register   MCR: 1.2
f 266

…

® Election of
the king

On the eve of St Edmund the King John Clutterbuck was elected as king for the coming year by the unanimous consent of the fellows.

…

® Coming of
the officers
to the hall

On 1 January town officers of Oxford came to the college to sing a song in the hall according to the ancient custom. When it was finished one noble was given to them from the pure benevolence of the fellows. They accepted it in a grateful spirit and, giving thanks, they departed.

…

1526-7
Merton College Register   MCR: 1.2
f 268v

…

® °King°

Election of
the king

On St Edmund's Eve Mr Ball was elected as king.

…

1527-8
Merton College Register   MCR: 1.2
f 270v

…

Election of
the king

On St Edmund's Eve Mr Tresham was elected as king.

…

f 271

®The coming of
the officers to
the hall

On 1 January town officers came to the high hall as is the custom and there
they sang a song. When this was done a noble was given to them from benevolence. They accepted it in a grateful spirit and thus they withdrew at once.

...

1528–9
Merton College Register   MCR: 1.2
f 272v

Election of
the king

On St Edmund's Eve Mr Bluett was elected as king.

...

Town officers

On the day of the Lord's Circumcision town officers came and had 6s 8d
from the bursar as they were accustomed.

...

1529–30
Cardinal College Expense Book   PRO: E/36/104
f 12v   *(1 November–1 November)*

...

Paid in reward to two entertainers, the duke of Norfolk's
servants, at the dean's command, 15 July   2s 6d

...

f 14

...

Paid for the battells of the minor canons when they were
preparing to put on a comedy last year as it appears in the
steward's bill   6s 11¾d

...

Magdalen College Liber Computi 1529–30   MC Arch
f 248   *(External payments)*

...

x   Paid to Merkame for wine given to the (St) Nicholas
     bishop in a bever   11d

...

++   Paid for gaudies given for the fellows and scholars in
     Christmas-time after the plays were performed and for
     other gaudies as it appears in the bill   [27s 7½d]

+   Paid for gloves given to the (St) Nicholas bishop   4d

...

Merton College Register   MCR: 1.2
f 273

®Election of
  the king   …
®Town officers On St Edmund's Eve Mr Reynolds was elected king.
                On the day of the Lord's Circumcision town officers came and had 6s 8d
                from the bursar as they were accustomed.
                …

1530–1
Magdalen College Liber Computi 1530–1   MC Arch
f 7v   *(External payments)*
…
Paid to the lady princess' performers   20d
…

f 8v

…
+   Paid for a bever given to the fellows and scholars
    after the interludes in Christmas-time   [6s 8d]
    …

Merton College Register   MCR: 1.2
f 274

…
®Election of   On St Edmund's Eve Mr Richard Ewer was elected as king.
  the king   …

1531–2
Magdalen College Liber Computi 1531–2   MC Arch
f 21*   *(External payments)*
…
Paid to the queen's players by the lord president's
command   12d
…
Bill   Paid for a bever given to the fellows after the bachelors'
          play in the great hall as it appears in the bill   6s 3d
          …

Merton College Register   MCR: 1.2
f 276

®Election of   On the eve of (St) Edmund the King, when the fellows had assembled
  the king   at the fire in the hall, by the old custom Mr Robert Tayler, registrar of the

University, principal of Alban Hall, and vice-warden in the college, was chosen and appointed as king for the coming year, taking the place after Clutterbuck's departure and (his) preferment to the chapel of Windsor by the warden.

...

Chancellor's Court Register   OUA: Hyp/A/4, Register EEE (or B reversed) f 248*

...

Lindsay con. Knyght

°Dr Lindsay died on 2 March 1534, Alumni Oxonienses, f 672°

On 7 June Master Doctor Lindsay, STD, claimed before the aforesaid lord substitute (judge) that he lent to Mr John Knight, MA, a certain pair of clarichords, which he asked be restored by the same (John Knight), and he (Mr Knight) did not wish to but said that the said Master Doctor Lindsay gave the said pair to the same (John Knight), agreeing that he had received it from him in the presence of the said doctor, who denied that he gave it but (said) that he lent it only, and he asked for justice to be done for himself in this matter together with expenses incurred and to be incurred. And then the said Mr John Knight asked for a term-day for proving that the said Master Doctor Lindsay gave the said pair of clarichords to him, and the lord (judge) assigned to him the next Monday and at 1 PM by the consent of the said master doctor, and he warned the parties to appear.

Lindsay con. Knight

On 9 June aforesaid, at the aforesaid hour, the aforesaid Master Doctor Lindsay appeared and asked the lord commissary to compel the said Mr Knight to restore the said clarichords and their true value, in the presence of Mr Knight who introduced no proof that the said master doctor gave him the aforenamed pair of clarichords. At his petition, indeed, the master (commissary) sentenced the aforesaid Mr John Knight to restore the said pair of clarichords within eight days in the same good condition in which they were at the time of their handing over, and to satisfy the parties, that is to say, Messrs Baldwin and Best, by whose consent the aforesaid pair of clarichords had been sequestered into the hands of the said Master Doctor Lindsay, also in the expenses to be assessed by the lord commissary and to discharge the said master doctor against (any claims of) the aforesaid parties by sufficient guarantors within the next eight days following under the aforenamed punishment as above.

1532–3
Merton College Register   MCR: 1.2
f 277v

...

Election of the king

On the eve of (St) Edmund the King, when the fellows had assembled at the fire in the hall, by the old custom Mr John Davy was chosen and appointed as king for the coming year.

...

1533–4
Magdalen College Liber Computi 1533–4   MC Arch
f 44   *(External payments)*

...

Bill +

Paid to Richard Alard for two meals after the fellows' and
scholars' plays as appears by two bills joined into one   12s 2d

...

Merton College Register   MCR: 1.2
f 279

...

Devenell is
elected as king

On 19 November, that is to say, on the eve of (St) Edmund the King, Mr Henry Devenell was elected as king because he has been preferred to the rectory of Bridport in the county of Dorset.

...

New College Bursars' Accounts   NC Arch: 7488
mb 7   *(Necessary external costs)*

...

...Paid in reward to the king's players at the warden's command, 3s 4d....

mb 8

...Paid in reward given to drummers (from) Calais at the vice-warden's command, 12d....

...

Chancellor's Court Register   OUA: Hyp/A/4, Register EEE (or B reversed)
f 257v   *(A Christmas play at Broadgates Hall)*

...

On the same day Robert Woodward, manciple of the house of Broadgates Hall, appeared and claimed that he had lent Sir John Moore, a scholar of the said hall, 15s for the purchase of specific clothing for the plays and stages in Christmas-time, which (money) he sought from the said Sir John Moore with legal expenses. And to prove the loan he brought in George Wimsley, LLB, and Thomas Burgayne, scholars of the said hall, who having sworn on the Holy Gospels deposed that the aforementioned manciple had lent the aforesaid sum, 15s, to the same Sir John Moore on this condition, (namely,) that he return the same sum after the collection usually held among the scholars of the said house to contribute to the payment. (This evidence was given) in the presence of the said Sir John Moore, who confessed that he had received the aforesaid sum from the said maniple, but he says that he has paid 7s to the aforesaid maniple, which sum, 7s, the aforesaid maniple confessed that he had received, and the judge found the aforesaid Sir Moore liable for the remainder, that is, 8s together with legal expenses, and he ordered the same to pay the said sum, together with legal expenses, to the aforesaid maniple within the eight days next following under penalty of law and without delay. The judge assessed the expenses at 10d.

…

1534–5
Magdalen College Liber Computi 1534–5   MC Arch
f 77   *(External payments)*
…

– Paid to a performer for diversions made for the fellows
in Christmas-time   4s 4d

…

– Paid for a light meal made after the performance of a
comedy as is entered in Alard's book   9s 3d

…

Paid to the lord king's jugglers at the lord president's command   20d

New College Bursars' Accounts   NC Arch: 7489
mb 8   *(Necessary external costs)*

…Paid in reward given to royal players, 2s.…

…

1535–6
Magdalen College Liber Computi 1535–6   MC Arch
f 67   *(External payments)*
…

Paid to a performer for diversions made for the fellows
and students in Christmas-time   4s
…

1536–7
New College Bursars' Accounts   NC Arch: 7493
mb 5   *(Necessary external costs)*

…Paid to the king's players by the vice-warden's hands, 20d.…

…

1537–8
Magdalen College Liber Computi 1537–8   MC Arch
f 120v   *(External payments)*
...

x   Paid to two drummers for (their) pains during Christmas-tide   4s 8d
...

f 122
...
Paid for sweetmeats given to the fellows when the comedy
was performed   6s 8d
...

Merton College Register   MCR: 1.2
f 283   *(November)*
...
Mr Ramridge was elected as king.

New College Bursars' Accounts   NC Arch: 7495
mb 4   *(Necessary external expenses)*
...
...In reward given to Lord Cromwell's entertainers, 7s....
...

1538–9
Magdalen College Liber Computi 1538–9   MC Arch
f 131v   *(Hall costs)*
...
Paid to Hammond for (his) labour for three days about the stage   18d
...

f 136   *(External payments)*
...
x   Paid for sweetmeats given to the fellows when the comedy
was performed   8s
...

Merton College Register   MCR: 1.2
f 284v
...
On the twentieth day Mr Borough, vicar of Croydon, was elected as king of
Merton.
...

1539–40
Magdalen College Liber Computi 1539–40   MC Arch
f 150v   *(External payments)*

...

Paid to two harpers in Christmas-time   4s 8d

...

Paid for a banquet given for the fellows at that time when
the tragedy was performed   8s 4d

...

– Paid for bread and drink given to the demies while they were
busy mounting a public comedy   20d

...

Merton College Register   MCR: 1.2
f 285v

...

Estwick was
elected as king

On 19 November Mr Estwick was elected as king on the eve of (St) Edmund
the King.

f 286

...

® Coming of
the officers
to the hall

On 1 January town officers of Oxford came to the college to sing a song in
the hall. When it was finished one noble was given to them from the pure
benevolence of the fellows. They received it in a grateful spirit and, giving
thanks, they withdrew.

...

1540–1
Magdalen College Liber Computi 1540–1   MC Arch
f 158   *(Hall costs)*

...

Paid for candles used in the hall during the time comedies
were performed   5s

f 162*   *(External payments)*

...

Paid for a bever given to the fellows after comedies
were performed   12s 4d

...

Paid to Mr Harley for a drummer hired during the
Christmas holidays   4s

...

1541–2
Magdalen College Liber Computi 1541–2   MC Arch
f 170v   *(Hall costs)*

...

– Paid for candles used while the comedies were performed   4s 4d

...

f 176   *(External payments)*

...

Paid to Mr Redman for a drummer   4s 8d

...

f 176v

...

• Paid for a light meal given to the fellows after the comedies
had been performed   13s 4d

...

New College Hall Book   NC Arch: 5530
f [167]   *(24–30 December)*

...

On Wednesday at dinner with the fellows:... two entertainers.

...

f [168]   *(31 December–6 January)*

...

On Sunday...
at supper with the fellows: two entertainers.

...

On Tuesday at dinner with the fellows:... two entertainers.
At supper with the fellows: two entertainers.

...

On Wednesday at dinner with the fellows:... two entertainers.
At supper with the fellows: two entertainers.

...

On Thursday at dinner with the fellows:... two entertainers....
At supper with the fellows: two entertainers....
On Friday at dinner with the fellows:... two entertainers.

f [169]   *(7–13 January)*

...

On Sunday...

at supper with the fellows:... two entertainers.
On Monday at dinner with the fellows:... two entertainers.

...

At supper with the fellows:... two entertainers.

...

On Wednesday...

...

At supper with the fellows: two entertainers.

...

On Friday at dinner with the fellows: two entertainers.

...

f [170]   *(14–20 January)*

On Saturday ... at dinner with the fellows:... two entertainers.

...

On Sunday...
at supper with the fellows: two entertainers.

...

f [173]*   *(4–10 February)*

...

On Friday at dinner with the fellows:... two entertainers of Lady Willoughby.

...

The Queen's College Long Roll   QC Arch: 2P131
single mb   *(1 July–1 July) (External expenses)*

...

...Likewise to pipers for the months of August and June, 20d....

...

Dedicatory Epistle to Gilbert Smith, Archdeacon of Peterborough
Grimald: *Christus Redivivus*
sigs A3v–4*

...But after I, having passed my time in the college of learned men that takes its name from the brazen nose for one month and likewise a second, had for my part adorned that Sparta, and after it so happened that the college youth, perhaps by fortune, were on fire to ascend the stage whereby they would both excite their own souls and show a certain image of life to be seen by the citizens, what I was working on and what I had in hand began to be known to many very quickly, from (being known by) the few who used to frequent my cubicle. And so Matthew Smith, warden of the college and your kinsman, a man furnished with marvellous modesty, generosity, and holiness of life, Robert Caldwell, a thoroughly honest man and remarkably | learned, (and) young men, most carefully chosen and of the greatest promise, (all) worked together with me with the result that I entrusted to them my offspring to be produced on the stage, and for this reason I dedicated and devoted my work to them. Since, moreover, it seemed difficult for me to refuse them sometimes striving for brilliant things, sometimes desiring things worthy of their own nature, I allowed indeed that this very comedy be publicly performed under their auspices in a gathering of the most erudite men. As soon as rumour resounding with a clamorous voice had poured this (news) out into your ears, you have continued not only to admonish me through my most diligent instructor John Airy but also yourself kindly to ask again and again for an edition of this play in verse. And indeed as often as I myself, being rather confused with amazement and embarrassment, have shown myself devoted to excuses and said that it was not possible that traces of ignorance would not appear everywhere in a youth of more or less twenty years, and regarded everything, which I have mentioned above, as an obstacle, just as often that man, my teacher – such was his assiduity both of obedience to you and of challenging me – stood firm and employed the examples, now of more recent (authors), now also of ancient ones, whose monuments are extant, written not without the highest praise at that age....

1542-3
Magdalen College Libri Computi   MC Arch: LCE/5
f 5   *(Hall costs)*
...
Paid for candles while the comedies were performed   4s
...

f 9v   *(External payments)*
...
x   Paid for a bever given to the fellows after the comedies
had been performed   13s 4d
...
Paid to Mr Ottley for a drummer during the Christmas
season   4s 8d
...

1544–5
Magdalen College Libri Computi   MC Arch: LCE/5
f 22   *(External payments)*

...

Paid to the drummer Tyllesley for his work during the
Christmas holidays   4s 9d

...

1545–6
Magdalen College Libri Computi   MC Arch: LCE/5
f 35v   *(External payments)*

...

Paid for a drummer during the Christmas holidays at
the hands of Mr Wodroffe   4s 8d

...

c **1546**
Christ Church Cathedral and College Foundation Statutes
ChCh Arch: D.P.vi.b.1
f 183*   *(Chapter 35) (On the disposition of bedrooms)*

...

In order that the bedrooms be prudently and well disposed, we establish,
ordain, and wish that everyone of our church conduct himself decently and
modestly in his dormitory both with his room-mate and with other neighbours, and that he hinder no one at any time from sleep, rest, or study by
excessive shouts, laughs, songs, clamours, dances, (or) playing of musical
instruments. But if at any time one is pleased to converse with others before
the fire elsewhere for the sake of relaxing the mind, the time is to be passed
with moderate silence in those things which pertain to virtue and learning,
and on those (occasions) there are not to be late feasts or drinkings, but
temperate and salutary (meals)....

ff 194–4v

...

48. On not delaying in the hall after meals
In order that, after the filling of the belly and thanksgiving, literary studies
or other works of piety be pursued, we establish, ordain, and wish that every
day after dinner and supper, when thanksgiving to God has been finished,
each and every canon of our church, of whatever degree they be, shall withdraw without any interval from our hall except when either meetings or
other important (*or* difficult) | business of the church has to be immediately
dealt with, or (when) readings, disputations, or expositions of the Bible are

to follow forthwith – when these are completed, they are to depart at once – or (except) when a fire is built on the more solemn feasts for the diversion of all the inhabitants there. Then we permit the canons of our church and the others aforesaid for the sake of recreation, modestly as is appropriate for clerics, to delay after the said meals and drinkings in the hall in songs and other suitable diversions, and also to pursue literary leisure amongst themselves, to discuss, read, and recount poems and histories and other things of this kind.

...

1546–7
Merton College Register   MCR: 1.2
f 299

...

® The arrival of the officers
On 1 January [town] city officers of Oxford came to the college to sing a song in the hall. When it was finished 6s with 8d were given to them from the pure benevolence of the fellows, and they accepted (the money) in a grateful spirit and giving thanks they withdrew.

...

1547–8
Exeter College Rectors' Accounts   EC Arch: B.I.16
mb 1   *(17 December–24 March)*

...

...Likewise 6s 8d paid for expenses of a comedy to be performed publicly....

...

Magdalen College Libri Computi   MC Arch: LCE/5
f 63v   *(External payments)*

...

Paid for candles used at the time of the tragedies and (for) torches	19s 8d

...

Paid for the fellows' light meal before the tragedies	10s

...

1549–50
Magdalen College Libri Computi   MC Arch: LCE/5
f 90v   *(External payments)*

...

Paid to a drummer in Christmas-time	4s 8d

...

Merton College Register   MCR: 1.2
f 302v

...

"City officers
of Oxford"

On 1 January city officers of Oxford came to the college to sing a song. When
it was finished 6s with 8d were given to them from pure benevolence. They
accepted (the money) in a grateful spirit and giving thanks they withdrew.

c 1550

Christ Church College Foundation Statutes   ChCh Arch: D.P.vi.b.1
f 55*   *(Chapter 35) (On the disposition of bedrooms)*

...

We establish, ordain, and wish that everyone of our church conduct himself
honourably and modestly in his bedroom both with his room-mate and with
other neighbours, and that he hinder no one at any time from sleep, rest, or
study by excessive shouts, laughs, songs, clamours, dances, (or) playing of
musical instruments. But if at any time one is pleased to converse with others
before the fire or elsewhere for the sake of relaxing the mind, the time is to
be passed with moderate silence in those things which pertain to virtue and
learning, and on those (occasions) there are not to be late feasts or drinkings,
but temperate and salutary (meals)....

...

f 60*   *(Chapter 53)*

...

On not delaying after meals

We establish and wish that every day after dinner and supper, when thanksgiving to God has been finished, each and every canon of our church, of
whatever degree they be, shall withdraw without any interval from our hall
except when either meetings or other important (*or* difficult) business of
the church has to be immediately dealt with, or (when) readings, disputations, or expositions of the Bible are to follow forthwith – when these also
are completed, they are to depart at once – or (except) when a fire is built
on the more solemn feasts for the diversion of all the inhabitants there.
Then we permit the canons of the church and the others aforesaid for the
sake of recreation, modestly as is appropriate for ecclesiastics, to delay after
the said meals and drinks in the hall in songs and other suitable diversions,
and also to pursue literary leisure amongst themselves, to discuss, read, and
recount poems and histories and other things of this kind. Further, in order
that there be no opportunity for wrongdoing available, (we grant) authority
to the dean and chapter to draw up (and) pass on rules and decrees in our

church, not to be violated without punishment, (provided) only that (these rules) not work against these our statutes.

...

1550–1
Exeter College Rectors' Accounts   EC Arch: B.1.16
mb 1*   (c *25 December–7 April*)

...

...Likewise of 5s 1d paid to Dolye painting those things that were needed for performing the comedies.... Likewise of 18s 7d paid for repairs on Lord's house and for expenses that were incurred in putting on the comedies....

...

Magdalen College Libri Computi   MC Arch: LCE/5
f 99v*   (*Hall costs*)

...

Paid on 17 January to Thomas Pickhaver for five days' work about the stage at 8d a day	3s 4d
Paid to Walter Oven working for the same time at 6d a day	2s 6d
Paid to Robert for three days' work about the same	2s

...

Merton College Register   MCR: 1.2
f 305v

...

On 1 January city officers of Oxford came to the college to sing a song. When it was finished 6s 8d were given to them from pure benevolence, for which they gave great thanks and departed.

...

1551–2
Magdalen College Libri Computi   MC Arch: LCE/5
f 125*   (*Hall costs*)

...

Paid on 23 January to Hickes constructing the stage for three days, (together) with half (a day), and for one night	3s
Paid for two dozen lamps, 9(s) 8(d) for each dozen	19s 4d
Paid for eight dozen candles	10s
Paid on 23 January to Hammond and (his) son working for six days on building the stage at 14d a day	7s

...

f 131v*   *(External payments)*

...

Bill

Paid for meals eaten by the fellows after the comedies
were performed as it appears in the bill   42s 6d

...

f 132v

...

Paid to a drummer in Christmas   4s 8d

...

1552–3

Magdalen College Libri Computi   MC Arch: LCE/5
f 148v   *(Hall costs)*

...

Paid for ropes for the use of those putting on the tragedies   14d
Paid to Mr Taynter for cord for the same use   6d
Paid on 28 January to Wilmot for his work with the
participants beforehand   3d

f 157v*   *(Store costs)*

...

Paid at the same time to Sutton (and) Wilmot for erecting
(and) replacing the boards and pulling down the stage for
three days   3s

...

f 159   *(Costs of internal repairs)*

...

Paid on 21 January to Robert Hammond and (his) son making
the stage, to (one of them) squaring timber, (and) to (the other)
making chests (*or* cupboards) in the kitchen for six days   7s

...

Paid to Robert Hickes working with Hammond for the
same number of days   4s
Paid on 28 January to Robert Hammond for his work of
pulling down the stage (and for him) squaring timber for
four days at 14d a day   4s 8d

...

Paid on 4 March to Robert Hammond and (his) son making
a table and other things in the musical pastime for four days   4s 8d

...

Bill

f 160v   *(External payments)*

...

Paid for meals spent on the fellows and the rest after the
comedies were performed as it appears in the bill   28s 6d

...

New College Bursars' Accounts   NC Arch: 7522
mb 7   *(Internal costs)*

...Paid for cleaning the houses after the plays, 4d....

...

1553–4
Magdalen College Draft Libri Computi   MC Arch: LCD/1
f 43*

...

[Paid to pipers for fourteen days during the Christmas holidays, 26⟨...⟩.]

...

f 56v   *(Hall costs)*

...

Paid on 3 February to Hickes working about the stage for
six days at 8d a day   4s
Paid at the same time to Hammond with (his) two sons
working for six days about the stage at 15d a day   7s 6d

...

f 60   *(External payments)*

...

Paid on 9 February to Sir Day for pipers in Christmas-time   4s

...

Bill   Paid on 13 January on the coming of the same (Lord Maltravers)
          to the tragedies for two nights according to the bill   42s 8½d
Bill   Paid for meals given to the fellows after the tragedies were
          performed according to the bill   10s 9d

...

1554–5
Magdalen College Libri Computi   MC Arch: LCE/5
f 187v   *(External payments)*

...

Paid to pipers during the Christmas holidays   4s 8d

...

1556–7
Magdalen College Draft Libri Computi   MC Arch: LCD/1
f 130v   *(Hall costs)*

…

Paid on 5 February to Hickes working about the stage for one day and a half	12d
Paid at the same time to Hammond working for half a day	4d
°Paid for half a dozen torches	2s 4d
Paid for rope at the time of the tragedies	12d°

…

f 134v   *(External expenses)*
…

Paid to pipers in Christmas-time	4s

…

Cardinal Pole's Statutes   Bodl.: MS. Top.Oxon b.5
f 85   *(6 November) (Chapter 17)*

…

With reference, moreover, to townsfolk, (enquire) whether the women (*or* wives) be disreputable, also (whether there be) games of chance, fencing schools, or swordsmen or dancing schools.
(Enquire) whether there are any who receive scholars in taverns or private homes and at feasts without a licence either of the warden of the college or the provost of the hall.

…

1557–8
Magdalen College Libri Computi   MC Arch: LCE/5
f 203v   *(Chapel costs)*

…

Paid on Maundy Thursday to twelve choristers	12d

…

f 205   *(Hall costs)*

…

Paid for rope acquired about the theatre	12d

…

f 213   *(External payments)*

…

Paid to piper/s in Christmas-time	4s 8d

…

Magdalen College Draft Libri Computi   MC Arch: LCD/1
f 147   *(Hall costs)*

…

Paid on 9 January to Oven and his servant working about the
stage for three days at 10d a day for one (and) 8d for the other   4s 6d

…

1558–9
Merton College Register   MCR: 1.2
f 320v

Given to the
city officers of
Oxford from
pure and volun-
tary generosity

On 1 January, that is, Circumcision Day, city officers of Oxford came to the
college to sing a song. It indeed did not quite fit the bill and not, however,
without just complaint, for the one of them who had sung was seized with
a sudden sickness, as everyone said with one voice. On that account we
determined to make allowance for them and nevertheless gave them, from
pure benevolence, 6s 8d. They accepted (the money) in a grateful spirit
and giving thanks they withdrew.

…

The Queen's College Long Roll   QC Arch: 2P146
single mb   *(7 July–7 July)* *(External expenses)*
…
…Likewise to pipers, 16d….

…

1559–60
Magdalen College Libri Computi   MC Arch: LCE/6
f 5*   *(Hall costs)*

…

Paid on 9 February to Oven and his servant working about
the stage for eleven days at 19d a day   17s 6d

°And so more
things regarding
the stage°

Paid to Webster busy about the same (task) for three days
at 9d a day   2s 3d
Paid to Cryspe engaged about the same (task) for the
same time   2s 3d
Paid to Wright and Cutberde carrying many things to
the same stage for five days at 14d a day   5s 10d
Paid to Welles and Heywood sawing various things for
the same stage for four days at 20d a day   6s 8d
Paid to John Willows and Henry Heywood on 26 January
sawing various things for the same stage for three days,
together with half (a day), at 20d a day   5s 10d

Paid at the same time for two dozen torches   8s

Paid to Alkot and Welles removing the stage   10d

Paid to Hickes repairing the benches and tables after the

comedies were produced   8d

...

f 8*   *(Internal repairs)*

...

Paid on 28 January to Oven and (his) servant busy for

five and a half days about Mr Atkinson's window and

the stage in the hall at 19d a day   8s 8d

...

f 8v*   *(External payments)*

...

+   Paid to the lord president for expenses on lords' sons at

the time of the shows   53s 4d

...

Paid to pipers in Christmas-time   4s

...

Magdalen College Draft Libri Computi   MC Arch: LCD/1

f 183

...

°Paid:° we gave pipers in partial payment of a greater sum   13s 4d

...

Merton College Register   MCR: 1.2

f 322v

...

On 1 January city officers of Oxford came to sing a song. When this was

done we gave them 6s 8d from pure benevolence.

...

1560–1

Magdalen College Libri Computi   MC Arch: LCE/6

f 17*   *(Hall costs)*

...

xx   Paid to Joynere, (a) painter, painting the names of the heresies

for the show which the choirmaster produced   3s 4d

...

f 21   *(External expenses)*

...

x   Paid to pipers in Christmas-time   4s

...

1561-2
Magdalen College Libri Computi   MC Arch: LCE/6
f 35v*   *(Hall costs)*

...

Paid on the last (day) of January to Squire and (his) son
sawing various things for the stage for five days and a half
at 20d a day   8s 4d
Paid at the same time to Oven and (his) servant con-
structing various things for producing the shows for six
days at 18d a day   9s
Paid on 7 February to Squire and (his) son sawing various
things for the stage for four days at 20d a day   6s 8d
Paid on 8 February to Oven and (his) servant erecting the
stage and constructing various things for the shows for five
days at 18d a day   7s 6d
Paid at the same time to Rixon and White working together
for the same number of days at 18d a day   7s 6d
Paid to Showsmythe repairing glass windows by agreement   6s 8d
Paid to the same in reward for glass broken during the shows   3s 4d
Paid for candles spent at the time of the shows   6s 8d

...

f 40   *(External payments)*

...

Paid to pipers in Christmas-time   4s

...

Bill   Paid for meals given to Mr Winchecombe and others at
the time of the shows as it appears in the bill   11s 10d

...

Magdalen College Draft Libri Computi   MC Arch: LCD/1
f 222   *(6 February)*

...

°Paid:° we gave as a loan to Sir Brasbridge on 6 February,
3s (of which was) for hair for women (*ie*, a wig *or* wigs)   £3 10s

...

f 223v

…

Paid for two dozen torches to put on the shows   8s

…

Merton College Register   MCR: 1.2
f 326

The college's
generosity to-
ward town of-
ficers of Oxford

On 21 October Mr Jones, the chief of the town officers of Oxford, readily
received 6s 8d, and that by the consent of the lord warden and the seniors,
from Mr Giffard, the bursar, in the place of Mr Atwood, who on the nineteenth of the same month declined of his own free will to be a fellow any
longer. The said Jones not only acknowledged that he and his (fellow officers)
had this sum not by right but from the pure generosity of the college, but
also declared (as much) to those present – Marshall, the vice-warden, and
Giffard, the bursar.

…

f 326v

…

The officers
did not see us
this year

On Circumcision Day the town officers of Oxford did not come here to us
from dinner (*ie*, after dinner (?)) at all, which could seem a wonder since
before this they were accustomed to take very eagerly those things which
our college conferred on them freely and voluntarily.

…

Letter of John Foxe to Laurence Humphrey   BL: MS Harleian 416
f [1v]*   *(January?)*

No indeed, I think that I should be thankful less on account of the scholarly
world, to which indeed no small part (of me) looks (with gratitude), than for
anything of use and profit that is hoped for from your honour. Anyway, while
I was writing these things to you and was wanting (to write) more on this
matter of gratitude, ⟨…⟩ occupying myself in the very wide and very joyful
field of writing, our Robert, servant of your Edward, whom as you know I
think as worthy now as I have always loved him from long ago in Basel on
account of a rare quality of piety and modesty, (and) whom you also benefited
in accordance with your richer ability, made an unexpected and timely arrival.
After him followed also your letter bearing not only the hand of my old
(friend) Laurence but also all the candour of (his) heart. In order that I might
write something in reply to that letter, since duty does not permit (me) to be
silent, regarding the show of which you write in it, *Christus Triumphans*, I pray
that Christ, the director of every good action, turns all to good for the men of

Magdalen if they have indeed decided (to put it on). But I am amazed at their reasoning in defence of this (choice) since there are so many comedies – Latin, Greek, sacred, and profane – available on which they perhaps could have exerted their efforts more usefully in other ways. But seeing that it so appears to them, even if it is not possible for me to be a spectator because of business, nevertheless I will not fail to be among those who always gladly applaud the excellent efforts of the men of Magdalen. Meanwhile I am very grateful for your graciousness in so lovingly inviting me there. As for inserting the conversion of (St) Paul, I am not yet certain what I should promise or what I should respond. For the one asking is someone whom I should not refuse. I am so detained by business at the moment that there is no time left over even if I should wish it. I hope, however, to write to you regarding this business more fully in a few days, our triumphant Christ permitting.

1562–3
Magdalen College Libri Computi   MC Arch: LCE/6
f 59v   *(External payments)*
…

Paid to pipers in Christmas-time   4s
…

1563–4
The Queen's College Long Roll   QC Arch: 2P150
single mb   *(7 July–7 July) (External expenses)*
…
…Likewise to a piper, 6d….
…

1564–5
Magdalen College Libri Computi   MC Arch: LCE/6
f 97   *(External payments)*
…

Paid to pipers in Christmas-time   4s
…

Paid to pipers on Pentecost Day by the vice-president's command   12d
…

Trinity College Bursars' Books   TC Arch: I/A/1
f 66v   *(External expenses)*
…

Paid for the show set forth on Trinity Sunday, namely, (for) the
oak placed in the deer park   6s 6d
…

1565–6
Magdalen College Libri Computi   MC Arch: LCE/6
f 106   *(Chapel costs)*

…

Paid to Showsmythe mending windows by agreement	6s 8d
Paid to the same repairing windows broken by balls and during the time of the shows	3s 4d

…

f 106v   *(Hall costs)*

Paid to Oven and two servants working about the stage at various times during the Christmas holidays for six days	14s

…

Paid to Oven and two servants working about the stage for six days	14s
Paid to Rixon and Morris doing the same thing for four days	6s
Paid to Squire and (his) servant sawing various things for the same project for four days	6s

…

Bill   Paid to Mr Brasbridge for expenses on the comedy   7s 10d

…

Bills | | |
|---|---|
| Paid for various things belonging to the shows according to the bills | £13 7s 11½d |
| Paid for candles used in the time of the shows | 15s |
| Paid to Oven and (his) servant working about the show for three days | 7s 6d |
| °Paid for coals used at the same time | £4° |

…

f 108v   *(Groundskeeping costs)*

…

Paid Oven and two servants trimming (*or* shaping) lumber for the new stage for three days	7s 6d
Paid Squire and (his) servant sawing at the same time for five days	8s 4d

…

f 109v   *(External payments)*

…

Paid to pipers in Christmas-time	4s

…

Paid to someone bearing a letter from the queen's counsellors   5s

...

Paid for expenses at the time of the queen's progress   £6

...

f 110

...

°Paid for meals given to gentlemen at the time of the shows   17s 4d°

...

Magdalen College Draft Libri Computi   MC Arch: LCD/1
f 293   *(Memoranda)*

...

°Paid:° we gave pipers in advance   43s 4d

...

We gave in advance to the bachelors for presenting the shows   £3 11s 8d

...

Letter of Guzmán de Silva to the King of Spain
Archivo General de Simancas: Estado, legajo 819
f [2v]   *(6 September)*

...

This queen has been received at this University in the manner princes are customarily (received) in the places that welcome them with all due applause and jubilation. They proffered four orations from various places upon her entrance, three in Latin and one in Greek, in which they praised her virtues and learning, demonstrating their jubilation and happiness at her visit. Included among the public functions on the days she has been here have been exercises in all areas of learning and, at night, comedies and tragedies (have been performed) in the Latin language and in English. Yesterday was the day on which the festivities ended, and the queen thanked them in Latin with good and solemn word⟨.⟩. No matters relating to religion, only ordinary ones, were treated in these functions, either in comedies or disputes, except the last one, which was about theology....

...

Nicholas Robinson's 'Of the Actes Done at Oxford'
Folger Shakespeare Library: MS V.a.176
f 158v   *(1 September)*

...

A story of a certain Geminus concluded this day. Some studious men of Christ College (*ie*, Christ Church) had turned this story into the form of a

comedy. But after they had dispensed with an oration, they performed the same (comedy) on a stage in the hall of the same college, where everything was very brilliant with respect to splendour and decoration with royal expenditures and with the help of Mr Edwards, who remained at the University for almost two months in order also to make a certain work in English, which on the following night he set forth. At this historical comedy the royal counsellors (and) noble men and women, together with the legate of the king of Spain, were present. The queen was absent either on account of fear of illness or (because) she was engaged in other business. The first hour after midnight had already sounded when an end was put to this show.
...

f 159   *(2 September)*
...

As on the previous night, on this one also this stage was decorated splendidly so that *The Knight's Tale*, as Chaucer calls it, translated from Latin into English speech by Mr Edwards and other students of the same college, was set forth to the public. *(blank)* After her royal majesty had entered onto the stage and all the entrances were closed, part of a wall by which one goes into the hall – by what chance or for what reason I do not know – fell down and crushed a scholar of St Mary's Hall and a townsman by the name of Pennye. They died there and also another scholar's leg was broken. And both of a cook's legs were shattered and his face was cut up, as if by blows, by the fall of stones. Nevertheless, the show was not interrupted but continued to midnight.
...

f 161v   *(4 September)*
...

On this night what had remained of the story or tale of *Palamon and Arcite* was performed with the queen herself present on the stage.
...

ff 164v–5   *(5 September)*
...

...afterward ǀ her royal majesty is conducted into the hall with wax torches lit, because the eighth hour had already sounded.

In the silence of this night it is shown on stage how King Tereus ate his son who was killed and prepared by his wife, Procne, on account of the rape of her sister. All (was put on) with the finest preparation and in truly royal style as was certainly proper. When this tragedy received its applause everyone went to bed.
...

Bereblock's Commentary   Bodl.: MS. Rawlinson D.1071
pp 13–15   *(1 September)*

...

...As night was approaching the most elaborate shows were given, which for many, I who being at leisure were anticipating them the whole day, were the pinnacle of reward in their distinction. And nothing indeed more precious or more magnificent could be devised than their provision and construction. First there was an elaborate approach (to the hall) by means of a doorway that was open in a large, solid wall and from it, a raised wooden platform placed on posts runs forward by a small (*ie*, narrow (?)) and skilful track across transverse steps toward the great hall of the college. It is equipped with a festive garland and an engraved and painted canopy so that by it, without the bustle and disturbance of the pressing crowd, the queen could make her way to the prepared shows with, as it were, an even step. There was the hall with a gilded panelled ceiling, a ceiling both painted and arched within, and you might say that it imitates the size of the ancient Roman palace in its grandeur and pride, and the image of antiquity in its magnificence. In its upper end, which faces west, a great and raised stage is built up, one also elevated by many steps. Along every wall raised steps and platforms have been constructed, benches were atop the same (raised steps and platforms) of many (different) heights, from which distinguished men and ladies might be admired, and the people all around were able to observe on all sides of the plays. Burning lamps, hanging lamps, and candles made a very bright light there. With so many lights arranged in branches and circles and so many torches (*or* chandeliers) providing flickering light here and there with unequal brightness, the place shone, so that like daylight, (the lights) seemed to sparkle and help the splendour of the shows with the greatest radiance. On either side of the stage, magnificent palaces and most sumptuous houses are constructed for the comedies and masques. A seat had been fixed on high, provided with pillows and tapestries and covered with a golden I canopy: (this) place was appointed for the queen, but she, in fact, was not present on this night. When everything had been prepared in this order and the house was quite full and occupied, one might have seen immediately on the stage Geminus Campanus accused falsely by Duillius and Cotta in the presence of Alexander Severus because of envy and emulation; slaves, farmers, and rustics ensnared by the allurements of bribes; (and) witnesses introduced. And nothing (was) more laughable than to observe those (characters) sordidly triumphing as if in certain victory, decreeing Geminus' punishment, squabbling over the division of his wealth, and fighting among themselves to a great degree, then deploring their misfortune with laments and tears like a woman's. When the play had gone on for some time like this, more honourable freedmen are later introduced whom neither penalty nor bribery could bring to an unjust accusation. Their written documents, testimonies,

evidences, (and) questionings made the truth clear. The accusing slaves, therefore, are then crucified at the emperor's command. Duillius and Cotta are
deservedly punished; the freedmen rewarded; Geminus is freed; great applause
is inspired from all. When it is finished everyone departs for bed.

...

pp 19–21   *(2 September)*

...While night was approaching they gather together for the prepared shows,
whose magnificent organization and refinement of incredible elegance had
so filled the minds and ears of all with their reputation, that an infinite and
innumerable multitude of people gathered together there out of an immense
and immoderate desire to see (them). The presence of the prince, of which
they were deprived now for two days, had added such desire for her to
the minds of all that their number had therefore been greatly increased and
larger. Hardly had the queen entered with her nobles, men of the first rank,
and sat down on an elevated seat, when everyone | flocked together to the
entrances of the theatre – it was in the hall of the college – with such a great
rush and the steps were now (so) completely filled with the people that in
their violence they spoilt the general joy with horrible destruction. There was
a wall of squared stones, with huge steps. On either side a barrier was placed
in order to sustain the rush of those going up. The crowd becomes more dense;
the rush greater; the wall, although it was very strong, could not hold. From
one side of the steps it fell. Three people were crushed by the collapse, as
many wounded. Of the those crushed, the one who survived the longest did
not live more than two days. The wounded recovered in a short time, when
remedies had been applied. Although this misfortune was able to spoil the
general joy, it was not able to ruin it (completely). And so everyone returns to
the shows, now more cautious because of the others' perils. There one could
observe the royal youths, Palamon and Arcite, whom the same land had long
held in concord, whom the same life-threatening danger and common prison
had joined together, whom the bond of affinity and the swearing of oaths had
made brothers. Those men were wretchedly perishing for the love of one and
the same maiden, Emily, sister(-in-law) of the duke of Athens. Here then in
them it was possible to see their souls agitated back and forth by motion, blow,
and thrust, hither and thither and, in prison, hardly in sufficient concord,
thrown into disorder by a stronger desire, fighting, battling – why go on?
They are prohibited by a command; they do not heed the command. They
are imprisoned; they break out; they go into exile. Love does not allow them
to go on | further: two days is too much; he cannot bear three. And so the
royal youth does not heed capital punishment. In a less proper style of dress
he returns; from being Arcite, by a change of name, he becomes Philostrates.
He instructs himself in every kind of duty; no service is so vile that he does

not pursue it. Nothing is so irksome by its nature that Emily's presence does not make it sweet and pleasant to him; without that most pleasant one, everything is laborious, tedious, and hateful. Palamon, meanwhile, tricks the guard with a potion, escapes from his troubles, flees by night, hides in the woods by day. At last he encounters his brother. Here Emily stirs up new commotions, and love had already caused such strong disturbances and affronts to the mind that soon they were fighting, but the fight is calmed immediately by the intervention of Theseus. Then Palamon tells (him) who they are (and) for what reason they were fighting. He begs, moreover, not (to be put to) death although he had gravely offended. Moved by the prayers of those (women) who had by chance been with him during the hunt, the duke decrees a duel. He orders that they prepare to fight on the fortieth day. He promises the maiden as a reward to the victor. It is not possible to say with what great pleasure indeed and joy the young people had departed. We also, after everyone had called on God together on behalf of the prince, departed on that night.

...

p 29   (3 September)

...no shows were given this night because the queen, having been detained before by an excessively long disputation, was not able to be present at the same (shows) without some jeopardy to her health.

...

pp 33–4   (4 September)

...This night, after the plays had been temporarily interrupted, they were begun again by agreement. We therefore returned to the theatre late at night with great contention (or exertion). The queen and the nobles are invited to the show; those invited arrive. Everyone sat down; a great silence followed. At that point both knights were present on the stage for the appointed day, each flanked by the strongest guard. On one side was Emetrius, king of India, under whose protection was Arcite. A hundred soldiers followed him. The Thracian Lycurgus, to whose virtue, faith, and good fortune Palamon was entrusted, had the same number on the other side. It seemed to Theseus that the battle should be waged by single combat (and that) the maiden would be his whose was the victory. By no means does this decision displease the kings, nor do the brothers object to it. Therefore three marble enclosures are made in the woods; there three most sacred altars are constructed. Emily goes in supplication to the one that was Diana's; here then she prays for a solitary life and perpetual chastity. The unhappy (maiden) was not able to gain very much by entreaty; the goddess proclaimed marriage. Arcite, on the other hand, sought victory from him in whose care are the defences of warlike

valour. Mars immediately thundered, 'Victory,' to him. Palamon prays to
Venus at her altar for the maiden, and she at once promises the maiden to him.
Here now a quarrel took place among | the gods; Saturn broke it up. Mean-
while each prince undertook the office of arming his knight. When this
was finished the song and noise of trumpets are heard. Then they battle fero-
ciously in close combat. As their armour rattled right from the first onrush,
and their glittering swords flashed, a monstrous horror grips the spectators
and, since hope has still inclined to neither side, the fighters, tired with ex-
haustion, rest twice. The third time, now when not only the movement of
bodies and brandishing of spears on both sides, but also blood and wounds
were a spectacle for all, Palamon collapses and is laid before his victorious
brother. Everyone acclaims Arcite with joy (and) rejoicing and giving thanks
they receive (him). Now all hope – though not all care – had deserted the
exhausted Palamon. Therefore he rages with more elevated speech and more
ardent action (*or* delivery) and curses Venus, whom he had served since infancy,
as having neither will nor power. Venus did not endure the aggrieved (Palamon),
and she could not with equanimity bear that Mars should take precedence
over her. She pleads her case like a woman with laments and weeping. Moved
by her tears Saturn strikes the victor with subterranean fire as he was triumphing
in his quite manifest victory. Thus Arcite dies on the spot. Then great preparation was made for his burial. He is honoured in a public funeral; nobles carry
his bier; kings follow (it); the body is cremated with great solemnity. Finally,
by royal counsel and the common consent of all, the maiden is given to
Palamon, and that deed performed before the now very crowded theatre
was approved with incredible shouting and applause from the spectators;
and on this night those shows were set forth.

p 43   (*5 September*)

...This was the sixth day after the prince's coming to the city. That (day)
now provided the fourth night of our plays on the stage. Then the fullest
and most sumptuous entertainment which the general expectation desired
is restored by a general effort. The queen and the nobles were marvellously
and exceedingly delighted by the elegance of its magnificent stage. Ovid
provided the story from the sixth book of the *Metamorphoses*. It is agreeable
to tell as much as we can of this (story)....

pp 45–6

...

That show was a remarkable likeness of the human race in its (depiction of)
depraved deeds, and for those watching | it was like a clear fable of all those
who indulge excessively in either love or anger, both of which, even if they
come to better (people), inflame (them) nevertheless with excessive appetite,

and render them far more intemperate and fierce than (they were) before and much farther removed in voice, face, spirit, words, and deeds from temperance and moderation. When the show was over, after the people in rising had given applause and approval in the prince's name, hastening they return home.

...

Camden, *Annales (1615)*   *stc*: 4496
p 103

...

® She visits the University of Oxford

Elizabeth, having at this time travelled into the country for the sake of relaxing her spirit, turned aside to the University of Oxford so that she would show herself no less well disposed to the muses of Oxford than to those of Cambridge, (who are) openly rivals of one another. There, being magnificently received, she stayed seven days, especially delighted by the charm of the location, the beauty of the colleges, (and) the talent and the meticulous learning of the learned students. They passed the night with theatrical plays and the days with learned disputations, for which she gave abundant thanks in Latin with singular sweetness of speech, and benevolently said farewell.

...

1566–7
Merton College Bursars' Accounts   MCR: 3932d
single mb   *(22 November–21 March) (External expenses)*

...

...To pipers by agreement when the students performed a play in the warden's lodgings, 5s.... To pipers when the students gave a comedy at the warden's lodgings, 5s....

...

Merton College Register   MCR: 1.2
f 347

® Comedy

On 3 January an English comedy, *Wylie Beguylie*, was performed at night in the warden's lodgings by the scholars, when the vice-warden, masters, (and) bachelors, with all the members of the house and some outsiders, were present. (The scholars,) who are deservedly to be praised for performing it correctly, displayed the greatest promise.

...

f 348

...

® Comedy

On 7 February Terence's *Eunuchus* was performed at the warden's lodgings

by the scholars, when all the members of the house and some outsiders
were present.

...

Episcopal Visitation to New College
Hampshire Record Office: 21M65/A1/26
f 55*   (18 March)   (Charges against Martin Colepeper)

...And that the same Mr Colepeper wickedly holds, or at least has held, the
aforesaid Davidic psalms in derision by calling the same 'Robin Hood
ballads' and (does so) continually....

f 56v   (Charges against Bartholomew Bolnye, Christopher Diggles, and
    William Browne)

Likewise that the aforesaid Bartholomew Bolnye, contrary to the form of the
statutes of the said college, is accustomed to fighting, and that, for the sake
of dancing, almost every day he betakes himself from dinner into the town
and to suspect places.... Likewise that the said Christopher Diggles and
William Browne in a similar way commonly frequent the town and the
aforesaid suspect places for sake of dancing....

Vice-Chancellors' Accounts   OUA: WP/β/21(4)
p 65   (21 December–21 December)
...
Paid to the dean and chapter of Christ Church for a third part
of their expenses in the past year for the reception of the queen,
on the strength of an order of a certain convocation, issued in
response to the consideration of a letter of the earl of Leicester,
chancellor of that University, as appears by a bill of Doctor
Westfaling, treasurer there: for the third part of the lumber sold
to Corpus Christi College, £4 3s 4d, and for the aforesaid expenses in the reception of the prince, £33 4s 8d, in total   £37 8s

1567–8
All Souls College Bursars' Accounts   Bodl.: MS. D.D. All Souls c.283
mb 6   (2 November–2 November)   (Various expenses)
...
And of 2s given to the waits at Christmas.

...

Magdalen College Libri Computi   MC Arch: LCE/6
f 129v   *(Hall costs)*

...

Paid to Oven and two servants busy about the theatre for
the (one) day   2s 6d

...

Paid to Oven and two servants working about benches broken in
the performance of the comedy for six days at 10d a day for each   15s
Paid to the same (men) doing the same and other things there
for four days (at the same amount) a day as above   10s

...

f 135v   *(External payments)*

...

Paid to pipers in Christmas-time   4s

...

Merton College Bursars' Accounts   MCR: 3932e
single sheet*   *(21 November–20 March)* *(External expenses)*

...

...To pipers and students putting on the play *Damon and Pithias* in the warden's
lodgings, 10s. To other pipers playing in the great hall on Circumcision Day,
2s. To pipers and students when they produced the comedy *Menaechmi*, 10s....

...

Merton College Register   MCR: 1.3
p 3

...

On 21 January, at night, Plautus' comedy *Menaechmi* was performed in the
hall by the students, although a few days before the same (students) had
performed the tragicomedy *Damon and Pithias* in English in the warden's
lodgings, while the masters, bachelors, and other members of the house,
with some outsiders, were present.

...

1568–9

Magdalen College Libri Computi   MC Arch: LCE/6
f 144   *(Hall costs)*

...

Paid to Hammond and (his) servant repairing benches and
removing the stage for three days   4s

...

f 147v   *(External payments)*

…

Paid to pipers at the time of the Christmas holidays   4s

…

1569–70
Magdalen College Libri Computi   MC Arch: LCE/6
f 168   *(External payments)*

…

Paid for pipers in Christmas-time   4s

…

1571–2
The Queen's College Long Roll   QC Arch: 2P156
single mb   *(7 July 1572–7 July 1573) (Expenses)*

…Likewise to the queen's pipers on 27 August, 10s….

…

1572–3
All Souls College Bursars' Accounts   Bodl.: MS. D.D. All Souls c.284
mb 4   *(2 November–2 November) (Various expenses)*

…

And of 3s 6d given to the waits.

…

Magdalen College Libri Computi   MC Arch: LCE/6
f 205v*   *(Hall costs)*

…

Paid to Oven and four servants making and removing the stage
for producing the shows   28s
Paid to those sawing various things at the same time for
the same stage   9s 8d
Paid to Mr Lister for two hundred boards   10s
Paid to Mr Gilbert for seven two-by-fours for the aforesaid stage   3s 4d
Paid to Younge for two hundred boards for the same work   10s
Paid for candles spent during the spectacles   10s

…

f 209   *(External payments)*

…

Paid to pipers   5s

…

Merton College Bursars' Accounts   MCR: 3944c
single mb   *(21 November–20 March) (External expenses)*
...
...To musicians of the town of Oxford, 12d....
...

The Queen's College Long Roll   QC Arch: 2P156
single mb   *(7 July–7 July) (Internal repairs)*
...
...Likewise for the construction of a stage in the hall for recounting a
tragicomedy, 3s 8d....
...

(Expenses)
...Likewise in expenses for the tragicomedy in Christmas, 7s 5d....
...

1573–4
Magdalen College Libri Computi   MC Arch: LCE/6
f 218v*   *(Hall costs)*
...

	Paid to Noke making a door for the shows	10s 9d
°Bill°	Paid to Oven making wainscot there °according to the bill°	37s 3d
	Paid to a smith for a lock and two pairs of hinges	10s 6d

...
Paid to Oven and (his) servants making, setting up, and
removing the stage for the shows   £5 3s
...

Paid to Noke and (his) servant for setting up pinnacles and
strengthening what had been either destroyed or weakened
at the time of the show   16d
...

f 223   *(External payments)*
...
+   Paid to pipers   25s 5d
...

f 223v*
...
Paid to trumpeters   *(blank)*
...

Magdalen College Draft Libri Computi   MC Arch: LCD/1
f 440v   *(External payments)*

…

Paid to the queen's [pipers] trumpeters
30 August   20s

…

1574–5
All Souls College Bursars' Accounts   Bodl.: MS. D.D. All Souls c.284
mb 5   *(2 November–2 November)* *(Various expenses)*

…

And of 12d for the torches at the play.
And of 6s 8d given to musicians at the same time.

…

1575–6
All Souls College Bursars' Accounts   Bodl.: MS. D.D. All Souls c.284
mb 4   *(2 November–2 November)* *(Various expenses)*

…

And of 2s given to the waits.
And of 2s 6d given to the musicians at Christmas and (All) Souls.

…

Magdalen College Draft Libri Computi   MC Arch: LCD/1
f 456v*   *(29 September–25 December)* *(External payments)*

…

+   Paid to Mr Lillie for the earl of Leicester's players
     (or entertainers)   20s

…

Paid to Wilson, a musician, for music in the hall
on the feast of the Annunciation to (St) Mary   10s

…

Merton College Register   MCR: 1.3
p 49

…

The regents' fire   [On 22 November the regents' fire, which for many years has lain hidden
                     in ashes and almost extinguished, again takes strength and bursts out with
                     such heat that its force could not be repressed, (even) without fruit, nuts,
                     wine, and the rest.]

…

New College Bursars' Accounts   NC Arch: 7553
mb 8   *(External expenses)*
…
…Paid to Wilson, a harper, 4s.…
…

Episcopal Visitation to New College
Hampshire Record Office: 21M65/A1/26
f 110   *(16 January)* *(Charges against Mr Smith)*

…Then the lord (judge) charged against Smith that he is accustomed to sing indecent songs and that he said he never wished to believe any preacher. And he denies the indecent speech. As to the rest he confesses *(English)*.…

1576–7
Magdalen College Libri Computi   MC Arch: LCE/6
f 236v   *(External expenses)*
…
+   Paid to musicians during Christmas-time and other times   28s
…

f 237
…
Paid to Lord Chandos' trumpeter during the Christmas
holidays   [18]s
…

1577–8
All Souls College Bursars' Accounts   Bodl.: MS. D.D. All Souls c.284
mb 5*   *(2 November 1576–2 November 1577)* *(Various expenses)*
…
And of 2s given to the waits.
And of 2s 6d given to musicians at the feast of All Saints.
…

1578–9
New College Bursars' Accounts   NC Arch: 7556
mb 6   *(Internal costs)*
…
…Paid to trumpeters at the Christmas holidays, 3s 4d.… Paid to musicians on Circumcision Day, 4s.…
…

Trinity College Bursars' Books   TC Arch: I/A/1
f 222   *(25 December–25 March)* *(External expenses)*
...

Paid to a mason working about the window in the hall at
the time of the plays   2s
...

1579–80
Magdalen College Libri Computi   MC Arch: LCE/6
f 260v   *(External expenses)*
...

Paid to musicians in the wake *(or on the eve)* and the
bursars' feast   16s
...

Magdalen College Vice-President's Register   MC Arch: VP1/A1/1
f 42v
...

Likewise at the same time the lord president and the remaining thirteen
seniors, agreeing together, have decided that the probationers are to pay
40s for the players' expenses. The rest, whether fellows or commoners, and
demies, together with the remaining multitude, are to completely satisfy
the remaining expense according to the dignity of (their) persons and
ranks.
...

Trinity College Bursars' Books   TC Arch: I/A/1
f 232v   *(25 December–25 March)* *(External expenses)*
...

Paid to musicians in the Christmas holidays   2s 6d
...

1581–2
Christ Church Treasurers' Account   Bodl.: MS. Top.Oxon c.23
f 46
...

And in expenses about the comedies and tragedies this year
as it appears in the same place   £7
...

Christ Church Computi   ChCh Arch: iii.c.6(b.)
mb 2
…
And in expenses about the comedies and tragedies this year
as it appears in the same place   £7
…

Magdalen College Draft Libri Computi   MC Arch: LCD/2
f 3v   *(External payments)*
…
Paid to musicians at the time of the shows and for the wake
(*or* eve)   13s 4d
…
Paid to musicians at Sir Foxe's direction   10s
…
Paid to musicians at the bursars' feast and for the wake (*or* eve)   13s 4d
…

OUM   ***Laurence Humphrey's Ash Wednesday Sermon (1582)***   STC: 13961
pp 163–5*   *(28 February)*

Laurence Humphrey's
sermon on
avoiding leaven

Mt 16, Mk 8, (and) Lk 12
Jesus said to them – the disciples – 'Take heed and beware of
the leaven of the Pharisees and Sadducees.'

® Comedies and tragedies in Oxford at the end of February

® The truth to be acknowledged

® Augustine

Enough already, enough, listeners, have we amused (our) ears and eyes with theatrical shows; enough have we seen, have we heard of masks (*or* demons) and of ghosts; enough have we indulged comic laughter and tragic sorrow. Now this day, this, as it were, ashen feast demands other behaviour, another regimen, another character from each one of us, in order that, forgetting the things which are behind us, we may proceed forward and do with sincerity those things which are before our eyes and before our hands, so that we may pass from playful things to serious, from comedy to sackcloth, from tragedy to ashes, from the profane to the sacred, from plays to the very search for and training in truth, since our representation of the truth is more brilliant than the entirety of the most ornate stage, and the truth of the Christians more beautiful and lovable than Helen of the Greeks. For if, as is rightly held by your philosophers, contraries are so constituted that you cannot know the one | unless you know the other, now after you have devoted (your) attention for a number of days and nights to plays, pleasant ones indeed and laudably acted, (but) plays nevertheless, greater zeal is most certainly to be placed in the knowledge and contemplation of the truth, and to be placed so that, (as) it

2. The truth to be loved

sufficed only to have seen and understood the former, one is bound to love and embrace the latter. For as there is no desire for the unknown, so, after we know it, it is to be longed for, desired, and loved. But he who loves coldly

3. Ardently

does not love; he who is not fervent, who is not ardent, who does not perish for love, does not love. This force is in love, and this is the nature, this the property of every ardent love, (whether) good (or) bad, considered (or) blind, that unless it is vehement, intense, burning, in the opinion of indeed all lovers, it is judged to be cold love or rather not (love) at all. This I believe you have seen and noted in these your plays, in which the flame of love appears and

Plays in the colleges of St John, Christ (Church), Mary Magdalen

bursts forth in such a way that it seemed to be not love but bitterness, not fervour but fury. Do you not remember that Euclio adored his pot (of gold) thus; Antony, Cleopatra thus; Alexander, his eunuch Bagoas thus; Philarchus, his Phaedra thus; Meleager, his Atlanta; Plautus' Menaechmus, (his) courtesan Erotium; Oedipus also, his mother Jocasta; Julius Caesar, (his) empire thus, so that he imagined that for the sake of a kingdom every binding oath was rather a bond to be violated? And will we not burn with the love of Christian truth whose face and form, if you are pleased to gaze (upon them) for (even) a little while with your mind's eyes, I will undoubtedly excite marvellous yearnings for her?

...

pp 175–6*

...

® 6. The worship of gods

The Jesuits offer worship (and) prayer not to God alone but to other gods. (This) was derived from the Pharisees who worshipped the dead, adorned the sepulchres of dead saints (*or* holy men), and celebrated (their) memory, I and ravaged, with every monstrosity of torture, the bodies of those whose survivors' (*ie*, descendants') opinions their fathers were not able to bear. The Romanists, in order that they might please all the gods for themselves (and) offend none, instituted the feast of All Saints, as it were, a morsel thrown to all, and they turned the Pagan Pantheon at Rome into a memorial of all these (saints). (They were)

Sophocles

terrified, I believe, by the pitiable example of King Oeneus, who when he had made sacrifices to all the gods omitted Diana alone. He, (his) wife, (and his) children paid the penalties of neglected duty as the stage has shown to you in tragedy.

...

pp 180–1*

...

Works pernicious to others

But are (the Jesuits) a general good? Are they useful to the church (and) to others? To whom? Surely not to widows? They devour their homes. Under the pretence of long prayers, confessions, (and) exhortations, they whisper the

Foolish women

In chapter four
of the first book
of Josephus on
the Jewish war

most inane and sophistical old wives' tales to them. Thus the Pharisees (did)
in the gospels and thus was Queen Alexandra made foolish by them and
deranged as if by a Circean potion, so that a marvellous, or rather, monstrous
metamorphosis of a woman occurred – not like Oeneus' three daughters
transformed into birds, as you have heard in the theatre, but a queen changed
into the Pharisees' servant and slave, so that she who had ruled all other
nobles was seen to serve the Pharisees | and do their wishes.

…

Epilogue to Caesar Interfectus   Bodl.: MS. Top.Oxon e.5
p 359*

> The epilogue of *Caesar Interfectus*; how that matter performed in Christ
> Church, Oxford, appeared on the stage; which epilogue was both written
> and spoken there on the stage by Mr Richard Edes. °1582.°

Caesar triumphed over the republic; Brutus over Caesar. The former was able
to do nothing more; the latter desired nothing more. Either the former ought
to have done nothing, or the latter ought to have done less. I have reason to
praise each; I have reason to find fault with each. The Caesar who seized the
republic (acted) wrongly; the Caesar who seized (it) without slaughter and
blood (acted) well. The Brutus who restored liberty (acted) rightly; he who
thought to restore it by Caesar's murder (acted) dishonourably. The temperance of victory drew, so to speak, a veil over the turpitude of the former crime;
unwelcome cruelty spread shadows over the latter deed of glory. The former
conducted himself very well in the worst cause; the latter, very badly in the
best (cause). Nor were there lacking those who, as if by applying torches near,
incited these very illustrious men, the one eager for a kingdom, the other for
liberty. Antony laid a fire under Caesar; Cassius under Brutus. Antony so
desired the royal diadem for Caesar that he handed (it) over; Caesar (so)
refused it that he desired (it). Whatever he wished for, Brutus wished for very
much; (whatever) Cassius (wished for, he wished for) excessively. Certainly
he was indeed the greater leader as Brutus was the greater man; in the one
strength (was) greater; in the other, virtue. You would prefer to have Brutus as
a friend; you would fear Cassius more as an enemy. The former hated tyranny;
the latter a tyrant. A just fortune followed Caesar if we look at his tyranny;
an unjust one if we look at the man. But the immortal gods do not tolerate
tyrants, even the best, and, as if in reward for such great virtue, it was granted
to him that he would foresee his murder, not that he would avoid it.

Gager, Meleager (1592)   STC: 11515
sig A2*

He (Gager) prays for a happy and favourable beginning of the new

year for the most illustrious and noble hero, Robert, earl of Essex,
knight of the golden garter, master of the royal horses.

The eleventh year is now almost gone, most noble earl, since *Meleager* first
came onto the stage, the eighth since it (was performed) again. And the first
time (it appeared) indeed willingly and of its own accord; (but) in the third
year afterward, it appeared a second time, invited and publicly called forth
with the most famous earls of Pembroke and Leicester, at that time our
chancellor, together with the most noble Philip Sidney and a number of
illustrious courtiers sitting there and watching. With what approval it was at
that time received, I do not now remember nor have I ever made much of
it. It was enough praise for *Meleager* – if indeed that was praise – that it was
twice subject to the discrimination of the most sophisticated ears with at any
rate no disgrace of noticeable distaste. Behold, now it goes out for a third
time, not indeed onto the stage but into the light that is your gaze....

1582–3
William Gager's Commonplace Book   BL: MS Additional 22583
f 63v*   (*26 September*) (*List of deans, prebendaries, masters, and students
then at Christ Church*)

...

Mr Leonard Hutten
Whether a comedy is be to written or acted,
    You, Hutten, are able to justly take first place.

...

f 64*

Mr John King
Your raging tragic parts are praiseworthy, King,
    A young man of what great promise? How great a star of the house?
Mr Thomas Crane
The second hope of our Rome and of great native talent,
    A comic role is more suitable for you, Crane.

...

Register of Congregation and Convocation   OUA: NEP/Supra/L
f 19v*   (*17 May*) (*Orders for plays for royal visitors*)

...

Likewise it has been decided that two stages are to be built, one in St Mary's
Church for public disputations, the other in Christ Church for stage plays, and
that no one from the University or anyone else, with foreigners (*or* strangers)
alone being excepted, should presume to mount the stages under penalty of

imprisonment for the space of one month and of a payment of 40s to the University and the proctors....

...

Likewise that stage plays be organized (*or* set forth) in the hall of Christ Church at the discretion of the dean, of the treasurers – or of (at least) one of them – and of the bursar, together with the consent of the vice-chancellor, Doctor Humphrey, Doctor Delabere, Mr Willis, (and) Mr Edes, the proctor, or with the consent of two of the above named, both regarding the argument of the plays and their participants and expenses.

...

Camden, Annales (1615)   STC: 4496
p 344

...

Albert Laski, a Pole, comes to England

Albert Laski, the palatine of Siradia, came to England this summer from Poland, neighbouring Russia, to visit the queen; an erudite man with a (fine) figure, a most promising beard, (and) seemly and very attractive clothing. He, after being received by (the queen) herself and (her) nobles with great honour and luxurious arrangements, and by the academy of Oxford with erudite amusements and various shows, secretly departed after four months, being oppressed by the foreign air.

...

Hannisters' Registers   OCA: A.5.3
f 17*   *(12 August)*

...

William Gibbons, musician, has been admitted into the liberty of this city on the same day and year, and he paid 4s 6d as a fee to the officer/s of the same city and he has been sworn.

...

1583–4
Christ Church Computi   ChCh Arch: iii.c.6(c.)
mb 2

...

And on the expenses of the comedies and tragedies produced
this year   £nil

...

Merton College Register   MCR: 1.3
p 94

...

Comedy performed

On the twenty-first of the same (month) the postmasters performed a comedy by Plautus, which is called *Captivi*, in the lord warden's hall. The lord warden, moreover, donated ⟨...⟩ 20s.

...

The Queen's College Long Roll   QC Arch: 2P161
single mb   *(7 July–7 July)*   *(External expenses)*

...

...Likewise to pipers on the feast of the Circumcision, 18d.... Likewise given to pipers on 2 February, 10s....

...

Register of Congregation and Convocation   OUA: NEP/Supra/L
f 241v*   *(24 July)*   *(Statutes in answer to royal complaints)*

...

3   Likewise it was decided that the vice-chancellor's licence may not be granted to players (*or* entertainers) to hold stage plays within the precinct of the University except by special favour of convocation.

...

City Memorandum Book   OCA: D.5.2
ff [1–1v]*   *(21 December)*

Let all know by the present (bond) that I, William Gibbons, of the city of Oxford, minstrel, am bound and firmly obliged to William Frere of the aforesaid city of Oxford, esquire, in (the amount of) £200 of good and legal English money to be paid to the same William Frere or to his assured attorney, his heirs, or assigns. Indeed, I firmly oblige myself, my heirs, executors, and administrators to make this payment properly and faithfully by the present (bond), sealed with my seal, given on 21 December in the twenty-sixth year of the reign of our Lady Elizabeth, by the grace of God, queen of England, France, and Ireland, defender of the faith, etc.

1584–5
Magdalen College Draft Libri Computi   MC Arch: LCD/2
f 20v col 1*   *(Charges of external payments)*

...

Paid for stage plays in the coming of the earl of Leicester	£3 19s 5d
Paid for the banquet in the coming of the same (earl)	£10

...

The Queen's College Long Roll   QC Arch: 2P162
single mb*   *(7 July–7 July) (External expenses)*

...

...Likewise given to Morris on the feast of Christ's Circumcision, 12d. Likewise given to pipers at the provost's command, 10s....

...

Trinity College Bursars' Books   TC Arch: I/A/1
f 276   *(25 December–25 March) (External expenses)*

...

Paid for plays   20s

...

Register of Congregation and Convocation   OUA: NEP/Supra/L
f 282v*   *(Visit of Lord Leicester, chancellor)*

...

At 1 PM on the aforesaid day, venerable men, appointed by the venerable house of convocation, according to the appointment entrusted to them, met in the house of the venerable man, Doctor Underhill, the vice-chancellor, and by common consent decided that sermons and debates should be held in each faculty and also that stage plays (should be held) at Christ Church and Magdalen College, for the expenses of which they will allow £20 to be divided equally between the said colleges.

...

1585–6
Exeter College Rectors' Accounts   EC Arch: A.II.9
f 105*   *(Memorandum)*

...Toward the expenses of the play in our hall, 10s....

The Queen's College Long Roll   QC Arch: 2P163
single mb   *(7 July–7 July) (External costs)*

...

...Likewise to musicians on 2 February, 12d....

...

1586–7
Magdalen College Draft Libri Computi   MC Arch: LCD/2
f 36v col 1   *(Charges of external payments)*

...

Paid to pipers on the bursars' feast   6s 8d

...

The Queen's College Long Roll   QC Arch: 2P164
single mb   *(7 July–7 July) (External costs)*

...

...Likewise to Morris, a piper, on the feast of the Circumcision, 12d....

...

1587–8
Vice-Chancellors' Accounts   OUA: WP/β/21(4)
p 111   *(17 July–16 July) (Extraordinary expenses)*

...

Paid to the earl of Leicester's players (*or* entertainers) so that they
would depart with their plays (*or* pastimes) without greater trouble
to the University   20s
Paid to the most honoured Lord Howard's players (*or* entertainers)   20s

...

1588–9
Magdalen College Libri Computi   MC Arch: LCE/7
f 15   *(Charges of external payments)*

...

To musicians on the bursars' feast   6s 8d

...

Vice-Chancellors' Accounts   OUA: WP/β/21(4)
p 114   *(10 July 1588–16 July 1589) (Extraordinary expenses)*

...

Paid to players (*or* entertainers) so that they would not perform
unseemly plays (*or* pastimes) within the University   *(blank)*

...

Robert Ashley's Autobiography   BL: MS Sloane 2131
ff [3–3v]*

...

...When I was just twenty-two years old and in the month of December, since
the Christmas holidays were on the point of being celebrated and a solemn
custom had developed in (my) college that someone would be elected out of
the outstanding young men among the fellows whom the rest would revere
and exalt as a lord with proclamations and praises, by whose commands, as
of a prince, would the rest of the crowd be ruled in triumphs, set dances, and
round dances, I was hailed as the lord and prince of the youth by reason of the
hope and expectation which I had aroused (in them) regarding myself. They
carry me on their shoulders in that cloistered kingdom, place me on a throne,
honour (and) grace me with encomia and speeches. I endeavour to acknowledge

with a grateful spirit the partiality of such ardent young men toward me, to
regard myself with modesty and humility, and to make much of their judgment
and estimation of me, as | it was the custom to indicate in a brief speech.
After that, I rule, I triumph.

...

1589–90
Magdalen College Draft Libri Computi   MC Arch: LCD/2
f 44v col 2   *(Charges of external payments)*
...
Paid to pipers on the bursars' feast   6s 8d
...

The Queen's College Long Roll   QC Arch: 2P165
single mb   *(7 July–7 July)*   *(External costs)*
...
...Likewise to Morris and his fellow, a piper, on the feast of the Circumcision, 12d....
...

Vice-Chancellors' Accounts   OUA: WP/β/21(4)
p 116   *(16 July–10 July)*   *(Extraordinary expenses)*
...
Paid to the queen's players (*or* entertainers) so that they would
leave the University without annoyance   20s 0 0
...

1590–1
Magdalen College Libri Computi   MC Arch: LCE/7
f 26v   *(Charges of external expenses)*
...
x   Paid for the binding of a book of poems presented to the queen   10s
...

f 27
...
Paid to pipers on the bursars' feast   6s 8d
...

Merton College Bursars' Accounts   MCR: 3.1
f 24v   *(20 November–19 March)*   *(External expenses)*
...
...To musicians of Oxford by agreement, 6s 8d....

Vice-Chancellors' Accounts   OUA: WP/β/21(4)
p 118   *(16 July–16 July) (Extraordinary expenses)*

…

Paid by Dr Edes, the vice-chancellor's deputy, to some
players (*or* entertainers) so that they would leave the
University without disturbance and noise   10s 0

…

1591–2
Christ Church Computi   ChCh Arch: iii.c.6(f.)
mb 2

…

And on the expenses of the comedies and tragedies held
this year as it appears in the same (bill)   £nil

…

Exeter College Rectors' Accounts   EC Arch: A.II.9
f 134v   *(1 November–1 November)*

…

Likewise of payments to the royal trumpeters when they came to the college,
for the honour of the college, 20s.

…

Magdalen College Libri Computi   MC Arch: LCE/7
f 38v   *(Charges of external payments)*

…

To Lord Howard's pipers   0 6 8

…

For lamps for the plays on the feast of Epiphany   0 4 0

…

To pipers on the bursars' feast   0 5 0
For the college's share in the lady queen's arrival   18 10s

…

Merton College Register   MCR: 1.3
p 158*

…

The queen's coming to the University

At this time we received a message that the queen was going to visit our
University in the month of September. Very many deliberations were held
both publicly and privately regarding the courtesy to be offered most
abundantly to the queen's majesty both by the University and by each college,
in proportion to our wealth. For this reason the vice-chancellor asked each
college to contribute specific sums of money, in proportion to (their) property

Taxation of the colleges

and revenues, to the common expenditures to be incurred by the University. Moreover, the prefects and fellows of the colleges establish that for each £100 of past revenue, 20s be paid to the University for the common use. Moreover, the property of each college had been reported to the vice-chancellor in this way: *(English)*

Allowance made to the warden for two courses for the courtiers' meals

It is particularly decided by us that, while (her) royal majesty is staying here, the warden shall cause two courses, properly arranged, to be prepared for each meal to oblige the courtiers of the nobility. One-third of the expenses incurred in this preparation is paid by the warden, the remaining two-thirds by the college. The tenants at farm from Kibworth, Barkby, Cuxham, Ibstone, Wolford, (and) Stratton St Margaret arranged these meals with various kinds of victuals.

...

On 22 September the queen came to the university; she departed on the twenty-eighth.

Dinner for the royal counsellors and nobles put on by the college, and disputations held

On 25 September, after more private meetings for (her) royal majesty, all the nobles and every lord, earl, (and) baron who was in hall come to a dinner having been invited by us, accompanied by all the famous courtiers of note, and all these, sixty in number, sitting in the high hall at one table, which is extended through the entire hall, partake of a banquet quite elegantly and magnificently prepared. When dinner was finished disputations were held, with Mr Cuff, Regius Professor of the Greek language, responding; Messrs Frenche, Trafford, Wilkynson, (and) Mason objecting; and Mr Savile, the proctor at that time, moderating. The question: whether disagreements among the citizens are useful to the state. When the disputations regarding matters pertaining to the state were finished, the royal counsellors withdraw with the ambassador of France, who was there at the feast at the same time, bound for Mr Colmer's chamber.

The queen makes a speech to the members of the University

When the leading men of the University and others assigned to offer the exercises had been assembled, the queen made a speech upon her departure, an example of which is found on page 160.

Oriel College Treasurers' Accounts OC Arch: S I.C.1
f 49 *(External expenses)*
...

Likewise to the queen's trumpeters 10s
...

f 49v
...

Likewise to the University at the queen's arrival £3
...

The Queen's College Long Roll   QC Arch: 2P167
single mb   *(7 July–7 July)* *(External costs)*

…

…Likewise to the earl of Cumberland's trumpeters by order of the provost, 5s…. Likewise to Morris and his sons, pipers, on Circumcision Day, 2s. Likewise to pipers on the day next after the Purification of the Blessed Virgin (Mary), 10s…. Likewise to trumpeters, 2s….

…

Vice-Chancellors' Accounts   OUA: WP/β/21(4)
p 119   *(16 July–13 July)* *(Extraordinary expenses)*

…

Paid to certain players (*or* entertainers) so that
they would leave the University without noise
and annoyance   10s

1592–3
Magdalen College Libri Computi   MC Arch: LCE/7
f 48   *(External payments)*

…

To pipers on the bursars' feast   6s 8d

…

To trumpeters at various times   12s

…

Merton College Bursars' Accounts   MCR: 3.1
f 33v   *(28 July–24 November 1592)* *(External expenses)*

…

…To royal trumpeters by the warden's command, 20s….

…

The Queen's College Long Rolls   QC Arch: LRA
f 3   *(7 July–7 July)* *(External costs)*

…

…Likewise to royal trumpeters by the provost's command, 20s.

…

Likewise to certain trumpeters by the provost's command, 3s 4d. Likewise to pipers from Oxford, 10s….

…

Vice-Chancellors' Accounts   OUA: WP/β/21(4)

p 122   *(13 July 1592–17 July 1593)* *(Extraordinary expenses)*

…

Paid to players (*or* entertainers) of various nobles so
that they would leave the University without noise
and annoyance   20s

…

Camden, Tomus Alter Annalium (1627)   STC: 4496.5

p 53

…

® The queen visits the University of Oxford

The queen, having gone into the country for the summer months,
made her way through Oxford where, delighted by the most refined
speeches, stage plays, (and) learned disputations, she remained for a
number of days, received by Buckhurst, the chancellor of the University, with lavish banquets. While departing she bid farewell in a Latin
speech, in which she professed that she placed (her) very well-known
love for the members of the University far before all the other delights,
even the most charming. For this she gave abundant thanks, made a
prayer, and gave advice. (Her) prayer was that she desired nothing
more than the well-being of the whole realm with the most prosperous
security and honour, and so also (that) the University, as much as any
other light of the realm, would daily shine more bright and flourish for
eternity. (Her) advice was that they should worship God above all, not
according to certain people's refined ingenuity, but according to the
laws of God and of the realm; (that) they should not go before the laws,
but follow them; (that) they should not dispute whether better (laws)
could be prescribed, but observe those which have been prescribed, obey
their superiors, and finally embrace each other in brotherly respect and
harmony.

…

1593–4

Magdalen College Libri Computi   MC Arch: LCE/7

f 57   *(Charges of external payments)*

…

To pipers on the bursars' feast   0 5 0

…

To trumpeters in Christmas-time   [5] 5 0

…

Merton College Bursars' Accounts   MCR: 3.1
f 40   *(23 November–22 March)* *(External expenses)*
...
...To musicians by agreement, 6s 8d....
...

The Queen's College Long Rolls   QC Arch: LRA
f 5 col 2   *(7 July–7 July)* *(External payments)*
...
Likewise to pipers from Oxford   10s
Likewise to trumpeters by order of Mr Airay, deputy   3s 4d
...

1594–5
Magdalen College Libri Computi   MC Arch: LCE/7
f 68   *(Internal payments)*
...
To pipers on the bursars' feast   0 5s 0
...

Merton College Bursars' Accounts   MCR: 3.1
f 44   *(22 November–21 March)* *(External expenses)*
...
...To musicians by agreement, 6s 8d....
...

The Queen's College Long Rolls   QC Arch: LRA
f 7 col 1   *(7 July–7 July)* *(External expenses)*
...
Likewise given to a musician on 1 January   2s
...
Likewise given to trumpeters from Oxford   10s
...

St John's College Computus Hebdomalis   SJC Arch: Acc.v.E.1
f 19v   *(17–23 February)*
...
Bestowed for musicians, 36s 6d.
...

Vice-Chancellors' Accounts   OUA: WP/β/21(4)
p 124   *(12 July 1594–5 August 1595)* *(Extraordinary expenses)*

Paid to the lady queen's players *(or* entertainers) so that they
would leave the University without noise and trouble   20s
...
Paid to Lord Morley's players *(or* entertainers) so that they
would leave the University without noise and trouble   10s
...

1595–6
Magdalen College Libri Computi   MC Arch: LCE/7
f 79   *(Internal and external payments)*
...
Paid to Buckner, a musician, on the bursars' feast   5s
...

Merton College Bursars' Accounts   MCR: 3.1
f 48v   *(21 November–19 March)* *(External expenses)*
...
...To musicians by agreement, 6s 8d....
...

The Queen's College Long Rolls   QC Arch: LRA
f 8v col 2   *(7 July–7 July)* *(External expenses)*
...
Likewise to pipers on the feast of the Circumcision   2s
Likewise to pipers from Oxford on 26 January   10s
...

Vice-Chancellors' Accounts   OUA: WP/β/21(4)
p 128   *(5 August–17 July)* *(Extraordinary expenses)*

Paid to the lady queen's players *(or* entertainers) so that they
would abstain from public activity *(or* performance)   0
...

1596–7
Magdalen College Libri Computi   MC Arch: LCE/7
f 91v   *(Internal and external payments)*
...
To pipers on the bursars' feast   5s
...

Merton College Bursars' Accounts   MCR: 3.1
f 53   *(19 November–18 March)*   *(External expenses)*

...

...To musicians by agreement, 6s 8d....

The Queen's College Long Rolls   QC Arch: LRA
f 11v col 2   *(7 July–7 July)*   *(External expenses)*

...

Likewise to Morris and other fiddlers   2s
Likewise to pipers from Oxford   10s

...

Vice-Chancellors' Accounts   OUA: WP/β/21(4)
p 129   *(17 July–14 July)*   *(Extraordinary expenses)*

...

Paid to certain players (*or* entertainers) so that they would
leave the University without noise   20s

Hannisters' Registers   OCA: L.5.1
f 245v*

...

George Buckner, musician, has been admitted to the liberty of the aforesaid
20s   city on the said 24 November in the aforesaid thirty-ninth year. And he paid
20s to the use of the said city and 4s 6d for the officer's/officers' fee, and he
was sworn, etc.

Leonard Major, musician, has been admitted to the liberty of the aforesaid
city on the same 24 November in the aforesaid thirty-ninth year. And he paid
20s to the use of the said city and 4s 6d for the officer's/officers' fee, and he
was sworn, etc.

...

1597–8
Christ Church Computi   ChCh Arch: iii.c.7(a.)
mb 4*

...

And on the expenses of the comedies and tragedies
produced this year   £nil

...

Magdalen College Libri Computi   MC Arch: LCE/7
f 105   *(Internal and external payments)*
...
To pipers on the bursars' feast   0 5s 0
...

Merton College Bursars' Accounts   MCR: 3.1
f 59v   *(18 November–24 March) (External expenses)*

...To musicians by agreement, 6s 8d....
...

New College Bursars' Accounts   NC Arch: 7586
mb 6   *(Internal expenses)*
...
...Paid to George Buckner, a musician, 6s 8d....
...

The Queen's College Long Rolls   QC Arch: LRA
f 14 col 1   *(7 July–7 July) (External expenses)*
...
Likewise on 2 January to Morris, a fiddler   2s
...
Likewise on 16 February to pipers from Oxford   10s
...

St John's College Computus Hebdomalis   SJC Arch: Acc.v.E.1
f 57v   *(16–22 January)*
...
A tragedy of Astiages
Acted after thirty years in
the president's house
...

f 58   *(23–9 January)*
...
The same tragedy
of Astiages performed publicly
in the hall
...

f 59   *(27 February–5 March)*
…
Bestowed for musicians   21s 9d
and for others   5s 6d
…

1598
Hentzner's Travels in England   Hentzner: *Itinerarium*
p 214

…The remains of a fortification, quite large but entirely ruined, are seen
at an intersection (*or* in an out-of-the-way place) in the town. We were
received at supper with very excellent music made with various and diverse
instruments.
…

1598–9
Christ Church Computi   ChCh Arch: iii.c.7(b.)
mb 3d
…
And on the expenses of the comedies and tragedies
produced this year   £nil
…

Magdalen College Draft Libri Computi   MC Arch: LCD/2
f 91 col 1   *(Charges of internal and external payments)*
…
To pipers on the bursars' feast   5s
…

Merton College Bursars' Accounts   MCR: 3.1
f 65v   *(24 November–23 March)* *(External expenses)*

…To musicians by agreement, 6s 8d.…
…

The Queen's College Long Rolls   QC Arch: LRA
f 16 col 1   *(7 July–7 July)* *(External expenses)*
…
Likewise to town fiddlers   10s
…

St John's College Computus Hebdomalis   SJC Arch: Acc.v.E.2
f 5v   *(15–21 January)*

...

Tenants with   Bestowed for shows   22d
New Year's gift
...

f 7v   *(5–11 March)*

...

Paid for a comedy and a tragedy performed by scholars
and fellows   54s

Vice-Chancellors' Accounts   OUA: WP/β/21(4)
p 134   *(18 July–17 July)* *(Extraordinary expenses)*

...

Paid to royal players (*or* entertainers) and others in order that
they would leave the University without noise and trouble   25s

...

1599–1600
All Souls College Bursars' Accounts   Bodl.: MS. D.D. All Souls c.287
mb 11   *(2 November–2 November)* *(Rewards)*

...

And of 6s to trumpeters at various times.

...

Magdalen College Libri Computi   MC Arch: LCE/7
f 117v*   *(Internal and external expenses)*

...

To trumpeters of the earls of Southampton and Nottingham
in reward   0 6s

...

To pipers on the bursars' feast   0 5s

...

Merton College Bursars' Accounts   MCR: 3.1
f 70v   *(23 November–21 March)* *(External expenses)*

...

...To musicians by agreement, 6s 8d....

...

New College Bursars' Accounts   NC Arch: 7588
mb 7   *(Internal expenses)*

...

...Paid to trumpeters in reward, 4s....

...

Oriel College Treasurers' Accounts   OC Arch: S I.C.1
f 93   *(Internal expenses)*

...

Likewise to Lord Mountjoy's trumpeters on Christmas
by agreement   5s

...

The Queen's College Long Rolls   QC Arch: LRA
f 18 col 1   *(7 July–7 July) (External expenses)*

...

29 December	Likewise handed over to trumpeters	2s
31 December	Likewise to clarioners	2s
	...	
1 January	Likewise to Morris, a fiddler	2s
	...	
17 January	Likewise to pipers from Oxford	10s

...

St John's College Computus Hebdomalis   SJC Arch: Acc.v.E.2
f 18v   *(7–13 January)*

...

And for trumpeters   2s 6d

...

f 23   *(5–11 May)*

...

Bestowed for (Lord) Monteagle's trumpeters   2s

...

Baron Waldstein's Diary   Biblioteca Apostolica Vaticana: Reg. lat. 666
f 167*   *(12 July)*

...

    Saturday, 22 July
The beginning of the Oxford commencement: in the morning lectures were

held by each professor. We were present at the theology lecture of a certain Holland, a very learned man. After midday theological disputations and outstanding declamations on travel (are held). The Windischgraetzes join us, with whom we travel by boat in the evening with music.

...

AC   ***Proceedings Regarding George Buckner***   Bodl.: MS. Twyne-Langbaine 3
ff 121–1v*   *(20 August)*

Proceeding of the court held before Thomas Edwards and Robert Master the vice-chancellor's deputies

...

®*(English)*   Proceedings concerning the goods of George Buckner, a suicide, taken from the Acta Book, specifically among the Acta of Trinity term, AD 1599, and the Acta of Michaelmas term of the same year, in the long vacation in the month of August.

...

Today and in this place the said venerable men, Thomas Edwards and Robert Master, deputies of the aforesaid venerable man, going to the house of a certain George Buckner, a suicide, in the name of the University of Oxford took possession of (a) house or a tenement in the parish of St Mary Magdalen outside the North Gate of the city of Oxford, and of all and each of the goods, rightful possessions, and loans which were in the said house or tenement, or otherwise belonging to the same George Buckner during the time of his life and death as forfeit to the University and pertaining to the same (University) by reason of (its) privileges and charters, by which every and each of the goods, rightful possessions, and loans of any persons dwelling within the precinct of the aforesaid University who do violence to themselves and kill themselves are granted to the said University. | In their judgment, since the aforesaid George did violence unto himself and was a suicide in AD 1598 in the month of January last past, the aforesaid venerable men, deputies of the aforesaid Thomas Thornton, entering into the vacant possession of the same house and tenement of the late George aforesaid, took (it) in the above name (*ie*, of the University). And moreover, in the name of (his) goods, rightful possessions, and loans, and of (their) possession of the same, they took from the hand of Ursula Buckner, widow of the aforesaid George *(English)*.

In the presence of Mr Thomas Frenche, notary public, and John Wodson ⟨...⟩ of the said University

(English)

...

1600–1

Christ Church Computi   ChCh Arch: iii.c.7(c.)
mb 3d

...

And on the expenses of the comedies and tragedies
produced this year   £nil

...

Magdalen College Libri Computi   MC Arch: LCE/7
f 130*   *(Internal and external payments)*

...

To royal trumpeters, 20s, to Lord Compton's
(trumpeters), 5s   £1 5s

...

To musicians on the bursars' feast   0 5s
To the steward for the duke of Bavaria's feast by the bill   £10 10s 9d

...

Merton College Bursars' Accounts   MCR: 3.1
f 76   *(21 November–20 March)* *(External expenses)*
...

...To musicians by agreement, 6s 8d....

New College Bursars' Accounts   NC Arch: 7590
mb 5*   *(24 June–29 September)*

...Paid to trumpeters in reward, 2s 5s.
...

The Queen's College Long Rolls   QC Arch: LRA
f 19v col 2   *(7 July–7 July)* *(External expenses)*
...

26 December   To trumpeters by order of the provost   2s 6d
...

1 January   To Morris, a piper   18d
29 January   To pipers from Oxford   10s
...

St John's College Computus Hebdomalis   SJC Arch: Acc.v.E.2
f 31v   *(5–11 January)*

...

An interlude upon the new year's first day by scholars and fellows while dining
(*or* among the diners).

f 33   *(16–22 February)*
...
Bestowed for lesser (*ie*, in skill *or* in importance) pipers   21s 4d
...

f 33v   *(23 February–1 March)*
...
(English)
Bestowed for greater (*ie*, in skill *or* in importance) pipers   37s [⟨.⟩d]
...

1601–2
Christ Church Computi   ChCh Arch: iii.c.7(d.)
mb 3*
...
And on the expenses of comedies and tragedies produced this year   £nil
...

Magdalen College Libri Computi   MC Arch: LCE/7
f 141   *(Internal and external payments)*
...
To musicians on the bursars' feast   0 5s 0
...

Merton College Bursars' Accounts   MCR: 3.1
f 81v   *(20 November–19 March)* *(External expenses)*
...
...To musicians by agreement, 6s 8d....

The Queen's College Long Rolls   QC Arch: LRA
f 21v col 2   *(7 July–7 July)* *(External expenses)*
...
Likewise to the queen's trumpeters   20s
...

28 January   Likewise to pipers from Oxford   10s
             Likewise to Morris, a piper   18d
...

1602–3
Exeter College Rectors' Accounts   EC Arch: A.II.9
f 179v   *(1 November–1 November)*
...
Likewise of payments and a gift given to royal trumpeters   20s
...

Magdalen College Libri Computi   MC Arch: LCE/7
f 151v*   *(Internal and external payments)*

...

To Sir Richard Lucy's trumpeters in reward   0 6s 0

...

Merton College Bursars' Accounts   MCR: 3.1
f 86v   *(19 November–18 March)* *(External expenses)*

...

...To musicians by agreement, 6s 8d....

Merton College Register   MCR: 1.3
p 202

...

At the same time it was agreed that the bursar in the customary manner
would pay 6s 8d to the pipers who pipe for us in the morning.

...

New College Bursars' Accounts   NC Arch: 7593
mb 4*   *(25 December–25 March)* *(Internal expenses)*

...

...Paid to trumpeters, 3s.... Paid to Leonard and (his) fellows, musicians,
6s 8d....

(24 June–29 September)
...Paid to trumpeters in reward   10s

...

The Queen's College Long Rolls   QC Arch: LRA
f 23v col 1*   *(7 July–7 July)* *(External expenses)*

...

Likewise to Morris, a piper   18d

...

Likewise to pipers of Oxford   10s

...

St John's College Computus Hebdomalis   SJC Arch: Acc.v.E.2
f 60v   *(14–20 February)*

...

Given to greater (*ie,* in skill *or* in importance) pipers, 42s 6d.

...

1603–4
Christ Church Computi   ChCh Arch: iii.c.7(e.)
mb 3*

...

And on the expenses of comedies and tragedies produced
this year   £nil

...

Magdalen College Libri Computi   MC Arch: LCE/7
f 163   *(Internal and external payments)*

...

To pipers on the bursars' feast   0 5s

...

Merton College Bursars' Accounts   MCR: 3.1
f 93   *(18 November–23 March)* *(External expenses)*

...To musicians by agreement, 6s 8d....

...

Merton College Register   MCR: 1.3
p 209

...

Granted to   Then also it was agreed there that the bursar should bestow 6s 8d upon
musicians   the common musicians of the University and of the town, according to the
             usual custom.

...

New College Bursars' Accounts   NC Arch: 7595
mb 5   *(25 December–25 March)* *(Internal expenses)*

...Paid to town musicians, 6s 8d....

...

The Queen's College Long Rolls   QC Arch: LRA
f 25v col 1*   *(7 July–7 July)* *(External expenses)*

...

Likewise to Morris, a piper   18d
Likewise to pipers from Oxford   10s

...

St John's College Computus Hebdomalis   SJC Arch: Acc.v.E.2
f 72v   *(16–22 January)*

…

For pipers   5s 2d

…

f 73v   *(20–6 February)*

…

(English)
Bestowed for the expenses on the tragedy and the musicians
for the whole year   £3 7s 5d
apart from coin.
Whereof 43s were paid to musicians, apart from 9s 6d in coin.

Vice-Chancellors' Accounts   OUA: WP/β/21(4)
p 148   *(23 July–14 July)* *(Extraordinary expenses)*

…

Paid to royal trumpeters being at Woodstock   20s

…

p 149

…

Paid to the queen's players (*or* entertainers) so that
they would leave without noise   40s

…

1604–5
Christ Church Treasurers' Accounts   ChCh Arch: iii.c.1
f 124

…

And on the expenses of comedies and tragedies produced this year   £nil

…

Exeter College Rectors' Accounts   EC Arch: A.II.9
f 187v   *(1 November–1 November)*

…

Likewise of 10s given to royal trumpeters

…

Magdalen College Libri Computi   MC Arch: LCE/7
f 170 col 1   *(Internal and external payments)*

…

To trumpeters of Sir William Monson   0 6s 0d

To trumpeters of Lord Cromwell, in reward | 0 5s 0

…

To the lord vice-chancellor, Doctor Abbot, for
the college's contribution at the coming of
the king | £36 0 0

…

For two pairs of gloves for the prince and for
one (pair) for the lord chancellor of Oxford | £10 15s 0

…

To the king's and the prince's musicians
in reward | £2 0 0
To the prince's yeomen in reward | £2 0 0

…

To Mr Castilion producing a comedy at the
coming of the prince (and) for candles and
drink at the time of the repetition (*or* rehearsal) | 0 10s 0

…

col 2

…

To Dr Hood bringing globes (*or* bowls) from the
most noble lady, Lady Arabella, in reward | £2 0 0
To Billingsley for gloves given to Lady Arabella | £2 10s 0
To musicians on the bursars' feast | 0 5s 0

…

Merton College Bursars' Accounts MCR: 3.1
f 98v *(23 November–22 March) (External expenses)*

…

…To the common musicians by agreement, 6s 8d….

…

New College Bursars' Accounts NC Arch: 7596
mb 4 *(25 December–25 March) (Internal expenses)*

…Paid to the town musicians, 6s 8d….

(25 March–24 June) (External expenses)

…

Paid to royal trumpeters, 10s….

…

Oriel College Treasurers' Accounts   OC Arch: S 1.C.1
f 119   *(External expenses)*
...

Likewise to the vice-chancellor for expenditures on the
coming of the king, made according to the decree of the
University and by the agreement of the provost and college   £6
...

f 120v   *(Internal expenses)*

Likewise to royal trumpeters   10s
...

The Queen's College Long Rolls   QC Arch: LRA
f 27 col 2   *(7 July–7 July)* *(Internal expenses)*
...
25 December   Likewise to the piper, Morris   2s
...

f 27v col 1
...
3 July   Likewise delivered for a trumpet and (its) carriage from
London and (its) repair   28s
...

f 28 col 1*   *(External expenses)*
...
Likewise to pipers from Oxford   10s
Likewise to trumpeters from Barnard Castle   3s
Likewise to three clarioners   3s
...

f 30 col 2*   *(7 July 1605–7 July 1606)*
...
1 August   Likewise delivered to the vice-chancellor at the coming
of (our) most serene king   £7 16s
...
Likewise to six clarioners   3s
...
25 (August)   Likewise delivered for two pairs of gloves for (our) most
serene queen   £14 10s
...
Likewise to (our) most serene king's trumpeters   20s
...

St John's College Computus Hebdomalis   SJC Arch: Acc.v.E.4
f 7   *(25 February–3 March)*
…
Bestowed for the tragedy of Lucretia, £3 17s 8d, apart from 22s 4d paid
in coin.
   In decrements, 11s 9½d
…

(4–10 March)
Bestowed for musicians for the whole year and for two nights   £3 2s
Whereof paid to musicians   £3
…
apart from 11s 6d in coin given to those musicians
…
   In decrements, 32s 9¾d

f 13   *(12–18 August)*
…
Levied upon the fellows individually by decree of convocation in the
coming of the king, namely, upon a knight's son, 3s 4d; upon an esquire's
son, 20d; upon a gentleman's (son), 12d; upon a commoner's (son), 4d;
in total 53s 4d.
Whereof paid to the University °by G.R.°, 40s, and by the college, £5.
…

f 13v   *(2–8 September)*
…
For decrements, £35 14s
(English)

Vice-Chancellors' Accounts   OUA: WP/β/21(4)
p 152   *(14 July 1604–17 July 1605)*   *(Extraordinary expenses)*
…
Paid to royal trumpeters being at Woodstock   20s
…

Letters of the Venetian Ambassador Nicolò Molen to the Doge
Archivio di Stato: Senato, dispacci ambasciatori Inghilterra, filza IV
f 72   *(10 August)*
…
On Tuesday, at eight in the morning, the second of the present (month), I
went to see His Majesty at Theobalds, Lord Cecil's place, as ordered....

f 72v

...the king ... then proceeded to discuss his trip with me and invited me
to go to Oxford, which is a University town where masters and scholars
are preparing several disputations and comedies to entertain His Majesty,
who despite not having visited the city for some time, nevertheless has the
pleasure of being received with great joy, solemnity, and all requisites of
honour....

f 82   *(14 September)*

...

In these past few days I have been in Oxford on His Majesty's invitation,
which I told Your Serenity in my other (letters) I had to do. The king, along
with the queen, prince, and the entire court, entered the city with great pomp
on Tuesday, the sixth of the current (month), where he stayed for three days,
which were entirely filled with comedies in the evening after dinner and with
various disputations in the daytime....

Wake, Rex Platonicus (1607)   STC: 24939
pp 18-19*   *(27 August)*
...

An ancient story, well known among the Scottish Britons, concerning
the royal lineage, offered an opportunity for the play. It tells that once three
sibyls encountered two Scottish nobles, Macbeth and Banquo, and predicted
that the former would be a king but would beget no king; the latter would
not be a king but would beget many kings. Events have confirmed the truth
of the prophecy, for the most powerful James is descended from Banquo's
stock. Three young men, cleverly dressed in sibyls' costumes, coming from |
the college and singing charming songs by turns, declare to the king that
they are those sibyls who had once predicted reigns for Banquo's offspring,
and that they now appear again to predict with the same truth of prophecy
for James that he is now, and will be for a long time, the most fortunate
king of Britain and the father of many kings, so that the British crown will
never lack an heir from Banquo's offspring. Then softly singing threefold
sweet (words) of blessings in a threefold turn of song to the three princes,
and begging pardon because the students of the college of St John, who
was the forerunner of Christ, had, with a forerunner's greeting, preceded
the students of Christ Church where the king was then going, they left the
princes, who were delighted with this little pretence. The whole crowd
of bystanders, expressing their desire for the happy fulfilment of these
predictions with vows and prayers, followed them from there as far as the
city's North Gate.

...

pp 45–8*

…

i A great part of this (wall at Christ Church) fell down when the Lady Elizabeth attended a show here in the year 1566, from the onrush and weight of a
countless multitude. By its collapse very many people were killed (and) the
limbs of many others were crushed pitiably, although for the whole duration
of the present royal visit, God so willing, no one either here or anywhere
suffered even the slightest wound, which is unusual in so great a crowd. †

But to move on according to plan, while these things are being finished in
Magdalen College, other labour calls members of the University eager for the-
atrical preparation, where they were going to receive the princes after dinner. |
A site for the stage had been provided, the hall of Christ Church, because it
(was) both the most spacious and close to the royal lodgings. For they both[i]
have a common gateway, to which one climbs by a double flight of very wide
steps, that holds the most expert architects astonished on account of the lofty
size of the tower and arches resting on a single column. It is not clear whether
the interior of the hall is more ample in the extent of its site because of the
founder's generosity or the artisans' skill. The eighteen tall windows filled
with painted work; the circle of the whole hall above,

k The book I of
Manilius
[k](like) the zodiac, shines in a vast circle, glittering with the bands,
as it were unending, of sculpted shields of the heraldic art; hangings from the
painted ceiling gilded at threefold intervals (and) glowing with a variety of
every emblem – these things, (even) if there had not been other shows here,
would have been enough of a show. The stage occupied the upper part of the
hall, (and) its proscenium, gently sloping, came to an end in a level surface –
it lent much dignity to the actors' departure as if they were coming down
a mountain. Embroidered hangings and stage houses were artfully prepared
with devices for the variety of every setting and action, so that the appearance
of the whole stage would suddenly become new, to the amazement of all, not
only for the change for each show each day but also for the change of scene in
one and the same play. The devices by which all these things were concealed
over a large area had been both hung and painted as if for (ie, to represent)
moving clouds by a very artful hand, so that you would suppose them fleeing
at once upon the imminent arrival of (our) British sun (ie, King James) and so
that you would believe you were looking at the sky itself, if you did not soon
behold the moon and stars (ie, Queen Anne and her retinue) glittering below.
From the lowest floorboards of the hall | to the highest apex of the panelled
ceiling, wedge-shaped blocks of seats are fixed in a large circle to the walls. In
the midst of the auditorium, a royal throne surrounded by lattice-work is set
up for the princes, which the places of noblemen surround on either side; the
remainder, the space between the throne and the stage, an area set apart for
noblewomen, is a little lower down. When the king and queen had entered
together with Prince Henry – who drove there after dinner in a coach – and

while an incredible multitude of all estates was filling up the wedge-shaped blocks of seats and the auditorium − in such a way that the spectators themselves were part of the show − the witty comedy *Vertumnus* is put on to cheer the princes by students of the same college, who were always regarded as chief both in the tragic buskin and the comic slipper. In this (comedy) three rivals vie for Pomona's love: Chaerilus, a vain poet; Sylvanus, a great drinker; and Vertumnus. He ensnares her by a trick of many forms, dressing up first as a fisherman, then a courtier, and thirdly as a soldier, to trick her into love. But by no means is his prayer answered by these tricks. Finally he ceases to be a man, and as a woman assails a woman. And in that guise he awakens marvellous love for him in Pomona. Having done that he reveals himself and the real Vertumnus possesses the real Pomona.

Since no noble delight by which either the ears or eyes could desire to be soothed was absent from this play − which learned men will conjecture from its very argument and will easily understand if it should be printed, which is hoped for − then nothing could be more pleasing to all the members of the University and courtiers than that they should observe by such obvious signs that small streams of joy were flowing back in turn into the hearts − whence, God willing, all our joys pour forth. For to those who do not understand the great troubles of kings, (their) dispositions appear dull, but l anyone would understand that those people understand nothing who do not understand that their (*ie*, kings') consolations and, so to speak, diversions from such great troubles are necessary.

One (event), however, although it occurred by chance, should not be passed over. When a certain number of doves were released from a net, as the play required,

> You observe how doves come to shining roofs

one of them sought out the queen − truly a bright-shining and dovelike breast − and settled on her chair, as I have heard many asserting doves (do), either as devised with skill, like Archytas', or taught by skill, ^klike Muhammad's.

Why go on? Everything pleased everybody, except those who did not understand or were seeking sleep rather than wit. However, after the king, always wakeful in serious matters (and) also (wakeful) now for the plays, had commended everything with a fine clapping of his hands and by the testimony of his voice − the queen and the prince and the rest then follow him (in this) − everyone departs to refresh their eyes for tomorrow's shows for it was the middle of the night.

pp 78−9   *(28 August)*
...

 But brief is the pause in pleasure, which the very pleasing sights of a tragedy renew, and the seasoning, so to speak, of a serious disputation which precedes it. The name of the play, which young men chosen from the whole University

k Muhammad used to pretend that this dove, which had been taught to take a grain of wheat from his ear with (its) beak (and so) afterward frequently poked its beak within (his) ear, was the Holy Spirit, who was a messenger from God to him and whispered everything to him.

performed, (was) *Ajax Flagellifer*: although the title was borrowed from Sophocles, still (the play) was as different in matter as in expression. The choice of its argument was made not only because it provided, with a splendid and stately variety of representations, abundant delight for such great spectators, but because the matter also seemed to be very appropriate for both courtly and academic ears and minds. For that celebrated dispute over the arms of dead Achilles is represented. Ajax claimed those arms as a reward for military prowess, but Ulysses obtained (them) as the deserts of (his) wisdom and learned eloquence. The conquered soldier fills the stage and all (its) round with (his) furious bellow; he calls upon the Furies; he curses gods and men; he breathes nothing but threats and vengeance. But wrath indeed (is) vain without strength, and strength (is vain) without prudence; and a ferocity, which the cultivation of letters and learning does not temper, results in (its) possessor's destruction. After | the madman's various wicked deeds, after he had slaughtered a flock of sheep instead of the Greek leaders and had scourged a large ram savagely in the place of Ulysses, he, when finally restored to (his own) mind, kills himself, more insane (now) than when (he was) insane. Tecmessa most piteously mourns the death of her lord, but the shade of Hector, which completely undetectable to Ajax provided the function of the chorus, rejoices. It is not easy to say with how marvellous a variety all these things fed both the eyes and the ears, all the more so because, on account of the variety of the matter, the whole fabric of the stage and the artful apparatus of the embroidered hangings were renewed again and again to the amazement of all. Where just now you had gazed on the living image of Troy and the Trojan shore, soon afterward you would see woods and deserts, horrific caves and the dwellings of the Furies, and while these were immediately vanishing, (you would see) unexpectedly the very agreeable appearance of tents and of ships.

pp 112–13   *(29 August)*
...

But after dinner one must hasten to the stage where, in the usual place, *Annus Recurrens* is presented to the princes by men of St John's – a play with a comic slipper but a tragic foot (*ie*, a comedy written in tragic metre), for it is written in tragic senarii for a novelty (*or* for a surprise), with the scene, fashioned most precisely into the form of the zodiac and with the sun passing through all twelve signs with splendid artifice. By its course the four seasons of the year, the four | stages of human life, the four types of humours of the body, and other forms of diversity, whether of fortunes or of dispositions or of loves, or of plays (*or* games) – if there be any (such) anywhere – are all led forth onto the stage in a delightful harmony and represented in (the character) Microcosm, first a youth at the University, and then experiencing the diversity of every other (human) condition. But why do I (write) these things when that most amusing comedy itself has already emerged from the press? It began with the sun entering Aries and finished when Pisces was being cooked by the fire of the sun. It was worthy indeed of lasting for the cycle of a whole year but, so that leisure for resting might be granted the princes who were exhausted by the great weariness of that day, the sun seemed to have traversed its zodiac more quickly.

pp 134–6   *(30 August)*
...

    The members of the University, moreover, who had polished everything up to this point – whatever was done or said – for that sensitive and learned ear of the great arbiter (*ie*, the king *(?)*), judged this an especially opportune time to offer something also for the ears of the less learned men and, above all, of the noblewomen. They had no doubt that some (of the noblewomen), such as (were) shining among so many stars of our sun, were more assiduous in the writings of our Sidney and Chaucer than in those of Plautus or Aristotle – for not everyone belongs either to Arabella or to Lucy (*ie*, to Arabella Stuart or to Lucy, countess of Bedford). They judge this to be an especially opportune time to charm (Queen) Anne's holy clemency and, along with Prince Henry, the whole beauty of the female court. And this (they do) not only with the native (*ie*, English), but also with the pastoral pan pipe, with which the choicest men among the Arcadians of the Isis have sung *Arcadia Restaurata*. And with one work they affected the minds of the princes and of all the spectators with great pleasure beyond belief, and at the same time taught actors in our native tongue, even if the most experienced, how great a difference there is between the commercial stage and the learned (stage). It is difficult to say which was the greater glory: that of the action or that of the verse. It is not difficult to judge, however, how much it captivated the ears of all. For both the court and the University speak of the former, and they speak as if they could never say enough. The thing itself speaks of the latter, and the book has already been worn out by everyone's hands.

    Our Thalia is not ashamed to dwell in the woods.
Especially our Daniel's woods; you will not think cities themselves more urbane than they. From the divine ark of his genius | our *Arcadia* and other writings fly up, very highly praised with such great praise. Our University rightly gives thanks for so great (a play) to her own foster son; so much the more, since he at least exists, may contemporary poets and all those coming after him learn from his example that there is not such a great war between mental acuity and the purity of the page but that they are able and ought to embrace each other.

    If anyone not fluent in English should wish to know from me the circumstances of this Arcadia, let him think of anything that can happen either by deception or love-philtre, so that thereby evil loves may be cemented; of anything (that can happen) either by falsities or jealousies, so that thereby even good and true loves may be ripped apart; of anything (that can happen) so that thereby young men may burn for lust (and) maidens for wantonness of minds and of dress. And let him understand how much the republic of the Arcadians is inflamed by the torches of lascivious debauchees and of corrupting procuresses. Those who were best able to remember the former probity of Arcadia because of their age, to long for it because of their virtue, to restore it because of their authority and wisdom, were eager to hold out a healing hand to these. And other bad (habits), no less pernicious than this evil behaviour, had invaded Arcadia: wicked corruptions of sacred rituals under a pretext of piety, the smokey frauds of fly-by-night hucksters (hiding) under the honoured name and feigned dress of doctors, and finally the tenpenny dregs of hack lawyers, who boast of being jurists among shepherds (but) among jurists are not even esteemed as shepherds. In the meantime all their tricks are represented and, after the earlier form of the republic has been restored, are punished by laws and penalties. If I say that (this) marvellously pleased the queen, the prince, and all the spectators, I shall only have said what the queen, the prince, and all the spectators both displayed with great applause I then and also bear witness to (it) still with marvellous praise.

But why am I seized, like a fool, by these fleeting names of pleasures and glory when no one suffers misfortune more unhappily than one who has known the peak of happiness? And why would I boast that the glory of utopian Arcadia has been restored when I see the glory of (our) Arcadia on the Isis and (their) pure pleasure disappearing? Thus all human things have been put on the stage and with the very brief comedy of our joy finished, tragedy and imminent grief waits for the University. For if[f] our ancestors rightly supposed that the sky should be mourned and that they should shake (it) with loud lamentation when they saw the bright face of the sun or moon disappearing, what great sorrow awaits us who, since (our) sun, and Cynthia, and the bright Julian star (ie, the king, queen, and prince) are about to take the presence of their splendour away from us at any time now, are oppressed more heavily by shadows than we have been surrounded by shining light? But stay, our delight, stay! If, moreover, you remain as long as you find us to be not unappreciative, not inattentive hosts, you will remain here eternally. But we who devoutly imitate that grief of our ancestors resort to their superstition in vain. For our light cannot be recalled by (our) laments, nor does anything remain for us, except to envy others who are able to see the same light which we ourselves cannot.

...

[f] Boemus relates that this is a customary practice (or a solemn observance) among the Germans

Gwinne, Vertumnus (1607)   STC: 12555
sigs B3–4

Thalia to the most illustrious earl of Montgomery,
Lord Philip Herbert

Earl Philip, dear to the king, whose harvest is (yet) on the stalks,
Thalia, pleasing to you,
invites, honours, greets, and adores you, earl of Montgomery, as her patron.
She, suffused with the blush of modesty, asks
will she, who once pleased when seen, be pleasing when she comes to be read?
They saw her – as she triumphantly recalls and remembers –
they, the darlings of the human race, the ornaments of the city and globe,
gods upon the earth, and the most celebrated lights of the world.
The king, an Augustus, the equal of Jove, (and his) offspring worthy of Jove,
the prince; the latter, a miracle among youths, the former, among men.
Earls, an assembly worthy of Apollo, saw her:
first and foremost, Dorset, an Apollo, governor of the muses.
And then three Howards by name – I would say divinities –
distinguished in counsel (and) command, supreme in (high) office,
Northampton, Nottingham, and Suffolk, know (her).
The first presides over ports; the second, ships; the third, buildings.
Then – but forgive me if the order, being inverse, fails in verse;
hardly anyone has been seated in the order of the stage –
he to whom famous Worcestershire gave its name was present,
or rather he was pre-eminent, for (his) dear devotion gave (him) the first place.
Rutland, (a man) of old-fashioned (moral) rectitude was there with them.
(Their) great friend Cumberland was near at hand, but Mars
or rather the Muses weep for him (now) because (their) friend died.
Then Southampton and then the hero Devon:
may the gods wish that the former lives on; the aether has carried the latter away.
The latter was, the former remains – and may he remain – a support to the
poet. |
And then my Maecenas, your brother, a second
Phoebus, Pembroke, for whom once (there was) a serious little book
thirteen years before, in the manner of one reading medicine:
he wrote such things about the macrocosm (and) microcosm,
as Thalia has now recalled playfully on the stage.
You, earl, gracious above all others, as Adonis (saw) Venus,
joyfully saw (and) joyfully listened (to the play), unless I am deceived by love;
but in your feelings, which demonstrate true love,
you were doubtful whether it would please, until you saw that it had pleased.
In this spirit, among many (others), the hero Danvers

and Effingham are noted to have watched and listened.

May others forgive, greater or lesser,

Scots or English, dukes or earls, barons

or knights, renowned in wealth or understanding,

supporters of the muses, whom the muses honour and celebrate in return,

if out of reverence Thalia fails to mention any with whom she is not acquainted.

May countesses, your stars equally pardon –

(they are) both the objects of your desire and the wonders of our heaven,

and the illustrious mistresses of (our) souls, dare I say, or (our) love,

ready to be looked at as they deserve – or to look –

if Thalia modestly passes over in silence those whom she does not know.

Above the rest, like the moon among lesser orbs,

Thetis among the water nymphs, Juno among (the) goddesses,

the pearl, the gem of gems, and the first goddess of goddesses,

Anna, (the same) backward and forward, like a little ring, the image of love,

descended from kings, parent of kings, the queen of Britain,

eagerly expected – would that she had joyfully looked on! But

Melpomene had exhausted her the previous day (and) Ajax had vexed her,

the following day the waiting Arcadian (muse) Euterpe charmed her.

She would like Latin less well, as she would like the vernacular better:

although the latter would have been more, the former less, appropriate for the scholars.

Of the others absent for a similar reason, he

that earl of Salisbury, the Hermes of the English race,

(its) tongue, head, heart, mind, hand, a hero second only to Jove, |

and she, the excellent Lucy, (countess) of Bedford, the glory of womanhood,

a pillar for the muses, a patroness of the poet:

would that only they had been spectators! For if Thalia desires

to please anyone with our art, she desires to please them.

However, she was able to please hardly anyone, and not (at all) them.

Nor can she fail to mention you, O highest chancellor,

when she speaks of illustrious friends of the muses,

for she and her poet, insignificant though he may be, are indebted

to (you,) Egerton.

But neither the very great business of the realm allowed (him) to attend,

nor (did his) authority (sit so) lightly, however greatly it would have pleased Thalia.

You, however, (Montgomery,) were then a witness or perhaps (its) source or (its) performer,

that she gave pleasure (to her audience),

for she attributes that pleasure to you. But indeed she who pleased when seen

and heard
asks further: will she please when she is read?
May Thalia, who will be silent at your bidding, be read at your bidding.

Why, you ask, is Thalia not in comic verse?
Let her seek to be equal to heroic (matter) by means of heroic metre.

sig C2v

...

A proscenium suitable for the four seasons. A palm in the middle with
twelve branches (and) the same number of lights. The area above the stage (*ie*,
the ceiling *(?)*) in the form of the zodiac with the image of the sun running
through the twelve signs, three for each subsequent act. The voice, action,
role, gesture cannot be expressed in writing. Imagine them.

sigs H3–3v*   *(27 August)*

At the king's entrance from (St) John's College, situated outside the
North Gate of the city, three in the role of sibyls greet (him) thus,
as if from a wood.

® The kings:
Duncan of the
Scots; Cnut
of England;
Llywelyn ab
Seisyll of Wales

1. It is said that prophetic sisters once sang
of your offspring's endless rule, O famous king.
Noble Lochaber acknowledged Banquo as thane.
They prophesized immortal sceptres, not for you,
Banquo, but for your immortal descendants.
Now, Banquo, you retreat from the court to hide in the forest,
we three equally sing the same fates for you and yours.
Now, O one expected by your (subjects), you approach the city from the forest.
And we greet you: greetings to you whom Scotland obeys.
2. To you whom England obeys, greetings. 3. To you whom Ireland obeys,
greetings.
1. To whom France gives titles, territories, and more, greetings.
2. To you whom one Britain, previously divided, worships, greetings,
3. Highest British, Irish, and French monarch, greetings.
1. Anne, mother, sister, wife, daughter of kings, greetings.
2. Greetings, Henry, heir, most handsome prince. Greetings.
3. Duke Charles and the very charming Polish prince, greetings.
1. And we put neither limits nor terms to those fates,
except to the kingdom of the earth; may the stars be the limit of fame.
Recall Cnut famous for a fourfold kingdom.
O greater than your forebears, worthy to be raised by your (subjects) with the
diadem of the sun. |

Nor do we sow slaughters, nor wars, nor anxious hearts;
nor is there fury in us, but we are excited by the agency of that
divine will by which Thomas White was moved in a dream;
a knight of London, he dedicated these buildings to the muses.
To the muses? No rather, to God, and (their) guardian, John:
he, the forerunner of Christ, has bidden (us) to go to greet the one dear to God
and His care, as he passes close by, on his way to Christ Church.
Therefore, after the greeting has been spoken,
continue on your way. May the University be joyful in your sight, continue
on your way.

M.G.

...

1605–6
Christ Church Computi   ChCh Arch: iii.c.7(g.)
mb 3d*

And on the expenses of the comedies and tragedies
performed this year   £6 12d
...

Magdalen College Libri Computi   MC Arch: LCE/8
f 3v col 2   *(Internal and external payments)*
...
To musicians on the bursars' feast   5s
...

Merton College Bursars' Accounts   MCR: 3.1
f 102   *(26 July–22 November) (External expenses)*
...
...To the lord vice-chancellor in the coming of the king by agreement, £12....
...

f 103   *(25 November–25 March) (External expenses)*
...
...To the common musicians by agreement, 6s 8d....

New College Bursars' Accounts   NC Arch: 7599
mb 5   *(25 December–25 March) (Internal expenses)*
...
...Paid to the town musicians, 6s 8d....
...

The Queen's College Long Rolls   QC Arch: LRA
f 30v col 1*   *(7 July–7 July) (External expenses)*
…

Likewise to Morris, a fiddler   2s
…

Likewise to pipers from Oxford   10s
…

St John's College Computus Hebdomalis   SJC Arch: Acc.v.E.4
f 15v   *(14–20 October)*
…

Paid out by the decision of convocation a second time for
the University's expenses in the coming of (his) royal majesty   57s 4d
…

Vice-Chancellors' Accounts   OUA: WP/β/21(4)
p 154   *(17 July–17 July) (Extraordinary expenses)*
…

Paid for the remainder of the money laid out during
the reception of (his) most serene royal majesty   £151 9s 6d
…

Hannisters' Registers   OCA: L.5.1
f 275   *(9 December)*
…

John Smith, musician, recently an apprentice of Leonard Major of the city of
Oxford, has been admitted to the liberty of the aforesaid city on 9 December
in the aforesaid third year, and he paid the officers' fee and 2s 6d for the
corporation treasury and was sworn.
…

1606–7
Christ Church Computi   ChCh Arch: iii.c.8(a.)
mb 3d
…

And on the expenses of the comedies and tragedies
produced this year   £nil
…

Magdalen College Draft Libri Computi   MC Arch: LCD/2
f 142   *(Repairs)*
…

For expenses incurred for the shows this year   £22 19s 8½d
…

(Internal and external payments)
To musicians on the bursars' feast   0 5s 0 0
...

To trumpeters of Lord Oxford and Lord Compton
in reward   0 5s 0 0
...

Merton College Bursars' Accounts   MCR: 3.1
f 109v   *(25 November–20 March)* *(External expenses)*

...To musicians by agreement, 6s 8d; on their supper, 2s....
...

New College Bursars' Accounts   NC Arch: 7600
mb 8   *(25 December–25 March)* *(Internal expenses)*
...
...Paid to trumpeters in reward, 3s.
Paid to the town musicians, 6s 8d....
...

The Queen's College Long Rolls   QC Arch: LRA
f 32 col 2*   *(7 July–7 July)* *(External expenses)*
...
Likewise to pipers   10s
...
Likewise to Morris, a piper   1s 6d
...

1607–8
Christ Church Computi   ChCh Arch: iii.c.8(b.)
mb 3d
...
And on the expenses of the comedies and tragedies
produced this year as it appears in the same place   £6 12s 4d
...

Lincoln College Calculus 1607–8   LC Arch
f 5*   *(7 December–6 March)*

           feast of the Purification of (St) Mary   18s
...
Musicians   of the house, 7s 1d
...

Magdalen College Draft Libri Computi   MC Arch: LCD/2
f 149v   *(Internal and external payments)*
...

To the lord king's trumpeters in reward   10s
...

f 150
...

To musicians on the bursars' feast   5s
...

Merton College Bursars' Accounts   MCR: 3.1
f 115v   *(20 November–18 March)* *(External expenses)*

...To musicians by agreement, 6s 8d; on their supper by agreement, 18d....
...

New College Bursars' Accounts   NC Arch: 7603
mb 6   *(25 December–25 March)* *(Internal expenses)*
...

...Paid to the town musicians in reward   6s 8d

The Queen's College Long Rolls   QC Arch: LRA
f 35 col 1*   *(7 July–7 July)* *(External expenses)*
...

Likewise to trumpeters from Oxford   10s
...

St John's College Christmas Prince   SJC Library: MS 52
pp 5–10*   *(Election of the Prince)*

(English)

> I believe, electors, most illustrious men, that these benefits – which
> bring more difficulty and responsibility when conferred than they can
> (bring) honour when properly administered – are to be undertaken
> more with caution at the first threshold than they are either to be
> avidly sought with the expectation of great dignity or recklessly seized
> with the blind desire for an unknown good. Since, conscript electors,
> I have always registered dignities of that kind carefully in the roll of
> these (benefits), it seems to me that you – with all due respect to your
> diligence, allow me to say – should not expect thanks so much as I,
> who am about to undertake that responsibility, deserve them. For
> only that benefit is accepted with thanks – I speak with reference to

the times – which neither solicitude I nor duty urges. Moreover, there are such infinite anxieties which surround that model, if you like, of lordship that few would freely wish them to be included in lordship, none can avoid (them), none endure (them). For when the appearance of true power is to be shown, some proportion of cares is always to be expected. But when electoral dignity, the regard of the electors, the applause of the people, (and) the consensus of all call (me) to pre-eminence with a view to promoting democracy, willingly I shall temper the impetus of our strenuously resisting soul, and earnestly devote care to satisfy the state as a whole, (even) if I am less able (to satisfy) each individual one of you. I do not therefore regard it appropriate to reply to the adversaries of our advances, who praise the disordered and confused care of power, or to agree with those extolling (*or* exaggerating) the necessity of a monarchical constitution. I have not come as the judge of your debates: I am sent for as (your) emperor (*or* commander). I willingly attribute the rising of our glory to your love, men especially dear to us; I do not judge that (our) august and glorious advance will require (anything) from you, out of your sense of duty, beyond love for us. I do not profess tyranny (but) I will exercise rule. In order that the happier advances of this (rule) be promoted and stabilized day by day, you ought to be more lavish with money than with (your) mouth. Wherefore I establish that the first fruits of love and of your duty are to be exacted immediately, lest I myself should appear to rule without authority or to have seized power without glory. We follow the Athenian polity, to whose standard I, appointed now to the task of kings, with the curators of plays, will take care, as my first responsibility in these sacred observances, that the observances sacred to Minerva, Vulcan, and Prometheus take place according to customary usage. But meanwhile, men already (made) greater by our authority, according to the image of the aforesaid republic, I desire producers, or assistants, who shall not only be put in charge of the plays but also, using liberality in the republic's expenses according to the proportion of wealth, shall partly offer rewards from the public purse and partly spend from their own (funds) for this reason: that they are prefects over those (plays). You will furnish when warned those other things that pertain to your duty, you will offer voluntarily, as I hope, the things that pertain to your love.

(English)

pp 47–9

...

(English)

I doff the tyrant Tereus by Fortune's leave.
I go on to be tongueless in Fortune's way.
® Of Philomela   Thus a mute punishment for a mute crime follows.
May another Tereus appointed be pleasing, I pray.
(English)

pp 111–16

(English)

Since it has never been a hindrance in any way to the majesty of the greatest
princes that several times they stood in need of more friends and their help
and support, and since each most noble one (of the princes) was accustomed
to owe much to a certain particular privilege, I, lest I should appear to be
lacking in the smallest entitlement of majesty or not to enjoy any privilege of
nobility, being forced and compelled by very many constraints – which we do
not judge honourable enough to explain according to the custom of princes
or safe enough for your duty to investigate – send this mandatory letter to
you, by virtue of which a sum of money is exacted, which you will present to
this our collector according to the proportion and substance of your love.
This (sum) I bind myself and my successors to repay faithfully and without
any fraud or evil trickery to you or your heirs on the Greek calends. Given
and sealed | with our privy seal, from the white hall of Alba Fortunata, on
1 February in the first year of (our) reign.
(English)

pp 169–78

(English)

Now we are replete with rich food.
We bear to you a flowing abundance.
Playfully we sing joy to you.
                    Live joyfully.
They call you a god, venerable Bacchus.
They call you a goddess, reverend mother.
Cast away heavy sorrows from yourselves.
                    Live joyfully.
Ceres gives strength and strengthens
human bodies, and he, Bacchus, the father of wine,
frees our souls from troublesome worries.
                    Live joyfully.
Lest sadness tire your souls,
this happy throng bids you put aside your worries,

and the holiday urges rejoicing.

Live joyfully. |

Behold, Ceres the creator of fertile crops
and the father of wine and peaceful sleep
merrily offer this cup to you.

Take, { Monarch.
       { Master.

They all drink in order while the actors repeat these last songs very often.
Soon each person in the whole gathering is thus wished joy in order.

Tenor

If abundance can make anyone happy,
abundance bids (us) to have the name, happy.
Joyful abundance bids (us) dispel sad worries,
abundance, whom Bacchus and nurturing Ceres embrace.

Counter tenor

Who is not delighted by the cup taken in moderation?
Whose soul is not delighted by sweet wines?
Sweet wines delight; wines bring sweet sleep;
sweet wines enhance magnificent food.

Mean

Nurturing Ceres nourishes mortal hearts with crops.
Nurturing Ceres adorns the field with crops.
If anyone lacks Ceres' gifts, he is not
pleased by father Bacchus' welcome gifts either.

May you not be lacking Ceres' or Bacchus' gifts.
May Jupiter himself answer my prayers.

Treble

Nurturing Ceres is gladdened by your feasts, and lo,
abundance and Bacchus sing of glad rejoicing.
Presently, they all exit singing.

Mean

We sing of glad rejoicing; we will sing
this the same always, for grieving is not
permitted now. A joyful holiday is celebrated here.
Live joyfully.
More often may the holiday return to us.
More often may the drinking of wine be permitted.
More often may we merrily sing to you.
Live joyfully.   They exit. |

(English)

I believe those were the suitors of Penelope,

whom the perhaps just anger of Telemachus
drove out of Ulysses' house. |

(English)

1608–9
Christ Church Treasurers' Accounts   ChCh Arch: iii.c.1
f 152
...

And on the expenses of the comedies and tragedies
produced this year   £5
...

Magdalen College Libri Computi   MC Arch: LCE/8
f 15   *(Internal and external payments)*
...

Paid | To the earl of Pembroke's trumpeters   6s
...

f 15v
...

To musicians on the bursars' feast   5s
...

Merton College Bursars' Accounts   MCR: 3.1
f 127v   *(18 November–24 March)* *(External expenses)*
...

...To musicians by agreement, 6s 8d, and for the same (musicians) on (their)
supper, 22d....
...

Merton College Register   MCR: 1.3
p 229   *(Allowances)*
...

On 29 January we allowed to pipers as usual, 6s 8.
...

New College Bursars' Accounts   NC Arch: 7604
mb 8   *(25 December–25 March)* *(Internal expenses)*
...

(English).... Paid to the town musicians, 6s 8d....
...

The Queen's College Long Rolls   QC Arch: LRA
f 36v col 2   *(7 July–7 July)* *(External expenses)*
…

Likewise to trumpeters   2s 6d
…

Likewise to the king's trumpeters   10s
…

Likewise to pipers from Oxford   10s
…

Vice-Chancellors' Accounts   OUA: WP/β/21(4)
p 160   *(17 July–14 July)* *(Extraordinary expenses)*

Paid to the king's trumpeters   20s
…

1609–10
Christ Church Treasurers' Accounts   ChCh Arch: iii.c.1
f 164
…

And on the expenses of the tragedies and comedies
performed this year   £nil
…

Letter of Henry Jackson to D.G.P   CCC: MS 304
ff 83v–4*

®10.   D.G.P.
   –Recently the king's stage actors were here. They performed to great
applause, the theatre being full. But they rightly seemed impious to pious
and learned men because, not being content to injure alchemists, they
most foully sullied the Holy Scriptures themselves. Of course they carped
at Anabaptists so that (their own) audacity would hide under this mask.–
   –(They say that) our theologians, who, I'm sorry to say, gathered (there)
very eagerly.–
   –(They say that) our stage has never sounded with greater applause
than when that masked scoundrel entered, who impiously and extravagantly
defiled the Scriptures so as | to place the Anabaptists' feigned sanctity
before the spectators to be derided. They also held tragedies which they
acted decorously and aptly. They moved (the audience to) tears in these
(tragedies) not only by what they said but also by what they did.–
   –But indeed that Desdemona, who was slain before us by her husband,
although she always pleaded her case very well, nevertheless moved (us)

more after she was murdered, when lying on the bed she appealed to the spectators' pity with her very expression.–

September 1610.

Exeter College Rectors' Accounts   EC Arch: A.II.9
f 207v   *(1 November–1 November)*

...

Likewise of 10s paid and given to royal trumpeters.

...

Magdalen College Libri Computi   MC Arch: LCE/8
f 25v   *(Internal and external payments)*

...

To the king's trumpeters in reward   £1 0 0

...

f 26

...

To trumpeters in reward   0 6s 0
To musicians on the bursars' feast   0 5s 0

...

Merton College Bursars' Accounts   MCR: 3.1
f 132v   *(24 November–23 March)* *(External expenses)*

...

...To musicians by agreement, 6s 8d; for the same (musicians') supper, 2s 6d.

New College Bursars' Accounts   NC Arch: 7606
mb 9   *(25 December–25 March)*

...Paid to the town musicians, 6s 8d....

...

Oriel College Treasurers' Accounts   OC Arch: S I.C.1
f 152v   *(Internal expenses)*

...

Likewise to the king's trumpeters   5s

...

The Queen's College Long Rolls   QC Arch: LRA
f 38v col 1   *(7 July–7 July)* *(External expenses)*

...

Likewise to trumpeters   2s 6d

Likewise to Morris, a fiddler 18d

...

Likewise to pipers from Oxford 10s

...

The Queen's College Long Rolls QC Arch: LRB
f 4v col 2 *(7 July 1610–7 July 1611) (External expenses)*

...

Likewise to the king's trumpeters on 29 August 20s

...

1610–11

Magdalen College Libri Computi MC Arch: LCE/8
f 35v *(Internal and external payments)*

...

To various nobles' trumpeters in reward 0 6s 0

...

To musicians on the bursars' feast 0 5s 0

...

Merton College Bursars' Accounts MCR: 3.1
f 140 *(23 November–22 March) (External expenses)*

...

...To musicians by agreement, 6s 8d; for the same (musicians') supper, 2s 6d....

The Queen's College Long Rolls QC Arch: LRB
f 4v col 2 *(7 July–7 July) (External expenses)*

...

Likewise to pipers from Oxford 10s

...

Likewise to Morris, a fiddler 18d

...

1611–12

Christ Church Computi ChCh Arch: iii.c.8(d.)
mb 2d*

...

And on the expenses of the comedies and tragedies
produced this year nil

...

Exeter College Rectors' Accounts   EC Arch: A.ii.9
f 216   *(1 November–1 November)*
...
Likewise of 38s paid to the king's and prince's trumpeters.
...

Magdalen College Libri Computi   MC Arch: LCE/8
f 45   *(Internal and external payments)*
...
To musicians on the bursars' feast   5s
...

f 45v
...
To royal trumpeters in reward   20s
...
To the prince's trumpeters in reward   20s
...

Merton College Bursars' Accounts   MCR: 3.1
f 146v   *(22 November–20 March) (External expenses)*
...
...To musicians by agreement, 6s 8d; for their supper, 2s.... To royal trumpeters, 6s....
...

The Queen's College Long Rolls   QC Arch: LRB
f 7 col 1   *(7 July–7 July) (External expenses)*
...
Likewise to pipers from Oxford   10s
...
Likewise to Morris, a fiddler   18s
...

f 9 col 2   *(7 July 1612–7 July 1613) (External expenses)*
...
Likewise to the king's clarioners on 28 August   20s
...
Likewise to the prince's trumpeters on 27 September   10s
...

1612-13
Christ Church Computi   ChCh Arch: iii.c.8(e.)
mb 2d*

...

And on the expenses of the tragedies and comedies
produced this year   nil

...

Magdalen College Libri Computi   MC Arch: LCE/8
f 55v*   *(Internal and external payments)*

...

To musicians on the bursars' feast   5s

...

Paid x   To Mr Oates for the comedy to be held before the
prince palatine, by (his) bill   £5 9s

...

New College Bursars' Accounts   NC Arch: 7611
mb 8   *(29 September–25 March)* *(Internal expenses)*

...

...Paid to the town musicians, 6s 8d.

...

The Queen's College Long Rolls   QC Arch: LRB
f 9v col 1   *(7 July–7 July)* *(External expenses)*

...

1 January   Likewise to Morris, a fiddler   18d

...

18 February   Likewise to pipers from Oxford   10s

...

1613-14
Christ Church Treasurers' Accounts   ChCh Arch: iii.c.1
f 198

...

And on the expenses of the tragedies and comedies
produced this year   nil

...

Exeter College Rectors' Accounts   EC Arch: A.II.9
f 224   *(1 November–1 November)*

...

Likewise to the king's trumpeters   1   2   0

...

Magdalen College Libri Computi   MC Arch: LCE/8
f 63v   *(Internal and external payments)*

...

To musicians on the bursars' feast   5s

...

To the king's trumpeters   20s

...

Merton College Bursars' Accounts   MCR: 3.1
f 155   *(19 November–18 March)* *(External expenses)*

...

...To musicians by agreement, 6s 8d....

New College Bursars' Accounts   NC Arch: 7614
mb 9   *(29 September–25 December)* *(Internal expenses)*

...

...Paid to a musician playing in the hall, 6d....

...

(25 December–25 March)
...Paid to a musician, 12d.... Paid to the town musicians, 6s 8d.

...

Oriel College Treasurers' Accounts   OC Arch: S I.C.1
f 180v   *(Internal expenses)*

...

Likewise to royal trumpeters, 10s....

...

The Queen's College Long Rolls   QC Arch: LRB
f 11v col 2   *(7 July–7 July)* *(External expenses)*

...

Likewise to pipers from Oxford on 4 February   10s
Likewise to Morris, a piper   18d

...

f 14 col 1   *(7 July 1614–7 July 1615)*

...

Likewise on 18 September to royal pipers   20s

...

Vice-Chancellors' Accounts   OUA: WP/β/21(4)
p 172   *(2 August–27 July)* *(Extraordinary expenses)*

...

Paid to the lady queen's players *(or* entertainers)   20s

...

1614–15
Christ Church Treasurers' Accounts   ChCh Arch: iii.c.1
f 205

...

And on the expenses of the tragedies and comedies
produced this year   nil

...

Magdalen College Libri Computi   MC Arch: LCE/8
f 71v   *(Internal and external payments)*

...

To musicians on the bursars' feast   5s

...

f 72*

...

To Mr Powell for expenses on a comedy held in the
lord president's lodgings   £1

...

To trumpeters at commencement   5s

...

Merton College Bursars' Accounts   MCR: 3.1
f 161v   *(17 March–28 July)* *(External expenses)*

...

...To musicians by agreement, 6s 8d....

New College Bursars' Accounts   NC Arch: 7615
mb 9   *(25 December–25 March)* *(Internal expenses)*

...

...Paid to the town musicians, 6s 8d....

...

The Queen's College Long Rolls   QC Arch: LRB
f 14 col 1   *(7 July–7 July)* *(External expenses)*
...

Likewise on 1 January to John Morris, piper   18d
...

Likewise on 1 February to pipers from Oxford   10s
...

col 2

Likewise on 11 July to royal pipers   10s
...

Vice-Chancellors' Accounts   OUA: WP/β/21(4)
p 174   *(27 July–20 July)* *(Extraordinary expenses)*
...

Likewise paid to royal trumpeters at Woodstock   22s
Likewise paid to those serving the lord vice-chancellor,
the doctors, and proctors at the time of the dinner at
Woodstock   22s
Likewise paid to royal trumpeters at the time of the
last commencement   10s
...

1615–16
Christ Church Computi   ChCh Arch: iii.c.8(f.)
mb 2d
...

And on the expenses of the tragedies and comedies
produced this year   £6 13s 4d
...

Magdalen College Libri Computi   MC Arch: LCE/8
f 80   *(Internal and external payments)*
...

To musicians on the bursars' feast   5s

f 80v

...

To the king's trumpeters   £1 2s
To the queen's trumpeters   £1

To the queen's drummer/s   10s

…

To trumpeters   5s

…

New College Bursars' Accounts   NC Arch: 7617
mb 7   *(25 December–25 March)* *(Internal expenses)*

…

…*(English)*…. Paid to town musicians, 6s 8d….

The Queen's College Long Rolls   QC Arch: LRB
f 17v col 2   *(7 July–7 July)* *(External expenses)*

…

1 January	Likewise to a fiddler, William Morris	18d
	…	
24 February	Likewise to four pipers, strangers	5s
2 March	Likewise to pipers from Oxford	10s

…

f 20v col 2   *(7 July 1616–7 July 1617)* *(External expenses)*

…

23 (August)	Likewise to the queen's trumpeter/s	10s
24 (August)	Likewise to the king's trumpeters	10s

…

Vice-Chancellors' Accounts   OUA: WP/β/21(4)
p 176   *(17 July–17 July)* *(Extraordinary expenses)*

…

Likewise paid to trumpeters   10s
Likewise paid to the lord king's players (*or* entertainers)   40s

…

p 179*   *(17 July 1616–17 July 1617)* *(Extraordinary expenses)*

…

Likewise given to the lord king's trumpeters on
24 August 1616   22s
Likewise given to the lady queen's trumpeters on
23 August 1616   22s
Likewise given to the lord king's drummers   21s
Likewise given to the most illustrious Prince Charles'
servants 28 August   22s

…

Hannisters' Registers   OCA: L.5.2
f 29v

…

Leonard Major
® Edward
Heywood

Memorandum that on 13 August in the aforesaid year, Edward Heywood, son of Walter Heywood of Cokethorpe in the county of Oxford, yeoman, placed himself as an apprentice to Leonard Major of the city of Oxford, musician, to learn his art which he practises. And he stays with him as an apprentice and serves from the feast of St Michael next to come after the date of the present (indenture) up to the end and completion of seven years thence next following, etc. And at the end of said term he will give the same, his apprentice, two sets of clothing (*ie*, one for daily use and one for holiday use) appropriate for such an apprentice, etc.

Hugh Bosle
® Roger Bates

Memorandum that on 24 August in the abovesaid year, Roger Bates, son of Edmund Bates of Norton in the county of Oxford, yeoman, placed himself as an apprentice to Hugo Bosle of the city of Oxford, musician, to learn his art which he practises. And he stays with him as an apprentice and serves from the day of the issuing of the present (indenture) up to the end and completion of seven years thence next following. And at the end of the said term he will give the same, his apprentice, two sets of clothing (*ie*, one for daily use and one for holiday use) appropriate to such an apprentice, and one treble viol, in English, 'one treble violin,' etc.

1616–17
Christ Church Treasurers' Accounts   ChCh Arch: iii.c.1
f 212

…

And on the expenses of the tragedies and comedies held
and produced this year   nil

…

Exeter College Rectors' Accounts   EC Arch: A.ii.9
f 236   *(1 November–1 November)*

…

Likewise of £1 2s paid and given to royal pipers.
Likewise of 11s 5d paid for the repair of a trumpet.

…

Magdalen College Libri Computi   MC Arch: LCE/8
f 85v   *(Internal and external payments)*

…

To musicians on the bursars' feast   5s

…

Twice to the earl of Essex's trumpeters   10s

…

To the queen's trumpeters   10s
To the lord king's trumpeters   £1 2s

…

To musicians and for the burning of perfume in
the bishop of Winchester's supper   5s 6d

…

f 86

…

To Hoby by (his) bill for various (expenses) in the
tragedy by poor scholars   8s

…

Merton College Bursars' Accounts   MCR: 3.1
f 174   *(21 March–25 July)   (External expenses)*

…

…To musicians by agreement, 6s 8d.…

New College Bursars' Accounts   NC Arch: 7619
mb 6*   *(25 December–25 March)   (Internal expenses)*

…

(English).… Paid to the town musicians, 6s 8d.…

…

(24 June–29 September)
(English).… Paid for gloves given to the bishop of Winchester, £3 2s.…
Paid to royal trumpeters, 11s. *(English)*

…

The Queen's College Long Rolls   QC Arch: LRB
f 21 col 1   *(7 July–7 July)   (External expenses)*

…

1 January   Likewise to Morris, a fiddler   18d

…

17 February   Likewise to pipers from Oxford   10s

…

f 22v col 2   *(7 July 1617–7 July 1618)*

…

Firstly, to royal clarioners, 8 September   20s

…

1617–18
Christ Church Treasurers' Accounts   ChCh Arch: iii.c.1
f 220

...

And on the expenses of the tragedies and comedies held
and produced this year   nil

...

Magdalen College Libri Computi   MC Arch: LCE/8
f 93v   *(Internal and external payments)*
...

To the earl of Essex's trumpeters   3s
To certain nobles' trumpeters   11s
...

To diverse (persons) by (their) bills (*or* for various
(expenses) by bills) for the comedy and tragedy
beyond the £22 17s 4d deducted from battells   £24 9s 5d
...

New College Bursars' Accounts   NC Arch: 7621
mb 8   *(29 September–25 December) (Internal expenses)*
...
...Paid to the earl of Essex's trumpeters, 2s....
...

(25 March–24 June)
...Paid to trumpeters, 12 d....
...

(24 June–29 September)
...Paid to trumpeters, 5s....
...

The Queen's College Long Rolls   QC Arch: LRB
f 22v col 2   *(7 July–7 July) (External expenses)*
...

Likewise to Morris, a piper   18d
Likewise to pipers of Oxford on 4 February   10s
...

TRANSLATIONS 1617–18

1049

Vice-Chancellors' Accounts   OUA: WP/β/21(4)
p 181   *(19 July 1617–20 July 1618)* *(Extraordinary expenses)*
…

Likewise given to royal servants waiting on
the lord vice-chancellor and the doctors at
Woodstock at dinner-time   22s
…

Likewise paid to the king's trumpeters   22s
Likewise paid to royal fiddlers *(?)*   5s
…

Burton, Anatomy of Melancholy (1624)   STC: 4160
p 124
…

aI have not so long ago touched on those (philosophasters) in a Latin comedy *Philosophaster*, which was held publicly at Christ Church, Oxford, in the year 1617 (*ie*, 1617/18) on 16 February †
…aPhilosophasters are those who are licensed in the (liberal) arts (but) do not have art, +and they bid those be wise who are endowed with no wisdom, and they contribute nothing to (this) position except the desire (to be wise)….

+Menippean
satire

Robert Burton's Philosophaster   Harvard Theatre Collection: MS Thr.10
p 8*   *(Prologue)*
…

Let it be known that it was written eleven years ago;
it hid away among bookworms and maggots until this day,
condemned by the author to eternal obscurity.
By the importunity of others, it comes now to the stage.
…

pp 89–90*   *(Epilogue)*
…

If (there is) anything aberrant or hackneyed which excessively offends the ears, we warn that this play was written eleven years ago.
…

They applauded.
16 February.
At Christ Church.
1617 (*ie*, 1617/18). |

The names of the actors.

(English)

The author was Robert Burton
of Lindley in Leicestershire.

Hannisters' Registers   OCA: L.5.2
f 401*

...

John Baldwin, the son and recently the apprentice of John Baldwin of the
aforesaid city, musician, has been admitted to the liberty of the said city on
20 July in the aforesaid year and sworn likewise.

...

1618–19
Christ Church Treasurers' Accounts   ChCh Arch: iii.c.1
f 227

...

And on the expenses of the tragedies and comedies held
and produced this year   nil

...

Exeter College Rectors' Accounts   EC Arch: A.II.9
f 246v   *(1 November–1 November)*

Likewise to royal trumpeters   0   11   0

...

Magdalen College Libri Computi   MC Arch: LCE/8
f 103   *(Internal and external payments)*

...

To trumpeters at various times   0   16   00
To the king's trumpeters   1   2   0

...

To various persons by (their) bills (*or* for various
(expenses) by bills) for the tragedies beyond £18 9s
deducted from battells   £13   18s   ½d

...

To musicians on the bursars' feast   0   5   0

...

New College Bursars' Accounts   NC Arch: 7623
mb 5   *(29 September–25 December)*   *(Internal expenses)*

...Paid to a certain old poor man singing in the hall, 4d....

...

(25 December–25 March)
…Paid to trumpeters, 5s…. Paid to the town musicians, 6s 8d….
…

(25 March–24 June)
…Paid to trumpeters, 2s 6d….
…

(24 June–29 September)
…Paid to royal trumpeters, 11s….
…

Oriel College Treasurers' Accounts   oc Arch: S 1.C.1
f 216   *(Internal expenses)*
…
Likewise paid to royal trumpeters   10s
…

The Queen's College Long Rolls   qc Arch: LRB
f 25 col 1*   *(7 July–7 July) (External expenses)*
…
| | | |
Likewise to Morris piping   18d
20 March   Likewise to pipers from Oxford   10s
…

f 27 col 1   *(7 July 1619–7 July 1620) (External expenses)*
…
23 August   Likewise to royal pipers   20s
…

1619–20
Christ Church Computi   ChCh Arch: iii.c.9(a.)
mb 4*

⟨…⟩ of the tragedies and comedies performed
and produced this year   nil
…

Magdalen College Libri Computi   mc Arch: LCE/8
f 113v   *(Internal and external payments)*
…
To the earl of Rutland's trumpeters   2s 6d

To the count palatine's trumpeters   2s 6d

…

To a little boy who drummed in the hall   10s

To royal trumpeters and (those of the earl
of) Buckingham   11s

…

To musicians on the bursars' feast   5s 6d

…

Merton College Bursars' Accounts   MCR: 3.1
f 189   *(24 March–29 July) (External expenses)*

…To musicians by agreement, 6s 8d.…

…

New College Bursars' Accounts   NC Arch: 7624
mb 5   *(25 December–25 March) (Internal expenses)*

…

…Paid to the town musicians, 6s 8d. *(English)*.…

The Queen's College Long Rolls   QC Arch: LRB
f 27 col 1*   *(7 July–7 July) (External expenses)*

…

Likewise to Morris piping   18d

21 February   Likewise to royal pipers about to set off into Bohemia   10s

Likewise to pipers of Oxford for (their) annual payment   10s

…

Vice-Chancellors' Accounts   OUA: WP/β/21(4)
p 185   *(17 July 1619–21 July 1620) (Extraordinary expenses)*

…

Likewise to those waiting on the vice-chancellor and
the rest of the doctors at dinner-time at Woodstock   53s

…

Likewise to royal trumpeters   22s

…

p 186

…

Likewise to players (*or* entertainers) so that they
would leave the University   22s

…

Hannisters' Registers OCA: L.5.2
f 63

…

Leonard Major

®Francis Jones

Memorandum that on 3 November in the seventeenth year of the reign of King James of England, etc, and in the fifty-third (year of his reign as king) of Scotland, Francis Jones, son of John Jones of the parish of Appleton in the county of Berkshire, husbandman, placed himself as an apprentice to Leonard Major of the city of Oxford in the county of Oxford, musician, to learn his art which he practises. And he stays with him as an apprentice and serves from the feast of All Saints which was in AD 1618 up to the end and completion of seven years thence next following, to be fully completed and finished. And at the end of said term he will give to the same, his apprentice, two sets of clothing (*ie*, one for daily use and one for holiday use) appropriate to such an apprentice.

…

f 395v

…

George Payne, recently apprentice to Leonard Major of the city of Oxford, musician, has been admitted to the liberty of this city according to custom, on 22 November in the abovesaid year, and he swore his oath.

…

1620–1
Christ Church Computi ChCh Arch: iii.c.9(b.)
mb 3d

…

And on the expenses of the tragedies and comedies held
and produced this year   nil

…

Magdalen College Libri Computi MC Arch: LCE/8
f 120v   *(Internal and external payments)*

…

To Lord Stanhope's trumpeters ⟨…⟩
To trumpeters at commencement ⟨…⟩
To the prince's trumpeters ⟨…⟩
To the king's trumpeters ⟨…⟩

…

To musicians on the bursars' feast   5s

…

Merton College Register   MCR: 1.3
p 268

On 11 February, when the fellows met in the vestry after evening prayer, we allowed according to custom 6s 8d for pipers.
…

New College Bursars' Accounts   NC Arch: 7626
mb 6   *(25 December–25 March)* *(Internal expenses)*
…
…Paid to the town musicians, 6s 8d.…
…

Oriel College Treasurers' Accounts   OC Arch: S 1.C.1
f 226v   *(Internal expenses)*
…

Likewise paid to royal trumpeters	10s
Likewise paid to the prince's trumpeters	5s

…

The Queen's College Long Rolls   QC Arch: LRB
f 29 col 2   *(7 July–7 July)* *(External expenses)*
…

Likewise to Morris piping	18d
Likewise to pipers from Oxford	10s

…

f 31v col 1   *(7 July 1621–7 July 1622)*
…

Likewise on 22 August to the prince's trumpeters	20s
Likewise on 27 August to the king's trumpeters	20s

…

Trinity College Bursars' Books   TC Arch: I/A/2
f 231v   *(25 March–24 June)* *(Reparations)*
…

Likewise to trumpeters from the king	10s
Likewise to trumpeters from the prince	10s

…

1621–2
Christ Church Computi   ChCh Arch: iii.c.9(c.)
mb 3*
...
And on the expenses of the tragedies and comedies held
and produced this year   nil
...

Magdalen College Liber Computi   MC Arch: LCE/9
f 4v   *(Internal and external expenses)*
...
To the earl of Oxford's trumpeters   3s
To the earl of Essex's trumpeters   6s
To unknown trumpeters   2s 6d
...

f 5
...
To musicians on the bursars' feast   5s
...

Merton College Register   MCR: 1.3
p 283
...
Granted to   Then also it was agreed that the bursar should pay 6s 8d of college funds to
musicians   the common musicians of the University and the town according to the usual
              custom.

New College Bursars' Accounts   NC Arch: 7629
mb 6   *(25 December–25 March) (Internal expenses)*
...
...Paid to the town musicians, 6s 8d....
...

The Queen's College Long Rolls   QC Arch: LRB
f 31v col 1   *(7 July–7 July) (External expenses)*
...
Likewise on 1 January to Morris piping   18d
...

col 2

Likewise on 11 March to pipers from Oxford   10s
...

Vice-Chancellors' Accounts   OUA: WP/β/21(4)
p 189   *(20 July–18 July)* *(Extraordinary expenses)*
...
Likewise given to those waiting on the lord vice-chancellor
and the rest of the doctors at the time of the dinner at
Woodstock   40s
...

p 190

Likewise to royal trumpeters   20s
Likewise to royal players *(or* entertainers) that they
would leave the University and not play *(or* perform)   20s
...

1622
A ***Jesus College Statutes***   JC Arch: ST4
p 94   *(Chapter 26)* *(Weapons not to be carried and hindrances to study to
be removed)*

...We wish also that none of the fellows or scholars or servants of the said
college, or those living in it, shall feed or maintain any dog, or any kind of
bird, or any animal whatsoever, within the said college or outside it to the
loss or detriment of the college or to the harm, disturbance, or distress of
any of the fellows or scholars of the same, or also in any way hinder any
fellow or scholar of the said college whatsoever with singing, noise, shouting,
a musical instrument, or any kind of commotion from being able to study
or sleep under penalty to be inflicted by the principal or, in his absence, the
vice-principal at (his) discretion.

1622-3
Christ Church Computi   ChCh Arch: iii.c.9(d.)
mb 3d*
...
And on the expenses of the tragedies and comedies held
and produced this year   nil
...

Magdalen College Liber Computi   MC Arch: LCE/10
f 4v   *(Internal and external payments)*

...

To Lord Stanhope's trumpeters	5s

...

To unknown trumpeters	5s

...

To musicians on the bursars' feast	5s

...

New College Bursars' Accounts   NC Arch: 7631
mb 6   *(25 December–25 March) (Internal expenses)*

...

...Paid to the town musicians, 6s 8d....

...

The Queen's College Long Rolls   QC Arch: LRB
f 34 col 2   *(7 July–7 July) (External expenses)*

...

8 February   Likewise to the trumpeters, or musicians,
from Oxford   10s

...

1623–4
Magdalen College Liber Computi   MC Arch: LCE/11
f 4v   *(Internal and external payments)*

...

To the king's trumpeters, £1; the prince's, 6s; the duke of Buckingham's, 5s; Lord Stanhope's, 1s 6d	£1 12s 6d

...

To musicians on the bursars' feast	5s

...

Merton College Register   MCR: 1.3
p 286

...

Granted to
musicians   Then also it was agreed that the bursar should pay 6s 8d to the common
musicians of the University and the town according to the usual custom.

...

New College Bursars' Accounts   NC Arch: 7633
mb 8   *(25 December–25 March)   (Internal expenses)*
...

...Paid to the town musicians, 6s 8d.
...

Oriel College Treasurers' Accounts   OC Arch: S I.C.1
f 243v   *(Internal expenses)*
...

Likewise to the king's and the prince's trumpeters   0 16 0
...

The Queen's College Long Rolls   QC Arch: LRB
f 36v col 2   *(7 July–7 July)   (External expenses)*
...

7 February	Likewise to trumpeters from Oxford	10s
	Likewise to Morris piping	18d

...

f 39 col 2   *(7 July 1624–7 July 1625)*
...

13 August	Likewise to the prince's trumpeters	10s
...		
25 (August)	Likewise to the king's trumpeters	20s

...

Vice-Chancellors' Accounts   OUA: WP/β/21(4)
p 198   *(31 July–27 July)   (Extraordinary expenses)*
...

Paid to royal trumpeters and other trumpeters at
another time   25s
Paid to certain players *(or* entertainers) so that they
would not play *(or* perform)   5s
...

1624–5
Magdalen College Liber Computi   MC Arch: LCE/12
f 4v   *(Internal and external payments)*
...

To royal trumpeters   10s 6d
...

Merton College Bursars' Accounts   MCR: 3.1
f 215v   *(19 November–18 March)*   *(External expenses)*
...
...To musicians by agreement, 6s 8d....
...

New College Bursars' Accounts   NC Arch: 7635
mb 8   *(24 June–29 September)*   *(Internal expenses)*
...
Paid to the town musicians, 6s 8d 0....
...

The Queen's College Long Rolls   QC Arch: LRB
f 39 col 2   *(7 July–7 July)*   *(External expenses)*
...

6 January	To Morris, a piper	18d
	...	
19 February	To pipers of Oxford	10s

...

Vice-Chancellors' Accounts   OUA: WP/β/21(4)
p 200   *(27 July–25 July)*   *(Extraordinary expenses)*
...
Paid to musicians at the funeral of James,
late the king, etc   20s
...
Paid to King James' trumpeters   22s
Paid to trumpeters of Charles, now the king   22s
...

1625–6
Magdalen College Liber Computi   MC Arch: LCE/13
f 4v*   *(Internal and external payments)*
...
Claimed by the bursars of the previous year for
the trumpeters returned from the naval fleet   3s 4d
...
To Lord Stanhope's trumpeters   3s
...
To musicians on the bursars' feast   5s
...

New College Bursars' Accounts   NC Arch: 7637
mb 8   *(25 December–25 March)* *(Internal expenses)*

…

…Paid to the town musicians, 6s 8d.…

…

The Queen's College Long Rolls   QC Arch: LRB
f 41 col 1   *(7 July–7 July)* *(External expenses)*

…

Likewise to the king's trumpeters   20s

…

20 December   Likewise to trumpeters from the royal fleet   5s

…

1 April   Likewise to flute players of the city of Oxford   10s

…

Vice-Chancellors' Accounts   OUA: WP/β/21(4)
p 202   *(25 July–22 July)* *(Extraordinary expenses)*

…

Likewise to royal trumpeters when the king
was at Woodstock   £1 2s 0

…

p 203

…

Likewise to royal trumpeters coming from the ships   0 10s 0

…

1626–7
Magdalen College Liber Computi   MC Arch: LCE/14
f 4   *(Internal and external payments)*

…

To musicians on the bursars' feast   0 5s 0

…

f 4v

…

To the king's trumpeters   £1 2s 0

…

To a certain magnate's trumpeters   0 2s 6

…

New College Bursars' Accounts   NC Arch: 7638
mb 8   *(25 December–25 March)* *(Internal expenses)*
...
...Paid to the town musicians, 6s 8d....
...

Oriel College Treasurers' Accounts   OC Arch: S 1.C.1
f 262   *(External expenses)*
...
Likewise to the king's trumpeters   11s
...

The Queen's College Long Rolls   QC Arch: LRB
f 43 col 1   *(7 July–7 July)* *(External expenses)*
...
Likewise to royal trumpeters   10s
...

col 2

Likewise to Morris, piper   18d
Likewise to trumpeters of Oxford   10s
...

f 44v col 2   *(7 July 1627–7 July 1628)* *(External expenses)*
...
1 August   To the king's trumpeters   20s
...

1627–8
Magdalen College Liber Computi   MC Arch: LCE/15
f 4   *(Internal and external payments)*
...
To musicians on the bursars' feast   5s
...

New College Bursars' Accounts   NC Arch: 7640
mb 7   *(25 December–25 March)* *(Internal expenses)*
...
...Paid to the town musicians, 6s 8d....
...

Oriel College Treasurers' Accounts   OC Arch: S 1.C.1
f 268v   *(Internal expenses)*

...

Likewise to royal trumpeters   0 5 0

...

The Queen's College Long Rolls   QC Arch: LRB
f 45 col 1   *(7 July–7 July) (External expenses)*

...

To Morris, a fiddler   18d

...

23 February   To pipers of Oxford   10s

...

To trumpeters   5s

...

1628–9

Magdalen College Draft Libri Computi   MC Arch: LCD/3
f 80v   *(Internal and external payments)*

...

To musicians on the bursars' feast   5s

...

To the king's trumpeters   £1 2s
To the queen's trumpeters   10s

...

Merton College Bursars' Accounts   MCR: 3.1
f 239v   *(31 July–20 November 1629) (External expenses)*

...

...To royal trumpeters, 6s. To the queen's trumpeters, 10s....

f 240*

...for the reception of nobles and ambassadors ... to musicians at the same
time, 10s. For the reception of the most serene king, Charles, and the most
illustrious queen, by bill, £9 10s.... To musicians at the same time, 10s....

...

New College Bursars' Accounts   NC Arch: 7642
mb 5*   *(25 December–25 March) (Internal expenses)*

...

...Paid to the town musicians, 6s 8d....

...

mb 6* *(24 June–29 September)* *(External expenses)*

…

…Paid to the king's and the queen's trumpeters, 20s.…

…

Oriel College Treasurers' Accounts   OC Arch: S I.C.1
f 276   *(Internal expenses)*

Likewise to royal trumpeters   £1   0   0

…

The Queen's College Long Rolls   QC Arch: LRC
f 3v col 2*   *(7 July–7 July)* *(External expenses)*

…

16 May   Likewise to pipers of Oxford   10s

…

Likewise to Morris, a fiddler, on 1 January   18d

…

f 5v col 2   *(7 July 1629–7 July 1630)* *(External expenses)*

…

19 (August)   Likewise to the king's trumpeters   20s

…

22 (August)   Likewise to the queen's trumpeters   20s

…

Hannisters' Registers   OCA: L.5.2
f 366v*   *(4 December)*

…

John Gerrard, Philip Golledge, Richard Burren, and Sampson Stronge,
musicians, were admitted freely to the liberties of this city, paying only the
officers' fees and each of them (paying) 2s 6d to the corporation treasury,
and they swore their corporal oath just as it appears more fully in the act
passed at the same council, etc.

…

1629–30
Christ Church Treasurers' Accounts   ChCh Arch: iii.c.1
f 276

…

And on the expenses of the tragedies and comedies held
and produced this year   nil

Magdalen College Liber Computi MC Arch: LCE/16
f 3v* *(Internal and external payments)*
…

To musicians on the bursars' feast	5s

…

To the earl of Warwick's trumpeters and (those) returned from the naval fleet	5s 6d

…

New College Bursars' Long Book NC Arch: 4200
f [182] *(25 December–25 March)* *(Internal expenses)*
…

Paid to the town musicians	6s 8d

…

f [182v] *(External expenses)*
…

Paid to trumpeters of the sheriff of the county of Oxford	5s

…

The Queen's College Long Rolls QC Arch: LRC
f 5v col 2* *(7 July–7 July)* *(External expenses)*
…

Likewise to Morris, a fiddler	18d

…

f 6 col 1
…

8 May	Likewise to pipers of Oxford	10s

…

1630–1
Magdalen College Liber Computi MC Arch: LCE/16a
f 3v *(Internal and external payments)*
…

To musicians on the bursars' feast	5s

…

To the king's trumpeters and to others (*ie*, other trumpeters (?))	£1 7s 6d

…

Merton College Bursars' Accounts   MCR: 3.1
f 247   *(18 March–29 July) (External expenses)*

...To trumpeters, 5s....

...

Merton College Register   MCR: 1.3
p 308

...

2 August

12d for each fellow has been granted to certain musicians, whom the University had hired not so long ago as different from the town (musicians) and permitted to rejoice in the badge and name of the University, and (the money) shall be deducted in the next term.

...

New College Bursars' Accounts   NC Arch: 7645
mb 10*   *(25 December–25 March) (Internal expenses)*

...

...Paid to the town musicians, 6s 8d....

...

Oriel College Treasurers' Accounts   OC Arch: S I.C.1
f 286v   *(Internal expenses)*

...

Likewise to royal trumpeters   00 010 00

...

The Queen's College Long Rolls   QC Arch: LRC
f 8 col 2   *(7 July–7 July) (External expenses)*

...

On 1 January to Morris, a fiddler   18d

...

On 7 March to pipers of Oxford   10s

...

f 10 col 1*   *(7 July 1631–7 July 1632)*

...

18 August   To the king's trumpeters   20s

...

To Morris, a fiddler   18d

...

Trinity College Bursars' Books   TC Arch: I/A/2
f 343*   (25 March–24 June) (Expenses)

...

To royal trumpeters   10s
To navy pipers on 25 May   6s

...

Hannisters' Registers   OCA: L.5.2
f 210v*

9 July 1631

(English)
°Memorandum that on 24 May in the tenth year of the reign of King Charles
(ie, 24 May 1634) both Christopher Palmer, who married Mary, lately the
wife of the said Richard Burren, and the same apprentice (John Hancocke,)
and Sampson Stronge, a citizen and musician of the city of Oxford, came
before Francis Harris, esquire, mayor of the same city and me, Timothy Cartar,
clerk of the commonalty of the aforesaid city. And then the same apprentice,
with the said Christopher's consent, placed himself as the apprentice of the
said Sampson Stronge for the remainder of the aforesaid term and from
the end of the same term up to 24 May then next following. And the same
Sampson at that time accepted the same apprentice into his service and undertook to give to the same apprentice on the same 24 May after the end of the
said term just what the aforesaid Richard Burren ought to give to the same
apprentice and just as is specified in the aforesaid enrollment (made) on ⟨..⟩
July 1631.
Likewise Timothy Cartar, clerk of the commonalty of the city of Oxford, is
(a witness to the enrollments (?)).°

...

f 361*

...

Robert Duke and Edward Golledge, musicians, have been admitted freely, as
others (have been) before, to the liberties of this city on 19 September in the
seventh year (of the reign) of King Charles, at the council held then; and they
were sworn.

...

City Waits' Obligations   OCA: F.5.2
f 51

Let all know by the present (bond) that I, John Baldwin the younger of the
city of Oxford, musician, am bound and firmly obligated to Thomas Cooper,

esquire, mayor of the aforesaid city of Oxford, (and) to William Potter, William Wright, Oliver Smith, William Boswell, and Henry Bosworth, aldermen of the same city, to (the sum) of £10 of legal English money to be paid to the same Thomas Cooper, William Potter, William Wright, Oliver Smith, William Boswell, and Henry Bosworth, or to any one of them, (or) hereafter to their assured attornies, executors, administrators, or assigns. Indeed I firmly oblige myself, my heirs, executors, and administrators to well and faithfully make this payment by the present (bond) sealed with my seal, given on 15 November in the sixth year of the reign of our lord Charles, by the grace of God, king of England, Scotland, France, and Ireland, defender of the faith, etc.

f 53

Let all know by the present (bond) that I, Sampson Stronge of the city of Oxford, musician, am bound and firmly obligated to Thomas Cooper, esquire, mayor of the aforesaid city of Oxford, (and) to William Potter, William Wright, Oliver Smith, William Boswell, and Henry Bosworth, aldermen of the same city, to (the sum) of £10 of legal English money to be paid to the same Thomas Cooper, William Potter, William Wright, Oliver Smith, William Boswell, and Henry Bosworth, or to any one of them, (or) hereafter to their assured attornies, executors, administrators, or assigns. Indeed I firmly oblige myself, my heirs, executors, and administrators to well and faithfully make this payment by the present (bond) sealed with my seal, given on 15 November in the sixth year of the reign of our Lord Charles, by the grace of God, king of England, Scotland, France, and Ireland, defender of the faith, etc.

1631–2
Magdalen College Liber Computi   MC Arch: LCE/17
f 3v   *(Internal and external payments)*

...

To musicians on the bursars' feast   5s

...

To trumpeters   10s

...

Merton College Bursars' Accounts   MCR: 3.1
f 250   *(29 July–18 November 1631) (External expenses)*

...

...To royal trumpeters, 10s....

...

Merton College Register   MCR: 1.3
p 311
...

16 August   By agreement of the wardens and fellows, 10s each year shall be paid hereafter to the new fiddlers of the University in place of the 6s 8d, which of old
the bursars were accustomed to pay to the town officers.
...

New College Bursars' Accounts   NC Arch: 7647
mb 8   *(25 December–25 March)* *(Internal expenses)*
...
...Paid to the University musicians, 6s 8d....
...

Oriel College Treasurers' Accounts   OC Arch: S 1.C.1
f 292   *(Internal expenses)*
...
Likewise to trumpeters   0 5 6d
...

The Queen's College Long Rolls   QC Arch: LRC
f 10 col 1*   *(7 July–7 July)* *(External expenses)*
...
To fiddlers of Oxford   10s
...

Brian Twyne's Notes on the History of the University Music
Bodl.: MS. Twyne-Langbaine 4
ff 105–7*

(English)
                Regarding musicians, or singers, of the University

From the register of the University of Oxford or the act book, page 93.1.
In AD 1501 and the sixteenth year of (the reign) of King Henry VII.

[Before the commissary, Thomas Bank, STD, rector of Lincoln College, at
the time when William Smith, the reverend father in Christ and bishop of
Lincoln, founder of Brasenose College, was chancellor of Oxford.] †®
On 29 May a certain William Jannys, a harper and a stranger, came before us
and he complained that two men, namely Pittes and Hawkinse of the parish
of St Michael at the North Gate, were unlawfully keeping his harp, claiming

service from him which he never owed nor promised them. And to prove this he brought in John Huskinse of the parish of St Mary, who promised and gave surety that he would prove precisely this, namely that the aforesaid William did not promise the aforesaid Pittes and Hawkinse any service, but promised service to himself, John Huskinse, and to his fellows. And therefore the aforesaid William as well as the aforesaid John asked me that it be registered that the oftensaid William pleaded his case before the commissary of the University, so that they would not be unjustly harassed by the town bailiffs or by the mayor of the town because he was a stranger, promising on his oath that he would respond, obey, do, and accept what justice required if an agreement were made in this regard.

®Case

      William Jannys, John Huskinse, Pittes, and Hawkinse

These things were done in the presence of Mr Thomas Bank, STD, rector of Lincoln College, and the deputy of Mr William Atwater, STD, commissary general of the reverend father in Christ, William Smith, then bishop of Lincoln, chancellor of the University of Oxford, and founder of Brasenose College.
(English)

(English) on the feast of St Matthew the Apostle, after a citation of the community of the town had been held beforehand and after an innumerable multitude both of locals and of outsiders had been brought together (and) after the common bell had been rung, the aforesaid burgesses in an armed band attacked the scholars of the aforesaid University with the sounding of horns, in a hostile manner, with malice aforethought, etc. *(blank)*
(English)

1632–3
Magdalen College Liber Computi MC Arch: LCE/18
f 3v *(Internal and external payments)*
...
To musicians on the bursars' feast   5s
...
To the king's trumpeters   £1
...

New College Bursars' Accounts NC Arch: 7650
mb 9 *(25 December–25 March)* *(Internal expenses)*
...
...Paid to the town musicians, 6s 8d....
...

Oriel College Treasurers' Accounts   OC Arch: S I.C.1
f 297v   *(Internal expenses)*
…

Likewise to royal trumpeters   0 11 0
…

The Queen's College Long Rolls   QC Arch: LRC
f 11 col 2   *(7 July–7 July) (External expenses)*
…

To Morris, a fiddler, on 1 January   0 1 6
…

To pipers of Oxford   0 10 0
…

Trinity College Bursars' Books   TC Arch: I/A/3
f 22   *(24 June–29 September) (Expenses)*
…

To royal trumpeters   0 10 0
…

1633–4
Magdalen College Liber Computi   MC Arch: LCE/19
f 3v   *(Internal and external payments)*
…

To musicians on the bursars' feast and the founder's obit   10s
…

Merton College Bursars' Accounts   MCR: 3.2
f 2v   *(26 July–22 November 1633) (External expenses)*
…

…To royal trumpeters   10s

New College Bursars' Accounts   NC Arch: 7651
mb 8   *(25 December–25 March) (Internal expenses)*
…

…Paid to the town musicians, 6s 8d….
…

The Queen's College Long Rolls   QC Arch: LRC
f 12 col 2   *(7 July–7 July) (External expenses)*
…

To the king's trumpeters   1 0 0
…

To Morris, a fiddler   0 1 6

...

To pipers of Oxford   0 10 0

...

OUS   ***Chancellor Laud, Corpus Statutorum (1634)***   STC: 19005
      sig Hh2v*   *(Of forbidden amusements)*

...

2) L.241.b.   Likewise that neither tightrope-walkers nor entertainers, who go onto the
L.262.a.   stage for the sake of profit, nor contests nor shows of fencers shall be permitted
             within the University of Oxford or its precinct without the special permission
             of the vice-chancellor. Nor should members of the University or students
             be present at the same. Indeed, entertainers, tightrope-walkers, and fencers
             contravening (this order) shall be imprisoned. And let undergraduate students –
             if any gathering at this kind of show should be apprehended – be punished
             or chastised according to the judgment of the vice-chancellor or proctors; let
             each graduate, however, pay 6s 8d to the treasury of the University as often
             as this occurs.

...

1634–5
Magdalen College Liber Computi   MC Arch: LCE/20
f 3v   *(Internal and external payments)*

...

To musicians for the bursars' feast and the
boys' interlude   10s

...

To the king's trumpeters   13s 4d

...

New College Bursars' Accounts   NC Arch: 7653
mb 6   *(25 December–25 March)* *(Internal expenses)*

...

...Paid to the town musicians, 6s 8d....

...

Oriel College Treasurers' Accounts   OC Arch: S 1.C.1
f 308   *(Internal expenses)*

...

Likewise to royal trumpeters   0 10 0

...

The Queen's College Long Rolls   QC Arch: LRC
f 14v col 1   *(7 July–7 July) (External expenses)*
...
To Morris, a fiddler   1s 6d
...

Trinity College Bursars' Books   TC Arch: I/A/3
f 39v   *(24 June–29 September) (Expenses)*
...
To the king's trumpeters   10s
...

1635–6
Magdalen College Liber Computi   MC Arch: LCE/21
f 3v   *(Internal and external payments)*
...
To musicians on the bursars' feast   0 5s 0
...
To the lord king's trumpeters   £1 0 0
...

Merton College Bursars' Accounts   MCR: 3.2
f 15v   *(31 July–20 November) (External expenses)*
...
...For royal trumpeters, 6s....

f 18   *(18 March–29 July)*
...
...For the college to receive (his) royal majesty, £20....
...

New College Bursars' Accounts   NC Arch: 7655
mb 7   *(25 December–25 March) (Internal expenses)*
...
...Paid to the town musicians, 6s 8d....
...

Oriel College Treasurers' Accounts   OC Arch: S I.C.1
f 312v   *(External expenses)*
...
Likewise paid to the lord vice-chancellor at the
arrival of the most serene king for the use of the
lord provost and the fellows by acquittance   10 0 0
...

f 313   *(Internal expenses)*

...

Likewise to royal trumpeters   0 10 0

...

The Queen's College Long Rolls   QC Arch: LRC
f 15v col 2   *(7 July–7 July) (External expenses)*

...

To the lord king's trumpeters   1   0   0
To Morris, a fiddler   0   1   6

...

f 16 col 1

...

To fiddlers of the University for the present
and past year   1   0   0

...

f 17 col 2   *(7 July 1636–7 July 1637)*

...

On 24 August to the lord king's trumpeters   01 00 00

...

Trinity College Bursars' Books   TC Arch: I/A/3
f 51   *(Expenses)*

...

Paid for receiving the king and queen   10 0 0
Paid to royal trumpeters   0 10 0

...

Register of Congregation and Convocation   OUA: NEP/Supra/R
f 138*

...

(English). Dated 12 December 1636 (and reads in the) beginning, 'Who to our
advantage, as if,' etc, on page 128 in The Deeds of Laud's Chancellorship°
°19 December
1636°
An auspicious work in which our mother, the University, obtains thanks and
indulgence from the queen's most serene majesty.
On Monday, 19 December, AD 1636, the reason for the convocation was to
publish the letter of the following tenor, which the queen's most serene majesty
sent to the University.

...

The Great Charter   OUA: Long Box XIX
mb 14   (5 March)

...

°Contests and shows°

...Moreover, since Lord Edward, formerly king of England, the first (of his name), in a certain writ of his containing (the phrase) 'given at Chertsey on 12 November in the thirty-third year of his reign,' directed to the sheriff of the county of Oxford, had prohibited that jousts and tilts or any other feat of arms be conducted or held near the town of Oxford, whereby the repose of the scholars of the University of Oxford might in any way be impeded or disturbed, contrary to the liberties of the same University, just as it appears more fully in the same writ, we, from our more abundant grace and from sure knowledge and our instigation alone, by means of the present (letter) for our part and that of our heirs and successors, give and grant to the aforesaid chancellor, masters, and scholars, and their successors by means of the present (letter), that the chancellor, or vice-chancellor, or his deputy for the time being themselves (shall have authority to act in this matter), lest anything of this kind, (namely,) jousts, tilts, tourneys, feats of arms, tournaments, adventures, or idle and vain or contentious shows accustomed to be presented or exhibited to the people for the sake of profit, sport, or spectacle, whereby the scholars could be called away from their studies, be held or take place within the University of Oxford or its precinct, or within the city of Oxford and of its suburbs, or throughout a five-mile radius, without the special consent and assent, previously obtained, of the said chancellor himself, or of his vice-chancellor or his deputy, and of both or one of the proctors of this University for the time being. And as much for ourselves as for our heirs and successors in perpetuity we give and grant by the present (letter) full power and authority to the said chancellor, masters, and scholars, and their successors, to restrain or expel, by their own agency or by their officials or servants, all and every-one who will in future attempt to offer or present some or any of the afore-mentioned within the aforesaid limits without the assent and consent, previously obtained, of the chancellor himself, the vice-chancellor or his deputy, and of the proctors of the University or of one of them, as has been said above, and also to banish and remove immediately outside this precinct or jurisdiction stubborn and disobedient (persons), to be imprisoned at their (ie, the chancellor's, masters', and scholars') good pleasure....

...

Letter of Thomas Read to Sir Francis Windebank   PRO: SP/16/331
f [1]*   (8 September)

Most honoured uncle,

I have added these finishing touches to the comedy – (its) prow, if you will, and stern, which perhaps can please (even) without a stage. Although we may

not attain courtly elegance, yet who will refrain from imitation? We do not
challenge Apollo in the arena but venerate him as a tutelary god. The other
offspring of our muses still remain hidden. But if they should go forth at
some time to the public, I will commit (them) not to your censure but your
guardianship, since I know you will be not the Aristarchus of academic studies
but (their) Maecenas.

Your honour's most observant
kinsman
Thomas Read

From New College, 8 September
   1636

1636–7
Merton College Bursars' Accounts   MCR: 3.2
f 21   *(29 July–18 November 1636)* *(External expenses)*
…
…To royal trumpeters, 10s.…

New College Bursars' Accounts   NC Arch: 7656
mb 9   *(25 December–25 March)* *(Internal expenses)*
…
…Paid to the University musicians, 6s 8d.…
…

The Queen's College Long Rolls   QC Arch: LRC
f 17 col 2*   *(7 July–7 July)* *(External expenses)*
…
To Morris, a fiddler   00 01 6
…

f 17v col 1
…
On 7 April to pipers of the University
of Oxford   00 10 00
…

St John's College Computus Annuus   SJC Arch: Acc.I.A.21
f 22   *(25 December–25 March)* *(Allowances)*

Likewise in the same (week)
for plays   £3 18d
…

Likewise in the thirteenth (week)
to musicians   £13 6s 8d
...

Vice-Chancellors' Accounts   OUA: WP/β/21(4)
p 234   *(22 July 1636–7 August 1637) (Debits)*
...
Likewise of coin received on the first and
second occasion from the colleges and halls
in receiving (his) royal majesty   718   9   4
...

1637–8
Balliol College Bursars' Accounts   BC Arch: Computi 1615–1662
f 134v   *(7 July–18 October 1638) (Expenses noted)*
...
Likewise to royal trumpeters   0 10 0
...

Magdalen College Liber Computi   MC Arch: LCE/23
f 3v   *(Internal and external payments)*
...
To the king's trumpeters   £1 0s 0d
...

New College Bursars' Accounts   NC Arch: 7657
mb 7   *(25 December–25 March) (Internal expenses)*
...
...Paid to the University musicians, 6s 8d....
...

Oriel College Treasurers' Accounts   OC Arch: S I.C.1
f 323   *(Internal expenses)*
...
Likewise to royal trumpeters   00 10 00
...

The Queen's College Long Rolls   QC Arch: LRC
f 18v col 2   *(7 July–7 July) (External expenses)*
...
On 2 January to pipers of Oxford on that day
when we entertained guests   0   5   0
...

To pipers of Oxford for predawn music in winter 0 10 0

...

To Morris, a piper, on 1 January 0 1 6

...

f 20 col 2 *(7 July 1638–7 July 1639)*

...

Firstly on 21 August to the lord king's trumpeters 1 0 0

...

St John's College Computus Annuus sɪc Arch: Acc.ɪ.A.22
p 44 *(25 March–24 June) (Allowances)*

...

Likewise for musicians £17 9s 4d

...

Trinity College Bursars' Books ᴛc Arch: I/A/3
f 72 *(25 March–24 June) (Expenses)*

...

To royal trumpeters 10s

...

Archdeacon's Court Book ᴏʀᴏ: ᴍs.Oxf.Arch. papers Oxon.c.13
f 306* *(16 December)*

Against Edward Brookes of St Michael's parish for working upon St Andrew's
Day last past
(He was) cited in person on the last day of March by Tomlinson, who was
sworn, etc. When the third call had been made, etc, he appeared. After he
was sworn, etc, and when he had been charged as above, he denies *(English)*.

On the next
(court day)

The lord therefore decreed that (his) servants should be cited, etc.
Against James Dudley of the same parish in like manner
(He was) cited in like manner, etc. When the third call had been made, etc, he
appeared and confesses *(English)*. The lord (judge) therefore admonished him
(English) and to appear on the next (court day) to see the further procedure, etc.
Against John Watson of St Thomas' parish in like manner
(He was) cited in like manner, etc. When the third call had been made, etc, he
appeared and responds in like manner in every respect and was admonished
in like manner, etc.
Against John Symmonds and Thomas Cox of the same parish
Having been sought on the aforesaid day, etc, sworn by Tomlinson, who was

sworn, etc, they appeared and confess in like manner and the lord (judge) admonished (them) in like manner as above.

...

1638–9
Magdalen College Liber Computi   MC Arch: LCE/24
f 3v   *(Internal and external payments)*

...

To musicians for the bursars' feast   0   5   0

...

Merton College Bursars' Accounts   MCR: 3.2
f 32v   *(27 July–23 November 1638) (External expenses)*

...To royal trumpeters, 10s....

...

New College Bursars' Accounts   NC Arch: 7660
mb 8   *(25 December–25 March) (Internal expenses)*

...

...Paid to the University musicians, 6s 8d....

...

The Queen's College Long Rolls   QC Arch: LRC
f 20 col 2   *(7 July–7 July) (External expenses)*

...

On 1 January to Morris, a piper   0   1   6
To pipers of Oxford for predawn music in winter   0   10   0

...

St John's College Computus Annuus   SJC Arch: Acc.I.A.23
f 71v*   *(25 December–25 March) (Allowances)*

Likewise in the eleventh (week) for musicians   £20 2s 4d

...

Likewise in the twelfth (week) for stage plays   £5 5s

...

Hannisters' Registers   OCA: L.5.2
f 340

...

William Hilliard, John Hilliard, and William Stronge, musicians, have been freely admitted to the liberties of the city, paying only the officers' fees and each of them (paying) to the corporation treasury. And they have sworn their corporal oaths, etc.

...

1639–40
Magdalen College Liber Computi   MC Arch: LCE/25
f 3v   *(Internal and external payments)*

...

To musicians for the bursars' feast   0 5s 0

...

New College Bursars' Accounts   NC Arch: 7661
mb 9   *(25 December–25 March) (Internal expenses)*

...

...Paid to the University musicians, 6s 8d.

...

The Queen's College Long Rolls   QC Arch: LRC
f 21v col 1   *(7 July–7 July) (External expenses)*

...

On 1 January to Morris, a piper   0   1   6

...

To pipers of Oxford for predawn music
in winter   0 10   0

...

1640–1
New College Bursars' Accounts   NC Arch: 7663
mb 9   *(25 December–25 March) (Internal expenses)*

...

...Paid to the University musicians, 6s 8d.

...

The Queen's College Long Rolls   QC Arch: LRC
f 23 col 1   *(7 July–7 July) (External expenses)*

...

To Morris, a piper, on 1 January   0   1   6
To pipers of Oxford for predawn music
in winter   0 10   0

...

St John's College Computus Annuus   SJC Arch: Acc.I.A.25
f 24*   *(25 December–25 March) (Allowances)*
...
Likewise in the twelfth (week) for musicians   £6 15s 8d
...

1641-2
Magdalen College Liber Computi   MC Arch: LCE/27
f 3v   *(Internal and external expenses)*
...
To royal trumpeters   £1
...

Merton College Bursars' Accounts   MCR: 3.2
f 56   *(18 March–29 July) (External expenses)*
...
...To trumpeters by the vice-warden, 6s 8d....
...

New College Bursars' Accounts   NC Arch: 7665
mb 10   *(25 December–25 March) (Internal expenses)*
...
...Paid to the University musicians, 6s 8d.
...

Oriel College Treasurers' Accounts   OC Arch: S I.C.1
f 341   *(Internal expenses)*
...
Likewise to certain nobles' trumpeters   00 05 00
...

The Queen's College Long Rolls   QC Arch: LRC
f 24v col 2   *(7 July–7 July) (External expenses)*
...
To pipers of Oxford   0 10 0
...
To Morris, a piper, on 1 January   0 1 6
...

St John's College Computus Annuus   SJC Arch: Acc.I.A.26
f 24*   *(25 December–25 March) (Allowances)*
...
Likewise in the eleventh (week) for musicians   £5 9s 8d
...

1642–3
Merton College Bursars' Accounts   MCR: 3.2
f 61v   *(18 November–24 March)*   *(External expenses)*
...
...To trumpeters of his royal majesty by agreement, 10s.... To royal drummers by agreement, 5s. To Prince Rupert's trumpeters by agreement, 10s....

...

APPENDIX 5

c 1400–22
Mock Letter from Neptune to the Nobles of the Kingdom of Beans
BL: MS Royal 10.B.IX
f 129v
...

Neptune, the offspring of heaven and son of great Diana, ruler, lord, and patron from Dis' palace to greatest Jove's citadel, to each and every noble of the kingdom of the bean, (wishing them) good health with peace and that they may listen attentively to the precepts of the everlasting republic, set (their) hands (to do them), and gather soon (to obey them) on the feet of affection as if on feathered wings. The highest maker of all things and father of what is caused has established the lower globe of the earth under the state of this condition, (namely) that, although it is the base, as it were, and stable foundation of all the spheres, it would suddenly be dissolved into the dust of division if it were not continually possessed of the moisture of our magnificent bounty. Thus if at any time any region stabilized by royal nobility should be deprived of the same, it turns into division and falls into ruin. Hence it is that a trustworthy report very recently now thundered in our ears that your excellent king, brother of the noble Atlas, about to renounce the world, has resigned the sceptre and arms of your most renowned kingdom. Lest the community of so great a region – from the beginning, especially dear to us – like a nation without a head, a people without a prince, or sheep with the shepherd taken away, should fall into depredation and ruin equally, we enjoining you command that, with every delay put aside, you hasten quickly to the election of a new king, proceeding by this counsel so that, after Golias four times acts as a restraint against his brother's madness, you may steer the oarsmen of your ship into the port of unanimous concord. (You shall write) imparting faithfully to us whatever you have done in the foregoing when next the feast of Clement dawns. Written in the port of Pelion at the time when Thetis was rejoicing everywhere with Bacchus in honour.

...

APPENDIX 13

1635-6
Entertainment of King Charles   Wood: *Historia et Antiquitates*
p 343 col 2   *(29 August)*
...

   When supper was finished on the same night, the august guests attended
an English comedy which students of Christ Church and other colleges were
performing in the refectory of their hall. Strode, the public orator whom we
have often mentioned, wrote it and gave it the name *The Passions Subdued*, or
The Floating Island Made Fixed. But, because of (its) too serious and severe
argument, it displeased the courtiers as much as some public lectures in stoic
(philosophy) did, even though both the industry of the actors and the very
large structure of the wooden stage – indeed, it stretched from the highest part
of the refectory nearly to the fireplace – greatly commended the same (play)
up until these things first began to be used.
   ...

p 344 cols 1–2   *(30 August)*
...

   When they had dined in this way, the archbishop led the king and the
queen and all the nobles separately into various rooms where they spent a
whole hour in leisure and conversation. But he meanwhile took care that
the windows of the refectory would be closed and, after the lamps had been
lighted, that everything that related to the theatrical performances would
be prepared, intent, with his full attention on the comedy, the greatest part (of
which was), they say, written by Mr George Wild, a fellow of the college,
and (is) called *Loves Hospital*. When everything was ready the chancellor
accompanied the king and queen together with the lords and ladies as they
walked by a new path, which was completely private and subject to no
disturbances – in as much as it offered an unimpeded passage from the
chamber of the royal presence, as we say, to the refectory – since while they
themselves were entering the houses designated for the shows (*ie*, stage
houses *(?)*), everyone else was kept out lest any injury from the summer
heat, intensified by the multitude of those flocking in, should befall such
great guests. After that, when the lower door had been closed and the spectators of greater note had been sent in, the actors chosen from that college
only came forth onto the stage. Since they brought skill in executing drama
to an amusing and delightful subject (*or* plot) and not, however, a smutty
or irreverent (subject *or* plot) – I say nothing of profanity, for a very few years
ago it was unheard of for God and religion to be made sport of – they filled
everyone with great pleasure. Somewhere around the middle of the shows

the archbishop took care that the choicest food would be placed before the king and queen and also all the nobles. But when the comedy was finished the august guests returned to Christ Church and, after dinner was finished in private, they proceeded around the eighth hour to the refectory of the college to receive far more abundant delight from another play – Mr William Cartwright had written this one and called it *The Royal Slave*. It surpassed the one previously mentioned in subject (*or* plot) and in wit, and especially in theatrical apparatus. Behind double doors placed together nearer the centre and at the back of the proscenium – it should be noted that these were used then for the first time – (and) linked together, moreover, by bars so artfully that they could be opened as quickly as possible, a very wide and very pleasant view was revealed. For verdant woods and a beautiful temple bathed from above by the rays of the sun feasted the eyes of the spectators, to whom also little towns presented themselves lavishly, when people were seen moving to and fro and going about their business. In a word, Inigo Jones – who used to adapt as well as possible every kind of spectacle, but especially those masques that are full of dances, to the disposition (*or* wit) of the courtiers – had seen to it that every part of the play would be adorned with vivid images of places and people and the remaining apparatus. Equal thanks were due also to Mr Busby, to whom Roscius would yield the palm on the stage. But then many as were there took so much pleasure from it, both from the highly trained actors and the Persian costumes full of novelty, that they said that they had experienced nothing more beautiful or more ingenious with (the) eyes or ears. And this was the ending of that day, which the chancellor observed had been named after St Felix and on which everything had turned out favourably.

...

Endnotes

4   OUA: SEP/Y/12a   mb [3]
This riot occurred between 21 and 24 February and caused two deaths, many injuries, and property damage. Although referred to in letters and chronicles, most information comes from a collection of ten legal documents now in OUA: SEP/Y/12a and 12b and edited by Salter in *Mediaeval Archives*, vol 1, pp 43–81. These documents include the king's Latin letters patent appointing two men to investigate and judge in the matter (dated 27 February, 26 Edward I (1297/8) and also found in the patent roll of 26 Edward I, mb 27d); five Anglo-Norman documents, all apparently drafts of the town's complaint against the University; an Anglo-Norman document giving the official University response; an Anglo-Norman document containing the pleading of the town's proctor; and two Latin documents giving articles and positions presented by the University's proctor. Because of jurisdictional disputes the case was heard by a panel of arbitrators rather than secular judges; the dating of the actual hearings is obscure. The three documents from the University's side all argue that the townspeople involved were acting as a body with official knowledge and consent, and, to that end, that they were summoned by the town bells and the town horn and used a common cry. We have excerpted from the University's official response. Brian Twyne cites one of the Latin documents as evidence in Bodl.: MS. Twyne-Langbaine 4, ff 105–7 (see p 503).

4–5   OUA: NEP/Supra/A   f 63
This statute, in the oldest part of the volume, is dated '1250?' by Anstey (ed), *Munimenta Academica*, vol 1, p 18, and 'before 1350' by Gibson (ed), *Statvta Antiqva*, p 82.
     The text of 'De modo' was later copied in nearly identical form in Bodl.: MS. 337, with 'Statutum' where NEP/Supra/A reads 'De modo' (p 4, l.30) and an explanatory marginal note (in the same hand as that of the main text), which reads 'Statutum ante modo interdicendi festa nacionum.' A collation is given by Gibson, pp 82–3.

5–6   Bodl.: MS. Twyne 4   pp 32–3
The reference 'Aaa' (p 5, l.27m) is to the chancellors' register, OUA: Register Aaa. The Drapery (p 5, l.29m) was on the west side of Northgate Street (now Cornmarket), north of Great Bailey Street (now Queen), very close to the northern edge of St Martin's churchyard (H.E. Salter, *Map of Medieval Oxford* (Oxford, 1934)).

7   EC Arch: A.1   single mb
The parishes of Long Wittenham and Little Wittenham, now in Oxfordshire, were in historic Berkshire.

They are located just north and east of Didcot. No relevant records survive from either parish, making this the only evidence of parish playing from the more westerly parish, Long Wittenham.

8–10   PRO: JUST 3/180   mbs 2c–d, 3d, 5d

The excerpts from mbs 3d and 5d are portions of indictments similar in breadth and detail to the indictment transcribed from mbs 2c–d. There are seven defendants against the charges described on mb 3d and eight against those from mb 5d, although the actions described in the passage excerpted here relate to charges against a Nicholas Stanley alone.

Deep Hall (p 8, l.27) was a tenement on the south side of the High Street between the present Magpie Lane and University College. Salter does not identify a 'Neville's Entry' ('Neuylesentre,' p 9, l.1) but Neville Hall was on the south side of the High Street, almost at the corner of Magpie Lane, and Neville Inn was in south 'Shipyerd Street' on the site of the present southwest corner of Merton Field. Salter does not identify a 'sent Agase halle' (p 9, l.6) but Agase Hall was near the corner of Vine Hall Lane and Little Jury Lane (the present corner of Alfred Street and Bear Lane). On the north side of the High Street and the west side of St Mildred's Lane (Turl Street), now the site of the Covered Market, were Pyry Hall, Mildred Hall, and Bastaples Entry (p 9, ll.12, 16, 17). Hampton Hall (p 9, l.16) was on the east side of St Mildred's and is now part of the site of Lincoln College. Charlton's Inn (p 9, l.23) was on the corner of Catte Street and the High Street (the present site of All Souls). The felons barricaded the High Street from the corner of Catte Street to Penchurch Lane (p 9, l.24), which in the early modern period was called Horsemill Lane and is now Logic Lane, intersecting with the High Street from the south on the east side of University College. See H.E. Salter, *Map of Medieval Oxford* (Oxford, 1934); and Salter, *Survey of Oxford*, vol 1.

10   BL: MS Royal 17.B.xlvii   f 44v

The phrase 'licet alias vobis consulerim' (l.26) refers to an earlier letter (f 44), in which the same writer had counselled the father to send his son to Oxford.

11–13   NC Arch: 9429   ff 24, 34v–5

This record of ceremonies on Holy Innocents' Day contains the earliest known reference to the boy bishop in Oxford. The 'saltus' ('leaping dances') (p 13, l.13) recall Absolon in Chaucer's *Miller's Tale* (ll.3328–30): 'In twenty manere koude he trippe and daunce/ After the scole of Oxenforde tho,/ And with his legges casten to and fro.' (*The Riverside Chaucer*, 3rd ed, Larry D. Benson (ed) (Boston, 1987), 70.)

13   Durham University Library: Durham Cathedral Muniments, Oxford Ac. 1399–1400   single mb

This account runs from the Translation of St Thomas to the day after Ascension. The feast day of the Translation of Thomas the Apostle is 3 July and that of St Thomas of Canterbury is 7 July.

14   MCR: 4114   single mb

This expense was incurred by John Mory, who may have been the same as the 'John Emery' incurring a like expense in 1410–11 (see p 1086, endnote to MCR: 4115 single mb, single mb dorse).

14   Bodl.: MS. Tanner 165   f 147

A marginal note dates this entry 'Anno gracie millesimo CCCCmo.' but the date appears to have been left incomplete. The degree candidates were Richard Godmersham and John Langdon (see Pantin (ed), *Canterbury College*, vol 3, pp 63–8).

14   MCR: 4115   single mb, single mb dorse
The first expense was incurred by John Emery, who may have been the same as the 'John Mory' incurring a like expense in 1400–1 (see p 1085, endnote to MCR: 4114 single mb). The second expense was incurred by Thomas and Edmund Tank.

14   Bodl.: MS. Twyne 23   p 242
Twyne dates this excerpt by regnal year only (2 Henry v). Civic accounts for this period are usually from Michaelmas to Michaelmas but whether this falls under 1413–14 or 1414–15 cannot be determined.

15   ORO: PAR 211/4/F1/1, item 5   single mb
The significance of the boughs is unclear. The entry occurs with expenses for candlewax and may represent payment for the material for a bower – a feature of the Whitsun festival elsewhere in the upper Thames Valley including nearby Woodstock. See Alexandra F. Johnston, 'Summer Festivals in the Thames Valley Counties', *Custom, Culture and Community* (Odense, Denmark, 1994), 44–5.

15   Bodl.: MS. D.D. All Souls c.268, no 210   mb 2 col 1
The roll is undated but its heading refers to Henry Chichele, archbishop of Canterbury and founder of the college. Since the college was founded in 1438 and officially opened in 1443, this record has been dated *c* 1440.

17   ORO: PAR 213/4/F1/1   single mb
The heading of this roll (mounted on sheet 3) is missing from the MS; the date has been taken from later ink marginalia reading 'ab an*no* 1461 ad an*num* 1462.' This date is repeated in modern pencil at the top of the MS. The account for 1466–7 (sheet 5) is illegible.

18   ORO: PAR 214/4/F1/3   single mb
This year, besides the Pentecost ale, St Peter le Bailey earned 11d from other ales at unspecified dates.

18   Bodl.: MS. Top.Oxon c.403   f 42
After this entry Salter writes, 'the rest illegible,' in brackets.

18   ORO: PAR 214/4/F1/4   single mb
The heading indicates this account was made on 20 October 1465 ('lxv') with the words 'p*ro* Anno p*re*dict*o*' interlineated. The interlineation replaces the phrase 'proximo precedente.' The account preceding this one (ORO: PAR 214/4/F1/3) is dated 1464–5 and the account following this one (ORO: PAR 214/4/F1/5) is for the year 1466–7. It seems likely then that this is the account for the year 1465–6 although the heading as it stands suggests otherwise. The scribe having made one revision to the MS heading apparently failed to add an 'i' to 'lxv' of the rendering date.

19   ORO: PAR 214/4/F1/5   single mb
Besides the money earned at the Pentecost ale, the parish raised 4s 1d at ales 'Alia vic*e*.'

19   Bodl.: MS. D.D. All Souls c.278   mbs 4, 5
In the draft version, a paper roll in the same box and with the same reference number, the 'Rewards' entry occurs on sheet 8, the 'Various expenses' entry on sheet 10.

20   oro: PAR 214/4/F1/7   single mb
John Rogers (l.12), a brewer, appears again in 1472–3 and 1474–5 (p 22). The lion and dragon (l.19) may have been depicted on banners; 'lyuerye' (l.21) refers to the Thames Valley custom of selling badges at the Whitsun festivals. See Alexandra F. Johnston, 'Summer Festivals in the Thames Valley Counties,' *Custom, Culture and Community*, T. Pettitt and L. Søndergaard (eds) (Odense, 1994), 51–2.

21   oro: PAR 211/4/F1/1, item 42   single mb
Salter (ed), *The Churchwardens' Accounts*, pp 78–9, dates this 1471–2 but the ms heading states that the account runs from 20 March, 10 Edward iv, to 7 March following. The next account runs from December 1471. An interim account may have been lost.

21   oro: PAR 211/4/F1/1, item 43   single mb
This marks the beginning of the parallel accounting stream for St Michael at the North Gate (see p 724). From 1471–2 to 1484–5 the Hock and Pentecost entries appear in the chantry chapel accounts and the churchwardens' accounts in alternating years, giving first the parish finances in general and then the chantry chapel income from the fundraising events. The chantry chapel accounts run from Christmas to Christmas, the churchwardens' from the feast of the Purification to the same.

22   oro: PAR 211/4/F1/1, item 46   single mb
The occasion of the donation of ale from John Rogers is not clear. It may have been St Anne's Day as in the 1474–5 account.

22   oro: PAR 211/4/F1/1, item 49   single mb
The account for 25 December 1473 to 25 December 1474 is not extant and thus no Hocktide 1474 receipts are represented in the Records.

23   oro: PAR 214/4/F1/10   single mb
John Holywode (l.18) rented various properties in the parish of St Peter le Bailey (Salter, *Survey of Oxford*, vol 2, pp 118, 137, 140). 'Iohanne Smyth' (l.21) is possibly the John Smith named as bailiff in a lease arrangement on 24 June 1459 (Salter (ed), *Properties*, p 373); two John Smiths, one a skinner and one a baker, were 'supervisors of nuisances' for the city in 1472 (Ellis and Salter (eds), *Liber Albus Civitatis Oxoniensis*, p 79).

24   Bodl.: ms. D.D. All Souls c.278   sheet 9
This is the draft account on a paper roll; the fair parchment account has not survived. Presumably 'evissam' (l.32) is Evesham, Worcestershire, which contained a large Benedictine abbey, but no other known connection between the abbey and All Souls exists. The players may well have been visitors from Evesham, particularly as All Souls had no known performance tradition of its own at this date.

25   oro: PAR 214/4/F1/13   single mb
John Robyns (l.19), a tanner, rented the property at what is now 33–5 Queen Street from the parish of St Peter le Bailey (Salter, *Survey of Oxford*, vol 2, p 140).

25   oro: PAR 213/4/F1/1   single mb
The part of the heading that contained the date of rendering is missing. 'AD 1481,' which is visible,

apparently indicates the end of the accounting period, so the year 1480–1 has been assigned to this MS. Since the next two accounts have no rendering dates and only a single year date, the accounts mounted on sheets 9–13 may be for the period 1481–4 rather than 1480–3. The accounting term, not evident from the MS heading, presumably remains 8 December to 8 December.

26   ORO: PAR 213/4/F1/1   single mb
This MS (mounted on sheet 11) bears the single date 1482 and no rendering date. The accounting term, not evident from the MS heading, presumably remains 8 December to 8 December.

26   Bodl.: MS. Wood D.2   p 328
The date of Wood's transcription is given on p 323: 'May 27 1667.' The accounting year for these accounts is not known in this period; Wood, however, does supply the rendering date. The term 'kinge game' (l.21), familiar for the summer festivals in the Thames Valley, suggests that a major feature of the festival was a mock king. See Johnston and MacLean, 'Reformation and Resistance in Thames/Severn Parishes,' pp 182–3.

26   ORO: PAR 213/4/F1/1   single mb
This MS (mounted on sheet 13) bears the single date 1483 and no rendering date. The accounting term, not evident from the MS heading, presumably remains 8 December to 8 December.

28   MC Arch   f 68v
This item is included on the slight possibility that the tabernacle of or for prophets was dramatic (or quasi-dramatic) rather than sculptural or pictorial.

29   MCR: 1.2   ff 18, 18v
The ceremony involving the 'fire' was probably a winter gathering of members of the college for warmth and refreshments, perhaps the revival of a more ancient, albeit undocumented, ceremony.

29   MC Arch   f 100v
The interpretation of what exactly the 'satrape' were is a matter of controversy among the editors. The interpretation presented here is that reached by Alexandra F. Johnston and Abigail Ann Young. Alan H. Nelson, noting the persistent references to music and a final reference to 'satrape,' again in a musical context, in 1631–2 (see p 497), reserves the opinion that the 'satrape' in the Records were in fact town musicians. Johnston and Young have concluded that the 'satrape maioris' (l.35) refers to one of the town serjeants, as the word 'satrapa' within the context of the Oxford city records means 'serjeant.' Beginning with the Latin Vulgate, the original meaning of the word (a borrowing from Persian) as a provincial governor was expanded to include 'military official' and 'count.' In a further development the word became an Anglo-Latin administrative term for 'serjeant'; in Winchester it referred to a town serjeant, in Canterbury, a serjeant at arms. Developments in English usage acted also on the usage of the Latin word: as English writers extended the meaning of 'serjeant' (originally someone holding land from the king by personal attendance and military service) to refer to an officer who protected a court and brought in the accused or was the administrative subordinate of a mayor or bailiff, so some Anglo-Latin writers called such persons 'satrapae.'

There were two sets of serjeants in Oxford – the mayor's serjeants and the bailiff's serjeants. One of the serjeants is named in the entry for 1561–2 as 'Mr Jones, the chief of the town officers.' Carl Hammer in private correspondence has identified 'Mr Jones' as Richard Jones, listed as mayor's serjeant in 1555–6 and again in 1568–9 (OCA: C/FC/1/A1/001, ff 88v, 114). The entries from the Merton College accounts have been included in the Records because the New Year's payment is ostensibly for a song that the serjeant or serjeants sang during the college New Year's celebration. Payments of one noble (6s 8d) occur in the Merton accounts in the period from 1505–6 to 1561–2. Most notations of payments are accompanied by wording that suggests that the payment is not simply for a song sung by an amateur. The 1508–9 entry reports that the officers received the money 'from the bursar in the college's name from kindness, to answer on our behalf … for our possession in the town.' This formula recurs, but with variants as in 1518–19: not 'as an obligation of any kind … but only from our kindness and generosity.' That the payment is more important than the song is shown by the 1558–9 entry where the one serjeant who could sing was taken sick but the payment was made anyway (see p 101). On 21 October 1561 Mr Jones was paid the regular 6s 8d perhaps for the previous year (see pp 105–6), for which accounts do not survive. However, the entry for 1 January 1561/2 notes that the officers did not come, 'which could seem a wonder since before this they were accustomed to take very eagerly those things which our college conferred on them freely and voluntarily.' Thereafter any payments made by the college for their New Year's celebration were made to musicians not to the town officers.

30 MCR: 1.2 ff 22, 23
The entry on f 22 constitutes the earliest reference in the Records to Merton's 'king of beans' ceremony (see Appendix 5), which seems to have been distinct from the 'fire' ceremony recorded on f 23 and first mentioned the preceding year (see p 29).

30 MC Arch f 130v
These fully itemized entries, divided into terms, also occur on a separate paper computus, now bound in with the parchment fair copy. Consolidated entries of the itemized hall costs appear on f 119v of the fair copy, where the first excerpted item under 'Hall Costs' omits 'vjo die Ianuarij' (l.30) but includes 'regardo *tempore* nati*uitatis* do*mi*ni.'

35 Bodl.: MS. Twyne 23 p 560
The internal date (6 Henry VII) is confirmed by the names of the mayor and bailiffs.

37–8 BL: MS Arundel 249 ff 52v–3, 85v
These two entries constitute the only record of a King Solomon play at Oxford. Based on More's letter (f 85v), we attribute the play to More himself. *The Correspondence of Sir Thomas More*, E.F. Rogers (ed) (Princeton, 1947), 3–4, dates this letter '*c* November 1501,' on the basis of references to Thomas More's life at Furnivall's Inn and St Lawrence Jewry in London. The letter is addressed to John Holt, school-master at Chichester Cathedral School since 1500, formerly usher at Magdalen College School in Oxford. For more on these entries and this play, see p 659 and Appendix 6:2 under *King Solomon*.

38 NC Arch: 5529 f [208v]
The week is called the ninetieth ('septi*mana* nonagesi*ma*'), clearly an error for nineteenth (the subsequent week is the twentieth).

39 ORO: PAR 213/4/F1/1 single mb
The MS mounted on sheet 19 is an undated fragment containing only expenses. It would fall between

the account for 1495–6 (sheet 17) and this account (sheet 21), which is also fragmentary and very fragile. The heading of the latter account is missing, but two antiquaries have made marginal notes speculating on the date. One, by W.H. Turner, dates the account 1501–2. The other, in an unidentified hand, refers to Bodl.: MS. Wood D.2, p 45, where Anthony Wood imputes these expenses to the year beginning in 1498. The next MS (sheet 23), also a fragment of expenses only, bears the date 1502–3. Given the uncertainty of the dates of the fragmentary membranes (sheets 19 and 21), this account has been assigned to the widest possible span of years, 1496–1502.

41   ORO: PAR 214/4/F1/14   single mb
The accounting year changes this year to 25 November–25 November and remains so until 1542–3.

41–2   OUA: Hyp/A/2, Register D (or D reversed)   f 93
This document was cited as evidence in Bodl.: MS. Twyne-Langbaine 4 ff 105–7 (see pp 498–9).

43   LC Arch: Computus 1   f 155
These entries are also recorded and cancelled on f 156.

44   Bodl.: MS. Wood C.1   p 78
Only a single year date (1504) is given by Wood, who made this transcription on 3 July 1665. He notes against the hocking entry, 'ye first time yat it occurs in these accompts as I remember.' There is, in fact, a Hocktide entry in 1499–1500 (p 41). The accounting term for St Peter le Bailey was normally 25 November to 25 November in this period. If by 1504 Wood meant a year ending 25 November 1504 then this is Hocktide, 15–16 April 1504. If he meant the year 1504–5 then this is Hocktide, 31 March–1 April 1505.

44   MCR: 1.2   f 151v
The marginal '.A.' (l.35m) matches a marginal '.B.' adjacent to another entry on this folio. The entries are out of chronological order and the two letters seem to indicate the proper sequence.

45   LC Arch: Computus 2   p 19
Decay has rendered the entry incomprehensible: compare to subsequent entries for 1506–7 (p 46) and 1507–8 and 1508–9 (p 49).

46   MC Arch: CP 8/51   f 63
Term 1 this year began on 8 November because of plague.

46–7   MC Arch   ff 200, 201
John Burgess was apparently interrogated concerning this play during this same year (p 47, ll.26–7). His play was evidently repeated in 1517–18 (see p 61).

47   Hampshire Record Office: 21M65/A1/18   ff 47, 58v, 69
An article on f 46 (#19) inquires about the playing of cards, dice, knuckle-bones, 'aut quencumque alium ludum noxium inordinatum et illicitum,' but all replies to it involve card games or (in one case) a ball game, which is probably tennis ('ludum sperilarium,' f 62v).
    Some of Mr Burgess' replies are misnumbered, eg, article 39 is a reply to article 40 while reply 40

('xl,' l.26) seems to answer article 41. Sir Burgess' reply (ll.32–3) seems to belong to article 45. For Mr Burgess' involvement in plays this same year, see p 1090, endnote to MC Arch ff 200, 201.

49–50   LC Arch: Computus 2   p 33
Of the three groups of entries, the first apparently refers to December 1508; the second to December 1507 and February 1507/8; and the third to 1 November, 17 November (the feast of St Hugh of Lincoln), and 6 December 1508.

50   MCR: 1.2   f 194
The first cross-reference, which has been left blank by the annotator (l.29m), may be to MCR: 1.2, f 158 (p 45); the second, '242.b' (l.30m), is to MCR: 1.2, f 241v (p 62); and the third (l.31m) is to MCR: 1.2, f 256 (p 65).

52   Bodl.: MS. Wood D.3   p 267
Wood adds under the hocking entry, 'This is ye first mention of hockyng *yat* I haue yet saw in these wrytings.'

53   Bodl.: MS. Wood D.2   p 301
The rendering date, supplied by Wood, is Rogation Sunday, which is the customary rendering date for these accounts until 1605.

53   ORO: PAR 213/4/F1/1   single mb
This account (sheet 39) and the account mounted on sheet 37 have identical headings but this one lacks a regnal year. Since the accounts for the periods 1507–9 and 1512–13 survive, these two accounts (sheets 37 and 39) must cover the period from 1510 to 1512. The account on sheet 37 is probably for 1511–12 based on the regnal year given, a fact confirmed by internal dating. Thus the account on sheet 39 is apparently that of 1510–11.

53   MC Arch   f 61
The sum is unusual. Possibly the first amount (6s 8d) is for fellows and the second (2s 8d) for scholars.

54   OUA: NEP/Supra/G   ff 143, 143v
Edward Watson's play is discussed in Appendix 12. It is noted also by Wood, *Athenae*, vol 1, col 32.

55–6   BL: MS Royal 12.B.xx   ff 39, 44
The 'sant mari … church' (p 55, l.29) was the University church of St Mary the Virgin, on the High Street. The possible real-life basis of this student composition can be seen in the records printed from the antiquarian St Mary's churchwardens' accounts, recording the wives' gathering at Hocktide in 1509–10, 1522–3, and 1527–8 (see pp 52, 65, 69). On the 'boye' who 'playd the lord' (p 56, l.11), see p 613.

57   LC Arch: Computus 3   f 28v
This entry occurs at the end of a list of payments of fellows' stipends for the first quarter of the accounting year, beginning on 21 December 1512. Entries beginning 'Domus' (l.5) are for expenses of the fellows as a corporate body.

58   Bodl.: MS. Morrell 9   f 8

The manuscript provides no concrete evidence from which to supply a dating sub-head but in later accounts (1567–8, 1572–3, 1619–20) the fiscal year appears to begin on or around the Monday after the Nativity of St John the Baptist.

The Tailors' accountants never give a date for the annual election dinner. However, a note in Thomas Crosfield's diary for 1630 suggests that the guild held its event on the feast of St Andrew, at least in the seventeenth century: 'The last of this moneth St Andrew when ye Talors vsually wont to haue their merry meeting…' (QC Library: MS 390, f 53v).

59   Bodl.: MS. Morrell 9   f 9

See above, endnote to Bodl.: MS. Morrell 9 f 8.

61   ORO: PAR 211/4/F1/2, item 97   pt 1, f [4], pt 3, f [1]

The heading does not survive but the account contains an internal date of 8 Henry VIII. The context suggests that 8 Henry VIII is the account end date. Assuming the standard March to March accounting year, the account ends in March 1517/18 and thus the Hocktide and Whitsuntide receipts are for 1517.

61   MC Arch   ff 123v, 126

John Burgess' play of *St Mary Magdalene* is first mentioned in 1505–6 (see p 46).

70   ORO: PAR 211/4/F1/2, item 108   single mb

The account began and ended on 12 March, St Gregory's Day, as did all the subsequent accounts until 1602–3. It begins a sequence of four accounts (items 108, 110, 111, 113) where the dating is uncertain. None has a year date. The heading of item 108 gives its date as St Gregory, 21 Henry VIII for one year; item 110, St Gregory, 22 Henry VIII for one year; item 111, St Gregory, 23 Henry VIII for one year. Item 113 also gives its date as 23 Henry VIII until St Gregory 24 Henry VIII. Judging from the names of the churchwardens and the sums carried forward, it seems fairly certain that these accounts run in sequence. The original numbering of item 108, 'xxti' Henry VIII, was altered to 'xxjti' Henry VIII with the addition of 'j.' Salter (ed), *The Churchwardens' Accounts*, p 187, assumed that the emendation was erroneous and that item 108 was for 20 Henry VIII. This would make item 110 21 Henry VIII and item 111 22 Henry VIII, thereby making the dating for item 113 correct as 23 Henry VIII. The assumption that the dating of item 113 is correct is strengthened by the definite dating of item 114 as 24 Henry VIII. Salter's dating has been adopted here.

71   ORO: PAR 211/4/F1/2, item 110   single mb

For dating of this account, see above, endnote to ORO: PAR 211/4/F1/2, item 108 single mb.

72   ORO: PAR 211/4/F1/2, item 111   single mb

The second sum is problematic. The final 'x' is smudged suggesting an intended deletion or correction to a previously written 'v.' Salter (ed), *The Churchwardens' Accounts*, p 194, prints the sum as 'xxxvi.' For dating of this account, see above, endnote to ORO: PAR 211/4/F1/2, item 108 single mb.

72   ORO: PAR 213/4/F1/1   single mb

After this year the accounts for ten years have been lost.

73   MC Arch   f 21
Among the external expenses is a payment of 2s to a Mr Engest 'pro noua tunica facta circa purificacionem beatæ Mariæ quam ad huc habet cum campanis.' The significance of the 'tunica' and the bells is not known.

73–4   OUA: Hyp/A/4, Register EEE (or B reversed)   f 248
The death of Martin Lindsay, here assigned by Twyne to 1534, is assigned by Foster (ed), *Alumni Oxonienses*, vol 3, p 915, to 1554.

78   ORO: PAR 211/4/F1/2, item 117   single mb
Following this account is ORO: PAR 211/4/F1/2, item 118, a paper account with payments only. The next full account is for 12 March 1543/4 to 12 March 1544/5.

80   ORO: PAR 214/4/F1/21   single mb
The item recorded here under 'Payments' may have no mimetic relevance, but a similar reference in 1540–1 (p 83) suggests that this may be the costume of the lady of the summer festival (see below, endnote to ORO: PAR 214/4/F1/24 single mb).

81   Bodl.: MS. Rolls Oxon Box 1, #15   sheet 1
This entry also occurs in Wood's transcription in Bodl.: MS. Wood D.3, p 273. Wood saw a 'qu' for a farthing at the end of the Hocktide expense.

82   MC Arch   f 162
The entry for 'biberio dato sociis' (l.26) is repeated on f 162v with the sum erased.

83   ORO: PAR 214/4/F1/24   single mb
The reference here to mending the queen's gown and her kirtle (l.11) probably refers to the costume of the parishioner who played the role of the queen of the summer festival. Evidence from Thames Valley parishes indicates that members of the parish were chosen to preside over the festival. See p 1086, endnote to ORO: PAR 211/4/F1/1, item 5 single mb. This more specific reference clarifies the entry in these accounts for 1537–8 (see p 80).

85   NC Arch: 5530   f [173]
Regarding 'domine Wylloby' (l.11), no Lord Willoughby existed at this date. Both titles, Willoughby de Eresby and Willoughby de Broke, had fallen into abeyance. This company of entertainers might possibly have been patronized by Elizabeth Willoughby, eventual sole heir before 1545 of her grandfather Robert Willoughby, 2nd Lord Willoughby de Broke. She married Fulke Greville in 1526 but he did not assume the Willoughby title in her right. This would be the only known performance of any company under her patronage. Alternatively the company could be that of Katherine Willoughby to whom the Willoughby de Eresby title descended on the death of her father, William Willoughby, 11th Lord Willoughby of Eresby, in 1526. She married Charles Brandon, duke of Suffolk, in 1533. Her uncle Sir Christopher Willoughby claimed Willoughby estates but apparently not the title; his son, William Willoughby, ultimately became Lord Willoughby of Parham in 1547. Players under the patronage of Katherine, as the duchess of Suffolk, were touring as early as 1546–7 after the duke's death in 1545 (see James M. Gibson (ed), *Kent*, vol 3, REED (Toronto, 2002), 1481; and Cameron Louis (ed), *Sussex*, REED (Toronto, 2000), 327). No instances of the duchess' players have yet been found before the duke's

death, so it seems probable that, during that time, such a company might have toured under her patronage as the Baroness Willoughby. See G.E. Cockayne, *The Complete Peerage* (London, 1910–50; rpt Gloucester, 1982) under Willoughby.

85–6   Grimald: *Christus Redivivus*   sigs A3v–4
The word 'tuus' (p 85, l.31) refers to Gilbert Smith, archdeacon of Peterborough, Grimald's patron, to whom the Preface is dedicated. 'Robertus Cauduuellus' (p 85, l.32) was Richard (not Robert) Caldwell, senior bursar of Brasenose College 1540–2. No other reference to 'Iohannem Aërium' (p 86, l.2) is known; Boas, *University Drama*, p 27, speculates that his surname may have been 'Airy' and he is so listed in the University Index. If the performance of the play was at Easter it cannot have been before 1541 but may have been in 1542. The college venue is not known. For a comprehensive note on Grimald, see Appendix 14, pp 898–9.

86–7   ORO: PAR 207/4/F1/1, item 6   single mb cols 1, 2
The account began and ended on St Catherine's Day. This was the accounting day of the parish until 1574–5.
    John Barry (p 87, l.9) of St Martin's parish was first named alderman on 29 September 1537 and served as mayor for two terms (1539–40 and 1540–1). He was appointed one of the town's arbitrators in a dispute with the University on 12 February 1540/1. Thomas Popyngaye (p 87, l.10), a carver, became a member of the common council in 1541–2. William Jones (p 87, l.11), a parishioner of St Martin's, had held a tenement in the parish before 1549. John Hore (p 87, l.12), also of St Martin's parish, was a member of the common council 1535–6. See Turner (ed), *Records of the City of Oxford*, pp 150, 156, 160–1 (for Barry), pp 111, 162 (for Popyngaye), p 198 (for Jones), p 134 (for Hore).

88   ORO: PAR 207/4/F1/1, item 8   single mb dorse
William Kyrkeman (l.8), baker, served as chamberlain in 1544–5. James Clarke (l.9), capper, was admitted to his freedom in 1543–4. William Joynere (l.10), a painter, was admitted in 1546–7. John Northe (l.12) is named as a glazier in 1542–3. Gerard Plowghe (l.14) was a member of the common council in 1536–7 and again in 1542–3. See Turner (ed), *Records of the City of Oxford*, pp 94, 175 (for Kyrkeman), p 174 (for Clarke), p 189 (for Joynere), p 173 (for Northe), pp 140, 167 (for Plowghe).

89   ORO: PAR 214/4/F1/27   mb [1]
The accounting year has changed to the Sunday after the feast of the Conception of the Virgin (8 December).

89   ChCh Arch: D.P.vi.b.1   f 183
These statutes were reissued, with revisions, *c* 1550: see p 91 and below, endnote to ChCh Arch: D.P.vi.b.1 ff 55, 60.

90   ORO: PAR 207/4/F1/1, item 9   mb [1]
It is not clear if the bread and ale entries (ll.30–1) have any connection with either the Whitson supper or the shooting day. No customary activities are recorded in accounts for the years before 1553.

91–2   ChCh Arch: D.P.vi.b.1   ff 55, 60
While Chapter 35 was carried forward essentially unchanged from *c* 1546 (compare p 89), Chapter 53 (renumbered from 48) was more heavily revised (compare pp 89–90).

93   EC Arch: B.I.16   mb 1
The entry on ll.6–7 may have been truncated by a tear, as the colon-like mark that habitually terminates each entry is wanting. Both entries appear to belong to accounts for the term running from approximately Christmas 1550 to the ninth day after Easter, 29 March 1551; the exact date in relation to Christmas is missing due to another tear in the membrane.

Robert Dolye ('dolye,' l.5) was a painter who was admitted to his freedom in 1538–9 (Turner (ed), *Records of the City of Oxford*, p 156). He is mentioned twice in the All Souls College accounts for 1555–6 as being employed in painting a canvas for the college chapel (Bodl.: MS. D.D. All Souls c. 283). As no contemporary member of Exeter College was surnamed Lord or Lordes, 'domo lord*es*' (ll.6–7) may be a theatrical term.

93   MC Arch: LCE/5   f 99v
Walter Oven ('gualtero oven,' l.15) was a carpenter who was admitted to his freedom in 1560–1 (Turner (ed), *Records of the City of Oxford*, f 284). This is the first of many entries regarding the construction of a theatre or stage at Magdalen College (see p 608).

93–4   MC Arch: LCE/5   ff 125, 131v
The draft computus (f 4) for this year contains the same entry as transcribed on f 131v but with 'ludos' for 'comedias'; in the draft the entry is dated '7o febr*uarii*.'

'Hamonde' (l.36) is possibly Robert Hammond, carpenter, admitted to his freedom in 1537–8 (Turner (ed), *Records of the City of Oxford*, p 150).

94   MC Arch: LCE/5   f 157v
'Sutton' (l.22) may be the John Sutton, occupation unknown, admitted to his freedom in 1550–1 (Turner (ed), *Records of the City of Oxford*, p 204).

95   MC Arch: LCD/1   f 43
The account is very long and all items are individually cancelled. The cancellation is probably administrative, indicating items had been transferred to a fair copy.

96   ORO: PAR 207/4/F1/1, item 22   single mb
The grammatical oddity of the second entry (ll.5–6) may be explained by the fact that the ink of 'gyuen…' is lighter than that of 'Item for,' suggesting that the formulaic opening words were written automatically, the scribe pausing before simply copying what was in front of him without worrying about the grammar. Bread and ale were provided this year for ringers at Queen Mary's accession.

96   ORO: PAR 209/4/F1/1   mb [1]
The parish paid for three copes this year, including a white one trimmed with red velvet and 'Images of gold' that cost 40s. They also repaired the Easter sepulchre, as well as the nose and the staff of an image of St Thomas.

96   ChCh Arch: D&C.i.b.2   p 93
The decree is signed by Richard Marshall, William Tresham, Thomas Day, Henry Siddall, Alexander Belsire, 'Richard B(..)arne,' Thomas Kent, James Cinthopp, and Richard Smith.

97   *stc*: 20175   pp ix–x

'Thy boke' (l.10) is *A Traictise declaryng and plainly prouyng, that the pretensed marriage of priestes and professed persones is no mariage* (London, 1554; *stc*: 17517), to which Ponet's book was an answer. Thomas Martin was the collective pseudonym of a group of authors, identified on Ponet's title-page as 'D. Step*hen* Gardiner/ nou Lord chauncelar and D. Smyth of Oxford/ and other Papists.' As Gardiner was a Cambridge man, reference is apparently to Richard Smith, Regius Professor of Divinity at Oxford. Smith entered Merton College as a fellow in 1527 and was deprived of his professorship in 1547 (*DNB*); the events referred to might have taken place any time between these two dates. Since Smith had no connection with New College, however, the charge may be a fiction.

98–9   Surrey History Centre: LM/41/8   f [1]

The letter cannot have been written later than December 1557 since Sir Robert Rochester, one of the signatories, died on 28 November 1557. The phrase 'the newe College *yn* Oxford' (p 98, l.31) apparently refers to Trinity College, whose statutes were signed on 30 May of that year. The possible date and location of the performance are discussed in Elliott, 'A "Learned Tragedy" at Trinity?,' pp 247–50; and by Feuillerat in 'Performance of a Tragedy,' pp 96–7.

99   OCA: P.5.1   f 15

An entry five lines below the entry for the earl of Oxford's players is dated 20 July.

99   ORO: PAR 214/4/F1/29   sheet [1]

The MS heading is fragmentary but enough survives to identify the accounting year as beginning the Sunday after the feast of the Conception (8 December). The regnal year is also visible – 3 & 4 Philip and Mary (1556–7) – but whether this accords with the beginning or ending of the accounting year is uncertain. It has here been treated as the year when the account began. The annotator of these accounts who habitually provides the beginning dates has written 'December 13' on the roll in pencil. This was the Sunday after the feast of the Conception in 1556. Also, the feast of the Conception fell on Sunday, 8 December in 1555 so the formula 'the Sunday after the feast of the Conception' would make no sense if this were the account for 1555–6.

100   ORO: PAR 207/4/F1/1, item 28   single mb

The dating of this roll is somewhat uncertain. '1557' is written on the roll in a slightly later than contemporary hand although the account heading dates the year from 25 November, 5 & 6 Philip and Mary, to 25 November in the next year. The regnal year 5 & 6 Philip and Mary ran only from Mary's Accession Day, 25 July, until her death, 17 November. The next account is clearly dated 1558–9. The second hand was probably clearing up confusion surrounding the Philip and Mary regnal years.

102   MC Arch: LCE/6   ff 5, 8, 8v

These expenses also appear in the draft computus on ff 185v, 190, and 191v. On f 185v the draft has 17s 5d for the first hall cost (ll.5–6), 10s for the seventh (l.16), and 4d for the eighth (l.17). On f 191 the draft for ll.30–1 has 'tragoedia*rum*' for 'spectaculo*rum*' and shows a sum of only 3s 4d.

103   OCA: P.5.1   f 26

The phrase 'mr Cogans house' (l.12) refers to the King's Head in Cornmarket, one of the three known playing venues in the city (see p 617 and Figure 5, p 618). Thomas Coggan, mercer, served as bailiff in

1552–3. He was a keykeeper in 1554–5, was elected 'assistant' on 4 September 1561, and served as a member of the mayor's council until his death before 16 September 1588. He was named one of the four aldermen on 16 September 1562. By 1567 he held the King's Head and in December 1575 he was licensed to sell wine. (Ellis and Salter (eds), *Liber Albus Civitatis Oxoniensis*, p 111; Salter (ed), *Oxford Council Acts 1583–1626*, p 42; and Turner (ed), *Records of the City of Oxford*, pp 212, 227, 282–3, 295, 337.)

103   ORO: PAR 209/4/F1/2   single mb
The PAR 209/4/F1 series places the hocking receipts under the heading 'Recept*es* by Casualtie' to distinguish them from the annual receipts from rents.

103   MC Arch: LCE/6   f 17
This payment also occurs in the draft account (MC Arch: LCD/1, f 204v), with 'portenta religiosor*um* in spectaculo baulino' for 'no*mina* ... ædidit' (ll.32–3). Details of the entry (and of the draft) suggest that the play may have been John Bale's *Three Laws*: see Appendix 9. 'Ioyner pictori' (l.32) was William Joynere, painter, admitted to his freedom in 1546–7 (Turner (ed), *Records of the City of Oxford*, p 189).

104   OCA: P.5.1   f 30
The queen's jester (l.9) at this time was Robert Grene (Nichols, *Progresses of Queen Elizabeth*, vol 1, p 270). Her keeper of the bears and mastiffs (l.11) was Richard Dorrington (David Cook (ed), 'Dramatic Records in the Declared Accounts of the Treasurer of the Chamber 1558–1642,' *Collections* 6, Malone Society (Oxford, 1962 for 1961), xii). The payments for the queen's bearward are listed under a section of the accounts headed 'Charges of my lord of Bedford.' The significance of this is not known.

104   ORO: PAR 214/4/F1/31   single sheet
The feast of the Conception fell on a Sunday this year. The Sunday after the feast, therefore, is a full week later, 15 December.

104–5   MC Arch: LCE/6   f 35v
The hall costs are found in the draft computus (MC Arch: LCD/1, f 223v). In the first payment (p 104, ll.39–40) the daily rate is given as 18d for six days for a total of 9s; in the third payment (p 105, ll.3–4) Squire and son are paid for three days at a daily rate of 18d for a total of 4s 6d; and in the fifth payment (p 105, ll.7–8) 'white' is referred to as 'henrico white' and he and Rixon are paid for four days at a daily rate of 20d for a total of 6s 8d.

106–7   BL: MS Harleian 416   f [1v]
This letter by John Foxe is a reply to an invitation from Laurence Humphrey, president of Magdalen College, to attend his college's performance of Foxe's play, *Christus Triumphans*. Magdalen College records contain no independent references to a performance. The play was, however, performed at Trinity, Cambridge, the following year (see Nelson (ed), *Cambridge*, vol 1, p 221; vol 2, p 979).

107   OCA: P.5.1   ff 33, 33v
The election and dinner occurred on the Monday before St Matthew's Day, when the mayor and bailiffs for the next year were elected. The day began with a peal of the bells rung by the mayor's serjeant at St Martin's, where the council gathered for morning prayer before commencing their business with the

selection of two candidates for mayor from among the thirteen 'assistants.' The two were then announced to the larger council who made their choice. This election was followed by the election of the serving bailiffs for the year (Salter (ed), *Oxford Council Acts 1583–1626*, pp xxxii–xxxiii). For 'wilson the mynstrell' (l.32), see p 1103, endnote to MC Arch: LCD/1 f 456v.

108–9   OCA: P.5.1   ff 38, 39v–40
The queen's jester and bearward (p 108, ll.20, 23) were Robert Grene and Richard Dorrington. The election dinner was held on 20 September 1563.

Regarding possible dates for 'Sainte tedward*es* daye' (p 108, l.21), the feast of Edward the Confessor was 5 January and his Translation was 13 October, while the feast of Edward 'king and martyr' was 18 March with two Translation dates, 18 February and 20 June. Given where this entry comes in the accounts – soon after Michaelmas and before St Andrew's Day – reference is probably to the Translation of Edward the Confessor, 13 October.

109–10   ORO: PAR 214/4/F1/32   single sheet
This account and the one immediately following (ORO: PAR 214/4/F1/33) are clearly dated for the seventh year of Elizabeth, ie, they both claim to run from December 1563 to December 1564. As there is a gap in the run of surviving accounts immediately preceding ORO: PAR 214/4/F1/32 (ie, there are no extant accounts for the period 1561–3) and none following ORO: PAR 214/4/F1/33 for the period 1564–72, it is impossible to tell which of these has been wrongly dated.

110   STC: 4088   pp 151–3
This anecdote about an Abraham and Isaac play in Oxford is part of an attack by Edmund Bunny (1540–1618), a Protestant preacher, against the Jesuit Robert Persons, a member of Balliol College from 1564 to 1574. According to J.P. Driscoll, Bunny's point is that Persons, in *A Christian Directorie* (Rouen, 1585; STC: 19354.1), tries to disguise his popery under cover of devotion but the disguise keeps slipping off (Driscoll, 'A Miracle Play at Oxford,' p 6).

111–12   OCA: P.5.1   ff 43, 44v–5v
The queen's bearward (l.14) was Richard Dorrington. The election dinner was held on 17 September 1565.

113–22   Bodl.: MS. Rawlinson C.878   ff 1–9
This is one of three surviving manuscript expense accounts for carpentry work in and around Christ Church at the time of Queen Elizabeth's visit to Oxford in 1566. The other two are Bodl.: MS. Top.Oxon e.9 and Bodl.: MS. Top.Oxon c.22.

MS. Rawlinson C.878 appears to be a rough draft while MS. Top.Oxon e.9 is the corrected copy. Significant water damage and tearing have made parts of Top.Oxon e.9 illegible but substantive differences have been noted where possible. Most of the items marked with a marginal '+' in the Rawlinson MS do not appear in Top.Oxon e.9 nor do cancellations and corrections.

Among minor variations the following substantive differences occur: Myles and his man (p 113, ll.23–4) are said to be due 'v s. iiij d.' for 'sawinge iiij C. di. of elme borde' (f 1); in the payment to Myles and his three men where the Rawlinson MS omits the 'd.' (p 116, ll.1–3), it is present in Top.Oxon e.9 (f 3), and the sum of the payment to Bladen and Pemberton for sawing rafters (p 116, ll.12–13) is legible as 'xviij s.' (f 3); 'Beryll' (p 116, l.17) is identified as 'Iohn Berill' and not the Thomas named elsewhere (f 3v); 'crosse garnett*es*' (p 116, l.34) reads simply 'garnett*es*' (f 3v); the total amount due the carpenters (p 116, l.36–p 117, l.5) is given as 'vj li. xiij s. iiij d.' (f 4); 'Richarde Emans' (p 118, l.7) is given as 'Richarde Evans' (f 5); Thomas Tymberley (p 119, l.34) is paid at a rate of xij d. by the 'hundred' (f 6); 'Edwarde Tanner' (p 120, l.22) is given as 'Edmunde Tanner' (f 6v); Mr Coggan (p 120, ll.25–6) is paid for 'ij C of borde,' Pickhaver (p 120, ll.26–7) receives 'xij d.' for carriage of boards, and the total amount is 'xix s. ij d.' (f 6v); even though the 8d payment to Fyshe has a '+' next to it (p 121, l.7) it was copied into Top.Oxon e.9 and then cancelled there (f 7v); the total payment to the clerks that is not legible (p 121, ll.34–6) is given as 'xviij s.' (f 7v); Henry Towe (p 122, l.23) is paid a total of 'xiiij li. xiiij s. vj d. ob. qua.' (f 8); and finally, the sum total of all the expenses (p 122, l.33) is given as 'Cxxxvij li. ij s. xj d. qua.' (f 8v).

The payment to Robert Mooneson for 'plumbe worke' (referred to on p 118, and entered at the end of the expense list on p 122, ll.34–7) is recorded in its appropriate place in Top.Oxon e.9, f 4v, but without correction to the number of men involved in hanging lights. There seems to be a direct correlation between Mooneson's work as described here and the first-person expense sheet, Bodl.: MS. Top.Oxon c.22, single sheet (see pp 122–3).

For an attempted reconstruction of the theatre, see pp 608–10.

122–3   Bodl.: MS. Top.Oxon c.22   single sheet
The last entry, written in the third person ('for hym & hys too men,' p 123, ll.23–4), is an interpolation in a different hand duplicating the final entry in Bodl.: MS. Rawlinson C.878, which records Robert Mooneson's expenses for 'hanginge vp lightes' (p 122, ll.34–7). This suggests that the 'he' of this first-person account may well be Mooneson (see p 644).

123   CCCA: C/1/1/4   f [9]
Examples of verses made to commemorate 'the Quenes cominge' can be found in CCC: MS 280, ff 170–86v.

126–35   CCC: MS 257   ff 115, 116v–17v, 118, 118v, 119–19v, 120v, 121, 121v, 122, 123, 123v
Miles Windsor was a fellow of Corpus Christi College at the time of the queen's visit in 1566. His MS account of the event remains in the library of his old college. For later copies (some of which are collated here) and for published versions based on them, see p 696.

Brian Twyne (in Bodl.: MS. Twyne 17, written in 1636, and not collated here) introduced three substantive errors perpetuated in Anthony Wood's histories of Oxford (see Appendix 13, p 877, ll.35, 36; p 878, l.19; and p 880, ll.23, 24) and subsequently in most modern accounts of the plays. They are 'Trecatio' for 'Trevatio' (p 129, l.4), 'St. Edward' for 'King Edward' (p 129, l.13), and the month of 'Marche' rather than 'maye' (p 133, l.10) as the setting for the story of Palamon and Arcite (from Chaucer's Knight's Tale).

Regarding 'ye King Edward cloake,' Windsor gives no indication of what the spectator who used this phrase meant by it. It may have been an old garment from the royal wardrobe, once belonging to Edward VI, loaned for the occasion by the queen (see Elliott, 'Queen Elizabeth at Oxford,' pp 223–4; and also Janet Arnold, 'Lost From Her Majestie's Back': Items of Clothing and Jewels Lost or Given Away by Queen Elizabeth I Between 1561 and 1585, Entered in One of the Day Books Kept for the Records of the Wardrobe of Robes, The Costume Society, extra series, 7 ([London], 1980), 14, 33).

Omitted from this transcription are an advance visit by the earl of Leicester (f 116); a list of noblemen attending the queen (f 116v); the queen's arrival at St Mary's Church (f 118); a list of sermons, lectures, and disputations (ff 118v–19); the queen's speech in Latin (f 121v); a convocation ceremony (f 122v); and a list of orators and disputants selected to appear before the queen (f 123v).

Regarding 'a fayre lardge scaffolde' (p 130, l.26), see pp 608–10 for an attempted reconstruction of the theatre.

The 'master Secretarye' (p 126, l.24) was William Cecil, Lord Burghley, secretary of State 1558–72 and chancellor of Cambridge University. 'Lord windsor' (p 130, l.2 and p 131, l.8) was Edward Windsor, 3rd Lord Windsor. The incident took place at Bradenham, Buckinghamshire, the Windsor family seat, on 7 September, the day after the queen left Oxford. On 'damon & Pythias' (p 130, l.11), Richard Edwards' only extant play, see Appendix 9. Edwards died a few weeks after the royal visit. On 'peter Carewe' (p 130, l.18), see Appendix 13, pp 876 and 878. Mr 'neele' (p 131, l.17) was Thomas Neal (1519–90), Regius Professor of Hebrew 1559–69. Windsor's narrative is sometimes erroneously attributed to Neal (see p 696). The 'Lord Chamberlayne' (p 132, l.9) was William Howard, Lord Howard of Effingham, lord chamberlain 1558–72.

Individuals named in the cast list (f 123v) are more fully identified in Appendix 7, p 843. Windsor does not say what part 'Rainoldes' (p 135, l.16) played in *Palamon and Arcite*, but Rainolds himself later said that he played Queen Hippolyta (see Appendix 11, p 870).

141–2   STC: 23322   ff 408v–9
Stow's account is repeated largely verbatim in Holinshed, *Third Volume of Chronicles* (London, 1587; STC: 13569), 1209, cols 1–2.

142–3   BL: MS Additional 26737   f 106v cols 1, 2
This is the only surviving fragment of Richard Edwards' *Palamon and Arcite*, performed for the queen's visit in 1566. The poem is divided into two columns on the top third of f 106v. A second poem occupies the same two columns on the lower two-thirds of the leaf. The columns are created by a vertical rule and the poems are separated by a thicker horizontal rule.

143–4   OCA: P.5.1   ff 51v, 54v
The entries in these accounts come near the end of the payments for the year, which fits with the bearward and players being in attendance on the queen at the end of August and early September, but surviving evidence does not confirm that the visits of the entertainers coincided with the queen's visit.

The queen's bearward (p 143, l.34) was Richard Dorrington. Richard Williams (p 144, l.3), baker and mayor, finished the term of William Matthew in 1564–5 (Turner (ed), *Records of the City of Oxford*, pp 308, 338, 398). Roger Taylor (p 144, l.4), brewer and possibly an innkeeper, was mayor in 1563–4 (P.W. Hasler (ed), *The House of Commons 1558–1603*, The History of Parliament, vol 3 (London, 1981), 480; Ellis and Salter (eds), *Liber Albus Civitatis Oxoniensis*, p 118). For 'v oxen to present the Quenes grace' (p 144, l.4), see p 127, ll.10–16m.

144   Pepys Library: MS 2502/15   f [1]
The letter is signed by Thomas Godwin, Thomas Bernard, Thomas Day, Henry Siddall, John Kennall, Robert Banks, James Calfhill, and Herbert Westfaling.

145   Hampshire Record Office: 21M65/A1/26   f 24
The initial charges were made by Thomas Greenway (president of the college) and others against Jerome Reynolds (fellow), George Atkinson (chaplain), and Richard Joynere (clerk of accounts). Reynolds brought the countercharges against Greenway, beginning with numerous accusations of consorting with prostitutes, converting college lands and goods to his own use, and preaching in a Catholic manner.

146   Hampshire Record Office: 21M65/A1/26   f 55
'Psalmos Daviticos antedictos' (l.25) refers to prior charges that the accused called translations of the
Psalms English 'rimes.'

147   PRO: C/115/L2/6697   p 23
This undated entry occurs between entries dated 3 January and 10 February 1566/7.

147   OCA: P.5.1   f 59
The queen's jester (l.25) was Robert Grene.

148   MCR: 3932e   single sheet
This account is in the hand of Sir Thomas Bodley, second bursar.

149   OCA: P.5.1   f 66v
The queen's bearward (l.13) was Richard Dorrington.

149   Bodl.: MS. Morrell 9   f 33
The MS account heading reads 'the year of our Lord 1568 and the vii day Iuly.' In later accounts of the
Tailors' guild the accounting year began and ended on the Monday after the feast of St John the Baptist.
If this is the case here, the accounting year ran from 30 June 1567 to 28 June 1568.

150   Pepys Library: MS 2503/273   f [1]
According to Boas, *University Drama*, p 158, the 'exercise' here called 'the destruction of Thebes' was to
be performed, along with sermons and disputations, on 15 May 1569, before the cardinal de Châtillon,
a French diplomat, and the earl of Leicester, chancellor of Oxford. The visit was apparently cancelled,
however, and no other record of a performance, or of a text, survives.

151   SJC Arch: Acc.I.A.1   p 6
The 'lord' (l.9) is the Christmas lord; see pp 612–13.

151   OCA: P.5.1   f 74v
The queen's bearward (l.22) was Richard Dorrington.

151   ORO: PAR 207/4/F1/1, item 17   mb [1]
This account is misbound. The original artifact was numbered '47' but the binder read it as '17' and
bound it out of serial order and thus out of chronological order. The only date on the roll is 'the yeare
of ower Lorde god 1569.' Since the accounts of the surrounding years are missing it is impossible to
tell if this is 1568–9 or 1569–70.

152   OCA: P.5.1   f 81v
Although this is definitely the account for 1569–70 the audit date is given as 10 November, 13
Elizabeth (ie, 1571). Either the scribe made a mistake entering the year of the audit date or this account
was audited a year later along with the 1570–1 account, which was also audited 10 November, 13
Elizabeth.

154   OCA: P.5.1   f 92
The queen's bearward (l.4) was Richard Dorrington.

155   MC Arch: LCE/6   f 205v
In the draft computus (MC Arch: LCD/1, f 407) the payment to 'oven' (ll.28–9) is marginally dated
'vltimo februarij.'

156–7   STC: 19392   ff 194v–5
The anecdote related here and in the following record concerns the struggle between two tutors at
Balliol College over whether one of their pupils should be allowed to attend plays at Christmas.
Robert Persons, bursar and dean of the college, accused his colleague Christopher Bagshaw of 'pupil-
poaching' because he took the pupil to 'certayne commedies' (p 157, l.5) over the Christmas vacation.
Bagshaw, however, brought countercharges of stealing from the bursary, and in February Persons was
forced to resign his fellowship. A year later Bagshaw himself was expelled for popery, and both men,
now Catholics, argued their case in controversial works published abroad as long as twenty-five years
after the event.
   In 1601 Persons' *Briefe Apologie* repeated the story about the part Bagshaw had played in corrupting
students with plays and causing his own expulsion from Balliol. Two years later Bagshaw struck back
with his own version, attached as an appendix to a treatise by Humphrey Ely, another exiled Oxford
Catholic, called *Certaine Briefe Notes* (Paris, [1602]; STC: 7628). Bagshaw's attack is titled 'An Answear of
M. Doctor Bagshaw to certayne poyntes of a libell called An Apologie of the subordination in England'
(see pp 633–4). Bagshaw says that he only took the student to a single play and does not reveal at
which college it was performed. For the background of the incident here reported, see Anthony Kenny,
'Reform and Reaction in Elizabethan Balliol, 1559–1588,' *Balliol Studies*, John Prest (ed) (London,
1982), 17–51.

157   STC: 7628   pp 32–3
See above, endnote to STC: 19392 ff 194v–5.

158   MC Arch: LCE/6   ff 218v, 223v
Christopher Noke (l.4) was a mason, admitted to his freedom in 1561–2 (Turner (ed), *Records of the
City of Oxford*, p 297). The item without a sum on f 223v of this fair account is possibly that which has
been transcribed fully in the draft account, MC Arch: LCD/1, f 440v (see p 158).

159   OCA: P.5.1   f 113
George Ewen (l.7), city musician, frequently played for special events in the 1570s (see pp 161, 163,
165). He gave up his scutcheon as wait along with George Buckner on 8 October 1577 (see p 167).
For 'Carfaxe' (l.10), see pp 584, 594.

159   Bodl.: MS. Morrell 9   f 37
Richard Floyd (l.20) was admitted to his freedom in 1572–3 (Turner (ed), *Records of the City of
Oxford*, p 349).

159–60   PRO: SP/46/15   f [4v] cols 4, 5
Folio [8] ('December') refers to 'the bookes sett forthe by the purytanes to the parlament.' The items

'newes of a rebellio*n*' and 'beseigid the adversaries force' (ll.40, 43) may be fictional exercises devised by the lord of misrule. For the format and dating of Richard Carnsew's diary, see p 692.

160–1   OCA: P.5.1   ff 118v, 119, 120–20v
Ralph Bowes (p 160, l.9) had become the keeper of the queen's bears and mastiffs in 1573–4 (David Cook (ed), 'Dramatic Records in the Declared Accounts of the Treasurer of the Chamber 1558–1642,' *Collections* 6, Malone Society (Oxford, 1962 for 1961), xii). The Accession Day expenses are entered twice. The first entry occurs at the foot of f 118v in the body of the 'Gifts and Rewards' section. It was cancelled and the 'Gifts and Rewards' account total altered to reflect the cancellation. The Accession Day expenses were then re-entered on f 119 under a separate heading, 'The charges bestowed on the daye of the change of the Quenes maiesties Raigne,' with a separate total. The election was held 19 September 1575.

162   MC Arch: LCD/1   f 456v
Thomas Wilson, musician, also received a small payment from the city in 1577–8 (see p 167). He may be 'wilson the mynstrell' paid in 1561–2 (see p 107). On 12 July 1575 the council leased twenty square feet of undeveloped property to Thomas Wilson for 2s annually on the condition that he build a house on the site (Turner (ed), *Records of the City of Oxford*, p 375).

163   OCA: P.5.1   f 128
The queen's bearward (l.24) was Ralph Bowes.

163   ORO: PAR 208/4/F1/15   single mb
The bullring where the civic baiting took place was outside the North Gate (see p 624), in the parish of St Mary Magdalen.

164   LC Arch: Computus 10   ff 1, 1v
The first payment to musicians (l.16) is for 19 May 1577, the second (l.24) for 31 May 1577. The payment to a minstrel (l.22) is for 28 May 1577.

165   OCA: P.5.1   ff 139, 139v
The countess of Essex (l.12) was Lettice Knollys, daughter of Sir Francis Knollys, high steward of Oxford from 1563 to 1592. The queen's bearward (ll.17–18) was Ralph Bowes. 'Yewen' (l.27) is George Ewen (see p 1102, endnote to OCA: P.5.1 f 113).

166   ORO: PAR 208/4/F1/17   single mb
'Mr Case' (l.9) may be Dr John Case who was a scholar and, until his marriage in 1574, a fellow of St John's College, which lay within the bounds of the parish. During Christmas 1577 Case was elected 'lord' of St John's College (see p 347). After his marriage Case moved to 2 Magdalen Street where 'he received pupils and his house was allowed to be reckoned almost a Hall' (Stevenson and Salter, *Early History of St. John's College*, p 337). The *Encyclopaedia of Oxford*, Hibbert and Hibbert (eds), p 403, calls him 'the most notable of the early members' of St John's, a 'theologian, philosopher, poet, political theorist and anatomist, whose commentary on Aristotle of 1585 was the first work to be published by the Oxford University Press.' Receipt for 18s rent from a Mr or Mr Doctor Case is recorded in several accounts from the 1570s onward. In 1598–9, the year before his death, the property at 2 Magdalen Street is described as 'the Churchowse.'

166   Bodl.: MS. D.D. All Souls c.284   mb 5
The waits' payment is undated but by virtue of proximity to the 1 November payment it has been treated as a post-Michaelmas expense and therefore also placed under 1577–8.

167   OCA: C/FC/1/A1/001   f 203v
This entry also occurs in OCA: C/FC/1/A2/1, f 67v. 'Bucknall' (l.11) is George Buckner (see p 1114, endnote to Bodl.: MS. Twyne-Langbaine 3 ff 121–1v).

167   OCA: P.5.1   f 147
The queen's bearward (l.20) was Ralph Bowes.

169   OUA: Hyp/B/11   mb 1
A copy of this inventory is preserved as OUA: Hyp/B/11, ff 114–18v.

169   Bodl.: MS. Rolls Oxon 66, roll 2   mb [2]
The occasion was an admissions dinner. Under 'Receipts' on the same mb, Thomas Collyns (l.22) paid 3s 4d for 'admittance into the company.' He was also admitted to his freedom that year (Turner (ed), *Records of the City of Oxford*, p 404).

170–1   OCA: C/FC/1/A1/001   f 221v
'Guilde Halls' (p 170, l.40m) presumably refers to the three spaces mentioned in the entry – the guildhall itself, the lower hall (a separate building to the south), and the guildhall court (see p 617). This entry also occurs in OCA: C/FC/1/A2/1, ff 82v–3.

171–2   OCA: P.5.1   ff 159v, 160–60v
The queen's bearward (l.13) was Ralph Bowes. The election was held 19 September 1580.

173   BL: MS Sloane 300   f 51v
Another version of this anecdote, but not referring to a specific location, occurs in BL: MS Sloane 1489, f 20v. J.O. Halliwell-Phillips claimed, erroneously, that it also occurred in William Vaughan's *The Golden Fleece* (London, 1626; STC: 24609), an error repeated by Warren B. Austin, 'William Withie's Notebook: Lampoons on John Lyly and Gabriel Harvey,' *Review of English Studies* 23 (1947), 297–309, who first published the version in MS Sloane 300.
    The year of this entry is derived from another entry on the same page, which is said to have been copied ('denuo rescriptum') on 23 September 1581.

175   ChCh Arch: xii.b.24   f 28
The three hands in this excerpt are apparently those of the accountant, the auditor, and Heton the payee.

176   SJC Arch: Admin.I.A.1   ff 204, 209v
Signatures on f 204 are those of Francis Willis (president), Roger Kiblewhite, John Rixman, Ralph Hutchinson, William Lee, Arthur Aubery, Matthew Gwinne, Edward Spratt, Thomas White, and Thomas Denham. The signatories on f 209v are the same, but in a slightly different order, with the addition of Jeremy Nashe and John Read and the omission of Denham and Hutchinson.

177–9 *STC*: 13961   pp 163–5, 175–6, 180–1

Humphrey's reference to Sophocles (p 178, l.33m) when mentioning Oeneus' sacrifice calls for comment. Oeneus was the father of Meleager, a Greek hero also mentioned by Humphrey along with Atalanta, the object of his love (see p 178, l.16); Humphrey also later mentions the metamorphosis of Oeneus' daughters into birds (p 179, ll.5–6). Since Sophocles' play of *Mealeager* survives only in fragments and the full form of the story developed subsequently, Humphrey must be referring instead to William Gager's version performed on 7 February (see pp 180–1).

The date of the sermon given on the secondary title-page (see p 686) refers to the 'historical year,' Ash Wednesday 1582 (ie, 28 February 1581/2).

179 BL: MS Cotton Appendix 47   ff 3–3v, 5

The day of the week is indicated in each case by the astrological symbol of the planet for which the day is named, ie, ♄ (Saturn) for Saturday, ☼ (Sun) for Sunday, ☽ (Moon) for Monday.

The right edge of each page is badly torn, resulting in many missing letters and words. Some of these have been supplied conjecturally by E.S. Donno in *An Elizabethan in 1582*, her edition of the MS.

In 1582 the city chamberlain was John Brush (l.14). Richard Madox's brother (l.16) was William Madox. Anthony and George Poulet, both members of Christ Church, were 'ye 2 paulets' (l.17). Presumably 'ye supposes' (l.29) was George Gascoigne's play of that name, first acted at Gray's Inn in 1566 (see p 854).

180 Bodl.: MS. Top.Oxon e.5   p 359

Richard Edes is said by Anthony Wood to have written several plays, 'mostly tragedies' (*Athenae*, vol 1, col 749), but only the Epilogue to *Caesar Interfectus* has survived (see Appendix 6:2). Boas, *University Drama*, pp 163–5, surmises that it was one of the three tragedies performed at Christ Church in February 1581/2 (see p 175 and Appendix 8, p 848).

180–1 *STC*: 11515   sig A2

This letter, published with the text of Gager's *Meleager* and dated 1 January 1592/3, fixes the first performance of the play in February 1581/2, at Christ Church (see p 175). The letter also refers to a second performance three years later, before the earl of Leicester, Sir Philip Sidney, and other notables, in January 1584/5, expenses for which are recorded in the Christ Church accounts for that year (see p 198).

182–3 ChCh Arch: xii.b.25   ff 51v, 52, 89

Albert Laski (p 182, l.4) was prince palatine of Siradia in Poland. He visited Oxford 10–13 June 1583 and was entertained with two plays at Christ Church, *Rivales*, a comedy, and *Dido*, a tragedy, both by William Gager (Boas, *University Drama*, pp 179–91).

'Chandense' (or Chandlings or Champoole) (p 182, l.15) is a wood in Berkshire, near Abingdon. It was bought by the dean of Christ Church from Abingdon Abbey in 1547.

The cancelled entry (p 183, ll.21–6) occurs with several similar ones on the last leaves of the book. All are cancelled and some torn or cut out. Other disbursement books of this period use their last leaves for the same purpose, ie, the collection of payees' signatures as a form of receipt. The entries were cancelled after the sums had been transferred to the finished accounts.

183–4   BL: MS Additional 22583   ff 63v, 64

These biographical notes were written by William Gager in his commonplace book for 1582–3. They describe some of his fellow scholars at Christ Church who, like Gager, composed and published literary works.

185–6   OUA: NEP/Supra/L   f 19v

Oxford's commencement stage merits comparison with that of Cambridge: see Alan H. Nelson, *Early Cambridge Theatres: University, College, and Town Stages, 1464–1720* (Cambridge, 1994), 10, 12, 14–15, 77–87.

192   OCA: A.5.3   f 17

William Gibbons (l.4), founder of a musical dynasty as father of Edward, Orlando (see pp 470, 489), and Ellis and grandfather of Christopher, was an Oxford man who had moved to Cambridge by March 1566. He first became master of the Cambridge University waits in the place of John Hewarden on 23 November 1566 and was appointed city wait the next year, receiving the five collars of the Cambridge waits on 25 November 1567. He returned to Cambridge in 1589–90, and in 1591 again became a University wait and head city wait. He died in 1595 (see Nelson (ed), *Cambridge*, vol 2, p 1004; see also pp 619, 621).

194–5   OUA: NEP/Supra/L   ff 241v, 242, 242v

Six Latin statutes (f 241v) were first decreed in response to a threatening letter from Robert Dudley, earl of Leicester, concerning lack of academic standards and discipline (ff 241–1v). Then follows a fuller English version in a different order (ff 242–2v), concluding with Leicester's confirmation.

A later copy of Leicester's letter to the University survives in OUA: NEP/Supra/A, ff 125–5v, with 'greatly complained' for 'complaned' (p 194, l.33), 'plaies' for 'players' (p 195, l.25), and 'Tragidies Commedies Shewes & other exercises' for 'tragedies commodies & other shewes of exercises' (p 195, ll.26–7).

195–6   OCA: D.5.2   ff [1–1v]

The documents in this MS are mounted in such a way that some parts of the originals are obscured. Such is the case with the names in the bottom left corner of f [1].

197   MC Arch: MS 655a   p 322

The hand is such that 'plaies' (l.19) might be read as 'places.'

198   ChCh Arch: xii.b.27   f 30

See p 180 and p 1105, endnote to STC: 11515 sig A2, for evidence that the tragedy performed on the occasion of Leicester's visit was William Gager's *Meleager*.

200   MC Arch: LCD/2   f 20v col 1

The first of the two payments was probably Magdalen's contribution to plays performed by Christ Church (see p 198).

200   QC Arch: 2P162   single mb

The Morris (l.12) family seems to have been employed by Queen's College as gardeners but regular payments to a Morris as a piper or fiddler occur on the feast of the Circumcision from 1584–5 to 1641–2. The payments to them as musicians are usually by last name only but a payment in 1614–15 is to John Morris and another in 1615–16 is to William Morris (see pp 408, 413). The Morrises do not seem to have been professional musicians but were sufficiently talented to serve as the college pipers or fiddlers for the Christmas season. Thomas Crosfield mentions the musical gardener in 1639–40 (see p 573). A gardener named William Morris and his son are also mentioned several times in the Oriel College accounts between 1600 and 1610 but without payments to them as musicians.

200–1   OUA: NEP/Supra/L   f 282v
This entry was transcribed in the 1630s by Brian Twyne into Bodl.: MS. Twyne 17, p 173. Twyne added, 'This is all that I finde of that entertainment, either in that Register or else where. Except that note of old Mr Wyndesores, touchinge ye disputation that then was openly in St Maries betwixt Dr Reynolds & his brother Edmund before ye saide Earle. &c.'

201   OCA: P.5.1   f 196v
The bullring lay outside the North Gate in the parish of St Mary Magdalen. John Massey (l.13) was a baker (Turner (ed), *Records of the City of Oxford*, p 272), listed among the mayor's council in the period 1583–5. On 26 May 1586 he was dismissed from the council but on 12 June a letter was sent to the mayor (Thomas Smith) from the privy council commanding him to reinstate Massey who had simply answered on his oath 'certain interrogatories' put to him by the vice-chancellor (Salter (ed), *Oxford Council Acts 1583–1626*, pp 2, 12, 20, 26).

201   ORO: PAR 209/4/F1/12   single mb
From this year until 1605 the accounting year was not Michaelmas to Michaelmas but St Andrew's Day to St Andrew's Day.

202   EC Arch: A.II.9   f 105
This entry occurs on an extra page containing corrections and additions for the years 1582–6.

203   OCA: C/FC/1/A1/001   f 284v
This entry also occurs in OCA: C/FC/1/A2/1, f 143.

203   OCA: P.5.1   f 203
On 26 January it was 'agreed That this Cytie shall geve Twentie mark*es* to two Preachers yearelie frome henceforthe to make one Sermon everie Sonndaye at Carfoxe to the Citizens: So longe as hit shall seeme goode vnto this howsse…. And it is agreed that Mr Potter and Mr Pryme, shalbe appoynted the said two Preachers, yff they will agree thereunto' (OCA: C/FC/1/A1/001, f 282). Prime (l.29) was appointed vicar of Adderbury in 1589 whereupon another fellow of New College, William Swaddon, became civic preacher (Salter (ed), *Oxford Council Acts 1583–1626*, pp xxviii, 53).

This entry may record an event that took place around the time of the anniversary of Elizabeth's coronation day, 15 January. It occurs between two items, well into the accounting year, that are specifically for the coronation celebration. It is also possible, since sermons and music were more common at the anniversary of the queen's accession (17 November), that the reference is to the November event and that the accountants were not following strict calendar order.

205   OCA: P.5.1   f 210v
Rowland Barber (l.11), a glover, served as town crier during the period 1583–92 (Salter (ed), *Oxford Council Acts 1583–1626*, pp 1, 72).

206   ORO: PAR 214/4/F1/37   single sheet
This account also includes the following: 'Item to a pore man for wearinge the parishe harness uppon Maye day xij d.'

206   OCA: C/FC/1/A1/001   f 302v
'Bucknall' (l.25) is George Buckner (see p 1114, endnote to Bodl.: MS. Twyne-Langbaine 3 ff 121–1v). '*Master* Chamberlen Goode' (l.31) is Richard Good, chandler and chamberlain in 1587–8 (Salter (ed), *Oxford Council Acts 1583–1626*, p 37). This entry also occurs in OCA: C/FC/1/A2/1, f 162.

207   ORO: PAR 213/4/F1/1   single mb col 1
The heading of this account (mounted on sheet 79) clearly dates it 1588–9 (31 Elizabeth); however, the next account (sheet 81) bears the same date. Two different sets of wardens imply different years. From the names of the outgoing wardens on sheet 79, 1587–8 is determined to be the correct year.

208   STC: 6238   pp 253–4
Chambers (*Elizabethan Stage*, vol 3, p 276) points out that 'the Apology is fixed by its own data to the autumn of 1604.' It was probably intended for the printed edition of Daniel's *Philotas* in 1605. Richard Latewar's play of the same title must therefore date before 1596. The phrase 'his Lords Chamber, and mine' (l.14) alludes to Charles Blount, Lord Mountjoy, Daniel's patron, to whom Latewar was chaplain (Wood, *Athenae*, vol 1, col 709). The 'late Tragedy' (l.22) was the earl of Essex's rebellion in 1601. The early date of the range given in Appendix 6:2 (*c* 1588–96) is conjectural but sorts with Latewar's entrance as a scholar in 1580.

209   BL: MS Sloane 2131   ff [3–3v]
This document is discussed further in Macray, *Register*, vol 3, pp 92–7; and Boas, *University Drama*, pp 195–6. Earlier entries in Robert Ashley's autobiography mention his participation in various plays as a schoolboy (see Rosalind Conklin Hays and C.E. McGee/Sally L. Joyce and Evelyn S. Newlyn (eds), *Dorset/Cornwall*, REED (Toronto, 1999), 170, 339).

210   ORO: PAR 211/4/F1/2, item 152   single mb
The account header reads 'the xxjth yeare' of Elizabeth's reign, but given the sequence of surviving accounts, '31' must have been intended.

211   OCA: P.5.1   ff 234v, 235v
A rough account (OCA: C/T/1/F/002) from this year includes the entries for the queen's players and the lord admiral's men (mb 1) with no substantive variants, as well as the payment for Essex's men (mb 2) specified as 'at the ber.' The seventeenth-century Bear Inn, built on the same site, still stands near the intersection of Blue Boar Street and Alfred Street, behind the guildhall and across the street from the Peckwater Quad of Christ Church.

   The entry for Essex's men (l.40) occurs at the end of the account under the heading 'At Mr Recorders' Diet' and may refer to his men of affairs rather than to his players. In the fuller rough account the payment for sugar and wine to the earl of Essex's men at the Bear comes under the heading of 'Mr Recorders charges for his dyet as foloth,' and although there is a space left between the item of 10s 10d for horsemeat and the payment for wine and sugar to the clerk of the council, they are part of the total for this section of the accounts. In the 'fair' version the two wine and sugar entries are not part of the total under 'Mr Recorders Dyet' but are totalled separately. Essex was only twenty-three at this time and not yet the high steward of Oxford.

212   OCA: P.4.1   f 60
William Gibbons (l.4) returned to Cambridge this year (see p 1106, endnote to OCA: A.5.3 f 17).

213   ChCh Arch: xii.b.33   f 28v
This entry was also written on f 91 and cancelled.

214   OCA: P.5.2   f 1
'George Bucknold' (l.4) is George Buckner (see p 1114, endnote to Bodl.: MS. Twyne-Langbaine 3 ff 121–1v).

214   ORO: PAR 214/4/F1/41   single sheet
The account was rendered 19 December. The scribe dated this account 'AD 1591' but also '33 Eliz.' (1590–1). Elizabeth's accession date was 17 November, so by 19 December, 34 Elizabeth had already begun. The confusion may be simply a scribal error.

215   Bodl.: MS. D.D. All Souls c.286   mb 11
The draft account to which this entry appears to refer is incomplete for this year and does not contain this entry.

215   ChCh Arch: xii.b.34   f 85
The Christ Church payment to Hammond cancelled here is presented correctly in 1592–3 (see p 228).

217–18   MCR: 1.3   p 158
This list is also found in OUA: NEP/Supra/N, f [iv], to which is added Jesus, Wadham, and Pembroke Colleges with no valuations given. Only Jesus had been founded by 1592. The list must have been copied from an earlier document between 1624, the date of the founding of Pembroke College, and 1628, the date at which NEP/Supra/N ceased to be used as a register. Sometime between 1636 and 1644 the entry was in turn copied by Brian Twyne into Bodl.: MS. Twyne 17, p 178. In the left margin Twyne wrote, 'payeable by ye colledges after 30s in ye hundred.' Twyne has also added in the right column below Balliol College the sum '7490' li. A version of the excerpt is also found in Bodl.: MS. Add. C.302 (correspondence and papers of Gilbert Sheldon, archbishop of Canterbury), f 90.

  With the exception of Barkby the manors and parishes listed were bestowed on the college by the founder c 1270. Barkby had been owned by the college since c 1265, owing to the connection with Simon de Montfort, earl of Leicester.

221   STC: 12900   pp 28–9
'Mr Greene' (l.35) is Robert Greene. 'Mr Pierce Penni-lesse' (l.37) is Thomas Nash; his 'supplication

to the Diuell' (ll.38–9) is *Pierce Penilesse his supplication to the diuell* (London, 1592; STC: 18371). For a history of the quarrel, see DNB under Gabriel Harvey.

222   STC: 12779   p 119
A similar point is made in Harington's Preface to *Orlando Furioso* (London, 1591; STC: 746): 'How full of harmeles myrth is our Cambridge Pedantius? and the Oxford Bellum Grammaticale?' (sig Pvj) (cited at length in Nelson (ed), *Cambridge*, vol 2, p 847).

222–4   Cambridge University Library: MS Additional 34   ff 4v–5, 6v, 8, 9
Philip Stringer, esquire bedell of Cambridge University, was dispatched to Oxford to report on the royal visit (see Nelson (ed), *Cambridge*, vol 1, p 347). He also reported on the royal visit of August 1605 (see pp 295–301; see also p 699). Sections of Stringer's narrative pertaining to disputations, public lectures, and sermons have been omitted. The progress was on its way from Woodstock toward London. Further details are given by Wood (see Appendix 13, pp 882–4). Plays performed during the visit are listed (with their dates) in Appendix 8, p 849.

224–5   OCA: C/FC/1/A1/001   ff 337v, 338
The 'Steward' (p 224, l.36) is Sir Francis Knollys, who became high steward of Oxford on 3 February 1632/3. 'Penyles benche' (p 225, l.2) had become a traditional gathering place in the centre of the city. It was built in 1545 against the east wall of St Martin's Church facing Carfax and 'was a lean-to with a leaded roof.' In 1578 the bench extended the width of the church and projected out into the street. Its upkeep was shared by the city and the parish (*VCH: Oxford*, vol 4, p 333; see also Figure 6, p 618). The mayor was Richard Browne, the town clerk John Hollway, who was admitted and elected on 2 August 1577 and served until 1610 (Salter (ed), *Oxford Council Acts 1583–1626*, pp 64–5, 194, 199; and Turner (ed), *Records of the City of Oxford*, p 392).

The 'monday next' (p 225, l.21) presents a problem. Because 13 August 1592 was a Sunday, Monday next would presumably mean the Monday of the next week (ie, 21 August 1592) as opposed to 'this Monday,' ie, the very next day, 14 August. The queen arrived, however, on Tuesday, 22 August.

226   OCA: P.5.2   f 12
Two of the four glovers named in this record – Edward Chiston ('Shisson,' l.24) and Robert Welles (l.27) – were not part of the ruling oligarchy. Henry Wilkes (l.19) had served as constable in 1579–80 and was this year (1592) made a member of the common council. He is last listed among the bailiffs in 1619. Edmund Barton (l.29) became a member of the common council in 1582, served as chamberlain during the period 1587–90, and is last listed among the bailiffs in 1593. Carpenter (l.35) is probably John Carpenter, son of Andrew Carpenter, who bought his freedom 5 May 1584. At the time of the queen's visit he was serving as the mayor's serjeant at mace. He is last listed among the bailiffs in 1621. Browne (l.39) is Richard Browne, 'Brown baker,' who was mayor for this year. He remained a member of the mayor's council until his death in 1607. On 16 January 1594/5 a John Willis (l.40) was left a message in St Peter le Bailey called the sign of the Talbot. See Salter, *Survey of Oxford*, vol 2, p 137 (for Willis); Salter (ed), *Oxford Council Acts 1583–1626*, p 47 (for Welles), pp 12, 74, 286 (for Wilkes), pp 32, 83 (for Barton), pp 9, 65, 302 (for John Carpenter), pp 64, 179 (for Browne); Turner (ed), *Records of the City of Oxford*, p 427 (for Chiston), p 410 (for Wilkes), p 319 (for Barton), p 205 (for Browne).

The keykeeper's accounts for 1593–4 (OCA: P.5.2, ff 17v–18v) list those citizens who loaned money to the use of the city for the queen's visit, giving particulars of how much was lent and when it was paid back. The sum total borrowed and repaid was £171 10s.

Bolt Shipton (ll.37–8) has not been identified but the villages of Shipton-on-Cherwell and Shipton Ho are slightly more than a mile east of Woodstock and four miles north of Wolvercote, the traditional place where the city and University officials met visiting monarchs. 'Bolt Shipton waye' (ll.37–8) may have been the local name for the road from Wolvercote to Shipton-on-Cherwell.

227 OCA: P.4.1 f 70v
Thomas Mundye (l.16), mercer, had been elected one of the 'Thirtene Associats of this Citie' on 26 March 1591 and was serving as a member of the mayor's council during the royal visit. He resigned his place on the council on 8 June 1595 and is last listed among the bailiffs in 1609 (Turner (ed), *Records of the City of Oxford*, p 376; Salter (ed), *Oxford Council Acts 1583–1626*, pp 61, 65, 92, 194).

227 Bodl.: MS. Rolls Oxon 66, roll 3 mb [2]
The three men honoured with guild dinners were made free during the accounting year: Simon Dobson (l.22), apprentice to William Tidiman, on 4 June; Oswald Belt (l.25), apprentice to John Wymans, on 19 January; and William Pearson (l.28), apprentice to Robert Gosson, on 9 March (Salter (ed), *Oxford Council Acts 1583–1626*, pp 61–2).

228 Bodl.: MS. D.D. All Souls c.286 mb 17
The entry occurs on sheet 28 of the paper roll of draft accounts for this year (also stored and catalogued as Bodl.: MS. D.D. All Souls c.286).

228–9 ChCh Arch: xii.b.35 f 27
The Christ Church payment to Hammond is presented incorrectly in 1591–2 (see p 215).

230–1 OUA: NEP/Supra/L ff 262–2v
The five-mile zone of University jurisdiction (p 231, l.19), absolute at Cambridge (see Nelson (ed), *Cambridge*, vol 2, p 779), here seems to have been subject to negotiation with the city.

Twyne added a marginal reference, 'playes and enterludes v. p. 242,' to f 242 (see p 194).

233 OCA: P.5.2 f 14
The payment to waits was presumably part of annual festivities for the queen's Accession Day as evidenced by the items preceding it – payments to the parson and clerk of St Martin's for bread and wine and to 'Becket,' the beadle of the beggars (Salter (ed), *Oxford Council Acts 1583–1626*, p xvii), both on St Hugh's Day (also 17 November).

These accounts are not in chronological order but jump from November to February to October to September. Following the entries for events in November are a block of payments for February including a payment dated specifically 'the iij of ffebruarie 1592' and the payment to the queen's men dated 25 February. Next comes the payment to Lord Strange's men on 6 October followed at the top of the next folio (f 14v) by two payments for the election day dinner in September. The next dated entry (on f 15) is for refreshments for the judges of the assize on 14 March followed two entries later by another date of 24 April. The accounts end on f 15v. There is little doubt that the date of the visit of Lord Strange's men was 6 October 1592 but it is possible that the block of February accounts are in fact for the preceding year. This would mean the visit of the queen's men took place on 25 February 1591/2 rather than 1592/3.

234   NC Arch: PA/L2   single sheet–single sheet verso
On salting money and saltings, see pp 613–14.

235   OCA: P.4.1   f 77
John Williams (l.35m), apothecary, was elected 'associate' on 1 September 1592 and served as a member of the mayor's council until his death before 25 May 1602. Richard Good (l.36), chandler, began his career of civic service as a member of the common council in 1583, becoming alderman in 1601 and serving as mayor in 1601–2. He died in July 1609. See Salter (ed), *Oxford Council Acts 1583–1626*, pp 3, 71, 138, 142, 146, 192.

239   ORO: PAR 213/4/F1/1   single mb col 1
This account (mounted on sheet 89) and the next (sheet 91) present a confusion in dating. The heading for this account gives the year as 1594 (36 Elizabeth) to 1595. However, 8 December was early in 37 Elizabeth. The next heading, originally 1594 (37 Elizabeth) to 1595, has been altered in a later hand to 1595–6. If this account is indeed for 1594–5 then the regnal year in the next account should have been changed to 38 Elizabeth. Since the next account after these two is unequivocally dated 1596–7, the accounts on sheets 89 and 91 have been here dated 1594–5 and 1595–6.

240   Bodl.: MS. Rolls Oxon 66, roll 4   mb [2]
Thomas Ewen (l.30) was admitted to the guild in this year and admitted to his freedom on 11 March 1595/6 (Salter (ed), *Oxford Council Acts 1583–1626*, p 99).

242   SJC Arch: Acc.v.E.1   ff 42v, 45
'Maio' or 'Mayo' (ll.16, 30) is possibly Thomas Mayo, who rented a tenement from the college on the site of what is now the Lamb and Flag public house (SJC Arch: Admin.I.A.2, p 548). This fiddler is mentioned by name (as 'Mais') again in 1598–9 when he received 22s 3d (see p 252).

242–3   OCA: L.5.1   f 245v
Leonard Major (p 243, l.4) was one of the assessors of George Buckner's estate in 1599 (see p 258 and p 1114, endnote to Bodl.: MS. Twyne-Langbaine 3 ff 121–1v). He played for the University and took his last apprentice, Francis Jones, in 1619–20 (see pp 267, 441).

243   OCA: P.5.2   ff 39, 39v
The date 2 July is written in the margin on the bottom of f 39 (next to the penultimate entry) between the two visits of the queen's men.

244   ChCh Arch: iii.c.7(a.)   mb 4
This entry also occurs in the draft treasurer's account (ChCh Arch: iii.c.1, f 60).

246–9   Hatfield House Library: Cecil Papers MS 62/16   single sheet
The document is not dated but was enclosed with a letter (Cecil Papers MS 62/15) dated 9 June 1598 from the University to Thomas Sackville, then Lord Buckhurst, the chancellor, and to Robert Devereux, the earl of Essex, who became high steward of the city in 1596. Although this deposition must have been written after the letter of complaint sent by the city on 3 June, it records the events of 28 May. The two documents have been placed here in their logical order.

This dispute went on over the summer months. On 26 August Essex was in the city apparently pursuing the suit. The city council minutes record for that day: 'It is also agreed that the char*dges* of the dynner made for the Earle of Essex gentlemen at his lordshipps late being here, and the char*ges* of the sute concerning the late wrong*es* done by mr Daniell and others of the Vniu*er*sitie vnto diverse of the Citizens and other controu*er*sies betwen the citie and the Vniu*er*sitie… Shalbe borne all att the char*ges* of this citie and shalbe paid out of the Com*m*on chest/' (OCA: C/FC/A1/002, f 48v). The chamberlain's accounts that year contain payments totalling £20 to Mr Dodwell and Thomas Harris for charges 'of them w*hich* went to o*u*r steward about businesse for the citie ˄⌈concerning the late⌉ iniurie done by mr Daniell & other schollers' (OCA: P.5.2, f 48).

The mayor was William Furness, senior, whose son William (p 247, l.22) drew his weapon on Master Daniel. The rowdy William Furness, junior, became a bailiff's serjeant in 1611. The town clerk (p 248, l.16) was John Hollway. See Salter (ed), *Oxford Council Acts 1583–1626*, p 205 (for Furness), p 114 (for Hollway).

249   OCA: P.5.2   f 45v
The queen's bearward (l.35) may still have been Ralph Bowes although this year 'the place reverted to John Dorrington' (David Cook (ed), 'Dramatic Records in the Declared Accounts of the Treasurer of the Chamber 1558–1642,' *Collections* 6, Malone Society (Oxford, 1962 for 1961), xii).

250   Bodl.: MS. Rolls Oxon 66, roll 5   mb [2]
The master this year was Thomas Collyns who had been admitted to the company in 1578–9 (see p 169).

250   ORO: PAR 213/4/F1/1   single mb col 1
The parchment has been torn and inaccurately repaired, with the result that the text is now out of alignment and difficult to decipher.

252   SJC Arch: Acc.v.E.2   f 6v
Mayo, the fiddler, is also paid 21s 10d by St John's in 1596–7 (see p 242 and p 1112, endnote to SJC Arch: Acc.v.E.1 ff 42v, 45).

255   MC Arch: LCE/7   f 117v
The entry also occurs in the draft computus (MC Arch: LCD/2, f 97) with 'Northampton' for 'Nottingham.' The former title was in abeyance in this period and therefore must be in error.

257   Biblioteca Apostolica Vaticana: Reg. lat. 666   f 167
The Windischgraetzes ('Windishgracij,' l.18) were brothers who had been friends of Waldstein since they were students together at Strasbourg University. They were also companions during part of his travels in France and elsewhere in England (G.W. Groos (trans), *The Diary of Baron Waldstein: A Traveller in Elizabethan England* (London, 1981), 70–1, 135, 137, 171).

257   OCA: P.5.2   ff 55v, 56v
Baldwin Hodges (l.25) became town crier on 13 September 1593 and served until 11 December 1610. He is listed among the former chamberlains in 1611 (Salter (ed), *Oxford Council Acts 1583–1626*, pp 80–1, 204, 217).

There is no way to identify the 'Lord*es* men' (l.30) but the 'men' are more likely to be servants than players. The entries that provide the context for the 'noble mens mucisions' (l.32) include wine and sugar on 18 July in the mayor's house for the justices of the assize and the rent of the Blue Boar tavern, presumably for lodging for the members of the circuit court.

258–9   Bodl.: MS. Twyne-Langbaine 3   ff 121–1v
George Buckner had been a city wait who also played for University functions (see pp 239, 245, 251). He gave up his scutcheon as wait along with George Ewen on 8 October 1577 (see p 167) but was appointed again 14 September 1588 (see p 206). He served as bailiff for the hundred of Northgate and was instructed to collect rents on 26 March 1591. (Salter (ed), *Oxford Council Acts 1583–1626*, p 61). He bought his freedom on 24 November 1596 (see pp 242–3). This document concerns the proceedings that followed his suicide (see p 621).

261   MC Arch: LCE/7   f 130
The 'ducis Bauariæ' (l.14) is Maximilian I, duke and later also elector of Bavaria.

261   NC Arch: 7590   mb 5
For 'the Duke of Bavare' (l.25), see above, endnote to MC Arch: LCE/7 f 130.

263   OCA: P.5.2   f 64v
There is no further information about why the city should be paying for musicians at the Bakers' dinner. From the surviving accounts of the Tailors' and the Cordwainers' guilds it is clear that it was the custom of the guilds to pay for musicians at their dinners. The fact that the city paid for this entertainment may have something to do with its dispute the preceding year with the University, involving a Mr Jackman and his fellow bakers over the issue of where their meal was to be ground (OCA: C/FC/1/A2/1, f 170).

264   ChCh Arch: iii.c.7(d.)   mb 3
The entry also occurs in the draft treasurer's account (ChCh Arch: iii.c.1, f 75).

265   ORO: PAR 208/4/F1/36   single mb
The date of rendering is almost certainly 29 May, which was Rogation Sunday. The damaged account header indicates only that the account was rendered '⟨...⟩ twenteth daye' of May. The lost text is very likely 'nine and.'

265   ORO: PAR 209/4/F1/18   single mb
The MS dating is clear. The heading states that the account runs from St Andrew's Day, 44 Elizabeth (1601), to the same feast, 45 Elizabeth (1602). The date 1603–4 is written on the dorse in a nineteenth(?)-century hand.

266   ORO: PAR 214/4/F1/49   single mb
The 'shooting daye' (l.14) is mentioned for the first time here. The parish paid a musician for the event in 1604–5 (see p 328).

266   MC Arch: LCE/7   f 151v
No Sir Richard Lucy (l.37) can be identified at this date. Sir Thomas Lucy (1551–1605), who had been sheriff of Gloucestershire in 1589–90, had a son Thomas who matriculated at Magdalen College

in 1601, and another son Richard who matriculated at the same college in 1607, both when they were fifteen years old. Richard, like his older brother, became prominent in public affairs and was knighted later on, but there is no compelling reason to question the dating of the record, and a confusion between the names of Richard and Thomas seems unlikely.

267 NC Arch: 7593 mb 4
'Leonardo' is Leonard Major (see p 1112, endnote to OCA: L.5.1 f 245v).

267 QC Arch: LRA f 23v col 1
These two entries occur among payments dated 1 and 10 July 1603. They must be for the end of the accounting year (ie, the July of 1603) because expenses are entered in month order and the two payments occur at the end of the block of external expenses.

268 SJC Arch: Acc.I.A.10 f 143
This entry is repeated verbatim in the annual account for 1603–4 (p 275). Henry Herbert (l.8) became the proprietor of the Lamb public house, on the south side of the college, on 24 May 1600. In 1613 he moved the establishment to its present site and renamed it the Lamb and Flag (Stevenson and Salter, *Early History of St. John's College*, pp 504–6).

268 SJC Arch: Acc.v.E.2 f 59
'Mr Langley' (l.17) is possibly Henry Langley, merchant tailor, whose son Adam was a student at the Merchant Taylors' School in 1603 and matriculated at St John's in 1610.

268–9 Bodl.: MS. Rawlinson poet.212 ff 82, 67
This work has been edited by Margaret L. Lee, who has demonstrated its connection with St John's (see Appendix 6:1 under *Narcissus*). 'Frances' (p 269, l.31) was Francis Clarke who became porter of St John's on 8 May 1601 (Clark (ed), *Register*, vol 2, pt 1, p 398).
    St John's lies in the parish of St Mary Magdalen (*VCH: Oxford*, vol 3, p 258) but is also associated with St Giles, which may be a more logical source of young male parishioners. Reference to a particular parish may also be part of the dramatic fiction.

272 OCA: C/FC/1/A1/002 ff 85, 85v
The entry on f 85 occurs in OCA: C/FC/1/A2/1, f 184v, with 'any other part' for 'any other sort' (l.8). The entry on f 85v also occurs in OCA: C/FC/1/A2/1, f 185v, where a cancelled phrase after 'at his owne Chardge' (ll.16–17) reads, 'as other musicions haue done.'
    John Baldwin, senior (l.14), along with his son John Baldwin, junior, was formally named one of the waits on 4 December 1628 (see pp 481–2). On 15 September 1604 he was granted a licence for a sign, 'The Bell' (Salter (ed), *Properties*, p 339).

272 OCA: P.5.2 f 76v
The proclamation of the king seems to have reminded city officials that the protocol for royal visits needed regularizing. As a result they recorded the following intention on 2 August (OCA: C/FC/1/A1/002, f 86):
> It is agreed At this Counsell That Whereas it is voyced abroad That the Kinges Maiestie entendeth shortly to comme to this Cytie/ master Mayor/ thaldermen/ the residewe of the thirteene/ and the bayliffes for the yeare shall bethinck themselues & sett downe in what

sort & order his Ma*ie*stie shalbe receaued/ And after such an order agreed vppon to *ce*rtifie
unto this howse of the Chardg*es* they shall thincke it will amount vnto/ And then to be sett
downe & agreed by this howsse what taxac*io*ns or impositions shalbe laid vppon the Citizens
& others for such his Ma*ie*sties receaving//

Substantially the same motion occurs in OCA: C/FC/1/A1/002, f 186. The king did not make a formal
visit to Oxford until August 1605.

273   ORO: PAR 208/4/F1/36   single mb
Regarding the date of this entry, see p 1114, endnote to ORO: PAR 208/4/F1/36 single mb.

273   ORO: PAR 211/4/F1/3, item 166   single mb
No rendering date is given. The MS is labelled '1603' on the dorse and is presumed to be the account
for the period from 12 March 1602/3 to 12 March 1603/4.

274   ORO: PAR 213/4/F1/2   single mb
This account was rendered 8 December. The next, mounted on f 3, runs from 8 December to Easter
week 1605. In 1605 the accounting year became Easter to Easter with the accounts usually beginning
and ending on the Wednesday after Easter.

274   ChCh Arch: iii.c.7(e.)   mb 3
The entry also occurs in ChCh Arch: iii.c.7(f.), mb 3d. Copies of the draft version (ie, the treasurer's
account) survive for this year. This entry occurs on ff 100 and 111 of the draft versions.

275   QC Arch: LRA f 25v col 1
The payment occurs among others dated 5 January; the next payment thereafter is for 12 February.

275   SJC Arch: Acc.I.A.10   f 164v
For Henry Herbert (l.24), see p 1115, endnote to SJC Arch: Acc.I.A.10 f 143, of which this entry is
a duplicate.

276   OCA: P.5.2 f 82v
Henry Niccolls (l.22) arrived in Oxford from London in 1591 and served as serjeant at mace for
the city from 4 February1593/4 until his resignation on 19 January 1613/14. He is listed among
the bailiffs from 1594 until 1615 (Salter (ed), *Oxford Council Acts 1583–1626*, pp 64, 84, 87, 155,
241, 248).

276   ORO: DD Par. Oxford St Aldate c.16/11   single mb
This year apparently marks the shift to an Easter to Easter fiscal year. An insertion in the account heading
indicates that the account was 'made' 2 April by the churchwardens who were chosen 13 February 1604/5.
As 2 April 1605 is just three days past Easter Sunday, it would appear that the new wardens began their
work at that time.

277   ORO: PAR 207/4/F1/1, item 102   single mb
This year marks a change in accounting period from November to November to Easter to Easter.

277   ORO: PAR 214/4/F1/51   single sheet
The accounting year changes with these accounts, which cover from December 1603 to the second
Sunday after Easter (ie, 10 April) 1605.

278   ChCh Arch: xii.b.49   f 60
The note of particulars (l.34) does not survive but see pp 610–11 and Appendix 1.

281   QC Arch: LRA   f 28 col 1, f 30 col 2
The expenses on f 28 col 1 are dated 28 January 1604/5. On f 30 col 2, the first payment to 'Clarionibus'
occurs between payments dated 17 and 20 August 1605, the second between payments dated 27 August
and 19 September 1605.

282–7   OUA: WP/γ/19/1   ff 1v, 2v–4, 4v–5
Omitted are lectures and disputations (f 3v); a list of authorities empowered to discipline violators of
public order (f 4); and regulations of behaviour on and around scaffolds during debates (ff 4–5v).
   The first section of the document, 'decrees & orders,' was copied in part in 1636 by Brian Twyne into
Bodl.: MS. Twyne 17, pp 181–3, from a common source and is collated here. Twyne's copy begins with
the specific agreement concerning stage plays (p 284, l.4ff.). He omits one other agreement (p 284,
ll.13–19) and reorders still others. Twyne also omits 'Advertismentes for the heades of houses' (p 285,
l.16–p 286, l.19) but includes the list of assessments upon the colleges and a selection of the agreements
that follow.
   The 'Advertisements' were copied in 1605 from a common source into Cambridge University Library:
MS Additional 34, ff 28–9, by an anonymous Cambridge man and are also collated here. Parts of the
document were copied by the Oxford antiquary William Fulman in 1662 into CCC: MS 301, f 93v. As
this MS has no independent authority it is not collated here. Two of Fulman's corrections of possible
mistakes deserve consideration: the exact punctuation of 'about ye Hall, Staires or within the Quadrangle'
for 'about ye hall stayres or within ye Quadrangle' (p 286, l.4), and 'upon paine of' for 'vppon of' (p 286,
l.5). Fulman also omits 'as vsually they weare wont to doe' (l.5).
   The 'dean of Christchurch' (p 282, l.34) was John King; 'ye greeke professor' (p 283, l.16), John
Perrinne; 'the Orator of the vniversitie' (p 283, l.18), Isaac Wake.

288–90   OUA: WP/β/P/5/3   sheet [1], f [1], ff [2–2v], sheet [3], f [1]
For a discussion of this document, see Boas and Greg, 'James I at Oxford,' pp 247–50.

294   Staffordshire Record Office: D649/1/1   paper fragment
The 'play which I made' (l.12) is the Latin pastoral *Alba*, performed on Tuesday, 27 August 1605 in
Christ Church (see Appendix 6:2). A complete transcription of the fragmentary letter is supplied by
Nochimson, 'Robert Burton's Authorship of Alba.'

294   PRO: C/115/M20, no 7594   ff [1–1v]
The 'one onely excepted' (l.31) presumably refers to Samuel Daniel's English comedy *The Queen's
Arcadia*, performed on Friday, 30 August 1605 in Christ Church (see pp 299, 304). Bodley goes
on to say that the king showed more interest in the disputations and orations than in other entertainments.

295–301   Cambridge University Library: MS Additional 34   ff 28, 30–30v, 32–4, 35, 37, 39v, 41, 42v–3v, 44, 44v–5v

Omitted are details of stops on the progress; a reiteration of the Advertisements (see p 285, l.16ff.); a summary of the speakers and subjects for the debates (f 28); the late arrival of Thomas Sackville, now earl of Dorset and chancellor of the University (f 30v); arrangements for events at St Mary's and inspection of lodgings (ff 30v–1); sermons and disputations on the days before the king's arrival (ff 31–2); prayers and services (f 34); meetings on order and discipline (ff 34–5v); more disputations (f 37); comments on availability of robes and gowns (ff 41, 43v); the king's behaviour at the disputations (f 44); and complaints about inflation in the market and the wearing of improper caps (f 45).

For more details on the theatrical stage, see pp 610–11 and Appendix 1. For *Alba*, see p 1117, endnote to Staffordshire Record Office: D649/1/1 paper fragment and Appendix 6:2. 'Mr. Iones' (p 301, l.10) is Inigo Jones.

301–4   STC: 18589   sigs A4–B2v, B3, C1v, E1v–2, E3–3v, E4v–F

Little is known about Anthony Nixon except that he was 'the author of many pamphlets in prose, with scraps of original and translated verse interspersed' (*DNB*). Omitted are events at Magdalen College Chapel and St Mary's Church (degree ceremonies, disputations, prayers, and speeches) and the king's tour of the new Bodleian Library, built over the Divinity School. For more details on the stage, see pp 610–11 and Appendix 1.

305–7   STC: 24939   pp 18–19, 45–8

Vertumnus (p 307, l.1) is evidently confused with *Alba*, as first noted by Chambers, *Elizabethan Stage*, vol 1, p 130. A marginal note in the fourth edition of *Rex Platonicus* (Oxford, 1627; STC: 24941) ascribes *Vertumnus* to Gwinne (see collation notes on p 307). See also Appendix 6:1 for *Vertumnus* and 6:2 for *Alba*.

Wake alludes to accounts of doves fashioned with skill like Archytas' dove, or trained with skill like Mahomet's dove (p 307, ll.21–2). Archytas of Tarentum (in Sicily) was well-known in antiquity as a Pythagorean philosopher and mathematician. In the *Noctes Atticae* (10.12.9) Aulus Gellius referred to a story that Archytas had built a mechanical dove that could actually fly. Mahomet is a Latinisation of the name of Muhammad. The story to which Wake refers comes from the 'Life of St Pelagius' in the *Golden Legend* of Jacobus de Voragine (*Legenda Aurea* 182.2). According to the hagiographer, a dove was trained to sit on Muhammad's shoulder and take grain from his ear in order to deceive people into thinking that the Holy Spirit was sitting on his shoulder and speaking the word of God in his ear.

'Germanis … Boemus' (p 310, ll.11–13m) presumably refers to Joannes Boemus, *Mores, leges, et ritus omnium gentium*, but the exact allusion remains untraced. For more details on the stage, see pp 610–11 and Appendix 1.

A translation of the lengthy collation (p 306) is here provided:

> Wolsey, moreover, wished the schools for professors of languages, of the three faculties, and also of the seven liberal arts to be as numerous as the vaults in that tower. For he had determined to establish here not so much a college as almost another university within the University, and to that end he transferred to this place the choicest picked flower of the University. (He transferred) some from Cambridge also, where they had not unprofitably applied themselves to letters, when on account of a paucity of funds they were not equal to pursue their studies. The cardinal, very moved by their humble prayers and the entreaties of (their) friends, generously granted (to them) a seat and assistance here among his own.

314–15   *stc*: 12555   sigs H3–3v
The reading 'Duncan' (p 315, l.3m) occurs on a cancel-slip appearing in some copies; the corrected reading is 'Donald' (see W.W. Greg, *A Bibliography of the English Printed Drama to the Restoration*, vol 2, (London, 1951), 937).

   'Llhewelyn ap Sitsylht' (p 315, ll.5–6m) is Llywelyn ab Seisyll (d. 1023), ruler of Gwynedd 1005–23 and of Deheubarth 1018–23. 'Polonice Regule' (p 315, l.16) is an undeciphered allusion. On 16 January 1604/5 Charles had been created duke of York.

315–19   Bodl.: MS. Ashmole 36, 37   f 259 cols 1, 2, f 259v col 1
Omitted are stanzas 11–12 (names of some of the nobility in attendance) and 23–5 (the king's breakfast). The poem seems incomplete but the word 'finis' does appear after stanza 25.

   In stanza 19 'Royston ⌊downe⌋' (p 318, l.22) is Royston, Hertfordshire, between London and Cambridge, where James I kept a residence and indulged his fondness for sports. The point is that the people of Oxford love the king so much that they do not begrudge his preference for spending leisure time closer to Cambridge. In stanza 21 'a pleasant pasto^⌈rall⌉' (p 318, l.39) is Robert Burton's *Alba*.

   The poem is listed as T3050 in Margaret Crum (ed), *First-Line Index of English Poetry, 1500–1800, in Manuscripts of the Bodleian Library, Oxford*, 2 vols (Oxford, 1969).

319–21   Bodl.: MS. Malone 19   pp 125–8
The poem is listed as N452 in Margaret Crum (ed), *First-Line Index of English Poetry, 1500–1800, in Manuscripts of the Bodleian Library, Oxford*, 2 vols (Oxford, 1969); also noted in Nelson (ed), *Cambridge*, vol 2, p 871.

322–4   OCA: C/FC/1/A1/002   ff 101, 101v–2, 103
The act on f 101 also occurs in OCA: C/FC/1/A2/1, f 203v, where it concludes, 'Lett the Later [act] ^⌈order made by the Maior aldermen & xiij^teene⌉ [entred] [made] the xxv^th of Iune bee entred heare./' The order is then written on ff 205–5v. The items from f 102 (20 and 25 June) and f 103 (29 July and 1 August) appear in OCA: C/FC/1/A2/1, ff 204–6.

   John Poole (p 324, l.6), cutler, is first listed among the bailiffs in 1596 and last listed in 1625. Henry Pigott (p 324, l.6), mercer, served as bailiff in 1603 and is last listed among the bailiffs in 1619. The chamberlains (p 324, ll.6–7) this year were William Tyrer, baker, and James Twayte. 'Master Alderman Levinz' (p 324, l.27) was William Levinz, apothecary, who served as alderman from 1582 to his death and as mayor in 1594–5. He was at the time of this royal visit one of the true elder statesmen of Oxford civic politics. Alderman Isaac Bartholomew (p 324, l.28), identified as a 'White baker,' was a member of the mayor's council from 1594 to 1618. He served one term as mayor in 1599–1600. John Hollway (p 324, l.28) was town clerk. See Salter (ed), *Oxford Council Acts 1583–1626*, pp 108, 335 (for Poole), pp 152, 170, 286 (for Pigott), pp 160, 163 (for Twayte), pp 2, 87 (for Levinz), pp 44, 128, 276 (for Bartholomew); Salter (ed), *Properties*, p 309 (for Tyrer); Turner (ed), *Records of the City of Oxford*, p 212 (for Levinz).

324–6   OCA: P.5.2   ff 86, 89v
William Potter (p 324, l.37), woollen-draper, was at the beginning of what was to be a long and in many ways controversial career in civic affairs. During this year he had taken his first significant office serving as bailiff. For Isaac Bartholomew (p 325, l.36), see above, endnote to OCA: C/FC/1/A1/002 ff 101, 101v–2, 103. William Wright (p 326, ll.7–8) was admitted to his freedom in 1581–2 as a shoemaker but at his son Martin's admission William was identified as a goldsmith. He served as bailiff in 1600–1.

See Salter (ed), *Oxford Council Acts 1583–1626*, pp 162–3 (for Potter), pp 135, 258 (for Wright); Turner (ed), *Records of the City of Oxford*, p 427 (for Wright).

326   oro: DD Par. Oxford St Aldate c.16/12   single mb
Mr Royce (l.36) was one of the churchwardens for the year. Several Royces lived in Oxford at this period – drapers and glovers – but none can be identified positively with St Aldate's.

327   oro: PAR 209/4/F1/21   single mb
Because the accounting year shifts from St Andrew's to St Andrew's to Easter to Easter, this account covers seventeen months. The rendering date is given as 23 April, which is three days after Easter Sunday, but the year is not specified. However, since the next account runs from Easter 1606, the hocking must be for 1605.

328   oro: PAR 214/4/F1/52   single mb
'Charles' (l.16) is probably Thomas Charles, who was later involved with John Bosseley, the wait, in the renting of the dancing school (see p 1122, endnote to oca: D.5.5 f 189).

328   stc: 772.7   sig A2
This work was issued in two earlier editions, in 1600 and 1605 (stc: 772.3, 772.5), under the title *Foole Vpon Foole*. The Dedication to the 'generous Gentlemen of Oxenford' does not occur in either of the first two editions. Armin's visit to Christ Church and All Souls may therefore probably be dated between 1605 and 1608. The king's men, for whom Armin was principal clown, received payments from the Oxford city council on 9 October 1605, 28 July 1606, and 7 September 1607 (see pp 333, 334, 337).

329   ChCh Arch: iii.c.7(g.)   mb 3d
This entry occurs in the draft treasurer's account (ChCh Arch: iii.c.1, f 140).

329   pro: SP/15/37   f [1]
The letter is signed by Richard Parry, bishop of St Asaph; Francis Godwin, bishop of Llandaff (l.20); and four others.

330   ChCh Arch: D.P.ii.c.1, item 6   single sheet
The memorandum is signed by John Howson, Leonard Hutten, John King, John Perrinne, Ralph Pickhaver, Richard Thornton, and John Weston.

331   qc Arch: LRA f 30v col 1
The payment to Morris ('Mauritio,' l.10) follows one dated 11 January 1605/6, while the 'Tibicinib*us*' payment (l.12) occurs shortly after that and before 2 March 1605/6.

331   sjc Arch: Acc.v.E.4 f 18v
The 'Christmas-Lord' entry (l.25) also occurs in the St John's steward's book for this week (sjc Arch: Acc.v.E.5, f 16), with the addition of the phrase 'strangers intertayned.'

332   Boughton House: Winwood Papers, vol 4   f [1]
For the complete text of the letter, see Chamberlain, *Letters*, vol 1, p 208.

332–3   OCA: C/FC/1/A1/002   ff 106, 109
The 11 December entry also occurs in OCA: C/FC/1/A2/1, f 209. The only substantive difference between the two versions is that OCA: C/FC/1/A2/1 gives £15 as the remuneration for the repair of the bridges where C/FC/1/A1/002 gives £16 (p 332, l.38).

Thomas Cossam (p 332, l.37), shoemaker, was near the end of a long career as a member of the Oxford governing elite that began with his election to the common council in 1576. On 15 September 1597 he was elected an 'associate' and for 1598–9 he was elected to the mayor's council, where he served until his resignation on 23 September 1608. He served as mayor in 1604–5 at the time of the king's visit (Turner (ed), *Records of the City of Oxford*, pp 88, 304; Salter (ed), *Oxford Council Acts 1583–1626*, pp 3, 107, 121, 163, 187). For the dancing school, see p 622.

333–4   OCA: P.5.2   ff 92, 93
24 March was James' accession day. The payment to the king's players (p 334, l.1) comes between two entries related to wine and gloves for the justices of the assize. The court sat on 28 July 1606.

336   QC Arch: LRA   f 32 col 2
The payments occur with others between 24 January and 3 September.

338–9   LC Arch   f 5
This entry (p 339, l.1) is added to the list of weekly commons for the fellows for the ninth week (1–7 February) of the first term, 1607–8. The term began on 7 December 1607.

340   QC Arch: LRA   f 35 col 1
The payment follows one dated 15 February. The next dated payment is in June.

340   SJC Arch: Acc.v.E.4   f 48
On St John's College 'Christmas sport*es*,' see p 613. For further discussion of The Christmas Prince, see Appendix 6:1 and the introductions there cited to the complete edition and to the facsimile.

340–54   SJC Library: MS 52   pp 5–10, 11–13, 26–39
Pages 10–11 contain a list of members of the college with amounts paid, for a total of £12 13s 7d. The musicians from Reading (p 354, l.14) were probably not town musicians but freelancers. The Reading town accounts survive in broken runs from 1413 to 1456 and again from 1587 to 1632 but the detailed corporation diary does not begin until 1622. There is nothing at all about musicians in the accounts from 1587 to 1628 (Berkshire Record Office: R/FCa 2/75–2/90). A very early record in the corporation diary for 29 October 1622 seems to refer to the setting up of a small group of town musicians (Berkshire Record Office: R/ACa 2 1622–28, f 2). These records are forthcoming in the REED series.

382   ORO: PAR 207/4/F1/1, item 107   single mb
The MS clearly states that the account was rendered on the 'Seaventh' of April, 1609. St Martin's churchwardens habitually rendered their accounts after Easter, which fell on 16 April that year. The scribe may have written the seventh in error for seventeenth. On the other hand, as the St Martin's churchwardens rendered their accounts on 7 April for the next two years, this may represent an attempt to standardize the rendering date.

387   CCC: MS 304   ff 83v–4
Henry Jackson was a fellow of Corpus Christi College. 'D.G.P.' is perhaps (Doctor) Griffith Powell of Jesus College. The letter has been published, in the original Latin with an English translation, by Salgado, *Eyewitnesses of Shakespeare*, p 30. For more on this letter, see p 648 and Appendix 10, p 857.

It is not known where in Oxford these performances took place but Jackson's reference to a 'pleno theatro' (l.22) suggests that one of the chambers in the Oxford guildhall was used (compare Nelson (ed), *Cambridge*, vol 2, pp 724–7).

389   OCA: C/FC/1/A1/002   f 132v
John Bosseley held a tenement in St Michael at the North Gate 'on the west side of Northgate' (Salter (ed), *Properties*, p 235). His interest in the dancing school located in the Bocardo is first mentioned on 8 September 1606 (see p 333; see also pp 390, 397–8). It was leased for the last time in the Records by his son John Bosseley, junior, 20 September 1636 (see p 550).

The Bocardo (l.31) was the city jail located at the North Gate of Oxford near St Michael at the North Gate. In 1231 the mayor and bailiffs were ordered to keep delinquent clerks there until they could be turned over to the University. By 1293 the building had two storeys and some attempt seems to have been made to segregate the sexes. In 1542 and 1543 a third storey was added at the cost of Thomas Mallynson, draper, who was elected alderman on 19 May 1549 and served as MP for Oxford in 1554 (Turner (ed), *Records of the City of Oxford*, pp 192, 216). It was here that Bishops Cranmer, Latimer, and Ridley were imprisoned in 1555–6 (*VCH: Oxford*, vol 4, p 334). This chamber 'at Bocardo,' which became the location of the dancing school, was not in the jail itself but in the same building.

390–1   OCA: D.5.5   f 180
'Dancing school north Gate' is written in the left margin in a nineteenth-century hand, possibly that of the antiquary George Parsons Hester.

391   ORO: DD Par. Oxford St Aldate b.17/1   mb [1]
The 'viij s.' is cancelled but the 'x d. ob.' was mistakenly allowed to stand.

392   ORO: PAR 214/4/F1/57   single mb
The Rowland Barber, glover and town crier between 1583 and 1592, who is mentioned in 1586–7 (see p 205), is probably not this man since the last mention of that Rowland Barber in Salter (ed), *Oxford Council Acts 1583–1626*, p 125, is dated 5 May 1599.

392   Bodl.: MS. Wood D.18, Pt 2   ff 1, 29
In his edition of *Mercurius Rusticans*, J.W. Binns argues that the author of the English verses on the last page of the MS was a student named either Henry or John Seller. For more on *Mercurius Rusticans* and Hinksey, see Appendix 6:1.

395   ChCh Arch: iii.c.8(d.)   mb 2d
This entry also occurs in the draft treasurer's account (ChCh Arch: iii.c.1, f 185).

397–9   OCA: D.5.5   f 189
Thomas Charles (p 398, l.36) may be the 'yonge Charles' paid by the parish of St Peter le Bailey for

music in 1604–5 (see p 328). A Thomas Charles, musician, was called before the court of quarter sessions in 1627 (OCA: QSC A2/001, pp 241–3).

399   ORO: PAR 207/4/F1/1, item 116   mb [1]
The Hocktide entry occurs as the second entry among the receipts. The first is merely the sum received from the previous year's wardens. The 'more' (l.19) must simply mean 'in addition to' the existing sum. The same formulation is used in the account for 1613–14.

401   ChCh Arch: iii.c.8(e.)   mb 2d
The entry also occurs in the draft treasurer's account (ChCh Arch: iii.c.1, f 192).

401   MC Arch: LCE/8   f 55v
On the prince palatine (ll.26–7), see pp 605–6.

402   OCA: P.5.2   f 126v
The Lady Elizabeth's players considered visiting Oxford this year. In a letter to Philip Henslowe about his new play, *The Arraignment of London*, Robert Daborne wrote, 'the company told me you were expected thear yesterday to conclude about thear comming over or goinge to Oxford…' (Dulwich College Archive: MS I.106, 357). Greg in his note to this letter writes, 'This "comming over" refers, I think, to the project of leaving the theatre in Whitefriars for Paris Garden, rebuilt and rechristened The Hope in 1614' (W.W. Greg (ed), *Henslowe Papers* (London, 1907), 72). The Lady Elizabeth's players are not recorded as ever visiting Oxford.

403   ORO: PAR 213/4/F1/3   f 1
This is the first year the same accounts occur in two MSS. ORO: PAR 213/4/F1/3 seems to have been the fair copy of the rough accounts (ORO: PAR 213/4/F1/2, f 10).

403   ChCh Arch: x(i).c.50   f 20
Both 'mr Browne' (l.37) and Edmund Trulocke (l.37) are listed as students elsewhere in the Christ Church battell book for 1613–14.

404   ChCh Arch: xi.b.16   f 3
Presumably the entry is cancelled to indicate return of the costumes.

405–6   OCA: P.5.2   f 132v
Thomas Brookes (p. 406, l.1) was admitted as a slater in 1591 but called an innholder when his son William was admitted in 1617. He served in the civic government, rising to the rank of bailiff. (Salter (ed), *Oxford Council Acts 1583–1626*, pp 62, 129, 154, 269). The Red Lion in this period was located in South Street opposite the guildhall (Salter, *Survey of Oxford*, vol 2, pp 102–3).

407   LC Arch   f 5
The heading to this section, 'festum Mildredae et carnisprivij,' refers to the expenses for the eleventh week of the first term, which began 3 December 1614. The feast of St Mildred is usually observed on 13 July. 'Carnisprivium' can refer to the first two days of Lent, to Septuagesima Sunday, or to Sexagesima Sunday. Here it probably refers to the latter, which fell on 11 February 1614/15, the first

day of the eleventh week of the first term. 'Mildredae' may be an error for 'Milburga,' whose feast was 23 February.

407   MC Arch: LCE/8   f 72
Ambrose Powell (l.28) left the college his bass viol and other instruments (see p 460).

409   PRO: SP/14/80   ff [3–3v]
John Howson, canon of Christ Church, wrote this account of his interrogation before King James at Greenwich on charges of papist leanings. Howson survived the interrogation and was made bishop of Oxford in 1619.

409   OCA: P.5.2   f 136v
Although 'Allhollowtyde' (l.28) could include more than the feast itself, Salter dates this performance 1 November (Salter (ed), *Oxford Council Acts 1583–1626*, p 445).

410   ORO: PAR 208/4/F1/45   single mb
It appears as if the barrels of ale were set up on trestle tables in the cellar of the church, possibly in an attempt to keep the ale cool.

411   ORO: PAR 213/4/F1/3   f 3
The inserted 'ale' (l.5) is in a different colour ink as is the total for the receipt column. It does not seem to be another hand but a scribal correction.

413–14   OUA: WP/β/21(4)   p 179
These entries also occur in Bodl.: MS. Add.c.206, f 123, with '*Venerabili* Regis' for '*Domini* Regis' (p 413, l.39).

414   OCA: P.5.2   f 145
The date of the audit was 7 November 1616. The other two dates specified in this account are St Scholastica's Day (10 February) and 5 August. The position of this entry makes it probable that the Marian festival intended is the Annunciation (25 March) although both the Salutation (25 June) and the Visitation (2 July) also fall within the possible date range.

414   OCA: P.4.1   f 157
There is no rendering date on this account, which is simply headed, 'Tempore Iohannis Bird Armigeri Maioris Ciuitatis Oxon.' John Byrd, mercer, was mayor in 1615–16 (Salter (ed), *Oxford Council Acts 1583–1626*, p 247). This is the last mention of William Gibbons' bond for the waits' scutcheons (see p 621).

415–16   Bodl.: MS. Wood F.29(a)   f 8c verso col 2
Folio 8c is an insert on which are recorded several notes about the conduit, which is itself mentioned on ff 9–9v.

417–18   NC Arch: 7619   mb 6
The bishop of Winchester (p 417, l.40) was the official visitor of both New College and St John's (*VCH: Oxford*, vol 3, pp 155, 252).

418   sjc Arch: Acc.i.A.11   f 24
The 'honourable Visitour' (l.38) is the bishop of Winchester, who appeared during the second week
of September 1617 (sjc Arch: Acc.v.E.6, f 48).

419–21   sjc Arch: Acc.iii.D.1   ff 23v, 24, 25, 34–4v
The heading for these entries assigns them to the first term, probably an error for the second. For 'our
Honourable Visitor' (p 420, l.8), see above, endnote to sjc Arch: Acc.i.A.11 f 24.
   William Chillingworth (p 421, l.21) was bailiff in 1614–15 and is listed among the bailiffs until 1643
when he was elected 'assistant' and then mayor in 1644–5 (Salter (ed), *Oxford Council Acts 1583–1626*,
pp 131, 239; Hobson and Salter (eds), *Oxford Council Acts 1626–1665*, pp 114, 121). 'Gennings' (p 421,
ll.23, 25) is William Jennings, tailor. It is impossible to tell whether he or his contemporary William
Jennings, mercer, served as constable in 1610–11 and became a member of the common council in
1617 (Salter (ed), *Oxford Council Acts 1583–1626*, pp 203, 273).

422   oca: P.5.2   ff 156v, 157
The two payments to the queen's and king's players (f 156v) are the last references to paid performances
by players in the Records (see p 615). Thomas Crosfield's diary, which begins nine years later in 1626
(see p 466), records the visits of many players to Oxford. From other evidence it is also clear that players
continued to perform in the region well into the 1630s. The Woodstock accounts, for example, record
payments to the prince's players in 1623–4 and the king's players on 22 November 1635 (Woodstock
Chamberlains' Accounts 1607–50, oro: B79 (1) 1, ff 72v and 131).
   The royal family was at Woodstock this year. The payment to the trumpeters (f 157) occurs among
a list of 30s to the queen's footmen, 18s to the queen's porters, 5s for the coachman, 30s for the prince's
footmen, 5s to the prince's coachman, and 7s to the 'lyttery men belonging to the Queene.'

422   oro: PAR 211/4/F1/3, item 181   mb [1]
The entry is in a different hand from the rest of the account and appears to have been squeezed into
the space between the final item and the total sum. The second clause appears to be written over
an erasure.

423   oca: QSC/A2/001   pp 51, 52
Since the Middle Ages the market had been held in the streets adjacent to Carfax spreading down the
High Street as far as St Mary's and by the early seventeenth century also into Queen Street. The cross-
streets – now Cornmarket running to the north and St Aldate's to the south – were also filled with
stalls (see *vch: Oxford*, vol 4, pp 305–6).
   William Steevenson (l.17), apprentice to Fulke Emerson, was admitted to his freedom 3 April 1618.
William Tilcock (l.29), painter, was admitted to his freedom 6 February 1614/15. The mayor was Richard
Smith who, like Emerson and Steevenson, was a tailor. See Salter (ed), *Oxford Council Acts 1583–1626*,
p 274 (for Steevenson), p 242 (for Tilcock), pp 54, 261 (for Smith).

427   Bodl.: ms. Wood E.4   ff 23v–4
For 'Whoop Holiday' (p 427, l.6) and other verses, see Appendix 2, especially Poem A.

427–8   Harvard Theatre Collection: ms Thr.10   pp 8, 89–90
The cast list is analysed in Appendix 7, pp 843–4.

429   *stc*: 13617   sig A2v
Barten Holyday wrote this play in hope of a performance before King James ('our Platonique King,' l.11).
Instead it received its first performance before the students of Christ Church on 13 February 1617/18.
It was finally performed before the king at Woodstock on 26 August 1621, to general derision (see
Appendix 2 and Appendix 13, p 886).

429   oca: L.5.2   f 401
John Baldwin, junior, was formally named as one of the waits on the same day as his father, 4 December
1628 (see pp 481–2). He may be the John Baldwin who was created Bachelor of Civil Law on 18 March
1646/7 although 'not educated in any university.'

430   oro: PAR 214/4/F1/63   f [1]
Goodman Turner (l.31) was probably Edward Turner, cordwainer, admitted to his freedom in 1617–18
(Salter (ed), *Oxford Council Acts 1583–1626*, p 269).

433   qc Arch: LRB   f 25 col 1
The payment to Morris (l.4) is preceded by an entry dated 18 January.

433   sjc Arch: Acc.i.A.12   ff 47v, 48, 50
These entries also occur in sjc Arch: Acc.i.A.13, f 22.

434   Harvard Theatre Collection: ms Thr.10.1   f 2
The memorandum, in the hand of Goffe, is in effect a 'to do' list ('An' being Latin for 'Whether,' here
meaning 'Have the following been accomplished?'). On this memorandum and the whole of the actor's
part for Amurath, see Carnegie, 'Hand of Thomas Goffe,' pp 161–5. See also Appendix 6:1 under
Courageous Turk.

437   oro: PAR 208/4/F1/48   single mb
No date is given for the rendering of the accounts but a memo at the foot of the account, concerning
arrangements for poor relief, is dated 18 April. Since Easter fell on the sixteenth this year an accounting
date on the following Tuesday would conform to the established pattern in this period.

437   oro: PAR 211/4/F1/3, item 184   mb [1]
The account was rendered in April (presumably after Easter, 16 April) but no day is given.

437–8   bl: Sloane ms 1457   p 17
The date range given to this excerpt is that during which Giles Widdowes was rector of St Martin's,
Carfax. Widdowes, as the rector of the 'city church,' appears with some regularity in the city records.
He performed services similar to those of a 'city chaplain,' being paid for administering the sacrament
and reading prayers on the election day in 1626–7 (Salter (ed), *Oxford Council Acts 1583–1626*,
pp 409–10). On 10 February 1641/2 the council decreed, 'Mr Widdowes shall haue ffive shillinges
eu*er*y of the said fast dayes soe long as the same shall continewe for readeinge prayers on the same dayes
to *Ma*ster Mayor & his Companie' (oca: C/FC/A1/3, f 121). He was briefly 'city lecturer' in 1618–19
and again in 1627–8 and 1638–9 (Hobson and Salter (eds), *Oxford Council Acts 1626–1665*, pp 413,

422). The picture of Widdowes derived from civic records is of a learned and dedicated clergyman, unlike the seeming buffoon of Wallington's partisan statement.

438   ChCh Arch: iii.c.9(a.)   mb 4
This entry occurs in the draft treasurer's account (ChCh Arch: iii.c.1, f 233), where the opening formula 'Et in expens*is*' and the first three letters of 'Tragœdiarum' remain intact.

439   QC Arch: LRB   f 27 col 1
The payment to Morris (l.28) is preceded by an entry dated 21 January.

439   SJC Arch: Acc.I.A.12   f 75
This entry also occurs in the weekly accounts (SJC Arch: Acc.V.E.6, f 82), where the sum is given as 'vij li. xiiij s. vj d.'

445   SJC Arch: Acc.I.A.12   f 101v
This entry also occurs in the weekly accounts (SJC Arch: Acc.V.E.6, f 95), where the sum reads 'ix li. iiij d.'

445   OCA: P.5.2   f 179v
The royal visit this year was to Woodstock, where Barten Holyday's *Technogamia* was performed before the king on 26 August (see Appendix 2).

446   ORO: PAR 213/4/F1/3   f 14v
On f 15 there occurs a payment of 20s to 'holbie and Abbot*es* for makinge the ‸⌈Queenes⌉ [queenes] Tombe.' The reference to the queen's tomb is of uncertain significance; 'holbie' is probably Richard Holbey, a painter, who served as constable in 1609–10 (Salter (ed), *Oxford Council Acts 1583–1626*, pp 108, 194).

447   ChCh Arch: iii.c.9(c.)   mb 3
This entry also occurs in the draft treasurer's account (ChCh Arch: iii.c.1, f 242).

448–9   SJC Arch: Acc.I.A.12   ff 130, 130v
All entries also occur in SJC Arch: Acc.I.A.14, f 23. With the exception of the item on l.35, they also all occur in the weekly accounts (SJC Arch: Acc.V.E.6, ff 107v, 109v).

449   SJC Arch: Acc.III.D.1   ff 69, 84, 85
These entries are part of a series of rough notes made between 6 December 1621 and 24 June 1622.

450–1   ORO: DD Par. Oxford St Aldate b.17/9   mb [1]
The MS gives the rendering date as 18 May. Easter Sunday was 18 April and the account runs Easter to Easter so either the account was rendered a month later than usual or May is an error for April.

452   BC Arch: Computi 1615–1662   f 45v
For Lord Stanhope (l.20), see Patrons and Travelling Companies. It may be more than coincidence that John and Henry, the two sons of Philip Stanhope, matriculated in November 1622 at Christ Church.

452   ChCh Arch: iii.c.9(d.)   mb 3d
This entry also occurs in the draft treasurer's account (ChCh Arch: iii.c.1, f 255), with 'habitar*um*' and 'factar*um*.'

452   ᴄᴄᴄᴀ: C/1/1/8   f [11] col 2
The number '40' looks suspiciously large and is perhaps an error for '4.'

454   ᴏʀᴏ: PAR 209/4/F1/27   single mb
The account heading states that the account runs 'from Easter weeke in anno Dominij 1622 vnto Easter weeke then next w*h*ich happen to be anno Dominij 1624.' It also gives a 5 April rendering date, which makes sense only for a year ending Easter 1624 (ie, 28 March). The account appears to be for one year only. It seems likely that '1622' in the account heading is an error for 1623.

455   ᴏʀᴏ: PAR 213/4/F1/3   f 17
No accounting date is given in the ᴍꜱ. The dates of the accounting period are derived from the end and start dates of the accounts that precede and follow this one.

455   Bodl.: ᴍꜱ. D.D. All Souls c.293   sheet 14
This is the draft account, on a paper roll. The parchment copy has not survived.

457–8   ᴏᴄᴀ: C/FC/1/A2/2   f 136
As the 1623 entry is written in acidic ink on paper, the resulting 'show through' makes transcription difficult. The corresponding entry in ᴏᴄᴀ: C/FC/1/A1/002, f 273v, does not mention music. For Carfax (l.37), see pp 584, 594. New Parks (p 458, l.2) is an open space in Holywell in the parish of St Cross, to the north of the city and slightly to the east on the west side of the Cherwell, bounded by the river, the wall of the city, and the Banbury Road. These grounds were used by the city for pasturage and other practical purposes, like Port Meadow farther to the west. The 'bench' (p 458, l.5) is Penniless Bench. The mayor this year was William Potter (Salter (ed), *Oxford Council Acts 1583–1626*, p 319).

458   ᴏʀᴏ: PAR 213/4/F1/3   f 19v
This entry also occurs in ᴏʀᴏ: PAR 213/4/F1/2, f 11 col 1.

459   ᴏʀᴏ: PAR 214/4/F1/67   single mb
Thomas Simpson (l.2), a mercer, served as chamberlain in 1623–4. Edward Warland (l.8) was a baker (Salter (ed), *Oxford Council Acts 1583–1626*, pp 292, 317, 321).

460   ᴏᴜᴀ: Hyp/B/17   f [1]
This inventory also occurs in ᴏᴜᴀ: Hyp/B/17, ff 77–7v, where it lacks a Latin note of exhibition.

461   ᴏᴄᴀ: C/FC/1/A2/2   f 159
As the text is written in acidic ink on paper, the resulting 'show through' makes transcription difficult. Charles ɪ succeeded his father on 27 March 1625. The bailiffs (l.6) were George Chambers and Robert Wilmot.
    Lord Wallingford (l.25) was William, Lord Knollys (1545–1632), second son and heir of Sir Francis

Knollys, Elizabeth's long-serving counsellor. He was created Viscount Wallingford in 1616. He served as high steward of Oxford (as his father had done before him) from 1611 until his death in 1632 (P.W. Hasler (ed), *The House of Commons 1558–1603*, The History of Parliament, vol 2 (London, 1981), 417–19).

462   OCA: C/FC/1/A1/002   f 285v
The tentative tone of these entries is explained by the circumstances of Charles' presence in Oxford. He resided in Christ Church, parliament having adjourned to Oxford because of the plague at Westminster (see *VCH: Oxford*, vol 4, p 78). The mayor was not allowed access to the king because of the danger of infection, and the pieces of plate (though purchased) were not presented. This was one of the occasions when the king's officers demanded 'very large fees beyond all precedents' and the mayor was authorized to grant them only 'such ancient fees as have been hitherto allowed' (Salter (ed), *Oxford Council Acts 1583–1626*, pp 332–4). The practice of royal officials persistently demanding unwarranted fees was finally dealt with by the city in 1638 (OCA: C/FC/1/A1/003, f 85) when it was decided 'That the kinge not Com*m*inge in State noe fees are due vnto them.'

The bailiffs were George Chambers and Robert Wilmot. The lawyer Thomas Wentworth had become recorder (l.17) in 1607. He was elected MP in 1604 and served continuously until his death in 1627. John Whistler, lawyer and deputy recorder (l.17), succeeded Wentworth as recorder in 1627 and served until 1646. See Salter (ed), *Oxford Council Acts 1583–1626*, p 328 (for Chambers and Wilmot), pp xlvi, 181 (for Wentworth), p 314 (for Whistler); Hobson and Salter (eds), *Oxford Council Acts 1626–1665*, p 7 (for Wentworth), pp 1, 8 (for Whistler).

462   ORO: DD Par. Oxford St Aldate b.17/11   single mb col 1
Richard Cooke, mender of drums (l.37), is likely Richard Cooke, skinner, admitted to his freedom on 17 January 1608/9 (Salter (ed), *Oxford Council Acts 1583–1626*, p 189).

463   ORO: PAR 213/4/F1/3   f 21
This account also occurs in ORO: PAR 213/4/F1/2, f 12 col 1.

463–4   ORO: PAR 214/4/F1/68   single mb
Goodman Owen ('Oven,' l.31) is probably the Richard Owen who served as constable in 1617–18. He had a house in the parish of St Peter le Bailey. Edward Warland (ll.22, 30) was a baker. See Salter (ed), *Oxford Council Acts 1583–1626*, p 271 (for Owen), pp 292, 317, 321 (for Warland); Hobson and Salter (eds), *Oxford Council Acts 1626–1665*, p 357 (for Owen).

464   MC Arch: LCE/13   f 4v
On the the payment to 'Buccinatoribus classe nauali' (l.25), see p 1133, endnote to TC Arch: I/A/2 f 343.

465   SJC Arch: Acc.I.A.12   f 226
The entry under 'Allowances' also occurs in the weekly accounts (SJC Arch: Acc.v.E.7, f 34).

466   QC Library: MS 390   f 17
This is one of the more cryptic entries in Crosfield's diary. Since '.3. maskes' follows 'librij .13.' reference is apparently to three performance texts (and not face coverings). The preposition 'with' probably signifies 'along with' (ie, in addition to) rather than 'including.' On the custom of circulating masques in manuscript, see Henry Lawes' dedicatory letter to the first edition of Milton's *Comus* (*The Poetical*

Works of John Milton, Helen Darbishire (ed), vol 2 (Oxford, 1955), 173); among REED volumes published to date, see David George (ed), *Lancashire* (Toronto, 1991), 252–66; and J. Alan B. Somerset (ed), *Shropshire* (Toronto, 1994), vol 2, 396. This interpretation of 'maskes' as 'masques' may be compromised, however, by uncertainty as to the meaning of 'points' in the phrase that follows (see OED for various possibilities). The phrase 'into ye North' probably refers to Crosfield's family home in Westmorland.

466–7   ORO: PAR 211/4/F1/3, item 190   single mb
The first sum of this entry is in a different ink and may be in a different hand.
    Goodwife Dewe (p 467, l.1) is probably the wife of Thomas Dewe, innkeeper (possibly of the Roebuck). In 1628 Thomas Dewe occupied a tenement belonging to St Michael at the North Gate (3–6 Market Street) (Salter, *Survey of Oxford*, vol 1, pp 16, 44). Mr Fletcher (l.3) is possibly John Fletcher, glazier and member of the common council between 1623 and 1636, or William Fletcher, baker, listed among the bailiffs between 1617 and 1632. See Salter (ed), *Oxford Council Acts 1583–1626*, p 322 (for John Fletcher), p 272 (for William Fletcher); Hobson and Salter (eds), *Oxford Council Acts 1626–1665*, p 71 (for John Fletcher), p 43 (for William Fletcher).

467   ORO: PAR 213/4/F1/3   f 22v
This account also occurs in ORO: PAR 213/4/F1/2, f 13 col 1.

469–70   SJC Arch: Acc.I.A.12   ff 227, 249
The payment to trumpeters (p 469, l.31) is entered under 'Expenses betweene Michaelmas & ye Auditt 1626.' On the 'Trumpeters yat came from Portsmouth' (p 470, l.5), see p 1133, endnote to TC Arch: I/A/2 f 343.

470   QC Library: MS 390   f 28v
Mr 'Gibbons' (l.36) is probably Orlando Gibbons (1583–1625), DMus Oxford 1622, one of the most celebrated composers of the period, who wrote thirty fantasies for viols. Wire, rather than gut, strings were still a novelty in 1627 (Crosfield, *Diary*, p 112). Gibbons was born in Oxford while his father, William, served as a city wait (see p 621).

471   OCA: P.4.1   f 193
The accounting year for this record is determined from the auditor's paragraph, which indicates that 6 December 1627 was the date the outgoing keykeepers were discharged and the remainder in the account was released into the hands of the new keykeepers.

471   ORO: PAR 211/4/F1/3, item 191   single mb col 1
Three John Stones appear in the civic records: one, a woollen-draper, admitted to his freedom on 25 October 1603; another, admitted 1617 (Salter (ed), *Oxford Council Acts 1583–1626*, pp 157, 266); and a third (not likely to be the one referred to here), a 'gentleman' who sold a property in Catte Street in St Michael's parish for £220 on 24 November 1648 (Salter, *Survey of Oxford*, p 81). The 'said parishe Clarke' (l.35) probably means 'the clerk of the said parish.'

472   ORO: PAR 213/4/F1/3   f 23v
This account also occurs in ORO: PAR 213/4/F1/2, f 14.

472   ORO: I 60/1/28   single mb

A John Stacy is mentioned in connection with John Bosseley's lease of the dancing school in 1609–10 and again in 1635–6 (see pp 390, 553). Stacy was one of the 'priuiledged men musitians & teachers of Musick' involved in establishing the University waits in 1631–2 (p 503). In 1633–4, 1641–2, and 1642–3, a John Stacy or Stacie signed for money lent to the musicians by St John's College (see pp 511, 578, 580).

472   Bodl.: MS. D.D. All Souls c.293   mb 9

This entry also occurs in the draft accounts (Bodl.: MS. D.D. All Souls c.294, sheet [18]). Neither version indicates which 'Duke' (l.17) patronized the trumpeters.

473   SJC Arch: Acc.I.A.12   f 270

The payment to musicians also occurs in the weekly accounts (SJC Arch: Acc.V.E.8, f 33).

474–7   QC Library: MS 390   f 33, f 35v col 2, f 36 cols 1, 2

References to performance in the city or elsewhere (p 474, ll.7–10) are included here to retain the integrity of the diary kept by Crosfield, who resided in Oxford. For more on Crosfield's versified text (p 474, l.21–p 477, l.8) of the puppet show called *The Chaos of the World*, see Appendix 10.

478   MCR: 3.1   f 240

These entries refer to three separate but related events. In an effort to conciliate the Puritan wing of the Oxford establishment, King Charles knighted the warden of Merton College, Nathaniel Brent, at a ceremony held at Woodstock Palace on 23 August 1629. The next day the French and Dutch ambassadors, on their way back from Woodstock to London with some of the English courtiers, were received with a banquet by Brent and his fellows at Merton. On 27 August the king and queen themselves were received at Merton, on their way to Abingdon, with a banquet in the warden's lodgings, where the queen would reside during the Civil War (George C. Broderick, *Memorial of Merton College*, Oxford Historical Society 4 (London, 1885), 75–6; Bernard W. Henderson, *Merton College University of Oxford: College Histories* (London, 1899), 108–9).

478–9   NC Arch: 7642   mbs 5, 6

This entry also occurs in the bursar's long book (NC Arch: 4200, f [140v]), reading 'buccinatoribus Regijs duabus vicibus xx s.'

479   QC Arch: LRC   f 3v col 2

The 1 January payment to Morris (l.17) is included in a block of payments, the first of which is dated 19 June 1628.

481   OCA: L.5.2   f 366v

Philip Golledge and Richard Burren, officially named at this time as waits (see p 482), took apprentices in April 1630 and July 1631 respectively (see pp 485, 490). Sampson Stronge (l.31), wait and father of William, is mentioned again in 1630–1 (see pp 491, 493). William is mentioned as a wait in 1638 and 1640 (see pp 568, 574) and with Sampson is listed as wait again 13 October 1661 (Hobson and Salter (eds), *Oxford Council Acts 1626–1665*, pp 17, 467).

481–2   OCA: C/FC/1/A1/003   f 1
For a discussion of the appointment of the waits this year, see p 621. On 25 August 1629 the council, anticipating a visit from the king and queen, made provision to borrow sufficient money for a 'faire guilt Cuppe worth betweene Thirtie & fforty Pound*es* ... and a payre of gloues about Twenty nobles price' (OCA: C/FC/1/A1/003, f 4v). The visit was not made.

482   OCA: P.5.2   f 209
For possible identification of Richard Cooke (l.38), see p 1129, endnote to ORO: DD Par. Oxford St Aldate b.17/11 single mb col 1. The word 'then' (l.39) probably refers to the riding of the franchises, a payment to a drummer being a typical expense.

484   MC Arch: LCE/16   f 3v
On the 'classe nauali reuersis' (ll.6–7), see p 1133, endnote to TC Arch: I/A/2 f 343.

484   QC Arch: LRC   f 5v col 2
The payment to Morris (l.24) is preceded by a payment dated 10 October.

484   SJC Arch: Acc.I.A.15   f 45v
The payment to musicians also occurs in the bursar's private accounts (SJC Arch: Acc.III.D.2, p 125), where it is dated 5 April.

485   QC Library: MS 390   f 50v
A 'prize' (l.23) was a contest, possibly a boxing or wrestling match (*OED*). Thomas Franklin was the owner of the King's Arms in Holywell, a venue for professional players (see p 514). No plays were performed this year because of plague (Crosfield, *Diary*, pp xxv–xxvi).

486   OCA: L.5.2   f 199v
Thomas Curtise (p 486, l.4) is named as one of the University musicians along with his master in 1631–2 (see p 503). He became a privileged person of the University on 3 June 1636 at the age of twenty. This may by the same Curtise who signed for money lent to the musicians by St John's College in 1638–9 and 1641–2 (see pp 570, 578).

486   OCA: P.5.2   f 213
The payment to the king's trumpeters occurs under the heading 'Item Moneys paid to Mr Henry Sowtham late Mayor w*hich* he disbursed as followeth.' Henry Southam, glover, was mayor in 1629–30 (Hobson and Salter (eds), *Oxford Council Acts 1626–1665*, p 21).

487   Bodl.: MS. D.D. All Souls c.294   mb 10
On the 'Trumpett*ers* for the Navy' (l.5), see p 1133, endnote to TC Arch: I/A/2 f 343.

488   NC Arch: 7645   mb 10
On the 'Trumpetters of his Ma*i*esties ffleete' (l.12), see p 1133, endnote to TC Arch: I/A/2 f 343. The 'streight*es*' (l.13) are presumably the Strait of Calais (ie, the Strait of Dover).

488   QC Arch: LRC   f 10 col 1
The payment to Morris (l.38), at the end of a block of payments the first of which is dated 22 September 1631, is probably for the year 1631–2 since he was usually paid in January and the next dated payment is for 28 February 1631/2.

489   SJC Arch: Acc.I.A.15   f 74
The missing sum (l.16) can be supplied from the bursar's private accounts (SJC Arch: Acc.III.D.2, p 178), where it is given as 'v s.'

489   TC Arch: I/A/2   f 343
'Tibicinibus nauticis' (l.31) represents one of many payments, starting in 1625–6, by the Oxford colleges to naval trumpeters and pipers, servants of the king. The payments seem to correspond to English expeditions against Cadiz in September and November 1625, and against La Rochelle in October 1627 and May through September 1628 (see pp 464, 470, 484, 487, and 488; see also David Loades, *England's Maritime Empire: Seapower, Commerce and Policy 1490–1690* (Harlow, England, 2000), 154).

489–90   QC Library: MS 390   ff 56, 57v, 58
'Allisons 5 parts & Gibbons 5 parts' (p 489, ll.38–9) probably refer to Richard Alison's *An Howres Recreation in Musicke, apt for Instrumentes and Voyces* (London, 1606; STC: 356) and Orlando Gibbons' *The First Set of Madrigals and Mottets of 5. Parts: apt for Viols and Voyces* (London, 1612; STC: 11826). For the 'history of some parts of ye bible' (p 490, ll.5–6), see Appendix 10 under *Chaos of the World*. The dancing horse (p 490, ll.7–8) performed at the Star Inn in Cornmarket (Crosfield, *Diary*, p 127). Mr 'Paine that dyed mare' (p 490, l.13) is somewhat cryptic and may refer to Walter Payne, cordwainer, who was mayor in 1617–18 and died before 20 January 1619/20 (Salter (ed), *Oxford Council Acts 1583–1626*, pp 114, 270, 289). The fact that Crosfield uses the verb 'translated' suggests that a body long buried is being moved. There is no relevant evidence from Abingdon in this period.

490–1   OCA: L.5.2   ff 201v, 210v, 361
Francis Taylor and Edward Golledge (p 490, l.24; p 491, l.25) are listed among the 'priuiledged men musitians & teachers of Musick' involved in establishing the University waits in 1631–2 (see pp 502–3). Taylor is listed as a wait in 13 October 1661 (Hobson and Salter (eds), *Oxford Council Acts 1626–1665*, p 467). Richard Burren (p 490, l.39) was made free and named one of the city waits in 1628–9 (see p 482).

491   OCA: C/FC/1/A1/003   f 26
Robert Duke later took John Payne, the son of George Payne, another Oxford wait, as his apprentice (see p 506).

494   Bodl.: MS. Morrell 20   f 78
Although the volume contains minutes of annual meetings beginning in 1534, itemized accounts begin only in 1631. The audit was taken 11 November; no inclusive dates are given.

497   QC Arch: LRC   f 10 col 1
The payment occurs in a block of payments, the first of which is dated 28 February 1631/2.

498   sjc Arch: Acc.i.A.16   ff 22, 22v
The payment in week seven (l.3) occurs in the weekly accounts (sjc Arch: Acc.v.E.10, f 22) as 'Set on for ye musitions.' The entry on f 22v (l.8) also occurs in sjc Arch: Acc.V.E.10, f 32.

498   qc Library: ms 390   f 60v
This entry follows an entry for St Stephen's Day and is itself followed by an entry for 6 January. For 'Cupids whirlegig' (l.14) see Appendix 10.

498–503   Bodl.: ms. Twyne-Langbaine 4   ff 105–7
Twyne's source for the chancellor's court case of 1501 is oua: Hyp/A/2, Register D (or D reversed), f 93 (see pp 41–2). The articles of 1297 'concerninge ye conflict … betwixt ye Scolleres and ye Townesmen' (p 503, l.10ff.) are found in oua: SEP/Y/12a (see p 4 and p 1084, endnote to oua: SEP/Y/12a mb [3]). The 'composition made in .37º. of .Henry .6. betwixt ye vniuersitie & ye Towne' (p 503, ll.38–9), an indenture (oua: WP/β/L/3), does not specifically mention musicians. The manuscript source for the petitions acquired in 1632 from Wadham College was not found.
    'Iarratt,' 'Garrett,' and 'Iarrett' (p 499, l.29; p 502, l.1; and p 503, l.4) are misreadings by Langbaine for Gerrard (see p 1137, endnote to oua: Hyp/B/13 f [1]). Edward Golledge (p 502, l.1) was named as a city wait when made free with Robert Duke on 19 September 1631 (see p 491). A Thomas Hallwood (p 502, l.2) received a 4s loan from St John's College in 1638–9 (see p 571). Francis Taylor (p 503, l.4) was apprenticed to John Gerrard on 15 October 1630 (see p 490) and is listed as a wait in 13 October 1661 (Hobson and Salter (eds), *Oxford Council Acts 1626–1665*, p 467).

505   tc Library: N.7.5   flyleaf
Arthur Wilson, gentleman-in-waiting to Robert Devereux, 3rd earl of Essex, entered Trinity College in 1631 at the age of thirty-six (*dnb*). On Edward Bathurst and this ms note, see p 703. The flyleaf also includes bibliographical notes in the hand of Thomas Warton the younger, fellow of Trinity during the period 1751–90.

505–6   oca: L.5.2   ff 213v, 215v
William Garrett may be the 'Will Garnet' named as one of the eight city waits on 13 October 1661 (Hobson and Salter (eds), *Oxford Council Acts 1626–1665*, p 467). Robert Duke (p 506, l.5) was named as a city wait when made free with Edward Golledge on 19 September 1631 (see p 491).

506   oro: PAR 207/4/F1/1, item 167   single mb col 1
The word 'more' (l.30) must simply mean 'in addition to' the existing sum. The same formulation is used in the account for 1611–12 (see p 399, l.19).

506   Bodl.: ms. D.D. All Souls c.295   mb 12
This entry occurs in the draft account roll (sheet [15]), stored in the same box.

508   uc Arch: BU3/F1/2   f [74v]
The payment on f [74v] is one of many described as 'Thomas Rockleyes expences from the Act till christenmas beeing one half yeere.' The whole of f [74v] is crossed through, presumably to indicate that payment was made.

510   ORO: PAR 214/4/F1/76–7   mb [1]
This roll lacks its first membrane, which would have provided the date and the names of the church-wardens. With no churchwardens named, the identity of the owner of the walls cannot be known. It appears he was prepared to share the expense of repairs with those who broke the walls. It is unclear whether 'my wals' (l.9) refers to the warden's own walls or the walls of the parish churchyard.

There are no dated rolls for 1632–3 or 1633–4. A modern hand has written 'c. 1633' at the top of the first surviving membrane. The presumption is that this roll is either 1632–3 or 1633–4. Since the total remaining in the hands of the wardens at the end of the account does not match the starting balance for 1634–5, 1632–3 seems more likely. Whit Sunday in 1633 was 9 June; in 1634 it was 25 May.

511   SJC Arch: Acc.I.A.18   f 22v
This entry also occurs in the bursar's private accounts (SJC Arch: Acc.III.D.4, ff 27v, 28).

512   STC: 19005   sig Hh2v
The section from which the excerpt derives is identified as 'Tit 15, Cap 7.' Marginal references ('L.241.b' and 'L.262.a') are to precedents for new statutes found in OUA: NEP/Supra/L, ff 241v, 262 (see pp 194, 230).

512–14   QC Library: MS 390   ff 65v, 67, 67v, 68–8v
All references to performance in the city or elsewhere (ie, 'the great maske or showe,' p 513, l.14) are included here to retain the integrity of the diary kept by Crosfield, who resided in Oxford. Omitted are various pieces of gossip.

For a commentary on the king's *Book of Sports* (p 512, l.27–p 513, l.4), see David George (ed), *Lancashire*, REED (Toronto, 1991), xcviii–xcix). The 'great maske' (p 513, l.14) is William Davenant's *Temple of Love* performed at court (Bentley, *Jacobean and Caroline Stage*, vol 7, p 96). The palsgrave (p 513, l.19) was the elector palatine, Frederick V, who once patronized a company of actors, but both that company and a successor were apparently extinct by 1631 (Bentley, *Jacobean and Caroline Stage*, vol 1, pp 135–54, 260–90); the meaning of his 'family' in this context is unclear. 'His ma*i*esties Hokus Pokus' (p 513, l.20) was William Vincent, a famous juggler who is named in the Reading records for 1625 as 'the Kinge's Majestie's servant' (J.M. Guilding (ed), *Reading Records: Diary of the Corporation*, vol 2 (London, 1895), 264). He appears frequently in entertainment records in the 1620s and 1630s (see Philip Butterworth, 'Brandon, Feats and Hocus Pocus: Jugglers Three,' *Theatre Notebook* 57 (2003), 89–106; see also p 518, l.5). For William Gosling's 'Hierusalem' (p 513, ll.22–3), see Appendix 10 under *Destruction of Jerusalem*. Boas, in his edition of Crosfield's *Diary*, p 135, suggests 'mr Camden' (p 513, l.24) is a mistake for John Tredescant, founder of the University Museum, which still displays a stuffed dodo. A dodo was apparently exhibited in London in 1638 (*OED* Dodo). For 'ye Kings Armes' (p 514, l.24), highlighted by a hand drawn in the left margin, see p 617.

514   OCA: P.5.2   f 225v
This excerpt comes from a block of entries headed 'By Bills of payment and Acquittances as followeth.'

515   ORO: PAR 214/4/F1/78   single mb
Thomas Byshopp (l.18), chandler, served as constable in 1625–6 (Salter (ed), *Oxford Council Acts 1583–1626*, p 334).

515–16   BNC Arch: U.B.21   f 35

The payment to the piper on Easter Monday (p 516, l.1) is bracketed by payments dated 1 and 20 January 1634/5. It may be a back payment for Easter 1634, or the others may be payments for Christmas 1634–5 that were recorded after Easter.

516   BNC Arch: A.8.7   f 24

The identity of 'Pigeon' (l.10) has not been fully established; in 1641 a man of this name was paid 'for sweepeinge ye Kitchen chymnies' (BNC Arch: A.8.11, f 21).

518   QC Library: MS 390   f 71v

This undated entry occurs between entries for 10 July and 1 August. In 1635 the Act took place on 13 July.

For 'Hokus pok*us*' (l.5), see p 1135, endnote to QC Library: MS 390 ff 65v, 67, 67v, 68–8v. 'The witches of Lancashire' (l.8) is *The Late Lancashire Witches*, by Thomas Heywood and Richard Brome, which was occasioned by the trial of witches in the Pendle district of Lancashire in 1633 (Bentley, *Jacobean and Caroline Stage*, vol 3, pp 73–6). For the Jerusalem play (l.10) and 'The beginning of ye world' (l.14), see Appendix 10 under *Destruction of Jerusalem* and *Chaos of the World* respectively.

The Blue Boar Inn (l.4) (now the site of the Museum of Oxford), the Fleur de Luce (l.5), the Crown Inn (l.7), the King's Head (l.8), and the Bear Inn (l.12) were all public houses, some still extant. For 'ye Kings armes' (l.7), see p 617. The Racket Court (l.4) (some tennis courts were also licensed as alehouses), the Moot Hall (ll.10, 13), All Saints' Church (l.6), and the intersection called Carfax (l.14) were all convenient gathering places in the centre of Oxford.

518   ORO: PAR 208/4/F1/62   mb [1]

The interpolated item looks as if it were inserted in the space left between the original last item and the total, to which this sum of £1 2s 10d has been added in the same hand. The mixture of roman and arabic numerals is unlike the rest of the account, which employs only roman numerals.

519   ORO: PAR 213/4/F1/3   f 41v

This account also occurs in ORO: PAR 213/4/F1/2, f 18 col 1.

519   Bodl.: MS. D.D. All Souls c.295   mb 9

These entries also occur in the draft account roll, sheet 20, where the interpolated payment to the king's trumpeters is marked with a marginal 'x.'

519–21   ChCh Arch: D.P.iii.c.1, item 27   p [1]

This document is a list of expenses incurred by Christ Church for the two plays performed in its hall before Charles I 29–30 August (see pp 851–2). It bears the signatures of the three delegates appointed by the University to oversee the entertainments: Samuel Fell, Daniel Escott, and John Saunders.

'Seuerall heades of haire' (p 520, l.12), or wigs, were used for the character Fancy in William Strode's *The Floating Island*, as was 'Fancies Picture' (p 521, l.4), which was 'crown'd with Gold' according to the stage direction (London, 1655; Wing: S5983, sig C3). The 'Sedan' (p 520, l.25), or chair, was used to carry the character Hilario in the same play; the 'Booke' (p 520, l.5) was probably a copy of the music composed for the plays by Henry and William Lawes. The 'Binding of Bookes for ye King & Queene' (p 520, l.38) may have been for presentation copies of the two play texts.

The court musicians, whose diet is provided for, are separate from the local musicians in the list. They are the Lawes brothers (p 520, ll.1, 7); Thomas Day, master of the children of the Chapel (p 520, ll.2, 7); Thomas Holmes, gentleman of the Chapel (p 520, ll.2, 7); Davis Mell, a player of wind instruments (p 520, l.3); and Peter Jones, a trumpeter (p 520, l.3). Of the locals, 'Mr Goodall' (p 520, l.4) is probably not a musician but Stephen Goodall, chaplain of Christ Church. Edward Lowe (p 520, l.4) is organist of Christ Church. 'Mr. Coleman' (p 520, l.5) is probably Simon Coleman, the organist of New College, and 'Mr. Iones Chanter of Christch*urch*' (p 521, ll.5–6) may be David Jones, subsequently vicar choral of St Asaph. See Elliott and Buttrey, 'Royal Plays at Christ Church,' pp 100–1; P.M. Gouk, 'Music,' *History of the University*, vol 4, p 611; and *A Biographical Dictionary of English Court Musicians 1485–1714*, Andrew Ashbee and David Lacocki (comps) (Brookfield, VT, 1998), vol 1, 338–41, 581–2, vol 2, 635–6, 706–9, 710–11, 795–6.

William Stokes (p 520, l.9) was John Bosseley's partner in the dancing school in 1635–6 (see pp 550, 565). Mr Taylor (p 521, l.2) may have been Joseph Taylor, principal actor with the king's men.

521   CCCA: C/1/1/9   mb 9 col 1
The payment is preceded by an entry dated 29 August.

523   SJC Arch: Acc.I.A.20   f 21
The week number '14^{tâ}' is an anomaly since each term usually had only thirteen weeks. However, 1636 being a leap year, Lady Day, normally the first day of the Easter term, fell on a Friday, creating a partial fourteenth week.

523–4   UC Arch: BU2/F1/1   pp 59, 61
These payments come from a long series of expenses for repairs and improvements in and around the college that, along with those transcribed here, may relate to the royal visit. UC Arch: BU3/F1/2, f 68, contains a series of undated but probably contemporary payments to labourers for sweeping the street and for mending the gates at the king's coming.

524–9   OUA: NEP/Supra/R   ff 132–2v, 133–3v, 134, 134v, 135, 138
Omitted are assignments of areas of jurisdiction to various doctors and masters (f 132v); appointment of overseers (f 133); direction to heads of houses regarding keeping the peace and entrance into the choir during service (f 134); provisions from the 'Orders ... for his Ma*ie*styes Entertainment' for locking the library door and appointing deputies in the colleges and halls (f 134v); protocol at convocation (f 134v); and restrictions on scholars approaching court officials or frequenting the kitchen and buttery (f 135).

The 'Gestis cancellariatus Laud' (p 529, l.10) is referred to several times by Langbaine and Wood in their notes on the University archives. Now lost, this manuscript served as the basis for the publication of Laud's *Remains* by Edmund Wharton (London, 1700; Wing: L596). The 'letter of thanks' (p 529, l.7) noted by Twyne as missing from OUA: NEP/Supra/R is printed in Wing: L596, pp 123–4.

After 'Auspicatum ... subsequentis' (p 529, ll.11–15) there follows a transcript of the letter to convocation from Queen Henrietta Maria (see Appendix 3, p 791).

530   OUA: Hyp/B/13   f [1]
John Gerrard was made a privileged person of the University on 21 January 1624/5 at the age of thirty-six and admitted to his freedom on 4 December 1628 (see p 481). He was at the same time named

one of the city waits (see pp 481–2). He took apprentices on 21 September and 15 October 1630 (pp 486, 490) and was one of the 'priuiledged men musitians & teachers of Musick' involved in establishing the University musicians in 1631–2 (p 499, l.29; p 502, l.1; and p 503, l.4; as 'Iarratt,' 'Garrett,' and 'Iarrett'). In the inventory heading, Gerrard is described as 'late of St. Michaels parishe.' The inventory was taken by 'Sollodell Lichfield yeoman Bedle in the Law and William Dauis Verger.'

530–1   PRO: SP/16/348   ff [2], [4]
Omitted are expenses for the feast including provisions and wages to kitchen staff.

531–2   PRO: SP/16/304   single sheet
A December 1635 warrant (PRO: SP/16/303, p 249) was issued to Thomas Welch to 'fetch vp' Thomas Warde, Martin Baccas, and John Watson. Also cited in Nelson (ed), *Cambridge*, vol 1, p 664.

532–4   PRO: SP/16/331   ff [1v–2], [2v], [3–3v]
Omitted are comments on changes in Oxford since Garrard's last visit and details about services and sermons, the convocation, and feasts. For the sequence of the plays with their dates, see Appendix 8, pp 851–2.
     Two letters regarding this royal visit were not located for this collection. The first is a letter of 31 August 1636 from Jonathan Edwards to his brother, John Jones, giving a detailed account of the king's reception (see The Historical Manuscripts Commission, Alfred J. Horwood, 'The Manuscripts of Colonel Myddelton-Biddulph, Chirk Castle, Denbyshire,' *The 2nd Report of the Historical Manuscripts Commission*, Appendix (London, 1871), 73). The second is a letter of 6 September 1636 from the earl of Newburgh to the earl of Middlesex. Newburgh observed that the archbishop's feast at Oxford was reported to have been very magnificent but that the University plays did not appeal to the courtiers (see The Historical Manuscripts Commission, Horwood, 'Earl de la Warr,' p 291).
     A letter from Francis Cheynell to Sir Gervase Clifton (Nottingham University Library: MS Cl C 84), with a lengthy description of the royal visit, will be published among the Clifton household records in the Nottinghamshire collection in the REED series. A letter of George Evelyn to his father, Richard Evelyn (formerly in ChCh Archives among Evelyn Papers since transferred to the BL), also describing the royal entertainment, has been excluded here in favour of its future publication with other family records in the Surrey collection in the REED series.

534   PRO: SP/16/331   f [1]
On the strength of this letter, which he had apparently seen only in summary, Bentley (*Jacobean and Caroline Stage*, vol 3, p 140) argues that William Cartwright's *The Royal Slave* was so renowned that individuals were collecting manuscripts or editions of the play, and that Windebank probably had attended the original performance or performances and was acquiring a copy through his nephew at New College. The full text suggests, however, that Read himself was the author of a play.

535–8   QC Library: MS 390   ff 77–8
'Camdens Elizabeth' (p 536, l.34) is William Camden's *Annales of Queen Elizabeth* (London, 1615; STC: 4496), perhaps in the French translation (London, 1624; STC: 4502) for Queen Henrietta Maria. The palsgrave (p 536, l.35) was Charles Louis, brother-in-law of Charles I, who came with his brother, Prince Rupert. For the sequence of the plays with their dates, see Appendix 8, pp 851–2. Omitted are academic and religious ceremonies and the king's visit to the Bodleian Library.

'Coll*egio*' (p 536, l.28) appears to refer to Queen's College alone, hence the expansion in the singular. Queen's, being assessed at £260, owed £13 at a rate of £5 per £100 assessed valuation.

538–42   Wing: L596   pp 100–1, 103–5
Neither the 'Inventory' (p 539, l.24) of stage materials and apparel (see p 607) nor Laud's 'Letters' (p 539, l.30) have survived. For the 'Accompt' (p 539, l.35), see p 519. For 'the Play ... Hampton Court' (p 541, ll.31–2), see Appendix 3. Omitted are descriptions of the king's visits to convocation and to a dinner in the Bodleian Library, and Laud's return from Oxford to Croydon.

542–5   Bodl.: MS. Twyne 17   pp 191–2, 193, 194, 199, 201
A description of disputations and speeches and of a convocation are omitted. Jasper Mayne (p 544, l.24m) wrote *The City Match* for the royal visit but it was not performed. For *The Royal Slave* (p 544, l.32) at Hampton Court, see Appendix 3. For the 'goodly stage' (p 545, l.6), see pp 606–7 and 611–12.

545–6   Wing: H1699   pp 318, 319
Anthony Wood copied parts of this description, without attribution, into his *History and Antiquities*, vol 2, pp 409, 411 (see Appendix 13, pp 888–95).

The 'great wit of Inigo Jones' (p 546, l.23) is illustrated in a poem by Thomas Gawen, fellow of New College, printed in a volume of poems – *Coronae Carolinae Qvadradutra* (Oxford,1636; *STC*: 19036) – dedicated to Charles I and Queen Henrietta Maria on the birth of Princess Elizabeth (28 December 1635), to whom the poem is addressed. Most of the contents must have been written (and perhaps presented in manuscript) soon after the event itself but Gawen's poem suggests a later date. It almost certainly refers to the plays presented in Christ Church during the royal visit. Internal evidence suggests that it was printed in December of the year of publication. A portion of the poem (here translated) praises the beauty of the newborn child above the other marvels available to the court:

> Now it will not be a matter for grief that
> the nobles have lacked (*or* have abstained from) the suspended device
> of the widowed theatre. The sight of you,
> which the court willingly buys
> with all (its) set dances
> and with all (its) jousts,
> outweighs the flowing scarlet robes of the final scene,
> the riches of the plaited (*or* woven) sea,
> and Inigo's wonders.

546–7   Wing: L373   pp 53–4
No contemporary source has been found for the assertion (p 547, l.3) that Richard Busby played the part of Cratander in *The Royal Slave*. The claim of Langbaine, Junior is repeated by William Bray in his 1819 edition of John Evelyn's *Diary* (vol 1, p 662). It is cited in turn by G.F. Russell Barker, *Memoir of Richard Busby* (London, 1895), 3; and G.F. Barker and Alan H. Stenning, *Record of Old Westminsters* (London, 1928), vol 1, 148–9). Bentley, *Jacobean and Caroline Stage*, vol 3, pp 136–7, noted the claim as in *Record of Old Westminsters* but was unable to corroborate what was by now a mythos. While Langbaine could have had this information from his father (provost of Queen's College and keeper of the archives, 1644–58) or from Busby himself, the loss of a cast list for *The Royal Slave* in the nineteenth century (see p 841) means that the claim can be neither proved nor disproved.

548–50   OCA: C/FC/1/A2/3   ff 12–12v, 13, 13v–14, 14v, 15
This is the second visit of Charles I to the city. Hobson and Salter (eds), *Oxford Council Acts 1626–1665*, pp xviii–xix, note that the city strove to make a strong impression on the king including incurring expenses of £46 and a 'general tidying up of the City.'

   The chamberlains this year were Thomas Pawlinge and George Potter. The mayor was Martin Wright, goldsmith. The bailiffs were Thomas Davis and William Stephens; the recorder was John Whistler. The town clerk was Timothy Cartar and the mace bearer, John Painton. (Hobson and Salter (eds), *Oxford Council Acts 1626–1665*, p 62.)

   Omitted from ff 13–13v is a two-column list of names of sixty-one citizens. As the text on f 15 (p 549, l.42–p 550, l.3) is both illegible and corrupt, no attempt has been made to rationalize its sequence.

550   OCA: C/FC/1/A1/003   f 68v
The scribe wrote the regnal year as 'decimo tertio' in error for 'duodecimo.' All the surrounding entries are for the twelfth year of the reign of Charles I.

550–1   OCA: E.4.5   f 7v
Eleven of the twelve members of the mayor's council are listed as riding to meet the king: William Potter, Oliver Smith, John Sare, William Good, Henry Southam, Thomas Cooper, William Charles, Francis Harris, William Boswell, John Dewe, and John Wilmot. The only member of the council missing is the mayor's father, William. The rest of the men named were members of the bailiff's court. Fewer than half the former bailiffs still alive are listed here. See Hobson and Salter (eds), *Oxford Council Acts 1626–1665*, pp 56–7, 62, 66–8. 'Carfax Churche' (p 551, ll.3–4) refers to St Martin's, Carfax (see pp 584, 594). The royal procession was met at the North Gate by the craft guilds (*VCH: Oxford*, vol 4, p 78).

552   OCA: P.5.2   f 232
John Paynton (p 552, l.7), gentleman, was chosen chief serjeant at mace to the mayor on 10 June 1634 (Hobson and Salter (eds), *Oxford Council Acts 1626–1665*, p 53).

552–3   OCA: D.5.6   f 5v
In the left margin opposite 'the said William Stokes' (p 552, l.34) is 'Dauncing School,' possibly in the hand of the nineteenth-century antiquary, George Parsons Hester.

553   ORO: PAR 207/4/F1/1, item 175   single mb col 1
The account was rendered after Hock Tuesday (18 April) and so includes the total receipts for the year.

554   ORO: PAR 213/4/F1/3   f 45
This account also occurs in ORO: PAR 213/4/F1/2, f 20 col 1.

554   ORO: I 144/3/13   single mb
George Payne, musician, was apprenticed to Leonard Major and admitted to his freedom on 22 November 1619 (see p 441). His son, John, was apprenticed to another Oxford musician, Robert Duke, in 1631 (see p 506). After his death George was replaced as a wait by William Stronge (see p 574).

554   Bodl.: MS. D.D. All Souls c.295   mb 11
This entry also occurs in the draft roll, sheet 14, with dittography of 'his.' As in the fair copy, 'patet' appears without 'ut.'

555   QC Arch: LRC   f 17 col 2
The payment to Morris ('Mauritio,' l.26) follows a December payment.

556   PRO: SP/16/344   f [2]
This letter, unknown to Bentley, confirms his conjecture of a St John's venue for *Grobiana's Nuptials*, as Richard Baylie was president of St John's. The letter disproves, however, Bentley's conjecture concerning the play's authorship and date of performance (see Bentley, *Jacobean and Caroline Stage*, vol 5, pp 1054–6; see also Appendix 6:1).

557   QC Library: MS 390   ff 176v, 79v
The 'abusiue booke' (l.13) is Henry Burton's *For God and the King* (see pp 557–8). Christopher Rogers (l.15) was the Puritan principal of New Inn Hall. Robert Lugge (l.28) was the organist at St John's (Crosfield, *Diary*, p 144).

557–8   STC: 4141   pp 49–50
Henry Burton (1578–1648), Puritan polemicist, suffered punishment in 1636 along with William Prynne for his attacks on bishops. The 'scurrilous Enterlude' (p 557, l.37) is William Strode's *The Floating Island*, with a satire of Prynne. The 'guelded Fast-book' (p 558, l.11) is *A forme of common prayer* (London, 1636; STC: 16553), which forbade plays on fast-days (sig N2v). Burton's sermons in November 1636 protested the alteration by the bishops of certain anti-Catholic phrases from this edition of the 'Fast-book.' The 'Proclamation' (p 558, l.11) was titled *By the King. A Proclamation for a generall Fast to be Weekely observed thorowout the Realme of England* (London, 1636; STC: 9075). Martin Butler, *Theatre in Crisis 1632–1642* (Cambridge, 1984), 94–5, argues that many Puritans like Burton were not opposed to stage plays per se, as Prynne was. Omitted is a general attack on bishops.

558–9   STC: 4140.7   pp 12, 46
This work was erroneously attributed to William Prynne in the first edition of the STC and numbered 20459. The second edition assigns it correctly to Burton under 4140.7. A second edition was published under the author's name in London in 1642 (Wing: B6161).
    Preceding this excerpt from p 12 is Example 31, which begins, 'At Oxford this last Sommer.' If the incident described in Example 32 likewise took place 'this last Sommer,' then it probably refers to the building of the stage for George Wild's *Love's Hospital* (see Appendix 8, p 851). 'Thomas Lovel his Dialogue' (p 559, ll.1–2) is Thomas Lovell, *A Dialogue Between Custom and Veritie Concerning Dauncing and Minstrelsie* (London, 1581; STC: 16860).

560–4   Bodl.: MS. Ashmole 47   ff 122v–6
The phrase 'annuall tributes to his crowne' (p 561, l.36) suggests that Mr Moore had cast himself in the role of 'Rex' or 'Princeps' of the festivities as by old custom in many Oxford colleges, particularly Merton. Thus it may have been a Christmas revel (see Salter (ed), *Registrum Annalium*, pp xviii–xix). See also Appendix 6:1 under 'Mr Moore's Revels.'

The word 'candidate' (p 562, l.16) involves a pun on white (l.17) as Roman candidates for office were so called because of the white togas they wore (*OED*, Candidate *sb* 2a; *Oxford Latin Dictionary*, P.G.W. Glare (ed) (Oxford, 1982), candidatus *sb*[1]).

The poem is listed as F16 in Margaret Crum (ed), *First-Line Index of English Poetry, 1500–1800, in Manuscripts of the Bodleian Library, Oxford*, 2 vols (Oxford, 1969).

565   OCA: C/FC/1/A1/003   f 75v
The item for 18 September also occurs in OCA: C/FC/1/A2/3, f 30.

567–8   STC: 15105   pp 22–3
Compare this anecdote to Thomas Goffe's poem on a cough (see pp 434–6).

568   OCA: C/FC/1/A1/003   f 85
'Sampsons sonne' (l.10) is William Stronge, son of Sampson Stronge, wait. William was admitted to his freedom on 3 September 1638 and elected wait in the place of George Payne on 17 February 1639/40. Both father and son are still listed as waits on 13 October 1661 (Hobson and Salter (eds), *Oxford Council Acts 1626–1665*, pp 17, 79, 89, 467). William Hilliard (l.10), made free in 1638–9 (see p 571, l.35), may be the William Hilliard who shared the rent of the Three Goats Head in St Michael at the North Gate near the dancing school (Salter (ed), *Properties*, pp 236, 238).

569   ORO: MS.Oxf.Arch. papers Oxon.c.13   f 306
It is not clear whether all four of these cases heard in the archdeacon's court had to do with building a stage at Balliol, or only the second one. Probably the stage was a scaffold for building constructions, but we cite the document on the remote chance that it was for a dramatic performance. Tomlinson (l.6) was an 'apparitor' of the deaneries of Oxford and Cuddesdon, whose job was to serve summonses to the archdeacon's court.

570   SJC Arch: Acc.I.A.23   f 71v
These entries also occur in the weekly accounts (SJC Arch: Acc.V.E.13, ff 25, 26). They read 'Set on for ye Musitian' and 'Set on for ye playes.' The entries also occur in St John's College bursar's private accounts (SJC Arch: Acc.III.D.3, f 64), with the following additional details: in the founder's show entry (l.18) 'allowed' is given as 'allowed by *Master* President'; the entry '*pro* Musicis' (l.22) is undated within the second term, reads 'Item for ye Musitians ⌈paide⌉,' and is signed '*Received* by us Thomas Halwood: Iohn Stacie'; and the twelfth week payment '*pro* Ludis Scenicis' (l.24) is described as 'for ye Playes' and is signed by 'Ioseph Crowther.'

570–1   SJC Arch: Acc.III.D.4   f 72
A Thomas Hallwood (p 571, l.1) is listed as one of the 'priuiledged men musitians & teachers of Musick' involved in establishing the University waits in 1631–2 (p 502).

572   BNC Arch: A.8.10   f 17v
'Whitney men' (l.32) refers to the Witney singers (see also pp 565, 575).

573   QC Library: MS 390   f 87
For 'Morrice ye gardiner,' see p 1106, endnote to QC Arch: 2P162 single mb.

574   oca: C/FC/1/A1/003   f 103
This entry also occurs in oca: C/FC/1/A2/3, f 71.

576   sjc Arch: Acc.i.A.25   f 24
This entry also occurs in the annual accounts (sjc Arch: Acc.i.A.26, f 27) and in the bursar's private accounts (sjc Arch: Acc.iii.D.4, f 18), which reads 'for ye Musick' and is signed by Thomas Hallwood and marked as paid.

576   jc Arch: BU:AC:GEN:1   p 125
Pembroke's men were evidently on their way to suppress the Irish rebellion of 1641 (see Tom Webster, 'Religion in Early Stuart Britain, 1603–1642,' *A Companion to Stuart Britain*, Barry Coward (ed) (Malden, MA, 2003), 266).

578   sjc Arch: Acc.i.A.25   f 25v
This entry also occurs in the annual accounts (sjc Arch: Acc.i.A.26, f 28v) and in the bursar's private accounts (sjc Arch: Acc.iii.D.4, f 19v).

578   sjc Arch: Acc.i.A.26   f 24
This entry also occurs in the weekly accounts (sjc Arch: Acc.v.E.14, f 26) and in the bursar's private accounts (sjc Arch: Acc.iii.D.4, f 53), where it is signed by Thomas Hallwood.

578   sjc Arch: Acc.iii.D.4   f 29
The loan comes from the account for 1640–1 but, as the loan was made after the November 1641 audit, the entry is included under 1641–2. The entry is cancelled, presumably to indicate repayment.

578–9   bl: Sloane ms 1457   f 67
See also Appendix 13, p 895.

579   oca: E.4.5   f 31
Hobson and Salter (eds), *Oxford Council Acts 1626–1665*, p 366, date this entry 25 May. See also p 578 and Appendix 13, p 895.

580   oro: PAR 211/4/F1/3, item 204   single mb col 2
Richard Swetnam and John Hamblin (l.16) were churchwardens this year. The memo concerning the Whitsun ale is in a different hand, on the left side of the membrane at the foot of col 1. It is clearly not part of the column and presumably refers to a situation that developed after the columns were totalled. To the right side of the membrane (under col 2) in the same hand and dated '29 May 1643' is further comment explaining that the sum of the receipts exceeded the sum of disbursements by £6 13s 6d. The note concludes that Richard Swetnam yielded the said amount to the new churchwardens and that the account was accepted by the auditors. The Whitsun receipts that were held back are either those of Whitsun 1642 (29 May–4 June), as the parish accounts usually record the receipts for the spring that is past and not the ensuing spring, or those of 1643 (21–7 May), given the specific date of the memo.

580   sjc Arch: Acc.iii.D.4   f 64
The loan comes from the account for 1641–2 but, as the loan was made after the November 1642 audit, the entry is included under 1642–3. The entry is cancelled presumably to indicate repayment.

Patrons and Travelling Companies

JOHN LEHR

The following list is an extension of the Index, which should be consulted in conjunction with it. Its first section lists companies alphabetically by patron, according to the principal title under which the companies (either troupes or individuals) appear. Cross-references to other titles by which patrons are referred to in the Records are also given. Its second section lists companies that have been identified by place of origin.

Research on patrons mentioned in REED collections is cumulative, and the list of patron profiles here depends heavily on work done for previous REED volumes by Margaret Owen, Arleane Ralph, Janet Ritch, and Elza Tiner. The accumulated profiles are collected in a master list that will be available eventually in a database linked to the REED Web site (http://eir.library.utoronto.ca/reed/). Ten of the following profiles appear in REED for the first time. The other profiles have been adapted from the database. One patron has been left unidentified.

The biographical information supplied here has come entirely from printed sources, the chief of which are listed below. In the case of differences between sources, the information obtained from contemporary records or the most recent scholarship is preferred. For example, information from the *Calendar of Patent Rolls* or P.W. Hasler's *The House of Commons 1558–1603* takes precedence over information from the DNB.

Normally each patron entry is divided into four parts. The first lists relevant personal data and titles of nobility with dates. Succession numbers follow the absolute sequence given in *The Complete Peerage* rather than the relative ones that begin afresh with each new creation. Knighthood dates are included for minor gentry not possessing higher titles.

The second part lists, in chronological order, court appointments, appointments to central government bureaucracies, and appointments that show local connections. Purely expeditionary military titles have been largely omitted, along with most minor Scottish and Irish office titles. Minor civil commissions have been omitted except for those concerning Oxfordshire and the geographically proximate counties of Berkshire, Buckinghamshire, Gloucestershire, Northamptonshire, Warwickshire, and Wiltshire.

For offices and commissions, dates of appointment and termination are given if available. Where possible, the date of an appointment is taken from the document granting that office or commission. The termination date, likewise, is taken from a document confirming the resignation or forfeiture of the office or from a document granting the office to a successor. Some offices are granted for life and, in cases where we know that the office was indeed held until the office-holder's death, the phrase 'for life' is retained in place of a termination date. If the original document has not been edited and a secondary source is used that states 'until death,' then this phrase is used. If the length of time that an office was held is unknown, then only the date of appointment is given. If the only evidence comes from a source dated some time during the period of tenure, then the word 'by' and a date appear. For all minor commissions such as commissions of array and musters, commissions of gaol delivery, and commissions of the peace (JP), years only are given. If the dates of these commissions cover several years in sequence, then the earliest and latest years of the sequence are separated by a dash.

The third part, for which information is often incomplete or unavailable, contains the names and locations of the patron's residences and the lands that he or she held in Oxfordshire and the proximate counties.

The fourth part lists the appearances of the patron's company or companies in the Oxford Records. The company type (for example, 'trumpeters') and the record dates, with page references in parentheses, are given. If a patron's company appears under a title other than the one under which the patron is listed, then the other title is given in parentheses next to the company type. Similarly, if the company type is expanded on in the Records, the extra information is given in parentheses: for example, 'players (men).' Companies named according to a patron's civil appointment are listed under the name of that post as it appears in the Records. If the patron sponsored more than one type of performer, all entries for a given type (both singular and plural forms) are grouped together in chronological order. The company type is only repeated within that grouping to indicate a change in number or to provide parenthetical information. Each group of entries is then listed according to the earliest year in which that company appears in the Records. If two or more companies first appear in the same year, alphabetical order is followed.

The reader may also refer to the Index for additional references to some of the patrons and to various unnamed companies.

Works Chiefly Consulted

Bindoff, S.T. (ed). *The House of Commons 1509–1558*. The History of Parliament. 3 vols (London, 1982).

Calendar of Close Rolls. PRO.

Calendar of Fine Rolls. PRO.

Calendar of Inquisitions Post Mortem (London, 1904–95).

Calendar of Inquisitions Post Mortem. Second Series (London, 1898–1955).

Calendar of Patent Rolls. PRO.

Calendar of State Papers. Domestic Series. PRO.

Cheney, C.R. (ed). *Handbook of Dates for Students of British History* (London, 2000).

Cokayne, G.E. *The Complete Peerage*. Rev and expanded ed. Vicary Gibbs, H.A. Doubleday, Duncan Warrand, Lord Howard de Walden, Geoffrey H. White, and R.S. Lea (eds). 6 vols (London, 1910–59; rpt Gloucester, 1982).

Dictionary of National Biography. Compact ed (London, 1885–1970; 1975).

Fryde, E.B., D.E. Greenway, S. Porter, and I. Roy (eds). *Handbook of British Chronology*, 3rd ed (Cambridge, 1986; rpt 1996).

Hasler, P.W. (ed). *The House of Commons 1558–1603*. The History of Parliament. 3 vols (London, 1981).

Le Neve, John. *Fasti Ecclesiae Anglicanae 1300–1541*. Rev and expanded ed. Vol 1. H.P.F. King (comp) (London, 1962). Vols 2, 3, 5, 7, 9, 12. Joyce M. Horn (comp) (London, 1962–7). Vols 4, 6, 8, 10, 11. B. Jones (comp) (London, 1963–5).

Letters and Papers, Foreign and Domestic, Henry VIII. 21 vols and Addenda (London, 1864–1932).

Roskell, J.S., Linda Clark, and Carole Rawcliffe (eds). *The House of Commons 1386–1421*. The History of Parliament. 4 vols (Stroud, 1992).

Wedgwood, Josiah C. and Anne D. Holt. *Biographies of the Members of the Commons House 1439–1509*. History of Parliament (London, 1936).

Wedgwood, Josiah C. *Register of the Ministers and of the Members of Both Houses 1439–1509*. History of Parliament (London, 1938).

Abbreviations

acc	acceded	jt	joint (two or more)
adm	admiral	KB	Knight of the Bath
bef	before	KG	Knight of the Garter
bet	between	kt	knighted
br	brother	lieut	lieutenant
capt	captain	m.	married
comm	commissioner	MP	member of parliament
cr	created	nd	no date
custos rot	custos rotulorum	NR	North Riding
d.	died	parl	parliament
da	daughter	PC	privy councillor
eccles comm	ecclesiastical commission	pres	president
ER	East Riding	succ	succeeded
gen	general	summ	summoned
gov	governor	Univ	University
JP	justice of the peace		

Companies Named by Patron

Archbishop (Canterbury)

George Abbot (29 Oct 1562–4 Aug 1633), son of Maurice Abbot of Guildford, Surr; pardoned for accidental homicide 24 Dec 1621; sequestered 5 July 1627–11 Dec 1628. Master of University College, Oxford Univ, 6 Sept 1597; dean of Winchester 6 Mar 1599/1600–3 Dec 1609; vice-chancellor Oxford Univ 1600, 1603, 1605; bishop of Coventry and Lichfield elected 27 May 1609, consecrated 3 Dec 1609, temporalities restored 11 Dec 1609; bishop of London elected 5 Jan 1609/10, enthroned 12 Feb 1609/10; archbishop of Canterbury elected 18 Mar 1610/11, confirmed 9 Apr 1611, temporalities restored 4 May 1611, held until death; PC 23 June 1611–5 July 1627, 11 Dec 1628–4 Aug 1633.

trumpeter/s	1622–3 (452)

Bedford

Jasper Tudor (*c* 1430–21 Dec 1495), son of Sir Owen Tudor; cr 16th earl of Pembroke by 20 Jan 1452/3; attainted 4 Nov 1461; restored 1470–1; attainted 1471; fled England after 4 May 1471; cr 3rd duke of Bedford 27 Oct 1485; restored to earldom 12 Dec 1485. JP Glouc 1470, 1485–90, 1493–4, Warw 1490–1, 1493–4, Bucks 1491, 1493–4, Northants 1491, 1493–4, Wilts 1491, 1493–4, Oxf 1493, Berks 1494–5; constable Gloucester Castle, Glouc, 14 Feb 1470/1; PC 27 Oct 1485; chief justice South Wales for life 13 Dec 1485; high steward Oxford Univ 1485–92; earl marshal of England 1492. Residence at Pembroke Castle, Pembrokeshire, Wales; lands in Glouc, Oxf, Warw, and Wilts.

performers	1495–6 (38)

Bishop (Hereford)

Thomas Millyng (bef 1445–by 12 Jan 1491/2). Prior Westminster Abbey Mar 1466–Nov 1469; abbot Westminster Abbey elected Nov 1469, confirmed 16 Feb 1469/70, vacated 21 Aug 1474; chancellor to the prince of Wales 26 June 1471–9 Apr 1483; PC after 26 June 1471–25 June 1483?; JP Glouc 1473–5, 1477, 1479, 1481, 1483–90; bishop of Hereford provided 22 June 1474, temporalities restored 15 Aug 1474, consecrated 21 Aug 1474, held until death.

singers	1490–1 (34)

Buckingham

George Villiers (28 Aug 1592–23 Aug 1628), son of Sir George Villiers of Brokesby, Leic; cr Viscount Villiers and Baron Whaddon 27 Aug 1616; cr 8th earl of Buckingham 5 Jan 1616/17; cr 1st marquess of Buckingham 1 Jan 1617/18; cr 4th duke of Buckingham and 1st earl of Coventry 18 May 1623; assassinated 23 Aug 1628. Chief justice in eyre north of Trent 23 July 1616–19; lord lieut Bucks 16 Sept 1616 until death; keeper Whaddon Park and Chase, Bucks, 1616; PC 4 Feb 1616/17; lord high adm 28 Jan 1618/19 until death; chief justice in eyre south of Trent by 20 Nov 1619 until death; high steward honour of Grafton, Northants, 1622; lord warden Cinque Ports, Kent and Suss, and constable Dover Castle, Kent, 17 July 1624 until death; constable Windsor Castle, Berks, 15 Jan 1624/5. Residences at Whaddon, Bucks, New Hall, Essex, Brooksby, Leic, Burghley House, Rut, and, from 1624, York House, Twickenham, Midd; lands in Bucks, Glouc, and Warw.

trumpeter/s	1619–20 (439)
	1623–4 (455)
trumpeters (duke)	1627–8 (472)

Chandos

Giles Brydges (*c* 1548–21 Feb 1593/4), son of Edmund, 2nd Baron Chandos; succ as 3rd Baron Chandos 11 Mar 1572/3. JP Glouc 1570–1; MP Cricklade, Wilts, 1571, Glouc 1572; chief steward manor of Hailes and hundreds of Gretton, Holford, and Kiftsgate, all in Glouc, for life 19 June 1573; keeper Braydon Forest, Wilts, for life 19 June 1573; steward hundred of Slaughter, Glouc, for life 19 June 1573; steward manors of Cricklade, Highworth, Long Compton, Staple, Winterbourne Bassett, and Wootton Bassett, all in Wilts, for life 19 June 1573; lord lieut Glouc 17 Nov 1586 until death. Residence at Sudeley Castle, Glouc.

    trumpeter   1576–7 (164)

Compton *see* Northampton

Council *see* Lords of Council

Count Palatine

Frederick Wittelsbach (26 Aug 1596–29 Nov 1632), son of Frederick IV, palsgrave of the Rhine, father of Prince Rupert, *qv*; succ as Frederick V, elector palatine and palsgrave of the Rhine, 19 Sept 1610; m., 14 Feb 1612/13, Elizabeth Stuart, *qv under* **Lady Elizabeth**; crowned king of Bohemia 4 Nov 1619; deposed 8 Nov 1619.

    trumpeters   1619–20 (438)

Cromwell

Thomas Cromwell (*c* 1485–28 July 1540), son of Walter Cromwell, alias Smith of Putney, Surr; cr 1st Lord Cromwell 9 July 1536; cr 16th earl of Essex 17 Apr 1540; imprisoned in the Tower 10 June 1540; attainted 29 June 1540; beheaded 28 July 1540. MP constituency unknown 1523, Taunton, Somers, 1529, Kent (?) 1536; PC by Jan 1530/1; chancellor of the exchequer 12 Apr 1533 until death; recorder Bristol, Glouc, 1533 until death; master of the rolls 8 Oct 1534–10 July 1536; constable Berkeley Castle, Glouc, jt 1535 until death; eccles comm Bristol 1535; lord privy seal 2 July 1536–2 June 1540; warden and chief justice in eyre north of Trent 30 Dec 1537 until death; JP Glouc 1537, 1539–40, Oxf 1537, Wilts 1537–9, Berks 1538, Northants 1538–9, Warw 1538–9, Bucks 1539, Peterborough, Northants, 1540, Salisbury, Wilts, 1540; lord chamberlain 18 Apr 1540. Residences at Austin Friars, London, and Oakham, Rut; lands in Northants, Oxf, and Wilts.

    entertainers   1537–8 (80)

Edward Cromwell (*c* 1560–27 April 1607), son of Henry Cromwell, 3rd Lord Cromwell; succ as 4th Lord Cromwell 20 Nov 1592.

    trumpeters   1604–5 (279)

Cumberland

George Clifford (8 Aug 1558–29 Oct 1605), son of Henry Clifford, 2nd earl of Cumberland; succ as 3rd earl of Cumberland and 13th Lord Clifford 2 Jan 1569/70. Member council of the north 1582; high steward honour of Grafton and ranger Salcey Forest, Northants, 1602; PC 10 Apr 1603; gov Harbottle Castle, Northants, 1603. Residences at Brougham Castle, Westmld, Londesborough, Yorks ER, and Skipton Castle, Yorks NR.

    trumpeters   1591–2 (218)

Derby

William Stanley (c 1561–29 Sept 1642), son of Henry, 13th earl of Derby, and br of Ferdinando Stanley, 14th earl of Derby, *qv under* **Strange**; succ as 15th earl of Derby 16 Apr 1594; confirmed in the lordship of the Isle of Man 7 July 1609. PC Mar–May 1603. Residences at Lathom, Knowsley, and New Park, Lanc.

    players   1595–6 (240)
    trumpeters   1597–8 (244)

Essex (countess)

Lettice Knollys (1539 or 1540–25 Dec 1634), da of Sir Francis Knollys; m. 1stly, bet 1560 and 1565, Walter Devereux, 18th earl of Essex, m. 2ndly, 21 Sept 1578, Robert Dudley, 14th earl of Leicester, *qv*, m. 3rdly, bef Aug 1589, Sir Christopher Blount (d. 18 Mar 1600/1).

    players   1576–7 (165)
                                            1578–9 (169)
    players (men)   1578–9 (168)
    players   1579–80 (171)

Essex (earl)

Robert Devereux (19 Nov 1566–25 Feb 1600/1), son of Walter, 18th earl of Essex; styled Viscount Hereford until he succ as 19th earl of Essex, 6th Lord Ferrers, and 9th Lord Bourchier 22 Sept 1576; beheaded 25 Feb 1600/1. Master of the horse 1587–97; PC 25 Feb 1592/3; high steward of Oxford 30 Aug 1596–25 Feb 1600/1; chief gov Ireland Mar–Sept 1599. Residences at Essex House, Midd, Lamphey, Pembrokeshire, Wales, and Chartley, Staff.

    players   1585–6 (203)
    players (men)   1589–90 (211)
    player   1596–7 (243)

Robert Devereux (bef 22 Jan 1590/1–14 Sept 1646), son of Robert Devereux, 19th earl of Essex, *qv*; styled Viscount Hereford until restored as 20th earl of Essex, 7th Lord Ferrers, and 10th Lord Bourchier 18 Apr 1604. PC 19 Feb 1640/1; capt-gen south of Trent July 1641; lord chamberlain of the household July 1641–2. Residences at Lamphey, Pembrokeshire, Wales, and Chartley, Staff.

    trumpeters   1616–17 (416–17)
                                            1617–18 (424)
                                            1618–19 (431)
                                            1621–2 (447)
                                            1625–6 (465)

Gloucester
Humphrey of Lancaster (3 Oct 1390–23 Feb 1446/7), 4th son of Henry IV; cr 2nd duke of Gloucester and 14th earl of Pembroke 16 May 1414. Constable Marlborough Castle, Wilts, and keeper Savernake Forest, Wilts, 1 Dec 1403; keeper Clarendon Forest, Wilts, 17 Mar 1409/10; keeper forests of Grovely, Wilts, 17 Mar 1409/10; lord chamberlain 7 May 1413, 30 Nov 1422; PC by 10 Apr 1415; JP Wilts 1415, 1417, Glouc 1416, Berks 1444; chief justice and warden of forests south of Trent for life 27 Jan 1415/16; regent 10 June 1421–1 Sept 1422; protector and defender of the realm 5 Dec 1422–15 Nov 1429; constable Gloucester Castle, Glouc, 10 Dec 1422; king's lieut 23 Apr 1430–9 Feb 1431/2; keeper castle and lordship of Rockingham and Brigstock Park, Northants, for life 4 Jan 1442/3; steward Rockingham Forest, Northants, for life 4 Jan 1442/3. Residences at Greenwich, Kent, and Baynard's Castle, London; lands in Berks, Glouc, Northants, and Oxf.

    entertainer/s   1431–2 (15)

Hertford
Edward Seymour (22 May 1539–6 Apr 1621), son of Edward Seymour, 5th duke of Somerset and 8th earl of Hertford; styled earl of Hertford 1547 until his father's attainder 12 Apr 1552; restored 1553 or 1554; cr Baron Beauchamp and 9th earl of Hertford 13 Jan 1558/9; imprisoned 1561; released after 27 Jan 1567/8. JP Wilts 1578, 1611; jt comm of musters Wilts 1579; lord lieut Somers and Wilts 24 Apr 1601 until death; comm custos rot Wilts June 1603. Residence at Elvetham, Hants; lands in Wilts.

    players   1605–6 (333)

Howard
Possibly
Thomas Howard (c 1543–1 Mar 1610/11), son of Thomas Howard, 1st Viscount Howard of Bindon, and br of Henry Howard, 2nd Viscount Howard of Bindon; succ as 3rd Viscount Howard of Bindon 16 Jan 1590/1; imprisoned briefly in the Fleet Feb 1591/2. KG 24 Apr 1606.

    pipers   1591–2 (216)

See also **Lord Admiral**

King
Possibly
Henry of Windsor (6 Dec 1421–21 May 1471), son of Henry V and Catherine of Valois; acc as Henry VI 1 Sept 1422; proclaimed king of France 21 Oct 1422; John, 1st duke of Bedford, appointed protector 5 Dec 1422; crowned king of England 6 Nov 1429 and of France 16 Dec 1431; deposed 4 Mar 1460/1; restored 3 Oct 1470; crowned 13 Oct 1470; deposed finally 11 Apr 1471.

    entertainers   1460–1 (17)

See also Edward of York *below*

Edward of York (28 Apr 1442–9 Apr 1483), son of Richard Plantagenet, 3rd duke of York, and

Cecily Neville; acc as Edward IV 4 Mar 1460/1; crowned 28 June 1461; fled England 3 Oct 1470–14 Mar 1470/1; restored 11 Apr 1471.

entertainers	1469–70 (21)
trumpeters	1471–2 (21)

Possibly
entertainers	1460–1 (17)

See also Henry of Windsor *above*

Possibly
Henry Tudor 'of Richmond' (28 Jan 1456/7–21 Apr 1509), son of Edmund Tudor, earl of Richmond, and Margaret Beaufort; acc as Henry VII 22 Aug 1485; crowned 30 Oct 1485.

bearward	1508–9 (50)

See also Henry Tudor *below*

Henry Tudor (28 June 1491–28 Jan 1546/7), son of Henry VII, *qv*, and Elizabeth of York; constable Dover Castle, Kent, and warden Cinque Ports 5 Apr 1492; cr duke of York 31 Oct 1494–18 Feb 1502/3; cr prince of Wales 18 Feb 1502/3; acc as Henry VIII 22 Apr 1509; crowned 24 June 1509.

players	1533–4 (76)
	1534–5 (77)
	1536–7 (79)
jugglers	1534–5 (77)

Possibly
bearward	1508–9 (50)

See also Henry Tudor 'of Richmond' *above*

Edward Tudor (12 Oct 1537–6 July 1553), son of Henry VIII, *qv*, and Jane Seymour; acc as Edward VI 21 Jan 1546/7; crowned 20 Feb 1546/7; Edward Seymour, 5th duke of Somerset, appointed protector.

minstrels	1554–5 (97)

James Stuart (19 June 1566–27 Mar 1625), son of Henry, Lord Darnley, and Mary Stuart, queen of Scots; acc as James VI of Scotland 24 July 1567 and as James I of England 24 Mar 1602/3; crowned 25 July 1603.

trumpeters	1602–3 (266, 268, 272)
trumpeters (at Woodstock)	1603–4 (276)
trumpeters	1604–5 (279–82)
trumpeters (at Woodstock)	1604–5 (282)
trumpeters	1607–8 (338–9, 382)
	1608–9 (384–5)
	1609–10 (386–90)

trumpeter/s	1611–12 (396)
trumpeters	1611–12 (395–7)
	1613–14 (403–5)
	1614–15 (407–8)
trumpeters (at Woodstock)	1614–15 (408)
trumpeters	1615–16 (411–13)
	1616–17 (416–18, 420, 422)
	1617–18 (426)
	1618–19 (431–2)
trumpeters (at Woodstock)	1618–19 (431)
trumpeters (royal navy)	1618–19 (431)
trumpeter	1619–20 (438)
trumpeter/s	1619–20 (439)
trumpeters	1619–20 (438, 440)
	1620–1 (443–5)
	1621–2 (450)
trumpeter/s	1623–4 (455–6)
trumpeters	1623–4 (455–7)
	1624–5 (460)
players	1603–4 (276)
	1605–6 (333–4)
	1606–7 (337)
	1609–10 (387, 390)
	1612–13 (402)
players (entertainers)	1615–16 (413)
players	1616–17 (422)
players (entertainers)	1621–2 (450)
musician/s	1604–5 (279)
pipers	1613–14 (405)
	1614–15 (408)
	1616–17 (416)
	1618–19 (433)
	1619–20 (439)
swordbearer	1613–14 (408)
drummers	1615–16 (414)
harpers	1617–18 (426)
Possibly	
trumpeters	1624–5 (459)

See also Charles Stuart *below*

Charles Stuart (19 Nov 1600–30 Jan 1648/9), son of James I, *qv*, and Anne of Denmark, *qv under* **Queen**; cr duke of Albany 23 Dec 1600; duke of York 6 Jan 1604/5; succ as duke of Cornwall 6 Nov 1612; cr earl of Chester and prince of Wales 4 Nov 1616; acc as Charles I 27 Mar 1625; crowned 2 Feb 1625/6; beheaded 30 Jan 1648/9.

players (prince)	1614–15 (409)
drummers (prince)	1615–16 (411)
drummers	1642–3 (580)
servants (prince)	1615–16 (414)
trumpeters (prince)	1615–16 (411)
	1620–1 (443–5)
trumpeter/s (prince)	1623–4 (455–6)
trumpeters (prince)	1623–4 (455–7)
trumpeter/s	1624–5 (461)
trumpeters	1624–5 (459–60, 462)
	1625–6 (465)
trumpeters (at Woodstock)	1625–6 (465)
trumpeters (royal navy)	1625–6 (465)
trumpeters	1626–7 (468–70)
	1627–8 (472–4)
trumpeter/s	1628–9 (479)
trumpeters	1628–9 (478–9)
	1629–30 (485)
trumpeter	1630–1 (487)
trumpeters	1630–1 (487–9)
trumpeters (royal navy)	1630–1 (488)
	1630–1 (487)
trumpeters	1631–2 (496)
	1632–3 (506–9)
	1633–4 (511)
	1634–5 (515–17)
	1635–6 (519, 521–3, 530)
	1636–7 (554–6)
	1637–8 (565–8)
	1638–9 (569, 571)
	1641–2 (577–8)
	1642–3 (580)
Hocus Pocus	1633–4 (513)
Probably	
trumpeters (royal navy)	1625–6 (464)
pipers (royal navy)	1630–1 (489)
Possibly	
trumpeters	1624–5 (459)

See James Stuart *above*

Lady Elizabeth
Elizabeth Stuart (mid-Aug 1596–13 Feb 1661/2), da of James VI (of Scotland) and I (of

England), *qv*, and Anne of Denmark, *qv under* **Queen**; m., 14 Feb 1612/13, Frederick v, elector palatine, *qv under* **Count Palatine**; crowned queen of Bohemia 7 Nov 1619.

    trumpeters   1620–1 (443)

Leicester

Robert Dudley (24 June 1532 or 1533–4 Sept 1588), son of John Dudley, 1st duke of Northumberland, br of Ambrose Dudley, *qv under* **Warwick**; imprisoned July 1553; attainted 22 Jan 1553/4; pardoned 18 Oct 1554; restored in blood 7 Mar 1557/8; cr baron of Denbigh, Denbighshire, Wales, 28 Sept 1564; cr 14th earl of Leicester 29 Sept 1564. PC 23 Apr 1559; lord lieut Warw 10 May 1559; lieut forest and castle of Windsor, Berks, 24 Nov 1559; master of the horse 1559–87; lord lieut Berks 1560?; constable Windsor Castle, Berks, 23 Feb 1561/2 until death; JP Warw 1562, 1564, 1584, Northants 1584; high steward Windsor, Berks, 9 Sept 1563; chancellor Oxford Univ 31 Dec 1564 until death; high steward the bishopric of Ely, Berks, 1565; high steward Reading, Berks, by 1566; high steward Abingdon, Berks, 1566; comm custos rot Warw 1568; lord lieut Worc 20 Nov 1569–15 Nov 1570; high steward Wallingford, Berks, 1569; high steward Bristol 1570 until death; high steward honour of Grafton, Northants, 4 Dec 1571 until death; keeper of Grafton and Hartwell Parks, and master forester of Salcey and Whittlewood Forests, all in Northants, 4 Dec 1571; lord steward of the household 1 Nov 1584–8; warden and chief justice in eyre south of Trent 25 Nov 1585 until death. Residences at Wanstead, London, Essex, Cornbury, Oxf, and Kenilworth, Warw; lands in Northants, Oxf, and Warw.

    players (Dudley)   1559–60 (103)
    players (Lord Robert)   1561–2 (107)
    players   1569–70 (152)
                                           1573–4 (158)
    players (entertainers)   1575–6 (162)
                                           1587–8 (206)
    players   1587–8 (206)
    musicians   1585–6 (203)

Lord Admiral

Charles Howard (*c* 1536–14 Dec 1624), son of William Howard, 1st Lord Howard of Effingham; succ as 2nd Lord Howard of Effingham 11 or 12 Jan 1572/3; cr 10th earl of Nottingham 22 Oct 1597. Chamberlain of the household 1 Jan 1583/4–July 1585; PC by 5 Mar 1583/4 until death; lord high adm 8 July 1585–27 Jan 1618/19; constable Windsor Castle, Berks, 5 Dec 1588 until death; high steward Windsor 15 Jan 1592/3 until death; chief justice in eyre south of Trent 15 June 1597 until death; lord steward of the household 24 Oct 1597–Nov 1615; queen's lieut and capt-gen in the south of England 10 Aug 1599 and 14 Feb 1600/1. Residence at Effingham, Surr.

    players   1586–7 (205)
    players (entertainers) (Howard)   1587–8 (206)
    players (men)   1589–90 (211)
    players   1590–1 (214)
                                           1594–5 (237)

	1595–6 (240)
trumpeter/s (Nottingham)	1599–1600 (255)
Possibly	
pipers (Howard)	1591–2 (216)

See also **Howard**

Lord Chamberlain *see* Sussex

Lords of Council
Various members of the king's privy council.

trumpeters	1621–2 (447)
	1622–3 (452)
	1623–4 (455)

Lucy
Richard Lucy, unidentified.

trumpeters	1602–3 (266)

Monson
Sir William Monson (*c* 1567–by 12 Feb 1642/3), son of Sir John Monson of South Carlton, Linc; imprisoned in Spain 1591–3; kt 22 June 1596; imprisoned in the Tower 12 Jan 1615/16–July 1616. MP Malmesbury, Wilts, 1601; adm of the Narrow Seas July 1604–Jan 1615/16; vice adm of fleet 1635; member council of war 17 June 1637. Residences at Charterhouse, London, and Kinnersley, Surr.

trumpeters	1604–5 (279)
	1609–10 (386)

Monteagle
William Parker (*c* 1575–1 July 1622), son of Edward Parker, 12th Lord Morley, *qv*; succ as 5th Lord Monteagle 12 June 1585; imprisoned in the Tower Jan 1600/1–Aug 1601; succ as 13th Lord Morley 1 Apr 1618. Residences at Shingle Hall, Epping, and Great Hallingbury, both in Essex, Hornby Castle, Lanc, and Martok, Somers, after 1605.

trumpeters	1599–1600 (257)

Morley
Edward Parker (*c* 1551–1 Apr 1618), son of Henry Parker, 11th Lord Morley; imprisoned Apr 1573; succ as 12th Lord Morley 22 Oct 1577.

players	1594–5 (237)
players (entertainers)	1594–5 (237)

Mountjoy
Charles Blount (*c* 1562–3 Apr 1606), son of James Blount, 6th Lord Mountjoy; succ as 8th

Lord Mountjoy 27 June 1594; KG 24 May 1597; cr 1st earl of Devonshire 21 or 27 July 1603.
Chief gov Ireland 21 Jan 1599/1600–c May 1603; PC 7 June 1603; jt earl marshal 5 Feb
1604/5; JP Wilts, nd. Residences at Canford Magna, Dors, and Wanstead, Essex; lands
in Northants.

    trumpeters   1599–1600 (256)

Norfolk

Thomas Howard (1473–25 Aug 1554), son of Thomas Howard, 7th duke of Norfolk; styled
Lord Howard 1483–1514; cr 14th earl of Surrey 1 Feb 1513/14; succ as 8th duke of Norfolk
21 May 1524; imprisoned in the Tower 12 Dec 1546; attainted 27 Jan 1546/7; released and
restored in blood and honours 3 Aug 1553. Lord high adm 4 May 1513–July 1525; PC by
May 1516 and 10 Aug 1553; chief gov Ireland 10 Mar 1519/20–after 21 Mar 1521/2; treasurer
of the exchequer 4 Dec 1522–Feb 1546/7; JP Northants 1524, 1526, 1528, 1531–2, 1536,
1538–40, 1543, Warw 1524, 1529, 1531–2, 1537–9, 1542, 1544–5, Berks 1525–6, 1530,
1532, 1538, 1541, 1543–4, Bucks 1525, 1530, 1532, 1536, 1539, 1542–3, Glouc 1525,
1528, 1531–2, 1537, 1539–40, 1542, 1544, Oxf 1525–6, 1531–2, 1536–7, 1541–2, 1544,
Wilts 1525–6, 1529, 1531–2, 1537–9, 1543; high steward Cambridge June 1529; earl
marshal 28 May 1533; comm oyer and terminer Glouc 1540; lieut-gen north of Trent 29 Jan
1540/1; capt-gen in the north Aug 1542; comm of array Berks, Northants, Warw 1545.
Residence at Kenninghall, Norf; lands in Berks, Oxf.

    entertainers   1529–30 (70)

Northampton

William Compton (bef 19 Feb 1571/2–24 June 1630), son of Henry Compton, 1st Lord
Compton; summ to parl as 2nd Lord Compton 19 Feb 1592/3; cr 10th earl of Northampton
2 Aug 1618; KG 21 Apr 1629. Lord lieut Warw 7 Oct 1603; high steward Henley in Arden and
Compton in Arden, Warw, Oct 1603; lord lieut Coventry and Warwick, Warw, 19 Feb 1603/4;
jt keeper Olney Park, Bucks, 27 Feb 1603/4; lord pres council in the Marches of Wales by
16 Nov 1617–14 June 1630; lord lieut Glouc 12 Mar 1621/2 until death; PC 10 Nov 1629;
high steward Gloucester, Glouc, nd; JP Warw nd. Residences at Bishopsgate Street, London,
the Savoy, Midd, and Compton Wynyates, Warw.

    trumpeters (Compton)   1600–1 (261)
    trumpeter/s (Compton)   1606–7 (336)
    trumpeters   1623–4 (457)

Norwich

Edward Denny (15 Aug 1569–24 Oct 1637), son of Henry Denny of Cheshunt, Herts, and
Waltham Abbey, Essex; kt 26 Oct 1589; summ to parl 27 Oct 1604–17 May 1625, whereby
he became Lord Denny of Waltham; cr 1st earl of Norwich 24 Oct 1626. Lands in Herts.

    trumpeters   1629–30 (485)

Nottingham *see* **Lord Admiral**

Oxford

John de Vere (*c* 1516–3 Aug 1562), son of John de Vere, 15th earl of Oxford; styled Lord Bolebec 1526; succ as 16th earl of Oxford 21 Mar 1539/40. PC 3 Sept 1553. Residence at Hedingham Castle, Essex; lands in Wilts.

    players   1556–7 (99)

Edward de Vere (12 Apr 1550–24 June 1604), son of John, 16th earl of Oxford, *qv*; styled Lord Bolebec bef 1562; succ as 17th earl of Oxford 3 Aug 1562; imprisoned in the Tower *c* Mar–8 June 1581. Lord great chamberlain 3 Aug 1562. Residences at Hedingham Castle, Essex, and Hackney, Midd.

    musicians   1584–5 (201)

Henry de Vere (24 Feb 1592/3–bet 2 and 9 June 1625), son of Edward de Vere, 17th earl of Oxford, *qv*; styled Viscount Bolebec bef 24 June 1604; succ as 18th earl of Oxford 24 June 1604; imprisoned in the Tower by 20 Apr 1622–30 Dec 1623. Hereditary lord chamberlain by 22 May 1619. Residences at Hedingham Castle, Essex, and Hackney, Midd.

    trumpeter/s   1606–7 (336)
    trumpeters   1621–2 (447–9)

Pembroke

Henry Herbert (after 1538–19 Jan 1600/1), son of William Herbert, 20th earl of Pembroke; styled Lord Herbert 1551–16 Mar 1569/70; succ as 21st earl of Pembroke and Baron Herbert of Cardiff 17 Mar 1569/70. Jt keeper Clarendon Forest, Wilts, and bailiff of the water of the Avon from Harnham Bridge, Wilts, to the sea 26 June 1553; comm of musters Wilts 1569, 1573, 1574; JP Salisbury, Wilts, 1569, 1570; lord lieut Wilts 4 Apr 1570; constable and keeper Bristol Castle 15 May 1570; keeper parks of Holm and West Park in the manor of Corsham, Wilts, 15 May 1570; warden of Pewsham and Blackmore Forests and steward of the manor of Devizes, all in Wilts, 15 May 1570; constable of St Briavels Castle, keeper of the forest of Dean, and bailiff of the manor of Lydney, all in Glouc, for life by 18 Nov 1577; high steward Salisbury, Wilts, by 16 Dec 1582; lord pres council in the Marches of Wales Mar 1586 until death. Residences at Ludlow Castle, Shrops, Cardiff Castle, Glamorgan, Wales, and Wilton, Wilts.

    players   1595–6 (240)

William Herbert (8 Apr 1580–10 Apr 1630), son of Henry Herbert, 21st earl of Pembroke, *qv*; styled Lord Herbert 1580; succ as 22nd earl of Pembroke 19 Jan 1600/1; imprisoned in the Fleet Mar–May 1601. Keeper Clarendon Park, Wilts, for life 17 May 1603; constable St Briavels Castle, Glouc, and warden forest of Dean, Glouc, 10 Jan 1607/8; PC 29 Sept 1611; lord chamberlain of the household 23 Dec 1615–26; jt earl marshal 25 Sept 1616; chancellor Oxford Univ 29 Jan 1616/17–30; lord lieut Somers and Wilts 14 Apr 1621 until death; jt comm of the great seal May–July 1621; lord steward of the household by 3 Aug 1626–30; jt lord adm 20 Sept 1628; chief justice in eyre south of Trent for life 8 Sept 1629. Residences at Baynard's Castle, London, and Wilton, Wilts; lands in Glouc and Wilts.

    trumpeters   1608–9 (383)

Philip Herbert (10 Oct 1584–23 Jan 1649/50), son of Henry, 21st earl of Pembroke, *qv*; cr earl of Montgomery and Baron Herbert of Shurland, Isle of Sheppey, Kent, 4 May 1605; KG 18 May 1608; succ as 23rd earl of Pembroke 10 Apr 1630. Jt steward Woodstock, Oxf, 5 Oct 1604; keeper Follie-John Park, Windsor Forest, Berks, 9 Dec 1611, manors of Combe, Handborough, Stonesfield, Woodstock, and Wootton, all in Oxf, 13 July 1615; high steward Oxford Univ 10 June 1615–41; PC by 18 Dec 1624; lord chamberlain of the household 3 Aug 1626–23 July 1641; lord lieut Bucks 28 Sept 1628–14 Feb 1632/3; lord lieut Somers, sole 12 Aug 1630, jt 26 Mar 1639–30 July 1640, and sole 13 Sept 1643; lord lieut Wilts 12 Aug 1630 until death; constable St Briavels Castle, Glouc, 26 Dec 1630; steward Devizes, Wilts, 5 May 1631; lord warden Devizes, Wilts, 15 June 1631; warden forest of Dean, Glouc, 1631; warden Clarendon Park, Wilts, by 21 Aug 1635; warden Wychwood, Oxf, 19 Jan 1637/8; chancellor Oxford Univ 1 July 1641–Oct 1643, 3 Aug 1647–50; capt-gen in the west 19 Oct 1642; constable Windsor Castle, Berks, 27 July 1648 until death; MP Berks 1649. Residence at Wilton, Wilts; lands in Glouc and Wilts.

    trumpeter/s   1641–2 (576)

Prince

Edward Plantagenet (2 Nov 1470–*c* Aug 1483), son of Edward IV, *qv*, and Elizabeth Wydevill; cr prince of Wales 26 June 1471; acc as Edward V 9 Apr 1483; protector, Richard Plantagenet, 3rd duke of Gloucester, appointed 30 Apr–25 June 1483; deposed 25 June 1483.

    entertainers   1479–80 (25)

Arthur Tudor (20 Sept 1486–2 Apr 1502), 1st son of Henry VII, *qv*; succ as 8th duke of Cornwall at birth; cr prince of Wales and 20th earl of Chester 29 Nov 1489. Warden-gen Marches of Scotland by 20 May 1490; JP Glouc 1490, 1493–4, 1496, 1499–1502, Northants 1490–1, 1493–4, 1496, 1500, Oxf 1490, 1493, 1496–7, 1501, Warw 1490–1, 1493–4, 1496–7, 1499, Wilts 1490–1, 1493–4, 1496, 1498–9, 1501–2, Bucks 1491, 1493–4, 1496–1501, Berks 1494–5, 1497, 1501–2; keeper of the realm and king's lieut 2 Oct 1492; justice of oyer and terminer Glouc 1493. Residence at Ludlow Castle, Shrops.

    performers   1492–3 (36)

Henry Frederick Stuart (19 Feb 1593/4–6 Nov 1612), 1st son of James I, *qv*; succ as 11th duke of Rothesay, Scotland, at birth; succ as 13th duke of Cornwall 24 Mar 1602/3; cr prince of Wales and 22nd earl of Chester 4 June 1610. Residences at St James, Midd, and Nonsuch and Richmond, Surr; lands in Oxf.

    musician/s   1604–5 (279)
    servants   1605–6 (333)
    trumpeter/s   1611–12 (396)
    trumpeters   1611–12 (395–7)

Charles Stuart (29 May 1630–6 Feb 1684/5), son of Charles I, *qv*, and Henrietta Maria, *qv under* **Queen**; succ as 16th duke of Cornwall at birth; styled prince of Wales and duke of

Cornwall and Rothsay on his Garter plate 21 May 1638, but generally known as prince
of Wales from bef 1637; exiled 2 Mar 1645/6–26 May 1660; became king 'de jure' 30
Jan 1648/9; proclaimed king 5 May 1660; acc as Charles II 29 May 1660; crowned 23
Apr 1661.

trumpeters   1641–2 (578)

Prince Rupert

Rupert Wittelsbach (27 Dec 1619–29 Nov 1682), son of Frederick Wittelsbach, king of
Bavaria and elector palatine of the Rhine, *qv under* **Count Palatine**, and Elizabeth Stuart, *qv*
under **Lady Elizabeth**; count palatine of the Rhine in Simmern; duke of Bavaria; imprisoned
at Linz, Austria, 1637–40; naturalized in England 19 Jan 1641/2; KG Aug 1642; cr 2nd earl of
Holdernesse and 1st duke of Cumberland 24 Jan 1643/4. General of the horse July 1642–
Nov 1644; king's lieut-gen 6 Nov 1644–Sept 1645; adm the king's fleet Oct 1648–Mar 1653;
master of the horse for the king's government in exile 1653– June 1654; adm of England
9 July 1673–13 May 1679.

trumpeters   1641–2 (578)
                                                    1642–3 (580)

Queen

Katherine of Arragon (16 Dec 1485–7 Jan 1535/6), da of Fernando V of Castile and Arragon
and Isabel of Castile and Leon, Spain; m. 1stly, 14 Nov 1501, Arthur, prince of Wales (d. 2 Apr
1502), *qv under* **Prince**, m. 2ndly, 11 June 1509, Henry VIII, *qv*; crowned 24 June 1509;
marriage declared null and void 23 May 1533.

players   1531–2 (73)

Mary Tudor (18 Feb 1515/16–17 Nov 1558), da of Henry VIII, *qv*, and Katherine of Arragon,
qv; acc as Mary I of England 19 July 1553; crowned 1 Oct 1553; m., 25 July 1554, Philip,
king of Naples and Jerusalem, and king of Spain from 16 Jan 1555/6.

performers (princess)   1530–1 (72)
minstrels   1556–7 (99)
players   1556–7 (99)

Elizabeth Tudor (7 Sept 1533–24 Mar 1602/3), da of Henry VIII, *qv*, and Anne Boleyn; acc
as Elizabeth I 17 Nov 1558; crowned 15 Jan 1558/9.

bearward   1560–1 (104)
                                                    1562–3 (108)
                                                    1564–5 (111)
                                                    1565–6 (143)
                                                    1567–8 (149)
                                                    1568–9 (151)
                                                    1570–1 (154)
                                                    1574–5 (160)

bearward *(cont)*	1575–6 (163)
	1576–7 (165)
bearwards	1577–8 (167)
bearward	1579–80 (171)
	1580–1 (174)
	1597–8 (249)
jester	1560–1 (104)
	1562–3 (108)
	1566–7 (147)
players	1565–6 (143)
	1567–8 (149)
	1569–70 (152)
	1571–2 (154)
	1585–6 (203)
	1588–9 (209)
players (entertainers)	1588–9 (211)
players	1589–90 (211)
	1590–1 (214)
	1592–3 (233)
	1594–5 (238)
players (entertainers)	1594–5 (237)
	1595–6 (240)
players	1596–7 (243)
	1598–9 (253)
players (entertainers)	1598–9 (253)
pipers	1571–2 (154)
trumpeters	1571–2 (154)
	1573–4 (158)
	1591–2 (215–16, 218)
	1592–3 (228, 230)
	1600–1 (260–1, 263)
	1601–2 (264)

Anne of Denmark (12 Dec 1574–2 Mar 1618/19), da of Frederick II of Denmark and Norway and Sophia of Mecklenburg; m., 20 Aug 1589, James VI of Scotland (later James I of England), *qv*; crowned queen of England 25 July 1603.

players (entertainers)	1603–4 (276)
players	1606–7 (337)
	1607–8 (381)
	1613–14 (405)
players (entertainers)	1613–14 (405)
players	1616–17 (422)
trumpeters	1605–6 (333)
trumpeter/s	1615–16 (413)
trumpeters	1615–16 (411–13)

trumpeters *(cont)*	1616–17 (417)
	1618–19 (431)
drummer/s	1615–16 (412)

Henrietta Maria (25 Nov 1609–31 Aug 1669), da of Henry IV of France and Mary de Medicis; m., 11 May 1625, Charles I, *qv*.

trumpeter/s	1624–5 (461)
	1628–9 (479)
trumpeters	1628–9 (478–9)
	1631–2 (495)

Rutland

Francis Manners (1578–17 Dec 1632), son of John Manners, 6th earl of Rutland, br and heir of Roger Manners, 7th earl of Rutland; imprisoned in the Fleet nd–31 Mar 1601; succ as 8th earl of Rutland 26 June 1612; KG 7 July 1616; cr Lord Roos of Hamlake 22 July 1616; succ as 17th Lord Roos 27 June 1618. PC 6 Apr 1617; chief justice in eyre north of Trent 13 Nov 1619 until death; comm custos rot Northants 7 Feb 1622/3; jt master forester King's Cliffe, Rockingham Forest, Northants, 25 July 1629. Residences at Belvoir Castle, Leic, and Helmsley, Yorks NR.

| trumpeters | 1619–20 (438) |

Sheriff of Oxfordshire

William Cobb (1591–bef 16 Mar 1657/8), son of William Cobb of London; kt 15 June 1624. Sheriff Oxf Nov 1629–6 Nov 1630; JP by 1636. Residence at Adderbury, Oxf.

| trumpeters | 1629–30 (484) |

Southampton

Henry Wriothesley (6 Oct 1573–10 Nov 1624), son of Henry Wriothesley, 3rd earl of Southampton; styled Lord Wriothesley 1573–4 Oct 1581; succ as 4th Lord Wriothesley and 4th earl of Southampton 4 Oct 1581; imprisoned in the Tower 8 Feb 1600/1–Apr 1603; attainted and all honours forfeited 19 Feb 1600/1; granted pardon and restitution 16 May 1603; KG 9 July 1603; cr Lord Wriothesley of Titchfield and earl of Southampton 21 July 1603; committed to close custody of the dean of Westminster 15 June –30 Aug 1621. PC 30 Apr 1619–15 June 1621. Residences at Beaulieu, Hants, and Southampton House, Holborn, London; lands in Glouc.

| trumpeter/s | 1599–1600 (255) |

Stanhope

Possibly

John Stanhope (*c* 1545–9 Mar 1620/1), son of Sir Michael Stanhope of Shelford, Nott; kt Aug or Sept 1596; cr 1st Lord Stanhope of Harrington, Northants, 4 May 1605. MP Marlborough, Wilts, 1572; master of the posts for life, sole 20 June 1590, jt with his son Charles 26 July 1607; treasurer of the chamber bef 7 Oct 1597–12 Jan 1617/18; treasurer of war for the armies 12 Aug 1599; steward Higham Ferrers and other duchy of Lancaster manors, Northants, 1600; vice-chamberlain bef 3 Feb 1600/1–Apr 1616; PC 29 June 1601; keeper of the game in the hundreds of Fawsley, Guilsborough, Huxloe, Orlingbury, and Rothwell, Northants, 14 Oct 1604. Residences at St Martin-in-the-Fields, London, and Harrington, Northants.

trumpeters	1620–1 (443)

See also Philip *and* Charles Stanhope *below*

Either
Philip Stanhope (1584–12 Sept 1656), son and heir of Sir John Stanhope of Shelford, Nott; cr Lord Stanhope of Shelford 7 Nov 1616; cr 1st earl of Chesterfield 4 Aug 1628. Residences at Bretby and Chesterfield, Derb, and Shelford, Nott.

or

Charles Stanhope (bef 27 Apr 1595–3 Dec 1675), son and heir of John Stanhope, 1st Lord Stanhope of Harrington, Northants, *qv*; KB 4 June 1610; succ as 2nd Baron Stanhope of Harrington 9 Mar 1620/1. Postmaster gen 7 June 1622–by June 1637. Residence at Harrington, Northants.

trumpeter/s	1622–3 (452)
trumpeters	1622–3 (453)
trumpeter/s	1623–4 (455)
trumpeters	1623–4 (457)
	1625–6 (464)
	1626–7 (468)
	1627–8 (472)

Possibly
trumpeters	1620–1 (443)

See also John Stanhope *above*

Stanley

Thomas Stanley (c 1435–29 July 1504), son of Thomas Stanley, 1st Lord Stanley; succ as 2nd Lord Stanley and sovereign lord of the Isle of Man 20 Feb 1458/9; cr 10th earl of Derby 27 Oct 1485. Lord steward of the household 14 Aug 1471–Oct 1485; PC 1471–1485; JP Warw 1473, 1493, Wilts 1473, Glouc 1474, Berks 1485, 1494, 1495, 1497, 1501, 1502, Northants 1493, Oxf 1493; constable of England for life 16 Dec 1483 and 5 Mar 1485/6; high forester north of Trent 7 Oct 1485; steward of the lordship of manor, master forester and keeper of the park of Sutton in Warw and Staff, 7 Oct 1485; comm of oyer and terminer Coventry, Warw, 1485, 1495, Glouc 1485, 1495, Warw 1485, 1493, 1495, Bucks 1493, 1495, Northants 1493, 1495, Oxf 1493, 1495, Berks 1495. Residences at Knowsley and Lathom, Lanc.

bearwards	1485–6 (29)
performers	1485–6 (30)

Strange

Ferdinando Stanley (*c* 1559–16 Apr 1594), son of Henry Stanley, 13th earl of Derby, and br of William Stanley, 15th earl of Derby, *qv under* **Derby**; styled Lord Strange from 1572; summ to parl as Lord Strange 28 Jan 1588/9; succ as 14th earl of Derby and lord of the Isle of Man 25 Sept 1593. Residences at Knowsley, Lathom, and New Park, Lanc.

    players   1592–3 (233)

Sussex

Thomas Radcliffe (*c* 1525–9 June 1583), son of Henry Radcliffe, 7th earl of Sussex; styled Lord FitzWalter 27 Nov 1542–53; succ as 8th earl of Sussex and 3rd Viscount and 9th Lord FitzWalter 17 Feb 1556/7. Chief gov of Ireland 27 Apr 1556–11 Nov 1557, 9 Mar–4 Aug 1558, 3 July 1559–17 Jan 1559/60, 6 May 1560–9 Jan 1560/1, 24 May–19 Dec 1561, 4 July 1562–1 May 1564; chief justice in eyre south of Trent 3 July 1557 until death; lord pres council of the north July 1568–Oct 1572; lord lieut of the north 15 Nov 1569; PC 30 Dec 1570; lord chamberlain of the household 13 July 1572 until death. Residences at New Hall and Woodham Walther, Essex, and Bermondsey, Surr.

    player/s (?) (lord chamberlain)   1572–3 (156)
    players   1575–6 (163)

Warwick

Ambrose Dudley (*c* 1528–21 Feb 1589/90), son of John Dudley, 1st duke of Northumberland and 19th earl of Warwick, and br of Robert Dudley, 14th earl of Leicester, *qv*; styled Lord Ambrose Dudley from Oct 1551; imprisoned and attainted 1553; pardoned 22 Jan 1554/5; cr 21st earl of Warwick 26 Dec 1561. Master of the ordnance for life 12 Apr 1560; JP Linc and Warw 1562, 1564; lord pres council of the north by 22 Feb 1563/4; lord lieut Coventry and Warwick, Warw, Nov 1569–Nov 1570 and by 9 Oct 1587 until death; comm of musters Warw 1569, 1579–80, Berks, Bucks, Northants, Oxf 1579, 1580; PC 5 Sept 1573; master forester Salcey and Whittlewood Forests, keeper Grafton and Hartwell Parks, all in Northants, 10 May 1589. Residence at Warwick Castle, Warw; lands in Warw.

    players   1561–2 (107)

Robert Rich (May or June 1587–19 Apr 1658), son of Robert Rich, 22nd earl of Warwick; styled Lord Rich 1618–19; succ as 23rd earl of Warwick 24 Mar 1618/19. Recorder Warwick, Warw, 1629–41; PC 27 Apr 1641; lord high adm 1 July 1642, 7 Dec 1643–9 Apr 1645, May 1648–23 Feb 1648/9. Residences at Leighs Priory and Rochford Hall, Essex, Warwick House, Holborn, Midd, and Wallington, Norf; lands in Northants.

    trumpeter/s   1629–30 (484)
    trumpeters   1629–30 (483)

Willoughby

Probably

Katherine Willoughby (22 Mar 1518/19–19 Sept 1580), da of William Willoughby, 11th Lord

Willoughby; 12th Baroness Willoughby de Eresby 19 Oct 1526; m. 1stly, *c* 7 Sept 1533, Charles Brandon, 4th duke of Suffolk, m. 2ndly, probably early 1553, Richard Bertie; fled England 5 Feb 1554/5; all lands seized by crown 1557; returned to England, lands restored, summer 1559. Residence at Westhorpe, Suff, from *c* 1528, and at Grimsthorpe and Tattershall Castle, Linc, from *c* 1536.

entertainers	1541–2 (85)

Windsor
Edward Windsor (*c* 1532–24 Jan 1574/5), son of William Windsor, 2nd Lord Windsor; kt 2 Oct 1553; succ as 3rd Lord Windsor 20 Aug 1558. JP Bucks 1562, 1564; comm oyer and terminer Bucks 1564. Residence at Bradenham, Bucks; lands in Berks, Bucks, Glouc, Warw.

minstrels	1564–5 (112)

Companies Named by Location

Abingdon, Berks
singer	1490–1 (33)

Barnard Castle, Dur
trumpeters	1604–5 (281)

Calais, France
drummers	1533–4 (76)

Evesham, Worc
players	1479–80 (24)

Hinksey, Berks
piper	1640–1 (575)

Ireland
trumpeter	1627–8 (473)

Kendal, Westmld
musicians	1621–2 (448–9)

London
singer	1490–1 (34)
players	1633–4 (514)

Portsmouth, Hants
trumpeters	1626–7 (470)

Wales
  harper   1615–16 (413)

Westbury, Bucks
  singer   1485–6 (29)

Witney, Oxf
  men   1639–40 (572)
  piper   1640–1 (575)
  singers   1640–1 (575)

Glossaries: Introduction

The purpose of the glossaries is to assist the reader in working through the text. The criteria for the selection of glossary entries are discussed below, under the headings Latin Glossary and English Glossary. The glossaries include words found in records printed or quoted in the Records, Introduction, Appendixes, and Endnotes. Definitions are given only for those senses of a particular word that are used in the records printed in this collection. For every word, sense, and variant recorded the glossaries cite the earliest example occurring in the Records as a whole. If a glossed word occurs twice in a single line, superscript numerals are used after the line number to distinguish the occurrences. Within references, page and line numbers are separated by an oblique stroke. Words occurring within marginalia are indicated by a lower-case 'm' following the page and line reference. Manuscript capitalization has not been preserved; however, if proper names are glossed they are capitalized in accordance with modern usage. Half-brackets used in the text to indicate insertions, and italics used to indicate expansions, are ignored.

There are no glossaries for the Anglo-Norman, Italian, and Spanish documents. Although sufficiently involved to qualify for translation by REED guidelines, they contain no vocabulary not found in standard reference works. Bibliographical information for the appropriate dictionaries will be found below, under Works Consulted. The few Greek words are found in the Latin Glossary alphabetized according to their Roman transliteration.

Latin Glossary

Words are included in the Latin Glossary if they are not to be found in the *Oxford Latin Dictionary (OLD)*, now the standard reference work for classical Latin. Words listed in the *OLD* whose meaning has changed or become restricted in medieval or Renaissance usage are also glossed. If a word is found in the *OLD* but appears in the text in an obscure spelling or anomalous inflectional form for which the *OLD* provides no cross-reference, that word has been included and its standard lexical entry form indicated without a definition. If the spelling variants or anomalous inflectional forms have been treated as scribal errors and more correct forms given in textual notes, the forms thus noted are not repeated in the glossary.

Most of the Latin words used in the Records are common classical words whose spelling has changed, if at all, according to common medieval variations. The results of these common variations are not treated here as new words, nor are forms of glossed words resulting from such variations normally cross-referenced. These variations are:

ML *c* for CL *t* before *i*
ML *cc* for CL *ct* before *i*

ML *d* for CL *t* in a final position
ML variation between *de-* and *di-* as a prefix
ML *e* for CL *ae* or *oe*
ML *ff* for CL *f*, common in an initial position
ML addition of *h*
ML omission of CL *h*
ML variation between *i* and *e* in unstressed medial positions, especially before another vowel
ML *n* for CL *m* before another nasal
Intrusion of ML *p* in CL consonant clusters *mm*, *mn*, *ms*, or *mt*
ML doubling of CL single consonants
ML singling of CL double consonants

No attempt has been made to correct these spellings to classical norms; rather, scribal practice has been followed in such cases. We have also not treated as significant variations caused by the Neo-Latin hyper-correction of 'm' to 'n' before a dental, eg, 'quorundam' rather than 'quorumdam.' Where the same word occurs in spellings that differ according to the list above, the most common spelling (or the earliest, when numbers of occurrences are roughly equal) is treated as standard and used for the headword. If a word appears sometimes in its standard orthography and sometimes in an over-corrected form (with 'ae' or 'oe' substituted for 'e'), it will be listed under the standard spelling regardless of the number of occurrences. However, we have conformed to the practice of the *OLD* as regards 'i/j' and 'u/v' variation: in this glossary only the letter forms 'i' and 'u' are used. If a noun of the first declension appears primarily in texts whose writers consistently used classical orthography, its genitive singular is listed as '-ae'; otherwise the ML '-e' is used. All listed variant spellings will be found under the headword, at the end of the definition, set apart in boldface type. Where the variant spelling would not closely follow the headword alphabetically, it is also listed separately and cross-referenced to the main entry.

It is difficult to know in some cases whether certain words are being used in a CL sense or in one of the modified senses acquired in Anglo-Latin usage during the Middle Ages. In these circumstances the range of possibilities has been fully indicated under the appropriate lexical entry. (When it seems useful to indicate the possibility that a given sense was intended in a given passage, even if no certainty exists, a '?' is added after the appropriate page and line reference under that sense.) In the Translations, unclear, technical, or archaic terms, especially those pertaining to canon or common law, performance, and music, are usually given a stock translation equivalent but receive a fuller treatment in the Glossary.

As a rule only one occurrence of each word, or each sense or form of each word, will be listed; 'etc' following a reference means that there is at least one more occurrence of that word, sense, or form in the collection. The one occurrence listed is either the sole occurrence or the first chrono-logically. Multiple occurrences of each sense may be listed for words defined in more than one sense; in fact all possible occurrences of a given sense may be listed if it is difficult to distinguish the senses in context.

All headwords are given in a standard dictionary form: nouns are listed by nominative, genitive, and gender; adjectives by the terminations of the nominative singular or, in the case of adjectives of one termination, by the nominative and genitive; verbs by their principal parts.

English Glossary

The English Glossary is not meant to be exhaustive but only to explain words, senses, or spellings apt to puzzle users not familiar with markedly provincial Late Middle and Early Modern English. Accordingly words and senses given in *The New Shorter Oxford English Dictionary (NSOED)* have nearly always been passed over, along with their obvious derivatives. Abbreviations have also been omitted if they are still current or widely known, as have forms whose only difficulty is a false word division, most errors corrected in the footnotes, and matter corrected and replaced by the original scribe. No attempt is made to gloss words left incomplete by damage to the source texts.

Readers are also expected to recognize such spelling variations as 'a/ai/ay,' 'a/au,' 'ar/er,' 'c/s,' 'ea/e/ei,' 'e/i,' 'ie/e(e),' 'i/j,' 'i/y,' 'oa/o,' 'o/oo,' 'o/ou,' 'o/u,' 's/z,' 'sch/sh,' 'u/v,' and the presence or absence of final 'e' in the contexts where they commonly occur in older literature. They are presumed to have read enough old-spelling texts to recognize forms in which the definite article is fused with a following noun (such as 'tharchangell' for 'the archangel' and 'thuniuersitie' for 'the university'), to know the values of 'þ,' '3,' and 'y' used for 'þ' (as in 'yeir' for 'their'), and to recognize commonly occurring spellings that are nearer to their Old English or Old French originals than the modern standard forms, such as 'brethern' for 'brethren' and 'embrodered' for 'embroidered,' and Renaissance etymological or pseudo-etymological spellings such as 'accompt' for 'account' and 'aucthorize' for 'authorize.'

A slightly fuller treatment has, however, been given to certain words and phrases likely to hold special interest for users of a REED volume. These are chiefly terms for musical instruments (eg, 'vilyn'), costumes and fabrics (eg, 'billament,' 'spang lace'), food and drink (eg, 'chewettes,' 'powder beef'), and the specialized vocabularies of Oxford University (eg, 'demy,' 'halliers'), Oxford civic government (eg, 'key kepers'), popular custom and pastime (eg, 'ffranches,' 'Hocke ayle'), and the performing arts (eg, 'wayghtes').

Normal headword forms are the uninflected singular for nouns, the positive for adjectives, and the infinitive for verbs, but nouns occurring only in the plural or possessive, adjectives occurring only in comparative or superlative forms, and verbs occurring only in one participial or finite form are entered under the form that actually occurs. A regularly formed adverb is subsumed under the root adjective when that also occurs in the Glossary (eg, 'strangly' under 'strang'), and a verbal noun is subsumed under the infinitive when other parts of the same verb are also entered (eg, 'pleainge' under 'pla').

The capitalization of headwords mostly conforms to modern usage. A word appearing in several noteworthy spellings is normally entered under the one most often found in the text or else – when two noticed spellings are equally or nearly equally common – under the one nearer modern usage, but a marginally less common spelling may be preferred to keep related forms together in the entry order of the glossary. Other noticed spellings are mostly entered in their alphabetical places and cross-referenced to the main entry. As a rule only the earliest occurrence is cited for each inflectional form entered and further occurrences are represented by 'etc,' unless the reader needs to be alerted that the sense in question applies in particular later passages. Since the documents in this collection are arranged chronologically, the occurrences cited are usually the first to appear in the page order of the text, unless they come from the Appendixes. Two citations given without 'etc' mean that the form or sense in question occurs only twice. The figure (2) after a citation means that there are two occurrences in the same line of the text.

Where the definition repeats the headword in a different spelling, the latter is normally the entry spelling in *The Oxford English Dictionary* and *The New Shorter Oxford English Dictionary* and further information can be found there. When that form is itself an archaism or ambiguous, a further brief definition usually follows. Any further citation of an authority or other succinct account of the glossarian's reasoning appears within square brackets at the end of the entry.

Works Consulted

Anglo-Norman Dictionary. Louise W. Stone and William Rothwell (gen eds) for the Modern Humanities Research Association in conjunction with the Anglo-Norman Text Society. Fascicles 1–7 (London, 1977– (in progress)).

Black's Law Dictionary. 5th ed (St Paul, 1979). [*Black's*]

The Catholic Encyclopedia. On-line edition, http://www.newadvent.org/cathen/ (2003; originally published New York, 1908–12). [*CEO*]

Cheney, C.R. (ed). *Handbook of Dates for Students of British History*. New ed rev by Michael Jones (Cambridge, 2000). [Cheney]

Covarrubias Orozco, Sebastián de. *Tesoro de la lengua castellana o española*. Felipe C.R. Maldonado (ed) (Madrid, 1994).

Dictionary of Medieval Latin from British Sources. R.E. Latham and D.R. Howlett (eds). Fascicles 1–6: A–N (London, 1975–2002). [*DML*]

The English Dialect Dictionary. Joseph Wright (ed). 6 vols (London, 1898–1905). [*EDD*]

Grande Dizionario della Lingua Italiana. Salvatore Battaglia (ed). 20 vols (Turin, 1961–2000).

Latham, R.E. (ed). *Revised Medieval Latin Word-List from British and Irish Sources* (London, 1965). [Latham]

Liddell, H.G., R. Scott, and H.S. Jones. *A Greek-English Lexicon*. 9th ed (Oxford, 1940; rpt 1996). [LSJ]

Middle English Dictionary. Hans Kurath and Sherman H. Kuhn, et al (eds) (Ann Arbor, 1952–2001). [*MED*]

The New Grove Dictionary of Music and Musicians. Stanley Sadie (ed). 20 vols (London, 1980). [*New Grove*]

The New Shorter Oxford English Dictionary. Lesley Brown (ed). 2 vols (4th ed, Oxford, 1993; 5th ed, Oxford, 1999). [*NSOED*]

The Oxford Classical Dictionary. N.G.L. Hammond and H.H. Scullard (eds). 2nd ed (Oxford, 1970). [*OCD*]

The Oxford Dictionary of the Christian Church. F.L. Cross and E.A. Livingstone (eds). 2nd ed with corrections (Oxford, 1978). [*ODCC*]

The Oxford English Dictionary. Compact ed. 2 vols (New York, 1971). [*OED*]

Oxford English Dictionary. J.A. Simpson and E.S.C. Weiner (eds). 2nd ed (1989). Additions 1993–7, John Simpson, Edmund Weiner, and Michael Proffitt (eds) and 3rd ed (in progress) Mar 2000–, John Simpson (ed). *OED Online*. [*OEDO*]

Oxford Latin Dictionary. P.G.W. Glare (ed) (Oxford, 1982). [*OLD*]

Page, Christopher. *Voices and Instruments of the Middle Ages*. Appendix 1 (London, 1987).

Ragazzini, Guiseppe. *Il nuovo Ragazzini: dizionario italiano-inglese, inglese-italiano*. 2nd ed (Bologna, 1984).

Simon and Schuster's International Dictionary. English/Spanish, Spanish/English. Tana de Gámez (ed) (New York, 1973).

Souter, Alexander. *A Glossary of Later Latin to 600 A.D.* (Oxford, 1949). [Souter]

Thesaurus Linguae Latinae. Vols 1–10.2.13: A–Propositio (Leipzig, 1900–). [*TLL*]

Young, Abigail Ann. 'Minstrels and Minstrelsy: Household Retainers or Instrumentalists?' *REED N* 20.1 (1995), 11–17.

– 'Plays and Players: the Latin Terms for Performance,' *REED N* 9.2 (1984), 56–62, and 10.1 (1985), 9–16.

Abbreviations

abbrev	abbreviation		LL	Late Latin
abl	ablative		m	masculine
acc	accusative		Mk	Mark
adj	adjective		ML	Medieval Latin
adv	adverb(ial)		Mt	Matthew
AL	Anglo-Latin		n	noun
art	article		nom	nominative
attr	attributive		nt	neuter
CL	Classical Latin		pass	passive voice
coll	collective		pa t	past tense
comm	common gender		per	person
comp	compound		pf	perfect tense
compar	comparative		pfp	perfect participle
conj	conjunction		phr	phrase
cp	compare		pl	plural
dat	dative		poss	possessive
decl	declension		pp	past participle
E	English		ppl	participial
f	feminine		pr	present tense
gen	genitive		prep	preposition
gd	gerund		pron	pronoun
gdve	gerundive		prp	present participle
imper	imperative		sbst	substantive
interj	interjection		sg	singular
intr	intransitive		superl	superlative
Kgs	Kings		tr	transitive
L	Latin		v	verb
Lk	Luke		vb	verbal

Latin Glossary

ABIGAIL ANN YOUNG

abbatissa, -e *n f* abbess, head of a house of nuns 3/7, etc

Abendonia *see* **Abundonia**

aberratus, -a, -um *adj* divergent (from a norm or standard), out of kilter 427/29 [*cp* OLD aberro]

abiuro, -are, -aui, -atum *v tr* to abjure, renounce 8/23

ablego, -are, -aui, -atum *v tr literally* to banish, *hence* to expel (ie, from university) 530/12

absento, -are, -aui, -atum *v intr* to be absent 3/11

absoletus, -a, -um *adj for* obsoletus [OLD]

Abundonia, -e *n f* Abingdon, site of an important Benedictine house 3/19; **Abendonia** 33/37

academia, -ae *n f* the university, whether considered as a physical site, an institution, or a community of persons 135/34, etc

academicus, -a, -um *adj* of or pertaining to the university 497/12, etc; *m pl as sbst* members of the university of whatever status 218/17m, etc; *f sg as sbst* the university 217/20

accepto, -are, -aui, -atum *v tr* 1. *literally* to receive or accept (something) 42/9, etc; 2. *by extension* to receive (someone) into a given status or relationship 491/15

Achilles, -is *n m* Achilles, a Greek hero of the Trojan War, *here named as* a character in the play *Ajax Flagellifer* 308/3

acquerenda *nt pl gdve for* acquirenda *from* acquiro [OLD]

acquietantia, -ae *n f* acquittance, a written receipt or discharge from debt 519/38, etc; **acquitantia** 522/23

acquieto, -are, -aui, -atum *v tr* to acquit (someone from a charge) 9/25

actito, -are, -aui, -atum *v tr* to put on (a play or the like), perform 136/22

actor, -oris *n m literally* participant, *hence* actor 37/36 (where 'actor' translates E 'player'), etc

actum, -i *n nt* 1. action, doing 542/21, etc; 2. *by extension* legal proceedings, action (sometimes used of the record of such proceedings) 258/39, etc; 3. administrative or legislative decision, act 481/34

actus, -us *n m* 1. action, activity 141/8; 2. *by extension* act, a subdivision of a play 310/31m, etc

ad *prep with acc* 1. (of space) to, toward 5/32, etc; (used figuratively, eg, of states or conditions, eg, **ad libidinem**) 4/7, etc; 2. (of spatial position) at 40/20, etc; (used figuratively of events or occasions) 29/20, etc; (expressing contact) at, against 8/25, etc; 3. (of time) at 16/17, etc; **ad duas uices** on two occasions, twice 19/32[1]; 4. (expressing manner) in accordance with, in harmony with 6/38, etc; **ad mandatum** 7/37, etc; 5. (expressing purpose) to 6/37, etc; *with acc of gd or gdve* 6/23, etc; *by extension* + E *participle* **ad mayynge** 8/5; **ad usum** + *gen* to the use (of) 94/16, etc; 6. (expressing goal of action) to, for 6/14, etc; **ad hoc** 9/27, etc; (expressing elevation to a status or office) 30/12, etc; 7. (with expressed or implied questions) in reply to, to 47/26; 8. (with numbers and sums of money) up to, to 8/29, etc; 9. (expressing indirect object, as a substitute for the dative case) 19/32[2], etc; 10. *in idiom* **ad manus** +

gen at the hands of (expressing agency) 88/37; *see also* **usque**

adiudico, -are, -aui, -atum *v tr* to sentence (an accused person to a penalty) 7/36

adiungo, -gere, -xi, -ctum *v tr literally* to join to, *here in idiom* **animos uestros adiungere** to set your minds (to something) 56/28

administrator, -oris *n m* administrator, one in charge of the estate of a deceased person or a minor 196/4, etc

admissio, -onis *n f* act of admitting (a person) to a status or office 54/12m

admitto, -ittere, -isi, -issum *v tr* 1. to admit (a person) to an office or responsibility 54/5, etc; 2. to admit (a person) to a legal status or condition (eg, burgess-ship) 192/4, etc

admoneo, -ere, -ui, -itum *v tr* to warn, admonish 86/3, *hence* to issue a formal legal warning to offenders 48/34

adscio, -ire, -iui, -itum *v tr* to hire 487/39 [*cp* OLD ascio²]

aduentura, -e *n f* joust, venture of arms 529/32

aedes, -is *n f (often in pl form with sg meaning)* 1. building 313/7; *hence* private house, residence 200/38, 313/7; *hence in pl* the lodgings of the head of a college 95/10?, 146/16, etc; 2. stage house, part of the traditional scenery used for Roman comedy 137/19, 894/12?; 3. community residing together, *hence* college: **Aedes Christi** Christ Church 305/17, etc; **Aedes Diui Iohannis** St John's College 305/17

Aedichristianus, -a, -um *adj* of or belonging to Christ Church 305/33

aedidit *3rd per pf over-correction of* edidit *from* edo² [OLD]

Aeneanasensis, -e *adj* of or pertaining to Brazen Nose, the eponymous emblem of Brasenose College; *see* **collegium**

aeneus, -a, -um *adj* made of brass, brazen; *see* **nasus**

aequester, -tris, -tre *adj literally* mounted on horseback, equestrian; *in* CL a reference to the equestrian class, a lesser aristocracy below the rank of senator, *hence in* AL knightly: **aequestris ordo** equestrian order, ie, the knightly class 217/37 [*over-correction of* OLD equester]

affabre *adv* in a craftsmanlike manner, artfully 894/29 [*cp* OLD affaber]

Aiax, -acis *n m* Ajax, a Greek hero of the Trojan War, *here named as* a character in the play *Ajax Flagellifer* 307/34, etc

Alba Fortunata, Albe Fortunate *n f* Alba Fortunata, imaginary kingdom of St John's Christmas Prince, so named because of a punning connection between the surname of the Prince (Tucker), the Greek word τύχη (luck), and the Latin 'fortunatus' (lucky) 360/38

Albanus, -a, -um *adj* Alban, *here* used in the name of an Oxford hall 73/19

alcumista, -ae *n m* alchemist, one who studies the supposed properties of elements with a view to their transformation, *here* used in reference to the play *The Alchemist* 387/23

aldermanus, -i *n m* alderman, a civic officer 493/9; **aldrimannus** 492/7

aleatorius, -a, -um *adj* of or pertaining to gambling, especially with dice; *see* **ludus**

Alexander, -dri *n m* 1. Alexander the Great (356–323 BC), *here likely named as* a character in a play 178/15; 2. **Alexander Seuerus** Severus Alexander (AD 208/9–35), Roman emperor AD 222–35, *here named as* a character in the play *Marcus Geminus* 137/24

Alexandra, -ae *n f* Alexandra Salome, queen of Judea 76–69 BC, who successfully ended a revolt of the Pharisees against her late husband Alexander Jannaeus 179/3 [*see* OCD JEWS]

allego, -are, -aui, -atum *v tr* to allege, to state or claim (something) formally in court as true or sufficient 73/27, etc

alligatus, -a, -um *pfp pass* allied, joined 8/16

allocatio, -onis *n f* allowance (of an expenditure as valid and subject to reimbursement) 217/36m

alloco, -are, -aui, -atum *v tr* to allow, provide 253/5, etc

alloquor, -qui, -cutus sum *v tr* 1. to converse (with), speak (to), address 3/9; 2. to state formally 9/25

Altissimus, -i *sbst m* the Most High, used as a divine title 11/7, etc

altus, -a, -um *adj* high, lofty; *see* **aula, uicus**

alueum, -i *n nt literally* a concave surface or

object, *in cl* a kind of gaming board used for throwing dice, *hence* a backgammon table or, *by extension*, the game of backgammon 56/23 (*cp* 56/31, where it is rendered by E 'tables')

alumnus, -i *n m literally* foster son, ward 309/20, *hence* student 136/10, etc

amasia, -ie *n f* (female) lover, mistress 4/6

amator, -oris *n m* lover; *see* **hospicium**

amodo *adv* from now on, hereafter 4/34

Anabaptista, -e *n m* Anabaptist, properly a member of one of several radically pietist Protestant movements in the sixteenth century that rejected infant baptism 387/24, etc [*odcc* ANABAPTISTS]

ἀνατύπωσις, -εως *n f* mould, model 343/7 [LSJ]

ancyle, -is *n nt literally* a waisted shield [*old* ancile], *here* a shield used as a decorative heraldic device 306/6

Anglia, -e *n f* England 3/7, etc

Anglicanus, -a, -um *adj* of or pertaining to England, English 893/28

Anglice *adv* in the English language 149/6, etc

Anglicus, -a, -um *adj* of or pertaining to England, English 135/35, etc; *nt sg as sbst* the English language 7/20

Angligena, -ae *n m* Englishman 314/11

Anglus, -i *n m* Englishman 313/30

annus, -i *n m* 1. year 3/15, etc; *hence* in a play title, *Annus Recurrens* 308/25; 2. *in various idioms*: **annus domini** year of the Lord, AD 126/7, etc; **annus etatis vicesimo tertio inchaoto** *literally* when the twenty-third year of (my) age had begun, ie (because of the inclusive counting methods used by cl writers), when I was just twenty-two years old 209/11; **annus gracie** year of grace, synonymous with AD 1085/43; **annus regni** (*with ordinal number*) *literally* the Nth year of a reign, expressing the regnal year 5/15, etc

antedictus, -a, -um *pfp pass* said or stated before 146/24, etc

Antonius, -ii *n m* a Roman gentile name or one of the holders of that name, *especially* Mark Antony, the triumvir, *here named as* a character in the play *Caesar Interfectus* 178/14, etc

anunciatio, -onis *n f* announcement, annunciation, *especially* the annunciation by an angel to the Virgin Mary of the impending birth of Christ (Lk 1.26–38), commemorated liturgically on 25 March 162/34; *see also* **festum**

apostolus, -i *n m* apostle, one of the first followers of Christ, often found in the names of saints' days 11/40, etc

applausus, -us *n m* applause, expression of approval 307/25, etc

appono, -onere, -osui, -ositum *v tr* to place, put 894/21; *in idiom* **manus apponere** to put one's hands (to something), apply oneself (to a task or the like) 799/9

apprenticius, -i *n m* (male) apprentice, one bound to a craftsman or other master for a term of years in order to learn certain skills 332/29, etc

apud *prep with acc* 1. at (locative) 8/16, etc; 2. among 305/4; 3. at (someone's) home, with (a person) 38/6; 4. before, in the presence of 137/24, etc; 5. for (someone's) part 307/6; 6. (of time) at, on (an occasion), during (an event) 18/6, etc; **aput** 21/11

arbor, -oris *n f literally* tree 5/4; *hence* timber, wood (for construction) 94/29, 94/35

Arcadia, -iae *n f* Arcadia, *literally* a region in the Peloponnese, *by extension* an imagined and idealized setting used in pastoral verse and other writing: referring to the title and setting of the play *Arcadia Reformed* 309/9, etc; *hence* **Arcadia Utopica** Utopian Arcadia, ie, the imagined pastoral setting of the play 310/8; **Isiaca Arcadia** Arcadia on the Isis, ie, Oxford 310/8–9

Arcas, -ados *adj* of or pertaining to Arcadia, Arcadian 314/7; *m sg as sbst* an inhabitant of (the imaginary) Arcadia 309/30; *hence* **Isiaci Arcades** Arcadians of the Isis, ie, Oxford men 309/9

archangelus, -i *n m* archangel, one of the highest order of angels 16/39

archipraesul, -ulis *n m* archbishop 894/4, etc

Architas, -ae *n m* Archytas of Tarentum, a Pythagorean mathematician who flourished in the first half of the fourth century BC and was believed to have built a mechanical dove 307/21

architectonex, -icis *n m* architect, builder 306/1

Arcitus, -i *n m* Arcite, a character in the play *Palamon and Arcite* 138/24, etc; **Arcis** 136/21

aries, -etis *n m literally* ram, *hence* Aries, the first sign of the zodiac, *symbolically* the beginning of the solar year 308/34

armiger, -eri *n m literally* one who bears arms, *in AL* used as an honorific, esquire 196/1, etc

armilausa, -e *n f* a sleeveless cloak 8/34

armum, -i *n nt* weapon 140/9, etc; *in various idioms*: **factum armorum** feat of arms, especially in a tournament or the like 529/24, etc; **resignare arma** to lay down one's arms, *hence* to stop doing some task 799/17

arraiatus, -a, -um *pfp pass* equipped, arrayed 8/16

ars, -tis *n f* 1. skill, craft 307/21, etc; especially that associated with a particular trade or guild 414/12, etc; *hence* **ars heraldica** heraldry 306/6; 2. *hence* an art, a branch of learning: **facultas arcium** faculty of arts, the lowest level of study, which students had to complete before continuing in one of the higher faculties (law, medicine, or theology); its curriculum was based on the seven liberal arts 52/18–19; **septem … artes liberales** the seven liberal arts, made up of the trivium (grammar, rhetoric, and dialectic (or logic)) and the quadrivium (arithmetic, music, geometry, and astronomy), that formed the university arts curriculum 306/30; *see also* **bacularius**

articulum, -i *n nt* article, part of a series of charges or allegations upon which witnesses are interrogated 47/26

aspiro, -are, -aui, -atum *v tr* to reach for, attain to 55/10, etc

assensus, -us *n m* agreement, assent, formal consent (eg, of a governing body) 38/33, etc

asser, -is *n m* plank, board 155/31, etc [*DML*; *but see OLD* asser]

assessio, -onis *n f* assessment, rating (eg, for taxation) 286/20

assignatus, -a, -um *pfp pass* assigned; *see* **iusticiarius**

assignatus, -i *sbst comm* assign, a person to whom another has assigned, or made over, rights in property or in receivable sums of money 196/2, etc

assistens, -entis *sbst comm literally* one who stands by or near, *here by extension* one present at a meeting 45/29

assumptio, -onis *n f* assumption, especially the liturgical festival commemorating the Assumption, or taking up, of the Virgin Mary into heaven, celebrated on 15 August 5/14

Astiages, -is *n m* Astiages, title character in the play *Astiages* 245/32

Atalanta, -ae *n f* Atalanta, legendary Greek huntress beloved by Meleager, *here likely named as* a character in Gager's *Meleager* 178/16

Atlas, -antis *n m* Atlas, *in classical mythology* a Titan who supported the world upon his shoulders, *here presented as* the brother of the king of beans (*see* **rex**) 799/16

attamen *conj* yet, nevertheless 10/29, etc [*see OLD* at¹]

attendens, -ntis *prp* waiting upon, attending 426/20, etc

attornatus, -i *n m* legal representative, attorney, proxy 196/2, etc

augustalis, -e *adj* pertaining to Augustus Caesar, imperial, *hence* royal 305/34, etc

Augustinus, -i *n m* Augustine, the name of several saints, eg, St Augustine of Hippo (AD 354–430), patristic theologian and exegete 177/37m [*OCD*]

auis, -is *n f literally* bird 6/24, etc; *hence* bird of prey, a hawk, especially one trained for hunting 64/36, etc; **auis reclamatoria** hawk trained to be recalled either by voice or a lure 6/26 [*see OEDO* reclaim *sb¹ and v*]

aula, -e *n f* 1. hall, dining area and centre of corporate activity in a college 6/33?, 6/34?, 10/41, etc, or in a royal or noble household 345/4, etc (referring to the fictive hall of the Christmas Prince); **alta aula** the high hall, name for the principal hall in Merton College 29/10, etc (**aula alta** 63/37–8; *also* **magna aula** 57/39, etc, *and* **aula magna** 51/8 the great hall), possibly so called in distinction to **aula communis** common hall 65/11, etc; 2. hall, a place of residence and instruction for students, technically distinct from a college in having no 'collegium' or corporate body of fellows but sometimes used synonymously 6/24, etc

auledus, -i *n m literally* one who sings accompanied by piping [*OLD* auloedus], *here* singer, musician (a synonym of **musicus**) 498/23

aulicus, -a, -um *adj* of or pertaining to court: *m sg as sbst* courtier 180/38, etc; *nt sg as sbst* the royal court 309/7

auris, -is *n f* ear 3/26, etc; in 364/4 the phr **aurium tenus**, *literally* up to one's ears, is rendered by E 'ouer shooes' as part of a punning speech [*see* OEDO over-shoe]

author, -oris *n m for* auctor [*OLD*]

authoritas, -atis *n f for* auctoritas [*OLD*]

autoritas, -atis *n f for* auctoritas [*OLD*]

bacularius, -i *n m* bachelor, one holding the lowest academic degree in a given faculty; unmodified, it probably refers to a bachelor of arts 31/1 (*in form* baccalarius), etc; *hence*: **bacularius artis** bachelor of arts, BA, one holding the lowest degree obtainable and the formal prerequisite for all higher degrees 428/17, etc; **iunior bacularius** junior bachelor, apparently the junior of two bachelors chosen as officers at Merton College 51/14, etc; **legum baccallaurius** bachelor of laws, LLB, one holding a bachelor's degree in both laws, ie, civil and canon law, but after the teaching of canon law was forbidden at the universities by Henry VIII, the degree was in civil law only and retained the pl by custom 76/27; **senior bacularius** senior bachelor, apparently the senior of two bachelors chosen as officers at Merton College 51/14, etc; **baccalaureus** 73/10, etc; **bacallarius** 31/2; **baccalarius** 45/26, etc; **bacchilarius** 58/38; **bachalarius** 62/29, etc; **bachillarius** 44/13

Bagoas, -e *n m* Bagoas, a Persian eunuch, a favourite of Alexander the Great, *here apparently named as* a character in a play 178/15

balliuus, -i *n m* bailiff, a civic officer: **uillanus balliuus** town bailiff 42/8, etc

Banquo, -onis *n m* Banquo, putative ancestor of the Stuart line, *here* named in a pageant for James I's arrival in Oxford 315/3, etc; **Bancho** 305/6, etc

baptista, -e *n m* baptist, one who baptizes; *always* in reference to St John the Baptist 5/23, etc

baro, -onis *n m* baron, lowest rank in the hereditary peerage 218/6, etc

baselardum, -i *n nt* dagger 9/14

Basilia, -ae *n f* Basel, a city in Switzerland 106/27

battellum, -i *n nt* battel, account for the provisions for members of a college 424/35, etc; *hence* the provisions themselves 70/23

Bauaria, -ae *n f* Bavaria, a German duchy 261/14

beatus, -a, -um *adj literally* happy, *hence* as the title of a saint, especially the Virgin Mary, blessed 3/14, etc

Bedfordia, -e *n f* Bedford, name of a dukedom 38/40, etc

bellum, -i *n nt* war, battle 309/23, etc; **Bellum Iudaicum** *The Jewish War*, title of a work by Flavius Josephus (AD 37–*c* 100) covering the history of Judaea from the capture of Jerusalem by Antiochus Epiphanes in 170 BC to its destruction by Titus in AD 70 179/6–7m

bellus, -a, -um *adj* pretty, charming, *hence in phr* **de Bello-Monte** Latinization of F Beaumont 349/4

benediccio, -onis *n f* blessing 3/8

beneficium, -ii *n nt* 1. benefit, freely bestowed gift 342/39, etc; 2. benefice, an ecclesiastical appointment, often one to a parish and involving a cure of souls 45/28

beneplacitum, -i *n nt* good pleasure, *in idiom* **ad beneplacitum suum** at his good pleasure (of the term of imprisonment ordered by a judge) 530/12 (written as two words)

biberium, -i *n nt* bever, *apparently* a light meal with wine served as a supper in the evening or after special events 29/10, etc; **bibesium** 60/14; *see also* **potacio**

Biblia, -e *n f* Bible 27/23, etc; **Biblium** 92/17

billa, -e *n f* bill, itemized statement of charges or expenses 30/4, etc

Boemus, -i *n m* Boemus, surname of Joannes

Boemus (c 1485–1535), author of *Mores, leges, et ritus omnium gentium* 310/13m

breue, -is *sbst nt* (legal) writ 529/22, etc

breuiuscula, -ae *n f* a short period of time 310/10

Brutus, -i *n m* a Roman cognomen, *or* one of the holders of that name, especially Marcus Junius Brutus (c 78–42 BC), one of the assassins of Julius Caesar, *here named as* a character in the play *Caesar Interfectus* 180/7, etc

Brytannus, -a, -um *adj for* **Britannus** [OLD]

buccinator, -oris *n m* trumpeter (*from* OLD bucina, a curved trumpet or horn, probably originally made from the curved horns of cattle); *probably* used generically for one who plays upon any wind instrument; *possibly* used to distinguish one who plays upon a curved wind instrument from one who plays upon a straight wind instrument 158/23, etc; **buccinitor** 256/4, etc [*the usual -cc- AL spelling may be influenced by* OLD bucca, cheeks, mouth]

burdeicia, -e *n f* tilting, joust 529/24, etc [*see* OEDO bourdis]

burgensis, -is *n m* burgess, one having the privileges, or freedom, of a city or town 503/17

bursarius, -ii *n m* bursar, a financial officer in a college or other corporation 30/31, etc; **secundus bursarius** second bursar, one of Merton College's three bursars 63/38, etc; **burssarius** 67/1, etc; *see also* **festum**

caena *see* **cena**

Caesar *see* **Iulius Caesar**

calculus, -i *n m literally* a pebble or stone, *also classically* a playing piece in certain board games, *hence* a chessman, *in pl* the game of chess 56/23

calendas, -arum *n f* calends, the first day of a month; in the Roman dating system all other days of a month were designated by counting backwards from three fixed points, the month's nones (the fifth or seventh day), its ides (the thirteenth or fifteenth day), and the calends of the following month 360/38, etc; **Graecae calendas** the Greek calends, a whimsical expression for never, like E '31 February,' since classically reckoning time by calends was unique

to the Romans 360/36; the phr **pridie Calendas** actually refers to the day before the calends, ie, the last day of the previous month, but on 363/30 it is used to make a pun on 'calendas' (which resembles a future participle in form) and the E participle 'Cald'; **kalendas** 41/36 [Cheney, pp 145–6]

caliga, -e *n f* stockings, hose 8/34

camera, -e *n f* room, chamber 8/31, etc; *in idiom* **presentiae camera** presence-chamber, one in which a monarch receives formal or state visits 894/11

campana, -e *n f* bell: 1. possibly a small bell used to decorate clothing 1093/3; 2. bell rung as a signal: **campana communis** common bell, ie, such a bell rung for official purposes, such as assembling a community 503/16

Campanus, -a, -um *adj* of or pertaining to Campania, Campanian; *see* **Geminus**

cancellariatus, -us *n m* state or office of being a chancellor, chancellorship 529/10

cancellarius, -ii *n m* chancellor: 1. another name for a vicar general, deputy of a bishop with primarily administrative and judicial responsibility, *hence* the chancellor of Oxford University, originally a deputy of the bishop of Lincoln, later head of the corporation composed of chancellor, masters, and scholars of the University 4/31, etc; 2. (royal) chancellor, originally the royal secretary, the post evolved to become that of the most senior administrative and judicial officer of the realm 7/23¹, etc; **chancellarius** 279/25 (*in sense 1*)

cancello, -are, aui, -atum *v tr* to obstruct (especially with a beam or block fallen or placed crosswise), block 12/32

Cancia, -ie *n f* Kent, name of a county 41/28

candela, -e *n f* candle, whether of tallow or of wax 34/19, etc

canis, -is *n m* 1. dog 6/23; as trained for bearbaiting 37/22; 2. *hence* hunting dog, hound 64/36, etc; **canis uenaticus** hunting dog 6/25

cano, -ere, cecini, cantum *v tr or intr* 1. to sing (*always here* of secular music) 56/23, etc; 2. to prophesy 315/1, etc; 3. to sound a tune 270/13?

(this CL sense was certainly known to the seventeenth century and the word play in this macaronic text suggests it may have been intended rather than sense 1)

canonicus, -i *sbst m* canon: 1. secular canon, a priest serving as a member of a collegiate church or similar body: **canonicus 2ⁱ ordinis** *literally* canon of second rank, *hence probably* minor canon, a canon chosen primarily to fulfil responsibilities in choir and usually not a full member of the college 70/23; 2. in the post-Reformation Anglican Church, a cleric belonging to a cathedral chapter 89/36, etc

Cantabrigia, -e *n f* Cambridge, name of a town and university 306/33

cantator, -oris *n m* singer, usually a choir singer 29/26, etc

Cantebrigiensis, -e *adj* of or pertaining to Cambridge 142/21

canticum, -i *n nt* song, whether secular or liturgical (eg, a canticle) 45/36, etc

cantilena, -e *n f* popular or folk song, ballad, probably one having a refrain, often but not exclusively with negative associations (especially associated with dancing) 4/6, etc; **cantulena** 28/3 [*see* REED *Herefordshire/Worcestershire* LG *cantilena and* EG carrall, *and* OLD cantilena]

canto, -are, -aui, -atum *v tr* 1. to sing (used of secular music) 4/7, etc; 2. to sing (liturgically), chant 12/10; 3. *prp as sbst* singer (*here probably* a choir singer) 33/32

cantor, -oris *n m literally* a man or boy who sings, *usually* a chorister or choir singer 33/37

cantrix, -icis *n f literally* a woman or girl who sings, *here* the chantress, leader of liturgical music, in a convent choir, who also acted as an administrative officer 3/16

Cantuaria, -e *n f* Canterbury, name of an archdiocese 42/20, etc

Cantuariensis, -e *adj* of or pertaining to Canterbury 3/6, etc

cantulena *see* **cantilena**

cantus, -us (*once with a 2nd decl abl ending*) *n m* 1. singing, *here apparently* raucous 13/7, etc; 2. an instance of such singing, a song: **cantus**

inhonestus a rude song 40/23; **cantus ritmicis** a song in verse, rhythmic song 7/20; 3. *by extension* the blast of a trumpet or the like 140/10

Canutus, -i *n m* Canute (*c* 994–1035), king of England from 1014 315/19

capa, -e *n f* cope, a liturgical vestment also worn by choir monks 47/27 [ODCC COPE]

capella, -e *n f* chapel 12/16, etc

capellanus, -i *n m* chaplain, a priest serving or having charge of a chapel 6/38, etc

capicium, -ii *n nt* hood 15/27

capio, -ere, cepi, -tum *v tr* 1. to take, receive 10/26, etc; 2. to take hold of, seize 310/7; 3. *hence* to arrest 8/13; 4. to get, grasp 10/27; 5. to hold (an inquest or other court session) 5/20; 6. *in various idioms*: **possessionem capere** to take legal possession (of property) 259/5, etc; **uires capere** to take fresh strength, revive 163/1

capitalis, -e *adj* 1. capital: **capitale supplicium** capital punishment 139/1–2; 2. capital, chief 12/18, etc

capitaneus, -i *n m* captain, leader 8/18

capitularis, -e *adj* of or belonging to a collegiate chapter, capitular 30/18m, etc

capitulum, -i *n nt* chapter: 1. a meeting of the members of a monastery, usually for administrative or disciplinary purposes 3/19; 2. an organized and partially self-governing body of clerics serving a cathedral or collegiate church 92/24, etc; *by extension* an organized and partially self-governing body of fellows of an academic college or a meeting thereof 29/11, etc; 3. one of the subdivisions making up a collection of canons or statutes, *hence* any subdivision of a longer work, eg, of a book 27/23, etc

capituus, -i *n m* captive, prisoner, *here* in play titles: **Captiuus** *The Captive*, a play by Plautus (d. *c* 184 BC) normally called *Captiui* [OCD PLAUTUS] 194/1; **Captiuus Regalis** *The Royal Slave*, a play by William Cartwright 894/25

carbo, -onis *n m* charcoal *or* coal 28/1, etc (without more context, it is often unclear which is being referred to: in the first instance the reference may be to mineral coal)

carcer, -eris *n m* 1. prison, gaol 7/37 *(in coll pl)*, etc; 2. *by extension* rendered *Castell* as part of a pun in a macaronic text on 363/34

cardinalis, -is *n m* cardinal, one of a group of senior bishops forming a council that elected and advised the pope 306/35

cardo, -inis *n m* hinge; *see* **par**

caritas, -atis *n f* love, loving kindness; *see* **potus**

carmen, -inis *n nt* 1. song 54/6?, 305/10, etc; 2. poem, verse 54/6?, 213/11

carnispriuium, -ii *n nt literally* removal of meat (from the diet), *hence* the beginning of Lent, often Shrove Tuesday, the day preceding Lent *or sometimes* either of the two Sundays preceding Shrovetide, Sexagesima Sunday (second before Ash Wednesday) or Septuagesima Sunday (third before Ash Wednesday) 1123/42 [*see* DML Carniprivium]

Cassius, -ii *n m* Cassius, a Roman gentile name *or* one of the holders of that name, *especially* C. Cassius Longinus, one of the assassins of Julius Caesar, *here named as* a character in the play *Caesar Interfectus* 180/16, etc

castimonia, -ie *n f* chastity 140/4

casualiter *adv* by chance, accidentally 12/31

casus, -us *n m* 1. *literally* event, occurrence 136/11, 270/6 (where the resemblance to E 'case' is used in a punning speech); 2. chance 347/20 (as part of multilingual puns on the E surnames Case and Tucker (*see* Τνχεϱος)

catallum, -i *n nt* chattel, moveable property 8/35, etc

causa, -e *n f* 1. law case, legal proceedings 42/7, etc, *hence by extension* cause, (one's) side 180/13, etc; **causam agere** to plead one's cause 140/20, etc; 2. cause, reason 29/12, etc; *hence* excuse 86/5 (*in form* **caussa**) 3. cause, sake 529/13; *hence in abl, with gen of sbst, gd, or gdve, to express cause or purpose* for the sake of, on account of 6/33, etc

causatus, -a, -um *pfp pass* caused, *hence nt pl as sbst* things caused, ie, the created order, the universe 799/10

cautela, -e *n f* warning, cautioning 40/34

celebracio, -onis *n f* celebration (of the Eucharist or another divine service) 3/8m

celebro, -are, -aui, -atum *v tr* 1. to celebrate the Eucharist or another divine service 3/17, etc; 2. to observe (an event or occasion), to keep as a day of special observance 4/34, etc; 3. to hold (a council or other meeting) 32/21, etc; 4. to celebrate, extol 305/5, etc

cena, -e *n f* supper, the latest of the three main meals of the day, usually less elaborate than dinner 10/41, etc; **caena Domini** the Lord's Supper, ie, Maundy Thursday, the festival, held the Thursday before Easter Sunday, commemorating the institution of the Eucharist 100/5; **caena** 6/14, etc; **coena** 251/6, etc

censura, -ae *n f* censure, rebuke, punishment 534/34

cepula, -e *n f* small cup 20/19

ceremonia, -ae *n f literally* a religious rite, *here* a customary or traditional practice 62/30, etc

cereteca, cerotheca, cerotica *see* **chirotheca**

certamen, -inis *n nt* 1. fight, struggle: **singulare certamen** single combat 139/34–5; 2. fight or bout staged as entertainment 529/21m; **gladiatorum certamen** fencing bout 512/13

ceruisia, -e *n f* 1. ale (not always clearly distinguished from beer) 13/14, etc; 2. **ceruisia ecclesia** 16/9 *or* ~ **ecclesie** 16/17, etc, church ale, a parish fund-raising event at which ale was sold; **seruicia** 25/29, etc; **seruisia** 22/6, etc (*both in sense 1*) [*see* MED āle, bēr]

ceruisium, -ii *n nt* church ale 20/19

chancellarius *see* **cancellarius**

charta, -ae *n f* sheet (of parchment), *hence* legal document written on such a sheet, a charter 259/10

chartula, -ae *n f literally* a small sheet (of paper or parchment), *hence* a short piece of writing, a little work (*here* used by an author with a deliberate assumption of modesty) 313/19

charus, -a, -um *adj for* carus [OLD]

chemisia, -e *n f* shirt 15/27

chirotheca, -e *n f* glove 279/24, etc; **cereteca** 14/26; **cerotheca** 26/15, etc; **cerotica** 28/11; **cheritheca** 281/15; **cyrotheca** 63/17

choraea *see* **corea**

choragus, -i *n m* (*from Greek* χοϱηγός) *in* CL *literally* one who contracted to supply a dramatic company with all necessary equipment, *hence* (play) producer, one responsible for putting on a play 343/31; *used figuratively* producer, orchestrator 106/35

chorista, -e *n m* member of a choir, chorister 103/33

chorus, -i *n m* 1. *literally* chorus, those who performed the choral passages in classical drama 308/13 [*OLD*]; 2. *by extension in later Latin* a choir, those who performed sacred music in a church or chapel *or* the section of a church or chapel in which the choir sat 3/11; **missa chori** choir mass, a mass sung or celebrated by or in the choir 3/14

Christianus, -a, -um *adj* Christian 178/19; *m pl as sbst* Christian people, Christians 177/38

cinctura, -e *n f* binding (of a book) 213/11

cineritius, -a, -um *adj* ashen, ashy; *see* **festum**

cinis, -eris *n m* ash, ashes 163/1; *figuratively* (in reference to Ash Wednesday and the start of Lenten observance) 177/35

circa *prep with acc* 1. around, near (of time) 5/17, etc; 2. in connection with, concerning 63/24, etc; 3. *of purpose* for (referring to a future event) 1093/2

circuitus, -us *n m* 1. a circular structure, circle 306/20 [*OLD* circu(m)itus]; 2. round dance 5/24m

circumcisio, -onis *n f* circumcision, the liturgical commemoration of Christ's circumcision on 1 January (Lk 2.21) 25/4, etc

circumquaque *adv* all around, on every side 5/19

cissor, -is *n m* tailor 5/21m, etc

citacio, -onis *n f* citation, summoning 503/15

citharaedus, -i *n m literally in CL* a singer who accompanies himself upon the lyre, *hence by extension* one who plays the harp, harper 42/34 (*in form* **cithereda**); *in later AL likely* a fiddler 426/25, etc; **cytharedus** 81/29, etc [*OLD* citharoedus]

citharista, -e *n m literally* one who plays upon a lyre, *hence by extension* harper; *possibly* a generic term applied to players of plucked-string instruments 30/30, etc [*OLD*]

cit(h)era, -e *n f literally* a lyre, *in AL usage often by extension* a harp (possibly used generically for

other plucked-string instruments) 9/8, etc; **cithara** 15/13; **cythara** 5/25 [*OLD* cithara]

citherarius, -ii *n m* harper 41/36, etc

cito, -are, -aui, -atum *v tr* to cite, issue a citation (to appear before an ecclesiastical or university court) 495/15, etc

clario, -onis *n f* 1. clarion, type of trumpet originally used for military signalling, *or* the sound of such a trumpet 6/15; 2. one who plays a clarion, clarioner 256/18, etc [*see OEDO* clarion *sb*]

clarus, -a, -um *adj* bright, clear, famous; *see* **de**

claustralis, -e *adj* enclosed, cloistered, *here* applied to a college community 209/18

Clementinus, -a, -um *adj* of or pertaining to St Clement; *see* **festiuitas**

clericalis, -e *adj* pertaining to or suitable for a cleric, clerical 11/19, etc

clericus, -i *n m* 1. cleric, one in holy orders 4/5, etc; 2. parish clerk, in pre-Reformation use, a cleric in minor orders assisting the priest of a parish in liturgy, et al 17/1, etc; **clericus parochialis** 35/35; 3. town clerk: **clericus communitatis** 491/11, etc

clocus, -i *n m* cloak 9/13

coelum, -i *n nt for* caelum [*OLD* caelum²]

coena *see* **cena**

coenaculum, -i *n nt literally* dining room, *here likely* lodging 305/34

collaboro, -are, -aui, -atum *v intr* to work together 105/7

collegium, -ii *n nt* college: 1. organized body of clergy and priests serving a particular church: **collegium Etonense** 30/12; 2. *hence* an academic college, viewed as a corporate body composed of fellows and scholars 11/13, etc; *with proper names or adj*: **collegium Aeneanasense** Brasenose College 498/31, etc; ~ **Christi** *literally* Christ's College, ie, Christ Church 135/31; ~ **Corporis Christi** Corpus Christi College 147/2; ~ **Diui Ioannis** 178/14–15m *or* **Ioannense** ~ 314/40 St John's College; ~ **Lyncolnense** Lincoln College 498/28–9, etc; ~ **Diue Marie Magdalene** 46/1 *or* ~ **Magdalense** 200/40, etc, *or* ~ **Mariae Magdalenae** 178/16–17m, Magdalen College;

~ **Mertonense** Merton College 525/36;

~ **Nouum** New College 525/37, etc;

~ **Wadhamus** Wadham College 525/36

colloquium, -ii *n nt* conversation 894/5;
forinsecum colloquium *either* conversation
about external topics *or* conversation with
outsiders 3/12

columba, -ae *n f* dove 307/17, etc

columbinus, -a, -um *adj* of or belonging to a dove,
dovelike 307/20

coma, -e *n f* hair, *by extension* a wig: **coma
muliebris** a woman's wig (either as representing
a woman's hair or possibly as made from
women's hair) likely used as a costume 105/26

comaedia, comedia *see* **comoedia**

Comberlandius, -a, -um *adj* of or belonging to
Cumberland, an English earldom and county:
m sg as sbst the earl of Cumberland 313/13

comes, -itis *n m* 1. earl, a peer ranking above a
viscount but below a marquess 146/43, etc; 2.
(continental) count; *see* **palatinus**

comicus, -a , -um *adj* of or pertaining to a comedy
or its performance, comic 177/30, etc

comitatus, -us *n m* 1. accompanying escort or
group, retinue 313/2; 2. county 8/14, etc

comitia, -iorum *n nt* (university) commencement
257/15, etc

comitissa, -ae *n f* countess, wife of an earl 313/34

comitiua, -e *n f* company, group 11/29, etc

commessacio, -onis *n f* dinner, banquet 60/37, etc

comminarius, -ii *n m* commoner: *normally* a
student at an Oxford college who is not a
member of the foundation and must therefore
pay for his commons, ie, his board, *but here
likely* one receiving full commons, *hence possibly*
a kind of fellow (*see* **semicommunnarius**) 170/25

commissarius, -ii *n m* commissary: 1. deputy or
representative of a bishop or other high ecclesi-
astic, often presiding as a judge on behalf of
his principal, *hence* **commissarius generalis**
commissary general, probably another title for
the vicar general of a diocese 499/13; 2. *by
extension* a judge presiding over a university
court as the deputy of the vice-chancellor
42/7, etc

commodatio, -onis *n f* loan 76/27

commodea *see* **comoedia**

communa, -e *n f* commons, the standard daily
provision of supplies, usually foodstuffs, made
for members of a college or the monetary value
thereof 13/25, etc

communicacio, -onis *n f* communication,
conversation 40/29

communio, -onis *n f* one's dealings with others,
social intercourse 11/29, etc

communis, -e *adj* 1. common, communal, of or
pertaining to a community, eg, a college or a
town 65/11, etc; 2. common, general 6/30, etc

communitas, -atis *n f* community, commonalty,
commons (eg, of a town or city) 799/18, etc

comoedia, -ae *n f* comedy, a play, usually in verse,
often of a humorous or satiric nature, sometimes modelled on ancient comedy but also
drawing upon scriptural and other sources, *or*
its performance 85/7, etc; **comaedia** 79/31,
etc; **comedia** 38/4, etc; **commodea** 54/7

compareo, -ere, -ui *v intr* 1. to appear, come into
sight 305/12, etc; 2. *hence as legal term* to appear
before a judge 73/39, etc

computus, -i *n m* account, formal accounting
made of the receipts and disbursements of an
institution 215/5, etc; **compotus** 7/10

concameratio, -onis *n f literally* vaulting, vaulted
ceiling, *hence* a vaulted room 306/29

concensus, -us *n m for* consensus [*OLD*]

concinnatus, -a, -um *pfp pass* produced, made
251/7 [*OLD* concinno]

concio, -onis *n f* sermon 177/23; **contio** 200/39

conclaue, -is *n nt* small private room 894/4

concubicularius, -ii *n m* one with whom one
shares a bedroom, room-mate 91/38 [*see DML*
concubicularius]

confeccio, -onis *n f* comfit, confection 51/19

confessio, -onis *n f* statement, acknowledgment,
confession, *here likely* alluding to the sacramental
rite of confession 179/2

confiteor, -fiteri, -fessus sum *v tr* to make a
statement, acknowledge, confess 76/33, etc

confluxus, -us *n m* confluence (of persons)
305/27

conquiror, -iri, -estus sum *v intr* to make a legal complaint 7/21–2, etc

conscriptus, -a, -um *pfp pass* enrolled, conscript, *hence* **electores conscripti** conscript electors, in a L speech by St John's Christmas Prince, imitating CL 'patres conscripti,' conscript fathers, a customary address to the (Roman) Senate 343/1 [*see* OEDO conscript *a and sb*]

consecrabilis, -e *adj* capable of being consecrated; *see* **panis**

conseruandus, -a, -um *gdve of* conseruo, to keep, preserve [OLD], *in idiom* **ad pacem … conseruandum** to keep the peace, part of the formal title of a JP 8/14–15

considero, -are, -aui, -atum *v tr* to make a judgment (that) 9/31

consiliarius, -ii *n m* counsellor, adviser 125/9, etc

consilium, -ii *n nt* 1. counsel, advice 3/16, etc; 2. deliberation 11/12, etc; 3. council, a group of advisers 7/23, etc (*in the occurrence at 313/5, a play on senses 1 and 3 seems intended*); 4. town council 481/35, etc

constitutio, -onis *n f* decision, decree 44/6

contesto, -are, -aui, -atum *v tr* to attest, approve 310/5 [*see* OLD contestor]

contio *see* **concio**

contrauenio, -ire, -i, -tum *v tr* to violate or contravene (eg, an order or decree) 512/15

contubernialis, -is *sbst m* fellow (of a college or hall) 51/19

contubernium, -ii *n nt* college, organized body of clergy and priests serving a particular church 41/27

conuentus, -us *n m* 1. assembly, group of people 370/1; 2. convent, religious house *or* the community living therein 3/8, etc

conuersio, -onis *n f literally* a turning in a new direction: 1. change, transformation: **humanae conuersiones** *Human Transformations*, used as alternate name for Ovid's *Metamorphoses* 141/3; 2. (religious) conversion 107/10

conuersor, -ari, -atus sum *v intr* 1. to talk (with), make conversation (with) 60/35; 2. to behave, act 11/26, etc

conuictor, -oris *n m* fellow (of a college) 253/4, etc

conuiuo, -are, -aui, -atum *v tr* to entertain (someone) with food and drink, to feast (someone) 44/13, etc

conuocatio, -onis *n f* meeting, assembly, convocation 4/33, etc; **domus conuocacionis** *literally* house of convocation, a deliberative assembly, *here either* the Oxford town council 50/30 *or* the University convocation 200/37

cooperans, -antis *prp* working together, cooperating 94/32

coquina, -e *n f* kitchen 94/29

corea, -e *n f* dance, originally a round dance; often used to describe a country dance held out of doors 5/29, etc; **choraea** 209/16, etc; **correa** 5/2

cornu, -us *n nt* animal horn: 1. ink horn 8/28; 2. a horn or trumpet, originally made from animal horn, used for military signals [OLD cornu], *here apparently* indicating an instrument used for ceremonial purposes 503/17

coronator, -oris *n m* coroner, a Crown officer whose responsibilities included jurisdiction over cases of accidental or violent death 5/18, etc

corporalis, -e *adj* bodily, physical; *see* **sacramentum**

corporatus, -a, -um *adj* of or pertaining to a (civic) corporation, corporate; *see* **sitella**

corpus, -oris *n nt* body 11/1, etc; *see also* **collegium**

correa *see* **corea**

creditum, -i *n nt* debt, money owed to a person or his estate 259/8, etc

crinis, -is *n m* hair, *by extension* a wig: **crines muliebres** a woman's wig (either as representing a woman's hair or possibly as made from women's hair), *likely* used as a costume 61/31

Cristus *for* **Christus**; *see* **aedes**

cronica, -e *n f* chronicle, annal 11/18, etc [OLD chronicum]

crucifixus, -i *sbst m* the Crucified, ie, Christ 12/21

crus, -ris *n nt* 1. (lower) leg, shin 136/14, etc; 2. *by extension* leggings, hose (in punning phr **crurum tenus** *literally* as far as the legs, rendered by E 'over bootes') 364/5 [*see* OLD cruralis, DML crurale, OEDO hose *sb* 1a]

crux, -cis *n f* cross: 1. as an instrument of execution under Roman law (represented in a play) 137/33; 2. symbol of Christ's death or of the Christian faith, *often* an article of church furnishing 12/21, etc; *likely* used in a play 63/23; 3. in the name of a festival; *see* **festum**

cubicularius, -ii *n m* one with whom one shares a bedroom, room-mate 60/31, etc [*cp* DML concubicularius *with* cubicularius]

culpabilis, -e *adj* guilty (as a plea or verdict in a court) 9/26, etc

Cumbria, -ae *n f* Cumberland, name of an earldom 218/33

curia, -e *n f* (royal) court 10/33

curialis, e *adj* of or pertaining to the court, courtly 534/30

custos, -odis *n m* warden, head of a collegiate chapter or similar body such as an academic college 13/26, etc

cyrotheca *see* **chirotheca**

cythara *see* **cit(h)era**

cytharedus *see* **cithaedus**

damarium, -ii *n nt* deer-park, an enclosure in which deer are kept 111/8

damnifico, -are, -aui, -atum *v tr* to damage 12/33

Damon, -onis *n m* Damon of Syracuse, famous for his friendship with Phintias (commonly but erroneously called Pythias), *named here* as an eponymous character in the play *Damon and Pithias* 148/37, etc [OCD DAMON (I)]

Danuersius, -a, -um *adj* of or pertaining to Danvers, a family name and barony, *hence m sg as sbst* Lord Danvers 313/27

datus, -a, -um *pfp pass* dated (of a document or letter) 196/4, etc [OLD do¹]

Daviticus, -a, -um *adj* of or belonging to David (*here* as putative author of the Psalms) 146/25

de *prep with abl* 1. about, concerning 3/8m, etc; 2. (in partitive sense) of, from 7/18, etc; 3. (expressing reason) from, of 47/32; 4. (expressing source, origin, or residence) from, of 5/24, etc; *as if synonymous with* 'ab' *or* 'ex,' out of 5/27, etc; 5. (expressing motion) from, down from 8/26; 6. (expressing connection of some kind) in regard to, of 9/29, etc; 7. (as a name element, likely

originally expressing place of residence or origin) of 5/15, etc; 8. for (a period of time) 9/24; 9. (expressing instrumentality) by 3/16, etc; 10. substituting for CL genitive 32/11, etc; with titles (usually landed) 447/30, etc; with vernacular expressions 8/32, etc; 11. representing E 'of' in expressions in which CL would use an appositive 3/8, etc; 12. *in other idioms*: **de bono et malo** for good or ill 9/26–7; **de cetero** hereafter, henceforward 28/35, etc; **de claro** clear, net (of accounts) 22/27, etc; **declaro** 45/4, etc; **de facili** easily 12/31 (*written as one word*), etc; *see also* EG **declaro**

deauratus, -a, -um *adj* covered or ornamented in gold 306/7

decanto, -are, -aui, -atum *v tr* 1. to sing (used of secular music) 163/17; 2. to chant (used of liturgical music) 3/13, etc

decanus, -i *n m* 1. dean, administrative head of a cathedral chapter 92/24, etc; 2. *hence* an administrative officer in a college 13/26, etc

decem-drachmarius, -ia, -ium *adj literally* worth ten drachma, *hence* ten a penny, common, cheap 309/36 [OEDO penny B 9o]

declamatio, -onis *n f* declamation, formal speech on a given subject, *possibly* a public lecture 257/17

declaracio, -onis *n f literally* the act of making clear or explaining, *hence* explanatory discourse on a text 27/24, etc

declaro *see* **de**

declinatio, -onis *n f literally* a swerving (away), *hence* avoidance, refusal (to engage in some activity) 6/37

decollacio, -onis *n f* beheading 7/11; *see also* **dies**

decrementa, -orum *n nt* decrements, a sum of money deducted from a scholar's foundation grant to pay for his share of common provisions such as fuel 262/38, etc [OEDO decrement 3]

defacili *see* **de**

defensus, -us *n m* defence: **in defensibus** + *gen* in defence (of), as a defence (of) 107/3

delegatio, -onis *n f* act of delegating (a task or the like), assignment 200/37

delibero, -are, -aui, -atum *v tr* to give, hand over, deliver 256/17, etc

dementatus, -a, -um *pfp pass* maddened, crazed 179/4

democratia, -ae *n f* popular rule 343/12

denarius, -ii *n m* a penny, one-twelfth of a shilling 62/5, etc

depono, -onere, -osui, -ositum *v tr* 1. to remove (someone) from an office, depose 7/31, etc; 2. to depose, make a formal statement or give evidence before a court or the like 32/21, etc

deposicio, -onis *n f* deposition, removal from office 7/39

deputo, -are, -aui, -atum *v tr* to appoint (someone) to a specific task or duty 6/16, etc; *m sg as sbst* deputy judge, one delegated by a superior to hear cases on his behalf 259/4, etc

desculptus, -a, -um *pfp pass* sculpted, carved 306/6

Desdemona, -ae *n f* Desdemona, wife of Othello, *here named as* a character in a play 387/32

detractio, -onis *n f* disparagement, carping criticism 11/2, etc

deuocio, -onis *n f* piety, devotion, *hence* devout observance 4/35

Deuonius, -ia, -ium *adj* of or pertaining to Devon, a county and earldom; *m sg as sbst* the earl of Devon 313/15

deuotissime *adv* very piously, in an extremely devout manner 12/25

diaeta, -e *n f literally* a day's supply of provisions, usually foodstuffs, *hence* one's daily regimen 177/32

Diana, -e *n f* Diana, *in classical mythology* the virgin goddess of the moon and the hunt, Apollo's sister 140/3, etc; in the deliberately skewed, invented mythology of the king of beans correspondence named as the mother of Neptune 799/6 (*in form* **Dyana**)

dies, diei *n m or f* 1. day 9/16, etc; 2. day of the week: *a.* **dies dominica** 5/14, etc, *or* ~ **dominicus** 6/6, etc, Sunday; *b.* ~ **Iouis** Thursday 5/22, etc; *c.* ~ **Lune** Monday 5/17, etc; *d.* ~ **Martis** Tuesday 569/6; *e.* ~ **Mercurii** Wednesday 29/20, etc; *f.* ~ **Sabati** Saturday 9/10, etc; *g.* ~ **Veneris** Friday 8/17, etc; 3. day

as a measurement of time 6/7, etc; 4. day set aside for a special purpose: *a.* referring to one or both of the Hock days: **dies nuncupatus hocday** 23/9–10 *or* ~ **hockeday** 24/6; *b.* ~ **capituli** chapter day, day of a chapter meeting 29/10–11m; 5. a saint's day: **dies decollationis Sancti Iohannis Baptiste** the Beheading of St John the Baptist, 29 August 7/11; ~ **Innocentium** Holy Innocent's Day, 28 December 3/22, etc; ~ **Purificationis Beate Marie** the Purification of St Mary, Candlemas, 2 February 40/21–2; ~ **Sancte Marie Magdalene** St Mary Magdalene's Day, 22 July 29/25; ~ **Sancti Nicholai** St Nicholas' Day, 6 December 16/32; ~ **Sancti Vlstani** St Wulfstan's Day, 19 January 53/13; 6. feast day, festival, celebration (religious or secular): **dies festi** festive days 55/6; *hence* ~ **Circumcisionis** Circumcision Day, 1 January 70/1, etc; ~ **Epiphanie** Epiphany, 6 January 46/27, etc; ~ **Natiuitatis** Christmas Day, 25 December 67/8; ~ **Pasche** Easter Day, Sunday after the full moon on or following 21 March 38/21, etc; ~ **Pentecostes** 111/1, *or* ~ **Pent(h)ecoste** 19/30, etc Pentecost, Whit Sunday, Sunday fifty days after Easter; 7. *other idioms:* **ante paucos dies** a few days ago 149/5 (*this adv phrase should not be confused with the prep phr* **ante paucos dies** before a few days (have passed), ie, in a few days 107/13); **crastinus dies** the morrow, tomorrow 29/13; **hic dies** today 56/25; **histerna dies** yesterday 55/20; **indies** daily, every day 232/40; **postremis his diebus** *literally* in these last days, *hence* recently 387/21 [*see* OEDO *last a* 3a *and* b]

dietim *adv* on a daily basis, by the day 93/14, etc

digladior, -ari, -atus sum *v intr* to fight with swords, fence 138/31

dii, diis *forms of* deus [OLD]

diocesis, -is *n f* diocese, administrative district under the authority of a bishop 4/36m, etc; *hence* **festum diocesium** a feast day observed locally within a particular diocese 4/35–6m; **dyocesis** 4/35

diolectalis, -e *adj* of or pertaining to dialectic,

one of the arts of the trivium, the first stage in the study of the seven liberal arts required for the medieval arts degree: **libri ... diolecticales** books on dialectic 9/7, etc

dirigo, -igere, -exi, -ectum *v tr* to direct (a letter or similar document) to someone *(with dat of person)* 529/23

diruo, -ere, -i, -tum *v tr* 1. to demolish, wreck 251/6 [OLD]; 2. to dismantle a previously assembled structure 94/23, etc

Dis, Ditis *n m* Dis, one of several names for the king of the underworld in classical mythology: **a Ditis palatio ad maximi Iouis arcem** from Dis' palace to great Jove's citadel, ie, from the westernmost shore of the encircling Ocean to the top of Mt Olympus, from one end of the earth to the other 799/6–7

discrecio, -onis *n f* judgment, discretion 13/25, etc

discumbo, -mbere, -bi, -bitum *v intr* to recline (for a meal), *hence* to sit down at table 364/16; *see also* **ostrum**

discupulus, -i *n m* student, follower, *here* used in reference to Christ's disciples 177/26 [OLD discipulus]

disputacio, -onis *n f* a formal disputation, an academic exercise in which the disputant resolves a difficult problem in fields such as theology or philosophy 11/13, etc

disputo, -are, -aui, -atum *v tr* to hold a formal disputation, either as a degree exercise or as an exhibition for a distinguished visitor 233/1

disrumpo, -umpere, upi, -uptum *v tr for* dirumpo [OLD]

dissentio, -onis *n f for* dissensio [OLD]

dissertatio, -onis *n f literally* disquisition, *here apparently* used for **disputatio**, a formal disputation 141/25

dissolucio, -onis *n f* dissolution, dissolving (of a meeting or the like) 51/8

dissoluo, -uere, -ui, -utum *v tr* to dissolve (a meeting or the like) 32/23

dissuetudo, -inis *n f* disuse 29/4

distractio, -onis *n f* (mental) distraction 6/28, etc

districtius *compar adv* more strictly 13/16

diuersus, -a, -um *adj* various, divers 5/25, etc

diuillo, -are, -aui, -atum *v intr* to go away from a town, leave town 197/19m

diuinus, -a, -um *adj* 1. divine, pertaining to or suitable for God 3/6, etc; *see also* **officium**

diuus, -a, -um *adj literally* divine; used as the title of a saint, holy 46/1, etc

doctor, -oris *n m literally* a learned person, *hence* doctor, one holding the highest academic degree in one of the superior faculties (eg, theology or law), often used as a title with names 73/26, etc; **doctor in medicinis** doctor of medicine, MD 48/1; **in sacra theologia ∼** 42/17–18 *or* **sacrae theologiae ∼** 498/28, etc, doctor of sacred theology, STD

doctrina, -e *n f* teaching, *hence often in* ML (Christian) doctrine, sound teaching 10/30, etc

dodecatemorium, -ii *n nt* 1. the zodiac 308/27; 2. one of the twelve signs of the zodiac 314/35

domesticus, -a, -um *adj* of or pertaining to a household or home, domestic, *by extension* of or belonging to a college [*see* OEDO house *sb*¹ 4b]: **pubes domestica** the youth of the college 85/26; *m pl as sbst* **domestici** those belonging to or residing at a college 146/10, etc

domina, -e *n f* lady, honorific for royalty, peeress, or peer's wife 72/4, etc

dominicus, -a, -um *adj* 1. of or pertaining to the Lord *(cp* **dominus** sense 3): *f sg as sbst* Lord's Day, Sunday 36/12, etc; *see also* **dies**

dominus, -i *n m* 1. lord, a ruler 799/7 *or* a member of the nobility 102/30; **agere dominum** to act the part of a lord in a play or game, play the lord 55/41; 2. the possessor of a quality or characteristic 308/8; 3. the Lord, title of God or Christ 10/31, etc; 4. lord: *a.* honorific for church dignitaries 34/12; *b.* honorific for secular dignitaries (kings and princes 5/18, etc; peers 15/20, etc); *c.* honorific for university officials or judges and college officers 4/31, etc; 5. Sir: honorific for knight 266/37, etc; *or* honorific for university student or graduate holding a BA degree 46/33, etc; 6. *by extension* husband 308/12; 7. lord, title of a mock ruler appointed in some colleges to oversee plays and other entertainments, often at

Christmas-time 209/14, 209/17

domus, -us *n f* **domu** *and* **domo** *found as abl sg*
1. building, house, home 93/6, etc; *hence* the
lodgings of the head of a college 40/20, etc; *by
extension* a structure within a building 137/23;
2. religious house 3/24; 3. a college 11/12,
etc; 4. *by extension of sense 1* one's substance,
possessions 179/1; *see also* **conuocatio** [*see*
OEDO house *sb*[1] 4b]

Dorsetia, -e *n f* Dorset, name of a county 76/6

Dorsettus, -a, -um *adj* of or pertaining to
Dorset, a county and an earldom; *m sg as sbst*
the earl of Dorset 313/3

draco, -onis *n m literally* dragon, *by extension* the
name of a banner or streamer, perhaps in the
shape of a dragon, traditionally carried in
liturgical Rogation processions, *here apparently*
a feature of a Whitsun ale 20/19

Draperia, -ae *n f* the Drapery, the Drapers' hall
in Oxford (*see* p 1084, endnote to Bodl.: MS.
Twyne 4 pp 32–3) 5/29, etc

duellum, -i *n nt* duel, a combat between two
persons 139/12

duodena, -e *n f* a group of twelve, one dozen
93/34

duodena, -orum *n nt* a group of twelve, one
dozen 93/33, etc

duplex, -icis *adj* double 305/35; *see also* **festum,
uestis**

dupplicatus, -a, -um *adj* lined (of garments)
8/34, etc

dux, -cis *n m* 1. leader 180/19, etc; 2. duke, ruler
of a duchy 261/14, etc; **dux Athenarum** duke
of Athens, a late medieval title for Theseus as
king of Athens 138/28; 3. duke, highest rank
of the hereditary peerage 10/33, etc

Dyana *see* **Diana**

dynastes, -ae *n m* nobleman, peer 894/21

dyocesis *see* **diocesis**

ebdomas *see* **(h)ebdomas**

ecclesia, -e *n f* church: 1. a specific church or
church building 4/34, etc; **ecclesia parochialis**
parish church 42/19–20, etc; 2. the church as a
corporate or spiritual body 3/6, etc; 3. **ecclesia**

Christi Christ Church, both a cathedral and
a college in Oxford 146/40, etc

ecclesiasticus, -a, -um *adj* ecclesiastical, of or
pertaining to the church 6/7; *m pl as sbst*
ecclesiastics, clerics, ie, those in holy orders
92/21; *see also* **officium**

Effinghamius, -ia, -um *adj* of or pertaining to
Effingham, the name of a barony, *hence m sg
as sbst* Lord Effingham 313/28

elabor, -bi, -psus sum *v intr literally* to slip away,
escape 139/6; *pfp with pass sense* elapsed, past
(of time) 146/41, etc

electio, -onis *n f* choice, election 799/21, etc;
elexio 69/12m

elector, -oris *n m* elector, *here* one of a group
entitled to elect St John's Christmas Prince
342/39, etc

electorius, -a, -um *adj* of or pertaining to an
elector, electoral 343/11

eleemosina, -e *n f* alms, charitable gift 6/22

elemosinaria, -ie *f sbst* almonry, department of a
chapter or similar corporation that dispensed
alms and sometimes also conducted a school
13/36; **elimosinaria** 14/13; *see* **episcopus**

elexio *see* **electio**

emendatio, -onis *n f* repair, act of mending
280/42, etc

emendo, -are, -aui, -atum *v tr* to mend, repair
105/9, etc

encomium, -ii *n nt* praise 209/19

ephydrias, -dis *n f literally* she who is above or
upon the water, *hence* water nymph, Nereid
314/1 [*see* LSJ ἐπί *(sense G)* + ὑδριάς]

epilogus, -i *n m* epilogue, a speech delivered at
the conclusion of a play 180/4, etc

epiphania, -e *n f* epiphany, revelation, *here* the
liturgical festival commemorating the revealing
of Christ to the gentiles (Mt 2.1–12), commemorated on 1 January 46/26, etc

episcopus, -i *n m* 1. bishop, member of the
highest of the major orders of clergy, the other
two being deacon (diaconus) and priest (presby-
ter *or* sacerdos) 34/12, etc; 2. boy bishop, a boy,
originally a choirboy in a cathedral or other
collegiate church or a student in an almonry

school, chosen to act as a mock bishop in liturgical and other observances on the feast of St Nicholas or of the Holy Innocents 16/33, etc; **episcopus Diui Nicholai** 63/18 *or* ⁓ **Nic(h)olai** 15/27, etc, (St) Nicholas bishop; ⁓ **elemosinarie** 13/36 *or* ⁓ **elimosinarie** 14/13 almonry bishop

eques, -itis *n m* knight 282/8, etc

equus, -i *n m* horse; *see* **magister**

erga *prep* 1. *of relationship* toward, with regard to 28/31, etc; 2. *of purpose* for, against (referring to a future event) 18/21

ergastulum, -i *n nt in* CL a prison farm for 'problem' slaves, *hence in* AL *by extension* a prison, *thence* a castle (as the site of a gaol) 37/21 (rendered by E 'castell' on 37/16)

Erotium, -ii *n nt* Erotium, the name of a character in Plautus' *Menaechmi* 178/16

essedus, -i *n m* carriage, coach 306/24

Essexia, -ae *n f* Essex, name of an earldom 180/29

ethnicus, -a, -um *adj* gentile, pagan 178/31

Etonensis, -e *adj* of or belonging to Eton, a town in Berkshire 30/12

euangelium, -ii *n nt literally* 1. gospel, one of the four New Testament books narrating the birth, ministry, death, and resurrection of Christ 179/3; 2. *in pl* a gospel book, ie, one containing all four canonical gospels, used in swearing oaths 76/28

Euclio, -onis *n m* Euclio, the main character in Plautus' play *Aulularia* 178/14

exagito, -are, -aui, -atum *v tr* 1. to disturb, harass 48/30; 2. to bait (eg, a bear) with dogs 37/22

exaltacio, -onis *n f literally* act of lifting up or raising, *here* in the name of a feast day, the Exaltation of the Holy Cross, often known as Holy Cross Day, 14 September 11/39

excerceo *see* **exerceo**

excessiue *adv* inordinately, excessively 40/21, etc

excessus, -us *n m* excessive behaviour, acts of misconduct, crime 11/4, etc

excommunicatio, -onis *n f* excommunication, ecclesiastical penalty under which the guilty party was punished by exclusion from the sacraments and especially the reception of

communion 5/4; at times further disabilities were imposed, such as exclusion from all social intercourse with other church members; this more severe form is also called greater excommunication: **maior excommunicatio** 5/2

execror, -ari, -atum *v tr see* ex(s)ecror [OLD]

executor, -oris *n m* executor, a man who oversees the due execution of the various clauses and bequests in a will and is accountable to the ecclesiastical authorities for so doing 196/3, etc

exequor, -qui, -cutus sum *v tr* 1. *treated as deponent* to carry out (an order), perform (a task or obligation) 12/6, etc; 2. *treated as pass* to be carried out, performed 12/8

exerceo, -ere, -ui, -itum *v tr* 1. to carry out, perform (an action or activity) 47/33, etc; 2. to pursue (an activity), devote attention (to) 48/28, etc; 3. to spend time at, frequent 11/28, etc; **excerceo** 90/7 [OLD exerceo]

exercitia, -orum *n nt* (academic) exercise, eg, a formal disputation or oration 218/16

exhibicio, -onis *n f* exhibition, a bursary or similar payment made to a student for his support 62/5

existo, -ere, exiti *v intr for* ex(s)isto [OLD]

exnunc *adv* from now on 5/5

exonero, -are, -aui, -atum *v tr* 1. to discharge (someone) from (an obligation) 74/10; 2. to discharge a debt or bill 114/2, etc

expello, -ellere, -uli, -ulsum *v tr* to throw (someone) out (eg, from a house) 371/13; *hence* to expel (a student) 48/35

expensus, -a, -um *pfp pass* spent (of sums of money): *f sg as sbst* that for which money is spent, expense 7/10, etc (*or nt as sbst* 188/25m, 189/33); *also in idiom* **expense facte** expenses incurred 43/18, etc

expositio, -onis *n f* exposition, explanation, *specifically* scriptural exegesis 60/19, etc

expulsio, -onis *n f* removal, expulsion: **expulsio a communis** removal from commons 28/34–5; **expulcio a communis** 40/28–9, 40/38–9

exspatior, -ari, -atus sum *v intr* to travel, journey 142/20, etc

extendo, -dere, -di, -sum *v tr literally* to extend, stretch out 218/9; *in idiom* **se extendere ad**

to amount to (of sums or money or the like) 16/33

extermino, -are, -aui, -atum *v tr* to put (someone or something) out of bounds, *hence* to expel 530/11

exto, -are, extiti *v intr for* ex(s)to [OLD]

extraneus, -a, -um *adj literally* external, foreign, *hence* from another college or town 41/37, etc

extunc *adv* from then on, thereafter 414/14, etc

faba, -e *n f* bean; *see* **regnum, rex**

fabula, -ae *n f* 1. *literally* story, tale 4/6, 136/21?, 141/2, 177/35?, 305/4; **aniles fabulae** old wives' tales 179/2; **fabula militis** *The Knight's Tale* 136/8; 2. *hence* a play 136/21?, 145/30, 148/37, 177/35?, 178/2, 178/3, 178/12, 178/13m, 306/14, 307/8, 307/17, 307/33, 308/25, 428/1, 894/19; 3. fable 141/9

factura, -e *n f* the act of making or constructing 61/30

facultas, -atis *n f* 1. ability, faculty 106/28; 2. *in pl* means, resources 137/28; 3. academic discipline, faculty 52/18–19, etc; *see also* **ars**

faelix *see* **felix**

familia, -e *n f* household 7/18

familiaritas, -tatis *n f* familiarity, over- or inappropriate friendliness 28/31

famulus, -i *n m* 1. servant, *especially* one who is a member of the 'familia,' the extended household or 'family' that comprises everyone living under the authority of the head of the house, household servant 36/12, etc; 2. *by extension* one who stands in an analogous relationship: *a.* workman in the service of a master craftsman, possibly living on his premises 100/21, etc; *b.* a personal servant of some kind 106/26

farculum *see* **ferculum**

fatidica, -ae *sbst f* seeress, (female) soothsayer 315/1

Felix, -icis *n m* Felix, the name of several saints, *here* an early Christian martyr whose feast was celebrated on 30 August 895/4

felix, -icis *adj* happy, fortunate, successful 232/39 (*in superl* **faelicissimus**), etc; **faelix** 343/22, etc; **foelix** 180/31

felo, -onis *n m* a felon, one who has committed a felony 8/16, etc; **felo de se** one who has committed suicide (*literally* a felon of self) 258/38, etc

felonia, -e *n f* felony, a serious and premeditated crime reserved to royal courts, in particular to the assizes 9/25, etc

felonice *adv* in a felonious manner, ie, so as to involve a felony offence 8/27, etc

feodum, -i *n nt* fee assessed for a particular service or procedure 192/5, etc

ferculum, -i *n nt* 1. (prepared) dish, usually of meat or fish 53/14, etc; 2. course (of a meal) 217/37, etc; 3. a mess, a group of persons who regularly take meals together at the same table and from the same dish 46/26 [*see* OEDO mess *sb* 4a]; **farculum** 59/12, etc (*all in sense 1*)

feria, -e *n f* 1. holiday, festival 369/34, etc; *in idioms*: **ferie natalicie** 87/27, etc, *or* ~ **natalitie Redemptoris** 209/11–12 *or* ~ **Natiuitatis Domini** 150/39–40 the Christmas season, the period from Christmas (25 December) to Epiphany (6 January); 2. a day of the week: **feria secunda tercia & quarta** Monday, Tuesday, and Wednesday 11/38; 3. a working day 55/7

festiuitas, -atis *n f* feast day, festival: **festivitas Clementina** the feast of St Clement, 23 November 799/24

festum, -i *n nt* feast: 1. celebration 261/14: **festum bursariorum** the bursars' feast, an annual celebration at Magdalen College 170/17, etc; 2. festival 4/29, etc: **festum maius duplex** major double, one of four classes of feasts designated as double because of the way in which the office was said or sung on those festivals 11/12; **festum principale** principal feast, a primary feast commemorating a central mystery of faith (eg, Christmas, the Incarnation) or the death of a saint 11/11–12 [*see* CEO Feasts, Ecclesiastical]; 3. a specific feast day or festival (secular or religious): **festa natalitia** the Christmas season, the period from Christmas (25 December) to Epiphany (6 January) 79/26, etc; **festum animarum** feast of (All) Souls, 2 November 162/19; ~ **Anunciationis**

Mariae the Annunciation, Lady Day, 25 March 162/33–4; ~ **Assumptionis Beatae Mariae** feast of the Assumption of St Mary, 15 August 5/14; ~ **Cineritium** Ash Wednesday, the first day of Lent 177/31; ~ **Circumcisionis** feast of the Circumcision, 1 January 25/4, etc; ~ **Epiphaniae** the Epiphany, 6 January 216/26; ~ **Exaltationis Sancte Crucis** the Exaltation of the Holy Cross, Holy Cross Day, 14 September 11/39; ~ **Hocktyd(e)** 39/13, etc, *or* ~ **Hoctyd(e)** 39/4, etc, *or* ~ **Hoktyde** 54/35 Hocktide, the second Monday and Tuesday after Easter; ~ **Innocencium** 3/20 *or* ~ **Sanctorum Innocencium** 11/37–8, etc, feast of the (Holy) Innocents, 28 December; ~ **Inuencionis Sancte Crucis** feast of the Invention (or Finding) of the Holy Cross, 3 May 11/39; ~ **Natiuitatis** Christmas, 25 December 162/19, etc; ~ **Omnium Sanctorum** feast of All Saints, 1 November 166/24, etc; ~ **Pentechoste** 22/15, etc, *or* ~ **Pentecoste** 18/27, etc, *or* ~ **Pentecostes** 16/17, etc, *or* ~ **Pentecosten** 23/10–11 Pentecost, Whit Sunday, Sunday fifty days following Easter; ~ **Purificacionis (Beate Marie)** the Purification (of St Mary), Candlemas, 2 February 338/39; ~ **Sancte Anne** feast of St Anne, 26 July 22/30; ~ **Sancte Katerine** feast of St Catherine, 25 November 5/1, etc; ~ **Sancte Magdalene** feast of St (Mary) Magdalene, 22 July 12/3; ~ **Sancti Andree Apostoli** feast of St Andrew the Apostle, 30 November 11/40; ~ **Sancti Bartholomei** feast of St Bartholomew, 24 August 12/1; ~ **Sancti Iacobi Apostoli** feast of St James the Apostle, 25 July 12/1; ~ **Sancti Iohannis Apostoli** feast of St John the Apostle, 27 December 11/37; ~ **Sancti Luce** feast of St Luke, 18 October 12/2; ~ **Sancti Marci Apostoli** feast of St Mark the Apostle, 25 April 12/1; ~ **Sancti Martini** feast of St Martin, Martinmas, 11 November 12/2; ~ **Sancti Mathei** feast of St Matthew, 21 September 12/2; ~ **Sancti Mathie Apostoli** feast of St Mathias the Apostle, 24 February 11/40, etc; ~ **Sancti Michaelis** feast of St Michael, Michaelmas, 29 September 12/2,

etc; ~ **Sancti Nicholai** feast of St Nicholas, 6 December 5/1, etc; ~ **Sancti Stephani** feast of St Stephen, 26 December 11/37; ~ **Sancti Thome Apostoli** feast of St Thomas the Apostle, 21 December 11/40; ~ **Sancti Thome Martiris** feast of St Thomas Becket, 29 December 11/38; ~ **Sanctorum Philippi et Iacobi** feast of Sts Philip and James, 1 May 12/1; ~ **Sanctorum Simonis et Iude** feast of Sts Simon and Jude, 28 October 12/2; ~ **Translacionis Sancti Swithuni** feast of the Translation of St Swithun, 15 July 12/2–3; ~ **Translacionis Sancti Thome** feast of the Translation of St Thomas Becket, 7 July 11/40; ~ **Trinitatis** feast of the Holy Trinity, ie, Trinity Sunday, the Sunday after Pentecost 111/7

fictiuncula, -ae *n f* a slight fiction, pretence 305/19

fidedignus, -a, -um *adj* worthy of confidence or trust 799/16

fideiussor, -oris *n m* guarantor 74/11

fideliter *adv* 1. faithfully, in a trustworthy manner 196/3, etc; 2. faithfully, exactly 799/24

fides, -ei *n f* 1. belief, conviction: **ultra fidem** beyond belief 309/10; 2. *hence* religious faith 196/6, etc; 3. oath 42/9, etc; 4. faithfulness, trustworthiness 139/33; 5. credit, credibility 271/5 (although this is likely the sense intended by Juvenal in the verse quoted on 271/4–5, in the context of the punning speech in which it is quoted the speaker is punning on 'fides,' 'fidicen' (fiddler), and 'fidis' (fiddlestring); 6. **fide iussit** *see* fideiubeo [OLD]

fidicen, -inis *n m literally* a lyre player, *by extension* a fiddler 242/9, etc

filia, -e *n f* daughter: 1. *literally* 179/6, etc; 2. of a symbolic or spiritual relationship between a bishop and nuns within his diocese 3/7

filius, -ii *n m* son 10/28, etc; *hence* **filii hominum** sons of men, usually a periphrasis for human beings but in this passage (alluding to Mt 15.26 and Mk 7.27) a periphrasis for children 6/23

finis, -is *n f* end 51/20, etc; *hence* a term 488/2

firmarius, -ii *n m* tenant at farm, lessee 33/31, etc [*see* OEDO farm *sb*²]

fiscus, -i *n m* treasury 512/18

fistulans, -antis *prp* playing upon a pipe, piping 439/28, etc

fistulator, -oris *n m literally* one who plays upon a 'fistula,' piper, *probably* a generic term for one who plays a wind instrument 10/17

flagellifer, -eri *n m literally* lash-bearer, *hence* madman; *see* **Aiax**

flagisiquus, -a, -um *adj* shameful, disgraceful 56/9

flatilis, -e *adj* produced by blowing; *see* **musica**

fluctans, -antis *prp* floating; *see* **insula**

foelicitas, -atis *n f over-correction of* felicitas [OLD]

foelix *see* **felix**

foemina, -e *n f over-correction of* femina [OLD]

foetura, -e *n f* child, offspring 85/33 [OLD fetura]

folium, -ii *n nt* 1. leaf (of a branch) 5/4; 2. leaf, folio (of a book) 44/7, etc

forensis, -e *adj* foreign, not native, *hence comm pl as sbst* non-natives, outsiders 503/16

forinsecus, -a, -um *adj* external; *see* **colloquium**

forisfactus, -a, -um *pfp pass* forfeited (of sums of money or the like) 259/9

fortuna, -e *n f* fortune, luck 85/26, etc; sometimes personified 347/20 (as part of a series of multilingual puns on the E surnames Case and Tucker (*see* **Τυχεϱος**)), etc

fortunatus, -a, -um *adj* fortunate, lucky, blessed; *see* **Alba Fortunata, Τυχεϱος**

frater, -tris *n m* brother: 1. *literally* 799/16, etc; 2. *by extension* a fellow member of the same community, *hence* member of the Franciscan order 3/6

Frauncia, -e *n f* France 196/6, etc

frons, -dis *n f literally* foliage, *hence* a garland of leaves or flowers 137/6

Gallia, -ae *n f literally* Gaul, *here used as* a name for contemporary France 218/14, etc

Gallicus, -a, -um *adj* French 315/13

gardianus, -i *n m* warden, guardian, *hence* a churchwarden 495/11, etc

gaudimonium, -ii *n nt* gaudy, a festive meal often held annually in a college in commemoration of some important event or anniversary 71/1, etc [*see* OEDO gaudy *sb* 4 *and* 5]

gaudium, -ii *n nt* 1. joy, happiness 128/21, etc; 2. gaudy, a festive meal often held annually in a college in commemoration of some important event or anniversary 8/5 [*see* OEDO gaudy *sb* 4 *and* 5]

Geminus, -i *n m literally* a twin, *here* the name of the title character of the play *Geminus Campanus* 135/30, etc

generalis, -e *adj* general, common; *see* **commissarius**

generosus, -i *n m* gentleman 125/16, etc

genuflecto, -ctere, -xi, -xum *v tr* to cause (someone) to kneel 8/23

gerens *see* **uicis**

gladiator, -oris *n m literally* a gladiator, *hence* swordsman, fencer 512/13, etc

gladiatorius, -a, -um *adj literally* of or pertaining to a gladiator or gladiatorial shows, *hence* of or pertaining to fencing; *see* **ludus**

globi, -orum *n m either* globes (ie, a set of terrestrial and celestial globes) *or* balls for playing bowls, bowls 279/37 [*DML* globus *and* OEDO globe *sb*]

Golias, -e (*abl* **Gole**) *n m* Golias, *either* the Vulgate spelling of the name Goliath, a Philistine warrior killed by David (*see* 1 Kgs 17) *or* the name of the legendary patron of the goliards and their verse; given the deliberately skewed nature of the mythological references in this text, the reference could be to either or to both 799/22

graduatus, -a, -um *adj* having graduated: **scholaris … graduatus** graduate student, one who is already a bachelor in one of the faculties and still pursuing a higher degree 512/15–17; **scholaris … non graduati** undergraduate student, one who is not yet a bachelor in any faculty 512/15–16

grammatica, -e *n f* grammar, one of the arts of the trivium, the first stage in the study of the seven liberal arts required for the medieval arts degree 54/4, etc

grammaticalis, -e *adj* of or pertaining to grammar: **libri grammaticales** grammar books 9/2, etc

granditas, -atis *n f* size, grandeur 137/9

gratanter *adv* gratefully 63/39, etc

gratia, -e *n f* 1. mercy, forgiveness, favour 194/28; **gratia ex officio**, *literally* forgiveness as a courtesy, is rendered 'a groat out of mine office' as part of a punning speech on 270/28–9; 2. favour, goodwill 529/27; *hence* **in gratiam** (+ *gen*) to oblige (someone) 217/37; 3. *hence* grace, divine favour 196/5, etc; 4. *by extension of sense 3* grace, a divine gift operating in human beings to sanctify, regenerate, and strengthen (used in conventional salutation at opening of a letter) 3/8; 5. thanks 232/37, etc; **gratiarum actio** thanksgiving 11/8, etc; **gratias agere** to thank 63/39, etc; **gratias habere** 127/20 *or* **habere ~** 107/10 to be thankful; 6. *in abl + gen of gd, expressing purpose* for the sake of, so as (to do something) 11/16, etc

gratis *adv* freely, without penalty or payment 481/32, etc

grauamen, -inis *n nt* injury, harm, disturbance 13/20

gubernator, -oris *n m literally* steersman, pilot, *hence* organizer, ringleader 8/18

guerrinus, -a, -um *adj* warlike 8/16

gynaecaeus, -a, -um *adj* of or pertaining to women, female 309/10; *nt sg as sbst* **gynaecaeum** a section set aside or reserved for women 306/22

habitaculum, -i *n nt* dwelling, *hence* **scaenicum habitaculum** stage house, part of the traditional scenery used for Roman comedy 306/11

hacha, -e *n f* axe 6/4

hastiludium, -ii *n nt literally* a sport with spears, *hence* joust, tournament 529/32

(h)ebdomas, -de *or* **dis** *n f* week 6/6, etc; **ebdomas Pasche** Easter week, ie, Easter Sunday and its octave 11/39; **ebdomas ... Pentecostes** Pentecost week, ie, Pentecost Sunday and its octave 11/39

Hector, -oris *n m* Hector, a hero of the Trojan War, *here named as* a character in the play *Ajax Flagellifer* 308/13

heraldicus, -a, -um *adj* of or pertaining to a herald, heraldic; *see* **ars**

Herefordensis, -is *sbst f* Hereford, name of a diocese 34/13

heresis, -is *n f* heresy, heterodox teaching on some point(s) of Christian doctrine 103/32

Hermes, -ae *n m* Hermes, the messenger and herald of the gods, a type of eloquence 314/11

Hibernia, -e *n f* Ireland 196/6, etc

Hibernicus, -a, -um *adj* Irish 315/13

Hispania, -ae *n f* the kingdom of Spain 136/1

historia, -e *n f* 1. *literally* story, account, history 60/25, etc; 2. *by extension* a visual representation of a story 28/17 (*in form* **istoria**)

historialis, -e *adj* historical: **historicalis comedia** a historical comedy (*here* one set during the Roman Empire) 135/35

historiola, -ae *n f* little story, a short tale 305/4

histrio, -onis *n m* 1. *in AL usually* entertainer, *probably* one whose entertainment included music of some kind, often with a named royal, noble, or other patron 14/21, etc; 2. *in early modern AL usage (influenced by CL)* actor, player 162/31, etc

homo, -inis *n m* 1. *literally* human being, person 6/23, etc; this is the sense originally intended in the quotation from Virgil's *Aeneid* on 270/16 but the speaker quoting is apparently punning on L 'homines' and E 'ominous'; 2. *used as a synonym for* 'uir,' *usually referring to hired labourers, porters, and the like* man, male human being 28/16, etc

hospicium, -ii *n nt* 1. lodging, dwelling 5/15, etc; *specifically* the lodgings of a college officer 407/29; 2. hospice, hospital: **Hospitium Amatorum** *literally* lovers' hospice, translating the title of a play, *Love's Hospital* 894/8–9

humilis, -e *adj* humble, lowly (as embodying a Christian virtue) 3/7

humiliter *adv* in a humble manner 209/21

humor, -oris *n m* humour: **quatuor humores** the four humours, the four primary materials (earth, air, fire, and water) from which the human body and all other earthly things were believed to be made 308/29 [OLD umor]

iaculator *see* **ioculator**

idea, -ae *n f* form, appearance 308/17

idioma, -atis *n nt* manner of speaking, especially one characteristic of a region or its people 307/35;

hence a particular language: **ydioma maternum** mother tongue 27/28

Iesuita, -ae *n m* a Jesuit 178/25

ignis, -is *n m* fire, a celebratory occasion marked by the lighting of a fire around which a group gathered 11/15, etc; **ignis capitularis** 30/17–18m, etc, *or* ~ **capituli** 30/17 chapter fire, such a fire held by a college chapter; **ignis magistrorum regentium** 29/2–4m *or* ~ **regens** 57/34m *or* ~ **regentium** 29/3, etc, regents' fire, such a fire held by the regent masters in a college; 2. *by extension in pl* the glowing coals or embers in a fire 270/4

ignitegium, -ii *n nt* curfew, time at which fires are banked or extinguished 11/9, etc

immediate *adv* immediately, at once 11/13, etc; **inmediate** 27/22

immorigerus, -a, -um *adj* disobliging, disobedient 530/12

imperpetuum *adv for* in perpetuum [*OLD* perpetuus]

impono, -onere, -osui, -ositum *v tr* 1. to place or lay upon or over 137/4; 2. to fix, impose 136/2; 3. *hence* to impose a tax, to levy 282/7; 4. to assign, confer, *hence* to bestow (a sum of money), pay out 237/22, etc [*see DML* imponere 19 *and OLD* impono 14]

impraesentia *adv* at the present, now 107/12

imprecor, -ari, -atus sum *v intr (+ dat)* to curse, ill-wish (someone): *in impersonal construction* **uae sit eis imprecatum** woe betide them! 6/23–4

inaduertencia, -e *n f* carelessness, inattention 12/27

incarceratio, -onis *n f* imprisonment, a judicial sentence of imprisonment 5/6, etc

incarcero, -are, -aui, -atum *v tr* to imprison, impose a sentence of imprisonment 7/37, etc

incautus, -a, -um *adj either* imprudent *or* unsafe 12/30, 12/37

inclaresco, -escere, -ui *v intr* to grow bright, shine 232/40

incontinenti *adv* at once, without delay 77/1

incrementum, -i *n nt literally* growth, increase, *hence* the process by which something is increased, intake; *here by extension* proceeds, income 33/3

incumbens, -entis *prp* resting on, being supported upon 306/1

incurro, -rere, -ri, -sum *v intr* to incur, bring (a penalty) upon oneself 27/28

indempnitas, -tatis *n f* freedom from harm, safety 12/35

indictatus, -a, -um *pfp pass* indicted 8/13

indies *see* **dies**

indiscretus, -a, -um *adj* foolish, ill-considered 32/21, etc

induco, -cere, -xi, -ctum *v tr* 1. to bring in, introduce (eg, a witness) 42/2, etc; 2. to induct (someone) to a post or office 45/28

inexpectato *adv* unexpectedly, without warning 308/20

informo, -are, -aui, -atum *v tr* to make (something) known, to inform (someone about something) 10/29; *hence* to teach 54/12, etc

infra *adv* 1. below, lower down a page 50/29m; 2. within 13/21

infra *prep* within 1. of space 6/29, etc; 2. *by extension* of the boundaries of civil authority 194/27, etc; 3. of time 54/7, etc

infrascriptus, -a, -um *pfp pass* written within 11/37

ingero, -rere, -ssi, -stum *v tr* to place (something) before one's notice, bring to one's attention 894/22

ingratitudo, -inis *n f* ingratitude, ungratefulness 45/38

inhabilitans, -antis *prp* making unsuitable, disqualifying 7/35

iniunctio, -onis *n f* order, injunction 28/30m, etc

inmediate *see* **immediate**

Innocentes, -ium *sbst m* the (Holy) Innocents, the children of Bethlehem killed by Herod in an attempt to kill the infant Jesus (Mt 2.16–18), commemorated liturgically on 28 December 3/20, etc

inobediens, -ntis *adj* disobedient 3/28

inquietacio, -onis *n f* disturbance, agitation 28/34, etc

inquisitio, -onis *n f* inquest, a judicial inquiry made by a coroner into the cause of a death 5/20

insedeo, -edere, -edi, -essum *v intr (+ dat)* to sit upon 307/21

insensissimus, -a, -um *superl adj* completely unperceived by one's senses, completely unnoticed by one *(with dat of person)* 308/13

instans, -ntis *prp* (of dates) present, instant, *hence* **instanti** at this time 799/25

institutor, -oris *n m* teacher, instructor 86/2

instrumentum, -i *n nt* (musical) instrument 5/26, etc; **instrumentum musicale** 28/36 *or* ~ **musicum** 6/27, etc, musical instrument

insula, -e *n f* island, *here* in the translation of a play title: **insula fluctuans in fixam conversa** *The Floating Island Made Fixed* 893/31

insultus, -us *n m* attack, assault 5/35, etc [*from* insulto *OLD*]

interloquutor, -oris *n m literally* one who takes part in a conversation, *hence* speaking part, speaker 268/30

interludium, -i *n nt* interlude, a form of popular pastime or entertainment, sometimes used as synonym for 'ludus' 43/19, etc

intermedium, -ii *sbst nt* the mid-point, the middle: **in intermedio** (+ *dat*) in or on the middle (of) 12/18

intimans, -antis *prp* making known, informing 799/24

intrinsecus, -a, -um *adj* internal, private 3/24

intro, -are, -aui, -atum 1. *v intr* to go in, enter 9/16, etc; 2. *v tr in legal idiom* to enter into, take formal legal possession of (property or the like) 259/17

introitus, -us *n m* entry: 1. a hostel for students and other members of the university 9/1; 2. a formal entering into a city or the like 314/40 [*see OEDO* entry 1b *and* 8]

inuencio, -onis *n f* act of discovering, *hence* **inuencio … sancte Crucis** the Invention, ie, finding, of the Holy Cross by the mother of Constantine the Great, commemorated on 3 May 11/39

inuenio, -nire, -ni, -ntum *v tr* 1. to find 8/38, etc; 2. to find, to determine by investigation 3/18, etc; 3. to acquire, *hence* **nomen inuenire** to take one's name 85/24

inuito, -are, -aui, -atum *v tr* 1. to entertain 566/32; 2. to invite 51/15, etc; *hence in idiom* **non invitantes seipsos** (*literally* not having invited themselves) not having given warning of their arrival 36/27 [*see OEDO* invite *v* 1a]

Ioannensis *see* **Iohannensis**

iocale, -is *sbst nt* valuable or precious object, treasure 47/17 [*see DML* jocalis]

Iocasta, -ae *n f* Jocasta, the mother, and later the wife, of Oedipus, *here named as* a play character 178/17

iocor, -ari, -atus sum *v intr literally* to jest, joke, *hence* to engage in an amusing pastime, to sport 6/35

iocularis, -e *adj* of or pertaining to pastime or sport, entertaining 55/7, 56/29

ioculator, -oris *n m* juggler, entertainer 48/32 (*in form* **iaculator**); sometimes one under expressed royal or noble patronage (then possibly a synonym of **histrio** *sense 1*) 72/20

iocus, -i *n m (nt in pl) in CL* jest, joke (usually verbal), *hence in AL* sport, pastime 55/5

Iohannensis, -e *adj* of or pertaining to St John or a foundation named for him: **Ioannensis collegium** St John's College 314/40; *hence m pl as sbst* **Iohannenses** the men of St John's College 308/25

Iouis *see* **Iuppiter**

irregularitas, -atis *n f* a breach of canon law sufficiently serious to impede a priest from exercising his office, *here especially* one arising from exercising a judicial role 7/25, etc [*see CEO* irregularity]

irrotulamentum, -i *n nt* enrolment (of an indenture) 491/18

Isiacus, -a, -um *adj* of or pertaining to the Isis, the river flowing through Oxford; *see* **Arcadia, Arcas**

istoria *see* **historia**

iter, itineris *n nt* way, route 55/21; *hence* **iter habere** to make one's way 232/32

Iudaicus, -a, -um *adj* of or pertaining to Judea or its inhabitants, Jewish; *see* **bellum**

iudicans, -antis *sbst m* judge 495/17

Iulius, -a, -um *adj* Julian, pertaining to the

Julian gens or one of its members, *hence* imperial, princely 310/14

Iulius Caesar, Iulii Caesaris *n m* Gaius Julius Caesar (*c* 102–44 BC), the Roman dictator, *here named as* a character in the play *Caesar Interfectus* 178/17

iunior, -ius *compar adj* 1. junior, lesser 51/14, etc; *m pl as sbst* juniors, junior members (of a college or the like) 11/11, etc; 2. *hence* the younger of two persons having the same name or surname 492/4

Iuppiter, Iouis *n m* Jupiter, Jove, chief deity of the Roman pantheon whose name was also given to the fifth planet 799/7, etc; *with* 'dies' *understood* **Iouis** Thursday 42/34, etc

iuramentum, -i *n nt* oath 7/2, etc

iurator, -oris *n m* juror 5/21, etc

iuratus, -i *sbst m literally* one who has sworn an oath, *hence* witness 47/32

ius, iuris *n f* 1. law 77/1; 2. right, one's due 57/27, etc; *hence* one's rightful property or possession 259/7, etc; 3. **ecclesiastica iura** rites of the church 6/7

iusta, -e *n f* joust 529/24, etc

iusticiarius, -ii *n m* judge, justice (eg, of the peace or of assizes) 9/24; once in full formal title: **iusticiarius domini regis ad pacem in comitatu predicto conseruandam assignatus** the king's justice appointed to keep the peace in the aforesaid county 8/14–15

kalendas *see* **calendas**

laesiuncula, -ae *n f* slight hurt, small injury 305/30

laicalis, -e *adj* of or pertaining to the laity, laical 47/33

laicus, -i *n m* layman, one who is not in orders of any kind 9/23

Lancastria, -e *n f* Lancaster, name of a dukedom 10/33

larua, -e *n f* 1. *literally* an evil spirit, spectre 177/30?; 2. *hence* a mask, worn in unidentified entertainments or pastimes 5/3, 177/30?

laruatus, -a, -um *adj* wearing masks, masked 62/8; *nt sg as sbst* a masque 894/36

latomus, -i *n m* stonemason 168/37

latus, -a, -um *adj* broad, wide: **fons latus pedibus tribus** (*literally* a spring three feet wide) is rendered 'a fountaine to wash three mens leges' on 364/3–4, punning on 'latus' and 'lautus' (washed) as well as on the two senses of 'pes' (a foot)

lauticia, -ie *n f* luxurious entertainment, sumptuous feast 44/13, etc

lauticinia, -ie *n f* luxurious entertainment, sumptuous feast 49/20; **lauticina** 50/31

le form of the Romance definite art usually used to signal the beginning of an English word or phr in an otherwise Latin passage 14/38, etc; although **le** is formally singular it is not always in agreement with the noun it modifies: **le weates** 166/23

Lecestrensis, -e *adj* of or belonging to Leicester, a county and earldom 180/37, etc; *f sg as sbst* the earldom of Leicester 200/5

Lecestria, -ae *n f* Leicester, name of an earldom 146/43, etc; **Leicestria** 162/31

lectica, -ae *n f* bier 140/24

lectio, -onis *n f* 1. (public) reading, act of reading aloud 60/19, etc; 2. academic lecture 257/15, etc

lectura, -e *n f* (public) reading, act of reading aloud 27/30

legalis, -e *adj* lawful; *see* **moneta**

legatus, -i *n m* legate, ambassador 135/36, etc

lego, -ere, legi, lectum *v tr* 1. to read (aloud) 27/24, etc; 2. *hence* to read (a subject), to study: **medicinam ... legere** to read medicine 313/20; 3. *by extension of sense 1* to read or recite (eg, a liturgical office) 12/10

leguleius, -ii *n m literally* specialist in legal minutiae, *hence* a pettifogger, a hack lawyer 309/35

Leicestria *see* **Lecestria**

leo, -onis *n m* lion, *here apparently* a banner depicting a lion (by analogy with **draco** a dragon banner) 20/19

leporarius, -ii *n m* a dog trained to hunt hares, *hence* a greyhound 6/25

libertas, -atis *n f* 1. liberty, freedom 180/11, etc; 2. *hence collectively* the liberty of a borough, ie, its privileged legal and administrative status, and especially its right to self-government and its own courts, enjoyed only by those residents who were burgesses 192/4, etc; *or* the liberty of the university, especially its right to self-government and self-discipline by its own officers, courts, and procedures 529/25

libra, -e *n f* 1. pound (currency denomination) 9/9, etc; 2. pound (measurement of weight) 21/12, etc

licentia, -e *n f* permission, freedom (to do something), *hence* formal permission, licence 98/23, etc

licentio, -are, -aui, -atum *v tr* to allow, permit, license, *especially* to license (someone) to lecture in a given subject 427/16

lichnus, -i *n m for* lychnus [OLD]

liciscus, -i *n m* dog, hound 37/23

Linliacus, -i *n m* Lindley, a town in Leicestershire 428/35

linthiamen, -inis *n nt* length or piece of linen cloth 8/34 [OLD linteamen]

lira, -e *n f literally* lyre, *hence* harp 10/32

liripipium, -ii *n nt* liripipe, the long tail of an academic hood, *hence possibly* hood 47/21

littera, -e *n f literally* a letter of the alphabet: 1. *in sg or coll pl* letter, epistle 50/21, etc; **literae mandatoriae** mandatory letter, one containing an order or command 360/33; 2. literary works or pursuits 56/27; *hence* study, scholarship, learning, education 89/34, etc

litterarius, -a, -um *adj* of or pertaining to literature or literary studies, literary 106/20

litteratus, -i *adj* lettered, learned 90/7

locumtenens, -ntis *sbst m* lieutenant, deputy, representative, locum 529/31, etc; *written as two words* 7/1, etc

locus, -i *n m* place 6/15, etc; rendered as 'locke' as part of a pun in a macaronic text 363/34

Londinensis, -is *sbst f* London 315/24; **Londoniensis** 34/7

Londonia, -e *n f* London 7/22

Loquabria, -ae *n f* Lochaber, a region of the western Highlands 315/3

Lucanus, -i *n m* Roman cognomen or one of its holders, especially Marcus Annaeus Lucanus

(AD 39–65), Lucan, author of *Bellum Civile*, a poem on the Roman Civil War 304/5

Lucretia, -ae *n f* Lucretia, a (probably legendary) Roman noblewoman, whose rape by Sextus Tarquinius was believed to have sparked the rebellion that founded the Roman republic, *here* the title of a play 281/30

ludicer, -cra, -crum *adj* of or pertaining to entertainment; pleasant, entertaining *hence nt sg as sbst* 1. pleasantry, entertaining remark 381/19; 2. public entertainment, show, play 37/34; the occurrence on 177/34 represents a play on both senses, though the first is primary there

ludio, -onis *n m* player 309/11

ludo, -dere, -si, -sum *v tr* to play, with various significances: 1. play, sport, engage in diversions 6/24; 2. to play a sport or game, engage in a pastime 5/29, 19/12; *hence* to play, sport (used without specification, exact sense unclear) 19/17, etc; 3. to play music 404/29; 4. to play a play or interlude 137/30, 450/12, 457/29; 5. *with dat* to play a game (eg, of chance) 56/23; *prp as sbst* player, gambler 6/37; 6. *prp as sbst* player, participant in an unspecified sport, pastime, play, or interlude 24/32

ludus, -i *n m* 1. game, sport, play, pastime, with various significances (which are sometimes difficult to distinguish): *a.* game of chance or one on which wagers are laid (including some board games) 6/31, etc: **ludus aleatorius** dice game 98/20; **~ scaccorum** game of chess 6/31; **taxillorum ~** game of knuckle-bones *or* dice 6/31; *b.* game, sport: **ludus sperilarius** a ball game, *possibly* tennis [*see* Latham *s.v.* sphera] 1090/44; *c.* sport, (folk) game, popular pastime 5/2m, 12/16, 12/31, 12/37, 13/8, 13/14, 48/30, 55/5, 197/21m, 209/4? (properly an occurrence of sense 1.f but use of the phr **ludi inhonesti**, frequent in the prohibitions of such pastimes to clerics and students, is likely an attempt to explain the exclusion of external players on the same grounds); *d.* play on a biblical theme or subject 7/11?, 34/19?, 38/20?, 38/26?, 63/24? *(all possibly occurrences of sense f); e.* play apparently on a classical model (frequently used of university or college drama from the middle of the sixteenth century, probably under neo-Latin influence) 137/14, etc; **ludus scenicus** 232/33 or ~ **theatralis** 142/24–5 or ~ **theatricus** 185/34, etc, stage play; *f.* entertainment, 'play,' of an unspecified kind, sense unclear 30/30, etc; ~ **musicalis** an entertainment with music 94/38?; 2. act of playing a musical instrument: **ludus lire** playing the harp 10/32; ~ **musicalis** musical performance 94/38?; 3. sport, jest: **ludum facere** (+ *acc*) to make sport of 894/19; 4. school: ~ **gladiatorius** fencing school 98/21; ~ **saltatorius** dancing school 98/21

Luna, -e *n f* the moon 310/12, etc; *with* 'dies' *understood* **Lune** Monday 84/26

lusio, -onis *n f* performance (of music) 57/15

lusor, -oris *n m* player, participant in a sport, pastime, play, interlude, or other entertainment: 1. used absolutely, exact sense unclear 30/32, etc; 2. player under patronage, with the nature of the entertainment often unspecified 73/8, etc; 3. local player, usually with the name of the town or parish expressed 20/35

lusorius, -a, -um *adj* of or belonging to a player 61/25

lusus, -i *n m* play, pastime, entertainment 30/4, etc

Lyncolniensis, -is *sbst f* Lincoln, name of a college and a diocese 498/29, etc

Macbethus, -i *n m* Macbeth, a king of Scotland, here named in a pageant for James I's arrival in Oxford 305/6

Magdalenensis, -e *adj* of or pertaining to Magdalen: **Collegium Magdalanense** Magdalen College 200/40; *m pl as sbst* men of Magdalen 106/34, etc; **Magdalensis** 305/31, etc

magestas *see* **maiestas**

magister, -tri *n m* 1. one who has authority or rank, master, also used as a title of respect with names (especially of those holding an MA degree) 28/35, etc, or titles of office 16/34, etc; 2. master, a member of the university holding an MA or higher degree and exercising teaching duties in a college 4/33, etc; **magister regens** regent master, one holding a master's degree in a given faculty and appointed to teach in that faculty 4/31, etc; at Merton College the masters were divided into two groups, juniors (**iuniores magistri** 28/30, etc) and seniors (**seniores magistri** 28/31); 3. master, the head of a collegiate church 41/27 or academic college 48/34; 4. as a title of office: master, the head of an attached community of brothers at Godstow Abbey 3/16; **equorum ... magister** master of the horse, an officer of the royal household in charge of various aspects of travel and transport, especially the provision and care of horses 180/30

magnas, -atis *n m* magnate, member of the gentry, peer, or other person of importance 468/35

Mahometes, -is *n m* Muhammad (AD *c* 570–629), founder of Islam 307/22, etc

maiacio, -onis *n f* Maying 14/31

maiestas, -atis *n f* (royal) majesty, a title or form of address for the reigning monarch 136/10, etc; **magestas** 56/7

maior, -ius *compar adj* greater (in size, dignity, or worth), elder 5/2, etc

maior, -oris *n m* mayor 29/35, etc

maioritas, -tatis *n f* higher or greater status 12/5

Maius, -ii *n m* the month of May, *hence* a May game or other pastime 14/5

malitia, -e *n f* malice, *hence* **praecogitata malitia** malice aforethought 503/18

mancipium, -ii *n m* 1. servant 179/6; 2. manciple, a college officer responsible for purchasing provisions 76/23, etc

mandatorius, -a, -um *adj* of or pertaining to an order, mandatory; *see* **littera**

manica, -e *n f* sleeve 8/33

Manilius, -ii *n m* Manilius, Roman gentile name or one of its holders, especially Marcus Manilius, a poet of the early principate, author of the *Astronomica*, a treatise on astrology 306/5m

mansus, -i *n m* room, lodging 6/29, etc

mantellum, -i *n nt* cloak 47/23

manus, -us *n f* 1. hand: *a. literally* 5/30, etc; *in idiom* **manus uiolentas inferre** 259/14 *or*

uiolentas ~ inferre 259/13 to lay violent hands on, to assault; *by extension* **in manibus** to hand, available 107/1; **prae manibus** before one's hands, *hence* ready, available 177/34 *or* beforehand, in advance 125/22, 125/24; *b. in various figurative senses*: expressing possession or ownership 74/8, 259/19; expressing care or keeping 85/30; expressing agency 79/19, 88/37, 202/17; expressing craft or skill 306/16, 309/30; expressing power or strength 314/12; 2. something written by hand, handwriting 106/30; 3. band, gang (of people) 503/17; *see also* **ad, appono**

Marcurius *see* **Mercurius**

maremium *see* **meremium**

Mars, -rtis *n m* Mars, the Roman god of war, whose name was also given to the fourth planet 140/6, etc; *with* 'dies' *understood* **Martis** Tuesday 36/33, etc

Martonensis *see* **Mertonensis**

martyr, -tiris *n m* martyr, one who dies out of adherence to religious principles, usually found as attribute of a saint, *here* of St Thomas Becket 11/38

mater, -tris *n f* mother: 1. *literally* 178/17; in reference to the Virgin Mary (as the mother of Jesus) 11/14, etc; 2. *by extension*: addressing a deity 369/25; the University (in a symbolic relationship to its members) 529/11

materia, -e *n f* 1. material, stuff, whether physical or spiritual 6/36, etc; 2. subject matter *or* plot 308/1, 308/15 [*see* OLD materia]

matutinus, -a, -um *adj* of or pertaining to morning, *hence f sg as sbst* matins, one of the canonical hours making up the divine office of clerics; despite its name, matins is the night office, being said at midnight or 2 AM under strict Benedictine observance 12/10

medicina, -e *n f* medicine; *see* **doctor, lego**

medio, -are, -aui, -atum *v intr* to be in the middle of, to divide 12/20

medius, -a, um *adj* central, middle 306/20, etc; *nt sg as sbst* middle, mid-point 314/33; **media nox** midnight 5/27, etc

Meleager, -gri *n m* Meleager, a legendary Greek hero, *here likely named as* a character in Gager's *Meleager* 178/16, etc

melos, -odis *n nt* melody, song 190/33

memoratus, -a, -um *pfp pass* noted, mentioned 12/29, etc

Menechmus, -i *n m* Menaechmus, one of the twin brothers who are the title characters of Plautus' play *Menaechmi* 178/16, *hence* the play itself 148/9, etc

Menippeus, -a, -um *adj* of or belonging to Menippus, a Greek author of the third century BC, who originated a style of writing in which prose is interspersed with verse; *see* **satura**

mercenarius, -a, -um *adj* hired, paid; *see* **scena**

Mercurius, -ii *n m* Mercury, a deity of the Roman pantheon whose name was also given to the first planet: *with* 'dies' *understood* **Mercurij** Wednesday 37/1, etc; **Marcurius** 30/23; *see also* **rusticans**

meremium, -ii *n nt* timber, wood for construction 124/41; **maremium** 147/2

merenda, -ae *n f* a light midday meal 77/17, etc [*from* mereo, *apparently originally part of a labourer's wages; see* OLD]

Mertonensis, -e *adj* of or belonging to Merton: **Collegium Mertonense** Merton College 525/36; **Martonensis** 80/35

metamorphosis, -is *n f* transformation, change (apparently an intentional reference to Ovid's *Metamorphoses*) 179/5

metrifico, -are, -aui, -atum *v intr* to compose in metre, write verse 14/26

Microcosmus, -i *n m* Microcosm, name of a character in the play *Annus Recurrens* 308/32

miles, -itis *n m* 1. warrior, knight [*see* OEDO knight *sb* 4b] 139/30, etc; 2. knight 7/18 [*see* OEDO knight *sb* 4a], etc; *hence* **Fabula Militis** The Knight's Tale, one of Chaucer's *Canterbury Tales* 136/8

mimus, -i *n m originally in* LL performer, actor, *especially* in the often obscene farces and panto-mimes of the later Roman stage [OLD], *hence in* AL performer, but probably one whose performance included music: 1. used without specification, exact sense unclear 30/30, etc;

2. with a named royal, noble, or other patron, such a performer under his or her patronage 30/23, etc [*cp* OLD *mimus and* REED *Devon* LG mimus]

mina, -ae[1] *n f* a Greek unit of weight approximately equal to a pound, *hence* pound sterling 201/1

mina, -ae[2] *n f* threat 308/6 [OLD minae]

minoritas, -tatis *n f* lower or lesser status 12/5

misericordia, -e *n f* mercy 387/34

misericors, -ordis *n m* dagger 6/2 [*see* OEDO misericord *sb* 3]

missa, -e *n f* mass, liturgical celebration of the Eucharist 3/14

mitra, -e *n f* mitre, ceremonial headgear worn by a bishop 15/27

moderator, -oris *n m* head, leader: **choristarum moderator** choirmaster 103/33

modero, -are, -aui, -atum *v tr* 1. to direct, guide 209/16; 2. to moderate (a discussion) 218/12

monachus, -i *n m* monk 3/19, etc

monarcha, -ae *n m* monarch, an absolute ruler 315/13

monarchicus, -a, -um *adj* of or pertaining to a monarch, monarchial 343/17

monasticus, -a, -um *adj* of or pertaining to a monk, monastic 3/18

moneta, -e *n f* money currency 6/32; *in idiom* **legalis moneta Anglie** legal English currency 196/1, etc

Montgomeria, -ae *n f* Montgomery, name of an earldom 312/32, etc

mora, -e *n f* elapse of time, usually with negative connotation, delay 799/20; *hence* **moram facere** 10/41, etc, *or* **moram trahere** 60/8, etc, to delay

multifarie *adv* in many different ways, variously 12/26

musica, -ae *n f* music 162/33, etc; **musica flatilis** *literally* wind music, *here apparently* the name of a collection of music for wind instruments 557/23

musicalis, -e *adj* of or pertaining to music, musical; *see* **instrumentum, ludus**

musicus, -a, -um *adj* 1. of or pertaining to music, musical; *see* **instrumentum**; 2. *m as sbst* musician 156/4, etc; **musici academici** university

musicians 497/12, etc; **musici oppidani** town musicians 280/13, etc; **musici publici** common musicians, ie, town musicians 280/7, etc

mutilacio, -onis *n f* cutting short, curtailment 3/18

nacio, -onis *n f* (student) nation, one of the groups into which the student population of a medieval university was divided, originally reflecting their national origins; at Oxford there were two nations, northern and southern 4/30, etc

nasus, -i *n m* nose 8/26; **Aeneus Nasus** Brazen Nose, the eponymous emblem of Brasenose College 85/24

natalis, -e *adj* of or pertaining to birth; *by extension* of or pertaining to Christmas; *nt (occasionally m) sg as sbst* (often with **domini** or **Christi**) the Christmas season, the period from Christmas (25 December) to Epiphany (6 January) 19/12, etc

natalitius, -a, -um *adj* of or pertaining to Christmas 79/26, etc; *nt pl as sbst* the Christmas season, the period from Christmas (25 December) to Epiphany (6 January) 94/9, etc

natiuitas, -atis *n f literally* birth: *alone* 67/8, etc, *or with* **Christi** 81/29, etc, *or* **Domini** 31/22, etc, Christmas, the Christmas season; **Natiuitas sancti Iohannis Baptistae** the Nativity of St John the Baptist, 24 June 5/23

nauticus, -a, -um *adj* of or pertaining to the navy, naval 489/31

Neptunus, -i *n m* Neptune, Roman god of the sea, presented (with a mix of real and invented mythological attributes) as the overlord of the kingdom of beans 799/6; *see also* **regnum, rex**

nobilis, -e *adj* illustrious, noble 56/7, etc; *m pl as sbst* noblemen, peers 218/5, etc; *nt sg as sbst* noble, a coin most commonly valued at 6s 8d although it could be worth as much as 10s 45/36, etc [*see* OEDO noble *a and sb*[1] B.2.a]

noctanter *adv* at night, by night 8/30, etc

nocumentum, -i *n nt* injury, hurt, harm 64/38, etc

nonus, -a, -um *adj literally* ninth 332/30, etc; *in idiom* **hora nona** noon (this shift in meaning resulted from a change in religious practice whereby the prayers appointed for the third, sixth, and ninth hours of the day came to be said together at midday) 5/17 [*see* ODCC *under* TERCE, SEXT, NONE]

norit, norunt *contractions of* nouerit *and* nouerunt *from* nosco [OLD]

Northantona, -ae *n f* Northampton, name of an earldom 313/6

Northfolcia, -e *n f* Norfolk, name of a dukedom 70/18

notacio, -onis *n f* act of providing (musical) notation or the notation itself 47/3

notarius, -ii *n m* notary, person authorized to draw up and attest to various public and legal documents, thus giving such documents an authoritative status at law; often notaries served as registrars of ecclesiastical courts: **notarius publicus** notary public 259/22

Notinghamia, -ae *n f* Nottingham, name of an earldom 313/6

nox, -ctis *n f* 1. *literally* night, night-time 5/25, etc; 2. the eve of a feast day, so called from the liturgical convention of beginning the observance of a holy day at sunset on the previous day: **noctes solemnes** solemn eves, ie, the eves of principal feasts 28/33; **nox sancti Iohannis** St John's Eve, either 26 December (St John the Evangelist) or 23 June (St John the Baptist) 57/10; *see also* **medius**

obediencialiter *adv* obediently 3/12

obiectum, -i *n nt* objection 86/7

obiiceo, -icere, -eci, -ectum *v tr* 1. to put (something) before (someone) *(with acc of thing and dat of person)* 140/15; 2. to bring a charge (against) *(with dat of person)* 163/16, etc

obitus, -us *n m* obit, annual commemoration of the death of a college's founder or other benefactor 510/35

obligo, -are, -aui, -atum *v tr* + 'se' *or pass* to bind or obligate oneself or to be bound or obligated, either to keep certain conditions or for the compliance of another, under pain of the forfeit of a sum of money 195/39, etc

obprobriosus, -a, -um *adj* insulting, taunting 48/30

obsequium, -ii *n nt* service (eg, to an employer or lord), *hence* **per obsequium** by service 504/22

obsonium, -ii *n nt* provision of foodstuffs for a meal, *hence* a meal 51/19; *in pl* foodstuffs, victuals 218/1 *(in form* **opsonia***)*

ocillus, -i *n m literally* a little eye, *hence* a die: **ludere ... ocillis** to play dice 56/23

octava, -e *n f* octave, the eight-day period following a major festival: **octava Epiphanie** the octave of Epiphany, 6–13 January 57/15

Oedipus, -i *n m* Oedipus, legendary king of Thebes, *here named as* a play character 178/17

Oeneus, -i *n m* Oeneus, a legendary Greek king, *here likely named as* a character in Gager's *Meleager* 178/32

officiarius, -i *n m* officer, a functionary in the service of a city or town 192/5, etc

officium, -ii *n nt* 1. office, position of responsibility 7/31, etc; 2. duty, task, responsibility 7/30, etc; 3. helpful or courteous action, a courtesy 270/28 (*see* **gratia**); 4. a liturgical office 3/13, etc; **diuinum officium** divine office, set of daily prayers and scriptural readings to be said by religious at the canonical hours 3/9m, etc; **ecclesiasticum officium** divine office, set of daily prayers and scriptural readings to be said by religious at the canonical hours 3/9 *(likely a deliberate play on sense 2 as well)*

opero, -are, -aui, -atum *v intr* to work, labour 95/22, etc

oppidanus, -a, -um *adj* of or pertaining to a town; it continues to be used of Oxford in some University-related sources after its status had changed 251/40, etc; *m sg as sbst* inhabitant of a town, townsman 98/20, etc

oppidum, -i *n nt* town (as opposed to a city); it continues to be used of Oxford in some University-related sources after its status had changed 37/21, etc

oppono, -onere, -osui, -ositum *v tr* 1. to put in the way of, place so as to block or obstruct 138/17; 2. to take the opposing side, argue against (of the opposing side in a disputed question) 218/11

opsonium *see* **obsonium**

optimas, -atis *n m* nobleman, peer 140/24, etc

ordinacio, -onis *n f* a specific regulation, an order 13/25, etc

ordino, -are, -aui, -atum *v tr* 1. to order, direct 10/34, etc; 2. to order, arrange 13/4

ornamentum, -i *n nt* 1. ornament, adornment 47/17; 2. gear, equipment (eg, for players) 30/3, etc

ostrum, -i *n nt* the colour purple, *derived from CL* ostrea, 'oyster' (whose shells were a source of purple dye), *hence* on 364/16 **strato discumbitur ostro**, they recline to eat on a couch of purple, is rendered by E 'they straite sett downe att this oister table' in a series of puns

Ouidius, -ii *n m* a Roman gentile name or one of its holders, *especially* the poet Publius Ovidius Naso, Ovid (43 BC–AD 17), author of the *Metamorphoses* 141/3

Oxonia, -ae *n f* Oxford, name of a city 5/16, etc; **Oxonium** 513/21

Oxoniensis, -is *adj* of or pertaining to Oxford, especially Oxford University 142/20m, etc; *m pl as sbst* Oxonian, an inhabitant of Oxford, *especially* a member of Oxford University 131/10

pacifice *adv* peacefully, peaceably 6/35

paena, -e *n f over-correction of* poena [OLD]

pagina, -e *n f* page, applied especially to either side of a folio 54/6m, etc

Palamon, -onis *n m* Palamon, a character in the play *Palamon and Arcite* 138/25, etc; **Palemon** 136/21, etc

palatinus, -a, -um *adj* of or belonging to a palace or court, palatine: **comes palatinus** count palatine, a count of the Holy Roman Empire exercising quasi-royal jurisdiction within his territory 438/39 [OEDO count *sb* 2]; **princeps palatinus** prince palatine, palsgrave, one of the electors of the Holy Roman Empire 401/26–7 [OEDO palatine *a and sb*[1]]; *hence m sg as sbst* palatine, title of the governor of a province in the kingdom of Poland 191/35

palatium, -ii *n nt* palace: 1. an imperial residence

on the Palatine Hill 137/9; 2. a sumptuous residence, especially that of a ruler 799/6, etc

pallians, -ntis *prp* hiding, cloaking 7/39

pallinodia, -e *n f literally* a song sung over again, *hence* a round 51/20

panis, -is *n m* bread, loaf of bread 3/27, etc; **panis consecrabilis** bread suitable for Eucharistic consecration 28/16

pannus, -i *n m* cloth, a piece of cloth, *pl* clothing: **panni ... lanei** woollen clothing 8/39, etc; **panni linei** linen clothing 8/39, etc

papa, -e *n m* pope, the bishop of Rome 7/32, etc

par, paris[1] *n nt* pair 8/28, etc; **par cardinum** pair of hinges, ie, a hinge (as naturally composed of two matching pieces) 158/6

par, paris[2] *adj* equal 314/29, etc

parochia, -e *n f* parish, the smallest distinct unit of ecclesiastical jurisdiction and Christian ministry, each parish having its own church, priest, warden, and tithes 4/36, etc

parochialis, -e *adj* of or pertaining to a parish; *see* **clericus, ecclesia**

parochianus, -a, -um *adj* of or pertaining to a parish, parochial, *hence comm as sbst* parishioner, member of a parish 7/10, etc

Pascha, -e *n f* Easter, festival celebrating the resurrection of Christ, kept on the Sunday after the full moon on or next following 21 March 38/21, etc; **feria secunda tercia & quarta ebdomade Pasche** the Monday, Tuesday, and Wednesday of Easter week, kept as doubles, ie, major feasts 11/38–9

passio, -onis *n f* passion, strong emotion, here in the translation of a play title **passiones pacatae** *Passions Calmed* 893/31

pater, -tris *n m literally* father: 1. *hence* ancestor 178/28; 2. applied to a deity 369/29, etc; 3. describing the relationship between a bishop and those in his diocese 498/31, etc; 4. applied to one revered as a father: **pater fidelium** father of the faithful, applied to Abraham on the basis of New Testament passages such as Rom 4.16–17 475/26

patibulum, -i *n nt* a gibbet for executing criminals: **patibulum sancte Crucis cum imagine**

Crucifixi is thus an elaborate periphrasis for a crucifix 12/21

patria, -e *n f* 1. homeland, native country 131/7, etc; 2. countryside, the rural district round about a city or town and associated with it 11/25, etc; 3. local district, neighbourhood, *hence* jury (as a body originally speaking for a district): *in idiom* **ponere se ... super patriam**, to entrust oneself to the jury, a formula used by a defendant seeking trial by jury on a felony charge 9/26–7

pax, -cis *n f* 1. peace, *especially* a state characterized by peaceful relations among neighbours or the like 799/8, etc; *hence* **ad pacem ... conseruandam** to keep the peace 8/14–15; 2. *in idiom* **pace** + *gen* by the leave of, with all due respect to 343/2–3, etc

pecunia, -e *n f* 1. money, wealth 6/32; 2. *sg or coll pl* (ready) money, coin, cash 21/12, etc

pegma, -atis *n nt* 1. scaffold, platform (*originally in CL* a moveable or temporary platform [*see OLD*]) 137/12; 2. stage (*or possibly* pageant?) 76/25 [*see TLL* pegma]

Pelion, -onis *n nt* Pelion, a coastal range on the southwestern coast of Thessaly; its highest point (which is inland) is the Mt Pelion of mythology, atop which the Giants are said to have piled Mt Ossa; *here* **portus Pelionis**, the harbour of Pelion, is likely a deliberate inversion of classical mythology (in keeping with the rest of the king of beans correspondence) although it could refer to the ports on the Bay of Volo sheltered by the range 799/25

pellex, -icis *n m literally* thumb, *by extension* inch 5/19, etc [*see OLD* pollex]

Pembroc(h)ius, -ii *n m* Pembroke, name of an earldom 313/19, etc

Penbrochiensis, -e *adj* of or belonging to Pembroke, an earldom 180/36

penitencia, -e *n f* penance, act of contrition or restitution imposed by ecclesiastical authorities upon persons guilty of canonical offences 62/6

pennarium, -ii *n nt* pen-case, penner 8/28

pensio, -onis *n f* pension, regular payment for services 29/35; **pencio** 439/32

Pentec(h)ostes, -es *or* **-e** (*irregular gen ending in* **-en**) *n f* Pentecost, Whit Sunday, Sunday fifty days following Easter 16/17, etc; **feria secunda tercia & quarta ebdomade ... Pentecostes** the Monday, Tuesday, and Wednesday of Pentecost week; Whit Monday and Tuesday were kept as doubles, ie, major feasts, while the Wednesday was properly observed as an ember day, a minor fast 11/38–9; **Pentacostes** 33/1; **Pentechosta** 18/13, etc; **Penthacostes** 22/6, etc; **Penthecostes** 23/1; **Penticostes** 26/8

per *prep with acc* 1. (of an agent or instrument) through, by, by means of 5/16, etc; 2. by, by reason of 5/21, etc; 3. (of stages of a journey or passage) through, by way of 314/35; 4. through, across (a region, space, or area) 529/36; 5. during, throughout, for (a period of time) 3/14–15, etc; 6. in accordance with, according to 30/4, etc; 7. *in other idioms*: **per manus** + *gen of person* by one's agency, by (someone) 202/17; **per tempus** in due time, betimes 56/9; **per uicem** in turn 9/25

peramicus, -i *n m* close friend 313/13

perbellus, -a, -um *adj* very charming 315/16

perditio, -onis *n f* ruin, loss 6/32

peregrinatio, -onis *n f either* foreign travel *or* pilgrimage 257/18

peregrinus, -a, -um *adj* foreign, strange, outlandish 62/8; *comm as sbst* foreigner, alien, *hence* stranger, outsider 185/35

perhonestus, -a, -um *adj* extremely well respected, very honourable 85/32

peripetasmata, -um *n nt* embroidered hanging covers for furniture, *hence* embroidered hangings or curtains, *possibly* tapestries 306/11, etc

periscelis, -idis *n f* anklet, *hence* **aurea periscelis**, *literally* golden anklet, the order of the Garter 180/30

perornatus, -a, -um *adj* fully adorned, very ornate 12/25

personaliter *adv* in person, personally 569/6

personatus, -a, -um *adj* wearing a mask 387/28; *hence f sg as sbst* masque 137/19

peruenustus, -a, -um *adj* very attractive 191/36

petra, -e *n f* 1. rock, stone 9/21; 2. *hence* stone,

a unit of weight equal to fourteen pounds 14/38

Phariseus, -i *n m* Pharisee, member of a Jewish religious party prominent in the gospel accounts but going back to the period of the Maccabees 177/27, etc [*ODCC* PHARISEES]

philosophaster, -astris *n m* a second-rate philosopher, *hence* one who pretends to knowledge or skill they lack 427/16; also the title of a comedy by Robert Burton, *Philosophaster* 427/14

philtrum, -i *n nt* love-charm, (magic) potion 309/25

pila, -e *n f* ball 12/29, etc

pincerna, -e *n m* butler 56/2

pinnaculum, -i *n nt* a structure rising above the roof or coping of a building, such as a turret, spire, or even a weather-vane, *possibly* a gable-end 158/11

piscis, -is *n m literally* fish, *hence in pl* Pisces, the twelfth sign of the zodiac, *symbolically* the end of the solar year 308/35

pitancia, -e *n f* pittance, an allowance of food and drink 3/25

Pithias *see* **Pythias**

Plautinus, -a, -um *adj* of or belonging to the Roman comic writer Plautus 178/16

Plautus, -i *n m* Titus Maccius Plautus, elder of the two Roman comic writers whose works survive (*c* 254–184 BC) 149/5, etc

plebeius, -a, -um *adj in CL* belonging to the plebian class, *hence m sg as sbst* commoner 282/8

plenarie *adv* fully, completely 441/11

polecia, -e *n f* commonwealth, state 799/8

πολιτία, -ας *n f* commonwealth, state, or the government and organization thereof 343/26 [LSJ πολιτεία]

Polonia, -ae *n f* Poland 191/34

Polonicus, -a, -um *adj* Polish 315/16

Polonus, -i *n m* a Pole 191/35m

pomposus, -a, -um *adj* charcterized by pomp and grandeur, grand, stately 307/36

pondrans, -ntis *prp* weighing *(with gen of amount)* 21/11

pono, -nere, -sui, -situm *v tr* to put, place 44/7, etc; **ponere se(ipsum) apprenticium** to place

oneself as an apprentice, become an apprentice 414/11, etc

porta, -e *n f* gate 8/24, etc; **aula latarum portarum** Broadgates Hall 76/23–4

portionista, -e *n m* postmaster, a poor student at Merton College who received an allowance, ie, a portion, of food from the college for his support 193/39

possessio, -onis *n f* 1. right of possession of property 259/5, etc; **uacua possessio** vacant possession, possession unencumbered by a tenant or the like 259/16–17; 2. the property so possessed 50/30

potacio, -onis *n f* drinking, act of drinking, especially in a social group, *probably* a light meal accompanied by wine 11/9, etc; *see also* **biberium**

potus, -us *n m* drink 11/1, etc; *in idiom* **potus caritatis** loving cup, a common cup that circulated among the members of a community after a community meal 11/8, etc

praecognitus, -a, -um *pfp pass* thought in advance, preconceived; *see* **malitia**

praecursorius, -a, -um *adj* characteristic of a forerunner (referring to St John the Baptist, eponymous patron of St John's College, in his traditional role as the forerunner of Christ) 305/18

praefectus, -i *n m* 1. prefect, title of various senior government officials and military commanders in the Roman Republic and Empire, *by extension* referring to the director of a play 343/34; 2. *in pl* heads of colleges 101/34, etc

praefulgidus, -a, -um *adj* particularly bright 306/6

praehabitus, -a, -um *pfp pass* had in advance, held beforehand 503/15

praelectio, -onis *n f* (academic) lecture 893/33

praepositus, -i *n m* provost, title of chief administrative officer in several colleges 6/39, etc

praesto, -are, -iti, -itum *v tr* to furnish, provide 94/18, etc; **prestare sacramentum** to swear or take an oath 441/20, etc

prandeor, -eri, pransus sum *v intr* to dine, have dinner 101/35, etc

prandium, -ii *n nt* dinner, the second and most

elaborate of the three main meals of the day 3/25, etc

praxis, -is *n f* practice, experience 54/5

precinctum, -i *n nt* precinct: 1. area within the walls of a college 47/21; 2. the area within or near Oxford under the authority of the University and its courts 194/27, etc

precise *adv* precisely, exactly 3/13[1], etc

preconizacio, -onis *n f* summoning, a formal call made in a church or university court summoning a cited party three times by name in an audible voice to appear before the court 569/7, etc

predicator, -oris *n m* preacher 163/16

prelibatus, -a, -um *adj* aforementioned 76/36

premitto, -ittere, -isi, -issum *v tr* to mention before 530/9; *nt of pfp pass as sbst* what has gone before, the aforegoing the aforementioned 7/1, etc

premunicio, -onis *n f* forewarning, notice in advance 27/26

prenominatus, -a, -um *pfp pass* having been named or specified earlier 74/3, etc

presentes, -tium *sbst comm* the present document or letter 414/13, etc [OLD praesens]

preses, -idis *n m* 1. presider, one who presides 313/3; 2. president, the head of a college 73/8, etc

presidens, -ntis *sbst m* one who presides, presiding officer, president of a college or chapter 3/19, etc

pretermitto, -ittere, -isi, -issum *v tr* to let (someone or something) pass unnoticed, let go by 55/24

prex, precis *n f* 1. prayer 139/11, etc; 2. *in pl* one of the two post-Reformation offices of the Church of England: **preces uespertine** evening prayer, evensong, the evening office based upon the pre-Reformation offices of vespers and compline 443/40

primas, -atis *n m* primate, metropolitan bishop of an ecclesiastical province 3/7

princeps, -ipis (*irregular gen* **principis** 141/14) *n m* 1. prince, ruler 799/19, etc; as ruler of an independent principality 401/26, etc (*see also* **palatinus**); *hence* title of a college Christmas lord 209/15, 209/17; **princeps Natalicius** Christmas prince, title given to a Christmas lord at Trinity College 101/33; 2. title of

emperor in the early Roman Empire (the principate), *hence* used with deliberate reference to Caesar Augustus as a title of Queen Elizabeth 138/9, etc; 3. prince, son or son-in-law of the king 25/5, etc; 4. head, person in the first rank or position 105/37

principalis, -e *adj* chief, principal: *see* **festum**; *m sg as sbst* principal, head of a college or hall 9/3, etc

principissha, -e *n f* princess 72/4

priuatus, -a, -um *adj* private, privately owned 6/25; *see also* **sigillum**

priuilegium, -ii *n nt* privilege, a special right or exemption 7/29, etc

pro *prep with abl* 1. on account of, on the basis of, for 11/7, etc; 2. in payment for, for 7/10, etc; 3. in view of, as befits, for 3/22, etc; **pro eo quod** because 8/13; **pro mea uirili** for my part 85/25; 4. in the case of, for 3/23, etc; 5. (of time) for, on 32/12, etc; **pro tunc** then, at that time 11/26, etc (*written as one word* 15/35)

probationarius, -ii *n m* probationer, a candidate for a fellowship or the like 170/24

processus, -us *n m* (legal) process, proceedings 258/38, etc

procestrium, -ii *n nt literally* what stands outside or before a camp, *hence* an approach, entry 137/4

procurator, -oris *n m* proctor, a college or university officer 31/2, etc

professor, -oris *n m* professor: 1. professor, a senior instructor in a given subject 218/11, etc; 2. **sacre theologie professor** one holding the highest degree in the theology faculty, a doctor of sacred theology (STD) 73/26

profunditas, -atis *n f* depth 5/19

Progne, -es *n f* Procne, the wife of Tereus, king of Thrace, who was transformed into a bird; *here* named as an eponymous character in Calfhill's *Progne* 136/30

progressus, -us *n m* 1. forward motion, advance, progress (used figuratively) 343/15, etc; 2. (royal) progress 125/11; 3. one's progress through life, one's life 308/29

promano, -are, -aui, -atum *v intr* to flow forth, proceed 307/12

promississimus, -a, -um *superl adj* giving greatest promise, most promising 191/36

promus, -i *n m* steward, a college or household officer 70/25, etc

propheta, -e *n m* a prophet, *here apparently* one of the Old Testament prophets as a character in a show of some kind 28/6

propositio, -onis *n f* act of proposing or showing; *see* **titulus**

propylaeum, -i *n nt* gateway 305/35 [*see* OLD propylaea, propylon]

proscaenium, -ii *n nt literally* what is before the backdrop or background, *hence* the stage of a theatre 80/23, etc

protunc *see* **pro**

psalmum, -i *n nt* psalm, one of the 150 liturgical songs, attributed to David in the biblical Book of Psalms, and incorporated into Christian worship 146/25

pubes, -is *n f* the youth, the young men 85/26

pugnacio, -onis *n f* fighting 146/32

pulsacio, -onis *n f* 1. knocking, striking at a door or the like 40/22; 2. playing (of an instrument) 60/34, etc

pulso, -are, -aui, -atum *v tr* 1. to ring (a bell or the like) 503/16; 2. to play (a pipe) 148/38 [*see* OLD pulso 4]

purificatio, -onis *n f* (ritual) purification, *especially* the liturgical commemoration of the Virgin Mary's purification after the birth of Christ (Lk 2.22–4), celebrated on 2 February 19/17, etc

Pythias, ae *n m* Pythias (properly Phintias), famous as the friend of Damon of Syracuse, *named here as* an eponymous character in the play *Damon and Pythias* 149/6 [*see* OCD DAMON (1)]; **Pithias** 148/37

Quadragesima, -e *sbst f literally* fortieth (day), *by extension* Lent, the forty days preceding Easter 8/17, etc

quadratum, -i *n nt* quadrangle, quad 28/36

quarterium, -ii *n nt literally* quarter, a fourth part of anything, *hence*: 1. quart, a liquid measure, the fourth part of a gallon 33/3; 2. quarter, a

measure for cut timber, a two-by-four 155/32 [*see* OEDO quarter *sb* 19]

quercus, -us *n f* oak tree, *here perhaps* one used as a summer pole 111/7

questio, -onis *n f* 1. questioning, examination (eg, of a witness) 137/32; 2. (disputed) question, a formal disputation of a point of theology or philosophy, held either as an academic exercise or as a debate for distinguished visitors 218/13

quietus, -a, -um *pfp pass* acquitted, discharged (eg, from a court proceeding) 9/31m, etc

quita, -ae *n f* acquittance, release (eg, from a bond or a debt) 554/26

quouismodo *adv* in any way you please, however possible 259/8

ramulus, -i *n m* a small branch (eg, of a candelabrum or lamp-stand) 137/16

receptio, -onis *n f* 1. receipt (eg, of a payment) 21/26, etc; 2. receiving (of a guest) 146/41, etc

reclamatorius, -a, -um *adj* pertaining to the recall of a hawk; *see* **auis**

recreacio, -onis *n f* 1. refreshment, relaxation 6/33, etc; 2. activity tending to provide refreshment, *hence* entertainment 40/26?

rector, -oris *n m* 1. director, leader 799/7; 2. rector, head of an academic college 16/34, etc

rectoria, -e *n f* rectory, benefice accorded the rector of a parish 43/28, etc

redditus, -i *n m* return, report (eg, of income) 286/20

reditus, -us *n m* revenue 217/22, etc

refectio, -onis *n f* 1. refreshment 11/1, etc; 2. *hence* a meal 27/24, etc

refectorium, -ii *n nt* refectory, dining hall 893/35, etc

refocillo, -are, -aui, -atum *v tr* to restore (eg, to health), refresh 307/27

reformacio, -onis *n f* reformation, correction (of an abuse) 40/20

refractarius, -a, -um *adj* unruly, unrestrained 530/12

regalis, -e *adj* royal 799/14, *hence* of or pertaining to the king of beans, a Christmas king at Merton College 49/19, etc; *nt sg as sbst* royal, an English gold coin originally valued at 10s, although its value could vary, *here* used as a synonym for a noble 62/38 [OEDO rial *sb*¹ 3a]; *see also* **nobilis**

regardum, -i *n nt* reward, gratuity, customary payment 30/31, etc; **regarda** 20/35, etc; **regardium** 267/19, etc; **rewardum** 17/15, etc

regencia, -e *n f* regency, the period during which a master acted as a regent, or presider, over disputations and questions 52/18

regens, -ntis *prp* ruling, regent: **magister regens** regent master, a master in a given faculty acting as regent, or presider, over degree disputations 4/32, etc; *hence m as sbst* regent, regent master 29/3, etc

regina, -e *n f* queen: 1. the reigning monarch 125/9, etc; 2. wife of the king 73/8, etc

register, -tri *n m* registrar 73/18

registrum, -i *n nt* register book 498/25

regius, -a, -um *adj* 1. *literally* of or pertaining to a monarch, royal 799/14, etc; 2. *hence* **professor regius** regius professor, holder of a chair in a given faculty endowed by the monarch 218/11

regnum, -i *n nt* 1. reign 5/15, etc; 2. kingdom, realm 7/23, etc; *in idiom* **regnum fabe** *or* **fabarum** kingdom of beans, the mythical realm of Merton College's Christmas king 799/7, etc

regulus, -i *n m* petty king, *hence* prince 315/16

relicta, -ae *n f* widow 259/20

religio, -onis *n f* religion, *often specifically* Christian religious practice or devotion 894/19

reparatio, -onis *n f* repair, mending 14/38, etc

reparo, -are, -aui, -atum *v tr* to mend, repair, fix 102/18, etc

repello, -ere, reppuli, repulsum *v tr literally* to drive away, *hence* to expel (a student or other member) from the University 530/10

repititio, -onis *n f literally* repetition, *hence* rehearsal (of a play) 279/32

repletio, -onis *n f* filling up 89/34

repositorium, -ii *n nt* storage place, *hence* a chest *or* cupboard 94/29

resarcio, -cere, -si, -sum *v tr* to start fresh, renew 56/28

rescriptus, -a, -um *pfp pass literally* rewritten

(as correction), *hence* copied, recopied 1104/35

resigno, -are, -aui, -atum *v tr* 1. to hand over, give up 799/17; 2. *hence as intr* to resign an office 7/39

restauratus, -a, -um *pfp pass* restored, *here* in the translation of a play title **Arcadia Restaurata** *Arcadia Restored* 309/9

rewardum *see* **regardum**

rex, -gis *n m* 1. king, reigning or former monarch 5/14, etc; 2. king, one chosen by a college to oversee festivities during the Christmas season, *here* the king of beans at Merton College 799/16, etc; **rex fabarum** 30/10, etc; **rex regni fabarum** 36/20–1, etc

rithmicis, -e *adj* of or belonging to verse, especially rhyming verse 7/20

Romanista, -e *n m* Romanist, a Roman Catholic 178/29 [*according to the* OEDO, *coined by Martin Luther in 1520: see* Romanist *a and sb*]

Roscius, -ii *n m* Roscius, a Roman gentile name or one of its holders, *especially* the famous actor Q. Roscius Gallus 894/38

Russia, -ae *n f* Russia 191/34

rusticans, -ntis *prp* travelling or staying in the country, *here* in the title of a play **Mercurius Rusticans** *Mercury in the Country* 392/27

Rutlandius, -ii *n m adj* of or belonging to Rutland, an English dukedom and county: *m sg as sbst* the duke of Rutland 313/12

sabbatum, -i *n nt* sabbath, *hence* Saturday 36/27, etc

saccum, -i *n nt* sackcloth, a mourning or penitential garb, *by extension* state of mourning or penitence 177/34

sacellatum, -i *n nt* chapel 73/20

sacerdos, -otis *n m* priest, a member of the second of the three major orders of clergy, the other two being deacon (diaconus) and bishop (episcopus) 13/4, etc

sacramentum, -i *n nt* oath, *especially* the oath sworn by jurors to give true findings to the best of their ability 5/21, etc, or that sworn by newly admitted burgesses 441/20, etc;

sacramentum ... corporale corporal oath, one in which the swearer must be in bodily contact with the gospel book, or the like, on which the oath is taken 481/34, etc [OLD]

sacrista, -e *n m* sacrist, one responsible for the communion vessels, plate, and other sacred or valuable objects belonging to a church or other religious institution 47/26

Sadducaeus, -i *n m* Sadducee, a member of the conservative, priestly sect opposed to that of the Pharisees, prominent in the gospel accounts as opponents of Christ and his disciples 177/27 [ODCC SADDUCEES]

saepedictus, -a, -um *pfp pass* often said 42/6, etc

sagitto, -are, -aui, -atum *v intr* to shoot arrows at, attack with arrows 8/20

Salomon, -onis *n m* Solomon, king of Israel renowned for his wisdom, *here named as* a character in a comedy 37/37; **Salamon** 38/5

saltatorius, -a, -um *adj* pertaining to dancing; *see* **ludus**

saltus, -us *n m literally* a leap *or* step, *hence by extension* a dance 12/16, etc [*see* OLD saltatus, salto]

salus, -utis *n f in CL* health, well-being 139/22, etc; often used in conventional good wishes in epistolary salutations; in Christian usage, salvation, *hence* used in salutations in a play upon both senses 3/8, etc

sanctus, -a, -um *adj* holy, blessed 12/20 (*in superl*), etc; *with names as a title* Saint 3/21, etc; *m or f as sbst* holy one, saint 4/5, etc

Sarisburia, -e *n f* Salisbury: 1. name of a diocese (*in indecl form* **Sarum**) 12/11; 2. name of an earldom 314/11

satelles, -itis *n m in CL literally* henchman, body-guard, *likely by extension* yeoman (of the guard) 279/28 [*see* OEDO satellite *sb*]

satrapa, -e *n m literally* satraps, a Persian provincial governor, *by extension* serjeant, a civic officer (*see* p 1088, endnote to MC Arch f 100v) 29/35, etc; **satraps** 45/35, etc

satura, -ae *n f* satire, an ancient literary genre: **satura Menippea** satire in the style of Menippus, ie, written in prose interspersed with poetry 427/16–17m

scaccus, -i *n m* chessman; *see* **ludus**

scandalum, -i *n nt* scandal, discredit 11/31, etc

scannum, -i *n nt for* scamnum [OLD]

scena, -e *n f* stage: 1. stage, a platform upon which plays are enacted 93/14, etc; *used metaphorically* 85/34, etc; 2. *by extension* scene, subdivision of an act 310/30m, etc; 3. *generally* the stage, the theatre 178/34, etc; *hence* **scena mercenaria** *literally* the hired stage, a disparaging reference to the professional theatre 309/12; 4. scene, setting (eg, of a play) 392/28

scenicus, -a, -um *adj* of or pertaining to a 'scena' in whatever sense, dramatic 232/33, etc

sc(h)olaris, -is *sbst m* scholar, student (in contrast to a master or fellow), *likely referring to* one who was a foundation scholar, ie, a supported member of a college and part of its corporation 4/37, etc

scholasticus, -i *sbst m* scholar, student 78/12, etc (*apparently a synonym of* **sc(h)olaris**)

scola, -e *n f* school 10/28

Scotia, -ae *n f* Scotland 305/5, etc

Scoto-Britanni, -orum *sbst m* the Britons of Scotland, the Scots 305/4

Scotus, -a, -um *adj* Scots, Scottish 313/30; *m pl as sbst* the Scots 315/2m

Scriptura, -e *n f* 1. the act of writing or copying 32/11, etc; 2. Scripture, the Bible 10/31, etc

scrutinium, -ii *n nt* scrutiny, a college meeting held for elections of officers and disciplining of members 32/21, etc

sculptura, -e *n f* a piece of sculpture 12/22, etc

scurrilis, -e *adj* scurrilous, offensive, *hence nt as sbst* something offensive, scurrility 4/6

scurrilitas, -atis *n f* offensive or scurrilous behaviour 11/2, etc

sella, -e *n f* chair (for a dignitary), throne 137/20, etc

semicommunnarius, -ii *n m* (*literally* a half-commoner) demy, name for a foundation scholar at Magdalen College, so called because their support was originally half that accorded a fellow 81/34; **semicominarius** 170/25

semiduodena, -e *n f* half a dozen, six 98/8

senescallus, -i *n m* steward, college officer 67/8

senior, -ius *compar adj* 1. elder, senior (in rank) 13/26, etc; 2. *hence m pl as sbst* seniors, *apparently* a designation for senior members of a college 11/9, etc

senioritas, -tatis *n f* seniority 43/27

septimana, -e *n f* week 8/17, etc; *especially referring to* a feast day and its octave 21/27, etc

septrum, -i *n nt for* sceptrum [OLD]

sequutus, -a, -um *pfp for* secutus *from* sequor [OLD]

sera, -e *n f* lock 158/6

serenissimus, -a, -um *superl adj* most serene, used as an honorific for the monarch 217/18, etc

serrans, -ntis *prp* sawing 102/11, etc

sertatus, -a, -um *pfp pass* festooned, garlanded 5/4

seruicia *see* **ceruisia**

seruicium, -ii *n nt* 1. service, *especially* personal service provided by an employee or servant 42/1, etc; 2. service, liturgical rite 32/11

seruiens, -ntis *sbst m* 1. servant 5/39, etc; 2. serjeant, a civic officer 25/4

seruisia *see* **ceruisia**

seruus, -i *n m* 1. *referring to the classical period* (male) slave 137/25, etc; 2. *referring to contemporary events* (male) servant 18/35, etc

Seuerus *see* **Alexander**

shoppa, -e *n f* shop 5/24, etc

sigillatus, -a, -um *pfp pass* sealed, affixed with a seal 196/4, etc

sigillum, -i *n nt* 1. a seal used to authenticate a document *or* the impression thereof 62/4, etc; 2. *in idiom* **sigillum … priuatum** privy seal, *here* that of the St John's Christmas Prince 360/37

Siradiensis, -e *adj* of or belonging to Siradia, or Sieradz, a Polish district administered by a palatine 191/35

sitella, -e *n f* treasury: **sitella corporata** the city treasury 332/31, etc

situo, -are, -aui, -atum *v tr* to locate, place 8/31, etc

societas, -atis *n f* 1. partnership, association, *hence* a college viewed as a corporate body 280/26

socius, -ii *n m* 1. fellow, associate, partner 8/14, etc; 2. fellow (of a college), person holding a degree of MA or higher who is a senior member of a college with teaching or administrative

functions 6/34, etc; **sotius** 72/9, etc [*overcorrected form*]

sodalis, -is *n m* companion, *here* a member of the Order of the Garter 180/30

sodalitium, -ii *n nt literally* club, confraternity, *hence* college 894/16, etc [*over-correction of* OLD sodalicium]

solarium, -i *n nt* sollar, an upper room or loft, so called because it caught the sunlight 13/3

solatium, -ii *n nt* 1. *literally* comfort, solace 60/21, etc; 2. *by extension* recreation, entertainment 5/25, etc

solem(p)nis (*or* **solennis**), **-e** *adj* solemn, ceremonious, partaking of religious rites 28/33, etc; *hence n pl as sbst*: solemnities, solemn religious services 3/20 (used ironically); 2. customary, traditional 209/12; *nt sg as sbst* custom 310/12m

solidus, -i *n m* shilling, one-twentieth of a pound 8/29, etc

sonitus, -us *n m* act of sounding (a musical instrument), *here* a horn 503/16

Sophocles, -is *n m* Sophocles, second of the three great Athenian tragedians (496–406 BC) 178/33m, etc

sotius *see* **socius**

specialis, -e *adj* special 194/27, etc

specifico, -are, -aui, -atum *v tr* to specify, make a detailed list of 491/18

spectaculum, -i *n nt* spectacle, show, usually unspecified but probably dramatic 11/28, etc; the hostility shown to 'spectacula' in statutes derived from canonical sources probably arises from the term's associations with gladiatorial shows and the like [OLD]

spera, -e *n f for* sphaera [OLD]

sperilarius, -a, -um *adj* of or belonging to a ball (for play); *see* **ludus** [*cp* Souter sph(a)era]

spiritus, -us *n m* spirit 141/12; *hence* **Spiritus Sanctus** the Holy Spirit, the third person of the Trinity 307/33–4m

spondialis, -is *n m literally* one who plays the flute at a religious observance, *used generally by extension* a flute player 465/8 [*from* σπονδή, a drink offering, *and* αὐλητής, a flute player; *see* Souter spondiales]

sponsus, -i *n m* bridegroom, *by extension* (influenced by conventional exegesis of the *Song of Solomon*) Christ 3/9

spontaneus, -a, um *adj* voluntary, unprompted 101/8m

statutum, -i *n nt* statute, regulation, law 92/26, etc

strata, -e *n f* street 5/28

studens, -ntis *sbst m* student 4/9, etc

subdecanus, -i *n m* subdean, official in a cathedral chapter subordinate to the dean 199/15

substitutus, -i *n m* substitute, deputy judge acting on behalf of another 73/27

subtraccio, -onis *n f* removal, reduction 13/24

suburbium, -ii *n nt* outskirts, suburb 529/36

succinens, -ntis *prp* singing, or chanting, softly 305/16

suffitus, -us *n m* burning of perfume or other sweet-smelling substance 417/17 [*see* OEDO suffiment, suffite]

Suffolcia, -e *n f* Suffolk, name of a dukedom 313/6

suffragatorius, -a, -um *adj* of or pertaining to electors 343/11

super *prep with acc or abl* 1. about, concerning 40/29, etc; 2. upon, by virtue of (eg, an oath) 5/22, etc; 3. on, upon (of location) 8/24, etc; *hence* **impositi super capita convictorum** *literally* levied upon the heads of fellows, ie, levied upon the fellows individually 282/7; *see also* **patria**

superuiuo, -ere, -xi *v intr* to continue living, linger (eg, after an injury) 138/20

supradictus, -a, -um *pfp pass* said earlier, stated above 6/6, etc

surexio, -onis *n f* insurrection, riot 9/19

symphoniacus, -i *n m* musician, *especially* one that is part of a band or consort, *hence probably* a wait 274/35, etc [OLD]

symphonista, -e *n m* musician 100/5

taberna, -e *n f literally* a shop, *but usually in* AL a tavern, alehouse, inn 11/28, etc

tabernaculum, -i *n nt either* a tent or booth *or* a tabernacle, name applied to various articles of church furniture, such as a canopied recess or other repository for an image 28/16

tabula, -e *n f* 1. board, plank 9/21?, 94/23; 2. table 9/21?, 29/26

tabulatum, -i *n nt* 1. *literally* floor or platform made of boards, *hence* floorboard 306/19; 2. **tabulatum scaenicum** stage platform, stage 893/34

tactus, -a, -um *pfp pass here in idiom* **tactis sacrosanctis euangeliis** when the holy gospels had been touched, referring to the form of a corporal oath (taken while touching a gospel book) 76/28

tangens, -ntis *prp literally* touching, *hence* touching on, having a bearing on 11/13, etc

tapete, -is *n nt* woven hanging, tapestry 137/20

taxatio, -onis *n f* taxation, assessment 217/21m

taxillus, -i *n m* ('talus' + *diminutive suffix*) knucklebone, a small die or playing piece in the shape of a die 6/31, etc

tela, -e *n f* woven fabric, cloth, *hence* **linea tela** linen fabric 8/35

templum, -i *n nt literally* temple 894/30; *hence* a Christian church or chapel: **templum Diue Virginis Marie** church of St Mary the Virgin 55/20

tempus, -oris *n nt* 1. time, occasion 3/10, etc; *often with gen of specification defining the nature of the occasion* 30/30, etc; 2. period of time 11/8, etc; 3. the octave or liturgical season associated with a major festival 19/12, etc; 4. season of the year: **tempus brumale** 566/35, etc, *or* ~ **yemale** 11/15 winter; 5. *in various idioms*: *in attr phr* **pro tempore existens** for the time being 529/31, etc; **tunc temporis** then, at that time 31/1, etc

tenementum, -i *n nt* land holding, *or* a dwelling thereon 259/6, etc

teneo, -ere, -ui, -tum *v tr* 1. *literally* to hold, *hence* to hold (someone) in a certain condition (with predicative modifier) 306/1; 2. to have, keep (eg, a domestic animal) 6/25; 3. to hold (eg, a meeting or other event) 29/12, etc; 4. to have an obligation (to do something), have (to do something) 3/23; 5. *in pass idiom in bonds and the like* to be bound, held accountable (for a sum of money) 195/39, etc; *see also* **locumtenens**

tenor, -oris *n m* tenor, tone, slant (of meaning, eg, in a document) 529/15

tenus *prep with gen* (of extent) right up to, as far as; *see* **auris, crus**

Terentianus, -a, -um *adj* of or pertaining to Terence (Publius Terentius Afer, 195 or 185–159 BC), one of the two great Roman comedy writers 146/16

terminus, -i *n m* 1. limit, ending 315/18; 2. term, a set date fixed for some purpose 73/33; 3. term, a set period of time, eg, that for which an indenture runs 414/14, etc; 4. an academic term 30/3, etc

tessara, -e *n f literally* something square or rectangular, *by extension* a playing card 56/23

testa, -e *n f* head 10/27

theatricus, -a, -um *adj* of or pertaining to a stage or the theatre 177/29, etc; *m as sbst* player 170/24

theatrum, -i *n nt* 1. theatre, place or structure specifically intended for dramatic performance 138/13, 387/22; 2. stage, platform upon which drama is performed 102/5, etc; 3. used with a general application to all aspects of drama, the theatre, the stage 85/27, 179/5, 310/10, 387/27 *(in coll pl)*

theologia, -e *n f* theology, theological study, divinity 42/17, etc

theologicus, -a, -um *adj* of or pertaining to theological study 257/16, etc

theologus, -i *n m* theologian, a student or master in the theology faculty 27/24, etc

thesaurarius, -ii *n m* treasurer, a college or university officer 147/1, etc

Thetis, -idis *n f* Thetis, *in classical mythology* chief of the Nereids (or ocean nymphs) and mother of Achilles 314/1, oddly associated with Bacchus in the king of beans correspondence 799/25

tibia, -e *n f literally* a reed-pipe, *by extension* the shin bone, *hence* the shin 5/19, etc

tibicen, -inis *n m literally* one who plays a reed-pipe [OLD tibia], piper; *but possibly* a generic term for one playing a wind instrument rather than specifically one playing an instrument with a reed mouthpiece 85/17, etc; **tibicina** *(1st decl)* 280/37; **tybicen** 158/29, etc

timpanista *see* **tympanista**

timpanizo, -are, -aui, -atum *v intr* to beat a drum, drum 439/1

tinto, -are, -aui, -atum *v tr* to ring (a bell), strike (a beat) 378/18m

titulus, -i *n m* 1. title (of a literary work) 307/34; 2. identifying description, title 360/30, etc; 3. land title: **propositio tituli** exhibition of title, *apparently* an annual event at Merton College involving the administration of the college's property 28/36

toga, -e *n f in* CL the Roman toga [OLD], *by extension* robe, gown (referring to contemporary dress) 8/33, etc

torneamentum, -i *n nt* tourney, tournament 529/32

totalis, -e *adj* total, complete, entire 96/37, etc

totaliter *adv* totally, completely 3/22

totum, -i *sbst nt* the whole of something, the total 286/22; *in idioms*: **in toto** in all, in total 12/33, etc; **pro toto** entirely 281/36

tractus, -us *n m* track, path followed (eg, by an aisle or walkway) 137/5

tragaedia, tragaoedia, tragedia *see* **tragoedia**

tragice *adv* in the manner of a tragedy 178/34

tragicocomoedia, -ae *n f* tragicomedy, a play blending elements of classical tragedy and comedy 149/6

tragicus, -a, -um *adj* of or pertaining to a tragedy 177/31, etc; **tragica comedia** tragicomedy, a play blending elements of classical tragedy and comedy 156/10, etc

tragoedia, -ae *n f* tragedy, a serious drama having an unhappy outcome, *here probably more specifically either* an ancient tragedy *or* a modern work imitating ancient tragedy at least in form 136/32, etc; **tragaedia** 94/16, etc; **tragaoedia** 424/18; **tragedia** 81/32, etc

translacio, -onis *n f* translation, a festival commemorating the formal transfer of a saint's relics from one site to another 11/40, etc

transuersalis, -e *adj* transverse, at right angles to a stated or implied direction 12/18

trebalis, -e *adj* treble; *see* **uiola**

triatus, -a, -um *pfp* tried, tested 9/28

trihumphus *see* **triumphus**

Trinitas, -atis *n f* 1. the Trinity 12/21 [ODCC TRINITY, Doctrine of the]; 2. Trinity Sunday, the Sunday after Pentecost: **terminus Trinitatis** Trinity term, the academic term following Trinity Sunday 258/39; *see also* **festum**

triplicatus, -a, -um *adj* triple, threefold 305/16

triplicitas, -atis *n f* that which is threefold, triplet 305/15

tripudium, -ii *n nt originally* ancient Roman ritual dance, *in AL apparently* a dance containing formal or set elements 5/22m, etc

Trisantonius, -a, -um *adj* of or pertaining to Southampton, a town and earldom; *m sg as sbst* the earl of Southampton 313/15

triumphans, -ntis *prp* triumphing 137/27, etc; **Christus Triumphans** *Christus Triumphans*, title of a play by John Foxe 106/33

triumphator, -oris *n m* one who triumphs, *here* an allusion to the title of John Foxe's play *Christus Triumphans* 107/14

triumphus, -i *n m* 1. triumph, *literally* a quasi-religious Roman ritual celebrated by a victorious general, *by extension* any celebration of a victory: **agere triumphum** to celebrate a triumph, to triumph 180/7; 2. *hence* a celebration of some kind, perhaps including music or dance 209/16; 3. a victory 14/26 (*in form* **trihumphus**)

truncus, -i *n m* (wooden) box, chest 9/23

tuba, -e *n f in CL* a trumpet with a straight tube used for military signals, as well as in various civilian processions; *here probably* any straight wind instrument not having a reed mouthpiece 140/10, etc; **tubus** *(2nd decl)* 416/36

tubicen, -inis *n m* trumpeter, one who plays the 'tuba' (probably one who plays any straight wind instrument not having a reed mouthpiece) 21/19, etc; **tubicenibus** *(dat pl)* 279/4

tubicina, -e *n m* trumpeter, one who plays the 'tuba' (probably one who plays any straight wind instrument not having a reed mouthpiece) 387/40

Τυχερος, -ου *n m* the surname Tucker, rendered into Greek as part of a pun based on the resemblance in sound between it and τυχηρός, fortunate, lucky 347/20

tunica, -e *n f* 1. coat, tabard 57/17, etc; 2. tunicle 1093/2 (*possibly also an occurrence of sense* 1)

turpiloquium, -ii *n nt* rude, shameful, or crude speech, bad language 11/2, etc; **turpeloquium** 163/18

tutelaris, -e *adj* of or pertaining to a guardian, tutelary 315/25

tybicen *see* **tibicen**

tympanista, -ae *n m* drummer 79/26, etc; **timpanista** 82/28, etc

tympanistrius, -ii *n m* drummer 76/16

uacatio, -onis *n f* vacation 259/1

uacuus, -a, -um *adj* empty 60/10; *see also* **possessio**

ualencia, -e *n f* value, price, worth (+ *gen of price or value*) 8/29, etc

ualor, -oris *n m* value, worth 74/2

ualua, -e *n f* door, *especially* one of a pair of doors 894/27

uenaticus, -a, -um *adj* of or pertaining to hunting; *see* **canis**

uendico, -are, -aui, -atum *v tr for* uindico [OLD]

uendidus, -a, -um *pfp pass* sold 22/6, etc [*form of* uenditus *from OLD* uendo]

uenella, -e *n f* lane, side road 8/20

uentilo, -are, -aui, -atum *v intr* to play a wind instrument 267/10 [*see OLD* uentilo]

Venus, -eris *n f* Venus, Roman goddess of sexual love and generation, whose name was also given to the second planet 140/7, etc; *with* 'dies' *understood* **Veneris** Friday 84/20, etc

uerberum, -i *n nt* a blow 56/3

uerbositas, -atis *n f* wordiness 60/9

uernaculus, -a, -um *adj literally* native-born, indigenous, *hence f sg as sbst* native tongue 314/8

uersus, -a, -um *pfp pass* reversed, turned over or around, *hence* **verso folio** on the back of the sheet 571/8

uersus *prep* 1. to, toward (often with hostile sense) 5/31; 2. (of purpose) for, toward 202/23

Vertumnus, -i *n m* Vertumnus, Etruscan deity regarded by the Romans as the god of the

changing year, here named as the title of a
play, *Vertumnus* 307/1, etc (*but see* p 1118,
endnote to *stc* 24939 pp 18–19, 45–8)

uespera, -e *n f* vespers, one of the canonical
hours making up the divine office of clerics;
despite its name, also the L word for evening,
vespers was usually said before dark, in the
late afternoon or early evening 3/20, etc

uespertinus, -a, -um *adj* of or pertaining to
evening; *see* **prex**

uestiarium, -ii *n nt* vestry, a room adjacent to a
church or chapel in which vestments, linens, and
other liturgical requisites were stored 443/40

uestis, -is *n f* clothing, *in pl* clothes 13/10, etc;
duplices uestes *literally* double clothing, *hence*
two outfits *or* sets of clothing 414/15, etc

uetus, -eris *adj* old 86/9, etc; *m as sbst* old friend
106/29; *n as sbst* something old 3/17

uicaria, -e *n f* vicarage, a vicar's benefice 42/19

uicarius, -ii *n m* vicar, one who acts as a deputy
for a rector who cannot discharge his duties
in a parish 80/34

uicecancellarius, -ii *n m* vice-chancellor, deputy
of the (University's) chancellor 7/22, etc;
uice-cancellarius 512/12; **uicechancellarius**
281/10

uicecomes, -itis *n m* sheriff, an officer of the
Crown within a given county, having particular
responsibilities for the county court and other
aspects of the administration of justice
484/18, etc

uicecustos, -odis *n m* vice-warden, deputy warden
(eg, of a college) 13/26, etc

uicepreses, -idis *n m* vice-president, deputy president, *here* of Magdalen College 46/36, etc

uicepresidens, -ntis *n m* vice-president, deputy
president, *here* of Magdalen College 27/25, etc

uice-principalis, -is *n m* vice-principal, *here* of
Jesus College 452/14

uicis *(gen) n f (nom sg lacking)* 1. occasion, time:
alia uice on another occasion, another time
1086/41; **duabus uicibus** on two occasions,
twice 1131/33; **prima ... uice** on the first
occasion, the first time 556/24; **2da uice** on
a second occasion, the second time 556/24;

2. one's part: **triplicatae carminum uices** songs
in three parts 305/16; *hence* **uicem gerens** one's
deputy 48/34, etc; 3. *by extension of sense 2*
uice + *gen* in place of, instead of 308/14, etc;
see also **ad, per**

uicus, -i *n m* street 8/20; **altus uicus** high street
5/29, etc

uideo, uidere, uidi, uisus *v tr* 1. to see (physically
or intellectually) 37/34, etc; 2. (of a coroner)
to view (a dead person for the purpose of
determining the cause of death) 5/17; 3. *in pass
idiom* to seem 37/25, etc

uidua, -e *n f* widow 179/1 [*OLD* uiduus[1]]

uiella, -e *n f* fiddle, a stringed instrument usually
played with a bow 5/25

uigilas, -atis *n f* wake, apparently a night-time
observance at Magdalen College providing an
occasion for various popular customs 176/11,
etc; **uigelas** 170/17 [*likely derived from* **uigilia**]

uigilia, -ae *n f* 1. vigil, eve of a liturgical festival
5/22, etc; 2. wake, a night-time observance
providing occasion for various popular customs
(sense perhaps derived from the association of
certain liturgical eves, such as St John's Eve or
St Nicholas' Eve, with such customs, or from
the vigils kept with the body of a dead person
the night before the funeral, which provided
similar occasions for such customs) 40/21,
etc; **vigialia** 73/17

uigilo, -are, -aui, -atum *v intr literally* to keep
watch; *hence by extension either* to observe a
(liturgical) eve *or possibly* to hold a wake 5/24

uigor, -oris *n m literally* strength, vigour, *hence*
uigore + *gen* by virtue of 146/41

uilla, -e *n f* town 5/18, etc

uillanus, -a, -um *adj* of or pertaining to a town;
see **balliuus**

uiola, -e *n f* viol, a bowed stringed instrument:
trebalis uiola a treble viol 414/24; *see EG* vilyn

uirgo, -inis *n f* virgin, often used as an attribute
of a saint 3/14, etc

ullibi *adv* anywhere 305/29

ulna, -e *n f* ell, a measure of length 8/35

Vlysses, -is *n m* Ulysses, a Greek hero of the
Trojan War: *named as* a character in the play

Ajax Flagellifer 308/4, etc; *as* a character in the masque *Penelope's Wooers* 371/13

umbraculum, -i *n nt literally* something providing shelter or shade, *here by extension* a canopy 137/6, etc

unanimis, -e *adj* being in concord or accord, *hence* (of agreement or a decision) unanimous 57/25

uniuersitas, -atis *n f* the university, whether viewed as a physical site 11/26, etc, or as a corporate body 7/24, etc

univocus, -a, -um *adj* having a single voice, unanimous 799/22

uocatio, -onis *n f* calling, summoning 6/15, etc

ursa, -e *n f* (female) bear (for baiting or other entertainment) 50/14

ursarius, -ii *n m* bearward 29/20

ursus, -i *n m* (male) bear (for baiting or other entertainment) 37/21

usque *prep (and adv)* 1. (of time) until, up to the time of 491/14; 2. *in combination with other prepositions*: **usque ad** until (a point in time) 414/14, etc; up to, as far as (a point in space) 9/24, etc; 3. *adv* as long as one can, *hence* **usque morari** to delay as long as possible, to linger 270/10; **huc usque** until now 308/41

Vtopicus, -a, -um *adj* of or pertaining to Utopia, Utopian, ideal 310/8

Wallia, -e *n f* Wales 9/20, etc

Wallicus, -a, -um *adj* Welsh 8/19, etc

Windishgracius, -a, -um *adj* of or belonging to the Windischgraetz family: *m as sbst* a member of that family 257/18

Wintonia, -ae *n f* Winchester, name of a diocese 417/17, etc

wlnero, -are, -aui, -atum *v tr for* uulnero [OLD]

Woodstochia, -ae *n f* Woodstock, name of a parish 465/35

Worcestria, -ae *n f* Worcester, name of an earldom 313/11

Wynsoria, -e *n f* Windsor, name of a royal castle and chapel 73/20

ydioma *see* **idioma**

yemalis, -e *adj for* hiemalis [OLD]

ymago, -inis *n f for* imago [OLD]

zelus, -i *n m* eagerness, ardour, zeal 178/9

Zodiacum, -i *n nt* the zodiac, a band of twelve constellations, also known as signs of the zodiac, which define the sun's apparent path across the sky following the plane of the ecliptic 308/27, etc

English Glossary

WILLIAM COOKE

a *pron* he 774/14

a *prep* on, at 61/9

a brode *adv* abroad, ie, present and active 185/24

abut *prep* about 542/27, 543/22; **a bowght** 56/35

accompteantes *n pl* accountants 88/3

aell *see* **alle**

Æsclypead *n* Asclepiad, an ancient Greek metre 318/29

aholfe *n phr* a half 123/13

Alhalo day *n phr* All Hallows' Day, All Saints' Day 50/4

alle *n* ale 24/25, 70/32; **aell** 211/1; **all** 17/8; *see also* **Hocke ayle, Whytson alle**

Allhollowtyde *n comp* Allhallowtide, All Saints' Day and the seven days following 409/28

als *adv* also 480/27 [*OED* Als]

alyn *n phr* a line, ie, a piece or cloth of linen 38/20 [*MED* līn *n* 3(a)]

an odre *pron* another 50/4

'an'ts *in phr* **the breath 'an'ts venome** the breath on it's venom, ie, its exhalation is poisonous 378/25

a pease *adv* apace, quickly or immediately 55/13–14; **a pece** 56/37

apoulsterer *n* upholsterer 520/24

apprenteship *n* apprenticeship 513/35

aringoes *n pl* eryngoes, candied roots of sea holly 480/11

as't *conj phr* as to 561/8

axe *v* ask; **axe** *pr 3 pl* 88/3; **axid** *pa t 1 sg* 55/31

ayene *adv* again 75/28

ayenste *prep* against, in anticipation of 75/17

aylyt *v pa t 3 sg in phr* **what aylyt** what ailed, what harm would it have done 129/16

barands *n pl poss* barons' *but with pun on* barrens', *meaning* of persons of dull wit or discernment 316/13 [*OED* Barren *a and sb* 8]

barbaries *n pl* barberries 480/11

baye salt *n phr* salt obtained from pans set in a bay of the sea 112/16

baylives *n pl* bailiffs 883/9; **bayles** 537/8; **baylies** 300/24; **bayliues** 35/17; **bayliues** *pl poss* 35/11

be *prep* by 37/19, 56/18

bearebruer *n comp* beer-brewer 153/1

bearerode *see* **berward**

bee *adj* bay, reddish brown(?) 292/25

beffe *see* **bieffe**

bequest *n* gift 87/1

bere *n* bier 122/19

berward *n comp* bearward, bear keeper 143/34; **bearerode** 171/13; **berwode** 249/35

beshrowe *v pr 1 sg* beshrew, condemn 869/34

betwine *prep* between 152/40

bieffe *n* beef 171/19, 171/23; **beffe** 111/24(2); **biefe** 171/21; **byffe** 160/27(2); *see also* **powder beef**

billament *n* biliment, spreading collar or neckcloth 285/10; *in comp* **billament lace** lace to trim a biliment 296/33

black a more *n comp* blackamoor, dark-skinned person 564/28

blacklings *n pl* small, Black boys 564/25

blutt *see* **Gotes blutt**

botmen *n comp pl* boatmen 257/35

bousars *n pl* bursars 176/34; **bowsers** 346/26

bowez *n pl* boughs 15/6

breyd *n* bread 71/36

brode *see* **a brode**

bushel nayles *n comp pl* nails sold by the bushel 175/33, 182/40; **busshel nayle** 120/7; **busshell nayles** 114/30

bussel *n* bushel 112/16

buttyre *n* butter 111/35

byffe *see* **bieffe**

by hocke or by crocke *adv phr* by hook or by crook; by any means, fair or foul 55/36

bylyue *v* believe 75/24

cabbyshes *n pl* cabbages 161/3

Candilmes *n* Candlemas 50/2

capp mayntenaunce *n phr* cap of maintenance, a kind of cap worn by, or carried before, a person of dignity, such as the sovereign or a mayor, usually round with a tapering extension at the back, made of velvet and lined and generously banded with ermine or other fur; *here* as a property in a play 30/32–3

caprons *n pl* capons 111/31, 112/12

caroach *n* caroche, carriage 782/19

caryge *n* carriage, transport 78/27; **charriadge** 112/5

casement *n* case 41/5 [*OED* Casement 3a]

ceazed *pp* put in possession(?), *or* settled, appointed(?) 344/41 [*OED* Seize *v*]

ceke *see* **sache**

cetterne *n* cittern 381/32; **cyturne** 166/30; **cittarnes** *pl* 530/24

chambled *n* camlet, a fine fabric made of angora wool, pure or mixed with silk 292/16

chanons *n pl* canons 75/24

charriadge *see* **caryge**

chaundry *n* chandry: 1. place for storing candles 116/35; 2. household or college staff responsible for making candles **chaundrye** 130/26

checkyns *n pl* chickens 111/32; **cheekynges** 160/36

chestes *n* chess 56/32

chewettes *n pl* dishes of various kinds of meat and fish, minced and seasoned 172/7

chife *adj* chief 579/7

chouse *n* choose 341/23, 346/35

Christenmas *see* **Cristinmes**

cittarnes *see* **cetterne**

clacking *vb n* cleaning, making to work smoothly (of a keyboard instrument) 480/20 [*OED* Clack *v*² and Clag *v* 4(?); *cp also EDD* Clack *s and v* 10 'valve of a bellows']

clericordes *n pl* clavicords 74/3, etc; **clavecolles** 154/32; **clerycordes** 73/28, etc

cleyr *adj* clear, free of offsetting expenses 59/22, 63/10; **clare** 330/13; **clyre** 66/6

close *n pl* clothes 319/5; *in comp* **close keepers** clothes keepers 514/18

clubbyng *vb n* holding the yearly feast and procession of a fellowship(?) 179/17, 179/19 [*EDD* Club *sb*²]

color de roye *n phr* colour-de-roy, a bright, tawny colour 293/5

companyounce *n pl* companions 56/11

conseittes *n pl* conceits, witty tricks and devices 55/11

construction *n* mental reception or interpretation 294/29

cornish *n* cornice 420/26

cosseck *n* cassock 289/31, 289/32

counties *n* countess 165/12

cowcombers *n pl* cucumbers 161/3

cowles *n pl* coals 50/1, 50/4

crafyshe *n pl* crayfish 161/8

Cristinmes *n* Christmas 50/1, 50/2; **Christenmas** 1134/43; **Cristinnmes** 55/12

crocke *see* **by hocke or by crocke**

cyturne *see* **cetterne**

damsell *n* damson 480/11

declaro *quasi-adv* clearly, without offsetting expenses 70/9, etc; **declaroe** 77/32, etc; **declarow** 210/11; **declarowe** 238/23 [*L* de claro *treated as E*]

defendores *n* defendress 152/40

demy *n* a foundation scholar at Magdalen College, Oxford 197/31; **demyes** *pl* 197/28

determiner *n* a student performing his final exercises to qualify as a bachelor of arts 887/7

determining *prp* performing the final exercises to qualify as a bachelor of arts 887/12

deuide *adj* devoid, empty, ineffective 436/2

di *abbrev for L* dimidium, *used in E context for* (and) a half 113/23, etc

dialaughter *n jocular pseudo-learned compound of* laughter(?) 784/29

diaphange *n* diaphragm, midriff 784/28 ['diaphragm' confused with 'diaphane'(?)]

differre *v* defer 355/18, 355/24; **differed** *pa t 3 sg* 248/26; **differred** *pp* 365/12; **dyfferred** 132/22

dodar *n* dodo 513/24

dossen *n* dozen 111/22, etc

doulcemeryes *n pl* dulcimers 41/5

dou3t *v pr 1 sg* doubt 75/21

drainge *vb n* drawing and selling (ale from a cask)(?) 211/1

driue *v pa t 3 sg* drove 475/2

Dutch lyghtes *n comp pl for* douse lights *or* dout lights *meaning* extinguishers(?) *or* lights made from Dutch rushes(?) 288/30 [*OED* Douse *v*¹ 4d *and* Dout *sb and v*]

dyfferred *see* **differre**

endagine *n* indignation, umbrage 567/37 [*MED* endeine *n*]

epithite *n* epithet 785/2

fagg & rag *n phr literally* the last scraps of a bolt of cloth; *here* everyone to the last man 318/20 [*OED* Fag *sb*² 2 *and* Rag *sb*¹ 1]

farme *n in phr* **to farme lett** let or lease to farm, lease to a tenant for rent 390/25; **to ferme lett** 153/10; **to ffarme lett** 552/34; **to farme letten** leased out 390/24; **to ferme letten** 153/9; **to ffarme letten** 552/33

fauchion *n* falchion, curved, one-edged sword; **fachions** *pl* 288/10; **ffachions** 289/16

fayne *adj* obliged, constrained 55/33 [*OED* Fain *a and adv* 2b]

feaskettes *n pl* fescues, rushes or pieces of straw for strewing floors or lighting fires 109/15

ferme *see* **farme**

fers *adj* fierce 37/17

fersnes *n* fierceness 37/20

fett *v* fetch; **fett** *pa t 3 sg* 111/40, etc; **fett** *pa t 3 pl* 112/25 [*OED* Fet *v*]

feyve *adj* five 123/1

ffachions *see* **fauchion**

ffarme *see* **farme**

ffranches *n* franchise, the district within which a city could exercise its privileges; *hence* the public marking of its boundaries 572/9, 572/16; **ffranchises** *pl in same sense* 334/7, etc; **ffranchizes** 576/14, etc; **ffraunchisies** 406/2, etc; *in phr* **goeing the ffrenches** making the yearly ride round the franchise limits 471/4; **rydeing of a franchises** *in same sense* 409/33; **ryde the ffranches** rode round the limits of the franchise 257/35–6; **went the ffranchises** *in same sense* 574/15, 574/24; **went the ffranchizes** 466/11; **ffraunches dynner** *n comp* franchise dinner, held when the mayor rode round the franchise limits 112/1

fiuth *adj* fifth 195/25

flexen *adj* flaxen, pale yellow 288/6, etc; **fflexen** 289/12, 289/13

flyen *pp* flown 270/21

foloth *v pr 3 sg* followeth, follows 1109/2

formalities *n pl* dress robes 876/19, etc

forthe nighte *n comp* fortnight 294/11

fotyinge *vb n* footing, attaching feet to (trestles) 172/19

foures *n pl* fourpenny nails 114/30

fowrmes *n pl* forms, benches 131/15

franchises *see* **ffranches**

Frenchehood *n phr* French hood, a kind of head-dress worn by women, particularly when undergoing punishment for unchastity 865/2; **Frenchehoode** 864/41

fullyd *pp* filled 55/12

fyues *n pl* fives, ie, fivepenny nails 114/29, 120/7

gaderyng *vb n* gathering 52/25

game *n* troop of entertainers (*here* trained animals) 165/18 [*OED* Game *sb* 8a]

Gasscune *adj* Gascon, wine from Gascony 112/14; **Gascoigne** 186/23

geaven *pp* given 215/10(2)

geise *see* **gyese**

getheryd *pp* gathered 88/29

gigg *n* jig, a song and dance, often performed at the end of a play 319/1

gogs nowns *interj euphemistic distortion of* God's wounds 222/18

Gotes blutt *interj* Welsh or German pronunciation of 'God's blood' as an oath 129/6

Greene Cloth *n phr* the Board of Green Cloth, the department of the royal household controlling domestic spending 121/10; **Greene Clothe** 121/34

grett *adj* great 55/15, 55/29; **gret** 175/33; **grette** 56/31

guelded *pp* gelded, *literally* castrated; *here* mutilated 558/11

guile-halls *n pl* taverns or gambling-dens where the patrons were tricked and cheated, dens of iniquity(?) 868/10

gyese *n pl* geese 160/30, 160/38; **geise** 171/26

gyys *n* guise, custom 55/32

haith *v pr 3 sg* hath 197/35

hale *see* **Whytson alle**

halliers *n pl* students attached to a hall (rather than a college) 219/19, etc

harneyes *n* harness, armour 99/2

harpsichon *n* harpsichord 485/16, 485/18 [*OED* Harpsicon]

harreldes *n pl* heralds 144/8

hayll *see* **Whytson alle**

heare *n* hair 116/18; **here** 121/15; *in comp* **heare lyme** hair lime, lime mixed with hair for use as plaster 120/35

here *pron pl poss* their 8/21

hesterday *adv* yesterday 55/29 [*spelling influenced by* L hesterna dies(?)]

himpen *n* hymn 109/29

Hochtyde *see* **Octyde**

hocke *see* **by hocke or by crocke**

Hocke ayle *n phr* Hock ale, a church ale held in Hocktide 99/36; **Hoke ale** 90/38; **Ock ale** 82/11

Hocke Tewnes day *n phr* Hock Tuesday, the Tuesday in Hocktide 18/28

Hogtyde *see* **Octyde**

holbert *n* halberd 247/16; **holbeard** 773/26; **holberte** 247/14; **holbertes** *pl* 246/38

hollyn *n* holly 179/26

hoo be it *adv* howbeit, yet 56/16

Hoocke mony *n phr* Hock money, money collected at Hocktide 113/4

hoole *adj* whole 134/6, 134/30

horshyre *n comp* horse-hire, hire of a horse 420/24, 420/30

ho so *pron* whoso, whoever 8/21

howpe *n* hoop, *here evidently* attached ring for lifting a cover 112/11

hundreth *n* hundred 199/22; **hundarthe** 123/1, etc; **hundereth** 111/34

iacke *n* jack, short close-fitting jacket 320/31; **iak** 8/32

insignes *n pl* insignia 283/4 [*OED* Ensign 4]

it' *pron poss* its 436/16

kewe *n* (actor's) cue, prompt 129/5

key kepers *n comp pl in Oxford* the city treasurers, so called because they kept the keys to the chest where the city funds were stored 167/15, 167/31; **keykeepers** 325/37

kinderkin *n* kilderkin, half-barrel cask 576/17; **kinderkine** 171/42; **kynderkyne** 165/24; **kynderkyns** *pl* 111/21

kirfes *n pl* kerfs, cut lengths of timber 113/22, etc

knawe *n* knave, menial 56/18(2)

kniues *n poss* knife's 784/37

kynderkyne, kynderkyns *see* **kinderkin**

laicks *n pl* laics; *usually* persons not in holy orders *but here* non-members of the University 884/27

landskips *n pl* landscapes 890/4; **landscips** 545/21

lawers *n poss* lawyer's 435/14

lett, letten *see* **farme**

liff *n* life 145/30; **lyffe** 56/19

liuerie *n* badge to indicate payment at Whitsun festivals 20/21 [*DML* liberare 9]

loese *v* lose 131/5

lowde *adj* clamorously and insistently demanding 129/9 [*OED* Loud *a* 2]

ly *definite art m (French)* used to mark the presence of a vernacular noun or phrase in a passage of Latin 73/28, etc; **le** 14/38, etc

lycke *adj* like 127/18
lyffe *see* **liff**
lyme *see* **heare**

macharoing *ppl adj* macaronic, mixing English with Latin 778/4
Mallicoly *n* Melancholy, personified as a character in a play 311/2; **Mallicolie** 312/2
mare *n* mayor 490/13
marybons *n pl* marrow bones 160/33
meane *n* a middle part in a musical composition, falling somewhere below the treble 370/12m [*New Grove* Meane]
mearcement *n* amercement, fine 400/25
mearcer *n* mercer, dealer in silks and other fine fabrics and sometimes small goods 421/20, 421/21
meate prickes *n comp pl* skewers for cooking and/or eating meat 172/30
meight *v pa t 3 sg* might 132/21
meny *n* meinie, company 55/29
mey *pron poss* my 123/12, etc
minstreill *n* minstrel 53/23; **mynster** 35/15
Moare *n* Moor, dark-skinned person from North Africa, the Middle East, or India 560/35; *see also* **black a more**
morrish daunces *n comp pl* morris dances 246/20
mucisions *n pl* musicians 257/32; **musetions** 242/26; **mvsisiones** 149/26
mumchance *n comp* a dice game 868/9
muske bisket *n comp* biscuits flavoured with some musky fruit or herb(?) 480/8–9
mynster *see* **minstreill**

needles *adj* needless, unnecessary 769/11
nother *conj in phr* **nother … nother** neither … nor 55/30–31; **nider … nor** *in same sense* 129/22
nowns *see* **gogs nowns**
noysers *n pl* noisers, noisy persons 374/17
ny3the *n* night 64/12, 64/13

ob *abbrev for L* obolus, *used in E context for* halfpenny 34/32, etc
Ock ale *see* **Hocke ayle**
Octyde *n* Hocktide 61/9, etc; **Hochtyde** 72/30; **Hogtyde** 86/37; **Ocke tyde** 83/6, 88/29; **Octide** 71/19, etc
odre *see* **an odre**
of *adv* off 97/14, 143/21
off *prep* of 58/22, etc
on *pron* one 50/4, etc
one *adj* own 185/21
onles *conj* unless 75/19
ons *adv* once 869/18; **oons** 56/15
or *conj* before 55/14
out *adv and prep* (of an actor) out of one's part, unable to remember one's lines 355/4, 357/24, 392/36; **owte** 129/4, 129/6, 129/9
ou3t off tewen *adv phr* out of tune 75/17

panses *n pl* pansies 293/12
parych clark *n phr* parish clerk, person in minor orders who helped the clergy to carry out services 45/19, 51/35
peace *n in phr* **of peace coulor** piece-dyed, ie, dyed after weaving(?) 292/1
peadles *n pl* a disparaging name for bedels 316/7 [*cp EDD* Peedle *v* 'look or creep slyly about']
pease, pece *see* **a pease**
pertynyd *v pa t 3 pl* pertained 56/33
philbeardes *n pl* filberts 171/33
phillippe *n* fillip 270/12
pla *v* play 56/37; **pleainge** *vb n* 172/36
plaudity *n* plaudit 356/18 [*OED* Plaudite]
ploumes *n pl* plums 161/6
plumbe worke *n comp* lead work 118/1 [*OED* Plumb *v* 5 *and* 6]
potted *v pa t 3 sg in phr* **potted oute** improvised (verses) as a retort 173/35 [*OED* Pot *v*¹ 7]
poulderling's *n pl* a term for second-year undergraduates at St John's College, Oxford 340/36, 340/40 [*cp OED* Polder *sb*¹, *EDD* Polder *sb* 'marsh, bog'(?)]
powder beef *n phr* beef salted or mixed with powder as a seasoning or preservative 108/33
powederinge covere *n phr* perforated cover allowing seasoning to be sprinkled over food(?) 112/11
preethee *v phr* prithee, (I) pray thee 374/31, 377/11; **prethee** 378/4
presedent *adj* precedent, previous 359/17

presens *adj used as n pl* presents, ie, present circumstances or affairs 500/13 [*OED* Present *sb*¹ 2]

president *n* precedent 222/3

prethee *see* **preethee**

pricke madame *n comp* prick-madam, a herb growing on walls, more usually called stonecrop 116/18

princelick *adj* prince-like, befitting a sovereign
130/26

priviledgemen *n comp pl* privileged men; tradesmen
enjoying licensed privileges as suppliers of goods
or services to the University 498/15; *see also*
Introduction, p 586

purseauantes *n pl* pursuivants, heralds' assistants
350/7

qua. *abbrev for L* quarterium, *meaning* a fourth
part, *used in E context for* farthing 80/10, etc

quarter *n* 1. quarter barrel (of ale or beer) 111/20,
159/3; **quaerters** *pl* 108/30; **quarters** 111/19, etc;
2. quarter chaldron (of coal) **quarters** *pl* 112/3;
3. quarter log (of timber) **quarters** *pl* 117/29

quarterne *n* quartern: 1. quarter hundredweight
(of lead) 118/3; **quartarne** 123/11; **quartarnes**
pl 123/3; 2. quarter bushel (of hair) 120/34;
3. quarter barrel (of ale) **quarturne** 90/30

querister *n* boy chorister 428/31

quyne *n* queen 99/5; **quines** *poss* 122/42

requiret *v pa t 3 sg* required 185/21

resseuyd *pp* received 25/12, etc; **recewyd** 54/28,
54/29; **resauid** 66/12, 66/13; **resauyd** 72/30,
72/31; **reseuyd** 72/24, 72/25; **resiuyd** 61/9,
61/10; **ressayuyd** 43/5, 43/6; **reysevyd** 63/9,
63/10

riall *adj* royal 135/4; **ryall** 127/13 [*OED* Rial *a*]

riallthe *n* royalty, royal rank and power 56/17
[*OED* Rialty]

rickinge *n* rick stand, frame for building
hayricks or similar structure(?) 394/23 [*OED*
Rick *v*¹]

rid(e), ridd *see* **ryde**

riflinge *prp* gambling 868/11

Robin Whodes ballades *n phr pl* Robin Hood's
ballads, ballads about Robin Hood 146/25–6

roomthes *n pl* (vacant) places, *hence by extension*

absences, non-attendance (of persons at a play)
869/35

roye *see* **color de roye**

ryall *see* **riall**

ryde *v pa t 3 sg* rode 257/35; **rid** *pa t 3 pl* 875/26,
etc; **ride** 316/2, 551/10; **rid** *pp* ridden 537/2;
ridd 130/4

sa *v* say 56/35

sache *n* sack, white wine from Spain or the
Canary Islands 109/8; **ceke** 112/15

sadnes *n* seriousness, gravity 55/13

salting money *n comp* fee for matriculation,
called 'salting' in student slang, or else for
accompanying student initiation rites 234/28

sant *n* saint 45/17, etc; **sanct** 59/4, 81/24; **sent**
9/6, etc

saore *adj* sour 789/9

sapplins *n pl* saplings 255/6

sarmans *n pl* sermons 579/12

sawyres *n pl* sawyers 182/4

scedule *n* schedule, itemized list 525/12; **schedall**
536/21

schargys *n pl* charges, expenses 67/15

schenes *n pl* scenes, scenery 557/2

scutchin *n* scutcheon: 1. ornamental shield on a
hearse **scutchions** *pl* 372/12; 2. small ornamental shield worn by a city wait on a
chain or ribbon round his neck as a badge of
office 272/16, 272/17; **scutchen** 482/7, etc;
schutchens *pl* 482/9; **schutchins** 201/24;
scutchins 167/12, etc; **scuttchins** 192/14,
etc; **skutchyns** 167/32

sea *n* see 259/39

seeling *n* ceiling 325/5; **selinge** 151/7

sent *see* **sant**

sere *adj used as n in phr* in that sere in that single
(person) 142/4 [*OED* Sere *adv and a*² B1]

sessor *n* assessor, technical adviser to a judge
350/21

shewett *n* suet 160/28, 172/32; **shwett** 111/28

Shroftide *n comp* Shrovetide, the three days before
Ash Wednesday 253/22; **Shorfetyde** 228/39

shut *n* sliding panel 889/37; **shutt** 545/14; **shuts**
pl 891/17, 891/19; **shutts** 544/34, etc

shute *n* suit 359/26

shutour *n* suitor 150/17

shwett *see* **shewett**

sids men *n pl* sidesmen, churchwardens' deputies; *in phr* **towne sids men** those sidesmen of the church of St Mary Magdalen who represented and oversaw parishioners living within the city of Oxford 518/28

singinge breade *n comp* wafers of unleavened bread as used for Holy Communion 119/20 [*OED* Singing bread]

sixes *n pl* sixpenny nails 114/29, 120/6

sle *v imper sg* slay 8/20, etc

snew *v pa t 3 sg* snowed 191/14, 882/19

soudering *vb n* soldering 520/34

spang lace *n comp* lace adorned with spangles 292/29 [*OED* Spang *sb*¹ 1]

squadrant *n* quadrangle, square or oblong court-yard 304/25 [variant of 'quadrant,' influenced by 'square']

steres *n pl* stairs 118/15, etc; **steares** 114/4, etc

Steven testament *n phr* Greek New Testament in the edition of Robert Stephens (Paris, 1550) 316/19

stodd *v pa t 3 sg* stood 446/33

strang *adj* strange 882/1, 882/20; **strangly** *adv* 378/22

strangness *n* strangeness 891/23

strenght *n* strength 434/26

stwes *n pl* stews, ie, brothels 868/8

supposes *n pl* intended matters 179/29 [*OED* Suppose *sb* 4]

sutty *adj* sooty 560/34

swait *v pa t 3 sg* swayed, swerved 435/15

swarse *adj* swarth, dark 129/3

swineyard *n comp* swineherd 354/7

swipinge *vb n* sweeping 123/14, 123/20

swurne *pp* sworn 491/36

syxtens *n pl* sixteens, a kind of beer 111/20; **syxtenes** 171/41; **xvj** *sg* 108/32 [*OED* Sixteen 3]

tabine *n* waved or watered silk 292/6, 292/27 [*OED* Tabine]

taffatye *n* taffeta 289/35, etc; **tafaty** 354/17; **tafatye** 292/8, 353/30; **tafety** 359/26

tale *n in phr* **a tale vvithout head or feet** an incredible or nonsensical tale, a cock-and-bull story 157/23

tell *prep* till 362/26

tennes *n pl* tenpenny nails 114/29, etc

tewen *see* **ouȝt off tewen**

Tewnes *see* **Hocke Tewnes day**

the *pron* they 55/35, etc; **ye** 55/31; **yer** *poss* their 127/16, etc; **þer** 37/31; **theym** *obj* 87/36, 88/4; *see also* **thyare**

theys *pron pl* these 153/9

thorow *prep* through 223/18

thot *v pa t 1 sg* thought 130/3

threes *n pl* threepenny nails 120/7

thresure *n* treasure 177/7m

through *v pa t 3 pl* threw 887/8

thyare *v phr* they're, they are 770/31

to bete *v pa t 3 sg* thoroughly thrashed 56/14 [*OED* Tobeat *v*]

togated *adj in phr* **togated crew** gowned ones, ie, University men 889/26 [*OED* Togated]

toth *prep phr* to the 434/10

tourne broches *n pl* turnbroaches, persons who turned spits for roasting 112/22

tow *n* two 123/13, etc

traictise *n* treatise 1096/2

trowps *n pl* troops 316/41

tuckes *n pl* plaits or rats of hair for eking out heads of natural hair or wigs 288/7, 289/13 [*OED* Tuck *sb*¹ 1]

tuelf *adj in phr* **the tuelf signes** the twelve signs (of the zodiac) 310/32

Twelfe Day *n phr* Twelfth Day, the feast of the Epiphany 359/7–8; **Twelffeday** 150/27; **Twelthe Daye** 184/17; **Twelve Day** 194/8; **12 Day** 359/5

Twelfe Eue *n phr* Twelfth Eve, the eve of the Epiphany 359/7

Twelfnight *n phr* Twelfth Night, the eve of the Epiphany 252/5, etc; **Twelfe Night** 268/28, 369/7; **Tweluth Nyght** 425/26

Twseday *n comp* Tuesday 185/13; *see also* **Hocke Tewnes day**

varges *n* verjuice 172/26

vaute *n* vault 769/10

vautinge schoole *n comp* vaulting-school, school teaching vaulting and gymnastics 232/20

veile *n* light tint or colouring(?) 129/23 [*OED* Veil *sb*¹ 6a]

vellat *n* velvet 147/20

vented have *v phr* have ventured(?) *or* ventured to have(?) 774/17

vichauncellor *n* vice-chancellor 187/42, etc; **vichancellor** 283/5; **vichauncellors** *poss* 188/32

vilyn *n properly* violin, *but here* viol 414/25 [*OED* Violin *sb* 1b]

vm *pron* 'em, them 374/3

vnhollowed *ppl adj* unhallowed, unholy 435/7

wale *n* wall 141/32, 161/38

Walsh *adj* Welsh 8/21

wan *n* fan(?) *or variant of* wand(?) 367/14 [*OED* Wan *sb*² 1]

wan *v pa t 1 sg* won 788/6

wardropp *n* wardrobe, the department of a sovereign's household that kept and supplied clothes, bedding, and hangings 350/11

ware *v imper pl* take care, be on guard 8/20, etc

warkes *n pl* works 75/26

washed *pp* decorated with wash colour(?) *or* coated with size(?) 297/25; **wasshed** 188/26

wasseld *v pa t 3 sg* wassailed, drank together convivially from a common bowl 179/14

wayghtes *n pl* waits, musicians retained by a corporation 155/8, etc; **waytors** 512/5; **weates** 166/23

wemen *n pl* women 205/24, 250/12; **weemen** 477/25; **weomen** 273/12; **weemen's** *pl poss* 864/23, 864/26; **wemens** 210/33, 870/22

Wesontyde, Wettsontyd(e) *see* **Whysontyde**

wheat money *n comp* money paid to buy wheat or in lieu of wheat(?) 462/26

wher *v pa t 3 pl* were 55/35

whill *n* while, time 56/31

whirrytts *n pl* wherrets: light, sharp blows, such as a box on the ear or a slap on the face 864/4

Whisson aile *see* **Whytson alle**

whister *n* whisker(?) 378/4

Whodes *see* **Robin Whodes ballades**

Whysontyde *n comp* Whitsuntide, Pentecost and the seven days following 74/19; **Wesontyde** 17/8; **Wettsontyd** 108/7; **Wettsontyde** 152/4; **Wyssontyde** 21/37

Whytson alle *n phr* Whitsun ale, a church ale held at Whitsuntide 82/36, 88/30; **Whisson aile** 446/26; **Wysson ale** 68/6; **Wytson all** 61/10, 67/16; **Wytsune alle** 99/30; **Wytsun hale** 74/26; **Wyttson hayll** 72/31

wiffe *n* wife 172/21, 474/32; **wyeffe** 161/23; **wyff** 112/23

wifling shuts *n comp pl* whiffling suits; suits for whifflers, armed attendants who cleared the way for public spectacles 421/27

wodd *n* wood 112/1

wol *v pr 2 pl* will 75/24

woodenes *n* madness, frenzy 37/20 [*OED* Woodness]

wu't *v pr 2 sg* wilt 376/4

wyeffe, wyff *see* **wiffe**

wyen *n* wine 52/39, 58/22; **wyine** 70/32

wyllynes *n* wiliness, cunning 37/19

Wysson ale, Wytson all, Wytsun hale, Wytsune alle, Wyttson hayll *see* **Whytson alle**

Wyssontyde *see* **Whysontyde**

xvj *see* **syxtens**

yall *v* yawl, bawl 435/6

yats *pron phr* that's, that is 316/35, etc

ye *see* **the**

yea *pron pl nom* ye, you 375/6, etc

yelde *n* aisle 123/4 [*OED* Yelde]

yeld hall *n comp* guildhall, city hall 192/26, 203/18m

yer *pron* there 55/29, 490/13

yer *pron poss see* **the**

ygges *n pl* eggs 161/1

yi *pron poss* thy 129/8, 129/13

yle *n* aisle 118/4

þer *pron poss see* **the**

Index of Members of Oxford University

This index presents a skeleton of information for all persons named in the Records, Introduction, Endnotes, or Appendixes who had formal standing within Oxford University or its colleges or halls. Most names are recorded with far more abundant detail in Foster's *Alumni Oxonienses (Alum)* or, from before 1540, in Emden's *Biographical Register to A.D. 1500* (Emden) or *Biographical Register A.D. 1501 to 1540* (Emden2). Members of the English royal family and titled foreigners who received unearned degrees are not included here but are listed rather in the main Index (under their regnal names or titles of nobility). Several alumni from after 1642 are included because they are mentioned in the apparatus as authors, antiquaries, or owners of manuscripts. Individuals employed by academic institutions in non-academic roles appear in the main Index unless they held earned or unearned degrees.

The following information is supplied, in the following order:

Surnames. Individuals are grouped under shared surnames. The spelling of the head surname (in boldface) is determined, in order of priority, by DNB or E.B. Fryde, et al, *Handbook of British Chronology*, 3rd ed (Cambridge, 1986; rpt 1996), for ecclesiastical office holders; *Alumni* or Emden; or the dominant form which occurs in the Records. *The Historical Register of the University of Oxford* (Oxford, 1988) has been selectively consulted as an authority for spellings of surnames of members of the University not in the DNB who held high office (ie, vice-chancellors, proctors, esquire bedels, and heads of colleges) as has Harbage, *Annals of English Drama*, for playwrights also not listed in the DNB. Noblemen noticed under their titles in the main Index are cross-referenced there to the appropriate surname here. Variant spellings are supplied in parentheses with cross-references where appropriate. To enable the user to locate entries in *Alumni* and Emden as efficiently as possible a '#' is assigned to any variant that accords with *Alumni* and a '##' with Emden or Emden2.

Given Names and *Alumni* Numbers. Given names are normalized. As an aid to distinguishing among individuals listed in *Alumni* who share the same name, numbers within parentheses are appended to given names. Thus, for example, 'Atkinson, Thomas (4)' means the fourth Atkinson named Thomas in *Alumni*. A 'u' within parentheses confirms that the name occurs in *Alumni* but is unique. Early names are designated 'Emden' or 'Emden2' in brackets.

Titles of Nobility. Principal titles of nobility are supplied in all cases, immediately following the given name and *Alumni* number. Family relationships are noted as appropriate.

College Careers. College affiliations are given where known (see Symbols, p 2, for college abbreviations).

The date that follows the first college affiliation indicates the earliest known Oxford academic association, whether by matriculation in the University or by entry on a college book. Where that date is known to be late, and particularly later than the date in Records, an explanation follows within parentheses, for example the granting of a BA (which generally occurred three and a half years after first setting foot in Oxford) or a deferred matriculation. Some individuals migrated from one college to another, whether as students or later in their academic careers; accordingly, the sign ':' signifies 'migrated to.' Major college offices, particularly headships, are recorded, with inclusive dates.

Degrees and Incorporation. Advanced degrees, which account for the title 'Dr,' are listed particularly when granted before 1642: these include Civil Law (DCL), Canon Law (DCnL), Divinity/Theology (DD), Medicine (DMed), and Law (LLD). Also included are degrees signifying competence in music (BMus). Included infrequently are bachelor's degrees of civil law (BCL), divinity/theology (BD), and grammar (BGram). Unearned BAs and MAs were dispensed like sweets to visiting dignitaries: these are named along with a date. (Such degrees account for the inclusion of many non-academics in *Alumni* and hence in this University Index.) Individuals who held an MA from Cambridge gained privileges in Oxford by 'incorporation.' 'Oxon' means 'incorporated or supplicated for incorporation at Oxford' and is indicated here for individuals who appear in *Alumni* but did not take up residence in Oxford. This device explains why Philip Stringer of Cambridge appears in this University Index while his companion Henry Mowtlowe does not.

University and External Offices. Proctorships and vice-chancellorships within the University are listed next with dates; then professorships; then significant appointments outside the University including bishoprics or major government offices – but only when these have been deemed of probable interest to the principal readership of REED volumes or when University members are referred to in the Records by their office titles only. The single term 'statesman' rounds out a career too long and complex to be detailed here.

Doubtful and Duplicate Identifications. Oxford academics who cannot be matched to entries in *Alumni* or Emden are included but with cautionary rubrics within brackets such as 'Not identified.' Doubtful identifications or perceived errors in *Alumni* are similarly signalled. Cases where two identifications seem equally plausible are normally entered in the form 'Knight (Knyght##), John (1 or 2).' Brothers with similar or identical careers may be given one entry.

Supplemental Authorities. Individuals given primary listings in Wood's *Athenae Oxonienses* are flagged 'Ath' within brackets; similarly with DNB and with Chambers, *Mediaeval Stage (MS)* and *Elizabethan Stage (ES)* and Bentley, *Jacobean and Caroline Stage (JCS)*. The main Index is referred to as 'Index' and Patrons and Travelling Companies as 'PTC.'

Burton, Henry (2). Cambr; Oxon 1612, 1617. 557–9, 611, 702, 1141 [*DNB*]

– Robert (3). BNC 1593 (matr)›ChCh; author of *Anatomy of Melancholy*. 294, 427–8, 605, 690, 701, 704, 819–20, 825, 850–1, 897, 1119 [*Ath*, vol 2, col 652; *JCS; DNB*]

– William (4), brother of Robert. BNC 1591. 294, 690, 819, 825 [*Ath*, vol 3, col 153; *DNB*]

Busby, Richard (2). ChCh 1625/6; DD; Westminster School, master from 1638. 547, 821, 842, 894, 1139 [*Ath*, vol 4, col 417; *DNB*]

Buste (Bust), Henry (1). MC 1560; DMed; junior proctor 1567–8. 128, 135, 219, 283, 843

– John (2). ChCh (before 1561); senior proctor 1574–5. 128, 135, 843

Byrde (Birde), John. MtC 1482. 30 [Emden]

Caldwell (Cauduuell), Richard (1). BNC *c* 1530›ChCh; DMed. 85, 1094 [Emden2; *Ath*, vol 1, col 510; *DNB*]

Calfhill (Calfehill, Calfhille, Caulfyll), James (1). Cambr›ChCh 1548; DD; Prof Divinity. 122, 128, 133, 603, 832, 843, 848, 878, 897, 1100 [*Ath*, vol 1, col 377; *ES; DNB*]

Carew, George (1). Broadgates Hall 1522 (BA)›ChCh, dean 1559–61. 843, 876 [*DNB* under George, Baron Carew]

– Thomas (2). MtC 1608. 897 [*Ath*, vol 2, col 657; *JCS; DNB*]

Carnsew, Matthew (u), brother of Richard. Broadgates Hall(?) 1575 (BA). 692

– Richard, brother of Matthew. Broadgates Hall (*c* 1573–4). 159–60, 613, 692 [Not found in *Alum*]

Cartar (Carter), Robert (u). ChCh 1506 (MA), canon; DD. 75

Cartwright (Carthwright), William (2). ChCh 1628. 534, 543–4, 547, 606, 611, 790–4, 816, 821, 852, 891–2, 894, 897, 1138 [*Ath*, vol 3, col 69; *JCS; DNB*]

Carye, Mr. ChCh (1635–6). 520 [Not identified]

Case, John (1). ChCh, chorister›SJC 1564; DMed. 166, 347, 613, 624, 842, 1103 [*Ath*, vol 1, col 685; *DNB*]

Castilion, (Sir) Francis (1). MC 1581. 279, 850

Cauduuell *see* **Caldwell**

Caulfyll *see* **Calfhill**

Cecil (Cecyll), Robert (u), 15th earl of Salisbury, son of William (1), father of William (2). Cambr; Oxon 1605; statesman. 231, 293, 314, 532 [*DNB*]

– William (1), 1st Baron Burghley, father of Robert. Cambr; Oxford MA 1566 (unearned); secretary of state 1550–3, 1558–72; statesman. 126, 129–30, 224, 231, 876–7, 1100 [*DNB*]

– William (2), 16th earl of Salisbury, son of Robert. MA 1605 (unearned); statesman. 532

Chamberlayne (Chamberlen), Robert (1). SJC 1601. 346 [Perhaps father of same, also Robert]

Chambre (Chamber#), John. MtC 1492; DMed. 47–8 [Emden]

Chapman, George (u). No academic particulars in *Alum*. 896 [*Ath*, vol 2, col 575; *ES; JCS; DNB*]

Chaundler, Thomas. NC 1435, warden from 1454; DD; junior proctor 1444–5; University chancellor 1457–61, 1472–9. 837, 897 [Emden]

Cheke (Cheeke#), (Sir) John (2). Cambr; Oxon 1542. 878 [Emden2; *Ath*, vol 1, col 241; *DNB*]

Cheynell, Francis (u). Magdalen Hall 1624›BC›MtC. 1138 [*DNB*]

Cheyney, William (1). SJC 1611 (BA). 350

Chittye (Chitty), Henry (u). MC 1572; DMed. 198

Cinthopp, James. 1095 [Not found in *Alum*]

Clarke, Francis. SJC, porter. 268–9, 815–16, 849, 897, 1115 [Not found in *Alum*]

– Thomas (11). SJC 1604. 346, 350, 360

Dannay, William. Neville's Entry, principal in 1389–90. 9 [Not found in Emden]

Dannet (Danet), Audley (u). ChCh 1561. 128, 135, 843

Davenant (D'Avenant), (Sir) William (1). LC *c* 1620. 652, 896, 1135 [*Ath*, vol 3, col 802; *JCS; DNB*]

Davies (Davis#), (Sir) John (13). QC 1585›MC. 897 [*Ath*, vol 2, col 400; *ES; DNB*]

Davy (David##), John (2). MtC 1522. 75 [Emden2]

Day (Daye), John (1). MC 1544; DCL. 95 [ID conjectural]

– Thomas (1). ASC 1518›ChCh. 122, 1095, 1100 [ID conjectural]

Deale, Robert (u). NC 1562. 127, 135, 876 [ID conjectural]

Delabere (Dalaper, Dalavere, Dalober), John (1). ChCh 1561 (BA)›Gloucester Hall, principal 1581–93; DMed. 128–9, 135, 186, 219, 843

Denham, (Sir) John (2). TC 1631. 897 [*Ath*, vol 3, col 823; *JCS; DNB*]

– Thomas (u). SJC 1575. 1104

Denne (Den), Henry (1). ASC 1563 (BA)›NC, principal(?). 179 [ID conjectural]

Devereux, Robert (1), 19th earl of Essex. Cambr, MA 1581 (unearned); Oxon 1588; high steward of Oxford city 1596–1601. 180, 231, 246, 249, 505, 587, 616, 686–7, 1108–9, 1112–13, 1134 [*DNB*]; *see also* PTC *under* Essex

Devenell (Devynel, Devynell), Henry (u). MtC 1524. 76

Dewhurst, Giles (u). ChCh 1567. 166, 684

Dickonson (Dickenson), William (2). SJC 1605. 349

Dicus, Hugh (u). BNC 1596; senior proctor 1615–16. 408

Diggles (Digles), Christopher (u). NC 1562. 146

Dochen, Thomas (1). MC 1564. 219

Dorset (Dorcet), Robert (u). ChCh (1561). 128, 135, 843

Dowe, Robert (u). ASC 1574. 206, 684, 827

Dowman, John (u). Cambr; Oxon 1514; LLD. 47

Downer, Thomas (1). SJC 1601. 344, 349, 842

Dudley, Robert (1), 14th earl of Leicester. University chancellor 1564–88. 120, 123–4, 126, 134, 144–6, 150, 180, 185, 188, 194–5, 198, 200, 604, 614, 616, 645, 751, 813, 875, 879, 881–2, 1099, 1101, 1106 [*DNB*]; *see also* PTC *under* Leicester

Dunnet, John. College unknown 1570. 152, 685 [Not found in *Alum*]

Duppa, Brian (u). ChCh 1605, dean 1629–38; junior proctor 1619–20; vice-chancellor 1632–4; bishop of Salisbury 1634–8, 1641; of Chichester 1638–41; of Winchester 1660–2. 871 [*Ath*, vol 3, col 541; *DNB*]

Edes (Eds, Eedes#), Richard (1). ChCh 1571; DD; junior proctor 1583–4. 180, 186, 190, 202, 213, 809, 825, 827, 848, 853, 897, 1105 [*Ath*, vol 1, col 749; *ES; DNB*]

Edmondes (Edmonds), (Sir) Clement (u). ASC 1586. 546, 889 [*Ath*, vol 2, col 322; *DNB*]

Edrich *see* **Etherege**

Edwards (Edwardes#, Edwars), Jonathan (1). JC 1632. 1138

– Richard (1). CCC 1540 (scholar)›ChCh 1547; gentleman of the Chapel. 130, 132–3, 135–6, 141, 143, 603–4, 830–1, 843, 848, 853–4, 877–81, 897, 1100 [*Ath*, vol 1, col 353; *ES; DNB*]

– Thomas (4). ASC 1581; DCL. 219, 258–9 [ID uncertain]

Egerton, (Sir) Thomas (1), 1st baron of Ellesmere. BNC 1556; high steward of Oxford city 1601–10; University chancellor 1610–16; statesman. 128?, 135?, 314, 587, 843?, 884 [*Ath*, vol 2, col 197; *DNB*]

Eglesfield, Robert. QC, founder 1341. 670 [Emden; *DNB*]

Fulman (Ful(l)man#), William (u). MC>CCC 1647; antiquary. 648, 683, 856, 1117 [*Ath*, vol 4, col 239; *DNB*]

Fulwell, Ulpian (u). St Mary Hall 1579 (age 33). 897 [*Ath*, vol 1, col 540; *ES; DNB*]

Gager, William (u). ChCh 1574; DCL. 180–1, 183–4, 219, 605, 645, 804, 809, 813, 816–18, 823–5, 829, 833–4, 841, 848–9, 860–70, 882, 897, 1105–6 [*Ath*, vol 2, col 87; *ES; DNB*]

Gardiner, Richard (5). ChCh 1607, canon 1629–48; DD. 804 [*Ath*, vol 3, col 921; *DNB*]

Garrard, George (2). MtC 1594. 532–4, 691, 1138
  See also **Gerrard**

Garrett *see* **Gerrard**

Gawen, Thomas (2). NC 1633. 1139 [*Ath*, vol 4, col 130; *DNB*]

Gay (Gaye), John (1). EC 1634. 887 [ID uncertain]

Gayton, Edmund (u). SJC 1626; esquire bedel 1636–48. 835, 841, 893 [*Ath*, vol 3, col 756; *DNB*]

Gee, Edward (1). MtC 1582/3>LC>BNC; DD; senior proctor 1598–9. 246–7 [*Ath*, vol 2, col 258; *DNB*]

Gellibrand, Edward (u). MC 1571. 197, 660

Gentili, Alberico (u). Perugia; Oxon 1581; Prof Civil Law. 860–1 [*Ath*, vol 2, col 90; *DNB*]

Gerrard (Garrett, Jarratt, Jarrett), John (4). Pleb. Privilegiatus (as musician) 1625. 481–2, 486, 490, 499, 502–3, 530, 617, 621–2, 685, 1134, 1137–8

Gibbons, Orlando (u). Cambr>Oxford, DMus (1622). 470, 489, 619, 621, 1106, 1130, 1133 [*DNB*]

Gidding, William. MtC 1490. 44 [Emden]

Giffard (Gifford#), Roger (1). ChCh 1555>MtC>ASC; DMed; junior proctor 1562–4. 105–6 [*DNB*]

Gilton (Getton, Gitton), William. St Agatha's Hall 1388; scholar of Canon Law 1406. 9–10 [Emden]

Gittisham *see* **Jutsam**

Glasier (Glasyer), Thomas (1). ChCh 1561>EC, rector 1578–92; DCL. 128, 135, 843

Glove, John. St Agatha's Hall 1388. 9–10 [Emden]

Goad, John (u). SJC 1634. 841, 893 [*Ath*, vol 4, col 267; *DNB*]

Godmersham, Richard. Canterbury College 1393–4, warden 1403–10; DCnL. 1085 [Emden]

Godwin, (Goodwin#, Goodwyn#, Godwyn), Francis (1), father of Thomas (5). ChCh 1577; DD; bishop of Llandaff 1601–17; of Hereford 1617–33. 329, 645–6, 1120 [*Ath*, vol 2, col 555; *DNB*]

– John (4). ChCh 1617. 845 [ID conjectural]

– Thomas (2). MC>ChCh, dean 1565–7; DD; bishop of Bath and Wells 1584–90. 126, 134, 875, 1100 [*Ath*, vol 2, col 827; *DNB*]

– Thomas (5), son of Francis. ChCh 1604. 329, 645–6, 841
  See also **Goodwin**

Goffe (Gough), Thomas (u). ChCh 1609. 428, 434–6, 804–5, 808, 817, 820–1, 840–1, 844, 851, 897, 1126, 1142 [*Ath*, vol 2, col 463; *JCS; DNB*]

Gomersall, Robert (u). ChCh 1616. 838, 897 [*Ath*, vol 2, col 590; *JCS; DNB*]

Good, John (5). NC 1620; junior proctor 1636–7. 526, 528, 888, 891

Goodall, Stephen (u). ChCh, chaplain 1637 (death). 520, 1137

– Thomas (1). MC 1547>Magdalen Hall. 106

Goodhew (Goodhugh), John. MtC 1490. 41 [Emden]

Goodwin (Goodwyn#), William (2). ChCh 1573, dean 1611–20; DD; vice-chancellor 1614–16, 1617–18. 408, 426 [*DNB*]
  See also **Godwin**

Juxon, Rowland (u). sjc 1602. 344, 349
− William (1). sjc 1598, president 1621–33; dcl; vice-chancellor 1626–8; bishop of Hereford 1633; of London 1633–60; lord treasurer 1636–41. 533, 537, 544, 557, 792, 805, 812, 888, 893 [*Ath*, vol 4, col 818; *DNB*]

Kennall (Kenall), John (u). bcl 1540›ChCh 1559; vice-chancellor 1564–6. 116, 121, 126, 129, 134, 211, 875, 877, 879, 1100
Kent, Thomas. MtC 1480. 32 [Emden]
− Thomas (2). bcl 1543›ChCh. 1095 [Emden2]
Kettell (Ketle), Ralph (u). tc 1579, president 1599–1643; dd. 284, 505 [*DNB*]
Kiblewhite, Roger (u). sjc 1570. 1104
Kiete *see* **Kite**
Killigrew, Henry (2). ChCh 1628; dd. 897 [*Ath*, vol 4, col 621; *JCS*; *DNB*]
Kinaston *see* **Kynaston**
King (Kinge#, Kyng#, Kynge), John (2). ChCh 1577, dean 1605–11; dd; vice-chancellor 1607–11; bishop of London 1611–21. 183, 204, 282, 294, 363, 365, 428, 841, 849, 1117, 1120 [*Ath*, vol 2, col 294; *DNB*]
− John (7). ChCh 1608/9; dd; public orator 1622–5. 526, 886 [Younger brother of *Alum*'s Henry (1), hence 'junior' in Records]
− Philip (2), brother of Robert (3) and William. ChCh 1616›ec; public orator 1625–9. 401, 845
− Robert (1). 1507 (bd); dd; bishop of Oxford 1542–57. 592 [Emden; *Ath*, vol 2, col 774; *DNB*]
− Robert (3), brother of Philip and William. ChCh 1612. 428, 844
− Thomas. MtC 1484. 40 [Emden under 'Thomas *or* John']
− William (5), brother of Philip and Robert (3). ChCh 1616›asc. 845
Kingsmill (Kingsmyll#, Kyngsmell), Thomas (1). mc 1558; public orator 1565–9, Prof Hebrew. 128, 876 [*Ath*, vol 1, col 758; *DNB*]
Kite (Kiete), ... sjc 1582 (ba). 177, 346 [Not found in *Alum*]
Knight (Knyght##), John (1 or 2). lc *c* 1530. 73–4 [Emden2]
− Thomas (2). ccc 1569. 179
− William (1). MtC 1503; dd. 59 [Emden]
Knollys (Knolles#), (Sir) Francis (1), father of William. mc in or before 1564; ma 1598 (unearned); high steward of Oxford city 1563–92; statesman. 112, 127, 134, 587, 876, 879, 1103, 1110 [*DNB*]
− (Sir) William (1), Viscount Wallingford, son of Francis. mc in or before 1564 (probably); high steward of Oxford city 1611–32; statesman. 461, 587, 1128–9
Kynaston (Kinaston#), (Sir) Francis (1). oc 1601›St Mary Hall›tc›Cambr›oc. 897 [*Ath*, vol 3, col 38; *JCS*; *DNB*]
Kyng, Kynge *see* **King**
Kyngsmell *see* **Kingsmill**

Lake, Arthur (1). nc 1588, warden 1613–17; dd; vice-chancellor 1616–17; bishop of Bath and Wells 1616–26. 234–5, 669–70 [*Ath*, vol 2, col 398; *DNB*]
− (Sir) Thomas (2). ma 1592 (unearned); Latin secretary to James i; clerk of the signet. 329, 645–6 [*DNB*]
Lancaster, Francis (u). ChCh 1606. 404, 850
Langbaine, Gerard, Sr (1). qc 1625; dd; keeper of the archives 1644–58. 498, 503, 546–7, 680–1, 701, 703–4, 738, 860, 878, 1134, 1137, 1139 [*Ath*, vol 3, col 446; *DNB*]

Peele (Pille), George (u). Broadgates Hall by 1572›ChCh 1574–9. 183, 187–8, 604, 739, 809, 829, 834, 837, 849, 853, 898 [*Ath*, vol 1, col 688; *ES; DNB*]

Peirs (Peirse#, Perse, Piers), John (1). MC 1542›BC, master 1570–1›ChCh, dean 1571–6; DD; bishop of Rochester 1576–7; of Salisbury 1577–89; archbishop of York 1589–94. 128, 133, 878 [*Ath*, vol 2, col 835; *DNB*]

– William (2). ChCh 1599; DD; vice-chancellor 1621–4. 440, 450

Pelham, Herbert (u). Magdalen Hall 1619›MC; DCL; senior proctor 1634–5. 887

Penson, William (u). ChCh 1561. 127–8, 135, 843

Percy, William (u). Gloucester Hall 1589. 898 [*ES; DNB*]

Perrinne (Perin), John (2). SJC 1575›ChCh; DD; Prof Greek. 283, 298, 303, 317, 346, 884, 1117, 1120

Perrott (Porett), Robert (1). MC 1508 (BA); musician. 61 [Emden2]

Persons (Parsons#, Person#), John. MtC 1478. 30, 842 [Emden]

– Robert (1). St Mary Hall›BC 1568; the Jesuit. 156–7, 633–4, 857, 1098, 1102 [*Ath*, vol 2, col 63; *DNB*]

See also **Parsons**

Petre (Peter#), (Sir) William (1). EC›ASC 1523; DCL; second founder of EC. 649, 698 [Emden2; *DNB*]

Pett, Simeon (u). MC 1571. 197, 661

Pickhaver, Ralph (u). ChCh 1561; DD. 1120

Piers *see* **Peirs**

Pille *see* **Peele**

Pinck (Pincke#, Pink, Pinke), Robert (u). NC 1594, warden 1617–47; DD; senior proctor 1610–11; vice-chancellor 1634–6, 1642–5 (with gap). 501, 525–6, 887 [*Ath*, vol 3, col 225; *DNB*]

Pole, Reginald (u). MC 1515 (BA)› CCC; University chancellor 1556–8; cardinal of England 1536–58; archbishop of Canterbury 1556–8. 98 [Emden2; *Ath*, vol 1, col 278; *DNB*]

Poll *see* **Paule, Powell**

Pollarde (Pollard), Francis (1). MC 1506. 47 [Emden2]

Pollen (Pleyn, Poleyn, Pullain##) (alias Smith), John (1). MtC 1506 (BA). 61 [Emden2]

Pope, (Sir) Thomas (2). No academic particulars in *Alum*; founder of TC. 677

– Thomas (3). St Mary Hall 1572 (BA)›Gloucester Hall. 166, 685

Porett *see* **Perrott**

Portrey (Portry), Alexander (u). ChCh 1620 (BA). 428, 844

Potter, Christopher (1). QC 1606, provost 1626–45/6; DD; vice-chancellor 1640–1. 526 [*Ath*, vol 3, col 179; *DNB*]

– Richard (1). TC 1571. 1107 [ID conjectural]

Potticary (Poticary), Thomas (1). SJC 1575. 179

Potts (Potes, Pottes), Nicholas (u), ChCh 1561 (BA); or Thomas (1), ChCh 1555. 128, 135, 843

Poulet (Paulet), (Sir) Anthony (1) and George (1). ChCh 1580. 179, 1105

Powell (Poll), Ambrose (u). MC 1604. 407, 460, 685, 850, 1124

– (D.G.P.), Griffith (u). JC 1581, principal 1613–20; DCL. 387, 648, 859, 1122 [*Ath*, vol 2, col 283; *DNB*]

– Rice (1). ChCh 1567. 128, 135, 843

See also **Paule**

Poxwell, John (u). MtC 1503; St Alban Hall, principal 1510–14. 59

Price (Pryce), Edward (1). ASC (before 1568)›New Inn Hall, principal 1581–4. 179

– Francis (1). ChCh 1621. 428, 844–5

Rogers, Christopher (u). LC 1612 (BA)›New Inn Hall, principal 1626–43, 1646–62; DD. 557, 1141
Romans, ... 135, 843 [Not identified]
Rondell *see* **Randall**
Rookes, William (1). MC 1544. 128, 135, 843
Rouse (Rous, Russe#), John (u). Subscribed 1596; BC›OC, University librarian 1620–52. 526, 537 [*DNB*]
Russell, Robert (1). ChCh 1573. 282 [ID uncertain]
– (Sir) William (1). MC. 189
Ryley (Riley), Christopher (u). SJC 1610 (matr). 353
Ryves, George (1). NC 1579, warden 1599–1613; DD; vice-chancellor 1601–2. 284, 795

Sacheverell (Sachevorill, Sachewerill), Ambrose (u). NC 1581. 287
Sackville (Sackevile, Sackvile#), Thomas (1), Lord Buckhurst, 1st earl of Dorset. Cambr; University chancellor 1591–1608; lord treasurer 1599–1608. 216–17, 231, 248, 279, 285, 287, 295–302, 313, 315–16, 409, 587, 661, 884, 1112, 1118 [*Ath*, vol 2, col 30; *ES; DNB*]
– John (1). SJC 1608. 350, 587
Salisbury, (Sir) Thomas (2). JC 1642 (DCL). 898 [*Ath*, vol 3, col 55; *JCS*]
Sandsbury, John (u). SJC 1593. 818, 850, 898 [*Ath*, vol 2, col 58; *DNB*]
Sandys, George (1). St Mary Hall 1589. 898 [*Ath*, vol 3, col 97; *JCS; DNB*]
Saunders (Sanders), Hugh (u) (alias Shakspere alias Breakspear). MtC 1487›St Alban Hall, principal 1501–3; vice-chancellor 1501–3. 42 [Emden]
– John (4). OC 1598/9›St Mary Hall, principal 1632–44; DMed. 519, 539, 1136
Savile (Saville), (Sir) Henry (2). BNC›MtC 1565, warden 1585–1622; junior proctor 1575–6. 299 [*DNB*]
– Thomas (1). MtC 1580 (BA); senior proctor 1592–3. 217, 219, 223 [*Ath*, vol 1, col 591]
Scarsbrook (Skarysbryke, Skirsbreke), Thomas. MtC 1492; DD. 42, 45 [Emden]
Searchfield, Rowland (u). SJC 1582; DD; junior proctor 1596–7; bishop of Bristol 1619–22. 346
Searle (Serle), George (u). ChCh 1616. 428, 844
Sedgwick, Obadiah (1). QC 1619›Magdalen Hall. 467 [*Ath*, vol 3, cols 65, 442, 1090; vol 4, col 751; *DNB*]
Seller (Sellar#), Henry (u), CCC 1611; or John (4), CCC 1609. 392, 1122
– Thomas (u). TC 1600 (BA); senior proctor 1612–13. 885
Sheffield (Shefeild), John (2), 2nd Lord Sheffield. MA 1566 (unearned). 130
Sheldon (Shelden), Gilbert (u). TC 1617 (BA)›ASC, warden 1635–48, 1660–1; DD; archbishop of Canterbury 1663–77. 526, 1109 [*Ath*, vol 4, col 853; *DNB*]
Sherborne (Sherborn), William (u). SJC 1612; DD. 421
Shipman, Roger (u). SJC 1637. 811 [ID uncertain]
Shirley, James (u). SJC 1615 (matr?)›Cambr. 898 [*Ath*, vol 3, col 737; *JCS; DNB*]
Shorte (Short), Anthony (1). BNC 1570 (BA)›ASC. 179
Siddall (Syddall##), Henry (u). Crd 1531/2 (BA)›Broadgates Hall›ChCh; DD. 120, 122, 1095, 1100 [Emden2; *DNB*]
Simpson, John (3). EC 1565. 165, 686
Singleton, Thomas (1). BNC 1573, principal 1595–1614; DD; senior proctor 1585–6; vice-chancellor 1598–9, 1611–14. 219, 282, 885
Skarysbryke, Skirsbreke *see* **Scarsbrook**
Skelton, John (2). Cambr›Oxford; laureate 1488?. 896 [Emden; *Ath*, vol 1, col 49; *DNB*]
Smalwood, William (1). MC 1552›SJC. 154, 685

Index

MARION FILIPIUK

The Index combines subjects with non-University names, places, and book or play titles in a single listing. Persons associated with the University are listed in the Index of Members of Oxford University or – for short – University Index (UI). When identical headwords occur in more than one category, the order is as follows: persons, places, subjects, and titles of books or plays.

Place names and given names appear in modern form when that could be ascertained, titles and family names of nobility and other public figures in forms commonly used by historians. Other surnames are usually cited in the most common form occurring in the Records text except that capitalization and the use of 'i/j' and 'u/v' have been assimilated to modern usage. Place names and surnames are regularly followed by any variant spellings (in parentheses). Nobles are entered under their family names, with cross-references from any titles that occur in the text or apparatus, and royalty under their regnal or given names. Saints' names are indexed under the abbreviation 'St,' alphabetized as if spelled out. In a few cases (eg, 'Browne') it has been necessary to assign numbers to different individuals of the same name to distinguish them; those numbers are in parentheses following the names. Ellipsis dots are used in cases where a person's given name is not known.

Occupations or titles of office are given when known and considered relevant or to assist in distinguishing individuals of the same name. Apart from the Records themselves, the chief sources used for identifying individuals were the *DNB*; E.B. Fryde et al. (eds), *Handbook of British Chronology*, 3rd ed (Cambridge, 1986; rpt 1996); Harbage, *Annals*; John Le Neve, *Fasti Ecclesiae Anglicanae 1300–1541*, rev and expanded ed, 12 vols (London, 1962–7); and E.G. Withycombe (ed), *The Oxford Dictionary of English Christian Names*, 3rd ed (Oxford, 1977; rpt 1979). Sources for royalty, nobility, and other patrons are specified in the headnote to Patrons and Travelling Companies (PTC), to which the Index refers throughout. Place name spellings are based on those provided in Eilert Ekwall (ed), *The Concise Oxford Dictionary of English Place-Names*, 4th ed (Oxford, 1960; rpt 1980) and Ordnance Survey (comp), *Gazetteer of Great Britain*, 4th ed (Southampton, London, and Basingstoke, 1999).

To aid research, many entries have been collected under such general headings as 'costume,' 'musical instruments,' and 'trades and occupations.' Particular items are sub-listed alphabetically there and usually not cross-referenced in the main listing. In the cross-references that are supplied, bold type is used for main entries in this index, roman type for sub-entries and entries in PTC and UI. Entries in which entertainers are referred to by such Latin terms as 'histrio' and 'mimus' are indexed under the English equivalent used in the Translations.

For explanation of the college codes, see Symbols (p 2).

The Christmas Prince *(cont)*

financial arrangements for 344–6, 359–60, 1121

interludes and plays as parts of: 850; *Ara Fortunae* 346–7, 611, 806, 842; *Ira Fortunae* 371–2, 806, 819, 842; *Periander* 372–80, 613, 806, 818–19, 842; *Philomathes* 363, 806; *Philomela* 355–6, 806, 842; *Saturnalia* 354, 806; *The Seven Days of the Week* 361–4, 806; 'Somnium fundatoris' 361; *Time's Complaint* 357–8, 362, 806, 842

projected entertainments 380

songs and singing in 353–4

visit to ChCh, for burlesque, *Yuletide* 364–5

watch-night activities 365–70

Christus Nascens 602, 827, 899

Christus Redivivus 85, 602, 807, 899, 1094

Christus Triumphans 106–7, 690, 823, 853, 1097

chronicles 11, 28, 60, 90

churches

equipment of 168, 173, 596

See also **bells** *and specific churches*: **All Saints; St Aldate; St Martin; St Mary Magdalen; St Mary the Virgin; St Michael at the North Gate; St Michael at the South Gate; St Peter in the East; St Peter le Bailey**

Cicero, Roman orator 884

Pro Sex. Roscio 270

Circumcision, feast of *see* **New Year's Day**

Cistellaria see **Plautus**

The City Cozener see The Ordinary

The City Match 544–5, 606, 892

Civil War 505, 584, 589, 596, 604, 1131

Claphole, Oxf (?) 420–1

Clarke (Clarck, Clark, Clerke), Hugh, player 514

– James, capper 1094

– John, carrier 114–17

– Richard, joiner 421

– Thomas, brewer or innkeeper 421, 494

clay 115, 121

Cleopatra, queen of Egypt 547

See also **'Anthony and Cleopatra'**

clergy 70, 172, 438, 467, 512, 1111, 1127

Clerke *see* **Clarke**

clerks

parish 17, 23, 31–2, 35, 38, 43, 45, 49, 51, 53, 64–5, 172, 1111

See also members of *under* **royal household**

Cleydon, William de 5–6

Clifford, George, 3rd earl of Cumberland 313

See also PTC

Clifton, Sir Gervase 1138

Clinche (Clynch, Clynche), Henry, painter 198

– Ralph, painter 198

clothing *see* **costume; dress**

clowns *see* **jesters**

clubs and clubbing 179

Clynch, Clynche *see* **Clinche**

Cnut, king of the English, Danes, and Norse 594

Cobb, Sir William *see* PTC *under* Sheriff of Oxfordshire

Cockram, Samuel, woollen-draper 551

Coggan (Cogan), family, proprietors of the King's Head 617

– Thomas, bailiff 103, 117, 120, 1096–9

coins

kinds: angels 133, 224–6, 301, 883; groats 270–1; nobles 45, 62–3, 66–7, 69, 82, 514, 1089

Cokayne, Aston, playwright 896

Coke, George 62, 624

Cokethorpe (Cokthropp), Oxf 414

Cole (Coles), Philip 196

Coleman, Simon, organist of NC 520, 1137

Coleshill Hall 16

Collyns, Thomas, tailor 169, 1104, 1113

Colly Weston (Colli Weston), Northants 773

The Combat of Love and Friendship 807

comedies *see under* **plays, college** *and* **plays, professional**

commencement (the Act) 417, 420, 431, 433, 438, 444, 447, 449, 452, 455, 474, 484, 495, 497, 510, 513, 571, 594, 599, 694, 1134, 1138–9

at church of St Mary the Virgin 294–5

degree ceremonies 594, 599

disputations and lectures at 257

entertainments at time of 484, 505, 513, 518, 532, 1136

Huchins, ..., bearward 104
Huet, John, labourer 114–15, 117–21
Hulle, John, JP 8
Humphrey of Lancaster, 2nd duke of Gloucester
    614
    See also PTC
Hunsdon, Lord see Carey
Hunt, ... 83
hunters and hunting 129, 139, 191, 311, 878,
    880, 882
The Hunting of Cupid 837
Huskinse, John 42, 498–9
Hutchinson, Matthew 694
Hyncksey, Hynxhye see Hinksey

Ibstone (Ibston), Bucks 218, 1109
ink 124, 779
Inns of Court, London 328, 599, 854, 880, 1105
interludes and interlude players 42–3, 47, 57, 64,
    72, 174, 252, 546, 557–9, 602, 847–9, 851
    forbidden 231–2
inventories
    at ASC 15
    at St Martin 596
    in chancellor's register 15
    Laud's proposal concerning 539, 607
    of chancellor's court 106, 147, 152–4, 156,
        165–7, 169, 246, 1137–8
    of musicians' goods 472, 554
    of play materials 539
Iphigenia see Euripides
Iphis 801, 812, 872
Ipswich, Suff 559
Ira Fortunae 371–2, 806, 819, 842
Ireland 315, 473, 1143
Isaiah (Esay) 558
Isis River, Oxf 310, 620
Ithaca, Greece 864

Jackman, Mr, baker 1114
Jackson, ..., 199
– Henry, manciple of ASC 186, 189
James I (James VI of Scotland), king of Great
    Britain 412–13, 427, 429, 445, 460–1, 512,
    531, 545, 588, 606, 610, 693, 747, 765–6,

James I (cont)
    772–89, 793, 837–8, 845, 1124, 1126–7
    entertainment for: academic exercises 294, 299,
        1118; disputations 287, 293–4, 300–1, 332,
        885, 1117–18; lectures 1117; meals 294, 300,
        303, 884–5, 1119; music 885; plays 283–4,
        286, 293–5, 298–9, 305–15, 332, 605–6,
        841, 884; poems 286, 294, 300, 318, 884;
        speeches 283, 286–7, 297–8, 300–3, 316–17,
        884–6, 1117–18
    gifts to 283, 287, 297–8, 300, 302, 316,
        325–6, 884
    letter of 329–30
    proclamation of 272, 620–1
    rewards actor by making him king's scholar
        329–30
    visit to Oxford (1605) 277–327, 330–3, 409,
        605–6, 683, 687, 693, 699, 765, 884–6,
        1110, 1115–18, 1121
    See also under Accession Day and PTC under
        King
James II, king of Great Britain 890–1
    visit to Oxford 607
James (Jamys), Stephen 88
Jannys, William, harper 41–2, 498–9
Jennings (Gennings), William, city chamberlain,
    tailor 421, 1125
– William, mercer 1125
Jerome, ..., cook 161
jesters 321, 751, 1097–8
    payments to 104, 108, 147, 615
    See also Armin; Grene, Robert; Tarlton,
        Richard
Jesus College 283, 501, 567, 600–1, 650–1,
    1109, 1122
    Hocktide activity at 516, 521, 623
    levies for royal visits 521, 524, 536, 555
    officials: principal 452, 650; vice-principal
        452
    records: Bursar's Book 487, 496, 507, 510, 516,
        521, 554–5, 565–6, 569, 572, 575–6, 651;
        Statutes 452, 651
    See also gifts and payments to under musicians
        and trumpeters; and under statutes, college
Jewish custom 777

Oxford, city/town of *(cont)*

New Year's 106; *see also under* **mayors**
elections 107, 619, 1097–8, 1103–4, 1126
franchises of 257, 334, 406, 409, 436, 466, 471,
549, 572, 574, 576, 620
gates of: 8, 225, 295; East Gate 134, 142, 190,
247, 303, 560, 591, 815, 879, 881, 883;
North Gate 127, 191, 259, 305, 314, 324–5,
398, 548, 553, 589, 622, 624, 876, 883–4,
1103, 1107, 1122, 1140
government of: 589–90; common councils
589–90, 707, 1098, 1103, 1121; 'compounding' in 589–90; council of Thirteen 127, 296,
300, 322–3, 457, 461–2, 509, 543, 548, 565,
590, 620, 883, 1098, 1111, 1115, 1119, 1121,
1140; council of Twenty-four 589; elderly 590;
freemen in 589–90, 619–20; policing 249,
458, 589; wards 589–90; *see also* officials *below*
guilds and companies of: 588, 590, 620, 1140;
Bakers 263, 1114; clothmakers 584; Cooks
595; Cordwainers 494, 568, 574, 580, elections
711; Fullers 537; Guild Merchant of 584–5,
589; leatherworkers 584; musicians 492, 499,
619, 1112; Shoemakers 537; Tailors 58–9,
149, 159, 169, 227, 240, 250, 254, 394, 441,
537; *see also* **guild records** *and* gifts and
payments to *under* **musicians**
high stewards of 127, 134, 224, 246, 461, 552,
587, 884; *see also* **Carey**, Henry; UI *under*
Devereux; Egerton; Howard, Thomas; Knollys,
Francis *and* William
history of: Anglo-Saxon period 583–4, 588,
591, 593; Black Death's effect on 585; centre
of government and trade 583–4, 591; city
and diocese of, created 588, 590–1; Danish
raids on 584; decline of 585; defences of 584;
Dissolution of monastic establishments of
588, 591–2; early modern period in 586–9;
economy of, based on service trades 586,
588, brewing and victualling 593; fee-farm
of 584–6, 589; friaries in 585, 588, 591;
gaols in 584; increase of secular colleges in
588; land and water transport systems of
583–4, 588; later Middle Ages in 584–6;
monasteries in 585, 588, 591; Norman period

Oxford, city/town of *(cont)*

in 584; parliaments in 584; 'portmanmoot'
of 585; 'privileged persons' in 503–4, 586,
619, 746; prosperity of 593; Puritan lectures
subsidized in 588; relations of, with the Crown
585; religious centre 591, 623; religious history
of 590–7; royal charters for 584, 588, 597;
scholars' arrival in 583, 591, 597; scholars'
rents in, fixed 585; seat of government at 589;
seventeenth century in 588; site of national
meetings 584; site of royal mint 583, 589;
sixteenth century in 588; taxpaying population
of 586, 588; University's development and
effect on town 585–6; Wood's 873–4
inns and taverns of: 588; Bear 518, 1108–9,
1136; Bell, sign of 1115; Blue Boar 518, 1136;
Charlton's (Cherlton) 9, 1085; Crown 518,
751, 1136; Dolphin 449; Fleur de Luce 416,
518, 1136; Lamb and Flag 1112, 1115; Red
Lion 406, 1123; Roebuck 1130; Split Crow
(Chequers) 416; Star 490, 1133; Swindlestock
585, 594; The Tavern 416; Three Goats Head
1142; *see also* **King's Arms; King's Head**
liberties of 134, 142, 589, 592, 879
mace of 127, 226, 297–8, 300, 302, 492, 533,
549, 551, 621, 888
officials: 134, 142, 190, 297, 589, 707, 1111,
1115, 1126; aldermen 35, 127, 225, 249, 296,
298, 316, 322–5, 457, 461–2, 533, 537, 543,
548, 551, 589–90, 875, 883, 888, 1097, 1119;
bailiffs 4, 35, 42, 171, 225, 300, 322–3, 457,
461–2, 492, 499, 537, 548–9, 551–3, 565,
585–6, 589–90, 619, 883, 1088–9, 1097–8,
1110–11, 1119, 1125; chamberlains 35, 225,
322–5, 482, 509, 548, 709, 1110, 1113, 1119;
clerks 35, 190, 248, 297, 300, 324, 461, 491,
533, 549; constables 35, 589, 1110; criers 35,
1122; keykeepers 167, 226, 325, 709, 1097;
order of precedence for 35, 322–3, 457, 461,
548–9, 711; proctors 1084; recorders 144,
223, 297, 462, 533, 537, 543, 549, 551, 615,
620, 1108–9; 'satrapes' 29, 45, 50, 62–3,
65–7, 69–71, 82, 90–1, 93, 101, 103,
105–6, 612, 1088; serjeants 25, 1088–9,
bailiff's 35, 461, 1088, at mace 619, 621,

RECORDS OF EARLY ENGLISH DRAMA

York edited by Alexandra F. Johnston and Margaret Rogerson. 2 volumes. 1979.

Chester edited by Lawrence M. Clopper. 1979.

Coventry edited by R.W. Ingram. 1981.

Newcastle upon Tyne edited by J.J. Anderson. 1982.

Norwich 1540–1642 edited by David Galloway. 1984.

Cumberland/Westmorland/Gloucestershire edited by Audrey Douglas and Peter Greenfield. 1986.

Devon edited by John Wasson. 1986.

Cambridge edited by Alan H. Nelson. 2 volumes. 1988.

Herefordshire/Worcestershire edited by David N. Klausner. 1990.

Lancashire edited by David George. 1991.

Shropshire edited by J. Alan B. Somerset. 2 volumes. 1994.

Somerset including Bath edited by James Stokes with Robert J. Alexander. 2 volumes. 1996.

Bristol edited by Mark C. Pilkinton. 1997.

Dorset/Cornwall edited by Rosalind Conklin Hays and C.E. McGee/Sally L. Joyce and Evelyn S. Newlyn. 1999.

Sussex edited by Cameron Louis. 2000.

Kent: Diocese of Canterbury edited by James M. Gibson. 3 volumes. 2002.

Oxford edited by John R. Elliott, Jr, and Alan H. Nelson (University)/Alexandra F. Johnston and Diana Wyatt (City). 2 volumes. 2004.